digital
media tools

Second Edition

Nigel Chapman and Jenny Chapman

WILEY

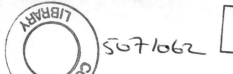

Second edition Copyright © 2003 John Wiley & Sons Ltd, The Atrium, Southern Gate,
Chichester, West Sussex PO19 8SQ, England
Telephone   (+44) 1243 779777

Email (for orders and customer service enquiries): cs-books@wiley.co.uk
Visit our Home Page on www.wileyeurope.com or www.wiley.com

First edition Copyright © 2002 by John Wiley & Sons, Ltd
Cover Illustration: Fernand Leger's *Study for 'Constructors': Team at Rest, 1950*
Scottish National Gallery of Modern Art/Bridgeman Art Library

Other Wiley Editorial Offices

John Wiley & Sons Inc., 111 River Street, Hoboken, NJ 07030, USA

Jossey-Bass, 989 Market Street, San Francisco, CA 94103-1741, USA

Wiley-VCH Verlag GmbH, Boschstr. 12, D-69469 Weinheim, Germany

John Wiley & Sons Australia Ltd, 33 Park Road, Milton, Queensland 4064, Australia

John Wiley & Sons (Asia) Pte Ltd, 2 Clementi Loop #02-01, Jin Xing Distripark, Singapore 129809

John Wiley & Sons Canada Ltd, 22 Worcester Road, Etobicoke, Ontario, Canada M9W 1L1

Wiley also publishes its books in a variety of electronic formats. Some content that appears in print may not be available in
electronic books.

British Library Cataloguing in Publication Data

A catalogue record for this book is available from the British Library

ISBN 0470 85748 X

Produced from authors' own PDF files
Printed and bound in Great Britain by Biddles Ltd, Guildford and King's Lynn
This book is printed on acid-free paper responsibly manufactured from sustainable forestry in which at least two trees are
planted for each one used for paper production.

digital
media tools

Second Edition

Contents

Preface

This book is intended as a lab work text for use in university-level multimedia courses. Most such courses deal with the preparation and manipulation of media, as well as with the bringing of media together into a multimedia presentation. Several quite different tools are therefore involved in the practical side of these studies. This presents an unprecedented learning and teaching challenge to students and tutors. Students typically require a fast way in to a basic mastery of the complex tools which are used to put their more intellectual studies into practice. Tutors are expected to provide instruction on half a dozen or so rapidly developing programs, but existing texts concentrate on a single program, and typically contain far more information than is required by students who are not intending to specialize in that program.

In contrast, this book brings together the major software tools for multimedia in one volume, and addresses the particular needs of multimedia students at an appropriate level of detail, within the context of their broader learning. It provides a strong, well-guided, and clearly focused introduction to each tool, with the acquisition of essential skills made as straightforward as possible, without unnecessary embellishments or over-refinement. Our approach is to encourage learning by doing, but not just by slavishly copying some project we have already done. Instead, throughout each chapter, we suggest exercises that develop the physical and mental skills necessary to use the tools. Then, at the end of the chapters devoted to each application, we set a number of more demanding exercises in which those skills can be applied. Finally, at the end of the book you will find a chapter of projects, each requiring the use of several programs in combination.

We should stress that we are addressing those students whose primary interest is in multimedia, not potential specialists in any single area. This book will not make anyone an expert user of any program, and it doesn't describe every single command and operation you can use in each program, but it should provide the basic skills necessary to perform everyday tasks. These skills may serve as a springboard for later specialization, but should be adequate in themselves for multimedia generalists to be able to make work using a combination of tools. The experience gained from using tools in this way should also provide an understanding of the potential of each tool, an appreciation of the skills of specialists, and a basis for communicating with them.

The book was written primarily as a complement to our previous theoretical work *Digital Multimedia* (John Wiley & Sons, Ltd., 2nd edition 2003), but it also serves as a stand-alone text for courses with a wholly practical orientation. It has no pre-requisite in computer science, and will be of value to all students undertaking practical multimedia work. We do assume students have some experience of using a computer system and know how to use menu commands, dialogue boxes, and so on. The book has been written from experience in teaching software tools to undergraduates at all levels, and it addresses the specific conditions of student learning, as opposed to the needs of the general or professional user.

The book is arranged as follows. The introduction expands on our view of the skills demanded by digital media tools, and the best way to acquire them. Chapter 2 provides a general description of the user interface elements that are found in all or most of the programs we cover. Chapters 3 to 8 are each devoted to a single program (although most of chapter 3 on Photoshop can also be read as a description of ImageReady). Chapter 9 describes a number of features which appear in almost identical form in two or more of the programs, and chapter 10 deals with the special topic of optimizing images for use on the World Wide Web, as it is performed in several of the programs we have covered. The book concludes with the projects mentioned previously. One way of reading the book would be to start with the introduction, skim through chapter 2 to make sure you are familiar with the standard interface elements, and then read the chapters for specific applications you are interested in, turning to chapters 9 and 10 when you find cross references. Alternatively, you could read all of chapters 2, 9 and 10 before you get on to any specific application.

A few aspects of our choice of included programs deserve comment. We have entirely omitted 3D programs. Although modelling and animation in 3D is likely to become increasingly important in multimedia and the Web, at present it is of fairly specialized interest. This situation does not seem to us to merit the space it would be necessary to devote to any 3D applications, in view of the complexity and difficulty of working with such programs, and the lack of any single dominant cross-platform application. More controversially, perhaps, we have not devoted a chapter to any sound application. Instead, we have confined our treatment of audio to a description of Premiere's recently improved facilities for sound processing. Our reasoning here is similar: dedicated audio applications, of which there is no identifiable leader, are intended for professional use, and resemble multi-track recording studios, with which most students will not be familiar. To perform at their best, they require specialized hardware. MIDI, which is often dealt with by the same programs, requires some musical knowledge and ability, which we cannot expect from most students. Hence, we have dealt with sound in the context of a program that offers a more familiar interface to basic operations that non-specialists should be able to master.

Finally there is (or rather isn't) Macromedia Director. For a long time, Director was synonymous with multimedia, and its omission may seem strange. Our main reason was that, in this case, we simply felt it was not possible to do justice to such a complex program in a single chapter of a book. This feeling has been reinforced by the release of Director 8.5, which has added extensive support for 3D, which in turn has required the addition of several hundred new commands to Director's scripting language, Lingo, and has made using Director to its full potential dependent on using 3D applications to make models. Although the effect of this addition is likely to be a rejuvenation of Director, it has moved it beyond the scope of a short introduction. Instead, we have described Flash, which does many things that Director used to do, and has rapidly achieved prominence on the Web.

In most cases, there was little room for argument about which program we should use for a particular media type. Flash, Photoshop, Premiere and (slightly less compellingly) Illustrator are all the clear leaders in their field. When it comes to Web graphics matters are less clear cut. We chose to describe ImageReady, because everyone who has Photoshop has a copy of ImageReady. However, Fireworks has a claim to be taken seriously as an alternative, so we have provided a version of the relevant chapter describing this program on the Web site which supports this book at WWWWWW.

There are, of course, many digital media tools in existence besides the few we have been able to accommodate in this book. Many of them have a thriving community of enthusiastic users, but none has the status of an industry standard. We would particularly note the programs which were formerly published by Metacreations – including Painter, Bryce and Poser – but which are now mostly sold by Corel under the procreate label. (Poser is now owned by Curious Labs.) Space and the intent behind this book did not permit their inclusion, but we recommend readers who are interested in digital media to investigate them.

It probably won't escape your notice that the programs which we have included are all made by either Adobe or Macromedia. This should not be construed as any sort of endorsement of our book by these companies, or of them by us. It is just a reflection of the domination these two companies have over the media tools market. Adobe and Macromedia both provided support and assistance with this project, though, and we gratefully acknowledge their help. We would also like to take this opportunity to thank everybody involved in the project at John Wiley & Sons, especially Gaynor Redvers-Mutton and Gemma Quilter, without whom this book would not have been possible.

Nigel Chapman
Jenny Chapman

Note on the 2nd Edition

An inevitable problem with a book of this nature is that, since new versions of the programs we describe in it are released at roughly fifteen- to eighteen- month intervals, it will become outdated within a relatively short period of time. Hence, there is a need for frequent revisions. In the case of a college textbook, the problem is compounded by the fact that some departments update their software as soon as new versions are released, while others prefer to stay one version behind the current one, others stick with a particular version they are happy with, and still others only update when their funding allows them to. Thus, we really need to cater to users of at least two different versions of every software tool.

We wanted to avoid trying to describe more than one version with the same text. This would have led to a great deal of writing along the lines of 'If you have version X, do this, but if you have version Y do that', or 'In version Y but not version X, you can do this', which would be tedious and hard to follow for users of any particular version. An alternative would be to produce a brand new edition of the book covering only the latest version of each media tool, while keeping the old edition in print, so that you could choose the one that matched your requirements but that would result in neither book being guaranteed to satisfy the needs of any reader on its own.

Our research shows that there is a demand for a teaching text, so that ruled out an otherwise perfect solution – a purely electronic work, consisting of chapters covering each version of each program, from which you could assemble your own book that met your exact requirements. Although the technology to produce such a book exists, the business model to sell it and support the authors (not to mention the publishers) doesn't.

So the solution we have adopted is to augment the first edition with supplements to the chapters covering tools that have seen a significant upgrade since it was originally published. The new versions we cover in this way are Photoshop 7, Flash MX, Illustrator 10 and Dreamweaver MX. We have not produced a supplement for ImageReady 7, since although the interface has been modified, the new features that have been introduced are minor (despite the big jump in the version number), and with the Web graphics support in Photoshop and a general backlash against Web animation, ImageReady has been somewhat sidelined. Premiere has only had a minor version update, to 6.5, which we did not consider to require a supplement.

With this arrangement, users of the old versions can just read the original chapters and omit the supplements, users of the new versions can read the original chapters and supplements together, and users who update after buying the book can read the chapters first and then the supplements when they need to understand the new versions. The arrangement is something of a compromise. We have added cross-references to the supplements in the margins of the main chapters, to try and point you to the areas where you need to consult a supplement if you have upgraded. For instance, in the chapter on Photoshop, the annotation you see in the margin here would mean that if you have version 7 you should go and read the section starting on page 146 before continuing.

7

→146

One of the noteworthy aspects of the upgrades is that they are all the first versions of their respective programs to run natively under MacOS X. Given the relatively high proportion of Macintosh computers in the digital media field, it seems likely that this will have triggered a wave of upgrades from users. You will probably notice, in fact, that the screenshots in the supplementary chapters are different in appearance from those in the rest of the book. This is because they were taken under MacOS X. The differences are purely cosmetic.

If it was a software package, this edition of the book would probably be version 1.1 or 1.5, rather than 2.0, but the book trade doesn't recognize these subtleties, so it has had to be packaged as a second edition. We hope that this note has clarified its actual content.

Finally, an important note. If you own the first edition of *Digital Media Tools*, you don't need to buy this second edition. All of the supplements are available as freely downloadable PDF files from the Web site www.digitalmultimedia.org.

Introduction

Much life of the hands is a form of knowledge: not a linguistic or symbolic knowledge such as you might use to read this book or write a computer program, but something based more on concrete action, such as sculpting plaster or clay.
Malcolm McCullough, *Abstracting Craft: The Practiced Digital Hand*, p2.

If **your** experience of using software has been confined to word processors, text editors, spreadsheets, database systems or compilers, Malcolm McCullough's words might seem, at first sight, to have little relevance to computer programs and their users. However, if you think for a moment about your experience of using the programs that you work with every day, you will see that many actions that contribute to your task have been internalized to such an extent that you don't have to think about what movements to make in order to pull down a menu and select a command to save a file, for example: you decide to save the file and your hands move to do so.

There's nothing scientific about ascribing knowledge to your hands – to the extent that we understand anything about knowledge, we know that it is the province of the brain. But the 'knowledge of the hands' is more than a metaphor for the absorption of knowledge so that actions become apparently automatic. It's what it feels like. This sort of knowledge is best appreciated when we consider highly refined physical actions. The playing of a musical instrument, for example, requires that the hands know what to do. A significant stage in the learning of an instrument comes when your fingers start to move to the next note in a scale apparently on their own. In a more mundane sphere, knocking in a nail or chopping vegetables are tasks that we do not think about in any detail, although they require continuous fine judgments of position, force and movement. In fact, if you try to think about what you are doing while performing some of these tasks – where to place the knife, how hard to swing the hammer – you will become confused and clumsy, and will probably hurt yourself. Not only can you let your hands work on their own, you have to. It's only when the knowledge has been acquired in the hands – or if you prefer, when the actions have become automatic and the decisions subliminal – that you really know how to do the job. In the context of actions in the physical world, we might say that you had then become *skilful* at the particular task.

In everyday computing, typing on a keyboard is the action that most obviously exemplifies the difference between knowing and not knowing with the hands. Even though many computer users cannot touch-type in the sense that secretaries can, experienced users can move their fingers without the laborious searching and poking that characterizes newcomers and occasional users. People who are experienced with a system with a command line interface, such as Unix, will be able to type common commands (such as ls -l) as if each were a single action, not a sequence of key presses: you want to find out what files are in the current directory, and your fingers just type the command. With command lines largely superseded by graphical user interfaces, control of the system is even more obviously in your hands, since it is the movements of the mouse that make most things happen. Although the graphical interface is supposedly more user-friendly and appealing to novices than the old-fashioned command line, to watch somebody who has never used a mouse before – even an experienced computer user – try to do something as simple as open an application program from the desktop can be a painful experience. The mouse runs away, the pointer moves slowly in jerks and misses the icon, a second click follows the first too slowly to be accepted as a double-click…. Using a graphical user interface to a desktop operating system requires a non-trivial level of coordination. It is a skill.

If this is so on the desktop, consider how much more so it is when we are using programs to create images or manipulate other digital media. Because, although they are computer programs and work with digital representations composed of bits, the programs that we describe in this book provide interfaces to these abstract media that bear more resemblance to the use of physical tools to manipulate physical media than they do to the use of symbolic notations to manipulate bit patterns. If the only way to make an image on a computer was to write a program to set the values of all the pixels making up the picture, there would be very little computer graphics in the world. It is only because programs like Photoshop and Illustrator provide a means of manipulating pictures directly on the screen using your hands that designers, illustrators and artists are able to work with computers.

It has become common to refer to computer programs that perform a single job as *software tools*, but our use of *digital media tools* as the title of this book is also intended to draw your attention to the similarities between the applications used to create work in digital media and the tools used to create work in physical media. Digital media tools are devices to shape bits into images, animation, video and other forms. And although present-day computers cannot provide us with the same contact with the medium we are working with as we are used to when working with real tools and real materials, they are largely controlled by the hand, using a mouse or a graphics pen and pressure-sensitive tablet, and provide visual, if not tactile, feedback. They are tools in the sense that they extend our capabilities to let us do jobs that would be difficult or impossible without them, in the way that a screwdriver does. But they are also tools in the sense that, in order to use them effectively, we need to learn them with our hands.

It is not just the hands that need to learn the tool. The eyes, too, need training. An experienced user will see something when they look at the screen of a computer running a program they know well, which is utterly different from what a novice will see. It's almost like the difference between what somebody who can read will see when they look at this page, and what someone who can't read will see. Almost every element of a program's user interface can tell you something, once you know what they mean. It may tell you something about the state of the document you are working on, or something about what you can do next. Part of the skill of using a program lies in being able to see the whole situation at a glance, without having to look at each individual icon or palette, in the way that chess grandmasters are said to be able to see the patterns of a game's possible evolution when they look at a chessboard, instead of an arrangement of pieces.

It's as well to remember that there are important differences between using physical tools and digital tools. Malcolm McCullough once again succinctly expresses the differences in the physical relationship. '…consider the example of a skilled computer graphics artisan – if we may use this word. His or her hands are performing a sophisticated and unprecedented set of actions. These motions are quick, small, and repetitive, as in much traditional handwork, but somehow they differ. For one thing, they are faster – in fact, their rates matter quite a bit. They do not rely on pressure so much as position, velocity, or acceleration. The artisan's eye is not on the hand but elsewhere, on a screen.'[*]

There are other differences, too. A program such as Photoshop is, in some ways, more like a whole workshop than a tool. Indeed, many of the operations you can perform in Photoshop are done by clicking on an icon that resembles a tool, such as a craft knife or a rubber stamp, in a palette suggestively called a toolbox, and then dragging the tool over the image you are working on. In terms of the muscular actions you are carrying out, and the specificity of the result achieved, these individual tools are closer to a craftsman's tools than the program considered as a whole is. Nevertheless, experienced Photoshop users can wield the whole program to alter images, using each of the tools in the toolbox in a coordinated fashion, so that, to them, Photoshop itself behaves as a single tool.

But the analogy should not be pursued too far. Photoshop, and all the other programs we will describe, are just that: computer programs. We cannot always control them using movements; often, it is necessary to interact through dialogue boxes. We can set options for tools and operations, so that it becomes necessary to think about parameters. Generally, there is a good deal of intellectual and symbolic activity involved in using a program. But these are programs of a special sort, whose interfaces need approaching in a different way from those of word processors and other office software or development tools.

Above all, to learn anything useful about a media tool, you must use it, and practise its use. We can tell you what the various commands and tools do, an instructor can demonstrate them to you, but if you don't try for yourself, you won't know anything. It would be as if you tried to learn to play the guitar by reading a book or watching a video without picking up the instrument. It's true that if you had the right sort of memory, you might be able to memorize the fingering for chords and scales, you might be able to describe to somebody how to bend a string, but you would not be able to play. It's the same with any of the programs we describe in this book: until you've tried it, you can't really say you can use it. You can only really know the important things about a program once you have tried, and made them part of your experience of that program.

[*]Op. cit., p19.

More than that, you still don't really know, in the way that someone who uses these programs knows, until you have practised, and repeated the actions. Learning, and hence teaching, of this sort requires a different approach from more conventional academic learning. If this was a book about programming or the theory of multimedia, we would probably try to stretch your understanding by asking you to think about difficult things. Here, though, what we want to try and make you do is practise basic operations until you can feel them. To this end, we have included simple practise exercises throughout each of the main chapters of the book. These are not in any sense intellectually demanding; you don't have to figure anything out. They don't have right answers, or even any answers at all. They may make you feel impatient or bored and want to get on to something more substantial. You may even feel that your intelligence is being insulted. Most of the time, though, we're not interested in your intelligence, we are trying to make your hands learn to move, your eyes learn to see and your brain learn how to coordinate them. You can think of the practice exercises more as a way of saying, 'Now would be a good time to practise what we just told you,' than as a test of your understanding. There are additional exercises at the end of each of the main chapters, which begin to demand more by way of intelligence, and the projects at the end of the book will definitely require you to direct the various software tools in an intelligent way. But don't skip straight to those.

We have made two assumptions. One is that you want to learn how to use the programs we are describing to you. We expect the learning to be an active process, and we assume that you will explore for yourself: try clicking on things to see what happens, move the mouse around and see what tool tips pop up, and so on. Our second assumption is that you are possessed of some common sense, and will be able to figure some things out for yourself. If a preferences dialogue has a checkbox with the words Show Tooltips next to it (as Flash's does), we aren't going to tell you that selecting the box will cause Flash to show tool tips. But we will tell you what tool tips are.

Even if you assiduously practise everything we suggest, this book is not going to make you an expert in any of the programs it describes. Our intention is only to provide the level of knowledge that is needed for somebody working in multimedia. This means enough working knowledge to be able to turn your hand to any of the tools when you have to and enough knowledge to be able to understand what specialists and experts are talking about and to make informed decisions about what the tools are capable of and which might be best for any particular job. We stress again, though, that even the knowledge you need to make what are essentially managerial decisions about the use of media tools cannot be an abstract knowledge, it must be based on experience. If you have read that it is possible to draw round an object with a tool called the background eraser in Photoshop, in order to extract it from its background, you know that extraction with the background eraser is an operation that a Photoshop user can perform. Thinking about that, you might see when it would be a useful thing to do, and how they could go on to put the extracted object into another image, and so on. Until you've actually tried to use the background eraser, you don't know how hard or easy it is, and what you might be asking of somebody when you tell them to do it. Try it once, and you'll have some idea. Try it lots of times, and you'll know.

There is one other thing about the effective use of media tools. Like a paintbrush or a guitar, you can become highly proficient at using the tool and still produce a terrible result. We have stressed the role of the hands and eyes, but as well as dexterity and coordination you need a sense of judgement, often based on observation, and a clear idea of what you are trying to achieve. You need the intelligence to choose the right tool for the job. We can't give you these things, we can only advise you to look at a lot of work that has been made with digital media tools, and learn what is good and bad about it. Follow links from the gallery pages on Adobe's and Macromedia's Web sites, and other sites that provide links to noteworthy Web pages. See – or guess, if you can't find out – what tools have been used to create Web sites, animations and images. On the basis of what you have learned from using the tools yourself, see how the tool has shaped the work. Always be on the lookout for original ways of applying tools.

Despite the extent to which computers are used in the design industry, outside it the machines are still often thought of as inhuman and far removed from creativity. Computerization is often equated with de-skilling. Computers are programmable, though: they can be almost anything you want them to be. If you run business software on them, they will be boring and alienating; if you run media tools on them, the same machines will provide a powerful means for expression and creativity, one that requires a high level of skill. This often comes as something of a revelation. For many people, media tools provide an exciting new way of looking at computers. As you work with the tools that we have today, you may lose sight of that excitement, and become frustrated by bugs, poor response, and technological limitations. It's worth trying to see past these annoyances, to the power and potential of digital media. And if an appreciation of what could be done, coupled with frustration at what can be done, leads you to contribute to the design or construction of better tools, so much the better.

Common Features

The burden of trying to cope with many different applications when you're working in multimedia is substantially reduced by the fact that most of them have many interface features in common. To begin with, all of the media tools which we describe in this book follow the standard model for a desktop application program. That is, each one opens documents – of a type appropriate to the particular application itself – in separate document windows, where they are displayed so that you can work on them. In each program, menus provide commands, many of which have keyboard shortcuts, for making changes to the document and performing other operations; dialogue boxes containing controls such as buttons, scrolling lists and pop-up menus are used to enter parameters. Standard file navigation dialogues are used to open and save files. Documents that are saved by an application become associated with it, so in future you can open them in the application that created them just by double-clicking on the icon representing the saved file.

There are, of course, differences between the appearance and functionality of applications on the two platforms on which these programs run – MacOS and

Windows. Figure 2.1 shows the different appearance of Flash's workspace on these two platforms. [*] Despite the heated emotions these differences sometimes excite, they are largely concerned with cosmetic features, such as the system fonts and the appearance of buttons and dialogue boxes. Even the fact that the Mac has a single menu bar at the top of the screen while Windows applications provide a menu bar in each window is not significant, since the former is context-sensitive and changes when a different window becomes active. Similarly, the functions of the PC's two-button mouse are now simulated by using a modifier key (ctl) with the Mac's standard single-button. Although the ctl key is used differently on the two platforms, and the keys that correspond to ctl and alt on Windows are called cmd and opt on the Mac, this is more of a nuisance to the writers of manuals than to users.

In fact, the manufacturers of media tools (which, for the programs described in this book, means Adobe and Macromedia) have gone to some lengths to produce interfaces to their programs which are not only platform-independent but are also consistent between programs produced by the same company. Increasingly, the interfaces produced by the two companies are converging (just as, in fact, the interfaces to the two main operating systems are converging). In particular, tabbed palettes (described below) have become a standard way of organizing the often large number of functions provided by these programs. Sadly, rather than accepting this convergence of interfaces as a benefit to users, the response of the manufacturers has been to sue each other for alleged patent infringements. Despite this, it seems safe to assume that, just as windows, menus and icons have now become standard elements of the desktop interface, tabbed palettes and other features we will describe in this chapter will become established as the standard way of providing an interface to media tools.

Menus and Commands

File Menu

You are probably used to applications that behave in the way described at the beginning of this chapter. If so, you will know that commands grouped together on a File menu provide operations on files stored on disk. The File menu will invariably provide a New command to create documents associated with the application. Several of the programs described in this book allow you to create more than one type of document, and these either have several commands (New, New Project, New Site, etc.) or a New sub-menu.

---

*There are now two distinct MacOS platforms: the 'classic' MacOS (up to MacOS 9) and the Unix-based MacOS X. As far as the interfaces to the programs we describe are concerned, the differences between the two are cosmetic: different system fonts, slightly different-looking controls in dialogue boxes, and so on (although there are substantial differences in what is going on beneath the interface). The screenshots appearing in the 2nd edition's supplementary chapters were made under MacOS X, those in the other chapters under MacOS 9.

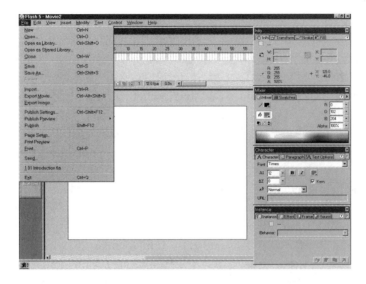

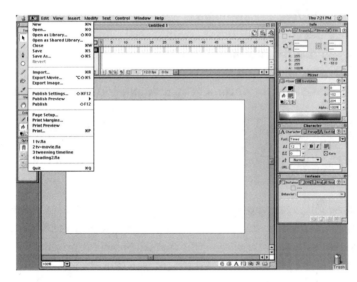

Figure 2.1   *The Flash workspace in Windows (top) and the MacOS (bottom).*

The File menu will also have an Open... command,[*] to reopen files you have saved previously, using a system-dependent standard file opening dialogue, which allows you to navigate through the directory structure to find the file you wish to open. Most programs nowadays (including all those described in this book) provide a means of opening files you have worked on recently that by-passes the Open dialogue. You will

---

[*]By convention, commands which cause dialogue boxes to open have an ellipsis (...) after their name in the menu. We have shown this wherever we mention such commands.

either find a Recent Files sub-menu on the File menu, or entries in the menu itself for each of the half-dozen or so most recent files. The feature is an invaluable one, sorely missed in programs that do not provide it. There is always a Close command on the File menu, which is used to close the current document window without saving it (although usually you are asked to confirm that that is what you want to do if there are any unsaved changes). However, every window comes with a close box in one of its top corners (its precise location and appearance are system-dependent) which provides a more convenient way of closing any window, including document windows.

The File menu is where the all-important Quit command, used to exit from the program, is located. The Save As... command can also be found on the File menu; it is used to save a file to disk while giving it a new name via a dialogue which is standard on each platform, and allows you to navigate to the folder where you want to save the file. The Save command is used to save a file to disk under its existing name. So, the usual pattern of using an application is to start it up, use File>New to create a document, then File>Save As... to store it safely on disk. You then begin working on the document, using the facilities your application provides, and saving it frequently using the Save command. You quit the application when you need to take a break, then start it up, open the file again, and continue working on it at a later date. When you have finished, you may need to export the document in a suitable format for its ultimate use.

> ☞ Start up each of the media tools programs you are going to learn. Pull down the menus to see what commands are provided. Find the standard commands on the File menu. Create a new document and save it under a suitable name. Close it and reopen it. Quit the program.

Many media tools create more than one type of file. For example, Flash creates *Flash movies*, which are the files that record the structure of a project so that you can edit it, but it also creates *Flash Player movies*, which are the real end-product, being the files that can be played in Web browsers. In a different vein, Photoshop can create images in many different file formats, as well as its own native format in which documents are saved by default. Two mechanisms are usually employed for saving files in different formats. The File>Save As... command causes an extended version of the standard dialogue to be displayed, which not only lets you choose the name under which to save your file and the location to save it in, but also lets you choose a file type. Figure 2.2 shows a typical example from Photoshop: a pop-up menu is used to select a file type. The other mechanism is to provide an explicit Export... command on the File menu. The resulting dialogue is similar: Flash provides an example in Figure 2.3. Whichever mechanism the application employs, we will refer to saving in this way as *exporting* a file in a certain format. Quite often the actual outcome of your work with a media tool will be an exported file, not the main document. For example, Premiere exports movies in various digital video formats. The file that is saved by the File>Save command is the project, which is a container for all the elements that are assembled to make the final movie.

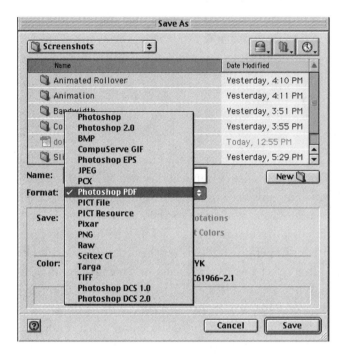

Figure 2.2   *Exporting via* Save As... *in Photoshop.*

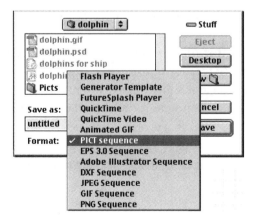

Figure 2.3   *Exporting via* Export Movie... *in Flash.*

As well as exporting files, media tools often *import* them, too. Again, there are two cases. Most applications allow you to use the File>Open... command to open files in formats other than their own. For instance, Photoshop will open image files in a host of different formats. It normally converts them to its own format when you save the document. It is also possible to import a file of some type so as to incorporate it into another document that is already open, rather than open the file in its own document window. For instance, Flash provides an Import... command on its File menu, which is used to bring data from files into a movie. Among other things, you can import a series of still image files, and they will be added to the movie as consecutive frames of the animation.

Edit Menu

The File menu is a standard interface component of every desktop application. The other standard menu that all such applications are supposed to provide is the Edit menu. At the very least, this menu should provide three commands: Cut, Copy and Paste, which are used to transfer data between a document and the clipboard. Again, this should be familiar to you from using word processors and similar applications. The Edit menu commands operate on the current selection in a document.[*] In a word processor, you often select a word, a sentence or a paragraph by clicking or dragging with the mouse. When we are dealing with media data, selection may be not be such a straightforward process and usually requires the use of specialist tools. However, every application allows you to make selections somehow, whether you are selecting characters in text, pixels in an image, frames in an animation, or whatever, and having done so, you can use the Edit menu commands on the selected data. The Edit menu usually provides a Select All command which allows you to select everything. Deselect, to select nothing, is also commonly provided, though it is not quite universal.

Edit>Cut removes the selection from the document and places it on the clipboard – a temporary storage space provided for the purpose – from which it can subsequently be retrieved using Edit>Paste, which copies the contents of the clipboard into the document. Edit>Copy copies the selection to the clipboard without removing it from the document. Precisely where pasted data is placed depends on the application – for some sorts of data, it isn't always obvious where it should go. You use the Cut, Copy and Paste commands to move and duplicate elements of a document. Most applications

---

*In a well written application they will also work on selections in text fields inside dialogue boxes.

also allow you to use *drag-and-drop* for this purpose, though sometimes the nature of the data makes this more complicated than it is in simple text applications.

> ☛ Verify that all the applications you are using provide the standard commands on the Edit menu. Practise cutting, copying and pasting. Observe whether the pasted data appears where you expected it to.

One other command that just about every application provides is Preferences..., which gives you access to various controls that affect the appearance and behaviour of your application. Interface guidelines for Windows and classic MacOS suggest that the Preferences... command should be on the Edit menu, but some applications put it on the File menu. Under MacOS X the Preferences... command will be under the application menu at the left of the menu bar. Naturally, the preferences you can set are highly dependent on the nature of the particular application, but the principle of using a Preferences dialogue to customize applications is one that is universally employed. For the most part, we will not describe preference settings in this book, assuming that you will start out using the defaults, and work out how to change them for yourself as you become more experienced. Preference settings persist until they are changed again, but changes to certain settings in some applications (for example, the scratch disks in Photoshop) will not take effect until you quit and restart the program.

> ☛ Open the Preferences dialogue in each application. See how many of the preference settings have evident meanings. Change any that don't suit you.

Some commands that you might expect to find on an Edit menu, on the basis of your experience with word processors and text editors, are concerned with searching: Find..., Find Again, and so on. These commands are rarely found in media tools (the major exception being Web design applications, such as Dreamweaver) because not only is searching in images, video and animation technically difficult, it is also rather difficult to define what to search for and what it means to find it. Hence, most media tools only provide specialized types of search. For example, Photoshop allows you to search for all pixels of a specific colour and Illustrator lets you carry out conventional text searches in any text that you have added to a picture. The commands to carry out these searches are not generally found in the expected place in the Edit menu.

Help Menu

Sometimes, an application's Help menu can be the most important menu of all. All Adobe and Macromedia programs now include an 'online help' system, which provides access to the full manuals on your computer. (This sort of online help system does not require connection to the Internet.) This offers more than the convenience of being able to bring up a manual on your screen while you have the application working in front of you. Increasingly, Adobe in particular are omitting sections of programs' documentation from the printed manuals, instead referring readers to the online version, which is the only complete documentation. (They have not yet gone as far as other software manufacturers, who no longer include printed manuals at all. However, if you are using a program under a site licence – for example, in a college – there may only be one copy of the printed manuals for the whole institution, so the online versions are invaluable.) Both companies now use HTML and other Web technologies to present the online manuals. Selecting a command from the Help menu launches your Web browser to display a welcome page and an outline list of the manual's contents. The precise command varies: Adobe favour Help Contents..., while Macromedia prefer the title of the manual, such as Using Flash.

The presentation and facilities are much the same, as shown in Figure 2.4. The manual is shown in frames. A scrolling list displays the chapter titles; clicking on a title reveals section headings, and clicking on a section name causes the first page from the corresponding section to be displayed in the main frame. Navigation buttons let you move forward and backwards within each section. As a compensation for having to read the manual on a screen, you are provided with extra means of accessing information. By clicking on the appropriate control, you can cause the index to be displayed as a set of hyperlinks, or start a search for a keyword. If you have used a Web browser before, you should not have any difficulty using the online help systems.

☛ Open the help systems for several applications. Practise using the navigation controls. Look up 'opening files' in the index. Search for some terms you would expect to be defined in the particular manual.

The use of 'online' to mean 'on the computer' in the expression 'online help' is somewhat old-fashioned. Usually, we think 'online' means 'over the Internet'. Additional online help in this sense is also available. You can visit the appropriate support sites directly, but it is also possible to reach them using commands chosen from the Help menu. Again, applications produced by both manufacturers offer similar, but slightly different, facilities. They all have menu entries which cause your Web browser to be launched and go to a support page – sometimes only one main page, sometimes a choice of sub-pages. Some also provide a special interface to the Internet resources that is activated within the application itself.

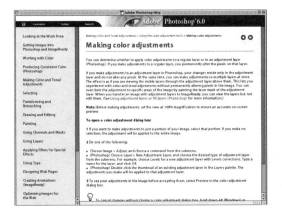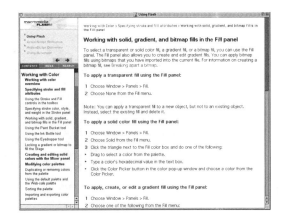

Figure 2.4   *Adobe (left) and Macromedia (right) Help systems.*

Macromedia call the interface they have developed for Flash the *Macromedia dashboard*. It is nothing more than a SWF movie that displays links to useful Internet resources for the application, with a bit of motion graphics to liven it up (see Figure 2.5). The dashboard movie is updated every month, which means that it can include links to details of relevant current events, such as conferences, and new technical notes and patches. Clicking on the Update button while you are connected to the Internet will load the latest version for you.

Figure 2.5   *The Macromedia dashboard in Flash.*

Adobe's equivalent, *Adobe Online*, which is available in all their applications, is a rather more sedate affair, as Figure 2.6 shows, but it provides the same function of giving access to useful links directly from inside the application. Like the Macromedia dashboard, Adobe Online can be updated to obtain the latest links. Both Adobe Online and the Macromedia dashboard launch your Web browser to actually display the pages that they download.

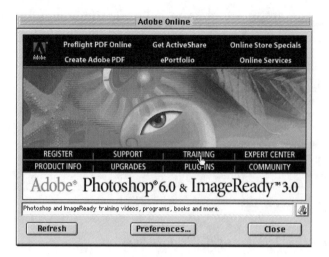

Figure 2.6   *Adobe Online in Photoshop.*

Among the Internet resources you can access, either directly or through the mechanisms embedded in the applications, are technical notes for each application. These are among the most valuable sources of information, since they often cover techniques that are not obvious from simply reading the manual, and provide news of updates and work rounds for bugs.

For it must be admitted that media tools are not exempt from bugs. Revisions to operating systems also lead to incompatibilities, so it is necessary for patches and updates to be applied from time to time, between version releases. The Web is now used extensively to distribute such updates. (Cover CDs on magazines such as Macworld are the other main distribution channel for updates.) It pays to keep an eye on the support sites for your media tools, and ensure that you have the latest versions.

☞ Visit the support sites for each application, using the commands on the Help menu to get there. Investigate the resources that are provided. If you maintain your own system, download any updates necessary to ensure that your programs are up to date. (If you have a system administrator, try to persuade them to do this for you.)

There are also newsgroups, mailing lists and online forums dedicated to every application. These can sometimes provide a useful source of help, but the signal-to-noise ratio is usually extremely low. The most useful forums are those to which technical support staff from the manufacturers contribute. You will find that there are those that do, and those that do not.

An additional source of help within the programs themselves is provided in the form of *tool tips*. A tool tip is a small label which pops up when the cursor is held over a tool or some other control element for a few moments, to tell you what it does. In most media tool applications, moving the cursor over almost any object on the screen which would make something happen if you clicked on it will cause a tool tip to be displayed. This can be invaluable – there are so many controls in each of the several programs you are likely to find yourself working with that sooner or later you are going to forget what clicking on some icon does.

☛ Move the cursor around the workspace of each application. See where tool tips appear. Become familiar with their appearance, and practise making them pop up. (If they don't appear, check that some preference has not been set to turn them off.)

Keyboard Shortcuts

Another universal feature of desktop applications that is shared by media tools is the use of *keyboard shortcuts* as an alternative to menu commands. Once you know what you are doing, it is quicker and less likely to lead to repetitive strain injuries to type [cmd/ctl] O instead of pulling down the File menu and selecting the Open... command. For the standard menu commands, there are standard shortcuts, which, apart from the use of a different modifier key, are the same on Windows and MacOS: [cmd/ctl] X, [cmd/ctl] C and [cmd/ctl] V for the standard clipboard commands on the Edit menu, for example. It is common practice for program developers to assign keyboard equivalents to other commonly used menu commands, and the use of these rapidly becomes second nature.

In many media tools the use of keyboard shortcuts is taken much further, with shortcuts being provided for many operations besides menu commands. In particular, in programs that provide tools for drawing and painting, including Photoshop, Illustrator and Flash, it is possible to switch between tools by typing a single letter instead of clicking on the tool's icon. This is much faster and allows you to leave the cursor where it was when you switch tools. It is also easier if you are using a graphics tablet and pressure-sensitive pen, which, although superior tools for drawing, can be rather clumsy and erratic for making menu selections and so on. Many professional users employ keyboard shortcuts almost exclusively. However, in an application with many different tools and commands it can become difficult to remember all the shortcuts, particularly if you don't use one program all the time. (It doesn't help that keyboard shortcuts are not always well documented. Indeed, some of them are only known to insiders.) Here again, though, programs are converging, with the same shortcuts being used wherever the same function is provided. For example, typing t will switch to the type tool in Photoshop, ImageReady, Illustrator and Flash.

☛ Find out where the keyboard shortcuts for your applications are documented. When you come to use any program in earnest, practise using keyboard shortcuts as an alternative to menu commands and other operations.

Despite the fact that if you become proficient in any of the media tools described in this book, you may well use keyboard shortcuts all the time, in our descriptions we have generally omitted them, since beginners will find it easier to use the menus and toolboxes most of the time.

Context Menus

One of the few user interface innovations made by the Windows operating system is the use of menus which pop up when the right button on the mouse is clicked, to provide immediate access to commands which are relevant to the object or window being clicked on. Such context-sensitive menus, usually simply called *context menus*, also became available on the Mac with the introduction of MacOS 8, using the ctl modifier key with the standard single-button Mac mouse. Figure 2.7 shows some of the context menus that pop up in different parts of the workspace in Premiere. (Of course, you can only have one context menu popped up at a time in reality.) Fairly fine distinctions between contexts are drawn: the two menus shown in the long window at the bottom are different, because in one case the click occurred in an empty space, and in the other, it was over an audio clip. In a program that provides tools the context menu displayed will take account of the currently selected tool. If the system of context menus is well designed, it should be the case that the commands that pop up in some part of the screen are those you are most likely to want to use in that context.

All the applications described in this book provide context menus. However, it is almost never the case that a context menu is the only place you can find a certain command. Some users never use context menus at all, while others rely on them as their primary means of invoking commands. In our descriptions, we will omit any reference to context menus, but if you like them you should find that the commands we describe as being on the menu bar or in palette menus can also be found by right-clicking or ctl-clicking in the appropriate context.

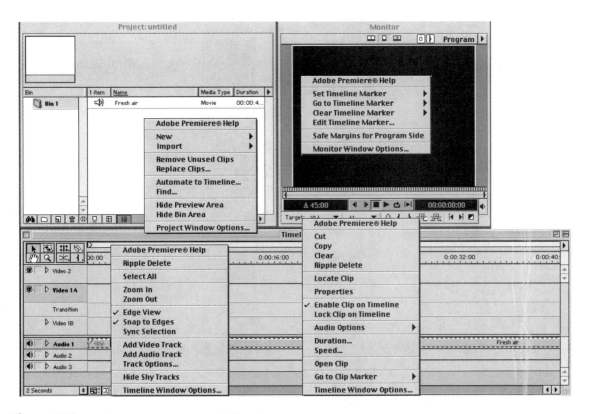

Figure 2.7 *Some context menus in Premiere.*

Tools, Toolboxes and Object Palettes

Selecting Tools

The metaphor of using tools to work on a document is a pervasive and intuitively appealing one. We are used to using tools (in a broad sense) such as pens, pencils, brushes, scalpels and so on when making work with physical media. The idea that you make a mark on an image by picking up a brush and dragging it over the picture is so familiar that it would be hard to imagine a different way of thinking about the process. In digital media, though, we cannot pick up physical objects. All we have for interaction with the program is the keyboard and mouse, or a graphics tablet and pen, at best.

Icons, grouped together into a floating window called a *toolbox* are used to stand in for physical tools. To pick up a tool, you click its icon in the toolbox. (Or, as we described earlier, use a keyboard shortcut.) Often, the cursor changes its appearance when you do

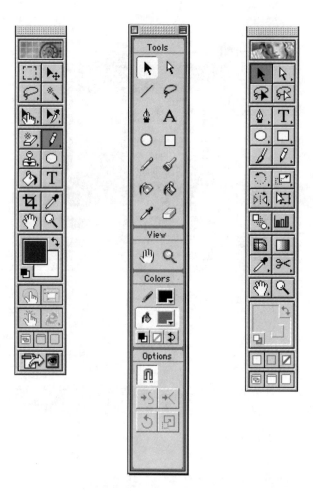

Figure 2.8   *The toolbox in ImageReady (left), Flash (middle) and Illustrator (right).*

so, to indicate which tool you are using at the moment. With the tool thus selected, you usually drag it in the document window to make a mark, or a selection or some other sort of change; the precise movement and its effect varies from tool to tool. Some movements resemble those you would use with physical tools, while others are uniquely digital. For example, to make marks with a brush in Photoshop you just drag the brush where you want the mark to appear, like a real brush; to draw a rectangle in Illustrator, you drag the rectangle tool from the point where you want one of its corners to be to the point where you want the diagonally opposite corner.

Figure 2.8 shows a few toolboxes from different applications. Notice that some of the same icons appear in all of them: the use of conventional symbols to stand for tools performing the same or similar functions is another way in which programs' interfaces have converged. Naturally, the use of familiar icons makes it easier to work with several different programs. Note also that some icons are immediately suggestive of the tool's function – brushes and pencils make marks, scissors cut, erasers erase – while others are purely symbolic and must be learned – what would you expect an arrow to do if you didn't already know?

☛ Compare the toolboxes in those programs that use one. Note which tools appear in more than one of them. Try to guess what each icon stands for. Make each tool's tool tip appear to see whether its name offers any further clue. Practise selecting different tools.

In order to keep toolboxes down to manageable proportions, it is sometimes necessary for some tools to share locations. That is, the icon for one tool is displayed, but holding down the mouse button while the cursor is over that tool will cause a menu to pop up, showing other related tools. (This convention is presently confined to Adobe products among those described in this book.) Figure 2.9 shows an example. Tools which conceal others in this way can be identified by the small rightward-pointing triangle in the bottom right of their icon in the toolbox. When you choose a tool from a pop-up menu, its icon replaces that of the tool that was originally shown in the toolbox – to access the original tool again you must make the menu pop up.

☛ Find all the tools in toolboxes which conceal others and make the hidden menus pop up. Practise changing between the different tools that share one location in the toolbox.

Objects

The tool metaphor doesn't always work. As we have seen already, some operations are naturally performed by menu commands. Others can be thought of in terms of placing an object of some sort on the document. This metaphor is especially popular in Web design software, where there is a multiplicity of types of object that can be added to a page. It is also used in some video applications to add transitions and other effects to a movie.

Objects are represented by icons held on a palette, and are added to a document just by dragging and dropping. If an object needs any parameters – for example, the name of a file – a dialogue box may be displayed when it is dropped on the document, or it may be necessary to set the parameters in a palette associated with objects of that type.

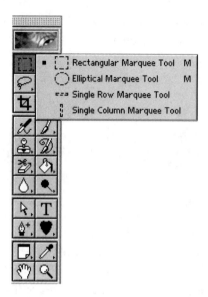

Figure 2.9   *Displaying hidden tools.*

Figure 2.10 shows Dreamweaver 4's object palette. Notice that there is a pop-up menu at the top, which allows you to select different classes of object. Also notice that the meaning of most of the icons on the palette is far from obvious. Tool tips are of great assistance here.

Figure 2.10   *Dreamweaver's objects.*

Tabbed Palettes

Many operations that you carry out in a program require *parameters* – values that affect how the operation is carried out. For instance, if you want to add some text to a document, you must choose a font to set it in: the font name is a parameter. Typically, parameter values are entered in text boxes, chosen from pop-up menus, or turned on or off using checkboxes and radio buttons.

There are two broadly different ways of allowing a user to enter parameters. The first is to use a *modal* dialogue box. A modal dialogue box will have a button, usually labelled something like OK, which you must click to dismiss the box and apply the values you have entered in it. Figure 2.11 shows an example. Until you click OK, you cannot do anything except change the values in the box. While you are interacting with the dialogue, the program is in a different mode (entering parameters) from its normal mode when you interact with the document. The alternative to modal dialogues is to use some *modeless* element. This may be a dialogue box, but it is distinguished from a modal one by the fact that you can leave it open while you are working on the document, and return to it when you need to. There may or may not be a button that causes values you have entered to be applied, but even if there is, clicking on it will not close the box, as it would with a modal dialogue. If there isn't, it is usually sufficient to make a choice from a menu or set of checkboxes or radio buttons, or to move the cursor out of a text field to cause any value just entered to be applied.

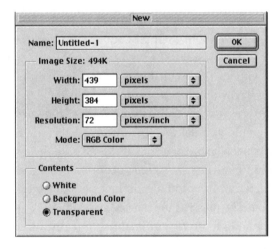

Figure 2.11   *A modal dialogue box.*

There is evidence from studies in the field of human-computer interaction (HCI) to suggest that users, especially novices, find modal dialogues confusing. The trouble with modeless alternatives is that they quickly clutter up the screen. *Tabbed palettes*[*] have

---

[*]In Flash and Dreamweaver, palettes are called *panels*, possibly in an attempt to avoid the litigation referred to on page 8, or perhaps to avoid confusion with colour palettes.

been developed as a form of modeless dialogue that is easy to manage and keep under control.

Tabbed palettes come in sets, which share a window. Figure 2.12 shows a typical example (from Illustrator). The window as a whole can be treated like any other: dragged to move it around the screen, minimized or closed using the controls in the title bar, or resized by dragging out its bottom right corner. The individual palettes are revealed by clicking on the tabs along the top of the window.

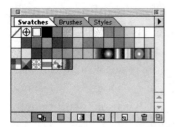 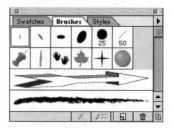 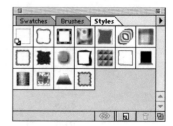

Figure 2.12   *A set of tabbed palettes.*

The arrangement of palettes into sets is not fixed. You can customize your workspace in any application by dragging palettes by their tabs out of their windows. If you let go while the dragged palette is in the window belonging to a different set, it joins the new set. It is said to be *docked* with the other palettes in the set. If you drop it anywhere else, it appears in a window of its own. In this way you can organize your palettes so that their grouping reflects the way you work with them. You can hide palettes you are not using just by closing the window containing them; you can also control their visibility using commands on the Window menu, which is available in all the applications in this book. Note that if you hide a palette using a menu command, all the palettes it is docked with will be hidden too. You can hide all the palettes by pressing the tab key, and then bring them all back by pressing the tab key again. In every application except Illustrator there is a command on the Window menu to reset the palettes to their original locations.

☞ Practise using and organizing tabbed palettes. In any application, bring each palette in a set to the front. Drag one palette out of a set; dock it with a different set. See what happens if you drag a palette out of a set and then back in. Hide and reveal individual palettes. Hide all the palettes, noting which interface elements remain. Put the workspace back in its original state.

Palette Controls

In the top right corner of every tabbed palette you will find a small right-pointing triangle. Clicking on this causes a pop-up menu, known as the *palette menu* to appear. Here you can find commands that are related to the functions performed by the controls on the palette. Sometimes, these are duplicates of commands found on the main menu bar, or controls on the palette itself. In other cases, the palette menu provides the only way of carrying out some operations. The function of the palette menu is to group together all the relevant operations in one place. (You may never use it, but it's as well to know it's there.)

☛ Practise making palette menus pop up. Note the commands that you find there, and see whether you can find them on some other menu.

In some applications, a pair of arrowheads can be found in the palette's tab. These are used to hide and reveal parts of the palette. (Although there are two arrowheads, they work as a single control.) Clicking on them causes the palette to cycle through different states, in which an increasing number of input elements is displayed. Figure 2.13 shows how ImageReady's Optimize palette changes as these controls are repeatedly clicked. Most palette menus have a command Show Options which works in a similar way, changing to Hide Options when the full palette is displayed. Unlike the arrowheads in the tab, the palette menu command only provides two different states, with a set of options hidden or revealed, respectively.

☛ Practise using the palette options controls for those palettes which have them. Use the palette menu to show and hide options, noting what is considered to be an option in each case.

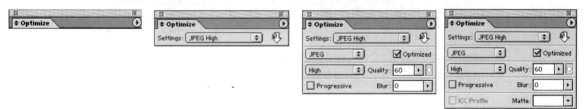

Figure 2.13　*Showing palette options in ImageReady.*

An important class of palettes is used to hold collections of things – layers, styles, swatches, actions and frames, among others. There are some operations that make sense for any palette that is used in this way, in particular, creating a new thing and deleting a thing. These palettes provide buttons along their bottom edges for quickly performing these operations. The palettes shown earlier in Figure 2.12 are all examples which include these buttons.

The New button is used to make a new entry in the collection, that is, a new layer on the Layers palette, a new style in the Styles palette, and so on. (The icon is supposed to represent tearing a new sheet off a pad of paper, we think.) The dustbin icon (or trash can, if you prefer) is used to delete an item. You can select the item in the palette and then click on the dustbin, or you can drag the item on to the bin. In Adobe applications, the difference is that in the latter case you will not be asked to confirm that you really want to delete it. (Macromedia applications don't bother to ask anyway.)

> ☞ Identify the New button and dustbin on any palettes that have them in each of your applications. Practise creating layers, styles, etc., and deleting them.

The Options Bar and Palette Well

Photoshop 6 and ImageReady 3 use a refinement of the usual tabbed palette interface, which will probably be incorporated into other media tools in the near future. An area called the *options bar*, shown in Figure 2.14, appears at the top of the workspace. (It can be moved to a different position by dragging the handle at its left end.) Controls and input fields appear in the options bar, as they do in palettes. The options bar is context-sensitive and displays options for the currently selected tool. In effect, it serves the same function as whichever tabbed palettes are associated with that tool. For example, the type tool's options can be set on the Character and Paragraph palettes; when you select the type tool, all the most commonly used typographic parameters can be set on the options bar instead. This means that most of the time you can hide all the palettes and just use the bar. (Press tab to hide everything, then select Show Options from the Window menu.) Where there are options on the palettes that don't fit on the bar, as in the case of text tools shown here, a button is provided to show the palettes.

> ☞ In Photoshop, select several different tools in turn and note how the options bar changes. Practise hiding all the palettes and displaying the options bar alone.

Figure 2.14   *The options bar in Photoshop 6.*

Flash uses the space at the bottom of its toolbox to present controls that alter the behaviour of the selected tool. You can see an example in Figure 2.8, where the buttons at the bottom of the toolbox allow you to set options for the way in which the selection

→49

tool behaves. The use of buttons in a restricted space means that these options are sometimes rather cryptic.

The dark grey area shown at the right hand end of the options bar in Figure 2.14 is called the *palette well*. This provides a means of keeping palettes available while still minimizing the space that they occupy on the screen. You can drag palettes and drop them in the palette well, in the same way as you drag them to palette windows to dock them. The palettes' tabs appear in the well, as shown on the left of Figure 2.15. When you click on a tab, the full palette pops up in place, as shown on the right of Figure 2.15. After you have finished using the palette, it pops back again, so it is only taking up space when you are actually interacting with it.

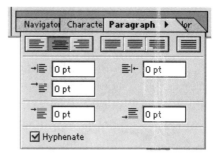

Figure 2.15   *The palette well.*

You can drag palettes back out of the palette well when you don't want them there any longer, or use the Window>Reset Palette Locations command to put everything back in its original place.

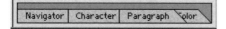
Practise dragging palettes into the palette well and making them pop up.

The reason for going to all the trouble of providing the options bar and palette well is that modern media tools all use a large number of palettes: Photoshop's dozen is about average. These all take up screen space and on a small monitor can easily obscure most of the main document window. A large monitor is really a system requirement for working with any of these tools – one capable of supporting a resolution of 1024 by 768 is an absolute minimum. A popular option on systems which have the capability is the use of two monitors, one using a relatively low resolution to hold all an application's palettes, the other, with a higher resolution to hold the document window. (The monitor with the palettes doesn't have to be particularly good quality; for image editing, the other should be as good as possible.)

History and Automation

Media tools provide considerable scope for making mistakes. As well as the usual slips of the hand, it is possible to make aesthetic misjudgments which need to be put right. The long-established method of making corrections is the Undo command. This is so well established that, like Cut, Copy and Paste it has a standard place in all conventional programs, in the Edit menu, and a universal keyboard shortcut: [cmd/ctl] Z. It does not have a universal semantics, though.

To be more precise, using the Undo command twice in a row does not have a universal interpretation. Does the second Undo undo the first, or does it undo the command before the one that the first Undo undid? In other words, do two Undo commands take one step back and then one forward, or two steps back? Taking the first view means that you can only ever undo one command. A single level of Undo like this, while it is popular with programmers because it is easy to implement, is unpopular with users, who usually want unlimited Undo levels. The second alternative, which provides this, is now more widespread, at least in media tools, and its absence is usually a source of users' grievance. Truly unlimited Undo is not possible, because of the finite size of even the biggest computer's memory, but in practice a hundred or so is usually enough to seem unlimited. Notice that if you have unlimited Undos you need a Redo command to undo an Undo. This, too, appears in the Edit menu, but there is no universal keyboard shortcut: shift-[cmd/ctl] Z and [cmd/ctl] Y are both popular, though other combinations are sometimes used.

In carefully written programs, the menu entry for the Undo command will change to show what will be undone if you select it. For example, in ImageReady, if you make a mark with the airbrush tool, the menu will change to Undo Airbrush. If you had done some drawing with the pencil before you picked up the airbrush, it will change to Undo Pencil if you undo the airbrush. At the same time, the command Redo Airbrush will appear, to show you what will happen if you want to undo the Undo. When you have gone so far back in undoing that there is nothing left to undo – which usually means as far as the last time you saved the document – the menu command changes to Can't Undo as well as being greyed out in the conventional way.

As well as allowing you to correct mistakes, Undo can be used as a way of judging the effect of some change you have made: make the change, then repeatedly undo and redo it, to get a quick impression of the state of the document before and after the change.

> ☞ Go through your applications and check how the Undo command operates in each one. Practise making some changes and then using Undo and Redo to judge their effect.

As a sort of emergency fall-back, programs also provide a Revert command on the File menu. Selecting this command causes any changes you have made since the last time you saved the file to be discarded (after you have confirmed that that is what you want to do). The effect of the command is simply to close the document without saving and then reopen it from disk.

History Palettes

It may come as something of a surprise to find that, by default, Photoshop only provides a single level Undo.[*] For many years that was all it provided, but since Photoshop 5 there has been an alternative mechanism for reversing the effect of changes to an image: the History palette. This has proved so popular and successful that it is being incorporated in some form into nearly every other media tool. (Flash and Illustrator are currently the exceptions among those we cover here.)

The basic idea behind the History palette is a simple one: it provides a record of each of the commands that you have executed. Figure 2.16 shows an example from ImageReady. History runs from top to bottom: the first thing that was done to this image was to make a selection with the rectangular marquee, then some levels adjustments were made, and so on. The latest operation shown is the application of a Resize Image command. Next to the entry for this command you can see a cursor. This is draggable, and by dragging it you can, as it were, turn back time, and revert to any of the previous states. Alternatively, just click on an entry in the History palette to return the image to the state it was in when the corresponding command was executed. In the instance shown in Figure 2.16, clicking on the entry for Rectangular Marquee would take you back to the point where you made the selection with that tool, undoing the Levels adjustments, the creation of a new layer and everything that followed after.

Usually, when you go back to an earlier state, it is because you wish to do something different instead of what is shown in the History palette. As soon as you make a change

---

[*]You change the behaviour to a multiple undo using the Redo Key pop-up menu in the general preferences dialogue.

Figure 2.16   *The* History *palette.*

after returning to an earlier state, any later states in the palette are destroyed. (As in tales of time travel, if you go back and change history, the present will end up different. In the History palette, though, this does not lead to a paradox.) If you make no changes, you can run forwards and backwards through the history, reviewing all the steps you have taken.

The History palette as described merely provides a shortcut for a series of Undo or Redo commands. This is actually more useful than it may sound, since each time you pick up a tool or perform a single operation with it, a new history state is created. For example, if you are erasing pixels in Photoshop, every time you release the mouse button you have, as far as Photoshop is concerned, carried out a new operation. Usually, erasing a detailed area is done using many such small operations, so if you wanted to reverse the effect of all your erasing, it would take many Undos. With the History palette, you can go back to the situation before you picked up the eraser with a single click. (Some operations, though, such as zooming in or rearranging the palettes are not added to the history, but you can't use Undo to reverse them, either.)

☛ Open an image in ImageReady and make some changes to it – adjust the levels, add a new layer and paint on it, and so on. Look at the History palette and see how your actions have been recorded. Practise going back in history to earlier states of the image. Carry out a similar exercise in other applications with History palettes.

The number of steps that are remembered in the History palette is limited, though. It is surprisingly easy to pass its capacity simply by a series of erase or paint actions, and then you can't get all the way back to the point before you started. You can increase the value using a preference, but you should realize that the more states you save in the history, the more memory will be needed.

Photoshop's History palette – the original of the concept – is actually more sophisticated than the imitators which have followed it. At any time, you can create a *snapshot* of the state of a document, using the New Snapshot... command on the palette menu. A snapshot is like a history palette entry except that it does not get destroyed if you return to an earlier state and make some changes. So, for instance, you might resize an image, adjust its levels, take a snapshot, return to the state where you resized it and have another go at adjusting the levels. If you decide that your first attempt was more successful, you just click on the snapshot to return to it. If you had not taken the snapshot, the state of the image with the first set of adjustments would have been lost when you made the second set. You can also use snapshots when you are making many detailed changes to an image, to preserve states which would otherwise be lost when the history overflowed. In this case, you take a snapshot whenever you think the image is in a state to which you might want to return. As Figure 2.17 shows, snapshots appear at the top of the palette, separated from the history proper, and a snapshot is automatically created by default corresponding to the state of the image when it was first opened.

☛ Practise taking snapshots in Photoshop and using them to remember history states which you feel it might be useful to return to.

Figure 2.17   *Photoshop's* History *palette, with snapshots.*

History states and snapshots are not saved with a document, so once you close a document you have lost the chance to go back. In Photoshop, though, you can create a new document from a snapshot (using the New Document command in the History palette menu) and save that, to provide yourself with alternative versions to reopen later.

Automating Repetitive Tasks

You sometimes find yourself performing the same task over and over again. This may just be the simple job of downsampling an image to 72dpi from some higher resolution, which you might need to carry out on a collection of a hundred files, or it may be a more complex sequence of operations, such as the alignments needed to centre a box around some text or draw a standard shape, which will be required many times in the course of a single project, such as the production of a set of diagrams for a technical book. It can get very tedious going through the same dialogues, typing the same value again and again.

Computers are well known to be good at performing repetitive tasks. With the exceptions of Flash and Premiere, currently, all the media tools in this book provide some way of recording a sequence of operations, saving the recording and playing it back.

The most elegant solution – although it is limited in what it can do – is Dreamweaver's.[*] The History palette has a button at the bottom labelled Replay, which executes any commands that are selected in the history. Figure 2.18 shows an example: the series of commands that is highlighted has the effect of inserting a horizontal rule (line) with default attributes in a document, then setting its width and height to new values, left aligning it and adding a paragraph break after it. Taken together, these commands insert a hairline rule (or the nearest thing to it that HTML provides) into the document. With the whole sequence selected as shown, clicking on the replay button will have the effect of adding another hairline rule. As you see, it also adds a Replay Steps entry to the history; undoing the Replay Steps entry undoes all commands contained in it, in a single step.

This is all very well, but since the history is lost when you close the document, you cannot replay the insertion after you reopen it; nor can you use it with a different document. For those occasions when you want to be able to use reuse some operations over a period of time, or in many different documents, you can save a sequence of

*The same mechanism is used in Fireworks, which is described on the Web site for this book.

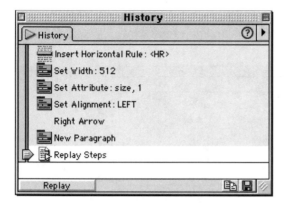

Figure 2.18 *Replaying history in Dreamweaver.*

history states as a command, by selecting them and choosing Save As Command... from the History palette menu. You can give your command a name, such as Insert Hairline Rule in this example, and subsequently it will appear in the Commands menu. It stays there permanently, even after you quit the program. (Choose Commands>Edit Command List... and use the resulting dialogue box to remove the command if you no longer need it.)

Commands which are applied to the current selection, such as Set Alignment, can be applied to different objects by selecting the object and then using the Replay button. For instance, if you wanted to set the size of a rule to 1pt, but leave its width as it was, you could insert the rule in the normal way, select it, and then select the Set Attribute and Set Alignment steps in the History palette and replay them. There is, however, no other way of parameterizing a recorded action. That is, whenever you play steps back, they are performed exactly the same way as they were when you first recorded them, with all the same settings. There is, for example, no way of making a command that inserts a rule, then asks you for the width, before setting its size and alignment.

☞ When you are familiar with using Dreamweaver, create a document and type a paragraph of text. Replay the actions from the History palette to make a copy of the paragraph. Select some words and set them in a different font at a larger size. Select some different words and set them in the same way by replaying actions from history. Save the actions to set words in that font at that size as a command, and use it to set the characteristics of some more text. Experiment further with replaying history, paying particular attention to how the current selection interacts with the replay.

Photoshop, ImageReady and Illustrator use a more elaborate method of recording actions, which does accommodate the use of parameters. The basic operation is not really different from Dreamweaver's, except that a separate Actions palette is used to record the steps to be replayed, and you must explicitly start and stop recording.

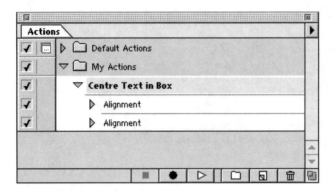

Figure 2.19   *The* Actions *palette in Illustrator.*

Figure 2.19 shows the Actions palette in Illustrator. Within the palette, actions are grouped into sets, which makes it easier to manage large numbers of them. Each application that provides an Actions palette comes with a set of default actions, which perform tasks that are widely used but not available as primitive commands on the menus. In Illustrator, for instance, the Default Actions set includes actions to export an image for the Web using several common combinations of optimization settings, set the transparency of a selected object to several useful values, reflect an object in the horizontal axis, and so on. You create new sets of actions by clicking on the New Set icon at the bottom of the palette. When you click on the standard New button, the dialogue shown in Figure 2.20 lets you give your new action a name and optionally assign a function key (with modifiers, if you wish) to it, so that you can replay it with a single keystroke. Otherwise, actions can be replayed from the palette, as we will describe shortly. In this example, we chose to use shift-F5 to trigger the command called Centre Text in Box.

After you click the Record button in the New Action dialogue, everything you do is recorded in the Actions palette, in the same way as it is in the History palette, under the heading for your new action. Figure 2.19 shows two alignment commands being recorded as part of the Centre Text in Box action. When you reach the end of the sequence that performs the desired action, you stop recording by clicking on the Stop button at the left of the bottom of the palette. (The three leftmost buttons here imitate the form and function of VCR or tape recorder controls.) You can then replay the action by selecting it and clicking on the Play button. (If you prefer, you can use commands on the Actions palette menu to create and record the action.) You can modify the

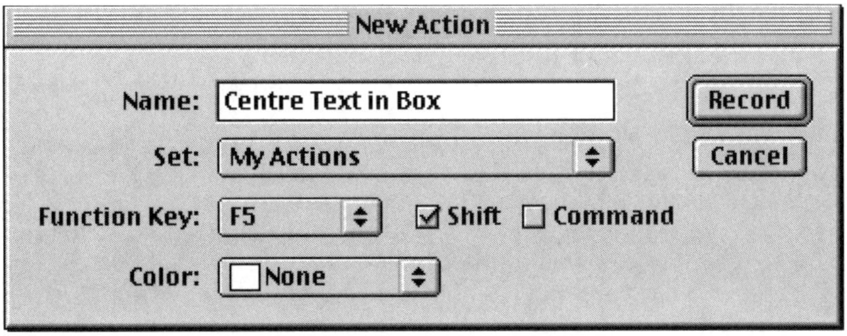

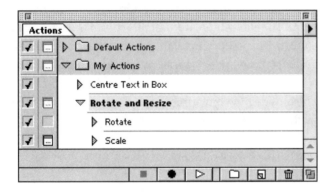

Figure 2.20   *Creating a new action.*

behaviour of an action by leaving out some steps: the tick marks in the boxes in the column at the left of the palette indicate the steps that will be included, by default all of them. To omit some steps, just untick their boxes.

Figure 2.21   *An action that displays a dialogue box.*

So far, then, the Actions palette is little different from the replayable History palette in Dreamweaver. The difference comes when you include commands in your action that bring up dialogue boxes. Suppose we recorded an action by rotating an object by 30° and scaling it down to 70% of its original size. By default, if we select another object and play back the action, it will be rotated and scaled by the same amount. However, if we click on the checkbox in the second column next to the Scale operation, this icon appears in it, as shown in Figure 2.21. This indicates that when the action is played back, the dialogue box associated with scaling will be displayed, so that we can enter a new factor to scale by. The rotation will be left at 30°, since the box is not checked for the Rotate step. In this way, you can create actions that have parameters, for which dialogue boxes will be displayed.

> ☞ Record an action in Illustrator by drawing a hexagon and setting its fill colour and stroke weight and colour. (Make a bright pink shape with a thick green outline, for example.) Play back the action to make another. Now, check the dialogue box option for the step where you drew the polygon. Play back the action, entering a new value for the number of sides, to make a triangle with the same fill and stroke. Practise creating similar parameterized actions in both Illustrator and Photoshop.

The little triangles next to entries in the Actions palette can be used to hide or show members of a set, hide or show the individual steps of an action, and hide or show details of each step, such as the values of any parameters that you set for it. You can delete individual steps, whole actions or complete sets of actions, using the dustbin icon.

Photoshop takes automation a stage further, by allowing you to apply the same action to a collection of files. The File>Automate>Batch... command lets you choose an action and apply it to all the files in a folder, or all the files you have open in Photoshop, saving the changed documents or saving new versions to a new folder under new names, whose form you can specify. The dialogue for setting up a batch action is shown in Figure 2.22, which should show how simple it is to process a set of files with a single command. This facility is invaluable to serious Photoshop users, but it has the potential to corrupt or overwrite a lot of files at once, so it should be approached with caution and we do not advise its use for beginners.

Layers

The concept of layers originally appeared in Photoshop 3, and has since become all-pervasive. Layers are popular because they allow you to perform complex operations, in particular compositing,[*] while at the same time being intuitively easy to understand.

Layers are pure metaphor: a layer is like a thin sheet of transparent acetate, on which an image has been placed. Layers can be stacked on top of each other and in the transparent areas the images on layers beneath them show through. You can build up a complicated composition by superimposing different elements on different layers. Separating elements on to layers in this way makes it easier to isolate them when this is

---

[*] 'Compositing' is the combining of two or more separate images using selective or partial transparency to create a single composite image.

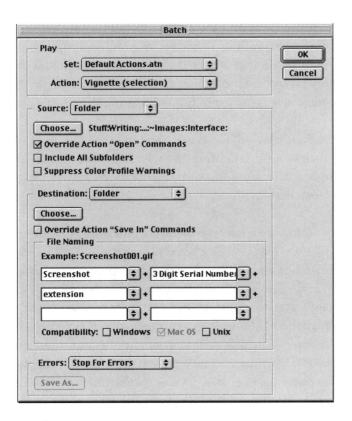

Figure 2.22 *Setting up a batch action in Photoshop.*

necessary. It is also possible to combine layers in more complex ways than simply superimposing their images on top of each other. For example, in Photoshop you can make images on two layers dissolve into each other. Since layers can be duplicated and selectively hidden, they also provide a means of making experiments by making different changes to different copies of a layer.

The metaphor of layers has been so successful that it has been applied even in areas where it is not really an accurate model of what is going on. HTML documents are not composed of separate superimposed layers, for example, but Web design software, including Dreamweaver, allows you to deal with absolutely positioned elements in a document as if they were independent layers. Photoshop has extended the layer metaphor in another direction, by allowing you to create 'adjustment layers', which behave like a special sort of acetate that distorts or transforms everything underneath it. (See page 115.)

Functionally, video tracks behave like layers, too, but they are based on a different metaphor deriving from traditional video editing and compositing, so we will not include them in this section. It is interesting to note in this context that Flash and After Effects both present compositions (movies) as layers, even though they are built on a timeline and might more logically be seen as tracks.

We describe the detailed use of layers in each of our applications in the appropriate chapter, since each uses them in distinctive ways, but some features are common to them all. In particular, facilities to manage a collection of layers are fairly uniform across all the programs.

The Layers palette is used to show you the layered structure of a document, and to allow you to add new layers, copy or delete layers or rearrange them in a new stacking order. Figure 2.23 shows the Layers palette in several different programs. ImageReady (which is identical to Photoshop) and Illustrator are basically the same, although there are detailed differences resulting from the different types of image these programs work with. A thumbnail image of each layer's contents appears besides its name in the palette. Dreamweaver's palette is quite a lot simpler, because of the underlying simplicity of the HTML constructs that it presents as layers. At the bottom right you see how layers are represented in Flash's timeline window, here performing essentially the same function of managing layers as the Layers palette does in the other programs.

In layered documents you always have at least one layer, of course. To add layers you can just click the New button at the bottom of the Layers palette. It is a good idea to give each layer a name that indicates what it contains, because in a document with a hundred or so layers (by no means an uncommon sort of document) it isn't very helpful to have the layers just called Layer1, Layer2,… as they are by default. In every program we are describing except Photoshop, you double-click the layer name in the palette – Illustrator and ImageReady then present you with a dialogue box, while Flash and Dreamweaver let you type the new name *in situ* – but in Photoshop you must hold down [opt/alt] while you do so.

At any time one layer will be the current, or active, layer – this is the layer on which you can draw or paint or whatever it is that the application you are using allows you to do. Any new elements you add to your document will be added to the current layer. In programs that provide a Duplicate Layer command, usually in the Layers palette menu, it is the current layer that is copied to make a new one. If you click on the dustbin icon, the current layer is deleted.

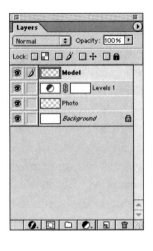

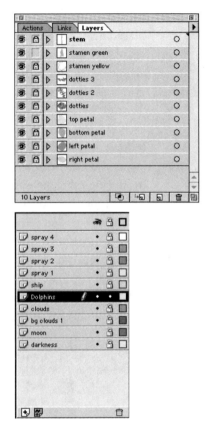

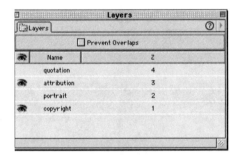

Figure 2.23   Layers *in (clockwise from top left) ImageReady, Illustrator, Flash and Dreamweaver.*

The current layer is usually highlighted, as you can see in Figure 2.23. (The Dreamweaver example shows no current layer, since none is selected.) You can make a layer current (or select it, as it is more usual to say) by clicking on its entry in the palette. If you make a selection of some element in the document window, the layer it is on automatically becomes selected too. Beware of accidentally making a layer current in this way, and then forgetting to switch back to the layer you were working on – check the Layers palette to make sure that you are working on the layer you think you are.

The order in which layers are stacked – their *z-ordering* – naturally makes a difference to the composite image that is produced. You can rearrange your layers by dragging them up and down in the palette.

All applications allow you to hide layers. In Figure 2.23, you can see an icon representing an eye in a column next to some or all of the layers in each of the palettes, except for the Flash timeline, where the eye is at the top of the column and dots are placed next to the layers. The presence of an eye or a dot by a layer shows that it is visible. It can be made invisible by clicking on that icon. Invisible layers can be made visible by clicking in the column where the eye appears. Hiding layers serves many purposes. The first, which may seem slightly frivolous until you have got lost in a document with dozens of layers, is to find out what is on each layer, and which layer each element is on, by observing what disappears when you hide it. Layers can also be hidden to get things out of the way so that you can see clearly what is on the layer or layers you are currently working on. Hidden layers allow you to experiment, by producing different versions of a layer and then making each one visible in turn to see which looks best, or by choosing different combinations of layers to try different compositions. Some users like to duplicate a layer when it reaches a certain stage of development, then hide it and go on working on the duplicate, keeping the hidden layer as a record of an earlier stage. Finally, a layer may be used during the creation of an image – as a tracing image or the source of a pasted element – without appearing in the finished result. It is sensible to hide such layers instead of deleting them, in case you need to go back to them.

☞ In every program that you are using, practise creating layers and placing objects or artwork on them. Try hiding individual layers, or hiding all layers but one. Duplicate a layer and make some changes to it, then try hiding each of the versions in turn to see how the changes affect the result. Experiment with moving layers up and down in the Layers palette to change their *z*-ordering.

You can usually lock layers, which prevents you from making any changes to them. This is a good thing to do once you are satisfied with a layer, because it is only too easy to select a layer accidentally. A padlock icon is used to show that a layer is locked. In Flash and Illustrator, the padlock works to denote a locked layer the same way as the eye denotes a visible one. In Photoshop and ImageReady, there is a slight difference because these programs provide a more elaborate locking system: each of three aspects of a layer can be locked separately, by selecting from the checkboxes along the top of the Layers palette. Checking the last box, with the padlock, locks everything in the more conventional way. In these programs, the padlock denoting a locked layer appears to the right of the layer's thumbnail (see, for instance, the ImageReady Background layer in Figure 2.23). The padlock may be black, to indicate a fully locked layer, or grey, to indicate a partially locked one.

Zooming and Navigator Palettes

Beginners sometimes overlook the fact that media tools let you work on a document at different magnifications. If you need to make precise adjustments to an image by eye, it is easier to do so accurately if you blow it up so you can see exactly what you are doing. (In fact, trying to make adjustments visually without blowing up the image is one of the most common ways of producing a sloppy result.) Since the size of your monitor is fixed, zooming in like this necessarily means that you can only see a smaller part of the document. Sometimes you therefore need to zoom out and work at a lower magnification so that you can fit an entire document into the window and see it all at once.

All programs that work primarily with images (including Flash) provide Zoom In and Zoom Out commands on a View menu to increase or decrease magnification in fixed steps. The keyboard shortcuts [cmd/ctl] + and [cmd/ctl] - are used by all programs. (Actually, + is a shifted = key on standard keyboards, but you don't have to hold down shift to zoom in. Flash, therefore, correctly, but not necessarily helpfully, shows the shortcut for Zoom In as [cmd/ctl] =.) You can also enter exact magnification factors numerically by typing a percentage in a field, usually at the bottom left corner of the document window, which always shows the current magnification. Flash also provides a pop-up menu from which you can choose one of a number of fixed magnifications, and most applications give you some way of choosing a magnification that makes best use of the available screen space: View>Fit On Screen in Photoshop, View>Fit In Window in Illustrator, and View>Magnification>Show Frame in Flash, for example.

> ☞ Open a document in an application that supports zooming and practise zooming in and out, and making changes at different magnification levels. For example, try erasing a small area in Photoshop or moving an arrowhead until it exactly touches the edge of a circle in Illustrator, at several different zoom levels. Try to get a feel for the appropriate magnification for different purposes.

It's possible to get lost in a document. For example, suppose you are working on a drawing in Illustrator and the objects that you are drawing only occupy a small part of the artboard (the notional piece of paper on which you are drawing). If you zoom in to work on the part of the image at very high magnification, it is perfectly possible to find yourself looking at a blank window, because all the objects are on parts of the artboard that isn't displayed. (It is harder than you might think to ensure that the area of interest is always in the middle of your window when you zoom.) You can then spend many fruitless moments scrolling back and forth vertically and horizontally in an increasingly desperate attempt to find some recognizable shape. A similar thing can happen in Photoshop, and in Premiere too, where you can lose yourself on the timeline.

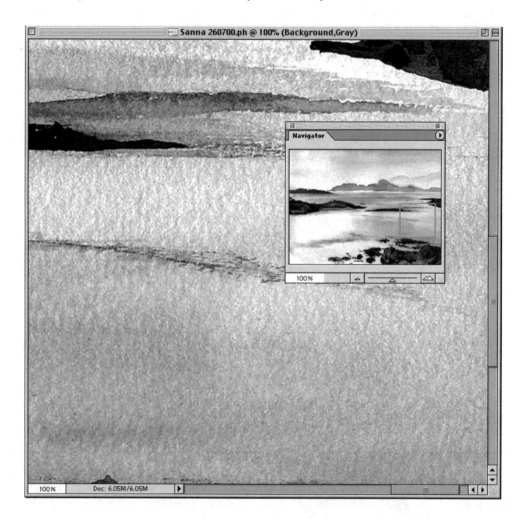

Figure 2.24   *The* Navigator *palette superimposed on the document window in Photoshop.*

To avoid such occurrences, Illustrator, Photoshop and Premiere all provide a Navigator palette. Figure 2.24 shows Photoshop's, with the document window corresponding to it behind, which may help you appreciate the need for the Navigator. The palette displays a thumbnail of the full image, no matter how much of it is visible in the document window – you can increase or decrease the thumbnail's size just by resizing the palette. The rectangle (it's actually bright red) that you can see towards the bottom right corner in the navigator is called the *proxy preview area*, and it shows you which part of the image is visible in the document window at the current magnification.

You can move the image in the document window in two ways from within the Navigator palette. Either drag the proxy preview area so it encloses the part of the picture you want to display, or click on a point in the thumbnail: the proxy preview area will jump so that it is centred on the point where you clicked.

The controls at the bottom of the Navigator palette provide an alternative way of zooming in and out. The two buttons with double triangle icons duplicate the Zoom In and Zoom Out commands on the View menu. The slider between them allows you to zoom continuously in either direction – the document window updates in real time as you do so. Alternatively, you can enter a percentage value in the field at the bottom left, just as you can in the document window.

> ☛ Open an image in Illustrator or Photoshop and observe how the Navigator palette changes as you zoom in and out. Drag the proxy preview area around to display different parts of the image in the document window. Zoom in to the maximum magnification, identify a feature of the image in the navigator thumbnail, and bring it to the centre of the document window.

Illustrator's Navigator palette is identical to Photoshop's, but Premiere's is slightly different, because it controls the display of the timeline, not of any image. Therefore, it only shows a schematic representation of each of the video and audio tracks, as shown in Figure 2.25. Dragging the proxy preview area scrolls the timeline in its window, and the zoom controls at the bottom of the palette only alter the length of each frame as it is shown in the timeline, and have no effect on their height. Instead of setting a zoom level in the input field in the bottom left corner, you can enter a timecode to position the proxy preview area and the timeline display numerically.

ImageReady does not provide a Navigator palette and Macromedia applications do not presently offer an equivalent.

Integration

Since you are likely to be using several media tools in the preparation of a single multimedia production, it is vital that they be able to exchange data. In practice, the extent to which this is possible varies considerably. Some programs can only read files in a few specific formats and can therefore only exchange data with programs that can

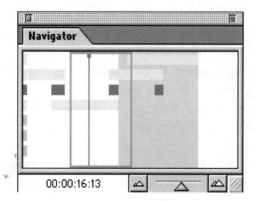

Figure 2.25 *The* Navigator *palette in Premiere.*

write in those formats, while others are fully integrated, to the extent that double-clicking an image or some other object in one application will immediately open it in another.

Even when we just consider the simple import of files, there is some variation in the extent to which programs can handle each other's formats. For instance, many programs claim to be able to import Photoshop files, but not all of them will preserve the layers, even if the importing program does support layers itself. Another way in which the exchange of files between programs may fall short of your expectations is in the version of the file format supported. Flash 5, for example, can import Illustrator files, but only up to version 6, so files that depend on facilities from later releases of Illustrator cannot be imported. In a similar vein, many programs can export SWF files, since SWF is an open file format, but usually the version they support lags one behind the current release of Flash.

Photoshop and ImageReady are integrated to the extent that clicking on a button in one of them will switch to the other with the same document. There is no need to save it to a file and then explicitly open the file in the other program. Any changes made in one program are reflected in the other when you switch back, so in effect all the Photoshop tools and commands are available to the ImageReady user, and vice versa. (The drawback to this sort of integration is that both programs must be running at once, and since each on its own requires a non-trivial amount of memory, they can only be run together on a machine with a substantial amount of RAM. At the time of writing, 256MB is a minimum; as time passes and the amount of RAM fitted as standard to machines increases, you can be fairly confident that the memory requirements of media tools applications will increase as well.)

In some cases, the nature of the data being manipulated by your programs will limit the extent to which it can be exchanged between them. Vector graphics and bitmapped images are fundamentally different, so it is not possible to simply open an Illustrator file in Photoshop, or vice versa, and expect to be able to edit it. If you import a bitmapped image into a vector graphics program, it will be treated as an indivisible object, which you can only work on in restricted ways. If you import a vector image into a bitmapped application, it will be rasterized, that is converted to a bitmap at a fixed resolution, and will no longer be capable of being treated as a collection of vector objects.

Web design programs offer a different sort of restriction. Usually, they only support the embedding of images in GIF, JPEG or PNG formats, since these are the only formats that most Web browsers can display unaided. At the same time, it is particularly useful to be able to double-click an image inside a Web design program and have it opened by an image editing program, since it is usually impossible to do any editing of images inside the Web application. Dreamweaver allows you to do this, but restricts you to the Web image formats. You can use any image editing program, but if you use Dreamweaver's companion Web graphics application Fireworks to prepare your images, it will open the original version of the image (a PNG file, since this is Fireworks' native format) when you double-click an optimized version (for example, a JPEG) that you have added to your Web page.

Adobe's Web design program GoLive does the same sort of trick, but in the opposite direction, as it were: you can embed Photoshop and Illustrator files in a Web page while you are constructing it, and open them in their parent application just by double-clicking. When you save the Web page as HTML, the images are converted to a Web image format (see Chapter 10) and optimized.[*]

As well as being integrated with each other, most media tools are integrated to some extent with Web browsers, reflecting the importance of the Web as a delivery medium for multimedia. The usual arrangement is to supply a button with a pop-up menu attached to it, or menu command with a sub-menu, showing all the browsers on your system, or that you have made known to the program via a preference setting. Choosing one of these causes the document you are working on – a Web page or an image – to be saved to a temporary file, which is immediately opened in the designated browser. Because of the idiosyncrasies of Web browsers, being able to preview images, in

---

[*]Fireworks and GoLive are not covered in this book, but Fireworks is described in an alternative version of Chapters 4, which can be downloaded from the companion Web site.

particular, without having to save them and create an HTML document to hold them is a considerable convenience.

Customizing

Most users of media tools, particularly novices, will be happy to use them just as they are, but all of the programs can be extended to provide extra facilities, and some of them can be extensively customized to provide a different interface.

The most widespread mechanism for extending applications, pioneered by Photoshop, is the *plug-in*. A plug-in is a software module, traditionally written in C or C++, which follows certain conventions so that it can be loaded by the main application when it starts up, called from within it and pass information to and from it. Usually, plug-ins are used to allow programs to import or export files in formats that are not otherwise supported, or to implement special effects that the program does not provide itself. Once a plug-in has been installed – usually just a matter of dragging it to the Plugins sub-folder of the application's folder – its name appears as a command in an appropriate menu. Selecting the command invokes the plug-in's code.

Generally speaking, when a plug-in runs, it opens a modal dialogue box to receive input from the user. What happens in that box, and what is done with the input, is up to the plug-in writer. Many plug-ins look just like built-in filters and import modules; others provide complex, sometimes unconventional, interfaces, which make them appear to be different applications running inside the program that called them. In fact, though, plug-ins must rely on the host program to make any actual changes to the document.

Plug-ins are obtained separately from the application itself, and often cost a substantial fraction of its price – although some perfectly good plug-ins are free or distributed as shareware at a nominal price. Writing and selling plug-ins has become a small industry in itself. Software Development Kits (SDKs) are available for each of the main applications. These provide documentation explaining the conventions that plug-ins must follow and the ways in which they can communicate with and control the host application, together with sample code to illustrate the construction of plug-ins of each of the types that the program supports.

A recent development is the use of JavaScript, XML and other Web technologies to provide extensions to programs, especially Web design programs. This approach, which means that you don't have to be a skilled programmer to extend your application, was pioneered by Dreamweaver. Almost all the elements making up Dreamweaver's user interface are described by HTML or XML documents. For example, the structure of its menus is defined by an XML document, from which the menu bar and the individual menus are constructed when the program starts up. By editing this document, it is possible to move commands to different menus, rename the menus and the commands on them, and add, remove or change keyboard shortcuts. Other aspects of the program's appearance and behaviour can be changed in a similar way.

Dreamweaver can also be extended with new commands or by adding new objects to its Objects palette (see page 22), since commands are implemented in JavaScript and can call methods on objects in the Dreamweaver Document Object Model, which allows scripts to control the application. Objects consist of some HTML which is added to the document when you insert an object, and a GIF image which provides the icon for the Object palette.

Dreamweaver can only be customized and extended so easily, using technology that will be familiar to many Web experts, because it already includes an HTML rendering engine and a JavaScript interpreter (it has to, it's a Web design tool) so it may not be so easy to provide a similar extension mechanism in other programs. Nevertheless, allowing knowledgeable users to customize their programs is one way in which software producers can make digital tools more comfortable for people who have to work with them every day, so it is to be hoped that the trend will continue.

Of course, you might make a terrible mess of everything. If you are going to try customizing an application, make sure you always keep a backup of any files you are going to change, so that you can get back to the standard configuration if things go wrong.

2a Macromedia MX Interface Elements

The set of upgrades to Flash, Dreamweaver and Fireworks released during the first half of 2002 all carry the suffix MX instead of a conventional version number. This is intended to emphasize that the programs can be considered as an integrated family of tools for Web application development. (The family also includes ColdFusion MX Server, for server-side scripting and integration with databases.) In practical terms, the most noticeable sign of this integration is an improved uniformity among the user interfaces of the three applications. Where it makes sense, they share the same tools, which can be found in the same place in the toolbox, and the same keyboard shortcuts. At the same time, a couple of interface innovations have been introduced into all three programs.

The Property Inspector

As we describe in Chapter 7, Dreamweaver has always had a context-sensitive *property inspector*, which changes depending on what you have selected in the current document. This concept has been extended and introduced into the other MX applications. (In the Window menus of these programs, the property

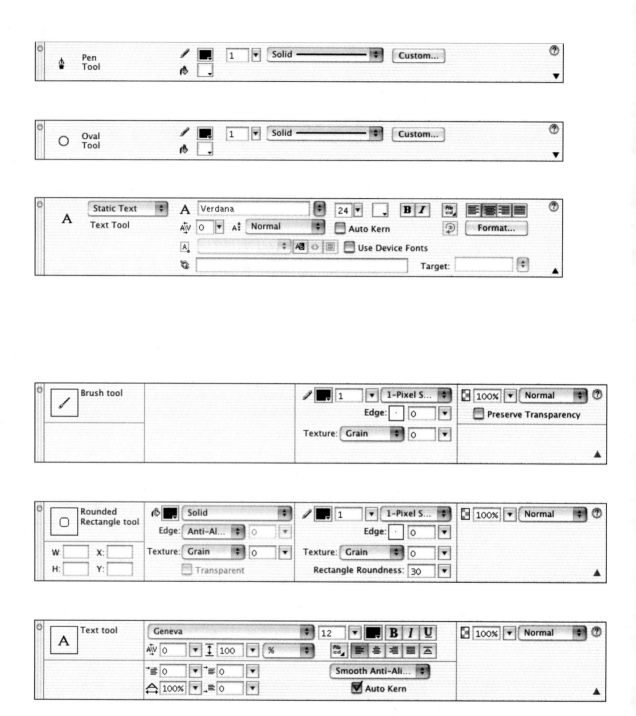

Figure 2a.1 *The Property Inspector displaying tool options in Flash MX (top three) and Fireworks MX (bottom three).*

inspector is identified as Properties.) Whenever you select a drawing or painting tool in Flash or Fireworks, the inspector shows an appropriate set of options for that tool. Figure 2a.1 shows some examples. This use of the property inspector to set tool parameters resembles the options bar found in Photoshop, and described in Chapter 2. Note that, in addition to options for the tool's behaviour, such as blending mode and transparency in the case of the brush tool, the inspector is used to set stroke and fill properties, so that separate panels are no longer required for this purpose. Similarly, when Flash MX's text tool is selected, character and paragraph attributes and text options can be set in the inspector, thus doing away with three of the panels found in Flash 5.

If you use one of the selection tools to select an object, the inspector displays the properties of the selected object – this is essentially the way Dreamweaver's inspector has always worked. Figure 2a.2 shows some examples in Flash MX, where the information that in earlier versions was displayed in the Instance, Frame, and Sound panels is all now shown in the inspector. As with the text tool, the use of the inspector here has removed the need for three panels. Together with the new design of dockable panel sets, described in the next section, the reduction in the number of panels that the inspector permits can save a fair amount of screen space.

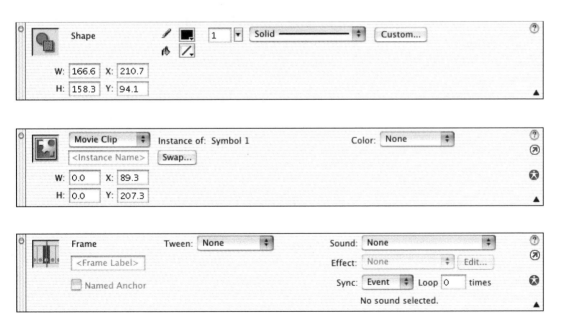

Figure 2a.2   *The Property Inspector in Flash MX with a shape (top), clip instance (middle) and frame (bottom) selected.*

Whether it is displaying tool options or object properties, the property inspector is divided horizontally into two panes so that it can show two levels of detail where this is appropriate. Figure 2a.3 shows the inspector for the paint bucket tool in Fireworks, at the top, with all the possible parameters displayed. By clicking on the upward-pointing triangle in the bottom right corner of the inspector, the lower pane is hidden, again saving screen space, as seen at the bottom of Figure 2a.3. The less commonly used Texture parameter can be revealed by clicking the triangle (which turns upside-down when the panel is collapsed). Figure 2a.4 shows the two states of the inspector when a shape has been selected; again some information which is less likely to be required can be hidden to save space. This method of hiding and showing the more esoteric properties is available whatever tool or object is selected, although sometimes the lower pane will be empty.

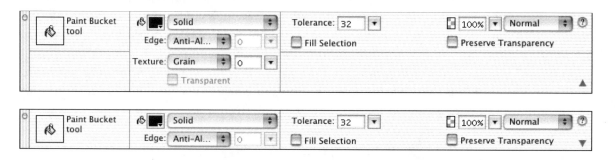

Figure 2a.3   *Displaying and hiding tool options in the Property Inspector.*

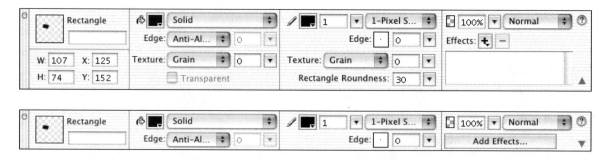

Figure 2a.4   *Displaying and hiding object properties in the Property Inspector.*

There is an inevitable problem with using the inspector for both tool options and object properties, which is that it cannot be used to display options for the selection tools: whenever a selection tool is active, the inspector is being used to show the properties of the selection. This is only really a problem in Flash, where, as we explain in Chapter 5, the arrow tool is also used for distorting objects. For this special case, the tool options are displayed in the options area at the bottom of the toolbox, as they were in Flash 5. (There are fewer options in Flash MX than there were in Flash 5, because a free transform tool has been added to the toolbox.) Although it is not strictly necessary (there could be separate tools) the same expedient is used to select magic wand options for the lasso tool.

> ☞ Thoroughly investigate the property inspector in Flash MX and/or Fireworks MX. Select each available tool and practise setting its options in the inspector. Create and select objects, and practise using the inspector to view and change their properties.

Dockable Panels

All the MX applications use a variation on the device of tabbed palettes, as described in Chapter 2. Despite the claim that all of these programs provide a uniform interface, there are actually small differences in the behaviour pf the panels in each of them. We will start with the most simple case, which is Flash MX.

Here, the difference between MX panels and the tabbed palettes found in Adobe applications and previous versions of Flash, is that each set of docked panels is arranged vertically, with their headings displayed, instead of horizontally, with tabs. The default configuration of panels in Flash MX is shown on the left of Figure 2a.5, which should make this clear. As you can see here, an advantage of this arrangement is that you can see more than one of the panels in the set at once. In fact, usually, all the panels you use can be arranged as a single set. Panels can be hidden or displayed by clicking on the triangle to the left of the panel name. The collection of panels in Figure 2a.5 is shown on the right after all the panels have been closed in this way. They don't occupy much screen space, but any panel can be accessed with a single mouse click. Although this arrangement takes a little while to get used to, it is at least as convenient as the more conventional approach.

> ☞ Practise hiding and displaying panels in Flash MX.

MX panels have the same features as other palettes, although the controls look a little different. You can drag an individual panel out of its set, but you must drag on the area to the left of the disclosure triangle, called the *gripper*. You can also drag a panel into a set, and, unlike tabbed palettes, you can rearrange panels by dragging them to a new location within the panel set. A set of panels can be resized by dragging its bottom right corner. When more than one panel in a set is open, individual panels can be resized by dragging the bar that separates it from its neighbour. The cursor turns into a pair of

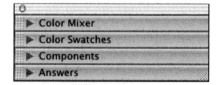

Figure 2a.5   *MX panels.*

arrows when it is over the divider. As one open panel is dragged larger, other open ones shrink to accommodate the expansion within the same total size.

> ☞ Drag a panel out of its panel set and back in again. Move a panel to a new position in its set.

Each panel has a panel menu, which pops up when you click on the icon at the right-hand end of the title bar. Although the icon looks different from the more familiar triangle used in other programs, the panel menu functions in the same way, to provide commands that are related to the operations provided by the panel.

In Dreamweaver and Fireworks, panels are slightly more elaborate, since each panel as described so far can itself be a set of tabbed panels. Figure 2a.6 shows this: the titles Design and Layers and Frames each refer to a collection of panels, with conventional tabs. When you click on the disclosure triangle for either of these panels, the entire set is hidden or displayed, as shown on the figure. The individual sub-panels work much like the familiar tabbed palettes with which you are familiar – clicking on a tab brings the attached panel to the front – except that docking them has to be done slightly differently to fit in with the behaviour of MX panels. You can't simply drag a tab; instead you must use the panel menu. When a tabbed panel, Frames, for example, is at the front of its set, the panel menu will have a sub-menu titled Group Frames With, listing all the sets of panels. If you choose one of these, the panel is moved to the corresponding set. You can also use the panel menu to give a new name to a panel set – this might be necessary after you have regrouped some panels in such a way that the old name (e.g. Layers and Frames) is no longer appropriate. In Dreamweaver, but not Fireworks, a context menu, displayed when you [right-click/ctl-click] on a panel tab, duplicates the panel menu.

> ☞ In Dreamweaver MX and/or Fireworks MX, find all the panels which have tabs. Practise bringing tabbed panels to the front. Move a tabbed panel to a different panel set and rename the set.

The Answers Panel

The Flash dashboard described in Chapter 2 has been superseded by the new Answers panel, which has been added to the interface of the other MX applications too. To begin with, the panel looks like Figure 2a.7, with a Learning... heading and three topics. Clicking on What's New plays a simple movie within the application, which highlights the new features; clicking on Readme displays the application's Readme file; clicking on Tutorials displays the tutorials from the online help system. When you click the Update

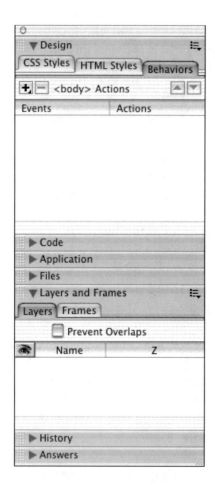

Figure 2a.6   *Tabbed panels within MX panels.*

button, if you are connected to the Internet, additional information is downloaded, and the panel's appearance changes. A pop-up menu is added, as shown at the top of Figure 2a.8, from which you can select different sets of information, as shown below in Figure 2a.8. After you have made a selection, you can click on one of the displayed titles, and your Web browser will be used to display the corresponding page from Macromedia's support site. As you can see from the example at the bottom left of Figure 2a.8, you can also search the site from within the Answers panel. The panel is just an interface to this site, which allows you to navigate it from within the application itself instead of using its own navigational structure within a browser.

☛ Investigate the use of the Answers panel in any MX application and assess its usefulness.

Figure 2a.7   *The* Answers *panel.*

Figure 2a.8 .   *The* Answers *panel after updating.*

Photoshop Bitmapped Images

Files and Formats Summary

Create documents with File>New and save them with File>Save As... (by default, as Photoshop – PSD – files).

Open image files using File>Open, in a wide range of formats, including GIF, JPEG, PNG, TIFF, PDF, BMP and PICT, and save to any of the same formats using File>Save As....

Scan images into Photoshop using a plug-in, usually supplied with the scanner.

Extract images from PDF files using File>Import>PDF Image....

Export optimized GIF, PNG and JPEG files using File>Save for Web....

Common Features
Used By This Program

Photoshop is the leading – we could even say the standard – program for retouching, editing and compositing bitmapped images. It is probably true to say that, of all the applications described in this book, it is the most difficult to master. This is not because of the sheer number of features it provides, although there are many, but because of the ways in which these features interact and must be used in combination to achieve the results that Photoshop is capable of. This is a program that offers little in the way of instant gratification. In fact, the newcomer to Photoshop may be hard put to see just exactly what all the fuss is about. Once you have played with some of the distortion filters and grown tired of the juvenile effects which these lend themselves to, there are few immediately understandable operations that you can perform – changing the size and resolution of images is perhaps the limit of the intuitively obvious. It is only by experience coupled with a certain amount of understanding of how bitmapped images can be manipulated that you come to realise why so many graphic designers and other visual artists working in digital media rely on Photoshop and rate it so highly.

There is a popular misconception that computers make life easier by automating tasks that must otherwise be performed by hand. While there are programs that take that approach, Photoshop is not one of them. It is not its business to provide shortcuts and quick solutions. Instead, it provides powerful tools to manipulate digital images that are equal to, or exceed in power, traditional darkroom tools used for photographs. Photoshop's tools require the same degree of patience, skill and visual sense, and will be just as frustrating if you approach them casually. Above all, remember that Photoshop is a professionals' tool. Use it professionally and you will get professional results.

Photoshop was originally designed at a time when the majority of images were ultimately destined to be printed. Print design and pre-press work remain important areas in which it is used, and many of the things you can do in Photoshop only make sense if your images are eventually going to be printed using ink on paper. For multimedia work, where images are only ever going to be displayed on a monitor, those features which are oriented towards print can be ignored, and we will do so. In fact, if you are purely concerned with preparing images for the Web, you may find it preferable to work with Photoshop's Web graphics companion application, ImageReady, from which these features are absent. ImageReady does many of the same things that Photoshop does, and it does them almost entirely in an identical way. This chapter can, for the most part, be read as a description of ImageReady as well as Photoshop. We will note where there are differences. Additional aspects of ImageReady will be described in Chapter 4 and Chapter 10. If you find that you need to use both Photoshop, for its advanced image editing features, and ImageReady, for its Web-specific features, you can switch between the two by clicking the Jump icon, which is at the bottom of the toolbox in both applications. This causes the document you are working on in Photoshop to be opened in ImageReady, or vice versa. When you jump back, the changes you have made in the second application are reflected in the first.

→145

We will describe Photoshop 6 or, if you prefer, ImageReady 3. We will, for the most part, concentrate on features that were already present in Photoshop 4 and 5, though, so if you only have access to an earlier version much of this chapter will still be relevant.

Fundamentals

What is it then that Photoshop does? The following are just a few examples of tasks that you might use it to carry out: removing a colour cast – that is, an unnatural predominance of one colour – from a scanned image; removing unwanted background objects from a photograph; superimposing text on a picture, and giving it a 3-D bevelled appearance; creating a collage from a mixture of scanned images, graphics created in some other program and stills taken from digitized video footage; increasing the contrast of a screenshot to make the text more legible; or just changing the resolution of a scanned image from 600 dpi to 72 dpi for display on a monitor.

On a more ambitious scale, Photoshop has been used for tasks such as the reconstruction of likenesses of historical personages, by adding make-up, clothes, accoutrements and detailed skin features, to models generated by 3-D applications, on the basis of archeological evidence and contemporary descriptions. For such reconstructions, a mixture of photographic material from different sources may be combined in various ways with computer-generated imagery and marks painted on by hand in Photoshop.

Opening and Importing Images

Photoshop has painting tools for creating images from scratch – we will describe them later – but it is more common to start with an existing image and alter it. There are two ways of getting an image into Photoshop, depending on whether it already exists in a file or is only available in some external medium.

The File>Open command can be used to open files in many bitmapped and some vector graphics formats, not just native Photoshop files – although, of course, you can open those in both Photoshop and ImageReady. Among the other formats which you can open are those used for Web images: GIF, JPEG and PNG. TIFF files, which are a common choice as an interchange format for bitmapped images, can also be opened and so can the platform-dependent formats which are most commonly used under Mac OS and Windows: PICT and BMP. Other, less commonly used, formats are also supported, although Photoshop is by no means able to open all of the hundreds of image file formats in existence. For this you need to use a specialised format conversion utility such as GraphicConverter or DeBabelizer.

7
→146

Files in vector graphics formats must be treated in a special way. PDF is an example of an essentially vector-based format that can be opened in Photoshop. (PostScript is another.) In general, a PDF file may include vector text and graphics as well as, possibly, bitmapped images. Since Photoshop deals with bitmapped images, any vector graphics must be converted to bitmaps, that is a PDF file must be *rasterized*. If you open a PDF file containing just a single page,[*] you will be prompted with the dialogue box shown in Figure 3.1 to set the resolution and size at which you want it to be converted to a

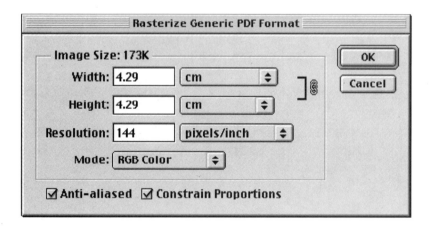

Figure 3.1   *Rasterizing a PDF file.*

bitmap. You can also specify a colour mode, which we will explain later. RGB is the appropriate choice for images to be displayed on a monitor. (In ImageReady, a resolution of 72 dpi and a colour mode of RGB are always used, so you are not given the option of setting them to any other value.) As a rule, it is a good idea to use a

---

[*]Adobe Illustrator 9 files are treated as one-page PDF files.

relatively high resolution – a rule of thumb is to use twice the resolution at which you will ultimately display the image – and not to alter the image's size at this point. This way, you have as many pixels available as possible while you're working on the image. You should only reduce it to screen resolution and its ultimate dimensions when you have finished, because in doing so you will usually be throwing away information.

☛ Open images in as many different formats as you can find. See what happens if you try to open a SWF file.

Most PDF files contain more than just one page. If you open a file with many pages the dialogue box shown on the left of Figure 3.2 will be displayed, allowing you to choose any single page to open. When you open a PDF file, everything on a page becomes part of your image. This may not be what you want to do, if the page includes text, since rasterized text is not much use to anybody. Photoshop also allows you to extract images only from a PDF file. To do this you use the File>Import>PDF Image... command. This leads to a similar dialogue box, shown on the right of Figure 3.2, from which you can choose one of the images embedded in the PDF document and open it. By clicking on the button labelled Import all images you can extract all the images included in the document and open each one in its own window.

☛ Open a page of a PDF document that contains some text. Zoom in and examine the quality of the text. Practise importing images from a PDF document.

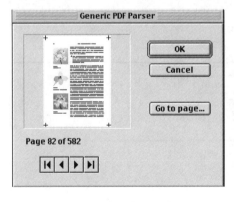 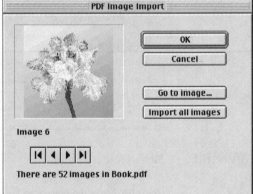

Figure 3.2   *Importing elements of a PDF file.*

You can only open an image if it has been stored in a file that already exists. It may have got there by being exported from some other application – perhaps it was an image of a scene rendered in a 3D program or a video frame exported from Premiere – or you may have downloaded it from a Web site or found it on a CD-ROM image library.

Frequently, though, Photoshop images are imported from an external device, often a scanner, although digital cameras are becoming increasingly common. Importing from external devices is done using plug-ins (see Chapter 2). These are not supplied as part of Photoshop, but must be obtained from the device's manufacturer and installed according to their instructions – normally just a matter of dragging a file into an appropriate folder. The name of any plug-in of this sort that has been installed will appear in the File>Import sub-menu. Usually, selecting a plug-in for a scanner, causes an elaborate dialogue box to be displayed, which is basically the interface to a scanning sub-application. Depending on the scanner's manufacturer (and its price) a range of facilities may be available from within the plug-in interface. There will certainly be a facility to preview a scan, from which you can usually select just part of the image to import. Some method of making colour adjustments is generally provided, too. This can vary from some very basic changes, which are usually better done in Photoshop itself, to highly sophisticated colour management systems, tuned to the particular model of scanner. When you are satisfied with the preview and any adjustments you have made, clicking the OK button is usually all that is required to start the scanning process, and when it is complete, the scanned image appears in a new Photoshop window.

☞ If there is a scanner attached to your computer, practise importing scans into Photoshop. Experiment with the options provided by your scanner's plug-in. Try scanning some unusual objects, such as some clothing or your hand, as well as flat images such as photographs and magazine pages. (*Never look at the scanner bed while it scans*. You can damage your eyes.)

Scanners do vary considerably in quality, and obtaining the best results from them, particularly from high-end models, requires some specialized skill and experience. For images that are going to be used on Web pages, inexpensive scanners can produce acceptable results, and do not require much by way of skilled operation, so they may actually be more appropriate for capturing Web images than more expensive models intended for the pre-press industry.

Although Photoshop is not an image file conversion utility, it can save images, using the File>Save As... command, in the same range of formats as it can import, so it can be used to translate among these. For Web formats it goes further, providing elaborate facilities for optimizing images through the File>Save for Web... command. These are described in detail in Chapter 10.

☞ Practise saving your scanned images in the different formats that Photoshop supports. Reopen each saved file and note any differences from the original.

Resolution

A bitmapped image is a rectangular array of values, each one representing the colour of a pixel – that is, a coloured dot on a screen or a dot of ink on paper. When it is stored in a computer system, such an image has no intrinsic physical dimensions. Its width and height are recorded as a number of pixels, but without knowing how many pixels are displayed in an inch or centimetre – the display *resolution* – this tells us nothing about how much space it will occupy on your screen. There was a brief moment, many years ago, when monitors and printers all used pixels 1/72 inch square – which, as we will explain shortly, is what we still pretend screen resolution is – and what you saw really was what you got, but printers now use much higher resolutions, monitors usually support several different resolutions, and scanners have entered the picture, with their own, sometimes very high, resolutions. There is considerable scope for confusion.

The confusion arises from two sources. First, the resolution of different sorts of device is quoted in different ways. For printers and scanners, the resolution is usually given as the number of dots printed or sampled per inch (or other unit of length). For digital cameras, video screens and monitors, though, it is more often given in the form of pixel dimensions. For example, a VGA monitor is usually said to have a resolution of 800 by 600, while PAL televisions are always 768 by 576. Obviously, a 20 inch monitor set to 800 by 600 is actually displaying fewer dots per inch than the 13 inch screen on a laptop set to the same resolution. However, the 20 inch monitor can be set to higher resolutions. When this is done, we don't expect the quality of images to improve, we expect to be able to fit more of them on to the screen. Hence, it isn't actually much use to quote monitor resolutions in dots per inch (dpi), the way printers' resolutions are. Instead, when it is necessary, it is (nearly) always assumed that monitors have a resolution of 72 dpi – even though very few actually do so nowadays.

The second source of confusion about resolutions arises from the fact we stated earlier: images in files and computer programs do not have any resolution, they just have pixel dimensions. Nevertheless, most original images have a natural physical size. For instance, if you were to scan a 6 by 4 inch photograph, irrespective of the scanner's resolution, you would only consider it to be the 'right' size if it was shown 6 inches wide and 4 inches tall. In that sense, a scanned image file does have a resolution: the resolution that the scanner used to create it. If images are created by programs, they can also have a resolution associated with them. This will not necessarily be the resolution of the monitor being used at the time. If an image is being prepared for printing, it will normally be created at a resolution appropriate to the device on which it will be printed. This means that when it is being worked on in Photoshop, or whichever program is being used, the image will appear too big, unless the user zooms out.

It follows from all this that when you open or create an image in Photoshop it will have a resolution and a set of pixel dimensions, which together specify a physical size. If the image's resolution does not match that of the device you want to display it on, you will have to change the resolution, and if it does not fit where you want it at that resolution you will have to change the size.

There are two interpretations of what it means to change an image's resolution. You can simply change the value stored in the image. For instance, if you had scanned a photograph at 300 dpi, you could change its resolution to 72 dpi, to see what it would look like in a Web browser. Since you haven't changed the pixel dimensions, it would look much larger than the original, since each pixel is bigger. More likely, what you intend to do is keep the image the same physical size (nominally, that is, given our earlier remarks about monitor resolutions) but only store 72 pixel values for each linear inch of image. This requires some pixels to be discarded, a process known as *downsampling*.

Changing an image's size can also be done with or without changing the pixel dimensions. If you keep all the same pixels, changing the size can only be done by changing the resolution – often to a meaningless value. If you want to change the size but maintain the resolution, you must either downsample (to make your image smaller) or *upsample*, that is, add extra pixels to make the image bigger. (You also need to upsample if you increase the resolution, but this is not something you often need to do for images that are not going to be printed.) Downsampling and upsampling are collectively referred to as *resampling*.

Because of the relationship between an image's size and its resolution, changing either of them (or both) is done in Photoshop in a unified dialogue box, which is shown in Figure 3.3. It is invoked by the Image>Image Size... menu command. The easiest thing to do is change the resolution, which is done by entering a value in the field labelled Resolution, towards the bottom of the box. (You can use the pop-up menu next to this field to choose between imperial and metric units.) Right at the bottom, you will see a checkbox labelled Resample Image. When this is selected, which it is by default, the image's size is left unaltered when the resolution is changed. In accordance with our earlier description, this means that the image must be resampled, and its pixel dimensions, shown at the top of the dialogue box, will change. The pop-up menu next to the checkbox allows you to select one of three resampling algorithms, which we will

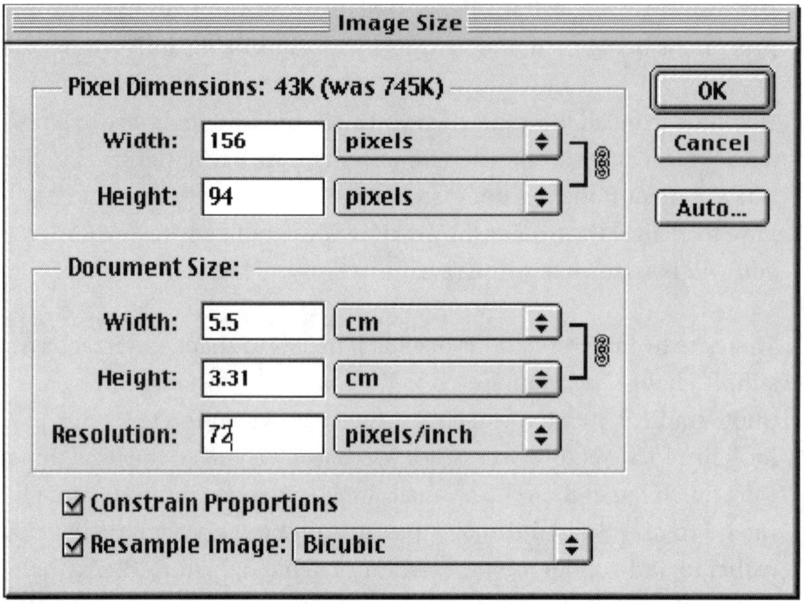

Figure 3.3   *Changing resolution and image size.*

describe shortly. If you deselect Resample Image, the pixel dimensions will not change, but the document size – its physical dimensions – will.

If it is the image's size that you are changing, you can again either select Resample Image or not. If you do, you can enter new values in the Width and Height fields for either the pixel dimensions (at the top of the dialogue box) or the document size (in the middle), whichever you need to fix. If you select the checkbox labelled Constrain Proportions, you only need to enter a value for one dimension (either one) and the other will automatically be set to preserve the image's aspect ratio (the ratio of its width to its height). This is indicated by the chain links connecting the height and width boxes. If you deselect Constrain Proportions, you can enter separate values for height and width, but this will generally result in a distortion of the image, which is rarely what you want to do. If you don't select Resample Image, the pixel dimensions text fields change to a read-only display of the values, and you can only enter new values for the document size. Doing so will, as we said before, change the resolution.

☛   Open any image file and experiment with changing its resolution and size, both together and independently. Use View>Actual Pixels to examine the changed image in detail.

In ImageReady, matters are somewhat simplified, because the resolution is always set to 72 dpi. If you open a file that was created at a different resolution, it is not resampled, the original pixel dimensions are preserved. The Image>Image Size... command brings up a simplified dialogue (shown in Figure 4.1 on page 170) which only lets you change the pixel dimensions. Images are always resampled, and sizes can only be specified as pixels. There is a separate option to scale by a specified percentage. (If you want to do this in Photoshop, choose Percent from the pop-up menu of units by the document size fields.) These limitations are sensible in an application intended for Web images only. It follows that if you open a high resolution image in ImageReady, it will appear to be huge. To downsample it, you would reset its size to correspond to its original physical dimensions (or, if you intend to make alterations to the image, twice its original dimensions, only reducing to actual size when you save it finally).

Resampling nearly always involves discarding some information. (The exception is upsampling to a resolution that is an exact multiple of the original.) The amount of information that is lost depends on how the new pixel values are computed from the old ones. This may be done in a naive way, that only takes account of one pixel at a time, or using more complicated algorithms that use information from neighbouring pixels. The three methods supported by Photoshop are *nearest neighbour*, the naive method just referred to, which almost always produces poor results, *bilinear* and *bicubic*, which are progressively better methods. (In ImageReady, the choice of algorithm is restricted to nearest neighbour and bicubic.) As you probably expect, the more complex methods require more computation, and so they take longer, but on a modern machine there is no real reason to settle for anything less than bicubic resampling. It is the default in Photoshop.

☛ Repeat the previous exercise, but use each of the different resampling methods in turn for each resizing and resolution-changing operation. Look at the differences in the actual pixels when you choose different methods.

It is always a good idea to use Photoshop to resample an image that was not originally made at screen resolution or is the wrong size, especially if you are going to use it on a Web page. In fact, for many images this may be the only thing you use Photoshop for. If you embed an image at a resolution other than 72 dpi in a Web page, or set its width and height using HTML attributes to some other values than those stored in the file, the Web browser will have to resample when it displays the page, and you can be sure that it will make a mess of it – and of your image. However, resampling is something you should leave until you have made any other alterations to your image, because you can never regain the information that is lost in the process. Furthermore, you should *always* keep a copy of the original image file.

Having said that, we must admit that high resolution images use up a lot of memory, and, because of the way Photoshop works, a great deal of scratch space on disk. This can slow down the program, too. If you have opened an image that was made at a very high resolution, such as those provided by image libraries for conventional design work, you may find it expedient to downsample it straight away. We would still recommend that you do not immediately go to 72 dpi, but work on the image at twice that resolution.

There is another situation where you need to think about an image's size and resolution, and that is when you create a new image from scratch, using the File>New... command. The dialogue box displayed when you do so is shown in Figure 3.4. Here you simply set the desired width, height and resolution. In ImageReady, you only have the chance to set the pixel dimensions. (At the same time, you can also specify whether the image should start out white, some other colour as set on the background colour swatch in the toolbox or transparent. Transparent areas are displayed as a chequer board pattern.)

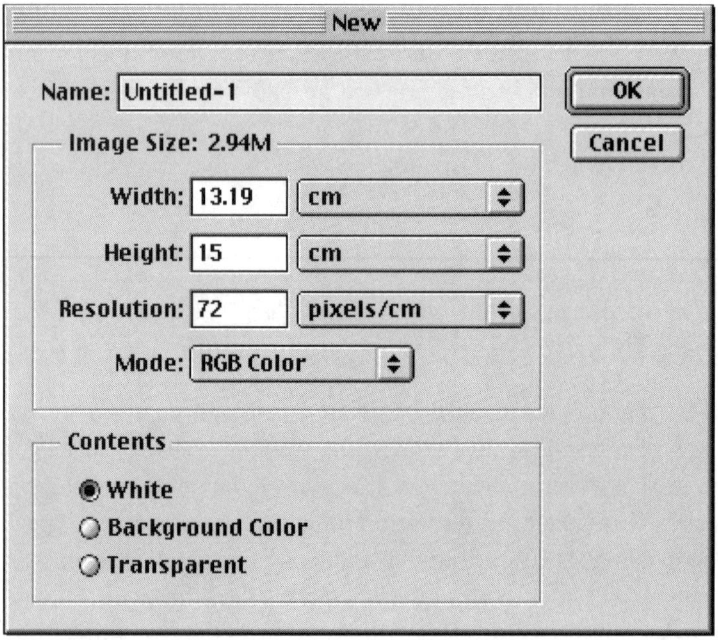

Figure 3.4   *Creating a new image.*

Modes and Colour Spaces

Looking at Figure 3.4, you will see that you can also set something called the Mode when you create a new image in Photoshop. This refers to the way in which colours are represented. The default mode, RGB Color, means that each pixel will be represented by three values, representing the intensity of red, green and blue light which, when mixed together, produce the colour at that pixel. This corresponds to the way in which colour is produced on a monitor, and so it is the natural choice for images for multimedia and the Web. It is the only mode supported by ImageReady, so you are not offered a choice when you create an image in that application. The other modes supported by Photoshop are mostly used in print, with the exception of Grayscale, which is used for black and white images, for which it affords a considerable saving in file size. It is not, however, supported by Web browsers, so it is less useful in that respect than it might have been. Discarding colour may be done for aesthetic reasons, though, and is sometimes a useful form of pre-processing before further manipulations of an image (for example, vectorizing it in Flash). Note that changing an image's mode is a one-way process: if you change it back, you won't get the same image you started with. In particular, if you change an RGB image to greyscale, you completely lose the colour information. (You can undo the change, though, until the image is saved.)

☛ Open a colour image and convert it to greyscale. Change the mode back to RGB. Does it make any difference at all?

Sometimes, if you open a file in Photoshop that you have not created yourself, you will find that its mode is something other than RGB Color. In particular, stock art collections that are intended for use in print will usually be in CMYK Color, or even, for high quality images, Lab Color. To change it to RGB, select RGB Color from the Image>Mode submenu. The range of colours that can be represented in RGB is greater than that which can be represented in CMYK, but it is not a superset, so changing modes may cause some colour shifts. It is best to trust Photoshop to take care of this for you, unless you know a great deal about colour.

You also need to know a certain amount about colour to understand the message shown in Figure 3.5, which you may see if you open an old Photoshop file. It concerns colour management, an attempt to compensate for the differences in the ways individual monitors and printers reproduce colour. Although we glibly talk about the values stored for each pixel in an image representing colours, the actual colour produced in response to any particular value will be different, to a lesser or greater extent, depending on the device being used to display or print the image. Colour management systems use *profiles*, which are coded descriptions of a device's colour characteristics, to try and produce consistent colour on every device. Files can have profiles associated with them, in the same sort of way that they can have resolutions associated with them, to specify an interpretation of colour values that corresponds to the device used to make the image in the first place. The message shown in Figure 3.5 is telling you that the file's profile does not correspond to the abstract device that Photoshop uses by default.

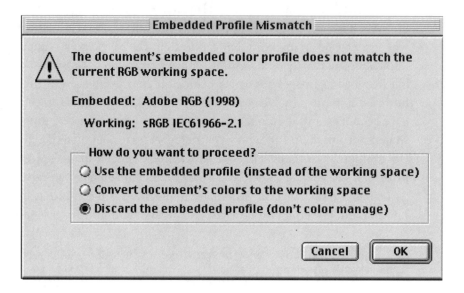

Figure 3.5   *An enigmatic message.*

There is no right answer to the question that Photoshop poses here. In theory, since the s in sRGB stands for *standard* and sRGB was devised for the Web, it would be a good idea to convert to sRGB, Photoshop's current default (the second option). However, not everyone believes that sRGB is an appropriate standard and Web browsers are no better at colour management than they are at resampling, so on the whole you might as well go along with the suggestion that the colour profile be discarded. That way, you are no worse off than you would have been if it hadn't been there in the first place.

Layers

Layers are pervasive in Photoshop, which has some claim to having originated the idea. As we explain in Chapter 9, layers can be thought of as sheets of transparent material, which can bear an image, like the sheets of acetate used on overhead projectors, or traditional animators' cels. Layers are overlaid; where a layer is transparent, the layers below it show through. If you are used to painting on paper or canvas, this may seem like an unnecessarily elaborate and artificial way of organizing a picture, but it allows you to manipulate digital images in ways that are not possible in physical media. By providing layers, which are a natural expression of the digital nature of bitmapped images, Photoshop can be more than just a poor substitute for natural media; it can open up possibilities that belong to the new digital medium.

Photoshop layers are used, broadly speaking, for two related purposes. They can be used to hold separate elements, often taken originally from different sources or created using Photoshop's painting and drawing tools, which are then combined into a composite or collage, or they can be used to separate different elements of an image, allowing them to be manipulated independently. This is required in image manipulation, because objects do not maintain their identity, in the way they do in vector graphics applications, such as those described in Chapters 5 and 6. What we can see as a vase, a football or a person is just an area of pixels, that we are able to interpret as an object, but Photoshop isn't. By placing such an area of pixels on its own layer, though, it becomes simple to deal with it as an object.

Layers are created in the Layers palette, which is described in general terms in Chapter 9. In Photoshop, a layer is also created automatically whenever you paste something into an image from elsewhere, or when you use the type tool (see page 90) to add some text. As in other layer-based applications, the Layers palette can be used to hide layers, allowing experimentation, and to lock them to prevent accidental changes. Layers can be re-ordered by dragging them up and down in the palette. Among Photoshop 6's innovations is the notion of a *layer set*: a collection of layers that can be manipulated as a single entity. This provides an additional level of organization for complicated images, but can safely be ignored by novices.

When an image is created in Photoshop, it consists of a single layer, designated the Background layer. As you add layers, they are stacked on top of the background. A common way of putting together a composite image is by opening several images – these might each have been scanned separately or obtained from an image library. You then create an empty image for the composite. Next, for each of the other images in turn, you select everything and copy and paste it into the new image. A new layer will be created each time you do this. You now have all the original images safely untouched in their own files, and a new image with copies of the originals on separate layers, so that you can alter them independently and then combine them into your final composition, possibly adding layers on which you have painted or set some text.

☛ Open between four and seven image files and shrink them all to a small size. Paste their contents into separate layers of a new full-sized image. Practise hiding and showing each of the layers (see page 39.)

Apart from the background, each layer has its own transparency setting and blending mode, which you can set by selecting the layer and using the controls at the top of the Layers palette, which are shown in Figure 3.6. These settings govern the way in which pixels on the layer interact with those on layers beneath it. You can enter any value in the Opacity field between 0% (entirely transparent) and 100% (entirely opaque). Intermediate values allow you to make the layer partially transparent, so you can build up an image out of translucent layers. If you hold down the mouse over the triangle to the right of the Opacity field, a slider appears as shown, which allows you to change the opacity by dragging. The document window changes as you do so, hence the slider gives you a way of setting opacity interactively by eye.

Photoshop goes rather further than this however, by allowing you to set the *blending mode* of your layers. The pop-up menu at the top left of the Layers palette shown in the margin allows you to choose between 17 different ways of combining the selected layer with the layer underneath it. The default Normal mode is what you expect: the underlying layer is obscured in proportion to the opacity setting. If the opacity has been set to 100%, it is entirely obscured (except where the selected layer is transparent). The other modes perform calculations which allow Photoshop to blend the selected layer with the layer beneath it in various different ways, some of them relatively straightforward, but some of them rather counter-intuitive if you are used to thinking in terms of physical media. For example, in the Luminosity mode, the hue of the colour of each pixel on the layer is ignored, but the brightness of the pixel beneath it is set to its luminosity. The Hard Light mode is described as producing an effect similar to shining a harsh spotlight on the image. Judge for yourself by experimenting. Modes other than Normal are used by experts to achieve effects that cannot easily be achieved otherwise, but using these modes effectively takes practice. (Even experienced Photoshop users find blending modes obscure and confusing.)

Figure 3.6   *Layer opacity and blending mode controls.*

When you set the opacity of a layer, the value is applied to every pixel on it that is not transparent and to everything that you subsequently paint on that layer, that is, the opacity is a property of the layer (the sheet of acetate, if you like) not the individual marks on it. In a similar way, you can apply certain special effects to an entire layer and the effects will be treated as a property of the layer. They are applied to any material on the layer, and to anything added to it subsequently. The image on the layer is not changed by the effect. If the effect is removed from the layer, the image is left behind without it. We will return to such *layer effects* later in the chapter. They are available not only in Photoshop, but in ImageReady, where they are an essential part of the way in which rollovers and Web animation are created, as we describe in Chapter 4.

☞ Open two images, both the same size, and paste one into a new layer on top of the other. Experiment with transparency settings to see how the lower image can show through the one on top. Try different blending modes to see how the layers can interact in more complex ways.

If you think about a layer as a sheet of acetate, then you can see that it makes sense to move layers about, each sliding over the one below it. Layers are not entirely like acetate, because they are, to all intents and purposes, infinite in extent. You can slide them about using the move tool: just pick up the tool and drag. The currently selected layer will be pulled around. (You can't move the background layer, though.) You can move several layers together by linking them. Click in the box in the second column of the Layers palette in a layer other than the currently selected one (which will have a paintbrush icon in its box). A chain link icon will appear in the box, to show that the layer is linked. Now, if you move a layer, all other layers that are linked to it will move as well.

☞ Use the move tool to arrange the small images that you pasted into separate layers, on page 74, so that they can all be seen at the same time.

Using the move tool you can only move layers vertically and horizontally – you can't drag them round to change their orientation. The Free Transform command, which is on the Edit menu can be used to rotate layers and to apply other geometrical transformations. (As we will see later, you can apply transforms just to selected parts of a layer.) When you choose this command, a *bounding box* is displayed, which surrounds the coloured pixels on the layer. Figure 3.7 shows a bounding box, which, as you can see, has small squares at each corner and in the middle of each side. These are called *handles* and are used to carry out transformations. You will also see a symbol that looks like the cross-hairs in a gun sight. This marks the centre of the layer, for the purposes of free transformation. To begin with, it is at the geometrical centre.

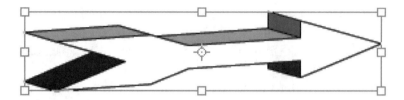

Figure 3.7   *A bounding box.*

If you drag one of the handles, the image inside the box is scaled: pulling one of the handles in a vertical side scales horizontally, pulling a handle in the top or bottom sides scales vertically, and pulling one of the corner handles scales in both directions. Hold down the shift key while pulling a corner handle to maintain the proportions. By pulling a handle all the way though an image and out the other side of the bounding box you can reflect the image.

If you position the cursor outside the bounding box, it changes appearance to a curved two-headed arrow, which indicates that you can use it to rotate the image, which you do just by dragging round, as illustrated in Figure 3.8. This works like a lever: the further away the cursor is, the further you have to drag to get the same amount of rotation, so if you want precise control you should move the cursor well outside the bounding box. You can drag the centre symbol to a different place, if you want to rotate the contents of the layer around a point other than its geometrical centre.

More esoteric transformation are performed by holding down modifier keys while dragging handles. The most general form of distortion is achieved by dragging a corner handle while holding down [cmd/ctl]. When you do this, the corner moves independently of all the others, which stay fixed, and the image inside the bounding box is distorted to fit in the box, as shown in Figure 3.8. If you hold down the shift key as well as [cmd/ctl] and drag one of the handles in the middle of a side, the image is skewed, as shown in Figure 3.8.

Whenever you use the Free Transform command, two things happen. First, the options bar changes as shown in Figure 3.9. You can apply precise transformations numerically by entering values in the boxes. Secondly, the menu bar changes, with most commands being disabled. This is because you must finish a sequence of transformations before you can do anything else – freely transforming is like using a modal dialogue box. When you have finished, you can press the return key or click on the tick mark at the

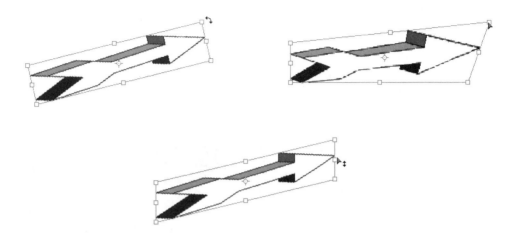

Figure 3.8   *Free transformation: rotation, distortion and skewing.*

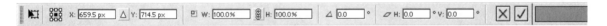

Figure 3.9   *Free transform options.*

right end of the options bar to confirm the operation, or press escape or click on the cross mark to cancel them.

> ☛ Draw a simple symbol or letter with any painting tool, select it and then practise scaling, rotating, distorting and skewing it with the Free Transform command.

When you use free transformation you should bear in mind that, in general, changing the geometry of a bitmapped image will require it to be resampled and this will usually cause a loss of quality – you can probably see this in the examples shown in Figure 3.8.

Linked layers can be arranged in various ways using the Layer>Align Linked and Layer>Distribute Linked sub-menus. Linked layers can be lined up along their left or right, top or bottom edges, or their vertical or horizontal centre lines. What is the edge of a layer, though, if it is an effectively infinite sheet of acetate? What is aligned by these operations is the areas of the layer which are not transparent, that is, those that you have painted on or pasted an image into. In effect, the objects on the layer are being aligned. The distributing operations equalize the space between layers' edges or centres in the same sense; the same options are available as for alignment. Note that you need at least three linked layers before it makes sense to distribute them.

You can use layer alignment to produce compositions with a grid-like layout. A specific example is shown in Figure 3.10. The small images have been arranged to look like negatives on a strip of film. This was done by aligning their centres and equalizing the space between them. While this could have been done by eye, it is quicker and more reliable to use the alignment commands.

> ☞   Arrange the small image you pasted onto separate layers on page 74 in all the different grid layouts their number permits. For example, if you have six images, arrange them as two rows of three columns, and three rows of two columns. (If you have a prime number of images, for instance, seven, place one of them on a row by itself in a neat way.)

Figure 3.10   *Aligned layers.*

Photoshop experts working on complex graphics often use a large number of layers – a hundred is not uncommon. Many of these may be hidden, having been used as experiments or interim stages. Each layer can occupy as much space as a single image of the same size, so using this many layers requires a machine with a lot of memory and a large scratch disk. Before saving a final version for display, it is common to flatten the layers, that is, combine them all into a single layer. (Be sure to make a copy of the image file in its layered form before you do this. You'd be surprised how often you need to go back to an image after it is supposedly finished.) This is done by selecting Flatten Image from the Layers palette menu or the Layer menu. (If you save the image in certain formats, including the common Web image formats, layers are flattened automatically, because those formats do not support them.) You can also selectively merge layers: the Merge Linked command (which also appears on both the Layers palette menu and the Layer menu) merges all linked layers. It is only available if any layers have been linked. If not, it is replaced by Merge Down, which combines the selected layer with the one below it. In the example in Figure 3.10, we merged the small image layers after they had been aligned, and then linked the merged layer with that containing the strip of black film stock, so we could centre the images within it.

A rather specialized way of using layers is as an animation medium. Animators who are familiar with Photoshop can create a sequence of frames on different layers of a Photoshop document, which can be saved in a file. The file can then be imported into various programs, including LiveMotion and After Effects, where each layer is made into a separate frame in the timeline. The resulting composition can then be exported as an animation in some suitable format. Animated GIFs for Web pages can be made by importing a layered Photoshop file into ImageReady, as described in Chapter 4.

Painting Pixels

Although work on many Photoshop images begins with the importing of a file, it is very common to subsequently paint other elements on to the imported image. Some images are created entirely by painting inside Photoshop. The tools provided for this purpose, although they offer a broad range of controls over the type of marks that can be made, should not really be thought of as substitutes for natural media such as oil paints, watercolours, pastels, charcoal and ink. They invariably produce a simple, graphic result, although this may be modified later to produce more painterly effects. If you want to use your computer to create art work that looks as if it was made with real media, and to do so by making marks as you would if you were really working with brushes and so on, then you would be better off using Corel's Painter program, which does an unequalled job of simulating natural media and their interaction with physical supports, that is, paper, canvas, etc.

→156

The Painting Tools

There are three different painting tools in Photoshop's tool box: the *paintbrush*, the *pencil* and the *airbrush*. (In Photoshop, the brush and pencil share a location in the toolbox; in ImageReady, all three are in the same place.) There is also an *eraser*, which behaves more like a brush than a real eraser, as we will see. Each of the three painting tools is used in the same way. You select a tool by clicking its icon in the toolbox, and then make marks by dragging in the image. Before doing this, however, you must set the colour: click on the foreground colour swatch in the toolbox, and then set a colour using the Color palette, or else double-click the swatch and choose a colour from the colour picker (see Chapter 9).

☛ Practise using each of the three painting tools in a range of different colours until you get a feel for which tool is suited to which type of job.

The names of the three painting tools give a broad indication of the nature of the marks they make. The pencil makes hard-edged lines, the brush makes softer strokes and the airbrush makes marks with diffuse edges. Each tool has many variants, differing in size, hardness, shape and the angle between the simulated brush head and the orientation of the image. You choose a variant – or create a new one – and set other brush characteristics in the options bar (see page 26) after you have selected the painting tool.

Figure 3.11   *The options for the painting tools.*

Figure 3.11 shows the options bar as it appears when a brush tool has been selected. At the left, next to the icon indicating the tool you have selected (here, the paintbrush), is a swatch representing the currently selected variant, with a downward pointing arrow next to it. Clicking on the arrow causes a palette to drop down, on which you can find swatches showing the shape of the tips of all the currently available variants of the brush. By default, an assortment of brushes, as shown in Figure 3.12, is available, including simple versions varying only in a diameter, and some more elaborate variants which make more of an attempt to mimic physical media. You can use the menu on this drop-down palette to load different libraries of brushes. The best way to understand the different brush variants, and the differences between the three types of painting tool, is by experimenting. We strongly urge you to do so.

☞ Choose one of the three painting tools and practise using its different variants to create a wide range of different marks at different sizes in the same colour.

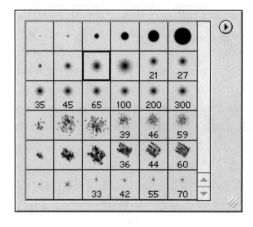

Figure 3.12   *The default assortment of brushes.*

A brush variant defines which pixels' colour will be changed in the region of the cursor when the brush is dragged across an image. This is determined by the brush's size, shape and hardness, the angle it makes with the path of the cursor, and the spacing between the individual strokes that make up a line. In Photoshop (but not ImageReady) all of these values can be changed. If you click on the swatch in the options bar representing the currently selected brush variant, the dialogue shown in Figure 3.13 drops down. Here you can change all the values that define the brush variant either numerically or graphically, by dragging sliders and squashing or rotating the ellipse that represents the shape and angle of the brush. (For the airbrush, the only value that you can change is the spacing. Increasing this value produces a more splattery effect.) Figure 3.14 shows the effect of changing some of the options for the paintbrush tool. From left to right it shows strokes made by a circular, hard brush, a soft brush of the same size and shape, the original brush with the spacing set to a high value, a flattened elliptical version, the same ellipse rotated through an angle, and finally all of the options varied at once, except for the size which we kept constant for all the example brush strokes. (Note that you have to use the brush to create the strokes. You cannot draw a path and then apply a brush stroke to it, or copy it and change the stroke, the way you can in Illustrator.)

☛ Practise creating a brush style of your own, until you feel confident that you are able to alter the values in such a way that you achieve the result you intend.

If you want to use again a brush with values you have changed, you can save it, by clicking on the button in the top right corner of the brush settings dialogue. You use the text field at the top of the dialogue to give your saved brush a name.

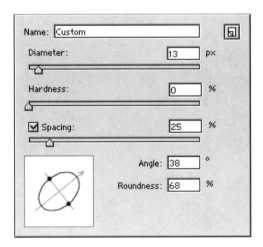

Figure 3.13   *Setting brush options.*

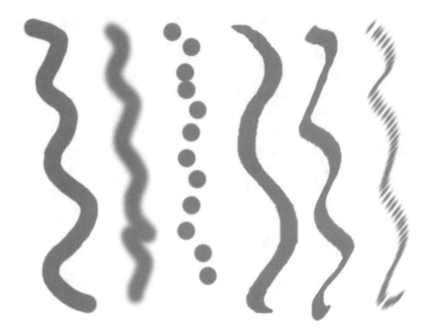

Figure 3.14   *Varying the hardness, shape, angle and spacing of the paintbrush tool.*

Figure 3.15   *A custom brush.*

You can go further in creating your own painting tools in Photoshop. If you use the rectangular marquee tool (which is fully described later on) to drag out a selection on an image and then choose the Define Brush... command from the Edit menu, a new brush is created which uses the shape within your selection as its tip. Usually, you will have made a simple shape inside the area to be selected. The custom brush can be selected and used to make marks like any other. Since the other parameters of the built-in brushes only make sense for elliptical tips, you can only change the spacing of a brush you have made in this way. Figure 3.15 shows, on the left, a shape that was used to make a brush, and to the right two strokes applied with this brush, using different spacings.

For most people, trying to produce controlled brush strokes using a mouse is not easy. The use of a graphics tablet and pressure sensitive pen is almost mandatory if you wish to make decent art work using these tools, especially if you are trying for a fluid line. If you click on the icon at the far right of the options bar or with a painting tool selected, a palette labelled Brush Dynamics, which is shown in Figure 3.16, will drop down. You can use this to specify which aspects of your brushes will respond to the pressure you use when you draw with a stylus. The precise characteristics vary with the tool. You cannot set brush dynamics in ImageReady. As you will have gathered, the brushes in Photoshop are more powerful tools than those in ImageReady, so you will generally find it better to use Photoshop for any projects that call for much painting on images.

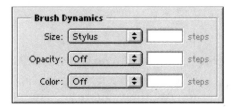

Figure 3.16   *Setting brush dynamics.*

The fact that Photoshop brushes are not real brushes has its advantages as well as its drawbacks. They can be made to do things which real brushes cannot. In particular the way in which the marks you make with a painting tool interact with the pixels beneath them can be altered in ways which physical media do not readily permit – the same ways in which layers can be made to interact. The transparency of the colour being applied can be set to any value between 1% (the marks are almost invisible) and 100% (any colour underneath the brush stroke is completely obscured). Intermediate values allow you to make partially transparent marks, so you can build up translucent layers of colour. You can also set the blending mode of your brush strokes.The Mode pop-up menu on the options bar allows you to choose between 18 different ways of combining the colour on your brush with the colour underneath it – the 17 available for blending layers, plus an extra mode, Behind, to simulate painting on the back of a layer considered as a sheet of acetate. Again, the default Normal mode is what you expect: underlying colour is obscured or allowed to partially show through depending on the opacity, while the other modes allow your brush strokes to interact with the pixels below them in more complicated ways.

> ☞ Use a large brush to paint an area of colour. Practise painting smaller brush strokes on top of this area using each of the different blending modes and observe the results.

A layer's opacity and the opacity of brush strokes you paint on it are applied cumulatively. For example, if you set a layer's opacity to 50% and paint using a brush whose opacity is also set to 50%, the resulting marks will only be 25% opaque. You can never create a mark on that layer which is more than 50% opaque – unless you change the layer's opacity. When you do so, the opacity of brush strokes will be changed proportionally, so if we increase our layer's opacity to 100%, the marks made by the 50% opaque brush will appear as 50% opaque.

> ☞ With the two-layered image from the exercise on page 75, experiment with applying brush strokes with different opacity, using different blending modes for brushes as well as for the layers.

Erasing

The eraser tool is used for removing colour from an image. You don't need this for correcting mistakes – you can use the History palette for that. The eraser is used either to remove areas from an imported image that are not wanted, or to produce an effect similar to that made by using a scalpel to scrape paint off a painting to reveal the paper beneath it. When you select the eraser, a pop-up menu labelled Mode appears in the options bar, from which you choose Block, Pencil, Airbrush or Paintbrush. These different modes determine which pixels are erased when you drag the eraser. In Block mode, a square block of pixels is erased, so this mode is rather like a conventional eraser. It is useful for removing large areas of an image. The other three modes behave just like the corresponding brush tools, except that they remove colour instead of applying it. In these modes, you can set the eraser's opacity and its size, just as you can with the painting tools. An eraser set to less than 100% opacity only removes some of the colour when you drag it over the image, so that it thins down previously painted strokes rather than removing them. (Remember that it is much easier to perform precise erasing if you blow up the image to a high magnification on the screen.)

☛ Choose a fairly complex image and practise using the different modes of the eraser to remove just the part of it that you want to. Practise erasing both large areas and small fine details.

 If you know that you want to erase only pixels of a particular colour, you can use the *magic eraser*. When you click with this tool, all pixels of the same colour as the one you clicked on are erased. You can specify whether only a contiguous area of colour around the pixel you have clicked on should be removed, or all pixels of that colour anywhere in the image. You can also set a tolerance, which determines how closely a pixel's colour must match before it gets erased. Choosing to anti-alias the erasure produces a smooth-looking edge to the erased area; if you don't do this, at low resolution, the edges may look jagged. Like the other erasers, the magic eraser can be set to an opacity less than 100%, for partial erasing. All of these options are set on the options bar, shown in Figure 3.17.

Figure 3.17   *The options for the magic eraser.*

We have been rather vague about what it means to erase colour from an image. Pixels that have been erased from a layer other than the background become transparent – or semi-transparent if the opacity of the eraser is set to less than 100%. Hence, in a layered image, erasing lets parts of the layers underneath show through. If you erase on the background layer, erased pixels are set to the current background colour (which you can set by clicking on the background colour swatch in the toolbox) unless you specified a transparent background when you created the image, in which case pixels are erased to transparency.

Fills

You can fill whole layers or selected areas (see page 92) with solid colour, a pattern or a colour gradient. While this may not be terribly useful in isolation, fills are often combined with other elements to make more interesting compositions.

The Edit>Fill... command provides an easy way to fill areas. When you select this command, the dialogue shown in Figure 3.18 appears. The pop-up menu at the top is used to choose between the foreground and background colours, black, white or a 50%

grey, a pattern, or a value chosen from the image's history – an option we will not describe. The simple colours are hopefully obvious; if you wish to fill with a particular colour, you merely need to set the foreground or background colour appropriately before applying the command. You set the opacity and blending mode for the fill as if you were using a painting tool.

☞ Create a new image and add layers to it, each filled with a different colour.

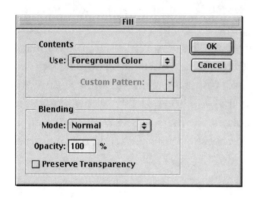

Figure 3.18   *Filling with colour or a pattern.*

If you select Pattern from the Use pop-up menu, the swatch below it becomes active, displaying a thumbnail of the current pattern. By clicking on the triangle to its right, you can make a palette of patterns drop down, from which you can select a different one. This is simple, if you are content with one of the default patterns, shown in Figure 3.19. You can load some additional patterns using the drop-down palette's menu, but the selection provided with Photoshop is limited. Making your own patterns is possible, but more difficult, and we will not describe it further.

7
→150

☞ Add some more layers to your image, each filled with a different pattern.

The *paint bucket* tool can also be used to fill areas with colour or patterns, but it doesn't behave in the way you might expect. The paint bucket looks as if it should just do the same as the Edit>Fill command and pour colour, the way paint buckets do in other programs. What it actually does, though, is apply colour to pixels that are adjacent to and the same colour as the one you click on with the bucket. The options bar for the paint bucket, shown in Figure 3.20, has a Tolerance field, which works in the same way as that for the magic eraser. Setting a very low value will cause the paint bucket to fill in a highly selective manner. Setting a high tolerance will allow it to fill larger areas.

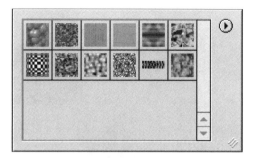

Figure 3.19   *The default collection of patterns.*

Getting the tolerance right to make the bucket fill an area that looks to you as if it is all the same colour can be tricky. The paint bucket can be used to fill with either the current foreground colour or a pattern, which you select from the drop-down palette on the options bar. The mode and opacity can also be set on the options bar, to the same values as those for any other painting tool. The remaining options resemble those for the magic eraser. In fact, you could imagine the paint bucket working by magically erasing and then filling the erased area with its colour or pattern.

☛ Open a photographic image, such as a landscape, and practise filling different areas with new colours using the paint bucket. See if you can set the tolerance so that the bucket fills identifiable areas of colour, such as the sky. Experiment with using different opacity settings and blending modes for the paint bucket.

Figure 3.20   *The paint bucket's options.*

Pleasing effects can be achieved by filling areas with *gradients*, where colours blend gradually into each other. Photoshop has five different sorts of gradient. In a linear gradient, the colours blend along a straight line, while in a radial gradient they blend outwards in a circular pattern. These two types of gradient are common to many graphics programs. Photoshop also provides angular gradients, in which the blend sweeps round a circle, reflected gradients, which are like linear gradients, but reflected to form a symmetrical blend, and diamond gradients, which are similar to radial gradients, but form a diamond pattern instead of a circle. Figure 3.21 shows these types more clearly than any description can.

You use the *gradient tool* to add gradient fills to an image. (It may be concealed underneath the paint bucket in the tool box.) The basic mode of action is as follows:

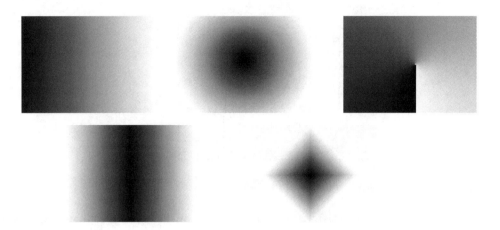

Figure 3.21   *Gradients.*

select the tool, select the type of gradient using one of the buttons on the options bar, select a preset gradient from the drop-down palette on the options bar, set the blending mode and opacity, and drag in the image with the tool to create the gradient itself. The role of the line you drag out depends on the type of gradient you are making.

For a linear gradient it defines the line along which the colours blend, with the line's end points defining the start and end points of the gradient. Beyond the ends, a solid fill of the ending colour is applied. For a radial gradient, the line is the radius of the circle; the starting point of your line acts as its centre, and is coloured with the starting colour for the gradient, the end point of the line defines the extent of the circle, beyond which the solid fill of the ending colour is used. For an angular gradient, the line is also the radius of a circle, but the gradient wipes round the circle, so the starting and ending colours appear on either side of the line. (You can see this clearly in the example in the top right corner of Figure 3.21.) If you choose a reflected gradient, the line is used in the same way as it is for a linear gradient, except that the resulting gradient is reflected about the starting point. In the example in the bottom left of Figure 3.21, for instance, the gradient tool was only dragged from the middle of the filled area to the right edge. Finally, for a diamond gradient, the line serves as a radius, as it does with a radial gradient, but the blended colours are arranged to form the diamond shape.

☛ Create a new image, and add five layers to it, each filled with a different type of gradient, but all based on the same preset gradient.

The selection of gradients provided with Photoshop may well not be adequate for your needs, but it is easy to adapt them to make new ones. With the gradient tool selected, click on the gradient swatch on the options bar instead of the triangle next to it that controls the drop-down palette. The Gradient Editor window, shown in Figure 3.22, will open. The top panel duplicates the drop-down palette from the options bar, complete with palette menu, which you can use, among other things, for loading different sets of gradients. The lower half of the window is used to modify the gradient.

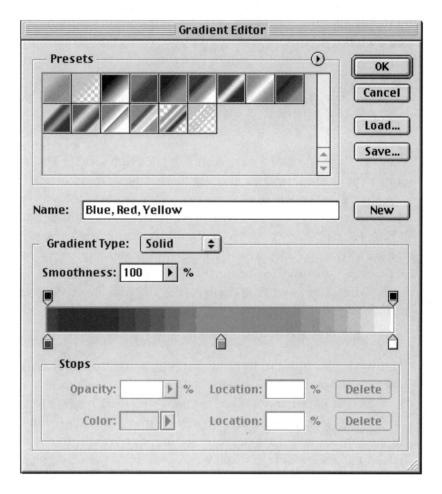

Figure 3.22 *The gradient editor.*

The gradient itself is illustrated in the bar running across the dialogue box – this shows a linear version of the gradient. The little markers above and below the sample are called *stops,* and they are used to set values for the colour (below) and opacity (above) at specific points in the gradient. These properties are interpolated between the stops, so you can alter the rate at which colours change by dragging the colour stops to different positions. If you double-click a colour stop, the colour picker opens, allowing you to choose a colour for the corresponding point in the gradient. In this way, you could take the basic black to white linear gradient from the default set and turn it into a red to yellow gradient. To make more complex gradients you can add extra stops. This is done by clicking below the gradient bar at the point where you want to set a value. In this way you can create very elaborate gradients. When you are happy with your gradient, you can click the New button, and it will be added to the gradient palette for future use like any other. In particular, any gradient you create can be applied as any of the five different types.

> ☞ Open the Gradient Editor window and practise adjusting the colours, opacity and rate of change of a gradient. Add extra stops to produce a more elaborate effect. Create a pleasing new gradient for yourself and then try applying it as each of the five different gradient types.

If all you want to do is create a layer entirely filled with a colour, gradient or pattern, the quickest thing to do is create a *fill layer*, of one of those types. The New Fill or Adjustment Layer button at the bottom of the Layers palette conceals a pop-up menu with entries at the top for each of the three types of fill. (We will deal with adjustment layers later.) When you select Solid Colour... from the pop-up menu, you are presented with the colour picker, using which you select the layer's colour. Similarly, if you select Pattern... or Gradient... you can select or create a pattern or gradient in a dialogue box which includes the appropriate drop-down palette. You will often want to set the opacity or blending mode of a fill layer to some value other than the defaults in order to combine it with other, more interesting, layers.

Once you have made a fill layer, you can't paint in it with other colours. If you select the layer, you will find that you can only paint on it with shades of grey and that doing so does not have the effect you expect: painting with black removes parts of the layer, painting with grey makes semi-transparent marks, and erasing has no effect on the fill colour, only on painted marks. This is because you can't actually edit a fill layer, you can only edit its associated layer mask. We will return to layer masks on page 110, but for now you should note that when you paint in a fill layer, you are effectively changing the shape of the visible fill. Later, we will show in more detail how this works.

Type

In Photoshop 6, adding text to an image is simple and intuitive: select the type tool, set the typographical properties, click in the image where you want the text to appear or drag out a text frame, and start typing. (This convenient method of adding type directly to the image is a long-overdue innovation in Photoshop 6. In earlier versions, it was necessary to enter the text in a dialogue box instead.) You will see that the menu bar changes: you are now in a restricted mode in which you enter and edit text. When you have finished, click the tick mark at the right hand end of the options bar to confirm the changes you have made to the text, or the cross to discard them, and return to normal image editing.

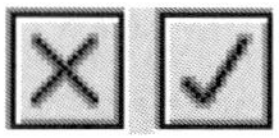

The text is automatically placed on a new layer, which you can position and transform like any other. Text can be selected and its properties can be set in the Character and Paragraph palettes, the same way as they can in most of the applications in this book, as described in Chapter 9. The options bar offers a more convenient interface to the most important properties, as shown in Figure 3.23. The palettes are still needed, however, if you wish to exert precise control over advanced features such as tracking and kerning, as well as more mundane, but less commonly needed parameters, such as the indentation of the first line of a paragraph, or the justification of its last line.

Figure 3.23 *Type options.*

In addition to the standard typographic controls, the Paragraph palette menu in Photoshop (and ImageReady) gives access to even more precise controls over hyphenation and justification, similar to those available in page layout programs such as InDesign, so experts can produce high quality typesetting within Photoshop.

> ☛ Practise adding type to an image you have already made. Experiment with the different character and paragraph layout options and with moving the type layer to different positions on the image.

On a less exalted level, the warped text button near the right hand end of the text options bar allows you to distort text in various ways. Clicking on this button brings up a dialogue box, whose main feature is the pop-up menu shown on the left of Figure 3.24, from which you can choose a warping method. The names and icons for each method are self-explanatory. Figure 3.24 shows the effect of some of the warping methods. Once you have selected a warping method you can set various parameters in the dialogue box: the extent of the bend and the degree of horizontal and vertical distortion. A little experimentation will show you what they achieve. You should be able to appreciate that discretion is needed in using warped text.

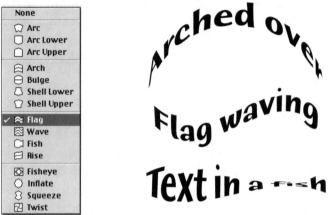

Figure 3.24   *Warped text.*

☛ Select some text and practise warping it, using all the available options. Consider where it would be appropriate to use each effect.

Selection and Allied Operations

You frequently need to select part of an image so that you can copy or move it to another position or another image, remove it from the image, make changes or apply a free transform only to the selected part, or protect the selected part from changes, or to create a mask to conceal parts of another image or layer. These last possibilities demonstrate how the familiar concept of selection is extended somewhat in the context of bitmapped images. You are probably accustomed to the idea of selecting some text in a word processor and applying a style, such as italicization, to it. In Photoshop, just about anything you can do will be applied only to selected pixels, if you have made a selection. For instance, if part of an image is selected and you paint with a brush tool, brush strokes will only appear in the selected area. Similarly, if you use the image correction and retouching tools described in a later section, your changes will only be applied to the selection. In other respects, selections in Photoshop are like selections in a word processor: you can delete, cut, copy and paste selected pixels in just the same way.

There are several different tools and methods of making selections, but conceptually there are really just three kinds of selection: selecting areas with a particular shape (for example, a rectangular piece of the image), selecting distinct objects (for example, a dog) and selecting parts of the image with common optical characteristics (for example, all the red bits).

Before we describe ways of selecting parts of an image, we should point out that sometimes you need to select all of it, or at least all of one layer. For this, use the Select>All command. This selects everything on the currently active layer. (If you switch layers, the selection moves to the new current layer. This is also the case with other more complicated selections.) You also often need to deselect whatever you have selected. The command to achieve this is Select>Deselect. Once you have done so, the menu command changes to Select>Reselect, which is useful on those occasions when you deselect a complicated selection and then discover you still need it.

Another generally useful command is Select>Inverse, which has the effect of deselecting everything that was selected and selecting everything that wasn't. Selecting the parts of the image you don't want and then inverting the selection can often be easier than trying to select the parts you do want directly.

Marquee Selection and Cropping

  The simplest of Photoshop's selection tools are the marquee tools, with which you can select areas of pixels that lie within a geometrical shape. Photoshop has four such tools: the rectangle, ellipse, single-pixel row and single-pixel column marquee tools. ImageReady has an additional marquee tool for selecting rectangles with rounded corners. This is often used for making buttons to provide navigation controls on Web pages.

To make a rectangular or elliptical selection with a marquee tool, select the tool of your choice – they all share the same location in the toolbox – and drag across the image diagonally. The shape of the selection is pulled out. (Making selections by dragging out a marquee is probably familiar to you.) When you release the mouse button, the outline of the selected area is shown as a dashed outline, which appears to move round slowly. This moving dashed outline is often referred to as 'the marching ants'. If you select either of the single-pixel marquee tools, you just need to click once, and every pixel in the row or column in which you have clicked is selected. This is useful for removing borders that may have been inadvertently introduced by a misaligned scan. Once you've made a selection you can move it by dragging with the selection tool inside the selected area. The area will remain selected until you make a new selection or explicitly deselect it.

☞ Practise making selections from an image of your choice with each of the marquee tools. Observe the effect of inverting each selection.

A common reason for making rectangular selections is that you want to crop an image, for example a photograph whose subject has been badly framed. That is, you want to remove everything outside the selected rectangle, giving you a smaller image from which unwanted elements have been removed, or which is just better proportioned. Inverting the selection and deleting everything outside the rectangle doesn't actually achieve this – it just erases the unwanted parts to the background but leaves the image the same size it was originally. To completely remove the extraneous parts of the image, use the Crop command from the Image menu. (You can use this command even if the selection is not rectangular, the effect is to crop the image to the smallest rectangle which encloses the selection, whatever shape it may be.) Figure 3.25 shows an example.

Figure 3.25   *Cropping an image.*

You may prefer to use the crop tool, which combines a selection with a cropping operation, and at the same time gives you extra control over the shape of the selected area. To begin with, you use the crop tool in the same way as a rectangular marquee, that is, you select it and drag out a rectangle. When you let go of the mouse button, though, you don't see a selection outlined by marching ants, you see a bounding box, which looks the same as if you are using a free transform (see Figure 3.7). You can pull the handles of this bounding box to position the edges of your rectangle precisely. You can also rotate the bounding box by dragging outside it (but you can't skew it as you can with a free transform). When you are satisfied with the position of the box, press return and the image will be cropped to the rectangle you have made.

☞   Select a suitable image – one that is badly framed or includes extraneous objects – and crop it to leave only the parts that you want. Use both a selection tool followed by the menu command and the crop tool.

Another way of cropping an image is based on its content. If you select Image>Trim, the dialogue box shown in Figure 3.26 is displayed. If you select the default option Top Left Pixel Color, then rows and columns of pixels which are the same colour as the top left-hand corner will be removed from the sides you have selected in the checkboxes in the lower half of the dialogue box. What this means is that if your image is an object on a plain background, empty background margins will be cropped off, leaving the object in the smallest rectangle that can contain it. You can base the trimming on the colour of the bottom right corner or trim off transparent borders, as appropriate. Because there is no tolerance in the trim settings, only pixels which match exactly will be trimmed. This means that trimming in this way works best with computer-generated images and is unlikely to work on photographic images, which will have natural colour variations, even in an apparently plain background. Figure 3.27 shows a successful example: a roughly framed screenshot of the trash can icon on a plain desktop was trimmed to leave a neat image with just the icon and its label.

☞ Practise using the Trim command to remove unwanted border pixels. Try it with both computer-generated images – such as screenshots or images made in a 3D application – and photographs. Try applying the command repeatedly to the same image.

Figure 3.26 *The* Trim *dialogue.*

Lasso Selections

If you want to select an object from an image, it is rarely the case that the part of the image that you want to select is a convenient geometrical shape that you can draw with a marquee tool. Freeform selections can be made in several ways, the most direct being by drawing round an object using the *lasso tool*. This sounds easy: select the tool,

Figure 3.27   *Trimming an image.*

position the cursor somewhere on the border of the area you want to select, and drag round to draw the outline. When you let go of the mouse button, the selection will be joined up in the most direct line possible, so usually you will draw all round the object you want to select, only releasing the button when you get back to where you started.

Whether this operation actually is easy depends on how good you are at precise freehand drawing. It is difficult to achieve accurate control using a mouse, a graphics tablet and pen are much easier to use for this job. It may be obvious, but it helps to zoom in on the image so that you can see exactly what you are doing. Because of the difficulty of achieving a precise result, the lasso tool is best used for the digital equivalent of rapidly cutting out an object from a picture in a magazine with scissors, so that you can discard most of its background, and if necessary, refine the selection later using more precise methods. (We will return to the subject of selecting objects on page 101.)

A variant of the lasso tool is the *polygonal lasso*, which is used to draw selections whose outlines consist of straight line segments. These are made by clicking at a succession of points with the tool. You can mix straight lines and freeform segments in the same selection: holding down [opt/alt] while you are using either the lasso or the polygonal lasso switches temporarily to the other.

A second variant is the *magnetic lasso*, which helps you select objects which appear against a background. It is used in a similar way to the ordinary lasso tool, that is, you draw around the object you are trying to select but, as you draw, the selection boundary snaps to the nearest clearly defined edge. If you're lucky, Photoshop's interpretation of a clearly defined edge will match yours.

In more detail, the magnetic lasso works as follows. The selection boundary is built up as a series of segments between what are called *fastening points*. You can imagine the fastening points as being pins that fix the selection boundary in place. In between the fastening points the boundary is like some flexible material that clings to the edges of objects – a sort of two-dimensional cling film. You select the magnetic lasso tool from the toolbox in the usual way and click to place the first fastening point. You then drag the cursor (you don't need to keep the mouse button pressed down) around the edge of the object you wish to select. Fastening points will be added automatically as you drag, at a frequency you specify in the options bar. If the selection boundary strays too far from where you want it, you can explicitly add fastening points by clicking. You can also delete fastening points by pressing the delete key.

There are two options which control the precise behaviour of the magnetic lasso. The Width is the maximum distance from the actual path you draw at which pixels are examined for an edge. The Edge Contrast defines what should be considered to be an edge, in terms of the minimum brightness variation it exhibits. Experimenting with these values may produce better results for particular images.

☛ Choose an image that includes a fairly prominent object (one that is simple enough to be easily drawn round). Experiment with using each of the three lasso tools to select this object. (Invert the selection, delete and deselect to see how successful you have been.)

Paths

If you are used to working with vector graphics applications such as Illustrator, you may find that the best way of making precise selections is by using the vector drawing tools that Photoshop provides. (If you are not used to vector graphics, stick to the lasso tools and skip this section.) Mixing vector graphics and bitmaps in the same program is never straightforward: they are two fundamentally different ways of representing images, which cannot be fully reconciled. This means that vector drawing cannot really be seamlessly integrated into a bitmap-based program like Photoshop, and instead vector elements are treated in a unique way.

Using vector drawing tools in Photoshop, you can construct a *path*, a slightly confusing name for a collection of curves and lines. You do this by clicking the Create New Work Path button in the options bar when you select a drawing tool. This path can then be used in several different ways. In particular, it can be converted to a selection.

The tools provided include several for drawing simple geometrical shapes: rectangles with or without rounded corners, ellipses and regular polygons. These are all used in the same way: select the tool and drag in the image. The shape is pulled out as you drag. Where appropriate you can set parameters, such as the number of sides of a polygon, in the options bar.

As well as the simple geometrical shape tools, there is a line tool, with which you can pull out straight lines to form irregular polygons. There is also a custom shape tool. When you select this, the options bar acquires a drop-down menu, illustrated in Figure 3.28, showing a selection of special shapes; you choose one of these, in the same way you choose a paintbrush, and then drag in the image to draw it, as you do with any other shape tool. You can create your own shapes, by making a path and then choosing Define Custom Shape... from the Edit menu. A dialogue box is displayed to allow you to give it a name and afterwards it will be added to the menu of shapes.

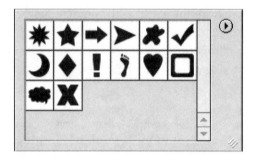

Figure 3.28   *The default collection of custom shapes.*

The most flexible way of creating paths is by using the pen, which is a standard vector drawing tool, as described in Chapter 9. That chapter also describes how you can alter paths once you have constructed them using the vector selection tools.

☞ Using the vector drawing tools, create a simple shape of your own and add it to the menu of custom shapes. Now select your shape from the menu and draw several versions of it at different sizes.

Paths are manipulated in the Paths palette. Most of the time, if you are creating paths to use as selections, you just work with a single path, known as the *work path*. (If you find yourself using paths a lot, you can create named paths using the New button at the bottom of the palette.) Once you have drawn a work path and adjusted it so that it encloses the area of the image you want to select, choose Make Selection... from the Paths palette menu. (For named paths, you must select the one you want to use in the palette.) The dialogue box shown in Figure 3.29 is displayed. By choosing an appropriate radio button you can combine the selection made from the work path with any existing selection. (See the following section for a description of the different options for combining selections.) You can also choose whether or not to anti-alias the selection, which has the effect of smoothing its edges. It is also possible to convert a selection to a path, using the Make Work Path command from the Paths palette menu.

You might do this, for example, so that you could use the direct selection tool to refine a lasso selection; after you had done so, you could turn the path back into a selection.

☛ Repeat the exercise on page 97, but try to select the object by drawing a path round it using the vector tools.

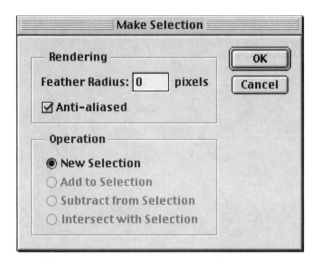

Figure 3.29 *Converting a path to a selection.*

Combining and Transforming Selections

Sometimes the best way of making a complicated selection is by building it up in pieces. If you look at the options bar when you are using any of the selection tools we have described so far, you will see a set of four small icons at the left hand end. These are used to control the way in which any selection you make interacts with any pixels that are already selected. Normally, the leftmost of the four buttons is selected, and this causes a new selection to replace any previous one. If you click on one of the other three buttons before making a new selection, this behaviour is altered.

The second button causes the new selection to be added to any existing selection. You can use this facility in two ways: either to build up a complicated shape by combining simpler shapes, or to select several different parts of an image.

The third button causes a new selection to be subtracted from the existing selection. That is, it allows you to deselect some pixels that you have already selected. Sometimes, this is the only way to make selections of a certain shape. For instance, the image on the left of Figure 3.30 shows a picture reflected in a mirror. Suppose you wanted to select just the bevelled edge of the mirror, in order to clean up the distorted reflection there. You could do so easily by making a rectangular marquee selection that enclosed the entire mirror, choosing the subtraction button from the options bar, and making a new selection just from the clear part of the mirror. Subtracting this from the original selection leaves just the bevel selected, as shown on the right of Figure 3.30.

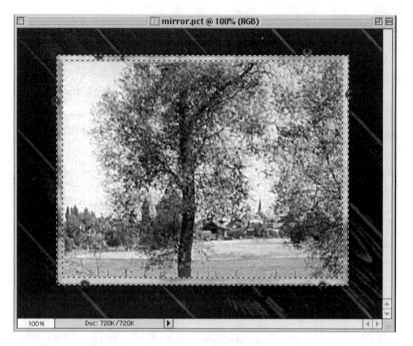

Figure 3.30   *Subtracting selections.*

The final option for these selection tools causes any new selection to be intersected with the existing one. That is, only pixels that lie within both the old selection and the new will be selected. (If you recognize the concept of intersection from set theory, you will also probably recognize that when we talk about adding selections we really mean forming their union, and that when we subtract them it is a set theoretic difference that we end up with.)

These four modifiers are arranged from left to right in decreasing order of usefulness, but all of them will occasionally prove helpful to you. In fact, you may well find that you spend more time combining selections than making entirely new ones, especially when you start using the magic wand tool, which will be described shortly. This being so you'll probably prefer to use keyboard modifier keys instead of the buttons on the options bar. You shouldn't be surprised to learn that holding down the shift key while you make a selection causes it to be added to the existing selection; the [opt/alt] key is used to subtract selections, and both of these keys together are used when you want to form an intersection.

> ☛ Make a rectangular selection in an image, then make an elliptical selection, using each of the modifiers in turn. Do this with selections that overlap, are completely separate and are enclosed in each other. Make sure you understand why the resulting selection is what it is.

Any selection can be transformed using the Select>Transform Selection command. This causes a bounding box to appear around the selection's outline, which you can manipulate in just the same way as when you use the free transform command on the image, to scale, rotate, skew and distort the selection. Although the method is identical, in this case it is the selection that is being transformed, not the selected pixels. When you have finished with the bounding box, you click in the tick or the cross in the options bar and the transformed selection will be shown in the usual way, by marching ants.

Extracting Objects

If you need to select an object and separate it cleanly from its background – in order to place it against a different background, for example – then you need to use specialized tools. The task is quite difficult, since in effect you are expecting Photoshop to perform some of the same processing tasks that go on in your brain when you look at an image and identify certain regions of it as being a person, a dog, a teapot or a bicycle. There is really nothing recorded in the array of pixels in which the image information is stored to identify any such object; it is only by looking at how colours and brightness change that it is possible to identify edges, and these changes can be subtle. Our brains make use of knowledge of the world to help interpret image information, but Photoshop knows nothing about the world. In other words, you should not expect selection tools to work miracles, and sometimes it will only be possible to extract an object from its background by painstaking use of the manual selection tools.

The oldest and simplest of Photoshop's tools for extracting objects is the magnetic lasso, which we described on page 96. It can perform quite impressively on certain types of image, but notoriously difficult objects, such as a person's head with loose strands of hair, usually defy it. Until Photoshop 5.5 was released it was necessary to use third-party plug-ins to help with such difficult selections, and these still give the quickest and best results. However, Photoshop now has its own tools for automatic extraction of objects, and these will sometimes suffice.

The *background eraser* tool is similar to the ordinary eraser, being a negative brush, which can be set to different shapes and hardness. It does not actually recognize backgrounds and erase them. What it does is erase all pixels within the area of the brush which are the same colour as the pixel under its centre, within a tolerance value you set in the options bar. This can be used to erase uniform backgrounds. If you drag the eraser so its centre, which is shown by a cross hair, is in the background but the brush intersects the edge of an object which is a different colour, all the background pixels under the brush will be erased, but the object will be left intact. Figure 3.31 shows the background eraser in action. Notice that the central object was roughly extracted from the background using the lasso tool before the background eraser was used. The chequer board pattern shows the transparent area being created by the eraser. To complete the extraction, the relatively easy job of removing the background beyond this area could be done with the ordinary eraser tool.

If an object is placed against a contrasting background of a more or less uniform colour that does not appear on the object itself, a single click of the magic eraser (see page 85)

Figure 3.31   *Using the background eraser.*

is all that is needed to delete the background. It is only for objects with less well-defined boundaries and more complex backgrounds that the background eraser is needed. Actually, it is never literally needed: by using a small eraser at high magnification, it is possible, with patience, to erase the most intricate outlines. The background eraser eases the task, though, since it does not require you to accurately follow every indentation of a complex outline, merely to keep the cross hair on the background. Even this requires care and patience.

The behaviour of the background eraser is controlled by several options. The Tolerance determines how closely a pixel must match the colour under the cross hair to qualify for erasure. If there is not much colour contrast between background and object, a low tolerance must be used, but this may lead to background pixels not being erased properly. (Provided the boundary becomes clearly defined after the background eraser has done its work, any extraneous background pixels can be tidied up with the ordinary eraser relatively easily.) The Limits option can be set to Contiguous, which causes blocks of pixels to be erased, Discontiguous, which causes all pixels within the eraser to be removed, and Find Edges, which attempts to do what it says. You can also vary the way in which the colour to erase is chosen, using the Sampling option. Setting this to Continuous causes the eraser to behave as we have described it, erasing all pixels which match the colour at its centre, so that the erased colour changes as the eraser moves. The Once setting uses the colour that was found when the eraser was first clicked on the image; Background Swatch uses the colour selected in the background swatch in the toolbox.

☛ Practise using the background eraser to isolate an object from its background. Experiment with different tolerance settings. Try to get as clean a result as possible.

The most intelligent facility for extracting objects from their backgrounds in Photoshop is a complete mini-application within the application, which is invoked by the Image>Extract... command. Figure 3.32 shows its interface. The mode of operation is quite simple. You begin by using the edge highlighter tool to draw fairly roughly round the edge of your object. The eraser tool within this dialogue can be used to erase the highlighting if necessary. You need to ensure that the actual outline of your object lies within the highlighted area, but otherwise you don't need to be too accurate. If you select the Smart Highlighting checkbox the highlighter will snap to edges. You can vary the size of the highlighter: it should be big enough to cover all the boundary region of your object, including loose strands of hair, fur, fuzzy twigs, and so on. Next you use the fill tool (paintbucket) to fill in the inside of the object – you just click with the tool inside any areas you wish to retain. To see the effect, click the button labelled Preview.

It will almost certainly not be perfect. You can touch up the results using the cleanup and edge touchup tools. The former behaves like an eraser, allowing you to remove extra pixels; if you hold down [opt/alt] while you drag it, it behaves in the opposite fashion, putting back pixels that have been excluded. The edge touchup tool is rather like the background eraser, and can be used to define edges more clearly.

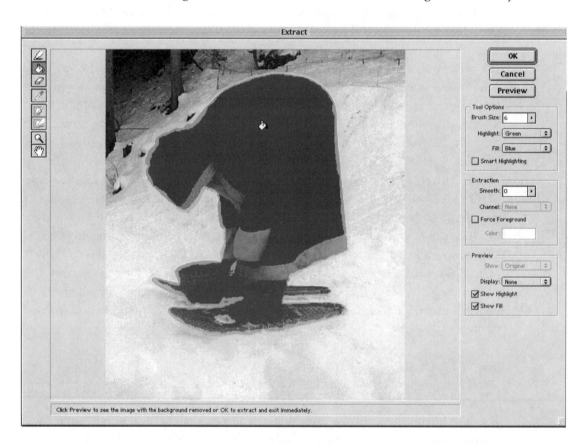

Figure 3.32   *Extracting an object from its background.*

For suitable images, this process can produce impressive results, as Figure 3.33 demonstrates. Where there is less contrast or extraneous details surround the object, the result is less satisfactory. It pays to be selective about the extraction tasks you attempt.

☞ Take an image containing an object with a poorly defined outline and extract it from its background. Try all possible methods.

Figure 3.33   *The extracted object.*

Selecting By Colour

We previously described the magic eraser, which removes pixels on the basis of their colour. A closely related tool is the *magic wand*, which selects pixels of a particular colour. To use it you just click somewhere in the image; all pixels of a similar colour to the one you have clicked on are selected. The magic wand takes the same options as the magic eraser (see Figure 3.17): a tolerance value to specify how closely a colour must match the one under the wand to qualify for selection, a checkbox to specify whether the selection should be contiguous – only pixels that are within the tolerance and adjacent to selected ones are added to the selection – or not, and another to specify whether the selection should be anti-aliased, that is, whether its edges should be softened. (We will look at anti-aliased selections in more detail in the next section.) A final checkbox, labelled Use All Layers allows you to choose whether the selection should be restricted to pixels on the active layer (deselect the checkbox) or should be extended to look at every layer (select it). It does not makes sense to consider the opacity of a selection, so the opacity field in Figure 3.17 is missing from the options bar for the magic wand.

The idea behind the magic wand is simple, but, like most of Photoshop's tools, using it effectively takes a bit of work. Once again, the problem is that Photoshop is dealing purely with numbers that represent colour values, whereas when we look at a picture we see it as a representation of something, or at least as a composition with some structure to it. For example, you might think that if you clicked somewhere on one of the stripes in a picture of a zebra, you would be able to select all of the animal's stripes. In fact, you wouldn't, unless you used a high tolerance, which might well select other parts of the picture, too. The reason is that, because of the differences in shading caused by the way light falls on the curved surface of a body, the actual colour values in a stripe vary quite widely. The situation is made worse by the fact that Photoshop does not always consider two colours to be close when we do, and vice versa. Again, this is because the computer program uses purely numerical calculations to determine the distance between two colours, but human colour perception is more complicated, owing to the structure of the eye and brain, and we distinguish more finely between shades in some parts of the spectrum than in others. It is usually necessary to experiment with the tolerance settings for each image individually to get the magic wand to make the selections you want. Nevertheless, with a bit of practice, the magic wand can be an effective selection tool, not only for selecting objects according to their colour, but for choosing ranges of colour for making tonal and other adjustments.

Because it is frequently necessary to refine magic wand selections, it is particularly useful to be able to use the add and subtract modifiers with this tool. You often make an initial selection and then add pixels by shift-clicking with the wand, or subtract them, until the selection based on Photoshop's interpretation of similar colours matches your own. You can also profitably use the intersection modifier: make a rough selection of the part of the image that you are interested in with a marquee tool, and then intersect that with a magic wand selection to pick out colours only within the selected region.

> ☞ Practise using the magic wand tool on different images with a range of visual characteristics, adjusting the tolerance to enable you to make the selections you want. Try greyscale images, portraits, landscapes, night scenes, and so on.

There is an alternative way of selecting colours in Photoshop (but not in ImageReady), which works in a slightly different way from the magic wand. The Select>Color Range... command brings up a dialogue box containing a preview of a selection (which is blank to begin with) and some controls, as shown in Figure 3.34. The pop-up menu at the top allows you to select a predefined range of colours: all the reds, greens, or blues, for example, which you might want to select if you needed to compensate for problems with a scanner. Most of the other options are directed towards printed material, apart from Highlights, Mid-tones and Shadows, although these only actually select a brightness range, which appears to approximate the sort of area indicated by the name.

The most usual option to use is Sampled Colors, which lets you choose the colours to select.

In this mode, the eyedropper tool is used to sample a colour from the main image; colours similar to it are then selected. You can add extra colours by sampling again with the eyedropper with a + sign attached to it, or remove colours from the selection by sampling with the eyedropper with a - sign. The Fuzziness slider is an essential part of the process; it is used to control how colours which are close to the sampled one are added to the selection.

☞ Practise using the Select>Color Range... command on different images, as you did the magic wand. Observe the effect of the Fuzziness slider.

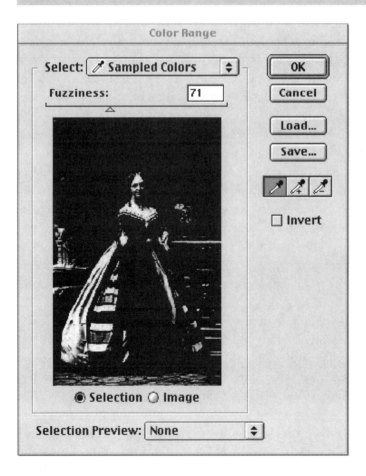

Figure 3.34   *Selecting a colour range.*

The Fuzziness slider appears to behave somewhat like the tolerance value for the magic wand, adding more colours as the value is increased, but actually it works in a different way, which introduces a new idea. With the magic wand, pixels are either selected or they are not. With a colour range selection, some pixels can be partially selected. Increasing the fuzziness value increases the extent to which colours that do not exactly match the sampled ones are selected. The dialogue box provides an immediate preview of the selection, so it is possible to adjust the fuzziness interactively to obtain the desired selection. Which is all very well, but what exactly does it mean for a pixel to be partially selected? To understand that, we must look at selections in a slightly different way.

Masks

We remarked at the beginning of this section that once you have made a selection, painting and other adjustments are applied only to the selected pixels and not the rest of the image. Looking at this another way, the area of the image outside the selection is protected from any such changes. The situation is analogous to the use of a stencil in conjunction with a paint spray. You place the stencil – typically a piece of card with some shapes cut out of it – on top of the picture you are creating and spray your paint. Where it strikes the card, it can't reach the paper to leave a mark. A similar technique is used by photographers, who place shapes on top of the paper onto which they are making a print, to protect parts of the print from the light projected by an enlarger. This way, unwanted parts of the image on the negative won't be printed. In this context the protective stencils are called *masks*. Unlike the masks used with a paint spray, which either completely stop the paint or let it all hit the paper, a photographic mask does not have to allow either none the light or all of it through; it can include partially transparent areas which just let some of it pass, and such masks are used to achieve some sorts of photographic effect, such as placing a soft edge around a portrait.

Thinking about these analogies, you can see that when we make a selection in Photoshop we are, in effect, defining a mask comprising the pixels which are *not* selected. Like the photographer's masks, Photoshop masks can be partially transparent. This is what it means for some pixels to be partially selected – the areas of the mask corresponding to those pixels are partially transparent.

Photoshop allows you to work directly with masks, providing several ways of creating them and editing them, as well as a range of different ways of using them. We will only describe some of the simpler aspects of masking, which is a complex subject.

If you think of a mask as something that allows light to pass through it in some places, and blocks it or allows it through partially in others, you may find yourself thinking about something like a sheet of acetate (like a layer, in fact) that has been blackened in some places to stop light passing through, left clear in other places to allow it to pass, and painted in shades of grey where light is to pass partly through. In other words, it is a greyscale image, and that is how Photoshop actually represents masks: as greyscale images which it uses in special ways to modify the associated layer. Since it is just an image, you can modify it the same way you can any other image, but since it is greyscale, if you use colours to paint on it, they are mapped to a shade of grey. By convention, if you paint on a mask in white, it allows the image to show through (in other words, it extends the selection to which the mask corresponds), and if you paint in black, it masks more of the image, with greys being treated as intermediate values in a straightforward way.

But how do you create masks and edit them separately from the image? There are several ways. The easiest way is to make a selection, and then click on the *Quick Mask* button in the toolbox. Two things happen when you do this. First, the mask becomes visible as a partially transparent red overlay covering the area outside the original selection. (This is not part of the image, it just shows you where the mask is, the same way the marching ants show you where a selection is.) Second, any painting you do, and any filters you apply (see below) affect the mask, not the image, so you can paint in new parts of the mask. It is common to use brushes with a soft edge for this purpose, to create masks which also have soft edges. When you have finished altering the mask, you return to ordinary image editing mode by clicking on the Standard Mode button, which is next to the Quick Mask button. Now, the mask you created in Quick Mask mode will be treated as a selection, so it will modify any paint or effects you apply to the layer. If, for example, you created a mask with soft edges, any effects you apply to the image will fade gradually over the edge. Alternatively, you can simply invert the selection and delete, to place the selected part of the image in a soft frame, in a manner made popular by Victorian photographers. We have done this to a detail from a photograph in Figure 3.35.

(Actually, there's an easier way of creating this effect, if you are happy to have the picture fade uniformly in every direction: make an elliptical selection, with the Feather option set to a suitable value. Feathering causes the edges of a selection to fade gradually. In effect, it is another way of creating a semi-transparent mask. Anti-aliasing a selection is similar. In this case, the potentially jagged edges of the mask are replaced by a mixture of grey pixels, which smooth out the jaggedness.)

Figure 3.35   *Fading with a mask.*

☞ Open any image and create a mask using the brush tools in Quick Mask mode. Experiment with painting over the masked image when you return to Standard Mode.

Masks you create using Quick Mask are transitory; like selections, they are lost once you have created another one. You sometimes want a mask to persist for longer. One way of making it do so is by associating it with a layer. Each layer of an image except the background layer[*] can have a mask – called its *layer mask* – associated with it. This lets you create transparent areas in the layer so that parts of those below show through it. There are several ways of creating a layer mask. The one that is most easy to understand in the context of our discussion of the relationship between masks and selections is by converting a selection into a mask. This can be done by clicking on the mask icon at the bottom of the Layers palette. When you create a mask in this way, it shows up as a thumbnail in the palette's entry for the corresponding layer, as shown in Figure 3.36. If you click on the layer mask's thumbnail, the paintbrush icon next to the current layer turns into a mask icon as it has in the illustration. This indicates that any painting, erasing or other changes you make will affect the mask, not the image. When you are working on the mask, you can even use the selection tools, but, like everything else, they

---

[*]The command Layer>New>Layer From Background can be used to create a regular layer from the background.

select areas of the mask, not the image. If you copy a selected area to the clipboard and then paste it into another image, you will see the greyscale mask.

☞ Create a simple circular layer mask, then use a painting tool to extend it into an irregular shape.

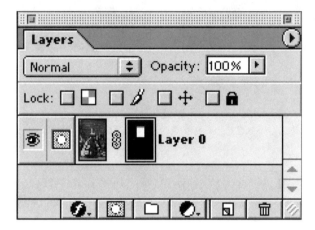

Figure 3.36   *A layer mask as shown in the* Layers *palette.*

We have made much of the link between selections and masks, but we should emphasize that, although you can convert between them, they are not the same thing. A mask is more permanent than a selection and, depending on the sort of mask it is, it will affect the appearance of an image in different ways, whereas a selection, in itself, makes no difference. In particular, when you turn a selection into a layer mask, all the masked pixels (the ones outside the original selection) become transparent. Unlike a Quick Mask, a layer mask is not shown as a red overlay, you just see the pixels become transparent.

Layer masks can be used to combine parts of different layers, since they allow you to mask out the parts you don't want, without actually deleting them, so you can return to the layer and alter the mask or restore all its contents at a later time. By using masks with soft edges or gradients, you can make images fade into each other. Figure 3.37 shows a straightforward example of how layers can be combined with a mask. A rectangular selection was made just outside the whole mirror, and then a smaller rectangle entirely within the bevelled edge was subtracted from it (cf. page 100). The resulting selection was turned into a layer mask, and a layer containing a wood-like texture was placed underneath the original image, to give the effect of a wood frame around the mirror.

Figure 3.37   *Combining layers with a layer mask.*

☞ Paste two different images of the same size into a document. Practise using layer masks with different shapes and characteristics to combine the two images into a composite.

As well as masks based on selections (i.e., areas of pixels), a layer can also have a *layer clipping path*, that is, a vector path which is used to define the visible region of the layer. This is done by creating a path with the drawing tools, and then choosing Layer>Add Layer Clipping Path>Current Path. Now, if you were to create a layer consisting simply of the foreground colour, which you can do with the Layer>New Fill Layer>Solid Colour... command, and then add a clipping path to it, you would end up with something that looked and behaved like a vector shape. You can perform these two operations in one by clicking the Create New Shape Layer button in the options bar when you pick up one of the drawing tools. In this way, Photoshop provides the illusion of combining vector graphics and bitmapped images in the same program. Since each type of graphics has its own unique characteristics, this may be considered valuable but only if you are proficient with the tools and techniques associated with both forms.

☞ Using the two layers you had in the previous example, practise creating layer clipping paths to combine them. Create some shape layers to add vector shapes to the resulting composition.

The last way of working with masks and selections which we will describe is to save them as what are sometimes called *alpha channels*. (Don't worry about the origin of the name.) The command Select>Save Selection... (which is only available if there *is* a selection to save) causes the dialogue shown on the left of Figure 3.38 to be displayed, where you can give the selection a name, so that you can easily identify it later. To reload the selection, you use Select>Load Selection..., which leads to the dialogue shown on the right of Figure 3.38. Any saved selections will be listed in the Channel pop-up menu.

When you choose a menu entry, the selection you saved with that name is reselected or combined with any current selection, depending on which of the radio buttons at the bottom of the dialogue box you choose.

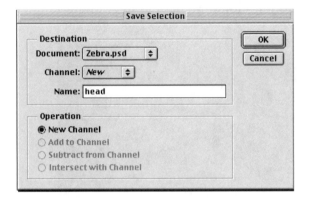
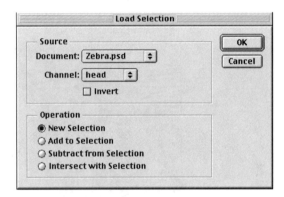

Figure 3.38   *Saving and loading a selection.*

You can use alpha channels in the obvious way, just to remember selections so that you don't have to go through the mechanics of selecting again later if you need to. It is especially useful to be able to load an alpha channel from one image into another, though you can only do so if they are both the same size. You do it by opening both images at once and using the Document pop-up menu in the Load Selection dialogue to choose a document to load the alpha channel from. If you have a set of images which are all the same size – for example, frames of an animation – you can quickly select the same part of each of them by making the selection in one file and saving it as an alpha channel which you load into each of the others in turn. (When you combine this facility with the automation features described in Chapter 9, you can apply a common process to selected parts of a set of images with relative ease.) Alpha channels can also be used in more imaginative ways. For instance, you can make a selection based on an image on one layer, perhaps using the magic wand, save it and delete the layer, then reload it as a selection on a different layer, and turn it into a layer mask. The outline of the mask will be the shape derived from the deleted layer. This is one way of achieving effects such as the one shown in Figure 3.39.

☛ Practise using saved selections to produce knockout effects. For example, make a picture of the place where you work shown through the logo of your college or company, or make a picture of the environment in which you would expect to find a certain animal shown through the outline of that animal.

Figure 3.39   *Using a saved selection as a layer mask.*

Photoshop has extensive facilities for manipulating alpha channels: they are displayed in the Channels palette, from which they can be selected and edited as greyscale images. ImageReady only allows you to save and load selections. If you need to do more, you will have to switch to Photoshop; alpha channels are preserved when you do so. Alpha channels saved with images in Photoshop can be used by other programs that can import Photoshop files. In particular, Premiere can use alpha channels from Photoshop, as described on page 518.

☞ Open an image, create a selection and save it as an alpha channel. Look at the Channels palette to see the alpha channel as an image. Practise loading the selection from the channel back into the original image and into other images the same size.

Adjustments and Retouching

Photoshop's name draws our attention to its traditional role as a digital image retouching application, incorporating many of the tools and techniques traditionally employed in a photographic darkroom for altering and improving the quality of prints.

Photoshop provides a host of ways of making adjustments to brightness and colour in an image. Any adjustment you make is applied only to selected pixels if you have made a selection; otherwise, it is applied to the current layer. Some of the adjustments which you can make, such as Selective Color..., are intended only for use by professional technicians who understand about process and spot colours, and other such esoterica of printing technology; they are much too specialized for novices and have no use in multimedia, so we will omit them from our descriptions. We will also ignore some of the options in the adjustments we do describe, for similar reasons.

ImageReady provides fewer and less detailed adjustments than Photoshop. Its more basic set may be adequate for Web design, although some of the missing facilities are valuable for the Web as well as print.

One of Photoshop's ideas that is sorely missed from ImageReady is *adjustment layers*. These are an extension of the layer concept; you can think of them as being layers that you look through and see an adjusted version of what lies beneath. Commands for making adjustments can be found in the Image>Adjust sub-menu, but for nearly all of them there is a corresponding entry in the Layer>New Adjustment Layer sub-menu. An adjustment layer carries just one kind of adjustment, as if you had applied one command. The dialogue boxes used to apply the adjustment are the same in both cases, but there are important differences between the two methods of application. When you add an adjustment layer, you are first offered the option of setting a blending mode and opacity setting for it, as you are with a normal layer, which affects how the adjustment is applied to the pixels on underlying layers. The adjustments associated with an adjustment layer affect any layers beneath it. By moving the adjustment layer up or down in the Layers palette, you can affect different layers. Most significantly, the adjustment is attached to the layer and is not actually applied to any pixels in the image. This means that you are free to experiment with adjustments, without having to worry about irreparably changing the image itself. You can always go back to an adjustment layer to change the parameter values. If you decide not to apply the changes, you can just delete the adjustment layer, or you can hide it and add another to try a different set of alterations.

An adjustment layer shows up in the Layers palette, as shown in Figure 3.40, with an icon representing a control panel instead of the image thumbnail you get for an ordinary layer. By double-clicking this icon, you can bring up the dialogue box for the adjustment on the layer and change its parameters. Like any other layer, an adjustment layer can have a layer mask, which prevents the adjustments being applied to parts of an image. If you add an adjustment layer when a selection is active, the selection is automatically converted into a layer mask attached to the adjustment layer.

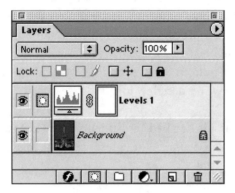

Figure 3.40   *An adjustment layer in the* Layers *palette.*

If you transfer an image with adjustment layers from Photoshop to ImageReady, which doesn't support adjustment layers, the layers' adjustments are still visible, but you cannot change their parameters until you switch back to Photoshop. We recommend the use of adjustment layers whenever possible.

Tonal Adjustments

The most basic adjustments you can make alter the distribution of light and dark tones in selected areas of an image. The crudest adjustments of all are made with the brightness and contrast sliders, shown in Figure 3.41, which are displayed when you add a Brightness/Contrast adjustment layer, or select Brightness/Contrast... from the Image>Adjust sub-menu. The sliders work like the corresponding controls on a monitor or television set. Brightness adjusts the value of each pixel up or down uniformly, so increasing the brightness makes every pixel lighter, decreasing it makes every pixel darker. Contrast is a little more subtle: it adjusts the range of values, either enhancing or reducing the difference between the lightest and darkest areas of the image. Increasing contrast makes the light areas very light and the dark areas very dark, decreasing it moves all values towards an intermediate grey. As with all the adjustment controls, if you tick the checkbox labelled Preview any adjustments you make are shown in the image window as you move the sliders, so you can judge your settings visually as you work.

☛ Choose an image that requires some adjustment to its brightness and contrast – an under- or over-exposed photograph, for example. Create a Brightness/Contrast adjustment layer and try to correct the image.

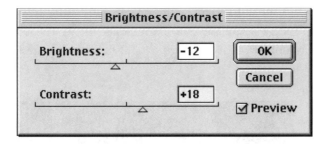

Figure 3.41 *The brightness and contrast sliders.*

More control over the tonal balance of an image is provided by the Levels dialogue, shown in Figure 3.42, invoked from either the Image>Adjust sub-menu or a Levels adjustment layer, which allows you to set the white and black levels in the image and adjust the mid-point. In terms of the content of the image, you are adjusting the tones of the shadows, highlights and mid-tones.

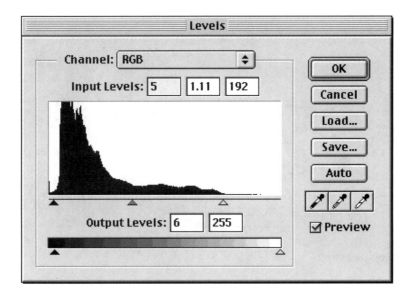

Figure 3.42 *The* Levels *dialogue.*

The little graph that occupies most of the dialogue box is called the *image histogram*. It shows how the different brightness levels are distributed among the pixels of the image (or selection). The horizontal axis represents the different possible brightness levels, with black (zero) at the left, and white (255) at the right. The height of the graph at each point indicates the number of pixels with that brightness, so in Figure 3.42 you can see that most of the pixels are rather dark, with none actually white. (If you just want to look at this graph, choose Histogram... from the Image menu. The resulting display provides some extra numerical detail.) Figure 3.43 shows two examples of images and their histograms.

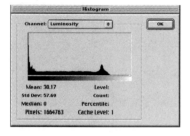

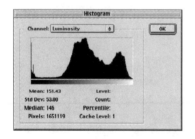

Figure 3.43 *Image histograms.*

In the Levels dialogue, the sliders immediately below the histogram control the range of input values. The slider at the left controls the pixel value that will be mapped to black. If you drag this slider to the right, say to 10, any pixels whose value is less than or equal to 10 will be displayed as black. The slider at the right controls the pixel value that is mapped to white, so if you drag it to the left, say to 245, any pixels with value greater than or equal to 245 will be displayed as white. In order to spread the range of tonal values evenly across the image, the input sliders are moved so that they line up with the lowest and highest values that have a non-zero number of pixels shown in the histogram. This will be done for you – unless your image has an unusual tonal distribution – if you click the Auto button. (The same effect is achieved by selecting Auto Levels from Image>Adjust. Most people prefer to adjust levels by eye, though, using the preview to judge the result instead of trusting Photoshop's mechanical adjustments.) Moving beyond these points will expand the dynamic range artificially.

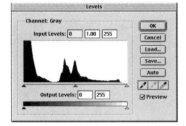

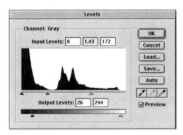

Figure 3.44   *Using levels adjustments.*

The values of pixels in between the black and white extremes are normally mapped linearly to intermediate shades. By dragging the middle slider, which represents the mid-point in the tonal range, you can affect the distribution of these intermediate pixels. If an image's brightness is concentrated in a particular range, you can move the mid-point slider under the corresponding point on the histogram, so that the brightness values are adjusted to put this range in the centre of the available scale of values. Figure 3.44 shows the effect that level adjustments can achieve in bringing out detail that has been lost in an under-exposed photograph. The top image was shot at dusk, with too short an exposure; the positions of the sliders that were used to produce the lower image and the changed image histogram can be seen in the lower Levels dialogue box.

The pair of sliders at the bottom of the Levels dialogue is used to control the range of displayed brightness. That is, they determine the appearance of the pixels that have been mapped by the input sliders to black and white. If, for instance, you drag the left (black) slider up to a value of 15, then any black pixels will actually be shown as a dark grey – the tone that would otherwise be used for pixels whose stored value was 15. Similarly, if you drag the right slider down to 240, white pixels will be displayed as a pale grey. These output adjustments can be used to compress the dynamic range of your image.

☞ Use a Levels adjustment layer to correct the image whose brightness and contrast you adjusted on page 116. Experiment with both sets of sliders to see the effect on the image and how this relates to the histogram. Try to duplicate the effect of your original brightness and contrast adjustment.

The pop-up menu at the top of the Levels dialogue can be used to select whether to apply the adjustments to the complete image, as tonal adjustments, or to one of the red, green or blue components of each pixel independently. Doing this alters the colour balance of the image. For beginners, this offers too much control and you will be better off using some of the more specialized colour adjustments to be described shortly.

If you are used to thinking about relationships as functions and to visualizing functions as curves, you will find the Curves dialogue provides a powerful way of manipulating the relationship between stored pixel values and displayed tones. (If you are not familiar with these things, you may prefer to stick with Levels.) It is displayed when you create a Curves adjustment layer or select the Curves... command from the Image>Adjust sub-menu.

To begin with, let's just consider greyscale images, where each pixel is represented by a single byte containing a value between 0 and 255. Normally, we consider 0 (no light) to be black and 255 white, with the values in between representing shades of grey. But we don't have to map those stored values to displayed shades in that way – they're just numbers. When we make adjustments in the Levels dialogue, we alter the mapping function from stored to displayed values. To begin with, when stored values are used directly to set the displayed brightness, the function is represented by a straight line, with a gradient of 1. In the Levels dialogue, the input slider at the left controls the pixel value that will be mapped to black, so, in graphical terms, it moves the bottom end of the mapping function's line along the horizontal axis. The input slider at the right controls the pixel value that is mapped to white, so it moves the top end of the line along the horizontal line corresponding to the maximum pixel value. In a similar way, the output slider controls move the end points of the line up and down. You should be able to work out how the brightness and contrast sliders move the line.

The Curves dialogue, which is illustrated in Figure 3.45, allows you to take detailed control of this graph. Manipulating the curve is straightforward. If you drag a point on the curve it is pulled out as if it was a piece of elastic. To fix a point in place, you click on it. If you wish, you can make completely arbitrary changes by completely redrawing the curve with a pencil tool: just click on the pencil icon in the bottom right of the dialogue and draw freely with it. To return to reshaping the curve by dragging, click on the curve icon next to the pencil. Whichever method of reshaping you choose, the curve does not have to be kept as a straight line, but can be any shape you like. The almost complete freedom to map grey levels to new values that this provides permits some strange effects, but it also makes it easy to apply subtle corrections to incorrectly exposed photographs, or to compensate for improperly calibrated scanners.

☛ Repeat the previous exercise, using a Curves adjustment layer. Create a second Curves adjustment layer and use it to experiment with the effect of making wild alterations to the shape of the curve by dragging or drawing.

An S-shaped curve such as the one illustrated in Figure 3.45 is often used to increase the contrast of an image: the mid-point is fixed and the shadows are darkened by pulling down the quarter-point, while the highlights are lightened by pulling up the three-quarter-point. The gentle curvature means that, while the overall contrast is increased, the total tonal range is maintained and there are no abrupt changes in brightness.

Colour Adjustments

Normally, curve adjustments are applied to all three colour components combined, which has the effect of altering the brightness levels without changing any colours. Like the Levels dialogue, the Curves dialogue has a pop-up menu that allows you to select one of the colour components to apply the adjustment to. This is probably the most flexible means of making colour adjustment that there is, but it is not easy to see in advance what the effect of any adjustment will be. If you need to make changes to colour balance, it is easier to use one of the dialogues that provide a higher level interface to the colours of the image. To appreciate how these work, it is necessary to understand a little bit about colour theory. If concepts such as the RGB and HSB colour models and the use of colour pickers are not familiar to you, you should read the short section on colour in Chapter 9, starting on page 559.

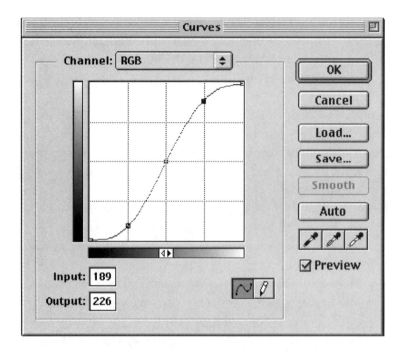

Figure 3.45   *Setting an S-shaped curve in the* Curves *dialogue.*

If you are new to colour adjustments, the most appealing interface may be that provided by the Image>Adjust>Variations... command, which allows you to change hue, saturation and brightness by selecting new versions of your image from a gallery of thumbnails that illustrates possible variations. An example is shown in Figure 3.46 (though some of the variations are not apparent in this black and white reproduction, of course).

The two thumbnail images at the top of the box show the original image, on the left, and the 'current pick', that is, the image with your currently chosen set of adjustments made to it. These adjustments are made by picking one of the thumbnails in the lower part of the dialogue box. The seven images on the left are used to adjust colour. With a little imagination, you can see these as comprising six variations arranged around the rim of a colour wheel at the positions occupied by the primary and secondary colours, with a seventh image in the centre, which is another copy of the current pick. To add more of a primary colour, click on the corresponding peripheral image: for instance, to add more red, click on the one at the right. To subtract some of a primary colour, click on the secondary opposite it, so to remove some red, click on the image at the left, labelled More Cyan. The slider at the top right of the dialogue is used to determine how much is more, that is, how big a step each of the thumbnails represents. When you click

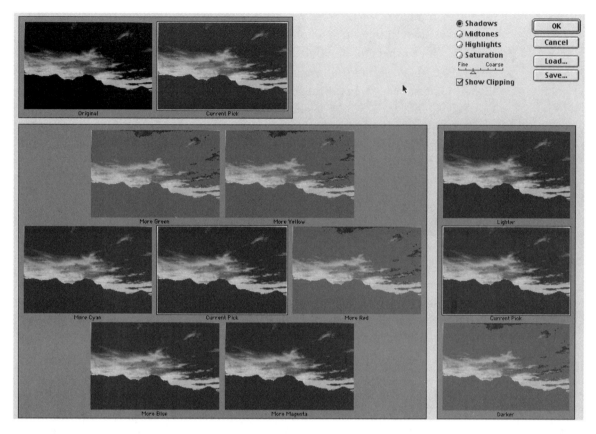

Figure 3.46   *Variations.*

on one of these small images, the current pick is replaced by the variation you have chosen, which is in turn replaced by a new variation with still more red, or whatever.

The three images on the right are used to adjust brightness in the same way. The radio buttons at the top right of the dialogue are used to apply the variations to the darkest (Shadows), lightest (Highlights) or mid-range (Midtones) tones of the image. If you select the last radio button, labelled Saturation, the display changes to show just three thumbnails which are used to adjust the saturation in the same way as the ones originally at the right are used to adjust brightness. Thus, in this one dialogue, you can adjust all three components using a simple interface that provides immediate feedback. As with other changes, if you had made a selection before bringing up the dialogue, the adjustments are only applied to the selected pixels; this is reflected in the preview images.

There is a limit to how much red you can add to any particular pixel: eventually the maximum amount that can be represented in a byte will be reached. When this happens, any further addition of red will have no further effect on that pixel, though it may affect others. Similarly, if you add too much cyan (i.e., subtract too much red), there will be no red left. In the same way, there is a limit to the amount of green or blue you can add or subtract, or the lightness or extent of saturation you can apply to any pixel. The pixels that have reached their maximum value are then said to be *clipped*. If you tick the checkbox labelled Show Clipping a fluorescent mask is used to show pixels that are clipped. You can see this in Figure 3.46.

☞ Choose an image with many different colours and practise using the Variations... command until you feel you have a reasonable understanding of how each variation affects the colour. Now take an image with a colour cast and try to correct it using variations.

The Variations dialogue is easy to use, but it only provides a crude interface to colour adjustment, even with the slider set to Fine. It also has the drawback that it cannot be used to create an adjustment layer. The Variations... command is only available in the Image>Adjust sub-menu and any changes made are applied to the pixels and can only be undone using the History palette.

If you wish to create an adjustment layer or you feel that the Variations dialogue does not offer you sufficient control, you can use the Color Balance dialogue, which can be brought up either from an adjustment layer or from the Image>Adjust sub-menu. It is shown in Figure 3.47. In effect, this performs the same job as the hue adjustments in the Variations dialogue. By dragging each slider towards either the primary or complementary secondary colour labelling its ends, you can add or subtract the corresponding colour component from the selected pixels in the image. If you tick the Preserve Luminosity checkbox, Photoshop will compensate for these colour adjustments so that the brightness is unaffected. (If you don't do this, since colour adjustment adds or subtracts light, the brightness will normally change as well as the colours.) Making small adjustments to the colour balance of an entire image is one way of compensating for colour casts introduced by a scanner.

☞ Use the same images you chose for the previous exercise and experiment with making adjustments to the colour balance, both to see their effect and to try to correct a fault in the image.

For still more control over colour adjustments, use the Hue/Saturation dialogue shown in Figure 3.48, which is also available both as an adjustment layer and as an adjustment

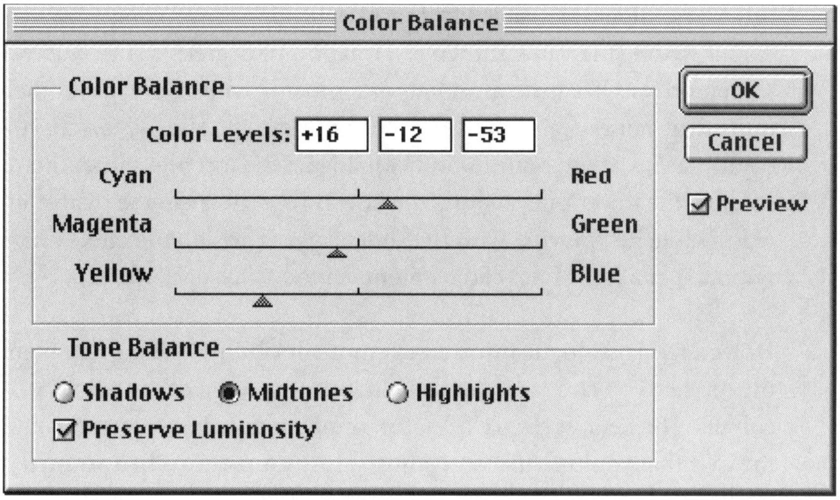

Figure 3.47 *Adjusting colour balance.*

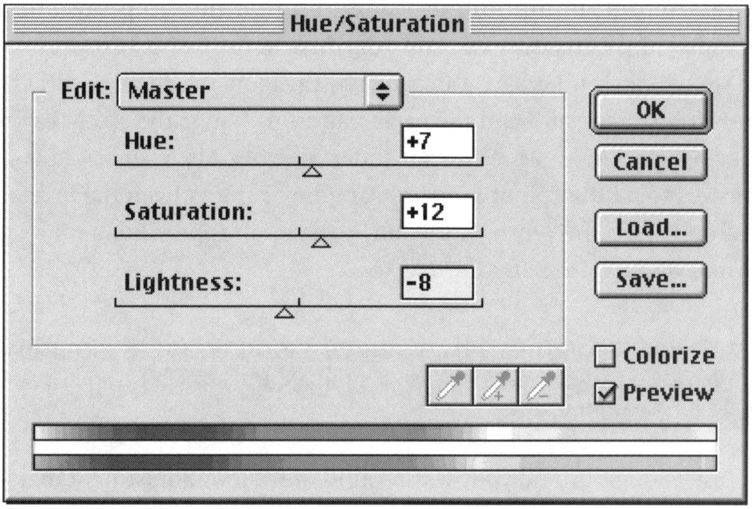

Figure 3.48 *The* Hue/Saturation *dialogue.*

to be applied to the image pixels. When it first opens, this dialogue provides a similar facility to Color Balance, but in terms of the HSB model of the colours in the image instead of the RGB model. This is in itself an advance if you find it easier to think about colour in terms of hue, saturation and brightness instead of the, essentially artificial, red, green and blue components. The interface to hue and saturation adjustments provides three sliders, one for each of the three HSB components (although the brightness slider is labelled Lightness). Dragging the top one moves colours around the colour wheel (the value shown is a rotation in degrees). The other two sliders change saturation and brightness, adding or removing white or black; in their case, the numerical values are percentages. As you move the sliders, the effect is shown in the colour ramps at the bottom of the dialogue: the top one shows the standard range of colours, the lower one changes to show how each is altered by the adjustments. (It's worthwhile just playing with the sliders and watching the effect on the lower colour ramp to get a feel of how adjustments in the HSB space work.)

However, this dialogue offers much more flexibility. The pop-up menu labelled Edit at the top lets you choose to apply changes to any one of the primary or secondary colours. The default choice of Master applies your changes to all colours, but it is often the case that you only need to adjust a limited range. When you select another value from the pop-up menu, some extra controls appear in the dialogue box, as shown in Figure 3.49. The grey bars that appears between the colour ramps show the range of colours that will be affected by the changes you make. The two light grey bars around the central dark grey bar indicate a fuzzy area, where changes will be partially applied. (Compare this behaviour with the fuzziness in the Select>Color Range dialogue.) You can stretch or shrink the colour range by dragging the small vertical bars between the central dark grey band and the fuzzy bands or change the extent of the fuzzy area by dragging the outermost triangular slider controls. Alternatively, you can use the eye droppers to set the colour range by sampling colours from the image: the plain eyedropper sets the centre of the range, the eyedropper with a plus sign extends it and the one with a minus sign shrinks it.

> ☞ Practise making hue and saturation adjustments to the two images you have used in the previous two exercises. Try to simulate the effect of colour balance adjustments using hue and saturation.

It's easy enough to find your way around the colour adjustment dialogues, but quite another thing to know how to achieve any particular visual adjustment using them. That takes practice.

Retouching By Hand

Making selections and then applying adjustments through the various dialogues we have described will suffice to improve or alter many images, but there are some jobs that are better done by working directly on the image using retouching tools. Examples of the sort of jobs that are best done that way include removing marks or blemishes from an image or reducing shadows under a person's chin in a badly lit portrait.

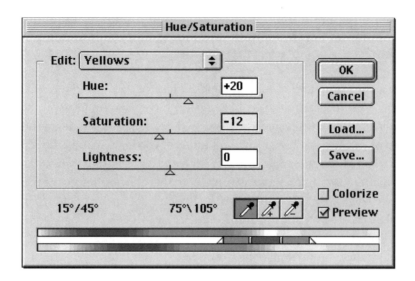

Figure 3.49   *Applying hue and saturation adjustments to a limited colour range.*

The dodge and burn tools (named after conventional darkroom techniques) apply tonal adjustments directly to pixels. They are used much like the paintbrush tool: you select a brush size and shape from a palette that drops down from the options bar and you can also set brush dynamics to make the tool respond to a pressure-sensitive pen. An option that is not appropriate for an ordinary paintbrush is a pop-up menu that lets you choose to apply the adjustments to shadows, midtones or highlights. You can also set the exposure, which is the amount by which the tool should lighten or darken the image. Having selected one of these tools and set its options, you just drag in the image, as you do with a paintbrush. The dodge tool lightens the pixels you drag it over, the burn tool darkens them. As you continue to drag over the same area the effect is increased. The dodge tool would be used to lighten shadows, or to remove bags from beneath someone's eyes if you wished to make them appear younger.

Figure 3.50   *Options for the dodge and burn tools.*

The sponge tool is used in the same way as the dodge and burn tools to desaturate colours, as if you were dragging a wet sponge over paint. Unfortunately for the analogy, you can set an option to make the sponge increase saturation instead.

☞ Experiment with using the dodge, burn and sponge tools on an image of your choice, to see how they work and what effect the settings have. Try to alter the image in precise ways, such as lightening or darkening an area of shadow.

The clone stamp tool is another hand retouching tool, which is used to make certain corrections that cannot easily be done any other way. Suppose you have scanned a watercolour painting on coarse paper with a visible grain and that there was a speck of dust or a scratch on the glass of the scanner. If you try to remove the resulting mark from the scanned image by painting or erasing, the corrected area will still show up because, no matter how careful you are, you will not be able to capture the texture of the paper where you have made your changes. The clone stamp is used to repair problems such as this. It paints a copy of part of an image onto a different part, so in this case, you could find an area of the image that was the same colour as the damaged area and remove the unwanted mark by cloning.

Like the other retouching tools, the clone stamp is a sort of paintbrush, so when you select it you can choose a brush size and so on. The next step is to [opt/alt] click at the point from which you want to start cloning. Once you have established this starting point you can paint with the stamp. As you do so, a cross-hair shows the point from which you are cloning; the cloned pixels are applied like any other brush strokes to the area over which you drag the tool. As well as correcting defects in an image, the clone stamp tool is often used for artificially improving images – faking, in other words. Figure 3.51 shows an innocuous example: we removed the peculiar ornament from the sideboard on the right side of the picture by cloning the wallpaper. The clone stamp is the secret of some models' perfect complexions. Like all the other retouching tools, it takes skill and a good visual sense to make a convincing job of such subtle alterations.

☞ Find an image with a clearly-defined subject, a background and some other objects and use the clone stamp tool to remove some of the extraneous objects.

Effects and Filters

The Filter menu provides commands for systematically changing the values of pixels in an image to produce effects reminiscent of natural art media and of special effects produced by the use of optical filters and other techniques in a traditional photographic darkroom. With one or two exceptions, filters are all applied in the same way. In all cases, they are applied to selected pixels, unless no selection has been made, in which case they are applied to the entire contents of the currently active layer. So, having made your selection if necessary, you choose a filter from one of the sub-menus of the Filter

Figure 3.51   *Retouching with the clone stamp.*

menu. Most filters have their own dialogue boxes, which allow you to alter various parameters controlling the extent of the alterations which the filter produces. (A few filters are always applied in the same way, with no variable parameters, so they skip the dialogue.) Figure 3.52 shows a typical example. Nearly all of these parameters are controlled by sliders, and although it is the case that each one really controls a clearly defined aspect of the particular filter it relates to, you don't need to understand in any detail what is being controlled, you can just fiddle with the sliders and see what happens. The effect of all filters with parameters can be previewed – they have a detailed preview within the dialogue box itself. The plus and minus signs underneath the preview box are used to zoom in and out, so you can see both the overall effect on a large area of the image and the detailed effect on a few pixels.

In addition to the filters supplied with Photoshop, many more are available as plug-ins from third parties. Sometimes, these duplicate the effect of one or more of the standard filters, but do the job better in some way, often by providing finer control or by using a more refined algorithm. Other plug-in filters provide distortions and effects that can only otherwise be achieved by careful application of a combination of filters, if at all. (The drawback to using plug-ins that produce a characteristic effect that cannot be achieved any other way is that everyone will know how you did it.) Plug-ins are usually

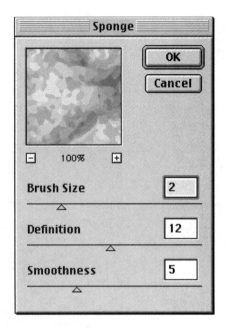

Figure 3.52   *A typical filter dialogue.*

supplied in collections. Kai's Power Tools (KPT) and Eye Candy are among the most widely used.

A filter can potentially alter every pixel in an image, and some filters perform fairly complex calculations using the values of several neighbouring pixels. As a result, applying a filter may take some time.

Blurring and Sharpening

Among the special effects and distortions there are two filters which are little less than essential, Gaussian Blur and Unsharp Mask, which are on the Blur and Sharpen sub-menus of the Filter menu, respectively.

Normally, you would not want a blurred picture, but when you are working with digital images, a slight amount of blur is often just what you need to remove characteristic digital artefacts, such as jagged edges caused by scanning at too low a resolution, Moiré patterns, which occur when a regular pattern interacts with the array of pixels, and, for Web images, the visible blocks that can result from excessive JPEG compression (see Chapter 10). When we talk about blurring in this context, we mean an operation that combines the value of a pixel with those of some of its neighbours, rather as if we were able to rub together the colour values of the pixels, in the same way as you blur edges in a pastel drawing by rubbing them with your finger. Taken to extremes, such an operation will produce a blurred image, but done more gently it will just remove the undesirable features just mentioned.

When you apply a Gaussian blur, each pixel is combined with several of its neighbours for some distance, the extent of the contribution of each neighbour falling off with radius. The falling off follows a 'bell curve', so that most of the contributions come from adjacent pixels, but those further away still contribute. (In theory, every pixel in the image will contribute something, but in practice the finite nature of computation means that only those within a radius of a few pixels will have any measurable influence.) Because of this spread-out influence, Gaussian blurring has a natural effect that is not visually intrusive.

The dialogue box for the Gaussian Blur filter, shown in Figure 3.53, lets you set the radius of the curve – a value which determines the width of the curve, although its exact relationship to the extent of the blurring is complicated. All you need to know is that higher values produce more blurring. A radius of 0.1 pixels produces a very subtle effect; values between 0.2 and 0.8 pixels are good for removing artefacts from low resolution scans and so on. Higher values are used to produce a deliberately blurred effect. A radius of 100 pixels or more blurs the entire image into incoherence; one of 250 pixels (the maximum) just averages all the pixels in the area the filter is applied to. This dialogue also has a Preview checkbox. If you tick this box, the effect is previewed in the main image window, not just in the small preview in the dialogue box.

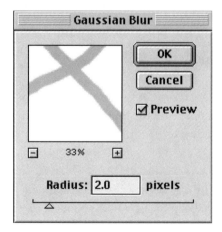

Figure 3.53 *Applying a Gaussian blur.*

Gaussian Blur is not the only filter on the Filter>Blur sub-menu. The simple Blur and Blur More filters apply a much more crude blur, which cannot be controlled by parameter settings and usually produce too coarse an effect. (They are more efficient than Gaussian blur, which is notoriously demanding of processing time.) Motion Blur and Radial Blur apply blurring in such a way as to convey a sense of movement. Like other filters, they are only occasionally useful. Smart Blur can be used to remove certain sorts of noise, such as film grain, from an image. It only blurs similar colours, while preserving edges.

☞ Practise applying Gaussian Blur to an image. Observe how the settings alter the appearance. Find values which (a) make no visible difference and (b) reduce the picture to incoherence. Try with another image with different visual characteristics, and see whether the same values have the same effect.

Sharpening up an image is a more obviously desirable thing to be able to do than blurring it. What is perhaps surprising is that it is possible to sharpen an image just by applying some algorithm to it, but it is. Like the Filter>Blur sub-menu, the Filter>Sharpen sub-menu offers several filters for performing this operation, but only one of them is generally effective at producing pleasing results and that is Unsharp Mask. This filter's curious name is derived from a photographic process, in which a positive image is masked with its blurred (unsharp) negative. The effect of adding a blurred negative is to subtract blurriness from the positive.[*] Photoshop's digital equivalent works by creating a copy of the image, applying Gaussian blur, and then subtracting it from the original. Although unsharp masking enhances features of an image, it should be understood that it can add no information to it. On the contrary, information is actually lost, although, if the sharpening is successful, the lost information will have been irrelevant, distracting or positively unwanted.

The parameters dialogue for Unsharp Mask is shown in Figure 3.54. The radius controls the amount of Gaussian blur applied to the mask; the amount determines by how much the contrast of edge pixels is increased. A threshold can also be specified: where the difference between the original pixel and the mask is less than the threshold value, no sharpening is performed. This prevents the operation from enhancing noise by sharpening it.

Unsharp masking can be used for the obvious purpose of enhancing detail in a poorly focused photograph or one that has been blown up. If you need to print from a scan,

---

[*]This really is essentially what happens, but if it sounds too far-fetched, you can describe unsharp masking more convincingly in terms of filtering of images in the frequency domain, if you understand such things. Consult Chapter 5 of *Digital Multimedia* or a book on image processing if you need to know the full story.

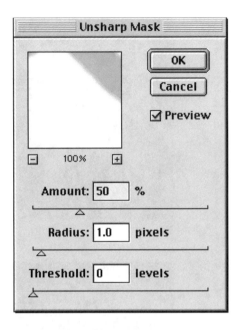

Figure 3.54 *Applying an* Unsharp Mask.

or display an image made by a cheap scanner on a Web page, you will have to sharpen it. Unsharp masking can also be used for putting back detail that has been lost by applying a Gaussian blur. If you apply a Gaussian blur followed by an unsharp masking you don't end up back where you started. The blur will remove unwanted artefacts and then the sharpening will restore detail at edges. Scanned images are often improved by this blurring and sharpening sequence.

Like other filters – in fact, like almost everything in Photoshop – obtaining good results with blurring and sharpening requires practice and a good eye. Every image will need slightly different treatment and it is not possible to come up with a set of infallible rules and formulas that will tell you which setting to use.

☞ Start with a scan or some other image of relatively poor quality. Practise using unsharp masking to create the sharpest possible on-screen image. Try both with and without a preliminary Gaussian blur. Try over-applying the unsharp masking and describe the resulting side effects.

Special Effects and Distortion

The majority of the filters that are available could be classified under this heading. The filters you can find on the Artistic, Brush Strokes, Pixelate, Render, Sketch, Stylize and

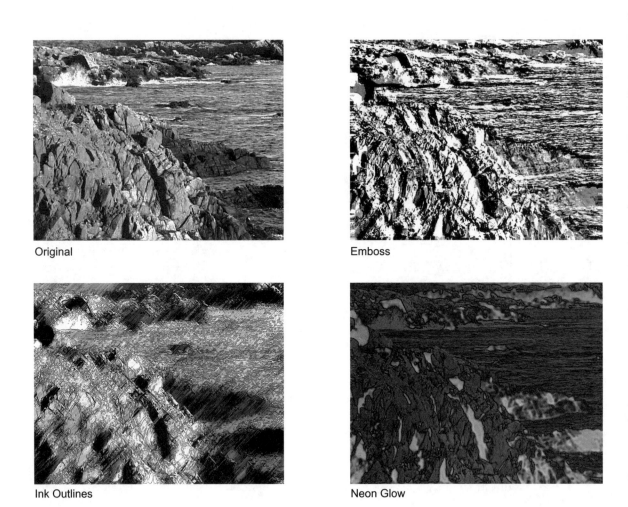

Original

Emboss

Ink Outlines

Neon Glow

Figure 3.55 *Filters.*

Texture sub-menus are all attempts to add the appearance of art materials or techniques of one sort or another, or traditional photographic effects, to an image. We will refer to these filters collectively as artistic filters, although we use the term in a broad sense. Artistic filters have evocative names such as Colored Pencil, Dry Brush, Palette Knife, Crosshatch, Spatter, Mezzotint, Pointillize, Lens Flare, Chalk & Charcoal, Conté Crayon, Water Paper, Solarize, Craquelure and Stained Glass. Some – mostly the ones based on photographic effects – produce an effect that does resemble their name, others are not so successful. Most of them work by identifying edges in the image and altering them in some way. Generally speaking, it's worth asking yourself whether it's really a good idea to try and make a photograph look like something it isn't before you apply one of these filters to an entire image. This isn't to say you can't have fun with artistic effects and everyone ought spend some time experimenting with them. Figure 3.55 shows a few examples.

☛ Choose several images of different types (e.g., a landscape, a portrait, a graphic design) and experiment with applying different artistic filters to them. Play with the controls in the filter dialogues to see how they affect the appearance of the filtered image.

Original

Diffuse Glow

Pinch

Polar Coordinates

Figure 3.56   *Distortions.*

The filters on the Distort sub-menu work in a different way from the artistic filters. Distortions are achieved by moving pixels to new positions, which makes it possible to apply ripples and waves, for example, to selected parts of an image. Again, you might well find that this isn't really something you wanted, although it can be entertaining, as Figure 3.56 shows.

☞ Repeat the previous exercise, using distortion filters on the same images.

One of the best ways of using distortions and artistic effects is less than obvious: try applying them to a layer containing a uniform colour. (Use Layer>New Fill Layer>Solid Colour... to create such a layer – see page 90.) Doing this can produce interesting textures, such as the ones in Figure 3.57, which you can use as Web page backgrounds and for similar purposes. If you experiment you will discover that some filters, for example Distort>Twirl, have no visible effect on a blank colour. However, the same filter applied on top of one such as Pixelate>Pointillize, which does produce an immediate and visible effect, will do something, so it is worth experimenting with applying filters in different orders.

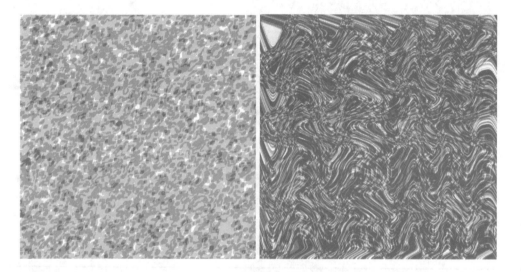

Figure 3.57   *Textures created by applying filters to a plain colour.*

☞ Try creating background textures by applying filters to a layer containing a plain colour and one containing a gradient fill.

The ultimate freedom in distortion does not actually come from a filter, but a sub-application, which you can access with the Image>Liquify... command. This opens a large window (which nevertheless behaves as a modal dialogue box) in which you can use brush tools to distort your image as if you were actually picking up its pixels and smearing them around. The Liquify dialogue closely resembles a stand-alone application which used to be available under the name of Kai's Goo, and the idea of spreading an image about like some gooey substance conveys quite well the essence of this facility (see Figure 3.58). Play with it –it's very easy to appreciate what's going on once you try, much easier than it is to get an impression from a description. The most popular application is in distorting pictures of people[*] –politicians being deservedly popular subjects for nose lengthening. As well as the basic smearing brush (which has several parameters you can vary), the dialogue provides additional tools for applying other distortions; you can also 'freeze' certain areas of the image to prevent them being liquefied. In the right hands it permits quite subtle and sophisticated distortions to be applied interactively to an image, but for most people it is classified as 'fun' – and since this is a college textbook, we must therefore leave the subject hastily.

Figure 3.58   *Use of the* Liquify *command.*

Layer Effects and Layer Styles

As well as the established method of altering images by applying filters to produce special effects, recent versions of Photoshop provide an alternative in the form of *layer effects*. These are applied to a layer – the layer itself, not the pixels it contains. This means, among other things, that the effect is not only applied to the pixels that are on the layer at the time, it is also applied to any marks you make on the layer, by painting, pasting or applying an ordinary filter, at a later time. You can combine several layer effects into a *layer style*, which you can store and then apply to other layers to achieve a consistent appearance. Several prefabricated layer styles are supplied with Photoshop

---

*The artist and illustrator Ralph Steadman experimented in the 1980s with applying similar gooey distortions to Polaroid photographs, by keeping them warm and smearing the gel with a pencil. The results can be found in a book, *Paranoids* (Harrap: 1986), which proves that this sort of distortion can be used for more than cheap caricature. (If you're as good as Ralph Steadman, that is.)

and ImageReady. While layer styles are fairly restricted in their creative possibilities, they provide a quick and easy way of creating stylized artwork to be used as furniture on Web pages.

The range of layer effects is much more limited than the range of filters. The basic effects can be found on the Layer>Layer Style sub-menu, the relevant part of which is shown in Figure 3.59. (This sub-menu contains some other commands that affect layer styles, which is presumably why it isn't called Layer Effects.) Most of these effects can be characterized as simulating light, textured surfaces and three-dimensionality. Figure 3.60 shows some examples. Nearly all layer effects work on edges between transparent and painted pixels. If you apply them to a layer containing no transparent areas, you won't see much happening, except at the very edge of the image. Layer effects work especially well on shape layers and type, as we have shown in Figure 3.60. By creating a shape or type layer and applying one or more layer effects to it, you can rapidly create buttons (for instance, for navigation in a Web page) or logos.

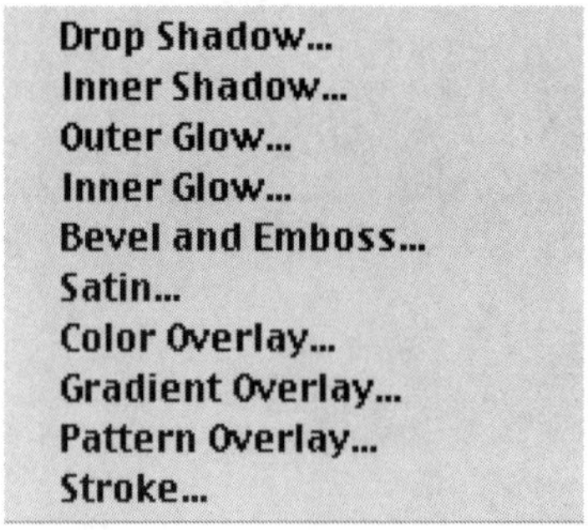

> **Drop Shadow...**
> **Inner Shadow...**
> **Outer Glow...**
> **Inner Glow...**
> **Bevel and Emboss...**
> **Satin...**
> **Color Overlay...**
> **Gradient Overlay...**
> **Pattern Overlay...**
> **Stroke...**

Figure 3.59   *The choice of layer effects.*

No matter which layer effect you apply, an elaborate dialogue box will open when you do so, giving you access to the full range of styles and, initially, the parameters for the style you selected. Figure 3.61 shows the dialogue as it opens when you apply a drop shadow effect. The main central area of the box is occupied by controls that allow you to alter various properties of the drop shadow, such as the angle from which it appears to be lit and the distance the shadow should be separated from the object throwing it. Every layer effect has its own parameters; as with filters, there is little point providing an exhaustive description of all of these and their results, since a little experimentation will soon show you how they work.

On the left of the dialogue is a list of all the layer effects, each with a checkbox. By selecting effects in this list, you can combine them. Ticking its checkbox adds an effect

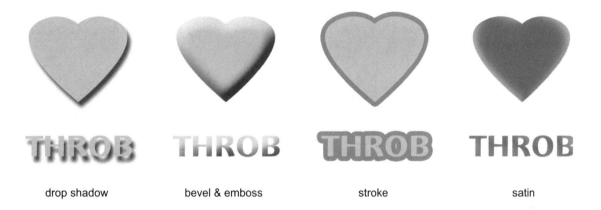

drop shadow   bevel & emboss   stroke   satin

Figure 3.60   *Some examples of layer effects.*

to the layer; selecting it in the list brings up its parameter controls so that you can make detailed adjustments to the appearance. If you come up with a combination of layer effects that you think you are likely to want to use again, clicking on the New Style… button allows you to name it and save it as a layer style.

☛ Create a shape layer and practise applying layer effects to it, singly (varying the parameters of each effect to see what they do) and in combination.

Styles that you have saved, along with some preloaded styles supplied with Photoshop, appear in the Styles palette.* Each style is shown as a button that illustrates its appearance. It is not always easy to identify styles shown in this way, but a tool tip appears when you move the cursor over an entry in the Styles palette, giving the style's name. To apply a style to a layer, you can simply select the layer in the Layers palette, and click on the style's button in the Styles palette. When you do this, any layer effects presently applied to the layer are discarded in favour of the new style. If you want to add the style on top of some existing effects which you wish to retain, then hold down Shift while you apply the style. As an alternative, while you are in the dialogue box of Figure 3.61, you can click on the word 'Styles' at the top of the list on the left, and the entries in the Styles palette will appear in the dialogue box, where you can select one directly. (Actually, the Photoshop manual offers no fewer than eight different ways of applying a style to a layer. The two we have described should keep you going for a while, though.)

---

*Not all the styles in this palette are layer styles; some are used for creating buttons. This is described in Chapter 4.

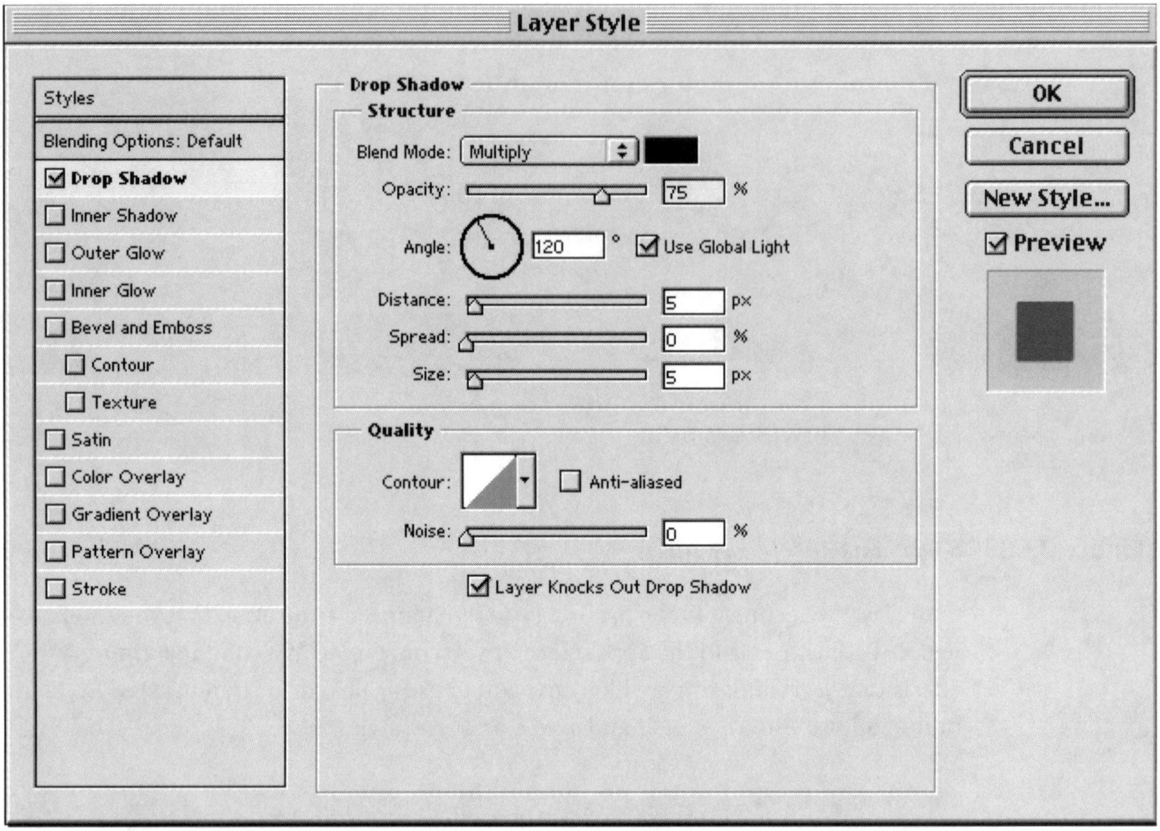

Figure 3.61   *Applying layer effects.*

☞ Choose several combinations of layer effects that you liked when doing the previous exercise, save them as layer styles, and try them out on different shape and type layers.

If a layer has one or more layer effects applied to it, these are shown in the Layers palette, in the manner illustrated in Figure 3.62. You can hide the effects by clicking the disclosure triangle by the circled letter *f* next to the layer's thumbnail. With the effects visible, though, you can double-click one of them to bring back the Layer Style dialogue box of Figure 3.61 and change any of its parameters you are not satisfied with. You can also temporarily remove a layer effect by clicking its eye icon, as if you were making a layer invisible.

If you are using ImageReady you should be aware that the manner of setting and changing the parameters of layer effects is different from that in Photoshop. There is no

Layer Style dialogue box; instead, each layer effect has its own palette, which appears when you select the effect in the Layers palette (by clicking on its name as if it was a layer). Figure 3.63 (which should be compared with Figure 3.61) shows the Drop Shadow palette; in general, the options that are available in ImageReady are somewhat more restricted than those available in Photoshop. If you want to add more than one effect to a layer, you must add them individually; there is no equivalent of the list in Photoshop's dialogue box.

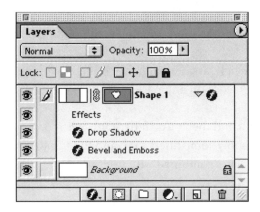

Figure 3.62   *Layer effects as shown in the* Layers *palette.*

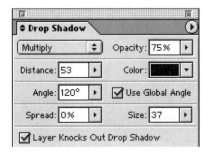

Figure 3.63   *A layer effect's palette in ImageReady.*

Further Exercises to do in Photoshop

1. (a) Scan a photograph at fairly high resolution. Make the best possible version of the resulting image for display on screen. Use any filters and adjustments you think appropriate and downsample as necessary. Try changing the order in which you carry out the steps in your work to see whether it makes any difference to the result.

(b) Start with a low resolution image and make any adjustments that you can, including changes to its dimensions, to improve its appearance when viewed on screen.

2. Using whichever means you think best, change all the blues in a coloured image to reds. How many different ways can you think of doing this?

3. Use the magnetic lasso to trace as accurately as possible around a figure in an image and paste the figure into a new document against a new background. (Why isn't the result convincing?) Repeat the extraction using the Image>Extract... command.

4. How would you make all the light areas in an image brighter without affecting the medium and darker tones? Practise on an image of your choice.

5. Open an image, select all of it and then paste it back into itself on a new layer. Lower the opacity of the top layer, apply some filters to it, and then change the blending mode so that the original image is combined with itself in all the possible ways. Which of these might be useful?

6. Open an image with a clear subject, such as a portrait, and use adjustments to accentuate the contrast to make selection easier. Use a selection tool of your choice to select the subject as accurately as possible. Save the selection to an alpha channel. Use the channel to allow a new image to show through in the shape of the selection against a background.

7. Take an image of an external scene that was photographed in the middle of the day and adjust its colours to make it look as if it was taken in the early evening. (Start by bringing up the yellows to simulate the glow of the sun low in the West.) What similar alterations can you make to scenes? Can you turn a sunny day into an overcast one, or vice versa? Can you turn day into night?

8. Scan a colour photograph and make a selection – a simple rectangle will do, or if you want to be more ambitious, select an object. Make the selected area stand out by desaturating the colours of the rest of the picture. (You have probably seen a similar effect used in advertisements.) Try making different adjustments to the selected and unselected areas to achieve similar effects.

9. Typeset each letter of the alphabet at a large size (about an inch) using as many fonts as you can, with each letter on a separate layer. Apply combinations of layer effects to

each letter, to change its appearance in a way that is sympathetic to the shape of the letter in the fonts you have used for it. Try arranging letters into words to see how they work together.

3a

Photoshop 7

A **s Photoshop** updates go, Photoshop 7 was a minor one. It introduced no major new features comparable to the introduction of layers, history or editable text in earlier releases. In fact, although advanced users and professionals will find some of the innovations to be invaluable time-savers, novice and intermediate users will, for the most part, be able to use this release in just the same way as we described for Photoshop 6 in Chapter 3. The area in which the update will make the most impact is the new brush engine, which expands the range of brushes that can be used and introduces an approximation to natural art materials into the program.

We will not attempt to describe the entire collection of new minor features added to Photoshop 7, any more than we attempted to describe the complete feature set of the earlier version, but will confine ourselves to a few aspects of the update likely to appeal to the intended audience of this book, before looking at the new brushes in more detail.

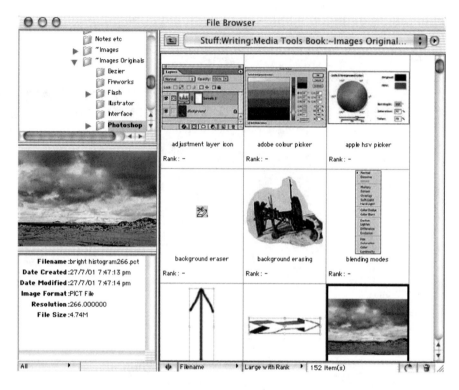

Figure 3a.1   *The file browser.*

Interface Enhancements

The File Browser

The single new feature which many users will find themselves using most is the file browser, which provides an alternative to the traditional file open dialogue. When you select Browse... from the File menu, a window, divided by default into four main regions opens, as shown in Figure 3a.1. In the top left corner is a schematic representation of the structure of the folders on your hard disks. To the left of each folder is a disclosure triangle, which can be turned down to reveal the contents of the folder, so you can work your way down through the folder hierarchy to any point. You select a folder by clicking on it. The main part of the browser window on the right shows thumbnails of all the files in the selected folder. (Files that do not contain images are not displayed. Sub-folders within the selected folder are represented by icons; double-clicking a folder here is an alternative way of selecting it in the browser.) The pop-up menu at the top of the browser window lets you move upwards in the folder hierarchy: its entries are the ancestors of the currently selected folder. The button to the left of the pop-up menu provides a quick way of moving up one level to the parent folder.

To open an image file in a Photoshop document window, you double-click its thumbnail in the browser display. It should be apparent that the browser provides a quick and easy way of finding images on disk (if not, it will become so once you start using the file browser). It is particularly useful if you have captured a set of pictures from a digital camera. The file browser enables you to quickly examine the images, and open any which you wish to edit in Photoshop.

> ☛ Practise using the file browser. Navigate through the folders on your hard disk looking for images, and open them in Photoshop from inside the browser.

If you just click once on a thumbnail, a larger version of it is displayed in the middle of the left column of the window, as Figure 3a.1 shows, and some basic information about the file – including the image format, file size, resolution and creation date – is displayed in the middle of the left column. If you don't like the split-pane arrangement of the browser, you can expand the preview pane to use the entire window, removing the structure tree and larger image, by clicking on the double arrowheads below the vertical separator between the two columns. Additionally, you can change the size of the thumbnails and elect whether to show the information about the file next to the thumbnail by choosing appropriate options from the pop-up menu beneath the arrow at the top right corner of the browser, shown in Figure 3a.2. Figure 3a.3 shows the browser's appearance with the left-hand column closed and details added to the thumbnails.

> ☛ Using the browser's menu and the controls in the browser window, experiment with the different thumbnail sizes and arrangements that are possible.

It is possible to rotate images from within the file browser. You can select several thumbnails by shift-clicking, and then rotate them by clicking on the icon at the bottom left of the browser window – this rotates 90° clockwise; hold down [opt/alt] while clicking to rotate in the opposite direction – or by choosing an appropriate rotation from the menu shown in Figure 3a.2. The image is not really rotated until you open it in Photoshop, but the facility is useful for turning images – again most often digital photographs – the right way round while you are browsing. As Figure 3a.2 shows, it is also possible to rename or delete files from within the browser, so that you never have to leave Photoshop and return to the desktop to perform these operations.

Dock to Palette Well
✓ Expanded View

Open
Select All
Deselect All

Rename
Batch Rename...
Delete
Clear Ranking

New Folder
✓ Show Folders

Rotate 180°
Rotate 90° CW
Rotate 90° CCW

Small Thumbnail
Medium Thumbnail
Large Thumbnail
Large Thumbnail with Rank
✓ Details

Refresh Desktop View
Reveal Location in Finder
Export Cache
Purge Cache

Figure 3a.2   *The file browser's menu.*

Workspaces

A small innovation is the ability to save named *workspaces*, which are arrangements of the palettes. Previously, if you moved palettes around and docked them in non-standard combinations, you could always clean everything up and revert to the default arrangement of the screen by selecting Reset Palette Locations from the Window menu. In Photoshop 7, this command can now be found on the Window>Workspace sub-menu, where you will also find the command Save Workspace.... If you select the latter command, you will be prompted for a name, which is used to identify the current arrangement of the workspace. This name will henceforth appear on the Window>Workspace sub-menu, and whenever you select it, the palettes will be moved to the locations you saved. If at any time you decide you no longer need a particular workspace, select Delete Workspace... from the Window>Workspace sub-menu, then choose the workspace to be deleted from the pop-up menu in the dialogue box that appears.

Workspaces are useful if several people use the same copy of Photoshop on the same machine. They may also be useful if you find yourself doing several different types of

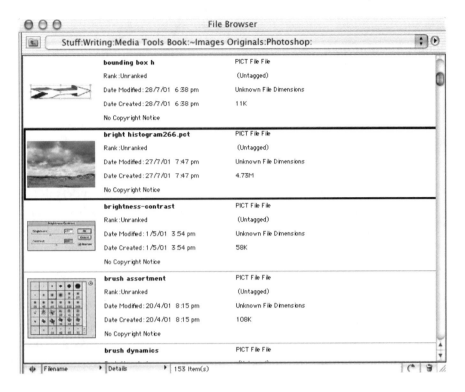

Figure 3a.3 *An alternative layout for the file browser.*

job, which use different palettes. You could, for example, define one workspace for photo retouching, with the palettes relating to type hidden, and another for poster design, with the type palettes conveniently placed to hand.

> ☞ Arrange the palettes in a way that suits your particular style of working and save the layout as a workspace. Define some other workspaces and practise switching between them. Delete some of your workspaces.

Tool Presets

In a similar manner to workspaces, *tool presets* allow you to tailor Photoshop 7 to your personal needs, by storing named sets of options for any of its tools. The options bar (see page 26) now has a drop-down palette at its extreme left-hand end, as shown in Figure 3a.4, where formerly it only showed the icon for the current tool. This palette can be used to create, manage and use tool presets.

To create a preset, you first set some options in the options bar in the usual way. You then click on the tool icon at the left end of the options bar to bring down the presets

Figure 3a.4   *Tool presets.*

 drop-down palette, and click on the New Preset icon on the right-hand side. A dialogue box opens, in which you can give a name to the preset – a default name based on the options settings is provided, but you can change it if you like. When you want to use the preset options, simply select the preset name from the drop-down palette. The palette menu provides the expected commands for managing presets, allowing you to rename and delete them, and so on.

Emphasizing the tools analogy, you could say that tool presets allow you to augment a single tool that has variable options, like an adjustable spanner, with a set of fixed special-purpose tools, like a set of standard spanners. The adjustable spanner is still there when you need it, but you don't always have to fiddle around setting it up correctly, if one of the presets fits the job. Unlike spanners, you can always create a new preset with arbitrary settings; you aren't constrained to the standard set that comes in your toolkit. In the special case of the type tool, presets allow you to approximate the use of *styles* in word processors and desktop publishing applications, since they allow you to create a collection of type attributes and give it a name, so that you can use it in a consistent way. Unlike styles, however, if you update a preset, type you created with it previously is not changed. A preset is just a way of setting a collection of options when you select a tool.

☞ Practise creating and using presets for all the tools you commonly use in Photoshop. Try to create a toolkit for the most common tasks you undertake.

Patterns

Photoshop's support for creating patterns has been enhanced. We described on page 86 how you could fill a layer with a pattern chosen from a default collection. In Photoshop 7, it is now easy to create your own patterns to use as fills. You can also use the *pattern stamp tool* to paint with a pattern. This tool behaves just like a brush, and has the same options for mode and opacity, but instead of painting with a colour, it paints patterns. When you select the pattern stamp, a pop-up menu of available patterns appears on the options bar, and you can use it to select the pattern you wish to brush onto your image. You might use the pattern stamp tool to remove unwanted elements of a picture that were in front of a regular background. For instance, you might be able to remove some graffiti from a brick wall in this way.

> ☞ Practise using the pattern stamp tool to paint with patterns from the default set. Experiment with using different options for the tool.

A pattern consists of a small image, called a *tile*, which is repeated in a regular grid layout to fill an area, just like a bathroom tile is repeated to fill a wall. You can make any rectangular area of an image into a tile that can be used as a pattern, simply by selecting the area with the rectangular marquee (the feather must be set to 0px) and choosing the Edit>Define Pattern... command. A simple dialogue appears, in which you can give your pattern a name. After that, it can be used like the built-in patterns. For instance, you can use the Layer>New Fill Layer>Pattern... command to create a fill layer containing your pattern, or you can select it for use with the pattern stamp tool.

> ☞ Open any image file and practise turning areas of it into patterns. Create fill layers filled with your patterns.

When you tried the preceding practice exercise, you will probably have found that most parts of an image don't make very good patterns – you can see the edges of the tiles and the repetition is obvious. The *pattern maker* filter is provided to help you make more pleasing tiles.

In the simplest case, the pattern maker can be used to replace a layer in an image with a pattern constructed from tiles which are created by rearranging the pixels in a selected area of the layer's original content. This rearrangement is performed in such a way that the resulting pattern has the general textural characteristics of the original selection. For example, if you select an area of wool in a picture of a sheep, you can create a woolly pattern, as shown in Figure 3a.5.

To use the pattern maker in this way, first select a layer from which the pattern is to be generated, and then choose Pattern Maker... from the Filter menu. A window opens, showing a copy of the chosen layer, together with some controls for making the pattern. In the top left corner are three tools; the topmost of these is a rectangular selection tool. You use this in just the same way as the rectangular selection tool in the main Photoshop application, to drag out a rectangular area which will be used as the basis

Figure 3a.5   *Making a woolly texture from a sheep.*

for the pattern. (The other two are a zoom tool and a moving tool, which allow you to adjust the visible part of the image to help you make a selection. These tools are also used like their counterparts in the main application.) With an area selected, click on the Generate button and a pattern will be created and used to tile the image area in the dialogue box. Figure 3a.6 shows this sequence of operations. In the top half of the figure you see the original image and the area selected for pattern making; in the lower half you see the pattern. You should be able to see that the image has been tiled and that the tile is not simply a copy of the selected area, but that it does retain its qualities, in terms of colour and contrast. (For this illustration, we have chosen an area of the image with high contrast, which does not make for very good patterns, but should help you to see how the patterns are related to the original selection.)

There is an element of randomness in the pattern making process, which means that different patterns can be generated from the same selection. If you do not like the first pattern that the pattern maker produces, you can click on the button now labelled Generate Again and another attempt will be made. You can also vary some parameters of the generation process, using the controls at the right-hand end of the dialogue. By increasing the Smoothness value, you can make edges in the generated pattern (within the tile, not between tiles) less prominent. The Sample Detail value controls the size of the elements that are rearranged to make the tile. If you want to preserve elements of the original sample, increase this value. Figure 3a.7 shows some more patterns

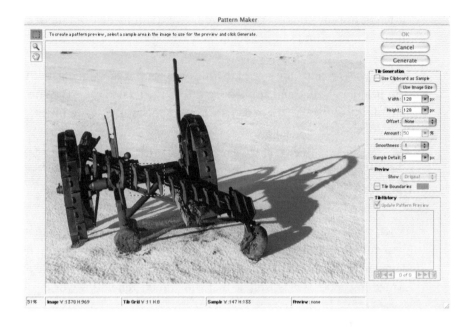

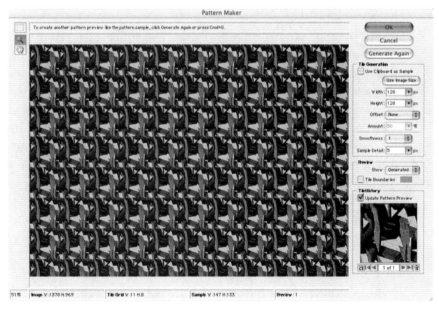

Figure 3a.6 *Making a pattern.*

generated from the selection shown in Figure 3a.6. The first was produced just by clicking Generate Again, leaving the parameters unchanged; this demonstrates that simply letting the pattern maker mix up the elements again can generate a quite different texture. The other two patterns were still made from the same selection, but the smoothness and sample detail were changed.

You can also change the size of the tile used for the generated pattern, using the Width and Height controls, and apply offsets to the generated tiles. The effects of the various parameters to the pattern maker are best understood by experiment.

> ☛ Apply the pattern maker filter to a variety of images. Try using some pictures with natural elements, such as landscapes, and some with artifical elements, such as buildings and machinery. Experiment with all the controls in the pattern maker dialogue.

When you did the previous exercise, you will probably have seen that generating patterns with this filter is a rather hit-and-miss affair. Typically, you fiddle with the parameters and then click on Generate Again a few times in the hope of coming up with something good. It may well be that you end up generating worse patterns than you started off with, and want to go back to an earlier one. For this reason, a method of reviewing patterns is provided.

In the bottom right corner of the Pattern Maker dialogue, you will see a small representation of the tile of the current pattern. (You can see it in the screenshots in Figure 3a.7, for example.) Beneath this are some controls for navigating through the list of patterns you have generated so far. The left and right triangles are the familiar previous and next buttons; the triangles with a vertical line at the end take you to the first and last pattern. When you use these controls, the preview of the entire pattern changes, not just the tile. You can also delete patterns that are no use at all, by clicking on the dustbin icon, and save particularly good ones, by clicking on the disk icon. A pattern saved in this way can be used in the same way as patterns created using the Edit>Define Pattern... command, as described earlier.

> ☛ Generate a series of patterns. Practise reviewing the patterns, deleting ones that you do not like and saving the good ones.

When you have a pattern you are satisfied with, click the OK button, and the active layer in your document will be filled with the pattern. Note that this destroys the original contents of the layer, so unless you are just making a background texture, it is advisable to copy the layer before using the pattern maker. If you want to make a new layer or a new image and fill it with a pattern, then you should select the area you want to use as the basis for the pattern from an existing layer and copy it to the clipboard. Then create an empty layer or a new document, invoke the pattern maker and tick the checkbox labelled Use Clipboard As Sample.

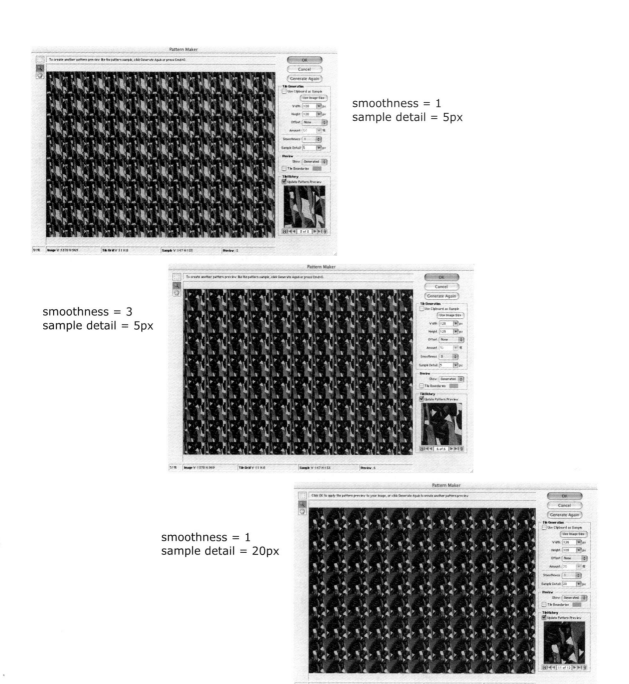

smoothness = 1
sample detail = 5px

smoothness = 3
sample detail = 5px

smoothness = 1
sample detail = 20px

Figure 3a.7   *Generating further patterns.*

Brushes

There have been major changes in the way the tools for painting pixels work in Photoshop 7. These have allowed a greater range of 'natural media' effects, which impersonate the appearance of physical art materials, to be achieved. This has led to the introduction of extra controls for changing newly available characteristics of brushes, which in turn has led to a change in some aspects of the way in which you work with brushes, notably the introduction of a new *brushes palette*. Because of this, we will describe the use of brushes in Photoshop 7 without reference to earlier versions. This will lead to some repetition, but this should only affect users who are upgrading from Photoshop 6 to 7. Photoshop 7 readers should consider the remainder of this section as a replacement for the material on pages 79 to 84. If you are using ImageReady 7, however, you will find that the painting tools still work as they did in ImageReady 3, as a limited version of the tools described on those pages.

The Paintbrush and Pencil

There are two different painting tools, which share the same location in Photoshop's toolbox: the *paintbrush* and the *pencil*. There is also an *eraser*, which behaves more like a brush than a real eraser, as described on page 84. Both of the painting tools are used in the same way. You select a tool by clicking its icon in the toolbox, and then make marks by dragging in the image. Before doing this, however, you must set the colour: click on the foreground colour swatch in the toolbox, and then set a colour using the Color palette, or else double-click the swatch and choose a colour from the colour picker (see Chapter 9).

The names of these two tools give a broad indication of the nature of the marks they make. The pencil makes hard-edged lines and the brush makes softer strokes. Apart from this, though, both tools can be used in the same way, with the same set of options. From now on, when we are describing features common to the pencil and the paintbrush, we will use the term *brush* to include both tools.

A brush can have many variants, differing in size, hardness, shape and the angle between the simulated brush head and the orientation of the image. You can also specify how a brush will react to pressure when you are using a graphics tablet, set semi-random variations in certain properties of the brush marks, associate a texture with the brush to simulate different types of support (paper, canvas, parchment etc.). You can even specify a second tip for a brush. Several libraries of *preset brushes* come with

Photoshop, and the easiest way to start working with painting tools is by using some of these presets.

Figure 3a.8 *The options for the paintbrush (top) and pencil (bottom) tools.*

Figure 3a.8 shows the options bar as it appears when each of the brush tools has been selected. In both cases, at the left, next to the tool presets drop-down palette, is a swatch representing the tip of the currently selected brush. Clicking on this causes a palette to drop down, on which you can find swatches showing a representation of the stroke made by each of the currently loaded preset brushes. By default, an assortment of brushes, some of which are shown in Figure 3a.10, is available, including simple round brushes, varying only in a diameter, and some brushes with more elaborately shaped tips, which produce more complex marks. You can use the menu on this drop-down palette to load different libraries of brushes, including calligraphics and natural media brushes. Note that each preset can be applied to either the paintbrush or the pencil tool, to produce either a hard or soft mark with the same characteristics. Figure 3a.10 shows the different strokes produced by the paintbrush and pencil with the same preset (Soft Round 100px) selected. This illustration demonstrates that the diameter of the brush tip is not necessarily equal to the width of the stroke for soft-edged brushes.

☛ Practise using the paintbrush and the pencil with a few different preset brushes in a range of different colours until you get a feel for which tool is suited to which type of job.

As you can see from Figure 3a.8, the options for the two painting tools are not quite identical. For both of them, as well as choosing a preset, you can set the blending mode and the opacity, which work for brushes the same way as they do for layers. The default Normal mode is what you expect: underlying colour is obscured or allowed to partially show through depending on the opacity, while the other modes allow your brush strokes to interact with the pixels below them in more complicated ways. Setting the opacity to less than 100% allows you to make brush strokes which allow the underlying colour to show through.

The paintbrush has two useful options that the pencil lacks. You can set the Flow to values between 1% and 100% to simulate different rates of application of paint. You can also make the paintbrush behave somewhat like an airbrush, by clicking on the

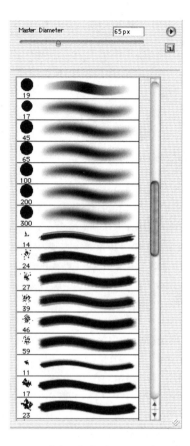

Figure 3a.9   *Some of the default preset brushes.*

 airbrush icon. With this option selected, if you hold the brush still (with the mouse button depressed, if you are using a mouse, or the pen in contact with the tablet if you are using one) paint will continue to build up around the cursor, as if you were spraying it from an airbrush or paint spraycan. This can be used to simulate an airbrushed style of painting or graffiti art.

> ☞ Use a large brush to paint an area of colour. Practise painting smaller brush strokes on top of this area using each of the different blending modes and different opacity settings, and observe the results.

The best way to understand the different preset brushes, and the differences between the paintbrush and the pencil, is by experimenting. We strongly urge you to do so.

☞ Select the paintbrush and practise using different preset brushes to create a wide range of different marks at different sizes in the same colour. Experiment with the different options in conjunction with the presets. Load different sets of preset brushes and explore the possibilities they offer. Repeat the exercise with the pencil.

Figure 3a.10 *Strokes made by the paintbrush (left) and pencil (right).*

As with any other tool, you can create a tool preset incorporating a set of options, as described on page 149. A tool preset for a brush is not the same as a preset brush – the terminology is confusing. However, if you think of a tool preset as being a saved set of values from the options bar, while a preset brush is a saved set of parameters set in the Brushes palette, as we will describe shortly, the difference should be clear.

The Brushes Palette

You can get a long way just using the preset brushes supplied with Photoshop, but if you are interested in simulating different sorts of brush strokes, you may want to customize some aspects of the preset brushes, or even build your own from scratch. The simplest change, and possibly the most useful for most users, is in the diameter of the brush's tip. Although a broad range of sizes is supplied, you can always change the size using the slider labelled Master Diameter at the top of the preset brushes drop-down palette. (As we remarked earlier, unless you are using a hard-edged brush with a simple tip shape, the diameter will not necessarily be the width of the brush stroke.) You can see this slider in Figure 3a.9, and you adjust the size in the obvious way by dragging it to the right to increase the diameter and to the left to decrease it. Alternatively, you can enter a numerical value in the field above the slider. The diameter can be any number of pixels between 1 and 2500. The change only affects the tool while it is selected – in effect, the slider is an additional option. If you want to keep a brush of a non-standard size for future use, you can click on the New Preset icon, and it will be added to the set of preset brushes (not the set of brush tool presets) after you have provided a name for it in the dialogue box that appears.

> ☛ Select a preset brush and practise changing its diameter. Observe the effect of changing the diameter on the strokes that the brush makes. Save some sizes of brush as presets.

To make more elaborate changes or to create a brand new brush, you must use the Brushes palette. A brush is just a metaphor for a set of values that, in conjunction with Photoshop's painting algorithm, define which pixels' colour will be changed in the region of the cursor when the brush is dragged across an image. This is determined by, among other things, the brush's size, shape and hardness, the angle it makes with the path of the cursor, and the spacing between the individual strokes that make up a line. All of these values can be changed.

Figure 3a.11 shows the Brushes palette, as it might appear when you first open it. As you can see, it duplicates the function of the preset brushes drop-down palette from the options bar, with the same list of previews of the strokes of the available presets, and a master diameter slider. At the bottom is an enlarged preview of the stroke of the brush currently selected in the palette. There is, however, much more to the Brushes palette. You can select any of the headings down the left of the palette in order to change different aspects of the brush.

Selecting Brush Tip Shape causes the palette's appearance to change as shown in Figure 3a.12. The panel at the top now shows all the available preset brushes' tip shapes, without the sample stroke, and the controls below it allow you to change the characteristics of the chosen brush tip. You can change all the values that define the brush tip either numerically or graphically, by dragging sliders and squashing or rotating the ellipse that represents the shape and angle of the brush. As you make changes, the sample stroke at the bottom of the palette is updated to demonstrate their effect. Any brush you have modified in the Brushes palette can be saved as a preset by clicking on the New icon in the bottom right corner of the palette.

> ☛ Select a preset brush and practise changing all the different tip shape options. Observe the effect of changing the values on the strokes that the brush makes.

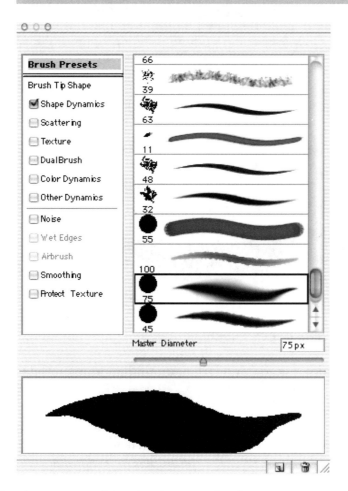

Figure 3a.11 *The* Brushes *palette, showing preset brushes.*

Figure 3.14 on page 82 shows the effect on a simple brush of changing some of these values. From left to right it shows strokes made by a circular, hard brush, the same brush with its hardness reduced, the original brush with the spacing set to a high value, a flattened elliptical version, the same ellipse rotated through an angle, and finally all of

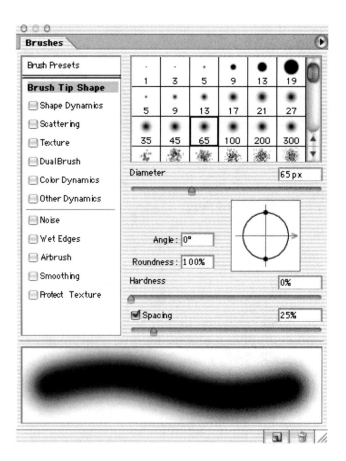

Figure 3a.12 *Changing brush tip shape in the* Brushes *palette.*

the options varied at once, except for the size which we kept constant for all the example brush strokes.

Marks made by Photoshop's brushes do not resemble those made with physical paint brushes very closely; they always have an artificial or mechanical character. To try and produce more realistic brush effects, the Brushes palette provides ways of introducing variations into brush strokes, either randomly or under the control of a pressure- and tilt-sensitive pen used with a graphics tablet. These options are set by selecting the headings Shape Dynamics, Scattering, Color Dynamics and Other Dynamics on the left of the palette. Note that to set options for these categories, you need to click on the name, which will then be highlighted. Clicking on the checkbox next to the name just activates the dynamic option with the current values.

The Brushes palette with Shape Dynamics selected is shown on the left of
Figure 3a.13. The term *jitter* is used in this context to refer to a pseudo-random
variation in some parameter; for example, at the top of the palette, you see a slider
labelled Size Jitter, which controls variations in the brush's size. This slider is used to
set a value that specifies the maximum percentage by which the size may vary. The
pop-up menu labelled Control is used to choose the method by which jitter is
controlled. If you set it to Off, the jitter is random; more interestingly, if you set it to
Pen Pressure, the amount of jitter is determined by the pressure you apply to the pen.
(You can only use this type of control if you are drawing on a graphics tablet; if you
don't have a tablet connected to your computer, a warning symbol will be displayed
when you select any option that requires one.) If this is the case, then the brush
diameter will vary within the limits you specify, depending on how hard you press
with the pen: press harder and the stroke will be wider, which is probably how you
would expect it to react. Within this pressure-sensitive variation, there is also some
randomness, so that the resulting brush stroke has some of the qualities of a real
brush wielded by an unsteady hand. This is the principle behind all the brush
dynamics settings. Instead of pen pressure, you can choose to have jitter controlled by
the pen's angle, if you have a tilt-sensitive pen, or by a stylus wheel. You can also select
Fade as the control value; this has the effect of fading out the jittered value along the
length of the stroke, perhaps as if the amount of paint left on the brush was becoming
less.

☛ Select a preset brush and experiment with changing size jitter. Use different sizes,
and if your input device permits it, all of the different control mechanisms. Observe
how the types of brush stroke you can make change when size jitter is used.

Within the shape dynamics category, you can also jitter the angle and roundness – the
values you can change in the Brush Tip Shape pane, as described above. The other sorts
of dynamics that you can add to the brush work in a similar way, using similar
controls. For instance, colour dynamics are changed by adding jitter to hue, saturation,
brightness and purity, and by jittering between the foreground and background
colours, using the controls shown on the right of Figure 3a.13. Scattering is controlled
similarly, and the Other Dynamics controls let you introduce variations into the
opacity and flow rate.

☛ Select a preset brush and investigate the use of all the brush dynamics settings.

There are two other sets of controls available in the Brushes palette. The Dual Brush
facility lets you create a brush with two tips, one of which paints in the foreground

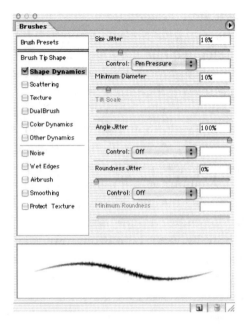 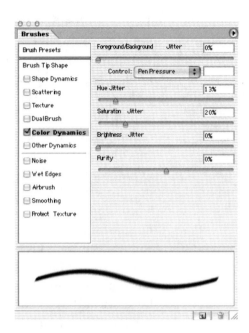

Figure 3a.13   *Shape dynamics (left) and colour dynamics (right).*

colour, the other in the background. The tips don't have to be the same shape, so you can create some highly elaborate patterns of paint in your brush strokes this way. We leave it to you to decide whether you can use such a tool effectively.

The final brush parameter you can select is a texture. This is a rather odd concept, at first sight – brushes don't tend to have textures. What is really being simulated is the texture of the surface to which the paint is being applied. It might be more logical to associate this texture with the layer on which you are painting, but in Photoshop, it is associated with the brush instead. The effect is the same: the way in which pixels are coloured as you drag the brush over them is modified as if there was a textured surface, such as canvas, beneath the paint. Figure 3a.14 shows the Brushes palette when Texture is selected.

The most prominent feature of the palette is a swatch of the chosen texture. As shown on the right of Figure 3a.14, a drop-down palette is attached to this swatch, from which you can choose a different texture. This palette of textures has its own palette menu, using which you can load different libraries of textures. Included with Photoshop are several of these, including many textures intended to model art materials, such as watercolour paper or canvas, and some other, more whimsical textures, for achieving special effects. To see textured effects, it may be necessary to reduce the flow rate of your brush in the options bar, otherwise the texture can get overwhelmed.

☞ Select a simple preset brush and set different textures for it. Observe the strokes produced. Do they resemble the way in which paint interacts with textured surfaces? Repeat the experiment with more complicated brush shapes.

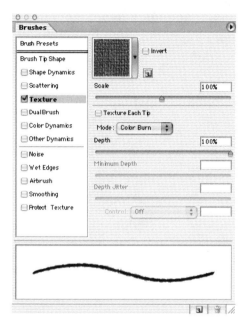
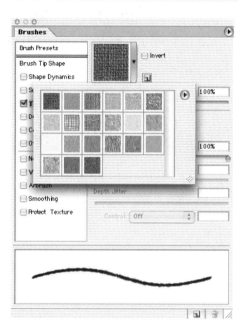

Figure 3a.14 *Specifying a texture.*

If you are trying to create something that looks like a painting, you will want to use the same texture with all your tools, so it looks as if the background is textured. To do this, choose Copy Texture To Other Tools from the Brushes palette menu. All the painting tools will then have a consistent texture.

Before leaving the topic of brushes, there are a couple of points that should be noted. First, brush dynamics and textures have improved the resemblance between Photoshop's brushes and real art materials, which means that using them effectively requires the same sort of talent and a similar set of skills. If you have such skills, you are almost certainly extremely familiar with using real materials. This being so, if you want to create an image with the visual characteristics of a piece of artwork in natural media, the best way to do so is probably to use real natural media and scan the result. It only makes sense to use digital art materials if you need to combine paint-like brush strokes with other sorts of digital image, for example, if you want to paint on to a still from a video.

Secondly, although in this section we have implicitly concentrated on using brushes to paint with, simple brushes, in particular the soft-edged and hard-edged round brushes, are as useful, if not more so, for creating masks with irregular shapes, for example in Quick Mask mode, as described on page 109.

ImageReady
Web
Graphics

Files and Formats Summary

- Create documents with File>New and save them as Photoshop (PSD) files with File>Save As....

- Open image files in a wide range of formats, including Photoshop, GIF, JPEG, PNG, TIFF, PDF, BMP and PICT, using File>Open and save them (always as Photoshop files) with File>Save As....

- Export optimized GIF, PNG and JPEG files using File>Save Optimized As....

- Create rollovers, image maps and slices by using File>Export... to create the images and an HTML file to put them together on a Web page.

Common Features
Used By This Program

Most images prepared on a computer have, until relatively recently, been destined for printing, and graphics programs have been designed accordingly. The popularity of the World Wide Web has led to a massive increase in the number of images that will only ever be displayed on a screen. Many of the problems of print are irrelevant to designers working for the Web – you no longer have to worry about the different colour models used by monitors and printers, or be concerned with colour separations, half-tone screens, dot gain, and all the artefacts of processes that use real ink and paper. Predictably, though, the Web has brought new problems, concerned with the low resolution of monitors, the necessity to transmit images over relatively slow networks, and new ways in which images can be used as dynamic page elements.

This change in the requirements placed on graphics applications has led to two responses. First, new features have been added to established programs to enable them to cater to the needs of Web graphics as well as established print media. Second, new programs have been produced, which are designed exclusively for producing graphics for the Web. These dispense with all the unnecessary baggage left over from print and concentrate entirely on supporting the requirements of the Web. One such program is ImageReady. We will describe ImageReady 3.0, the version bundled with Photoshop 6.

ImageReady occupies a rather anomalous position. Originally a stand-alone Web graphics application based on a cut-down version of Photoshop, with a virtually identical interface providing most of the same functionality, it is now only available as an integrated companion application included with Photoshop. Furthermore, some of ImageReady's Web facilities have now found their way back into Photoshop. While it seems almost inevitable that ImageReady will eventually be absorbed into Photoshop, it remains attractive on its own to Web specialists, who can get on nicely with the cut-down Photoshop core it provides for image editing, and appreciate the added Web specifics in the same application.

For a full description of ImageReady, you will need to refer to Chapters 3 and 10 as well as the present chapter. If you wish to use ImageReady for retouching scans or compositing, you should begin by reading about Photoshop in Chapter 3. Most of the tools, palettes and menu commands described in that chapter are present in ImageReady, where they are used for the same purpose. A few commands can be found in different places, but such differences are minor. Although ultimately ImageReady files will be saved in one of the Web image file formats, working versions are saved as Photoshop files. You can jump between the two applications to work on the same image, if you find it necessary, as described on page 44.

ImageReady has some features that Photoshop lacks and some of Photoshop's facilities are missing from ImageReady. In particular, the polygon and pen tools for adding vector graphic shapes are absent – you can only make ellipses, lines and rectangles (with or without rounded corners), on the assumption that you will be using vector shapes to define buttons – and the facilities for working with masks are more limited. Sadly, adjustment layers are also absent. ImageReady images always use a resolution of 72 pixels per inch, that is, they are nominally at screen resolution. The Image Size dialogue is therefore a much simplified version of Photoshop's, in which you can only change the pixel dimensions, as Figure 4.1 shows. There is also no provision for colour management. In fact, ImageReady only supports the RGB colour model. These omissions tell you quite a lot about its intended use. So does the fact that the customary Print... command on the File menu is replaced by a Preview In sub-menu containing the names of all the browsers installed on your system, which can be used to open an image in a Web browser.

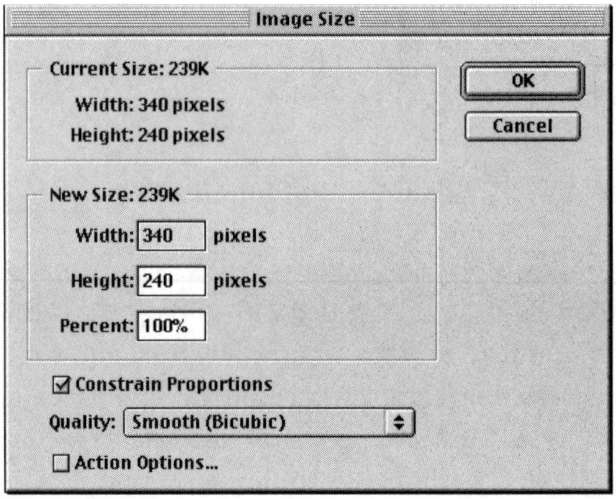

Figure 4.1   *Resizing an image.*

Image Optimization

The most characteristic operation that must be carried out on an image file before it can be embedded in a Web page is *optimization*, that is, converting it to a suitable file format and setting various properties related to compression and the representation of colour.

The intention is to reduce the file's size so that it can be downloaded over the Internet in an acceptable time. This type of optimization is performed in roughly the same way in ImageReady as it is in Photoshop and Illustrator, although it is more thoroughly integrated with the main application. Chapter 10 describes Web image file formats, the concepts behind image optimization, and the way in which it is done in all three of these programs. In ImageReady, optimization is integrated with the rest of the application, not confined to a special Save For Web dialogue as it is in Illustrator and Photoshop. The relevant settings can be found in the Optimize palette. The document window has four tabs to show the original, optimized, 2-up and 4-up views comparing the original with different optimized versions. You can paint, make selections and adjustments, and so on, only in the original image, but you can use any view in which it appears. For instance, you could work on the original in the 2-up view and see the changes reflected in the optimized version next to it. Figure 4.2 shows the document window and the Optimize palette in ImageReady. You should compare this illustration with Figure 10.2 on page 589.

☛ Open an image in ImageReady and experiment with using the Optimize palette – see Chapter 10 for further details and more exercises on image optimization.

Image Slicing

Slices

A technique that has become popular among Web designers is that of dividing an image into pieces – usually called image *slices* – that are stored in separate files and recombined on the Web page, either by placing them into table cells or using CSS positioning. Slicing an image may immediately improve download speed because browsers can usually keep more than one connection open at a time. This only works under some circumstances, though, depending on the available bandwidth and the complicated and largely unpredictable behaviour of a network as complex as the Internet. The main advantages of slicing come in different ways.

Web image files are usually stored in either GIF or JPEG format. (A third format, PNG, is becoming more common. It should eventually supersede GIF.) These are described in Chapter 10 but for now it is sufficient to know that GIFs are good for the efficient compression of areas of flat colour without any loss of quality, but using a limited number of colours (up to 256), while JPEGs permit millions of colours to be used and can effectively compress images with continuous tonal variations, such as photographs. They do so by discarding some information, which is generally undetectable (except at

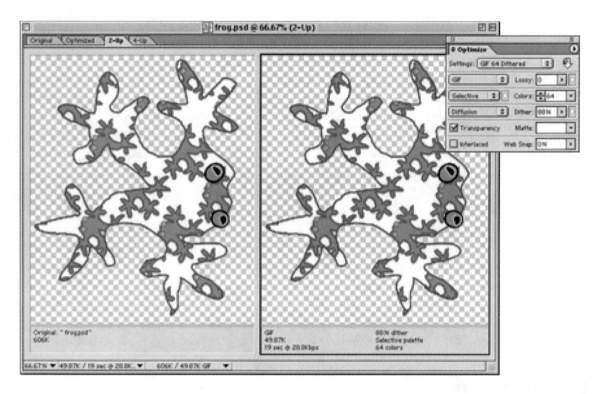

Figure 4.2   *The document window and* Optimize *palette.*

low quality settings used to achieve very small files) but can interfere with the legibility of text and the clarity of sharp edges. GIFs have some extra capabilities not provided by JPEGs. In particular, areas of a GIF image can be designated as transparent so that, when they are displayed on a Web page, the background colour or image will show through and GIFs may be animated (see page 192).

Slicing an image makes it possible to apply different levels of compression to each slice, or to save some slices as GIFs, others as JPEGs. It may be possible to replace some slices with HTML, allowing text to be added to the image without having to render it, and making it possible to design a whole Web page as a sliced image. With clever design, slices can be reused in more than one image; this will reduce download times, as slices that have been used once will be cached. Slices can also be used as an alternative to image maps (see page 180) to add hot spots that react to user input to an image.

Many photographs consist of an object in front of a background, such as the one shown in Figure 4.3 depicting an old agricultural implement in the snow. Most of the interest of pictures composed in this way is in the central subject, here the harrow (and to some extent, its shadow). The snow in the background could be more heavily compressed than the central image, because any loss of quality would be less noticeable. By slicing the image to separate the harrow from most of its surroundings, as indicated in the illustration, different levels of JPEG compression can be applied, and the total size of the resulting slices would be less than that of the entire image since, if it was not sliced, it would have to be compressed in its entirety at sufficiently high quality to preserve the important detail in the harrow. Note that image slices must be rectangular, so in this case it is necessary to piece together the central object with several slices.

Figure 4.3   *Slicing an image.*

Cutting objects, such as products or models, out of their background by masking and superimposing them on a plain colour is a common design idiom, seen widely in advertisements and magazines. (Figure 3.33 on page 105 could be an example.) The objects are usually taken from photographic originals, so they are best suited to JPEG compression. The large areas of flat colour that surround them will be compressed more efficiently as GIFs, so the image can usefully be sliced and most of the plain background can be stored in GIF files, leaving only the part that needs lossy compression as a JPEG. The GIFs can be made transparent, although since slices can only easily be rectangular, this does not help if you want to make the entire background transparent – to do that you must use GIF or PNG for the whole image.

GIF and JPEG slices can also be usefully mixed if text is superimposed on an image. JPEG compression interferes with the legibility of letters. It may not always be possible to superimpose the text using CSS layers (perhaps it is part of the original) but it is possible to confine it to slices that can be stored as GIFs. (This is only worth doing if the text is a small part of the image, of course.)

Slicing images by hand in a conventional image editing program is tedious. So is altering the slices afterwards – moving their boundaries or changing the compression quality, for example. Web graphics applications offer assistance with the task, automating much of the operation and providing a convenient interface with which to control the process.

Although the inspiration for image slicing was the desire to compress parts of an image in different ways, slices, rather like layers before them, have proved to be a more versatile concept, which is used in ImageReady in other ways. A sliced image is a way of presenting a collection of images so that, some of the time they can be treated as one, but at others they can be treated as individuals. In particular, individual slices can be made to change in response to events, such as the cursor moving over them. URLs can also be attached to slices, so that clicking in different parts of an image will cause a different document to be loaded into the browser. Combining these effects leads to some familiar Web idioms for navigation, as we will demonstrate later. Finally, individual slices can be animated, while the rest of the image stays still.

Creating Slices

ImageReady provides two distinct ways for you to divide an image into slices. The more intuitively obvious way is to use the slice tool to draw the boundaries of your slices. After selecting the tool,[*] move the cursor to where you want the top left corner of a slice to be, press the mouse button and drag. A rectangle is pulled out; its bottom right corner will be at the point where you release the mouse button. This rectangle is a *user slice* – that is, a slice that you have defined explicitly for some purpose. In the example shown in Figure 4.3, you might have started by dragging out the large rectangle enclosing the bulk of the harrow. In order to fit the image back together when it is displayed on a Web page, it is necessary to slice up all the remaining parts into rectangular areas. (Slices can only be rectangles – they are just images themselves.) ImageReady does this for you automatically. In this case, it needs to create three extra slices, as shown in Figure 4.4. The slices created automatically by ImageReady are called *auto-slices*.

An image may have more than one user slice. It might have more than one area of interest, or there may be areas you want to isolate for animation or for particularly low

---

*Although it looks like a dagger, we think it's supposed to be a cake knife.

Figure 4.4   *A user slice and auto-slices.*

quality compression as well as high, or, as in this case, it may be necessary to use several slices to cover an awkwardly shaped object. New user slices are added by dragging. Whenever you drag out a user slice, auto-slices are added or adjusted so that the entire image is divided into pieces that fit together. You can create overlapping user slices, which will automatically be sub-sliced to handle the region where they intersect.

By default, when you slice an image, the slices are shown in the document window as you see them in Figure 4.4. User slices are outlined with a solid line, auto-slices with dotted lines. Each slice is numbered, and the numbers are shown in the top left corner of the slice, together with some icons indicating other properties of the slice. Slices which are not selected (see below) are dimmed, auto-slices more than user slices. This display is somewhat cluttered; by choosing the Edit>Preferences>Slices... command, and selecting the Show Lines Only checkbox, you can remove most of the clutter, leaving just the slices' boundaries showing.

☛ Open an image with a clearly defined subject against a background and slice it to isolate the subject. Try adding extra user slices to this image and see how auto-slices are produced to accommodate them.

When you save an optimized version of a sliced image to be used on a Web page, ImageReady creates separate image files for each slice and an HTML file that contains the necessary code to put the sliced image back together. For more details, see Chapter 10.

If you are slicing your image in order to compress the parts differently, you will need to select each individual slice in turn. This is done with the slice select tool, which normally hides underneath the slice tool in the toolbox. To select a slice, click anywhere within it with the slice select tool. To select additional ones, shift-click them. Having selected some slices, you use the Optimize palette to choose a file format in which to save the slice and to set properties of the saved image. Chapter 10 describes how. If you want to apply the same settings to several slices you can link them together: select the slices and choose Link Slices from the Slices menu. After you have done this, whenever you apply optimization settings to one of the linked slices, they are applied to the rest as well. All the auto-slices in an image are linked automatically.

☞ Referring to Chapter 10 as necessary, specify appropriate optimization settings for each slice in the image you sliced in the previous exercise. Preview the optimized image in a Web browser.

The slice select tool is also used to move and resize slices. You move a slice simply by dragging when it is selected. To resize it, just drag one of the eight handles that appear when a slice is selected. You can also split slices vertically and horizontally, using the Slices>Divide Slice... command, which causes the dialogue box shown in Figure 4.5 to be displayed. Here you can enter numbers to divide the selected slice vertically, horizontally or both into even-sized slices, or into slices of a specified height or width (which need not divide the original slice exactly – any remainder is made into a smaller final slice at the bottom or right). All these operations affect the way in which the image is divided up into separate sub-images, but they have no affect whatsoever on the content of the image – for example, moving a slice does not move any pixels, it simply slices the image up in a different way. Slices can also be combined. If two or more slices are selected, the Slices>Combine Slices command creates a new slice in the form of the smallest rectangle that can enclose the selected slices. Any slices within the selection are discarded. Auto-slices are reconstructed whenever they need to be to accommodate any changes you make.

☞ Practise reslicing your image, by resizing some slices, dividing and combining slices. Try making slices of a specified height and width.

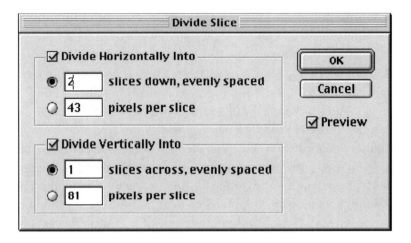

Figure 4.5   *Dividing slices.*

Basing slices on the content of layers provides an alternative to using the slice tool to create user slices. In some ways, such *layer-based slices* are easier to work with, especially for creating rollovers based on slices, as we will describe later.

Creating a layer-based slice is simple: select a layer in the Layers palette, and use the Layer>New Layer Based Slice menu command. The new slice will be the smallest rectangle that is required to enclose all the pixels on the layer that are not transparent. If you are constructing a collage or composite image, this means that you can easily send each element that you have isolated on its own layer to a slice.

Where layer-based slices differ from user slices is in automatically changing size to accommodate any changes you make to the image on the layer they are based on. Conversely, you can't resize a layer-based slice by hand or divide it. If you need to do so, you must convert the layer-based slice to a user slice, using the Slices>Promote to User-slice command. After that, the slice no longer adjusts itself automatically to changes on the layer, but it can be resized, moved, divided, and so on, like any other user slice.

☞ Open or create an image on several layers and make layer-based slices for each layer. Make some changes that affect the extent of one of the layers – paint or erase part of it – and see what happens to the slice boundaries.

If you decide that it wasn't a good idea to slice your image after all, the Slices>Delete All command can be used to remove all slices and restore it to a single image.

The Slice palette, shown in Figure 4.6, provides some extra operations. The most useful is the ability to attach a URL to a slice, so that whenever a user clicks anywhere in it a document will be retrieved. The URL must be entered in full in the text field labelled URL, with the leading http://, or whatever. There is no facility for browsing to a file to obtain a relative URL, but once you have used a URL in ImageReady it is added to the pop-up menu attached to the URL field so you can easily use it again. The field labelled Target can be used to specify a frame or window in which the browser should display the retrieved document. The pop-up menu offers the standard set of targets for working with framesets: _blank to open a new window for the new document, _self to display it in the frame or window containing the link, _parent to replace the frameset containing the frame containing the link, and _top to replace the entire window contents with the new document. You can also enter the name of a frame in the text box, on occasions when your sliced image is destined to be displayed in a frameset with named frames. This will often be the case if the image contains navigational links to help users find their way around a site.

☛ Turn one of the images you sliced in a previous exercise into a site map, by adding a URL to each slice. Test the map in a Web browser.

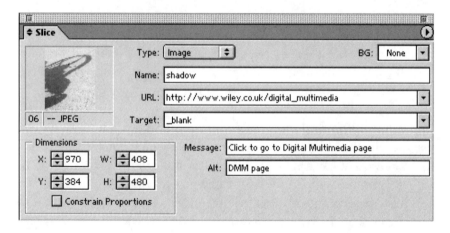

Figure 4.6   *The* Slice *palette.*

The Slice palette can also be used to set a background colour for a selected slice, using the BG pop-up menu in the top right hand corner – the background is not shown in ImageReady because it is added by the browser. You can give a slice a meaningful name, which can be helpful when you are dealing with several slices in an image. Using the fields in the bottom half of the palette you can set the size and position of a user slice precisely, by entering numerical values for its coordinates.[*] (You can't do this for a layer-based slice, without promoting it to a user slice.) You can also set a message to be displayed in the browser's status line when the cursor is over the slice and alternative text (an alt attribute, in HTML terms) to be displayed in place of the slice by browsers that cannot or do not display the image. Judicious use of alternative text for images can greatly increase the accessibility of Web pages.

Finally, you can use the Slice palette to replace the image in a slice with HTML text. If you use the pop-up menu labelled Type, at the top of the palette, to set the slice's type to No Image, the top half of the palette changes as shown in Figure 4.7. You can enter text with HTML tags in the text field now provided. When the sliced image is displayed, this text will appear in the position occupied by the selected slice in the image – it is simply placed in the table cell at that position instead of the image file. No assistance is provided with entering the HTML, you have to type everything by hand and no checking is carried out to make sure you haven't made a mistake. (It may be expedient just to type some place holder text in ImageReady and then edit the HTML file that is saved with the images in an HTML editor or a Web design program.)

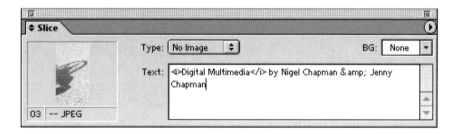

Figure 4.7   *Creating a text slice.*

If an image has not been sliced, you can use the Slice palette to set a background colour or attach a URL, status bar message and alternative text to the whole image.

> ☛ Practise using the Slice palette to add status messages and alternative text to slices, to set the background colour of transparent slices, and to create HTML text slices in an image.

---

[*]You may need to use the arrows in the palette's tab to display all the fields.

Image Maps

A way of using images that is unique to Web pages is as *image maps*. These are images containing active areas, called *hot spots*, which have URLs associated with them. Clicking on a hot spot causes the browser to load a new page from the associated URL. A classic example of an image map would be an actual geographical map, with hot spots surrounding tourist attractions. Clicking on one of these would cause the browser to go to a page containing more information about the particular attraction. Less literally, image maps based on abstract designs or appropriate representational images are often used to provide a navigational overview of a Web site.

Since the arrival of Web graphics applications that include tools for conveniently slicing images, it has become fairly common to implement image maps by attaching conventional HTML links to some or all of the slices an image has been divided into. (Technically, the img tag used to embed the slice image is surrounded by an a tag with an href attribute.) If you don't want to slice your image or want to use more elaborate shapes for your hot spots than slicing tools provide, you can use the tags and attributes provided in HTML for making image maps.

Without going into the details of the HTML code, what you need to do for image maps that are to be processed in the browser (nowadays the most common case) is define a map by giving the coordinates defining a set of hot spots, as rectangles, polygons and circles, and providing a URL for each. The map is then associated with an image, using an attribute provided for the purpose. It is perfectly possible to do all this by hand, entering the HTML with a text editor, but to do so – even if you are happy typing HTML tags and attributes – you need to work out the coordinates of all the hot spots geometrically. It is much quicker to draw hot spots on an image with conventional vector drawing tools and have a program translate your shapes into the necessary HTML. It is much easier to change the location or area of hot spots graphically, too. Utilities for creating image maps of this kind have been available almost as long as there have been image maps in HTML. Increasingly, the tools for doing this have been incorporated into conventional image manipulation programs, and are considered an essential part of any Web graphics application.

Insofar as an image map is an image with active areas, which cause a new page to be loaded into the Web browser when they are clicked on, a sliced image with URLs attached to some or all of its slices is an image map. Usually, though, as we explained earlier, this is not what is meant by 'image map'. More often, the expression refers to a single, unsliced, image which is associated with an HTML map element, which defines hot spots by their geometry. Unlike slices, hot spots can be circular or polygonal as well as rectangular.

ImageReady provides separate tools for defining hot spots in each of these three shapes. These three tools all share the same location in the toolbox, where you can also find a tool for selecting a hot spot (see Figure 4.8). You create hot spots by selecting the appropriate tool and drawing on the image. The circle and rectangle tools are used by dragging diagonally to define the area, in the same way as the slice tool is used to drag out rectangular slices. The polygon tool is used slightly differently. Position the cursor where you want one of the vertices (corners) to be, click the mouse button and move to the position of the next vertex. As you move the cursor, a line is pulled out, which will form one side of the polygon. You click again where you want the next vertex to be, then drag out the next side in the same way. To close the polygon you draw the last side so that it ends where it began, or double-click to have the polygon closed automatically. As you can see from this description, polygons can be irregular – the sides don't all have to be the same length.

Figure 4.8   *The image map tools.*

After you have drawn some hot spots on an image you can use the Image Map palette shown in Figure 4.9 to associate a URL with each hot spot. The values you enter in this palette affect the currently selected hot spot; the image map selection tool is used in the usual way to select hot spots. As you can see, the image map palette resembles a subset of the slice palette. A URL and a target frame are entered in just the same way; so is alternative text for the benefit of Web browsers which do not display images. You can also use this palette to set the size and location of rectangular and circular hot spots precisely, by entering numerical values in the left half of the palette. You cannot change polygonal hot spots this way though.

> ☛ Open any image and draw hot spots of all shapes on it; practise drawing polygons with different numbers of sides. Add a URL and alternative text to each hot spot. Test the image map in a Web browser.

The resemblance between image map hot spots and slices goes further than the similarities between their respective palettes. Just as you can create slices from layers, so you can create hot spots in the same way. That is, you select a layer in the Layers palette

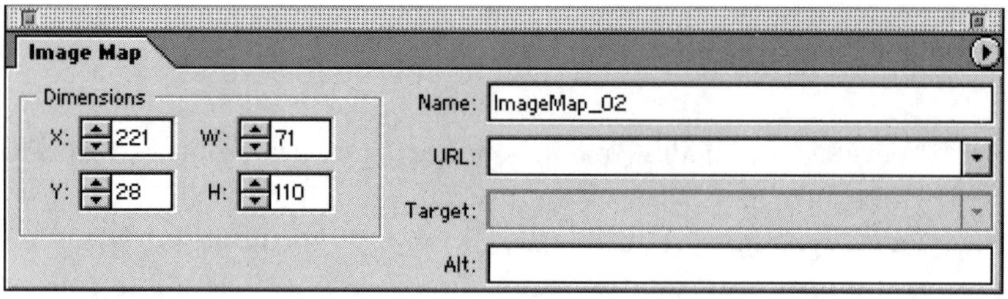

Figure 4.9   *The* Image Map *palette.*

and choose the Layer>New Layer Based Image Map Area command. This creates a rectangular hot spot enclosing all the pixels on the selected layer which are not transparent. When you select a hot spot that has been created in this way the image map palette gives you the option of changing its shape. As Figure 4.10 shows, a pop-up menu appears on the left of the palette, from which you can choose Rectangle, Circle or Polygon. With polygons you can set a tolerance value (actually the maximum number of sides) which determines how closely the polygon is drawn around the image on the layer. By using a large value you can create a hot spot that follows the outline of a shape very closely.

☛   Open an image containing several layers and base an image map on these. Practise using different tolerance values to fit hot spots to the contents of each layer. Add a URL and alternative text to each hot spot created from a layer.

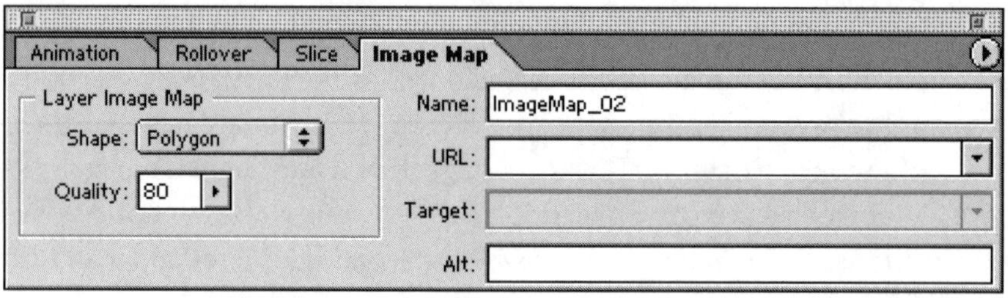

Figure 4.10   *Changing the shape of a layer-based hot spot.*

Given the extent to which hot spots resemble slices, you should not be surprised to learn that the image map selection tool can be used to move hot spots by dragging, and to resize them by pulling handles.

You can create overlapping hot spots but when you do so only the frontmost – that is, the one you added most recently – responds to mouse clicks in the area of overlap.

Normally, you use either slices or an image map, but there is in fact nothing to stop you using both at once. Hot spots can even overlap slice boundaries. ImageReady is clever enough to associate a suitable image map with each slice the hot spot intersects.

Rollovers

The introduction of JavaScript by Netscape in Navigator 2.0 and the more extensive scripting support and document object model (DOM) developed by Microsoft under the designation *Dynamic HTML*, and finally formalized by the World Wide Web Consortium in its DOM Recommendations has provided new roles for images on Web pages. Images can be changed dynamically. That is, if an image is embedded in a Web page, a script, triggered by some event, can substitute a different image in the same position. This is the basis of a Web idiom that has become almost ubiquitous: the *rollover*.

A rollover is an image that changes when some event occurs. The most popular form of rollover changes when the cursor moves over it – hence the name – to provide feedback to the user by indicating that something will happen if they click on the changed image. Such a rollover comprises two separate images, one for the original state and one for the rolled-over state, together with some JavaScript code that swaps the images when the cursor rolls over and swaps them back when it rolls off again. More elaborate rollovers that change in response to more events have more images and more complex scripts, but the principle is no different. It isn't difficult to make rollovers if you know some JavaScript (although getting them to work on all browsers and platforms is less simple), but like image slicing, it can be tedious and error-prone. And if you don't know any JavaScript and don't want to – as many people legitimately don't – some method that hides the scripting is required if you are to be able to make rollovers. Since the necessary scripts are just stereotyped code sequences, they are well suited to being automatically generated by computer programs, which can also handle the book-keeping needed to associate images with scripts to make a rollover.

The principle behind rollovers is easily adapted to produce an effect where the cursor's rolling over one image causes a change in a different image. This is called a *secondary* or *remote* rollover. Another variation on the technique is the *animated* rollover, where the image starts to move when the cursor rolls over it. This can be implemented either by using an animated GIF (described in the next section) as the replacement image, or by an additional script that animates the rollover by replacing the image by successive frames of an animation.

Probably the most common use of rollovers is to identify navigation buttons that are used to move between different areas of a Web site. They are often grouped together into a *navigation bar*. An easy way of producing a navigation bar in which the individual buttons are nicely arranged is by slicing an image, creating each button as a slice. With sliced images, it is also fairly easy to create secondary rollovers, with one slice responding to the rollover event by causing another slice to change its appearance. For instance, when the mouse rolls over a slice containing the name of a major section of a site, a menu containing the subsections of that section may appear in an adjacent slice.

The basic idea of a rollover is quite a general one – when an event occurs one image is replaced by another one. Actually, this idea is *too* general to be much use. Rollovers are normally used in a more systematic way. The replacement image is often a modified version of the image it is replacing. For instance, suppose you were using a rollover in connection with a button which was intended to take users to a Web page from which they could download software. The button could simply be labelled with the word Downloads. When the mouse rolls over the button, the word could change colour or be emphasized in some other way. This would let the user know that the button would now respond to a click. The same sort of feedback would not be provided if the word Downloads changed into a picture of a fish.[*]

It is possible in ImageReady to create rollovers with purely arbitrary image changes, but the program makes it convenient and relatively easy to create more structured rollovers of the kind that is generally encountered on Web pages.

Instant Rollovers

Rollovers in ImageReady are slices or image map hot spots which respond to events caused by mouse movements. (There is a degenerate case where a rollover can be applied to an entire unsliced image.) At any time, a rollover is in one of a set of *states*, depending on what has most recently happened to it. Most of the time, it is in its *normal* state, when nothing has happened. When the cursor moves over it, it changes to the *over* state; when the button is then pressed, it changes to the *down* state. For each state, a different appearance is defined by the contents of the Layers palette – which layers are visible, what effects have been applied to each, and so on. (You may find it helpful to review the description of Photoshop layers and layer styles in Chapter 3. ImageReady's Layers palette is the same as Photoshop's, although the palette menus have some minor differences.) In effect, each rollover state is an abstraction of the contents of the Layers

---

[*]People get used to anything, of course, but if you are interested in having users understand your site's navigation controls immediately without instruction, avoid the fish rollovers.

palette. To demonstrate what this rather enigmatic statement means, we will begin by describing how you can very easily create certain common types of rollover.

As an example, suppose we do want to place the word Downloads on a Web page, and make it into a rollover, such that it acquires a drop shadow when the cursor is over it, and turns a different colour when the mouse button is pressed (see Figure 4.11). We would proceed as follows. First, create a text layer containing Downloads in a suitable font. Next, create a layer-based slice (see page 177) from this layer. It is a good idea to use layer-based slices for simple rollovers, because then you don't have to worry if the changes you make when you define the different states change the size of the image that must be contained in the slice. It would be convenient to name the slice for future reference; let's call it Download Button. With the slice selected, the Rollover palette, shown in Figure 4.12, can be used to turn it into a rollover.

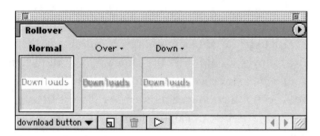

Figure 4.11   *A simple rollover.*

Figure 4.12   *The* Rollover *palette.*

To begin with, the Rollover palette contains a single thumbnail image, showing the slice we have just made, containing the plain text. This is the rollover's normal state. Extra states are added by clicking on the New button at the bottom of the palette. The first time you do so, the new state is headed Over, the second time, Down. These are the states that a simple rollover which responds graphically to the presence of the cursor and a mouse click requires. You can select a state by clicking on the corresponding thumbnail; it is then outlined to show that it has been selected. Any changes you make to the Layers palette when a state is selected will be reflected in the appearance of your image when the rollover enters that state but will not show in any other state. In particular, if you apply a layer style to the layer from which the rollover slice was made when the Over state is selected, the style will be applied when the cursor rolls over the slice.

For our example, we can select the Over state and use the Layer>Layer Style>Drop Shadow command to add the required drop shadow. Next, we select the Down state, and apply a colour overlay, using Layer>Layer Style>Color Overlay, to change the colour of the slice. That is all that is needed to create the rollover effect. Usually, though, we don't just create rollovers to look nice, but to provide an indication that something will happen in response to a click. To make something happen, we use the Slice palette to add a URL to the slice.

You can preview the effect of rollovers by clicking on the Play button at the bottom of the Rollover palette, and then moving the mouse over the image in the document window. After we have added states to the Download Button slice, when the rollover is previewed the word will acquire its drop shadow when the cursor is moved over it – the drop shadow was added to the Over state – and it will change colour when the mouse button is pressed, because the colour overlay was added to the Down state. In order to preview the operation of the button fully, it is necessary to use a Web browser. The browser preview button in the toolbox causes the slices of the image, together with an HTML file containing the tags to put the slices back together and JavaScript code to make the rollover work to be saved to a temporary location, and then opened in your default browser. The rollover should work the same way as it did when you previewed it in ImageReady and, when you click on it, a document will be loaded from the URL associated with the slice. It is a good idea to preview rollovers in as many browsers as you have access to, because they do not all implement JavaScript in the same way. (They all have different bugs.) The pop-up menu attached to the browser preview button shows all the browsers you have on your system, allowing you to select any of them for previewing.

☞ Practise creating rollover buttons by applying layer effects to text layers. Which effects provide the best rollover feedback? Preview your rollovers in any browsers available to you.

A navigation bar can be created out of suitably arranged slices of a single document, each of which is a rollover. When several rollovers are used together as a navigation bar, it is customary to use the same visual effects for each one. If a Downloads button acquires a drop shadow when the cursor moves over it, a neighbouring Contact Us button would be expected to behave in the same way. Instead of requiring you to repeat the procedure for creating a rollover in exactly the same way every time you want to apply the same behaviour to a different slice, ImageReady allows you to create *rollover styles*, which collect together all the aspects of a rollover – which states it has and the effects applied in each state. You do this by selecting a rollover slice and then choosing New Style... from the Style palette's menu. You are presented with the dialogue box shown in Figure 4.13. By selecting all the checkboxes you end up with a rollover style, which then appears as a swatch in the Style palette. A black triangle in the top left corner indicates that it is a rollover style.

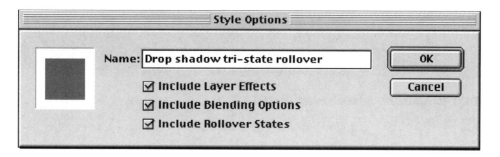

Figure 4.13   *Creating a new rollover style.*

Suppose that, having created a rollover for the Downloads button as just described, you make a rollover style from it, called something like Drop shadow tri-state rollover. To create another button that behaves the same way, all you need to do is create a new slice from a suitably positioned text layer containing the appropriate words, such as Contact Us. Select this slice, and click on the swatch representing Drop shadow tri-state rollover in the Style palette. (A tool tip with each style's name appears when you move the cursor over the style swatches.) That's all you need to do, apart from attaching a URL to the slice to make the rollover into a link.

☞ Choose a rollover effect from your attempts at the previous exercise, save it as a style and apply it to some other text layers to make a navigation bar.

The libraries of styles that are supplied with ImageReady include several rollover styles, some of which are perfectly serviceable, so the very simplest way to create a rollover is by applying one of these to a slice you have made containing some text or an icon. The next easiest way is to apply a library style and then make some small changes. For example, among ImageReady's style libraries is a set of quite classy glass button rollovers. When you apply one of these to some text, it takes on a translucent appearance in one of several different colours, and the lighting on the glass changes when you press the mouse button on the rollover. If you like the effect, but want the appearance to change when the cursor moves over the button, not when it is clicked, all you need to do is turn the Down state, which is created when you apply the style, into an Over state. If you look carefully at Figure 4.12 on page 185 (or the Rollover palette itself) you will see that, apart from the normal state, the labels above each thumbnail have a small triangle attached to them. As this suggests, there is actually a pop-up menu above the thumbnail, from which you can select a different state, that is, a different event that will cause the state to be entered. In this case, you simply need to choose Over instead of Down. You can create a new rollover style based on the button you just created, and use it to make more similar buttons.

☞ Use rollover styles from the library to create navigation bars. Make small changes to a library style, such as the one suggested in the text, save the modified style and apply it to some rollovers.

More Elaborate Rollover Effects

The method just described can be used to create rollovers where the superficial appearance of a basic image changes when the cursor moves over it. If you want to create a rollover where the actual image content changes you must work with additional layers. Remember that a rollover state maps to the state of all the layers in an image, that is, in effect, to the contents of the Layers palette. This means that each rollover state is associated with settings for the visibility, location and effects on every layer, but not with the layers' image content. This is always the same in every state – whichever state you have selected, if you paint on a layer the changes you make will appear in every state of the rollover. Consequently, in order to have some parts of an image visible in the Over state but not the normal state for instance, you must place them on a separate layer and use the visibility controls in the Layers palette to make that layer appear and disappear as the rollover changes its state.

A simple example should suffice to demonstrate how this works. Suppose we want to provide our own tool tips for navigation buttons on a Web page. That is, when the cursor is moved over a button some extra text should appear, telling the user what the button is for. Figure 4.14 shows an example. This was created in the following way. First, a text layer was made just containing the word Downloads. Next, a second layer was made containing a tool tip around which the speech bubble was drawn. Both of these layers were made into layer-based slices.

The Downloads layer was selected; in the Rollover palette its only (normal) state was selected. In the Layers palette, the layer containing the tool tip was made invisible. Next, a second state was added to the rollover. With this new (Over) state selected, the tool tip layer was made visible using the Layers palette. When the document is previewed in

Figure 4.14   *Tool tips.*

a Web browser the tool tip appears only when the cursor is over the word Downloads, as we intended.

> ☞ Try to duplicate the rollover shown in Figure 4.14 by following the description in the text. Make some similar rollovers with pop-ups of your own design.

Although it may be slightly counter-intuitive, this way of working with rollovers and layers makes it is relatively easy to create elaborate rollover effects within the conceptual framework of layered images that is familiar to many designers from Photoshop and other applications. It also leads to fairly efficient rollovers, usually with no duplication of image content in different files. It can be slightly confusing in more complicated cases, and it is worth doing some advance planning beforehand. You should determine how many layers you will need, what should be on each of them and under what circumstances each should be visible, invisible or displayed with some layer effect. A more elaborate example should give you some idea of what may be involved.

For a relatively large Web site it may be helpful to users to attach pop-up menus to some or all of the navigation buttons. The intention is that each button which is permanently displayed on the page identifies a major division of the Web site, and when the cursor moves over a button a menu pops up to show subdivisions within that major division. Figure 4.15 shows an example. To illustrate how such an effect can be achieved, we will just describe the implementation of a single button as shown in the illustration; we leave implementing an entire navigation bar are along these lines as an exercise. We should point out, of course, that we are only showing one way of going about this task.

Our first step is to decide how to distribute the content of the images among different layers. A little thought shows that each of the three words Downloads, Demos and Updates will have to be on its own layer, since each is going to have to respond to events, that is, each is going to be a rollover. Less obviously, the area enclosing the lines connecting the sub-headings to the main button will also have to respond to some events, as we will see, so this too must be placed on its own layer.

Downloads

Figure 4.15   *A rollover with a pop-up menu.*

We therefore began by creating four layers and adding text and graphics. At this stage we did not apply effects to any of the layers. We did, however, create layer-based slices from each of them. In order to create the rollovers, we can usefully tabulate the visibility and effects to be applied to each layer in each state. Table 4.1 shows this information. We have chosen to use two-state rollovers for now. The Lines layer has to respond to the cursor moving over it, because otherwise, when a user moves the cursor between the word Downloads and one of the sub-headings there is no way of ensuring the pop-up menu does not disappear while the cursor is in between the two words. As in previous examples we chose to add a drop shadow to each button when it is responding to the cursor. (The drop shadow is useful for these examples because it shows up well on the printed page. We do not suggest that it necessarily makes a good rollover.)

Table 4.1.   *State changes for the pop-up menu rollover.*

		Downloads	Lines	Demos	Updates
Downloads	**Normal**	Visible	Invisible	Invisible	Invisible
	Over	Visible + drop shadow	Visible	Visible	Visible
Lines	**Normal**	Visible	Invisible	Invisible	Invisible
	Over	Visible + drop shadow	Visible	Visible	Visible
Demos	**Normal**	Visible	Invisible	Invisible	Invisible
	Over	Visible + drop shadow	Visible	Visible + drop shadow	Visible
Updates	**Normal**	Visible	Invisible	Invisible	Invisible
	Over	Visible + drop shadow	Visible	Visible	Visible + drop shadow

Armed with the information in the table, it is very straightforward to create the rollovers we need to. We begin by selecting the Downloads slice; the Rollover palette shows its normal state. With that selected, we used the Layers palette to make sure that the Downloads layer is visible and the other three layers are invisible. Next we added the

Over state and, again using the Layers palette, we added a drop shadow layer effect to the Downloads layer and made the other three layers visible. This means that when the rollover is displayed in a Web browser the menu will pop up when the cursor is over the word Downloads, as we required it to.

We proceeded similarly to add rollovers to the other three layer slices, setting values in the Layers palette for each state of each rollover in accordance with the table.

When the result of these operations is previewed, a couple of shortcomings become evident. In the first place, the slice based on the Lines layer is too small: it only encloses the lines themselves. This means that if a user moves the cursor over the word Demos and then moves it horizontally until it is over the word Updates, while it is in between the two the pop-up menu disappears in a disconcerting fashion. To fix this problem we promoted the Lines slice to a user slice, and then used the slice selection tool to drag it out until it included the entire area through which the cursor is likely to move while a user is interacting with the pop-up menu.

The second problem with our initial attempt at this rollover is that nothing happens if you click on the word Downloads. This is consistent, but it may not conform to users' expectations. Generally, if you click on a button you expect something to happen. In this case, after a bit of experimentation, we decided that an appropriate thing to happen when you click on Downloads is for the pop-up menu to disappear. To add this feature we used some facilities of the rollover palette which we have not yet described.

First we added a state and used the pop-up menu to set its event to Click, since in this case it is the actual click we need to respond to, not simply the pressing or release of the mouse button. Now, we know that what we want to do when this click happens is return the rollover to its normal state. Instead of explicitly recreating that state, ImageReady allows us to copy it. To do this we simply selected the rollover's normal state, chose Copy State from the palette menu, selected our new state and chose Paste State from the palette menu. To complete the exercise for a real Web page we would select each of the Demos and Updates slices in turn and use the Slice palette to attach URLs to them.

☛ Try to produce your own version of the example just described. Devise your own variations based on the same technique, such as a menu in one place that controls the contents of a sub-menu elsewhere on the page.

Animation

The GIF file format provides animation. A single GIF file can contain many images. Most Web browsers, when they find a GIF with more than one image, show each one in turn. When images are shown in succession sufficiently rapidly, persistence of vision leads to an illusion of movement, or animation. GIFs thus provide a simple means of adding animated elements to a Web page, without the use of a plug-in. Web graphics programs generally provide some means of creating *animated GIFs*, as GIFs containing several images are called.

An animated GIF can include a specification of how many times the animation is to be played (including an infinite number) and the delay that the browser should allow to elapse between frames. This value sets the frame rate for the animation, though there is no guarantee that any browser will consistently maintain the specified rate. A value of zero is used to mean that the frames should be played as fast as possible.

There is an added complication in the case of images that include transparent areas. Usually, when a frame is displayed, you will want the page background to show through in the transparent areas. For this to happen, the previous frame must be discarded when a new frame is displayed. Sometimes, though, it is advantageous to have the previous frame showing through. This can be used deliberately as the basis of an animation in which a picture is built up incrementally over the course of several frames. In a less specialized way, not disposing of frames can be used to reduce the size of animated GIF files. If each image in the file contains, instead of a complete frame, just the difference between one frame and the one preceding it, then overlaying these successive images (which will usually be smaller, and possibly much smaller, than a complete frame) will produce the same animation as showing the complete frames in turn and disposing of each one before showing the next. Optimizing GIFs in this way is another function that is usually provided by Web graphics applications.

ImageReady can be used to create animations, which can be saved as animated GIFs or as QuickTime movies. An animation in ImageReady is a sequence of frames, which can be manipulated in the Animation palette. The approach taken to animation resembles that taken to rollovers. Each frame in an animation is associated with a configuration of the Layers palette the same way a rollover state is. While this approach supports a variety of animation styles and techniques, it is best suited to techniques which are based on layers, effects and compositing – the concepts which underlie Photoshop's (and therefore ImageReady's) approach to image manipulation.

Frame-at-a-Time Animation

One traditional animation technique – perhaps the most easy to understand – consists of drawing each frame on a separate sheet of paper, photographing each sheet in turn with a movie camera, then playing back the resulting sequence of frames. This technique can be simulated in ImageReady, by identifying each frame with its own layer, which is only visible in that frame. By drawing, painting, importing an image from a scanner, or otherwise creating an image on that layer, a frame can be created as if it was being drawn on its own sheet of paper. The mechanics of making this sort of animation in ImageReady are fairly straightforward, although it must be admitted the technique is labour-intensive. Later we will describe animation techniques in which the program does more of the work for you.

Frames can be created in the Animation palette, which is shown in Figure 4.16. This palette has the standard New button at the bottom and it is by clicking on this that you add frames. Every time you add a frame in this way it initially contains a copy of the one preceding it. So to make animation in the fashion outlined in the preceding paragraph, you could proceed as follows: first, make a new layer in the first frame and create the first frame's image on it. Next, add a new frame. The new frame will be selected when you create it. In the Layers palette add a new layer and make the layer on which the first frame was drawn invisible. Now create the image for the second frame on your new layer. Continue in this way, adding new frames on new layers while making all other layers invisible except for the one for the frame you are working on. As the Layers palette in Figure 4.16 shows, for each frame, one layer will be visible; the rest will be hidden.

ImageReady will give you some help if you want to animate in this fashion. If you select Add A Layer To New Frames from the Animation palette menu, then whenever you create a frame, a new layer will be created at the same time which, by default, will be invisible in all preceding frames. So now, when you add a frame you just need to make the preceding frame's layer invisible and create the new image in the new frame, on the layer that has been created for it. Actually, it will often be easier to carry out those steps in the reverse order. That is, draw the new frame while you can still see the one before, and only when you've finished make the preceding frame's layer invisible. This will make it easier for you to judge how to move elements of your animation in successive frames in order to produce a convincing illusion of movement. (Note that this is even more useful if you adjust the opacity of the preceding layer to fade it down before drawing on the new layer. This will not, of course, affect its appearance in the preceding frame.)

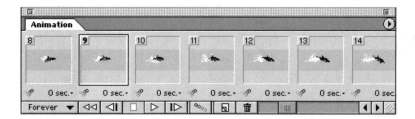

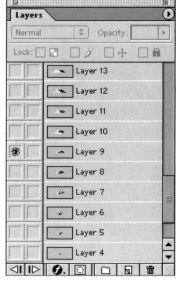

Figure 4.16   *The animation palette and corresponding layers.*

You can use the Animation palette to set various properties of your animation. In particular, you can specify the delay between successive frames. You do this by choosing a value from the pop-up menu displayed beneath the thumbnail on the palette. You can in fact set a different delay for each frame, but normally you will want the animation to play back at a constant rate. The easiest way to ensure this is by choosing Select All Frames from the palette menu; if you then choose a delay for any frame it will be applied to all of them, and to any frames that you add subsequently.

You can specify how many times the animation will play (loop) in a browser using the pop-up menu in the bottom left corner of the Animation palette. This offers three choices: Forever, Once and Other.... If you choose the last option you can set a number of times in a simple dialogue box that is displayed.

At the bottom of the Animation palette you can find a set of conventional VCR-style playback controls, which you can use to preview your animation in ImageReady. However, generally animations will not play back at the correct frame rate when you do so; it is usually better to preview them in a browser. Note that since the only Web image file format that supports animation is GIF, you must choose this format in the Optimize palette when you're working with animations (although you can ultimately save them as QuickTime movies using File>Export Original...). It is then sufficient to select Save Optimized from the File menu to create the animated GIF.

> ☛ Practise making simple animations a frame at a time. Start with just a few frames and some simple drawing to get used to the mechanics, and then, if you have a taste for animation, go on to something more ambitious – but try to keep the resulting file size down to manageable proportions.

An alternative way of creating the frames of an animation is by placing each image on a separate layer to begin with, either in ImageReady or in Photoshop, as if you were working on a single layered image. You can then open the file in ImageReady if necessary, and select Make Frames from Layers from the Animation palette menu. Each layer will be sent to its own frame. You can then edit the animation and its properties in the same way as one you created a frame at a time using the Animation palette as we described before.

As we described earlier in this section, animated GIFs can be optimized so that only the differences between successive frames are stored in the file. If you wish to do that, select Optimize Animation... from the palette menu. (Leave both options selected in the dialogue box that appears.) The effectiveness of optimization depends, as we explained earlier, on not disposing of each frame before the next one is displayed. Unusually, the only way in which you can set the disposal method for frames is by using a contextual menu. If you right-click/ctl-click on a frame, the disposal menu pops up; you can choose Restore To Background, Do Not Dispose or Automatic. For optimized images you should choose Automatic.

Animating Layer Properties

Making animations one frame at a time offers the greatest range of possibilities to the animator, but it is hard work and if you're going to animate in that way you'll probably prefer a more powerful animation tool. If you're animating in ImageReady, it is simpler to produce your animations by changing layer attributes over time, instead of actually trying to change the image content. Unlike frame-at-a-time animation, such animations are very easy to produce.

The simplest sort of animation that you can produce in ImageReady is made by moving the contents of a layer over successive frames. For this you do not want to create a new layer for every frame, so you must deselect Add A Layer To New Frames in the Animation palette menu. You then create a single layer and put an image of some sort on it. Using the move tool, if necessary, you position the layer where you want it to be in the first frame of your animation. You can now add frames to the animation; each time you do so, use the move tool to reposition the layer. To take the very simplest case as an example, if you place an image of a single object – say, a teapot – on your layer so that in the first frame it is positioned at the left and then move the layer a small amount to the right every time you add a new frame, when you preview the animation your teapot will appear to move across the screen from left to right. Remember that in ImageReady you can only move the layer – if you try to move the teapot itself, by redrawing it, its position will be changed in every frame of the animation.

In making animation of this sort you are not restricted to a single layer, of course. You can place different images on separate layers and move each layer independently to create complicated motions and interactions.

> ☞ Try making an animation by moving the contents of a single layer in successive frames. Start just by making an abstract shape on a layer and experiment with making it move. Try using more representational elements and try to make them move in a natural way.

You can animate other attributes of the layer besides its position. A popular effect that is achieved this way is the fade – out or in. Images can be made to grow dim and disappear by steadily decreasing the opacity of a layer over the course of an animation. Conversely, they can be made to appear and grow brighter by steadily increasing it. A very simple fade-out would be made by creating a new layer (this won't work on the background layer) and placing an image on it, then, in the Animation palette, adding a second frame and setting the opacity to 90%, adding a third frame with the opacity set to 80%, and so on. For this kind of animation you only need one layer, whose properties are altered to give it a different appearance in different frames. You can use a similar method to animate layer effects, just by setting different values for their parameters in each frame.

> ☞ Make an animation consisting of a shape or some text with a drop shadow, whose direction and intensity vary, as if the text was illuminated by the sun, which was moving around the sky from dawn to sunset.

Animating layer attributes depends on the fact that any changes you make to the Layers palette are only applied to the frame you have selected in the Animation palette. If you want to make changes that apply to all frames or apply some settings you have made in one frame to all of them, you should select Match Layer Across Frames from the Animation palette menu.

Varying parameters in a simple linear way, as in the suggested fade-out, is tedious; it is also just the sort of thing that computer programs are good at doing for you. In Web animation, automatic interpolation of frames is called *tweening*. ImageReady provides primitive tweening facilities for layers. It can automatically calculate intermediate properties for a layer's position, its opacity and the parameters to any effects applied to it, on the basis of their starting and ending values.

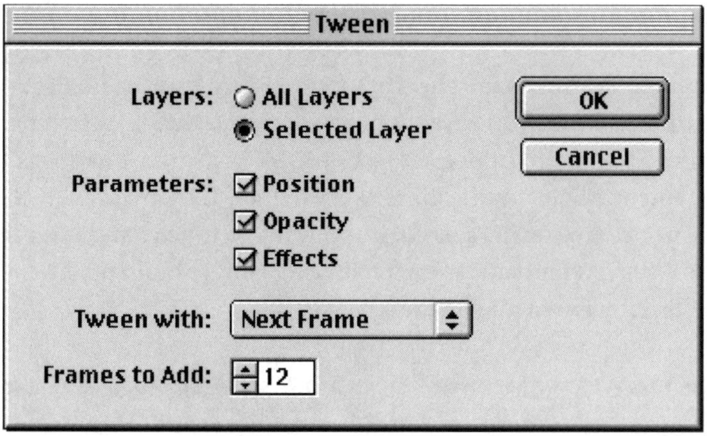

Figure 4.17   *The tweening dialogue.*

Returning to our example of a fading image, a much quicker way of creating this animation would be to use tweening. We would begin as before by creating a layer and placing the image we wish to fade on it, but then, after switching to the Animation palette, we would just make a single copy of this initial frame. We would select the copied frame – that is to say, frame 2 of the animation – in the Animation palette and set its opacity to zero in the Layers palette. Next, we would select the first frame and click on the tweening button at the bottom of the palette. The dialogue box shown in Figure 4.17 would be displayed. The options here are fairly self-explanatory. The two crucial ones are those at the bottom. The pop-up menu labelled Tween with lets us choose which frame is going to be the other end of the tweened sequence; in our case we want the next frame (that is, the second) to be the end of the sequence. (We could have chosen the second, and set the pop-up to Previous Frame if that had been more convenient for any reason.) The field at the bottom of the dialogue box lets us specify how many new frames are going to be inserted in between the first and last of the tweened sequence. Clearly, the number of frames we specify here, in conjunction with the inter-frame delay set for the animation, determines the speed at which the fading occurs.

The two options at the top of this dialogue box give you a choice of interpolating just one selected layer (in which case the other layers become invisible during the tweening, except for the background, which is held static) or all of them. The check boxes in the middle of the dialogue box let you choose which attributes of the layer are going to be tweened. These are the same attributes that you can vary in a handmade animation.

☛ Repeat the previous exercise, but use tweening instead of manually creating every frame. Practise using tweening to create animations.

Tweening in ImageReady has the effect of inserting new frames into the animation for which the attributes which you have specified are given values in between those you set in the start and end frames. (It doesn't just store some instructions about how to compute the intermediate frames, the way Flash does. They are actually there.) The intermediate values are equally spaced; if you want them to change over time in more sophisticated ways you must add extra frames explicitly, to build up the effect you want as a series of linearly tweened sequences.

☛ Make an animation using tweening, in which an image fades in quickly and then fades out slowly.

A consequence of the way in which ImageReady implements tweening is that once you have carried out the operation you are left with a sequence of frames which are in no way distinguished from any you might create explicitly yourself. You can therefore edit these frames. On the other hand, if you change the value of a parameter that you have already tweened, in the first or last frame of a tweened sequence, the intermediate values are not recalculated. For instance, you might make a fade by tweening as we described above, but then decide that you didn't want your image to fade down to nothing, after all, but only to fade down to half its original brightness. If you therefore selected the last frame and set its opacity to 50%, instead of achieving a less pronounced fade you will end up with an animation in which the image faded to almost nothing and then suddenly brightened up again. If you wish to change the start or end values in this way, you must redo the tweening process. You don't have to delete all the tweened frames, though. Instead, you only need to select them all before you click the tweening button. When you do that, the Tween with option in the tweening dialogue box is set to Selection and all the other options in that menu are disabled, as is the field for entering the number of frames to add. The interpolated frames replace the selection.

☛ Experiment with altering the values of the parameters for your tweening in the previous exercise, with and without re-doing the tweening.

There is one very useful refinement to the tweening process. If you select the last frame in an animation, you can then choose, when the dialogue box is displayed, to tween it with the first frame. The effect is to add frames after the last one which interpolate whatever value it is you are tweening to the corresponding values in the first frame. What this means is that, if your animation is played in a continuous loop, there will be no discontinuities between the last frame and the first frame when the loop completes itself.

☛ Create a cyclical animation in which some layer effect applied to text varies one or more of its parameters from an initial value, to some maximum and then back again. Make the animation loop forever and preview it in a Web browser. Use tweening to ensure that the loop completes without visible discontinuities.

Animated Rollovers

You can combine animation and rollovers to produce animated rollovers, but you need to keep a clear head when you do so. The basic idea is that, if you select a state in a rollover and then use the Animation palette to create an animation, that animation will be played when the state you selected is entered, that is, when a specified event is received by the rollover. To show how this works – and to consolidate our earlier descriptions of animation and rollovers – we will describe an example of a simple animated rollover.

If you are taken with the interface elements of MacOS X, you might like to add some pulsating translucent buttons to your Web pages. One way to go about doing so is by making a rollover and animating its Over state so that it appears to pulsate. You could proceed in the following way.

First, use the rounded rectangle tool to make a button shape on its own layer, and create a layer-based slice from it. Select this slice and apply one of the glass button styles to it, in a colour of your choice. (If the glass button rollovers are not shown in the Styles palette, select Glass Button Rollovers from the palette menu and they will be loaded into it.) When this style is applied, your button shape will have layer effects applied to it to make it appear glassy and translucent and a Down state will be added to the rollover, with the lighting subtly altered. It is this state which we're going to replace by a pulsating animation, but first we want to change the event which causes it to be entered, by selecting Over from the pop-up menu above its thumbnail in the Rollover palette.

Having done that we make sure that the Over state is selected and switch to the Animation palette.

There are several different ways in which you might make the button pulsate, but the most convincing appears to be by fading the opacity of the gradient overlay layer effect which is applied as part of the glass button style. Naturally, we will use tweening to help us.

Initially, the Animation palette shows a single frame identical to the Over state of the static rollover button. We add a second frame, select it, and also select the gradient overlay effect in the Layers palette, where it is shown applied to the button layer we started with. When the effect is selected, an effect palette is displayed in which its parameters can be set as usual (see Chapter 3). In this palette, we just set the opacity to a value of 50%. (See Figure 4.18.)

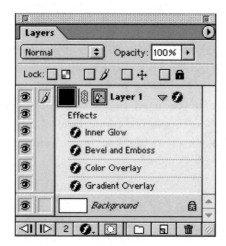
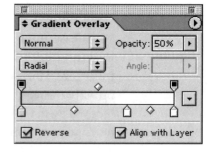

Figure 4.18   *Layer effects in a pulsating button.*

With this new frame still selected, we bring up the tweening dialogue box, choose to tween it with the previous frame, and add a suitable number of intermediate frames – half a dozen at least. When we have dismissed the dialogue box and the tweened frames have been added, we again select what is now the final frame of the sequence, and bring up the tweening dialogue once more. This time, we elect to tween with the first frame, thus completing the pulsating sequence to be looped. We set the number of frames to be added to the same value as we did before. We end up with an animation during which the overlaid gradient fades down and back up again.

To complete the animated rollover, we must set a suitable frame delay – a fifth of a second is the longest you can get away with if you want the button to appear to pulsate smoothly – and set the animation to loop forever. Making sure that we have chosen GIF as the file format in the Optimize palette, we can now choose Save Optimized As... from the File menu and save all the images that these processes have generated and the HTML file that glues them all together. When this is opened in a Web browser and the user moves the cursor over the button it will pulsate gently.

> ☛ Work through the example just described to make a pulsating button. Practise making similar animated rollovers, by applying different time-varying layer effects to a button or a text layer. Make sure that they loop smoothly.

To make a useful button, we would have to attach a URL to the slice out of which the rollover was built, and generally we would want to superimpose some text to indicate the function of the button. Sadly, you cannot save animated rollover styles. If you try to do so, the animation is lost and you just end up with a simple rollover style. If you want to create pulsating buttons of different shapes, you will have to repeat the process. (You can record an action to automate it, though, as described in Chapter 9.)

Further Exercises to do in ImageReady

1. Import a photograph of a friend or family member. Slice the image so that it may be efficiently optimized for the Web and preview the result in a browser.

2. Import an image related to a subject that interests you – e.g., music, sport, stamp collecting, or whatever – which is suitable for use as an image map. Create hot spots on appropriate parts of the image and add real URLs which link to live Web sites connected with the subject you have chosen.

3. Design and make some buttons that spin when the cursor is over them.

4. Make a rollover with a different image for every possible state. Test this rollover in a browser, making every different image appear.

5. Make an animated rollover in the form of a button that cycles through all the colours of the rainbow when the cursor is over it.

6. Create a navigation bar for a small Web site, featuring three or more buttons labelled with major divisions, each of which has a pop-up menu. For instance, for a typical

small software vendor's site, you might have major divisions Downloads, with sub-divisions Demos and Updates, Contacts, with sub-divisions Enquiries, Complaints and Brochure Requests, and Information, with sub-divisions FAQs, Company Profile and Products. Make sure that each pop-up menu only appears when the cursor is in the region of the appropriate main heading.

7. Place seven invisible buttons in random positions on a page and add rollovers so that when the cursor is over one of the buttons, one of seven related images appears somewhere else on the page.

8. Make a Web page for either educational or commercial use, designed to be perspicuous, easy to use and informative. It should consist of an unobtrusive background image and a set of buttons which change their appearance on rollover to provide feedback and, when clicked, cause an image and a short piece of explanatory text related to it to appear. For example, a commercial site might have buttons for each of a collection of products, which should bring up a picture of the product with price details and a brief description of the item.

9. Create an animation of about twelve frames by making successive adjustments or alterations to a single image. Do this first by hand and then by using tweening.

10. Make a little banner ad that has the characteristics of commercial ads used on the Web. Your ad should be the most popular banner size (468x60 pixels) and convey a short sharp message in nine frames or fewer.

11. Cut several figures or other objects out of a magazine, scan them and import the images into ImageReady. Clean them up and paste them on to separate layers in a single image. Make an animation by moving the different layers, so the figures and objects appear to move. (The early animation work of Terry Gilliam might provide you with some ideas for this exercise.)

12. Take a suitable image, slice it and animate one slice only. For example, you could slice an image of a dinosaur and make just its head move in some way.

13. Take eight small square images, all of the same size, place them on separate layers and align them so that they form the outside of a 3x3 grid, leaving a gap the size of an image in the middle.
    (a) Set up rollovers so that when the cursor is over an image a copy of it appears in the middle of the grid.

(b) Set up rollovers so that when you click on a square the image in it moves to the empty square leaving a gap behind it. The next click will cause an image to move into this new gap, and so on. (You might find it helpful to try this with just three images in a row with a gap first.)

14. Import or create an image which is suited to having elements in it animated. (This could be either abstract or representational.) Slice the image up in an appropriate way and turn two or three suitable slices into animated rollovers.

5 Flash Animation with Interactivity

Files and Formats Summary

- Create Flash Movies (FLA files) with File>New, and save them with File>Save As... and File>Save.

- Open FLA files that have been saved previously with File>Open.

- Create SWF files, also known as a Flash Player movies, using File>Export Movie....

- Create an SWF file and an HTML document that embeds it so it can be played in a Web browser, using File>Publish with its default settings.

- Export finished movies in other formats besides SWF, using File>Export Movie...

- Export single frames in various still image formats, using File>Export Image....

- Import images and movies in various formats, using File>Import....

Common Features
Used By This Program

Macromedia Flash is a program for creating animations, often with interactive features, usually to be played over the Internet. It provides simple tools for drawing individual frames and also allows artwork to be imported from other graphics applications. Animations can be constructed in a traditional manner by drawing frames one at a time, or semi-automatically by drawing only a relatively small number of keyframes and allowing Flash to interpolate movement and shape changes between them. Flash animations are fundamentally vector-based, although bitmapped graphics can be handled at the cost of efficiency and some flexibility. Completed animations can be exported in a compact form, embedded in Web pages and streamed over the Internet.

'Interactivity' means that the animation can respond to events initiated by a user, by clicking or dragging with the mouse, and so on. In early versions of Flash, events such as these were able to influence the playback of the animation, by causing it to jump to a specified frame, for instance. This was achieved by adding simple parameterized actions to special interface elements known as buttons or to frames of the animation. With each successive release of the Flash software, the repertoire of actions was enlarged, allowing more complicated computation to be performed in response to events. In Flash 5, this has been taken to its logical conclusion: a scripting language called ActionScript, which is closely related to JavaScript, is now incorporated in Flash. Events trigger the execution of scripts, which can perform arbitrary computation and control the playback of the movie. Additionally, a collection of built-in objects provides scripts with sophisticated mathematical and text-manipulating capabilities, and with facilities for communicating with a server in various ways, including via the exchange of XML data. It is thus slightly misleading to see Flash as simply an animation program with some interactive features, since ActionScript allows it to be used to build sophisticated front-ends to all sorts of distributed systems. Flash's distinguishing contribution lies in the combination of such computation with vector-based animations.

The version described in this chapter is Flash 5. The changes made to both the scripting facilities and the user interface with this release represent a radical departure from previous versions. Since, without exception, the changes are all improvements, earlier versions will not be considered here and we advise anyone still using Flash 4 or earlier to upgrade as soon as possible.

→275

Basic Concepts

Flash can be used in several different ways to create animation. The simplest way, corresponding to traditional methods, is to create each frame individually by drawing it or importing an image from a file. The completed animation is a sequence of frames, each one differing to a greater or lesser extent from the preceding one. The illusion of movement is created by persistence of vision when the frames of the sequence are displayed in rapid succession.

It is more usual to draw only certain *keyframes* and use Flash's interpolation – or *tweening* – facilities to insert additional frames by moving elements of the keyframes in easily specified ways. In the simplest case, a keyframe is created, containing a graphical object at a certain position. A second keyframe is created further along in the timeline as a copy of the first keyframe, the object is moved to a different position and Flash is instructed to tween its motion between the two keyframes. (The details of how this is accomplished will be described later.) When the movie is played, the frames between the two keyframes are automatically constructed, so that the object appears to move in a straight line between its two positions in the keyframes. (See Figure 5.1.)

In Flash, the term *motion tweening*, which is used for this process, encompasses more than just interpolating the position of an object on the stage. Its size and angle of rotation can also be tweened; so can its colour, brightness and transparency. By using a sequence of keyframes placed at different intervals, the object can be made to change direction and speed. By using layers, a whole collection of objects can be made to move independently. Finally, in addition to motion tweening, Flash supports *shape tweening*, or *morphing* as it is commonly known, whereby one shape can be transformed into a different one. (See Figure 5.2.) By combining the various types of tweening that Flash provides, animations can be produced in a range of styles.

The two most important components of the Flash interface are its *timeline* and a window called the *stage*, in which the elements of a frame are created and assembled. The timeline provides a spatial view of the temporal succession of frames making up an animation; the stage displays the contents of a currently selected frame. By default, these two components are docked together, as shown in Figure 5.3, but they may be pulled apart by dragging the blank area at the top of the timeline. This will usually provide a more convenient work area if you have two monitors. In addition to the timeline and the stage, the Flash interface consists of about twenty palettes – or *panels* as they are referred to in the Flash documentation – many of which will be introduced in the following sections. Most panels can be made active using the Panels sub-menu

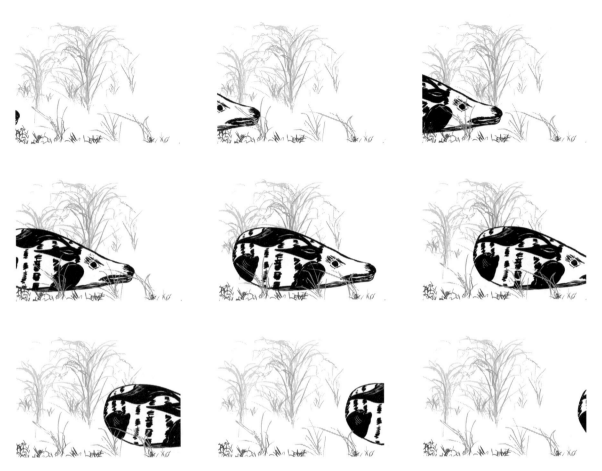

Figure 5.1 *A simple example of motion tweening.*

MX
→276

of the Window menu. Some of the more important have their own entries in the Window menu though (and the timeline and stage are hidden or revealed using commands in the View menu). A mini-launcher, in the form of the row of icons you see at the bottom right of the stage can be used to get at certain panels with a single click. Tool tips pop up if you hold the cursor over these icons to tell you which panels they launch.

The timeline and the stage work in conjunction with each other. The *current frame* is the one which is currently displayed on the stage. It can be set by dragging the marker attached to the vertical red bar through the frame numbers in the timeline. The stage is used for more than just displaying a frame. It is also the window in which a frame is created and modified. Often, Flash's drawing tools, which are described in the next section, are used for these operations, but it is also possible to import frames from a file created in some other program.

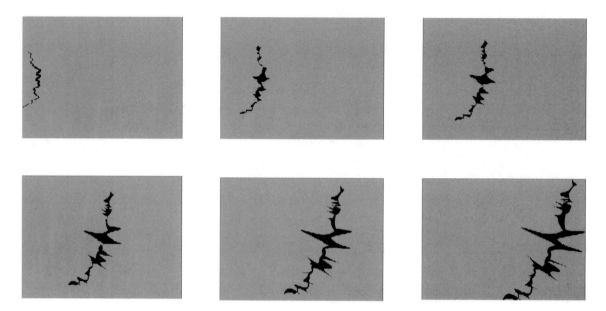

Figure 5.2   *A simple example of shape tweening.*

Some slightly confusing terminology is used to identify the various files that Flash creates. A *Flash movie* is, properly speaking, the equivalent of a project in Premiere and most other time-based media tools. It is the file in which you assemble and organize the various components of an animation. When Flash starts up, a new movie (called Untitled 1) is created by default. Movies can also be created using the File>New command, in the usual way. A newly created movie contains just a single keyframe on one layer. You can change the pixel dimensions of the movie in the dialogue invoked by the Modify>Movie command. (Clicking on the button labelled Save Default will cause all subsequently created movies to share the same dimensions. Originally, the default is set to the rather unusual value of 550 by 400 pixels.)

What many people think of as a Flash movie is the file that you find embedded in Web pages, which actually plays as an animation in your browser. This is properly a *Flash Player movie*, the most important of the formats in which Flash can export a movie so that it can be played. To avoid ambiguity, we will usually refer to a Flash Player movie by its alternative designation, an *SWF file* or *SWF movie*.[*] SWF files are created using the File>Export Movie... command. After you choose the destination in the usual file saving

---

[*]Clearly, SWF cannot stand for Flash Player by any stretch of the imagination. The initials SWF originally stood for Shockwave Flash, by extension of the Shockwave terminology used for the Web versions of Director movies. Since the two are not really the same, and the use of the name Shockwave caused confusion, SWF is now 'officially' just a name for a Flash Player movie and doesn't stand for anything. Many people like to pronounce SWF as 'swoof'.

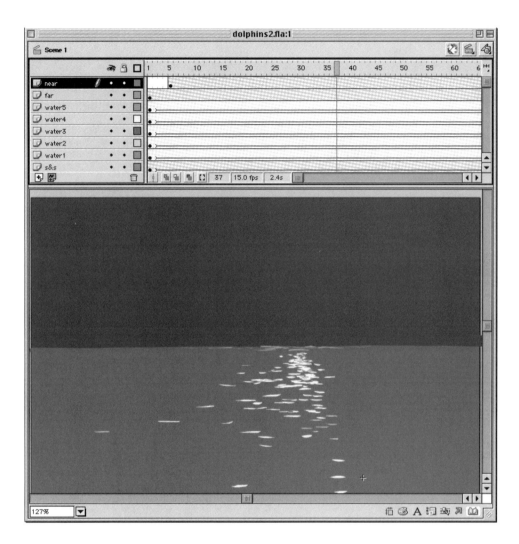

Figure 5.3 *The stage and the timeline.*

dialogue, a second dialogue box appears, which allows you to set various parameters of the SWF file. It is usually safe to go with the defaults.

Normally, when you have finished work on a Flash movie, you will want to export a SWF file and embed it in a Web page. The File>Publish command can be used to export a movie and the necessary HTML code to embed it in, in a single step. File>Publish Settings... can be used to set parameters for the SWF and HTML. It can also be used to select other formats for export and to set the appropriate parameters. As with movie exporting, it is safe to leave everything set to the default values to begin with, until you have a clearer idea of what is going on.

In between creating a movie and publishing it, you make an animation and add actions to it. The basis of any Flash animation is the creation of individual keyframes, so we must begin by looking at the facilities provided for doing that.

Drawing

Flash is fundamentally a vector graphics application. This means that a picture (that is, the contents of a frame) consists of a collection of shapes, each of which is made up of simple strokes and which may be filled with a colour or a more complex pattern. If you have used another vector drawing program, such as Illustrator (see Chapter 6) or Freehand, the principles behind Flash's drawing tools will be familiar, as will most of the tools. However, the tools in Flash's toolbox (shown in Figure 5.4) are slightly eccentric, sometimes behave inconsistently, and may hold some small surprises.

Figure 5.4   *The Toolbox.*

Lines and Shapes

The simplest thing you can draw is a line. For most people, the simplest way to draw a line is with the *pencil tool*. This is selected by clicking on its icon in the toolbox. Lines are drawn just by dragging the tool across the stage using the mouse, or a pressure-sensitive pen if you are using a drawing tablet. Flash inserts a straight line or Bézier path (see Chapter 9) that approximates the motion of the cursor. The style of approximation is determined by the option you choose for the pencil tool

In general, whenever a tool is selected, a set of options becomes available. These appear as buttons and pop-up menus in a small panel at the bottom of the toolbox. For the pencil tool, there is only one option, which controls the smoothing applied to the lines you draw. If you select Straighten, your movements will be approximated by straight lines or, if they are obviously curved, by segments of circles or ellipses. Furthermore, if your drawing looks like a triangle, rectangle, square, ellipse or circle it will be converted to a precise version of the shape it approximates. (An option, which can be set in the Editing pane of the preferences dialogue controls how good an approximation must be before Flash will substitute the geometric shape.) If you select Smooth instead of Straighten, Bézier curves with few control points will be used to approximate the line. Finally, if you select Ink the movements will be followed closely, using curves with many control points – generally, this will produce a somewhat ragged line if you are trying to draw with a mouse. No matter which smoothing option you select, holding down the shift key while dragging will force the pencil to draw a straight line that is either horizontal or vertical.

Alternatives to the pencil tool for drawing lines and curves are the *line tool* and the *pen tool*. The line tool can only create shapes made out of straight lines. After selecting it, you click at the point where you wish one end of the first line to be and then drag; the line appears to be pulled out of the starting point like a rubber band, so that you can easily see what its final appearance will be. When you let go of the mouse, the line is fixed with its other end at the point where the mouse button was released. If you now press and drag again, you can add a second line joined to the first. In this way, polygonal shapes can quickly be drawn. There are no options for the line tool, but holding the shift key while dragging constrains the lines to be at multiples of 45° to the horizontal.

The pen tool in Flash 5 behaves in a standard fashion, as described in Chapter 9. It can be used to draw straight lines, by clicking at successive end points, or Bézier curves, by dragging away from the end points towards control points. It is the most flexible curve-drawing tool in Flash's toolbox, but the least intuitive.

> ☞ Create a new movie and practise drawing lines on the stage with each of the pencil, line and pen tools. Try drawing a rectangular shape, a curvy line and a simple face, selecting the appropriate tool for each.

Stroke and Fill

→276

Any line or curve has a specific thickness and colour; it may also be drawn solid or in some other style, such as dots, dashes or spatters. These various properties of lines may be chosen using the Stroke panel, which is illustrated in Figure 5.5. At the top is a pop-up menu, from which the style of line may be chosen; Figure 5.6 shows the default set of available styles. Below this pop-up is a field for entering the thickness (weight) of the stroke. Units of pixels are used. A value between 0.1 and 10 may be entered, or a slider control, activated by clicking on the small triangle to the right of the text field, may be used to vary the width. The display at the bottom of the panel shows an example of the chosen values, so the slider can be used to set the width visually. The colour may be set by clicking on the swatch at the middle right of the panel and choosing a colour from the palette that is displayed. Choosing Custom... from the pop-up menu below the triangle in the top right corner of the panel allows you to construct your own preset strokes, which are then added to the pop-up menu.

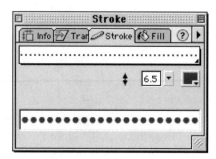

Figure 5.5   *The* Stroke *panel.*

When you draw a line, the values most recently set in the Stroke panel are used to control its appearance. You can change the appearance by selecting the line (see below) and changing the values. An alternative quick way of changing strokes is to select the ink bottle tool. When you click on a line using this tool, the values currently set in the Stroke panel are applied to it.

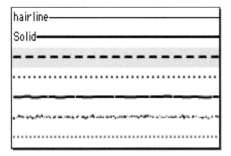

Figure 5.6 *Line styles.*

→277

If a line is closed, that is, if it joins back on itself, it can be considered to be the boundary of a shape. This means that it can be *filled* – or coloured in, as we might more familiarly put it. The way in which this is done depends on how the shape was drawn.

In all cases, the fill colour can be selected using the Fill panel, shown in Figure 5.7. For the simple case of a single solid colour chosen from the default palette it is sufficient to click on the swatch and choose a colour from the palette that pops up, as shown. If you need a wider range of colours than the default palette provides you can use the Mixer panel (shown in Figure 5.8) instead. This too provides a pop-up palette, but it also allows you to enter R, G and B values numerically and provides access (via a button on the pop-up palette) to the system's colour pickers, allowing you to select a colour graphically in one of several colour models. You can also enter a percentage value for the Alpha – or transparency – of the colour. Note that the mixer can be used to set either stroke or fill colours, depending on which of the two buttons at the top left you click. The colour you mix is applied immediately to any selection you have made on the stage. If you wish to reuse the colour, you can select Add Swatch from the pop-up menu under the triangle in the top right of the Mixer panel; it will then be available in the Swatches panel.

☛ Practise drawing shapes with different line styles and fills. Make a rectangular shape each of whose sides is created in a different line style and colour with a contrasting fill.

More complex fills can be created in the form of radial or linear gradients. Selecting one or other of these gradient types in the Fill panel, causes controls for building gradients to appear, as in Figure 5.9. Each of the markers below the bar represents a point at which the colour can be specified. Between markers, a gradual blend of colours is produced. New markers can be added simply by clicking below the bar. A marker may

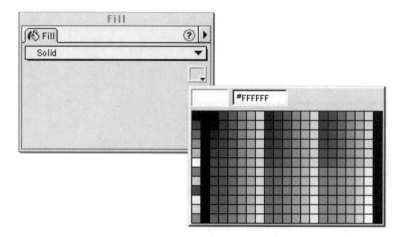

Figure 5.7   *The* Fill *panel.*

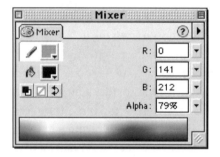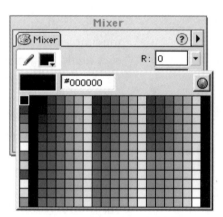

Figure 5.8   *The* Mixer *panel.*

be selected by clicking on it, and then the colour at that point can be chosen. Markers may be dragged to new positions to change the way in which the colours blend. As with solid colours, gradients will be applied to any selected object and will become the default fill for any subsequent drawing. They may also be stored in the Swatches panel using the Add Gradient command from the Fill panel's palette menu.

Shapes that are drawn with the pen tool are automatically filled with the currently selected fill when they are closed. Shapes that are drawn with the pencil or line tools must be filled explicitly by selecting the paint bucket from the toolbox and clicking inside the shape.

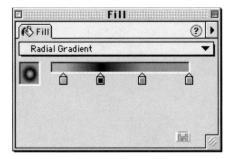

Figure 5.9   *Creating a gradient fill.*

The eyedropper tool can be used to apply the fill from one object to another. If you click on a filled area using the eyedropper, it sets the values in the Fill panel to correspond to the area you clicked on. At the same time, the tool changes into the paint bucket, so if you go on to click in another filled area it will be filled with the colour or gradient you sampled with the eyedropper. (If you use the eyedropper to sample a stroke, the tool changes to the ink bottle, so you can transfer that stroke to other objects.)

Shapes and Brushes

It is pretty difficult to draw a circle by hand. Like most drawing programs, Flash provides an ellipse tool for constructing oval shapes, including circles, directly. You simply select the tool and drag out the shape. Holding down the shift key forces a circle to be drawn; otherwise an ellipse is produced which fits inside the rectangle whose opposite corners are the start and end of the drag. (When you try this, you will see that it is more intuitive than it may sound.) The rectangle tool is used in a similar way to draw rectangles and squares, the latter when the shift key is held down. An option for this tool allows you to draw rectangles with rounded corners. Such precise geometrical shapes may not be much use for cartoons and similar animations, but they are often used to create user interface elements such as buttons, as we will see later. The outline of a rectangle or ellipse is always drawn using the current stroke settings and the shape is automatically filled with the currently selected fill colour or pattern.

At the opposite extreme to the formal geometry of rectangles and squares, the brush tool allows you to make marks in a fashion resembling painting with a brush. The brush tool has options to determine the profile and size of the brush and the way in which strokes interact with other objects on the stage. (The best way to find out what these options actually do is by experiment.) The brush tool, uniquely among Flash's drawing tools, can respond to pressure if you are drawing with a pen and pressure-sensitive tablet. Click on the pressure-sensitivity icon in the tool's options and the width of the stroke will be determined by the pressure you apply to the pen. Figure 5.10 shows the type of effects that can easily be achieved with the brush.

Figure 5.10   *Use of the brush tool.*

The brush is the most appealing way for people trained in traditional art materials to draw in Flash, especially if a pressure-sensitive tablet is being used. Its simplicity can be misleading: 'brush strokes' are actually fills. If, for example, you were to draw a ring with the brush, you would not have produced a thick circular line but a filled band, whose outline was a pair of concentric circles. The stroke is invisible; all you see is the fill of the shape. This has interesting consequences, as we will see shortly.

> ☞ Practise drawing with the brush tool, using different sized brushes and experimenting with pressure sensitivity if you have a graphics tablet. Draw a face with the brush, using different colours for the eyes, mouth, hair etc.

Selection

As we mentioned above, it may be necessary to select a line in order to change its stroke properties. There are many other reasons for selecting parts of a drawing. Not only do you often need to correct mistakes, when we come to animating in Flash you will see that a good way to proceed is often by moving or transforming selected shapes or parts of shapes. Flash's selection tool has some unexpected features.

First, strokes and fills can be selected independently. Second, by default only individual segments of a compound path are selected. Third, where shapes overlap, they are split into separate pieces.

Consider the drawing consisting of a triangle drawn with the line tool and filled with the paint bucket shown at the top of Figure 5.11. Clicking inside the triangle with the arrow tool does not, as you might have expected, select the entire filled triangle. Instead, it just selects the fill. Once it has been selected, the fill can be manipulated independently of the enclosing stroke that is apparently its boundary; for example, it can be dragged out of it, as shown. Similarly, clicking on any of the edges of the triangle will select just that edge, which can be moved independently, as also shown in Figure 5.11.

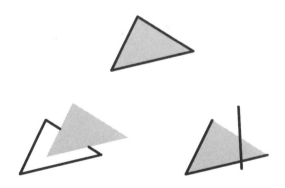

Figure 5.11   *Selecting lines and fills.*

If you want to select an entire shape, fill and stroke together, you must double-click in the fill. If you double-click a line, it and any lines connected to it will be selected, so in the case of a simple shape consisting of a filled outline, the entire outline will be selected in this way.

Things become more complicated when shapes overlap, because in Flash when a line crosses a shape it divides the shape into segments which will be selected separately by

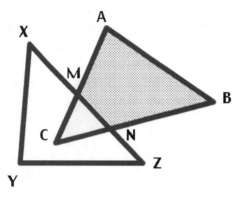

Figure 5.12   *Overlapping shapes.*

the arrow tool. The line too is divided into segments at the points where it crosses the shapes. Consider, for example, the picture shown in Figure 5.12, which we have annotated in the style of a geometric diagram. The hollow triangle XYZ was drawn over the top of the filled one ABC. If you click anywhere in the quadrilateral area ABNM, you will select just that four-sided fill, as shown by the shading in the figure, not the entire fill of ABC. Similarly, clicking within the area MNC selects just the fill of that small triangle. Double-clicking in either of these areas selects the fill and its surrounding stroke, but not the entire triangle. Clicking on the line AC will select only the segment AM or MC, depending on which side of M you click. (Clicking precisely at M selects the segment XM, in case you were wondering.) However, double-clicking any line segment at all will select all the lines in the picture, since these are connected to each other.

In order to select the areas or lines you need to, you can hold down the shift key while clicking or double-clicking. If you do so and click on an unselected object it will be added to the selection; if you shift-click on a selected object, it will be removed from the selection. Hence, to select the entire filled triangle, you could double-click in the small triangle, shift-double-click in the remaining quadrilateral and then shift-click on the line MN to remove it from the selection.

The easy way to avoid the complications of overlapping shapes is to place each shape on a separate layer, as we will describe later. If this is not possible, selected shapes can be combined into a *group*, which can then be manipulated as a single object. (Use the Modify>Group menu command to turn the currently selected objects into a group.) For instance, with the fill and stroke of the coloured triangle selected as just described, the Group command will combine all the elements, so that subsequently a single click anywhere in the triangle will select all of it.

The arrow tool can also be used to select several objects or parts of objects at a time. If you hold down the mouse button and drag with the arrow tool, a rectangle is pulled out, as when you use the rectangle tool. Any object inside the rectangle becomes selected when you release the mouse button. Where an edge of the selection rectangle passes through an object, both strokes and fills are split along the edge, and only the part that lies within the rectangle is selected. This is another potential surprise if you are used to the behaviour of selection tools in other programs but it is consistent with the way Flash treats overlapping shapes.

> ☞ Draw some shapes or a simple scene or object of your choice, using both strokes and fills. Experiment with altering the drawing by making selections with the arrow tool and changing line characteristics, fill colours and the arrangement of the shapes.

The behaviour of the rectangular selection tool is generalized by the lasso tool. If this tool is selected without modifiers, it can be used to draw a freehand outline in the same way as the pencil tool, and anything inside the outline is selected. If you select the polygon modifier, the lasso behaves like the line tool, enabling you to draw polygonal selection areas. In this case, you must double-click to close the selection polygon; for freeform selections it is enough to let go of the mouse button.

Infuriatingly, there is no way of inverting a selection, that is simultaneously selecting everything that is currently not selected and deselecting everything that is. If, for example, you need to delete everything outside a rectangular area, you must drag the arrow tool to select everything within the rectangle, cut that to the clipboard, select and delete everything left on the stage, then paste the clipboard contents back in place (Edit>Paste In Place).

Transformations and Reshaping

→279

Once you have selected an object on the stage you can transform it in various ways. Broadly speaking, there are two approaches you can take to transformation: either you can do it by hand and eye, manipulating objects directly on the stage, or you can do it numerically, by entering values in the Info and Transform panels. The first approach is probably more natural for artists and designers; the second provides greater accuracy.

Transforming by hand is done using the arrow tool and its options. The simplest form of transformation is movement. This is done by selecting the object or objects to be moved and then dragging with the arrow tool; holding down [opt/alt] while dragging causes the objects to be copied, as you would probably expect.

Objects can be scaled by clicking on the scaling icon in the toolbox's option area when the arrow tool is active and an object has been selected on the stage. The immediate effect is for eight drag handles in the shape of small squares to appear, at each corner and in the middle of each side of a rectangle enclosing the selected object, as shown on the left of Figure 5.13. Dragging one of the handles in the middle of a side causes the selected object to be scaled vertically or horizontally, expanding or contracting in the direction of the drag. Dragging one of the corners causes it to be scaled in both directions by the same amount (i.e., its proportions are preserved). The corner opposite the one being dragged stays fixed, so the object grows or shrinks in the direction it is pulled.

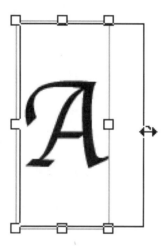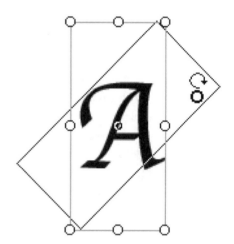

Figure 5.13 *Scaling and rotating.*

The rotation option works in a similar way. When it is selected, eight handles appear as before, this time in the shape of small circles, as on the right of Figure 5.13. Dragging on a corner causes the selected object to rotate (around its centre). Dragging one of the other handles skews the object horizontally or vertically. In this case, only dragging along the side has any effect – the direction of drag is indicated by the cursor turning into a pair of arrows when it is over a skewing handle. (The corner handles can be dragged in more or less any direction to make the object rotate, but moving them as if you were actually pulling the object round to its new position produces the most intuitive feedback.)

If you prefer using menus, the Modify>Transform sub-menu offers alternative ways of invoking the scaling and rotation tools. It also provides some further useful transforms, including reflections in the horizontal and vertical axes (Flip Vertical and Flip Horizontal respectively).

If you know the exact coordinates to which you want to move an object you can enter them in the X and Y fields in the Info panel (shown on the left of Figure 5.14). Clicking in the appropriate square in the little grid to the left of these fields allows you to choose whether to set the coordinates of the top left corner or of the centre of the object. Similarly, if you know the exact size to which you need to scale it, you can enter the width and height in the W and H fields.

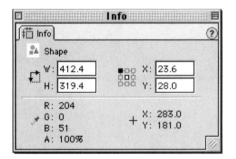 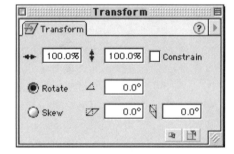

Figure 5.14   *The* Info *and* Transform *panels.*

The Transform panel, shown on the right of Figure 5.14, offers a numerical way of applying scaling, rotation and skew transforms to selected objects. The two fields at the top of the panel are for entering percentage factors by which to scale the object horizontally and vertically. By selecting the checkbox marked Constrain before you enter any values, you can ensure that the scaling is uniform – both height and width are scaled by the same proportion. In this case, you only need to enter one value, the other is automatically set to match it. The remaining three fields are for providing values, in degrees, for a rotation or skewing. Rotations are measured clockwise; you can use negative values to rotate objects anti-clockwise. Separate horizontal and vertical skewing can be applied, but rotation and skew cannot be applied at the same time.[*] (Use the radio buttons to select one or the other.) There are two easily overlooked buttons in the bottom right corner of the Transform panel. The one at the extreme right

---

[*]More precisely, skewing an object by the same amount vertically and horizontally is the same as rotating it.

can be used to reset all transforms – i.e., return the object to its original state – and the other is used to copy the object while transforming it.

☞ Draw a simple asymmetrical object and practise transformations by altering its scale, position on the stage and angles of rotation and skew. Try this out with the arrow tool, the Transform palette and the commands on the Modify>Transform sub-menu.

Yet another way of moving objects is by aligning them with each other. The Alignment panel, shown in Figure 5.15, provides a means of lining up objects in various ways. This panel is especially useful for laying out controls in a movie that provides interactivity via buttons. When you click on one of the icons in the panel all currently selected objects are moved to align in the way indicated. Most of the icons are self-explanatory. For example, clicking on the icon at the left of the top row causes all the selected objects to be aligned along their left edges – the selected object that is originally furthest to the left is used to set the position to which the others are aligned. Similarly, objects can be aligned along their right, top and bottom edges, or centred vertically or horizontally. They can also be distributed, so that the distance between corresponding edges is the same. Unless the objects are all the same size, this often produces unexpected results. More often, what you want to do is distribute the objects so that there is the same amount of space between them. This is what the two icons in the bottom right of the panel do. Selecting the button at the right of the panel, labelled To Stage causes the alignment or distribution to be performed relative to the stage. For example, if you select this option and then click the left align icon, all the objects will be lined up on the left edge of the stage.

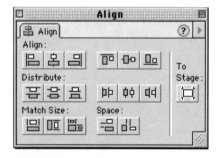

Figure 5.15   *The* Alignment *Panel.*

You can also use the Alignment panel to scale objects so that they are all the same size. This is done with the three buttons in the bottom left of the panel, which match the selected objects' horizontal or vertical dimensions, or both. In each case, the size is set to match the largest selected object. Again, you can select To Stage, in order to make objects as tall or as wide as the stage.

> ☞ Draw nine different objects and practise the different ways of aligning and distributing them on the stage. Finally, arrange them in an evenly spaced three by three grid, centred on the stage.

As well as transforming entire objects, you can modify shapes after you have created them. This is done by using the arrow tool to drag a point on a line or the edge of a fill, *without first selecting it*. Various different modifications can be made. Dragging the end of a line will extend or shorten it, and dragging a sharp corner will pull it, extending or shortening the lines that meet there. Dragging in the middle of a line or the edge of a fill will cause it to curve with the dragged point following the cursor until you let go. As the cursor approaches an object a small curve appears beside the arrow to indicate that dragging will reshape a curve; a right-angled bend appears to show that it will drag a corner or end point; a cross shows that it will drag the entire object – for example, if the cursor is in the centre of a filled area or among a group. Reshaping with the arrow tool can profitably be applied to brush strokes. In addition, Flash has a subselection tool which can be used to adjust anchor points of curves, as described in Chapter 9.

> ☞ Draw a circle and turn it into a star by using the arrow tool to reshape it.

Importing Artwork and Manipulating Bitmapped Images

Although Flash's drawing tools have some additional features beyond those described in the preceding sections they are not as powerful as those provided by dedicated drawing tools such as Illustrator and Freehand and, as noted, they have quirks which may interfere with the productivity of someone used to other applications. Nor does Flash provide any means of creating bitmapped images. It is common, therefore, to use other graphics applications in conjunction with Flash.

A range of different file formats can be imported into Flash, using the File>Import... command. The exact range available depends on the platform on which you are using Flash and whether or not you have installed QuickTime. Consult Chapter 5 of *Using Flash* for details. As you might expect, for vector drawings Flash works best with Macromedia's Freehand. If you prefer to use Adobe Illustrator for drawing, you must save any file you wish to import into Flash in the file format of Illustrator 6 or earlier.

Alternatively, recent versions of Illustrator can save files in Flash's own SWF format,[*] which may provide a more convenient route. We will see later that not just single images but animations built on layers in Illustrator can be imported into Flash.

As we have stressed, Flash is fundamentally based on vector graphics. It can, however, incorporate bitmapped images. The nature of bitmaps and their differences from vectors means that they cannot be as readily manipulated without loss of quality, they tend to increase the size of movies and they can slow down animations. Nevertheless, the greater expressiveness of bitmapped art means that it is often worthwhile combining them with vector graphics in Flash movies. In particular, bitmapped images can often be used effectively as static backgrounds. Additionally, Flash can convert bitmaps into vector drawings, which can be a quick and effective way of creating animations.

As with vector files, the range of bitmapped formats which can be imported into Flash is dependent on the platform you are using – for example, PICT files can only be handled on the Mac and BMP only on Windows. The range is extended if QuickTime is installed. The formats commonly used on the World Wide Web – GIF, JPEG and PNG – are supported on all platforms. When completed Flash movies are exported as SWF files, all images are converted to JPEGs. This means that any files that originate in JPEG form may be recompressed with an inevitable loss of quality. For that reason, uncompressed or losslessly compressed formats are to be preferred. Flash is well integrated with Macromedia's Web graphics application Fireworks, making PNG a good choice if you also use the latter program.

When you import a bitmap image, you can normally only treat it as an indivisible object. Transformations – moving, scaling, rotation or skewing – may be applied to it, although you should be aware that in general this cannot be done without some loss of image quality.

An image can be made editable to some extent by selecting it and choosing the Modify>Break Apart command. This makes some interesting effects possible.

Once an image has been broken apart you can select parts of it using the arrow and lasso tools. As with vector objects, these split objects into pieces where the selection boundary intersects them, so you can 'tear out' parts of a bitmapped image. (See Figure 5.16, where a screenshot of the Align palette has been ripped up using the lasso

*This facility is built into Illustrator 9. An SWF export filter is available as a free download for Illustrator 8.

and arrow tools.) If you reshape a piece of a bitmap after you have extracted it from the complete image, stretching the edges does not distort the image, it reveals more of it. This is because a bitmap is treated as a special kind of fill. Whenever you import a bitmap into a movie it is added to a list which appears in the Fill panel if you select Bitmap from the pop-up menu at the top. You can select a bitmap and use it to fill other vector objects as if it were a solid colour or gradient. (More directly, if you click on a bitmap with the eyedropper tool you can use it as the current fill.) The bitmap remains available as a fill even if you delete the imported artwork. Bitmap fills can be used in a variety of ways; one possibility is to use a bitmap as a texture. For example, you might scan a piece of cloth – for example, part of a pair of jeans – and import the resulting image into Flash. You could then use it to paint other objects with the colour, texture and pattern of the original cloth, creating blue denim shapes.

☛ Import a bitmap and practise breaking the image apart into several pieces using different selection tools. Draw one or two shapes and use your imported bitmap to fill them. Observe what happens if you now reshape and transform those filled shapes.

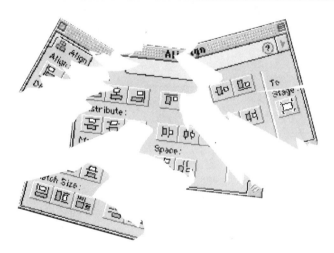

Figure 5.16   *Manipulating a broken apart bitmap.*

A different way of working with bitmapped images in Flash is to convert them into vector drawings, by tracing them. The effect of the Modify>Trace Bitmap command when applied to a selected bitmap is to convert areas of roughly the same colour into filled vector shapes. When the command is selected, the dialogue shown in Figure 5.17 is displayed. The four values that you can set in this dialogue affect the fidelity with which the bitmap is traced. The Color Threshold is the maximum difference there may be between two pixels' colour values before they are considered to be the same colour and combined into the same shape. The value may range between 1 and 500. If the threshold is set to 1, the colours of the original image will be preserved. As higher values are used the traced image becomes more posterized – areas of similar colours are merged, with a loss of detail and texture, rather like a badly printed screen print. The Minimum Area is the number of surrounding pixels which are considered when deciding whether a pixel's colour is closer than the threshold to that of another and thus whether to merge them into a single area. (The value is actually the radius of the area and ranges from 1 to 1000.) These two values control how areas are coloured; the remaining two control the shape of the outlines of these areas. The Curve Fit ranges in six steps from Pixels – the curve exactly follows contours in the bitmap – to Very Smooth – outlines are curves with few anchor points. The Corner Threshold can be set to Few Corners to produce undulating curves, Many Corners to produce an angular outline, or Normal, which is in-between.

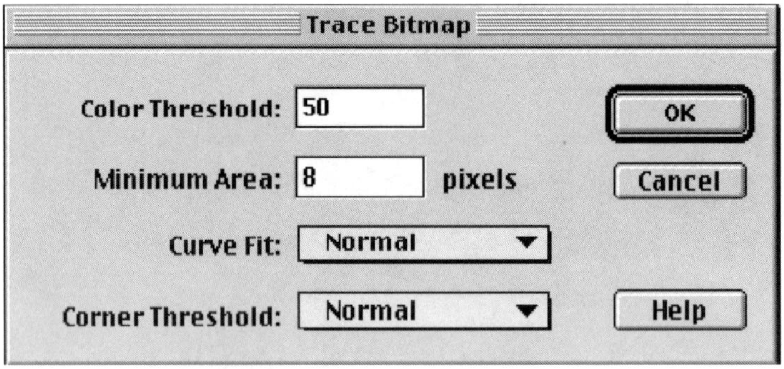

Figure 5.17   *The* Trace Bitmap *dialogue.*

Although it is fairly easy to see the general effect of each of these parameters, their combined effect on a particular image is hard to predict in detail, and experimentation is required to come up with suitable values for achieving any desired effect. Figure 5.18 shows examples of different values applied to the same bitmapped image, which is shown at the top left. Flash remembers the most recent values you have used to trace a bitmap, which makes it relatively easy to trace a series in the same way. (One of Flash's main shortcomings in its present version is that it provides no means of automating repetitive tasks comparable to actions in Photoshop.)

It may be obvious but it is important to remember that the more accurately an image is traced – using a low colour threshold, small minimum area, pixel curve fitting and many corners – the larger the resulting vector artwork will be. Flash can produce vector versions of bitmapped images which closely resemble the originals, but doing so

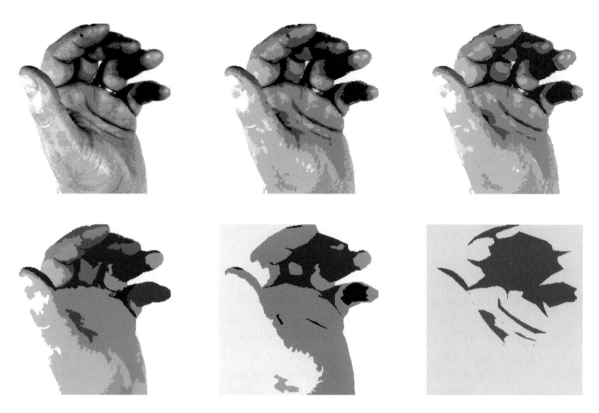

Figure 5.18 *The effect of different parameter values on tracing a bitmapped image.*

produces extremely large files, often several times larger than the bitmapped version. These traced images also take a long time to render, so it is generally a bad idea to trace bitmaps accurately. It is better to use the tracing facility to produce more stylized vector artwork based on bitmapped source images.

→286

☞ Import a bitmapped image of a relatively simple object (e.g., a hand, a house, an animal, etc.) and practise using Trace Bitmap with different settings to obtain both highly simplified and stylized vectorized versions of the image, and versions that are as close as possible in appearance to the original. Export each version as an SWF file and observe how the settings affect its file size.

Animation

The preceding descriptions of drawing and importing artwork into Flash should have provided enough information for you to create single pictures. We can now return to the subject of combining pictures into an animation, transferring our attention from the stage to the timeline.

The timeline provides a spatial representation of a sequence of frames. Flash's timeline is two-dimensional, since a movie can be arranged on separate layers (see Chapter 9). Layers are stacked vertically and frames are arranged horizontally. That is, time runs from left to right, with the scale at the top of the timeline measuring time in frames. The relationship between this and elapsed time in seconds is determined by the movie's *frame rate*, which can be set in the Modify>Movie dialogue. A value between about 24 and 30 will produce animation as smooth as film or TV, but older computers may not be able to play back movies at that rate. Values around 12 are more commonly used for Flash animations, especially if they are destined for the Web. This rate is sufficient to produce an illusion of movement, although it may sometimes appear jerky. Lower rates can also be used if stylized motion is adequate. A very low rate – less than one – can be used to make slideshow presentations.

Animating One Frame at a Time

Traditional animators working on film or videotape must create every frame of their animations, by photographing a drawing on paper or cel, a group of three-dimensional models on a miniature set, or some other less conventional arrangement of objects. Flash allows you to work in a similar way, by adding frames to the timeline and filling them by drawing on the stage or importing graphics. When you work in this way, creating your animation one frame at a time, each frame must be a keyframe.

The procedure is simple but time-consuming. Let's assume that you are starting from scratch with a new movie containing a single, initially empty, keyframe. By clicking the appropriate icon in the timeline you select this keyframe and then create an image that will be the first frame of your animation. The image is created on the stage using the tools and techniques described in the previous section. Once the first frame is complete, you click on the next frame position in the timeline and select Insert>Keyframe or use its keyboard equivalent (F6). This creates a new keyframe containing a copy of the keyframe to its left. In a typical animation, each frame will differ from the one preceding it only in a small way – that is how the illusion of continuous movement is created. Hence, starting a new frame as a copy of the one before it is an efficient way to proceed. Adjustments are made to the contents of the frame so that objects appear to move, fade in or out, or otherwise change. Once a frame is complete, you add a new keyframe after it and carry on in the same fashion. If the action of your animation cuts, you may wish to start over with an empty keyframe; the command Insert>Blank Keyframe is provided for this purpose. (In complicated animations you may prefer to divide your movie up into separate scenes, which is simply done. However, since we are only dealing with simple examples, we will not describe the use of scenes.)

Animation is about creating movement from still images, so you need to be able to see your work in motion. This can be done by using the Control>Test Movie command. Since you will be doing this a lot, you will find it worth using the keyboard shortcut ctl enter/cmd return. This opens the movie in a version of the Flash Player, running inside Flash. What you see is not exactly what a user will see when your completed movie is played back in a Web browser or the Flash Player. In particular, the window does not adapt itself to the size of the movie. For quickly checking the animation, you can play it on the stage (though some features which we will be describing later are disabled when you do so) using Control>Play or by simply pressing enter/return. You can also scrub through an animation by dragging the current frame indicator above the frame numbers in the timeline.

☞ Create a short animated sequence by making a simple drawing on the stage in frame 1 and changing it progressively in succeeding frames. For example, you could animate the transformation of a circle into a star or a face. Check that your animation works both by previewing it in Flash and by using Test Movie to preview it in the Player.

You may find it convenient to work on several layers when constructing an animation. This makes it easier to select and transform or modify elements of a scene independently. Layers are added by clicking the page icon labelled with a + sign at the bottom left of the timeline. (Refer back to Figure 5.3 on page 211.) It is a good idea to give meaningful names to your layers. This is done by double-clicking the layer name and typing a new name when it is highlighted. Layers are selected by clicking their names; shift-clicking selects a range of layers, and [cmd/ctl] clicking adds discontiguous layers to the selection. Layers can be deleted by clicking on the trash can icon below the timeline. This deletes the selected layer or layers.

☞ Try creating an animation frame by frame by moving and transforming objects on different layers.

When you draw, the lines and shapes you create are added to the currently selected layer. (If more than one layer is selected, all but one are deselected when you start to draw. Experiment suggests that if the selection is contiguous, the lowest layer is used, but if it is not, the highest is used. This behaviour is not documented, so it is probably a good idea to make sure you have only selected one layer before you start drawing.) Selecting an object automatically selects the layer it is on.

If your images are complicated and constructed on many layers, you may need to hide certain of them so that you can see what you are doing. This is done by clicking in the column headed with an icon representing an eye in the rows corresponding to the layers you want to hide. You can lock layers so that you cannot make any changes to them in a similar way, by clicking in the column headed with a padlock icon.

Traditional animators sometimes use a device known as a lightbox to help them draw successive frames of an animation. The frames are drawn on thin sheets of paper, sometimes called *onion skins*, which are laid on the surface of the box, which contains a light bulb. The top of the box has a translucent inset that allows the light to pass through. This makes it possible to place a completed frame on the top of the lightbox, put a fresh sheet of paper on top of it and see the frame below through it. Hence, elements of the first frame can be copied by tracing and the relative positions of objects in the successive frames can be seen. Flash provides a similar facility. By clicking on the Onion Skin icon below the timeline, a faded version of adjacent keyframes is shown beneath the current frame on the stage. By default, the two preceding and following frames are shown, if they exist. The extent of onion-skinning can be altered by dragging the markers above the timeline which show where it begins and ends. Generally, using more than one or two onion-skinned frames is confusing.

It should be stressed that although Flash provides a mechanism for creating animation quickly, with its tools for moving and transforming objects, and its onion-skinning facilities, and so on, it can't make you into an animator. In other words, Flash can't tell you how to change your images from one frame to the next so that a convincing or expressive illusion of motion is created. Just about anyone can produce bouncing logos, but if you want to produce more ambitious animation you will have to spend more time observing how things move and how to represent motion than you will spend mastering Flash.

If you prefer to make your images outside Flash and import them, there are several ways of creating animation sequences. Conceptually the simplest is to create each frame in a separate file. If the files are named following a consistent convention so that each one includes a sequence number in its name, Flash is clever enough to recognize the sequence and import it into successive frames of an animation. Various formats can be used for the file names. The most reliable consists of inserting a sequence number, padded with an appropriate number of leading zeros, before the file extension (if you use one), as in anim001.gif, anim002.gif, anim003.gif, and so on. To import such a sequence, choose the File>Import command and then, in the navigation dialogue that appears, select just the first member of the sequence and click Import. Flash will tell you that it thinks the file is the first in a sequence and ask whether you want it to import the lot. If you say that you do, each file will be imported into a new keyframe. Note that if there are any gaps in the sequence, Flash will stop importing at the end of a consecutive run of numbers. (For example, if you have a sequence of forty-nine images called anim001.gif to anim050.gif, with anim010.gif missing, only the first nine images will be imported if you select anim001.gif.)

Sequences of image files can be produced in various ways, the most obvious being by saving a sequence of images from a graphics program. A less obvious way is by exporting a QuickTime movie from the QuickTime Player[*] or a video application as an image sequence. This produces a sequence of bitmapped images, which can be imported into Flash and traced in order to create an animation based on live video footage.

As well as a sequence of image files, Flash can create a sequence of frames from an animated GIF or by importing an SWF file. This last method is not as pointless as it may sound, because Flash is no longer the only program that can create SWFs. Illustrator and Freehand can both export to this format, turning layers into frames. Macromedia's Web graphics programs Fireworks can also export images as SWFs, After Effects will save video as SWF, and Adobe's LiveMotion is an alternative to Flash as a way of creating animations which can be saved as SWF. For a host of reasons, any of these routes may provide a better way of creating the original artwork for a Flash movie than Flash's own drawing tools.

Motion Tweening

In many types of animation, objects often move in a predictable manner. For example, a cartoon character may fall off a tall building or a balloon might blow across the sky. In the production-line approach to animation, perfected by the Walt Disney studios and followed by most large-scale cartoon makers, only the key frames at the extremes of predictable movements are drawn by the head animators on a project; the frames in between are filled in by less experienced drudges, known as 'in-betweeners', a task sometimes called *tweening*. Flash is able to perform tweening semi-automatically for certain kinds of motion.

Keyframes in the Flash timeline correspond to the key frames drawn by senior animators. Tweening requires two keyframes to be created explicitly; the intermediate frames are interpolated by computation from them. Conceptually the process is simple: draw the keyframes at the beginning and the end of the sequence and tell Flash to tween them. However, Flash is rather particular about the order in which the necessary operations are carried out, and, although there are several ways of creating motion

*The Pro version only.

tweening that will work eventually, it can sometimes behave in a confusing fashion if you do not follow the procedures described below precisely, at least until you understand what is going on.

In a movie with several layers, tweening can be applied to each one separately. For the moment, assume that there is only a single layer. Insert a keyframe at the point in the timeline where you want the motion to begin and draw an object. (If you draw more than one object, they will automatically be grouped by the next step in this procedure and will move as one.) Select the keyframe in the timeline and then select the menu command Insert>Create Motion Tween. Next, select the frame position at which you wish the tweening to end and select Insert>Frame. You will see a dotted line in the timeline between the starting keyframe and the new frame, which signifies that the tweening has not been completed. With this new frame selected, move the object, apply transformations to it, or use the Effect panel to change its brightness, colour or transparency (alpha). The dotted line will turn into a solid arrow, and the frame will be converted to a keyframe. (See Figure 5.20 on page 236.) You can make several changes at the same time. For example, a combination of moving and scaling an object can be used to make it move closer or further away.

Once you have created a motion tween on a layer, you can continue to tween the motion of the object on that layer just by adding new frames in the timeline and moving it on the stage, and so on. You do not need to use the Insert>Create Motion Tween command again. To create any sort of interesting movement you will almost always have to use several keyframes with tweened motion between them in this way.

> ☞ Practise making a simple object move across the stage in 12 frames using the motion tween facility. Make it move back again in a further 12 frames. Now try overlaying two motion tweens on separate layers. (You don't necessarily have to place the keyframes in the same place on both layers.)

If you select any frame in the tweening and look at the Frame panel, you will see that motion tweening has been applied (see Figure 5.19). The controls in this panel enable you to modify the way in which tweening is applied. In particular, the Easing can be set to a value between -100 and 100, either by typing in the text field or using the slider that pops up from under the triangle to its right. *Easing in*, using a negative value, means that instead of starting to move instantaneously, the object accelerates steadily. *Easing out*, using a positive value is the reverse: instead of coming to an abrupt halt, the object decelerates.

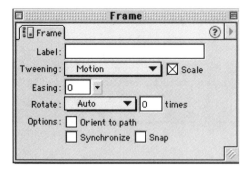

Figure 5.19   *The* Frame *panel and motion tweening.*

☞ Experiment with the Easing settings to control the beginning or end of each part of the motion.

The introduction of tweening complicates the way in which frames can be selected and manipulated in the timeline. When every frame is a keyframe, selection works in a fairly intuitive way that is an extension of the paradigm of clicking to select, familiar from the desktop. On each layer, a keyframe is represented as a closed rectangle; if it has any content, a small circle is shown inside it.[*] Clicking on such a keyframe icon selects the corresponding layer of the corresponding frame. Other keyframes and layers can be added to the selection by shift-clicking; a contiguous block of frames on adjacent layers can be selected by shift-dragging. With interpolation this does not work in quite the same way. If you click on the keyframe at either end of a tweened sequence or anywhere in the middle, the entire sequence is selected. A tweened sequence is shown in the timeline as a long arrow, so you can see where the interpolated frames are. If you want to select a frame from the middle of a sequence, you must [ctl/cmd] click. Once selected, frames can be copied, cut and pasted. Use the commands Edit>Copy Frames, Edit>Cut Frames and Edit>Paste Frames or their keyboard equivalents. Don't use Edit>Copy and so on. These work on the graphical objects contained in the frames, not on the frames themselves.

If you add frames after a keyframe without creating a motion tween, the contents of the keyframe are held for all the following frames, up to any following keyframe. This is how you would add, for instance, a static background to an animation. Figure 5.20 shows the various icons that are used in the timeline. If you hold the cursor over a frame for a moment, a tool tip will be displayed indicating the type of frame it is.

---

[*]This assumes you have left the display of the timeline in its default state. Using the pop-up menu at the right hand end of the scale of frame numbers you can change the display so that thumbnails of the frames' contents are shown. This rapidly becomes unwieldy and most of the time the iconic representation is easier to work with.

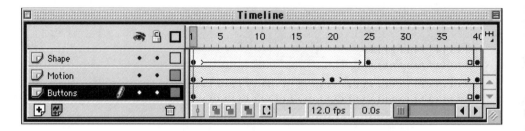

Figure 5.20   *Icons used in the timeline.*

Returning to motion tweening, you may not always find it adequate to move objects in a straight line. You can, of course, use lots of keyframes and combine simpler linear translational movement with rotation and scaling to produce movements more interesting than the simple motion in a straight line of Newton's first law. Flash lets you draw a path for objects to follow when they are motion tweened. This is simply done.

 First, create some tweened motion as before. Next, select the layer on which the tweened object has been placed and click on the Add Guide Layer icon. A new layer, with a special guide icon beside its name, is created above the selected layer, which is indented below it. Select the guide layer and draw a path on it using the pencil or pen tool. When you play the movie, the tweened object will follow this path. Normally, the object retains its orientation as it moves, rather as if it was a cork bobbing up and down as it moved. If you wish it to appear to follow the path, like a vehicle on an undulating road, check the box labelled Orient to path in the Frame panel. Be warned that it takes some practice to make this produce any realistic sort of movement. It is often easier to piece together short sequences of linear motion with rotation.

> ☛ Create a simple animation using motion tweening and a motion path to make a simple asymmetrical object trace a course around the stage. Practise changing the direction and speed of movement by using keyframes at appropriate points to achieve a more sophisticated animation. Experiment with the Orient to path option.

Symbols and Instances

You may notice if you try creating some motion tweening that when you select your object after you have created the motion tween it behaves differently from before. It is highlighted in a different way and a single click selects the whole object. This behaviour deserves explanation, as it introduces an important concept.

When an object is motion tweened, it is automatically converted into something known as a *symbol*, which is an element that can be stored and used repeatedly in a movie. The collection of symbols defined in a movie is known as the movie's *library*. Of course, any object can be reused by copying and pasting and so on. Symbols are reused in a different way. Whenever you use a symbol, a reference to the original symbol in the library is added to the movie, no copying is performed. This is efficient, because a reference is compact. If the concept of a reference is unfamiliar to you, you may be better able to appreciate what it implies if we consider a concrete example.

Suppose you wanted to animate a bicycle and you wanted the wheels to be identical. Without symbols, you would probably draw one wheel and then copy and paste it to use as the other. With symbols, you could create a symbol, called Wheel as likely as not, and then use it twice, once for the front wheel of the bicycle and once for the back. Each of these wheels is referred to as an *instance* of the Wheel symbol.

Suppose now that you decide to change the appearance of the wheels on your bike – giving them narrower profile tyres, perhaps. If you had created two separate wheels you would have to alter both of them (or, more economically, delete one, alter the other and copy it as a replacement for the deleted wheel). If the wheels were instances of a symbol, you would edit the symbol and both instances would be updated automatically with your changes.

Symbols have another advantage for this particular application: they can be animations themselves, so you could create wheel symbols that go round and add these to your bicycle, to make its wheels spin as it moves.

The mechanics of symbol creation are not complicated. As we just remarked, creating a motion tween is actually one way of creating a symbol. Normally, though, you create your symbols explicitly. The most straightforward way is by using the Insert>Create New Symbol menu command. The dialogue box shown in Figure 5.21 is displayed, giving you an opportunity to name the symbol. The radio buttons are used to specify the type of symbol. For now, we will only consider graphic symbols. After you have selected the Graphic type and dismissed the dialogue box, you are returned to the timeline and stage, but the timeline header shows the name of your symbol, and no frames from the main movie are visible – the timeline looks the same as it does when you create a new movie, with a single keyframe on one layer.

You create a graphic symbol in just the same ways as we have described creating an animation. As this implies, a graphic symbol can contain more than one frame, although you often use this type of symbol for single objects in just one frame. After creating your symbol you can return to working on the movie itself by choosing

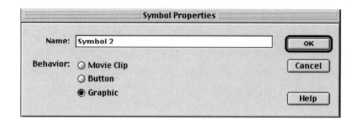

Figure 5.21   *Defining a new symbol.*

Edit>Edit Movie. To use the symbol you must open the Library window (by choosing it from the Window menu or using the mini-launcher). When you do so, you will see a scrolling list of all the symbols you have created in your movie. (You can edit a symbol at any time by double-clicking it in the library window, which returns it to the stage and timeline.) By dragging one of these onto the stage you can add an instance of it to your animation. You don't need to create instances only in the main movie: you can create instances of symbols within other symbols, allowing you to build up symbols hierarchically. For example, you could make a bicycle symbol containing wheel symbols and then create instances of the bicycle to make a bicycle race animation. Whether they are in another symbol or the main movie, instances can be scaled and rotated with the Transform panel and have their brightness and alpha values set in the Effect panel, independently, without altering the symbol in any way.

You can only create an instance of a symbol in a keyframe. In other words, when you drag it to the stage, the current frame must be a keyframe. The instance is only present in the keyframe and any static or tweened frames following it, like any element you have drawn explicitly. If a graphic instance contains more than one frame (i.e., it is an animation) then it will play in synchronization with the movie you have placed it in. That is, if you created an instance of a graphic symbol with six frames in the first frame of a 12 frame movie and the remaining frames on the layer containing the instance were static, the instance's first frame would be displayed in the first frame of the movie, its second frame in the second frame, and so on. By default, instances loop, so the first frame of the instance would be displayed again in the seventh frame of the movie and so on. It follows that if you want to see all of an animated graphic symbol, you must make sure it is present in sufficient frames.

Creating a motion tween converts the tweened object or group to a symbol because only instances of symbols can be motion tweened. (There are good technical reasons for this, which we will not go into.) If you want to tween the motion of an instance of a symbol that you have explicitly created and stored in the library, using Insert>Create

Motion Tween is superfluous, although harmless. You can tween the motion more directly by placing an instance of your symbol in a keyframe where you want the motion to begin. Then, go to the Frame panel (see Figure 5.19 on page 235) and select Motion from the pop-up menu labelled Tweening. Next, select the frame position where you want the tweening to end and insert a frame (not a keyframe). A dotted line will appear on the timeline where the tweening is supposed to take place, as before. If you select the ending frame and move or otherwise transform the instance that you are tweening, this line will turn into an arrow, to indicate that the tweening has been applied. You can use the Frame panel to adjust the easing in or out.

> ☞ Create a graphic symbol consisting of a simple animation – it can be as simple as a moving geometrical shape – and practise making different sized instances of this symbol placed at different points on the stage. Experiment with placing instances on different layers and at keyframes to create more complex animations from the interaction between the different instances. Create a new symbol from three instances of your original symbol and practise creating instances of this composite symbol in the same way.

Looking back at Figure 5.21, you see that as well as graphic symbols you can create symbols of type Button or Movie Clip. Buttons are special symbols, used to control movies in response to users' input. They will be described later on. Movie clip symbols are similar to the graphic symbols we have used so far: they are reusable pieces of animation. There are some important differences between movie clips and graphic symbols, though. A movie clip is a completely self-contained movie within a movie. It can be controlled – stopped, started, and so on – independently of the main movie and other clips. The full implications of this will only be realized when we describe actions and interactivity. For now, the difference can be demonstrated by stopping a movie while it is playing. Any animated graphic symbols will stop with the main movie; clips will continue to play. If you are just using Flash for animated cartoons and similar linear animations without interactivity, graphic symbols will be the appropriate choice. If you want to create non-linear interactive movies, clip symbols are immensely useful, as we will see.

Shape Tweening

Motion tweening is an efficient way of animating, both in terms of the effort needed on the part of the animator and the computational power needed to play it back. On occasion, you may prefer a more fluid kind of change, while still not wishing to draw every frame by hand. Shape tweening can sometimes provide a suitable alternative type of interpolation.

Shape tweening is a process of transformation, turning one shape into another, as for instance, a moon into a star or Dr. Jekyll into Mr. Hyde. This type of transformation is often referred to as *morphing*, and has recently enjoyed a vogue in films based on special effects, to the extent that 'shape shifting' has become something of a cliché, perhaps best avoided unless you are being ironic. However, shape tweening can be used more subtly to create interesting effects, such as ripples on the surface water or purely abstract transformations (see Figure 5.2 on page 210).

Whereas you can only apply motion tweening to instances of symbols, you can only apply shape tweening to objects that are *not* instances of symbols. (This does make sense if you think about what shape tweening is doing.) If you want to apply shape tweening to imported bitmaps, you must first break them apart; the results are likely to be disappointing, though.

Creating shape tweening is similar to creating motion tweening using symbols: first draw something in a keyframe where you want the tweening to begin, next create a new keyframe (not a simple frame, this time) where you want the tweening to end and draw the final image, then select the tweened frames and choose Motion from the Tweening pop-up menu in the Frame panel. You can set an easing value for shape tweening just as you can for motion tweening. You can also select between Distributive and Angular blending. The former is smoother, while the latter preserves corners and straight lines in the intermediate frames. It is worth experimenting to see the different effects of the two – sometimes they behave just the same as each other, other times they create quite different effects, depending on the starting and ending shapes of the tweening.

An attractive way of applying motion tweening is to create the first image by painting with the paintbrush and then create the final image by reshaping the brush strokes, as described on page 225. You can produce some pleasing effects in this way, but you should remember that shape tweening is a computationally intensive process. If you become enchanted with transformation and try to base an entire animation on it, with many independently shape-tweened layers, you will find that even the most powerful computers will struggle to play back your movie smoothly. Shape tweening must be used judiciously.

☞ Practise the process of shape tweening, starting with a simple transformation of an object on one layer. Try animating the transformation of a circle into a star with this method.

Like 'motion tweening', 'shape tweening' is a slightly misleading name, since it is not only the shape that is transformed; all aspects of the initial drawing, including its colours, size and position, are mutated into the final drawing. However, if all you want to do is create a gradual blend of colours, it is more efficient to use motion tweening and the Tint option of the Effect panel than to use shape tweening on identical, but differently coloured, shapes.

☞ Experiment with changing the colours, position and number of objects being morphed by shape tweening. For instance, try turning a red circle into four blue stars.

The appearance of the intermediate frames produced by shape tweening is not, except in simple cases, readily predictable. This is especially the case if you draw more than one shape on the tweened layer or transform a single shape into several. You can produce interesting effects serendipitously by experimenting with such unpredictable transformations, but if you insist on retaining command over your work you may prefer to use *shape hints* to control the morphing to some extent. Shape hints provide a means of identifying points that you wish to correspond in the initial and final images. With the start keyframe selected, choose the Modify>Transform>Add Shape Hint command. A small red circle labelled *a* appears; drag it to a point which you wish to constrain. Now select the final keyframe in the tween. The labelled circle appears again, and you drag it to the point you wish to correspond to the one you designated in the first keyframe. When the tweening is applied, the corresponding points will be translated in as direct a manner as possible. You can go back to the starting keyframe and add additional shape hints in the same way as the first. Figure 5.22 shows the effect of constraining shape tweening in this way – the upper row of frames shows the shape tweening without hints, the lower row shows it with hints. (You should be able to see the labelled circles in the first and last frames of the lower row.)

☞ Try applying shape hints to a simple shape tween and assess whether the result is more successful than tweening without hints.

It is a good idea to test the effect of shape hints as you go along, since they are by no means as predictable as you might think at first. Over-constraining, by adding too many shape hints, can have disastrous effects. If you find you need to remove a shape hint, just drag its circle off the stage. Don't expect shape hints to do too much for you. If you need to control any type of change closely – motion as well as morphing – add additional keyframes.

Figure 5.22   *The effect of shape hints on shape tweening.*

Sound

Flash animations don't have to be silent. You can add a synchronized soundtrack to provide backing music or dialogue and you can add 'spot sounds' – sound effects that play at specified points in the movie.

Adding sounds is a two-stage process. First, a sound must be imported into the movie. Flash can import sounds in several different formats: MP3 files can be used on any platform, AIFF on Macs and WAV on Windows; if you have QuickTime, WAV files can be used on Macs, too, and several other formats are then supported, including Sun AU files and QuickTime movies consisting only of a soundtrack. Flash cannot record sounds directly, though, it can only import them from a file already on disk. This is done in the same way as importing artwork, using the File>Import... command. Any sound you have imported appears in the Library window, as if it was a symbol. Sampling rates of 11, 22 and 44kHz are supported, in 8- or 16-bits. If your sound was recorded at a different sampling rate, for example, the 48kHz used by DAT, it will be resampled by Flash, which might cause a deterioration of quality. Try to avoid mixing sampling rates if you possibly can. Sound files can occupy a large amount of space, and if your movie is intended to be played over the Internet, you may find it is necessary to compromise on quality and use a lower sampling rate than the 44kHz used by audio CDs, in order to minimize the movie's bandwidth requirement.

To add a sound to a movie once you have imported it, you should first create a new layer to hold it. (This isn't strictly necessary, but it is more convenient and is strongly advised.) Make a keyframe in the new layer at the point where you want the sound to begin playing. With this keyframe selected, the Sound panel, shown in Figure 5.23, can be used to select a sound to add to the layer at that point: the pop-up menu labelled Sound at the top of the panel contains entries for every sound you have imported. To add a sound, just select it from this pop-up menu. When you do so, a waveform will appear in the timeline on the layer on which you have placed the sound, as shown in Figure 5.24. You can add several layers with sounds to a movie: they are treated like channels in a conventional audio recorder and are mixed down when the movie is exported.

Figure 5.23   *The* Sound *panel.*

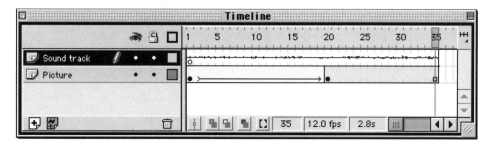

Figure 5.24   *A sound displayed in the timeline.*

Sounds can be synchronized with the movie's playback in one of two ways. *Event sounds* start to play when the frame at which the sound was added is displayed and continue to play until they reach their end or for a specified number of repetitions, irrespective of how the playback of the animation proceeds. For example, an event sound will continue to play if the movie is stopped, like a movie clip. *Stream sounds* are synchronized to the main movie: if it stops, they stop; if frames are being displayed at less than the movie's specified frame rate (because it is being streamed over a slow network connection or played on a slow machine), frames are dropped to ensure that the relationship between sound and picture set on the timeline is maintained. Stream sounds behave like still images in that they are only played during static frames following the keyframe in which they first appear. If a subsequent keyframe with a different sound, or no sound, is added to the layer, the first sound stops. Stream sounds are suitable for synchronized soundtracks, while event sounds are useful for providing ambient sound and spot effects. You use the pop-up menu labelled Sync on the Sound panel to choose whether a sound is an event or stream sound.

If you want to use an event sound, you first add the sound to your movie, as just described, and then select Event from the Sync pop-up menu. You can type a number in the Loops box, to specify a number of repetitions.

If, on the other hand, you want the sound to be synchronized to the playing of the animation, you choose Stream from the Sync pop-up menu. (It is not advised to set a number of loops in this case.) This will be appropriate for dialogue or a music track that has been fitted to the picture. Using Stream may lead to dropped frames in the animation, but this is usually less intrusive than either a loss of synchronization (for example, between speech and a character's lip movements in a cartoon-style animation) or interruptions to the audio.

☞ Practise adding sounds to movies. Import several sounds from disk and add them as both event sounds and stream sounds to one or more of the movies you have made for earlier practice exercises. Note the differences in behaviour between the two types of sound. Try creating a chorus effect by adding the same sound to several layers, offset by a few frames.

What if you want a sound to stop at a certain frame? This is easily achieved. Create a keyframe in the layer containing the sound at the point where you want it to stop, and select it. In the Sound panel, select the sound from the pop-up menu and select Stop from the Sync pop-up menu. The sound will stop at that keyframe, even if it is an event sound.

You can carry out some very simple editing operations on sounds that you have added to a movie. Select a frame that contains your sound and click the Edit... button in the Sound panel. A sound editing window, such as the one shown in Figure 5.25 appears, displaying the waveform of the sound. You can drag the vertical markers in the time display between the two channels to set the start and end point of the sound, allowing you to trim off superfluous parts of a recording. You can also change the envelope of the sound, that is the way the volume changes as it plays. You do this by dragging the square handles that appear in both channels. This moves the line representing the volume. You can add extra handles by clicking at a point on this line, and then drag them to create a complex envelope. In Figure 5.25, we have shaped the envelope in the lower channel to suppress noise, by pulling the volume down to zero in the places where there is no actual signal, just background noise. Notice that envelope handles have appeared in the corresponding points in the upper channel, too, although these have not yet been adjusted. It is not possible to create handles at independent points in the two channels, although, as you can see, the levels in the channels are set independently.

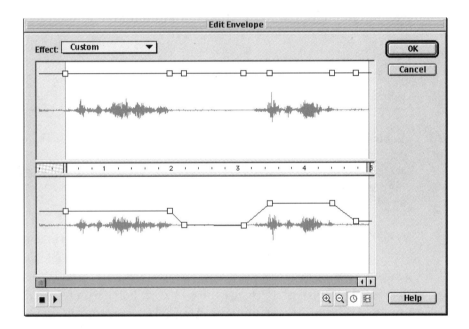

Figure 5.25 *Editing a sound.*

The pop-up menu labelled Effect at the top of the envelope editing window allows you to apply some classic effects with a single click. These include fading sounds in or out and fading between channels, from left to right or from right to left. These effects are achieved by shaping the envelopes in a simple way. For instance, the fade-in is achieved as shown in Figure 5.26. These effects can also be applied by selecting them from the Effect pop-up menu in the Sound panel. The advantage of applying them in the envelope editing window is that you can modify the basic effect to suit your particular sound.

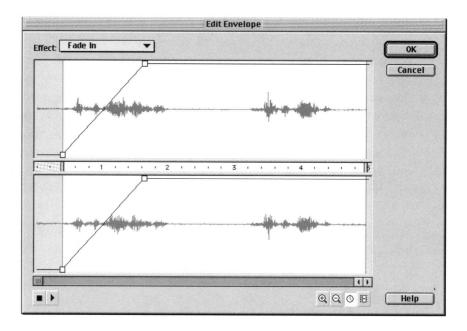

Figure 5.26 *Fading in.*

☞ Practise applying effects to the sounds you previously added to your movies. Use the standard effects, and try shaping the envelope by hand. Try to see what sorts of envelope would actually be useful.

By default, when you export a movie as an SWF file, any sounds in it are compressed as MP3 audio. Since this is the most compact sound format available for SWFs and achieves a quality that is generally felt to be acceptable, it is usually sensible to stick with this default. If you wish to change the format, or fiddle with the detailed settings, you can do so via a number of routes. To change the settings for all the sounds in a movie, first choose Publish Settings... from the File menu, then click on the Flash tab, and finally click the Set button next to either Audio Stream or Audio Event. The dialogue box shown in Figure 5.27 will appear. If you understand about audio compression, you can set the parameters or choose a different format from the pop-up menu at the top. You can also set the export settings of individual sounds, by double-clicking them in the Library window to get the Sound Properties dialogue shown in Figure 5.28. Normally, the compression is set to Default, which picks up the values set in the Publish Settings dialogue but, if you choose a different method from the pop-up menu, you can enter values for the parameters corresponding to your chosen method, as shown here.

Figure 5.27 *Setting sound properties for a movie.*

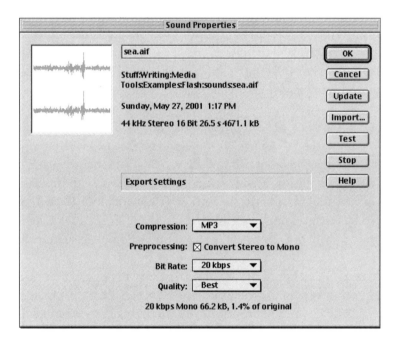

Figure 5.28 *Setting an individual sound's properties.*

Actions

The facilities described in the preceding sections allow you to create animation using Flash. The SWF format is optimized for playing over the Internet, but in other respects the resulting animations are no different from any you might produce on video (digital or otherwise). They start at the beginning and play through to the end and all anyone can do is watch them. If Flash could do no more than that, it is unlikely that it would have achieved the popularity it enjoys today. The power to integrate animation with computation and to have movies respond to events initiated by the user is what distinguishes Flash from conventional animation. It permits a Flash animation to operate as an interface to sophisticated distributed applications, including ecommerce, as well as making possible new and innovative forms of art or entertainment based on the combination of animation and interactivity.

Flash's model of interactivity is *event-driven*. That is, computational actions occur in response to events. This model will be familiar from the graphical user interfaces of modern operating systems. A user does something, such as double-clicking an icon on the desktop, and something happens in response, such as the launching of an application. In a Flash movie, special objects called *buttons* can be placed on the stage to receive events, such as mouse clicks. *Actions* – scripts that can be executed in the Flash Player – can be attached to buttons and associated with particular events so that the action is performed when the specified event occurs. For instance, you may attach an action to a button that stops the playback of a movie.

Matters are slightly more complicated than the previous paragraph suggests. Actions can also be attached to frames in a movie, to be executed whenever playback reaches that frame. This is incorporated in the event-driven model by saying that an event occurs whenever the playhead (a notional device that scans the frames of the animation causing their contents to be displayed) enters the frame. In Flash 5, events can also be received by instances of movie clip symbols. However, the use of such events is slightly tricky and we will not describe it in this introduction to Flash's interactive features.

In fact, there are many aspects of actions that we will not describe. An action may be an arbitrary script written in a language called *ActionScript*, a close relation of JavaScript. Although it lacks some of the features of conventional programming languages such as Java, ActionScript still offers a powerful collection of programming constructs, including support for (one style of) object-oriented programming. In other words, to make full use of ActionScript, you need to know a certain amount about programming, a topic which lies beyond the scope of this book. However, it is possible to add simple actions to Flash movies without any programming knowledge at all, and even that is sufficient to transform them from linear animations into something more lively.

Buttons

Before you can start using actions, you need to understand buttons. Buttons are a type of symbol, like the graphic symbols we have already described. They can be stored in a library and instances of them can be created by dragging them to the stage. They are created in the same way as other symbols, but they have a special structure: every button consists of exactly four frames, designated Up, Over, Down and Hit. When you select Button as the behaviour in the Symbol Properties dialogue when you create a new symbol (see Figure 5.21 on page 238), these four frames are shown with their names on the timeline, as shown in Figure 5.29. You can insert the actual frames and draw in them as you do for any other animation. You can even use tweening, though it isn't often going to be useful.

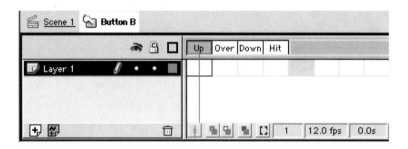

Figure 5.29   *A new button's timeline.*

The first three frames of a button correspond to its possible states with respect to the cursor. Up is the state the button is in when the cursor is not over it; Over is its state when the cursor is over it but the mouse button is not pressed; and Down is the state when the mouse button is pressed with the cursor over the button. The image in each of these frames is displayed when the button is in the corresponding state. That is, the button appears as the image in the Up frame when the cursor is not over it. Its appearance changes to the Over frame as the cursor rolls over and to the Down frame when it is pressed. (See Figure 5.30.) This sort of behaviour will probably be familiar. The Hit frame is different: its contents define the area that is considered to be occupied by the button, and hence the area within which the cursor must be to cause the rollover effect and for events to be passed to the button. This need not necessarily correspond to the shapes in the other frames. Sometimes it is convenient to extend the area beyond the visual elements of the button, so that a label can be attached to it and behave as if it was part of the button itself. Figure 5.30 shows an example, taken from the library of buttons provided with Flash.

Buttons are often designed to look like physical push-buttons, or at least the iconic representations of buttons that are commonly used in graphical user interfaces. They don't have to, though. A button is simply an area that is going to respond to events. Sometimes it may be appropriate to make an invisible button the size and shape of the

Up	Over	Down	Hit

Figure 5.30 *States of a button.*

whole stage. At other times, it may be more appropriate to use buttons that look like objects within a scene, for example, a door that opens when you click on it. Buttons don't always have to change their appearance when the mouse rolls over them. Often, rollover effects provide helpful feedback, but sometimes they may be intrusive. Since a button symbol is an animation, constructed on the timeline, there is no difficulty in making two or more of the frames the same – just clear the appropriate keyframes, so that the previous frame is held statically. This technique can be used to make the hit area match the graphic content of the Down frame, which will often be the same size as the Up frame. Within the constraints of their four frames, buttons can use all the animation techniques available in Flash. They can be built on layers and they can include instances of other symbols. In particular, any frame of a button can contain a movie clip symbol, so that it can incorporate animation.

> ☞ Practise making simple buttons, for example, one that changes appearance in every state and one that does not change when you click on it. Try making a button whose active area is larger than the visible graphics in the first three states. Create instances of your buttons and observe how they respond to cursor movements and mouse clicks.

A button can only respond to events when the frame being displayed contains it. That is, as we will prefer to say from now on, when it is in the frame under the playhead. Because of this rather obvious fact, it is a good idea to place buttons on their own layer in a movie, extending keyframes statically to cover the range of frames where the buttons are needed. Often, buttons used as controls must be present throughout the movie. You would therefore place them in a keyframe at the beginning of the movie, on their own layer, and add frames (not keyframes) so that they persist over the entire duration. Figure 5.20 on page 236 illustrates an appropriate structure for the timeline.

Button Actions

To make a button do something, you must associate an action with it and specify an event that will trigger that action. The Actions panel is used for this purpose. This panel is context sensitive: if you have a button or clip instance selected on the stage, its title shows as Object Actions, any actions you specify are attached to the selected object, and in its normal mode of operation the event that triggers the action must be specified at the same time. If you have a keyframe selected, the panel is titled Frame Actions and any action will be triggered when the playhead enters that frame.

The Actions panel can be used in either of two modes: Normal and Expert. In normal mode, actions are constructed by selecting building blocks from a list. The actual ActionScript code is inserted automatically and input elements displayed in the lower half of the panel are used to enter parameters where necessary. (See Figure 5.31.) In expert mode, the panel behaves more like an intelligent editor. Code can simply be typed directly into the script pane. For experienced programmers, expert mode is faster and more convenient to work with. However, it allows the possibility of certain sorts of syntax errors which are impossible using normal mode, since in the latter case Flash inserts all the necessary syntactic elements for you. To begin with, it is advisable to stick with normal mode. (If you become a real expert you may well find it best of all to work on scripts in an external editor, such as BBEdit, and import them into Flash. We will not deal with this possibility, though.)

Figure 5.31   *The* Actions *panel in normal mode.*

We will begin by considering attaching actions to buttons. First you must create an instance of a button symbol, either one you have created yourself or one taken from a library. (The Window>Common Libraries sub-menu provides quick access to the libraries supplied with Flash. These include one called Buttons, which contains controls resembling those of a VCR, arrows and push-buttons, in several different styles.) With the button selected in a keyframe, display the Actions panel if it is not already visible. (The arrow icon on the mini-launcher at the bottom right of the stage provides a quick way of doing this.) As you can see from Figure 5.31, the left hand pane of the panel contains a scrolling list. Initially the list shows a set of icons in the shape of closed books. These represent categories of actions. Clicking on one of these books causes it to open and show the individual actions within it; in Figure 5.31, the category of Basic Actions has been expanded in this way. The actions in this category are the only ones that can easily be used without any knowledge of programming, so we will confine our initial description to them. If you wish to pursue the use of actions any further, you will need to consult a more advanced book which covers the use of ActionScript as a scripting language.

With a button selected and a category of actions expanded, you can click on an action to attach it to the button. As a simple, but useful, example, suppose you wished to provide player controls within a movie, so that users could stop, play and rewind the movie without using the Flash Player's own controls. (This would be particularly useful if your movie was embedded in a Web page, since under those circumstances the Player's controls are only available through a contextual menu, which many Web users may not be aware of.) Looking at the list of basic actions, it is fairly clear what is needed for the stop and play buttons. When you click on the Stop action, the following code is added to the script pane at the right of the Actions panel:

```
on (release) {
    stop ();
}
```

The stop() does what is appears to do: it stops the movie. More interesting is the code that surrounds it. The keyword on specifies that the code between the curly brackets (in this case, just stop()) should be executed when a particular event occurs. The event is written in brackets; here it is release, an event which occurs whenever the mouse button is released. Conventionally, a mouse click is considered to occur when the user releases the button, so this is what we require: when the stop button is clicked , the movie will stop.

If you select the first line of code in the script pane (the one beginning with on) the bottom pane of the Actions panel will change, as shown in Figure 5.32. This provides you with an opportunity to change the event that triggers this action or to add additional ones. For instance, you might want the user to be able to use keyboard shortcuts as an alternative to your control buttons. If you click the checkbox labelled Key Press and type s in the text box next to it, your script will change to

```
on (release, keyPress "s") {
    stop ();
}
```

which means that the movie will be stopped when the user clicks the stop button or presses the s key on the keyboard.

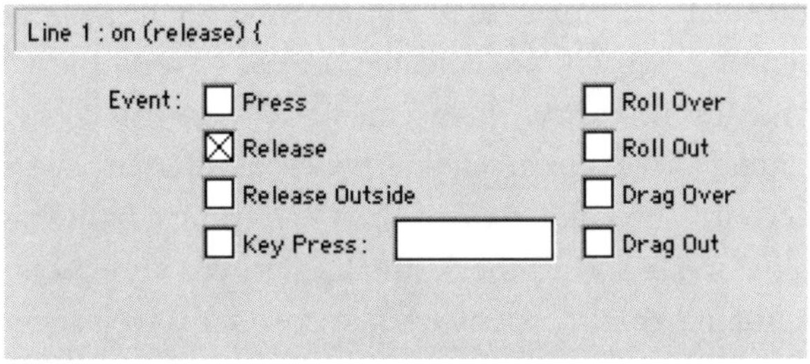

Figure 5.32 *Specifying events to trigger a button action.*

A button can potentially respond to the following events: a mouse button being pressed or released while the cursor is within its hit area, a mouse button being released outside its hit area, the cursor being moved over or out of its hit area, the cursor being dragged (i.e., being moved while a mouse button is held down) either over or out of its hit area, and a specific key being pressed. The check boxes in Figure 5.32 correspond to these events.

> ☛ Create a short movie with a simple animation, add a Stop and a Play button to it on a separate layer, and attach the action just described to the Stop button. Use the same procedure with the obvious change to attach an action to the Play button, so that the movie will restart when it is clicked or the p key is pressed. Test your movie controls.

Rewinding a movie is slightly more complicated. We need to make the playhead go to the first frame and stop there, because that's what rewinding is generally understood to mean. The Go To action is used for actions such as this, where it is necessary to transfer the playhead to a specific frame. This particular basic action can be used in several different ways, producing different ActionScript statements, depending on the values you set for some options and parameters. Figure 5.33 shows the controls displayed at the bottom of the Actions panel when you add a Go To action.

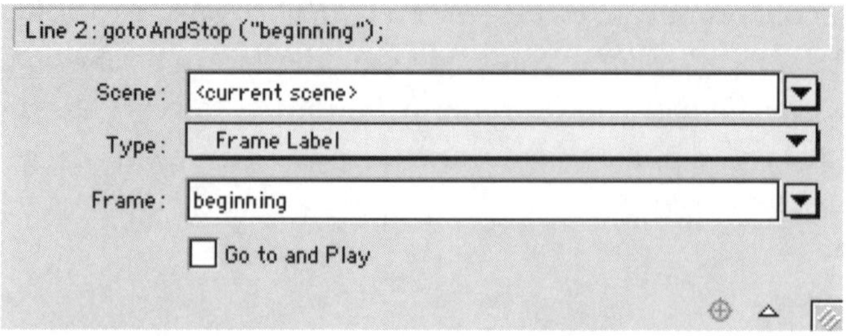

Figure 5.33   *Options and parameters for the* Go To *action.*

The first pop-up menu allows you to go to a frame in a specific scene, which is a named sub-sequence of a movie. We will not consider the use of scenes; leaving this value set to <current scene> is always correct when a movie only has one scene, as all of ours do. The next pop-up menu allows you to choose between different ways of specifying the frame you wish to go to. The main choice is between using a frame number or a frame label. It may seem natural to specify the destination using a number, since their number in a sequence is a fundamental property of frames – that is why frame numbers are displayed in the timeline. You know that to rewind a movie you need to send the playhead to frame 1. In this case, that is straightforward, but in general using frame numbers has a serious drawback. If you remove or insert frames when you edit a movie, the numbers of frames beyond the edit point will change, so any Go To actions you have added that use a frame number as their destination will send the playhead to the wrong place. You would have to change any such actions to reflect the change in numbering. (And to do that you would have to be sure you could find them all.) Using frame labels avoids this problem and we strongly recommend that you get into the habit of always doing so from the start.

A label is just a name that you attach to a frame so that you can identify it by name instead of by number. You attach a label by selecting the frame and then entering the label in the appropriate text box in the Frame panel. (See Figure 5.19 on page 235.) You don't have to, but it is good practice to add a layer specially for labels. Labels (and frame actions, which we will meet shortly) can only be attached to keyframes; if you use a separate layer for labels and actions you can insert keyframes wherever you need to, without upsetting any tweening. A label stays attached to its frame no matter where it is on the timeline, so Go To actions that use the label as their destination will always send the playhead to the right place. If you select Frame Label in the Type pop-up menu when you are setting the parameters to a Go To action using the dialogue in Figure 5.33, a pop-up menu is activated by the triangle to the right of the bottom field (labelled

Frame) in which all the labels you have set in the movie appear, so you can select the destination.

After the playhead has been transferred to a new frame, playback may continue from there or be stopped. The checkbox labelled Go to and Play at the bottom left of Figure 5.33 is used to choose between the two. For our rewind button we would deselect it, since we do not wish the movie to play automatically after rewinding. Assuming that the first frame of the movie had been labelled beginning, and we had selected a suitable keyPress event to match the other buttons, the code inserted would be:

```
on (release, keyPress "r") {
    gotoAndStop ("beginning");
}
```

☛ Add the rewind button to your movie with the actions as described. Following a similar procedure, make a button for jumping to the end of the movie. Use frame labels. Test the operation of your movie controls.

Frame Actions

Attaching an action to a frame is similar to attaching one to a button. As we noted before, you can only attach actions to keyframes and it is a good idea to reserve a layer for actions and labels. You can then create a keyframe wherever you need an action. With the keyframe selected, you use the Actions panel as before. Since frame actions are only executed when the playhead enters the frame to which they are attached, there is no question of selecting an event to trigger the action and so the on (...) boilerplate that is inserted when you attach an action to a button is not needed with frame actions. If, for example, you were to select a keyframe and then choose the Stop action from the list in the Actions panel, the entirety of the code created in the script pane would be:

```
stop ();
```

Compare this with the example on page 252.

☛ Make a movie with 25 frames and attach an action to frame 10 which causes the playhead to jump to the end and stop.

The fact that frame actions are only executed when the playhead enters the frame to which they are attached has some important implications for the way they can be used. For instance, suppose you had added a Stop action to a frame somewhere in the middle of a movie. Then the movie would always stop whenever it reached that frame, so that unless there was a button somewhere which could restart it, playback could never get past the stopped frame.[*] In general, the effect of frame actions can always be predicted by looking at their code and the timeline. Only button actions, which permit users' actions to influence events, can add an element of non-determinism.

A common use of frame actions is for making part of a movie loop repeatedly. By default, when a movie is played by the Flash Player or in a Web browser, it loops indefinitely, going back to the beginning as soon as it reaches the end. You can change this behaviour when you publish a movie for the Web, by deselecting the Loop checkbox in the HTML tab of the Publish Settings dialogue. Alternatively, you can add a Stop action to the final frame. But what if your movie consists of a short introductory section – perhaps a title or credits sequence – followed by an animation that you want to loop?

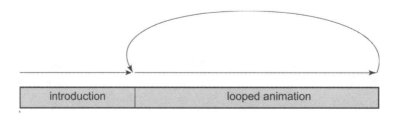

Figure 5.34   *An introduction followed by a loop.*

Figure 5.34 shows the intended behaviour in schematic form and it probably suggests a way of making it happen using basic actions. The first frame of the looped section is given a label, say loop, and then a Go To action is attached to the movie's final frame, with loop as its destination and Go to and Play selected, so that the code inserted will be:
        gotoAndPlay ("loop");
It should be evident that this will achieve the desired result: as soon as the playhead reaches the last frame of the movie, it is sent back to the beginning of the loop. (If you want the repeated section to loop for just a specific number of times you need to use a variable to keep track of the number of iterations. We will describe this possibility briefly later.)

> ☞   Make a short movie with the structure shown in Figure 5.34 and add an action to make the latter part loop as described.

Another very common use of frame actions is in making a *preloading movie*. This requires a short digression.

---

[*]This is not strictly true, because some actions are executed when an asynchronous operation, such as the loading of data from a remote server, finishes. The use of such actions is a bit advanced for an introduction such as this.

When SWF movies are embedded in Web pages to be played over the Internet, they are *streamed* from a server. This means that each frame is played as soon as it arrives; the browser does not wait for the entire movie to be downloaded to the local hard disk before beginning to play it. Provided data is arriving faster than it can be displayed, this is an efficient way to proceed, since it avoids delays. However, if data is not arriving fast enough – that is, if the contents of a frame do not arrive by the time it has to be displayed at the movie's frame rate – there will be pauses in playback as the player waits for data. Such pauses destroy the illusion of motion that is the essence of animation and are often less acceptable than waiting for the entire movie to download.

A widely adopted solution is to structure a movie so that it consists of a short introductory loop, which is very simple and therefore compact, which is played continuously until enough of the rest of the movie has arrived to permit it to play back smoothly without pauses. That is, the movie is *preloaded* before it is played. The short section that is displayed while the preloading goes on can be as plain as a message that says Please wait, or it can be a simple animation that serves to indicate that something is happening. (This section serves the same function as the holding music on telephone help lines and suchlike services. A certain amount of care is needed to ensure that it doesn't become as annoying.)

You can use the *bandwidth profiler* to determine whether it is necessary to preload your movie. Use the Control>Test Movie command to open up the Player within Flash, and then choose View>Bandwidth Profiler and View>Streaming Graph. Figure 5.35 shows an example of the resulting display, which takes over the top half of the Player window. On the left is a summary of various properties of the movie, including its size and duration. The last line in the first section of this summary indicates how many frames must be preloaded before the whole movie can play back smoothly. In this case it is four. The figure given for bandwidth in the section headed Settings shows the value that has been assumed in calculating the movie's behaviour. This can be altered using the Debug menu in the Player. In this example, we have told the profiler to assume that the movie is being streamed over a 56K modem. The bottom part of the profiler's textual display gives a dynamic report of the status of the movie: which frame is being displayed, how much has been downloaded, and so on.

The main part of the profiler's display is a graphical summary of the way the data contained in each frame is streamed. In this particular example, which uses motion tweening to animate several movie clip symbols, the data is concentrated in the first frame, during which the symbols are loaded. After that, very little data is needed in each frame, since all they contain is instructions that position the symbol instances in

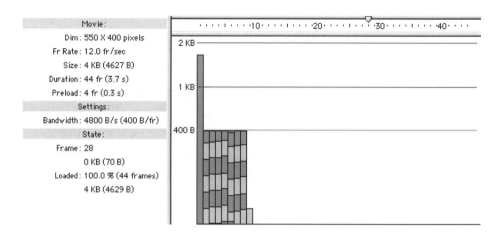

Figure 5.35   *The bandwidth profiler.*

accordance with the specified motion tweening. The vertical bars show how much data is loaded while each frame plays. The stripes in the bars represent frames, so for example, while the second frame is playing, there is time for nearly five more to come down the connection. The horizontal line at the 400 mark (it is red in the actual display) shows the assumed bandwidth. Whenever the bar representing a single frame goes above this line, you know that it will not be possible to obtain the data for that frame in time to display it at the correct frame rate, so there will be a pause in playback. In this example, the only pause occurs while the first frame loads, which is acceptable. By selecting Show Streaming from the View menu, you can see how the movie will play when it is streamed over a connection with the assumed bandwidth. If you select Frame By Frame Graph from the View menu, instead of Streaming Graph, you get a simpler display which just shows the amount of data in each frame, so that you can identify potential bottlenecks.

> ☛ Choose one simple and one complex movie from your earlier exercises (or from some other source) and practise using the bandwidth profiler to assess the movies' potential performance over different network connections.

The bandwidth profiler is a very helpful device, which often demonstrates just how small a movie must be before it will stream smoothly over present-day Internet connections. It is only a simulation, though, and the real network is subject to additional delays beyond those due to restricted bandwidth. In particular, insufficiently powerful servers may not be able to supply data as fast as the network can transmit it. The profiler makes some attempt to allow for this, but, it is wise to add some extra to the its estimate of the number of frames that need to be preloaded. In fact, for many movies you might as well preload the lot.

The initial loop of a preloading movie must contain at least two frames. In the first, we test to see whether the preloading is done; in the last we loop back to the first so the test will be repeated. There can be frames in between if you want to play an extended animation while the preloading takes place, but obviously, the holding animation should not be too elaborate or else you will need to preload it in its turn, and it should not be very long because you will want to test frequently to see whether the movie is ready to play. However, you can't get away with using a single frame that tests and then jumps back to itself. The reason is slightly subtle: frame actions are only executed when the playhead *enters* a frame. If you jump back to the same frame, the playhead doesn't move, so no actions are executed.

You know how to make the holding section loop using a Go To action. In order to break out of the loop when enough of the main movie is loaded, a new action is required. If you are confining yourself to basic actions, you should select If Frame Is Loaded from the list of actions. This inserts the following incomplete code into the script pane:

```
ifFrameLoaded (1) {
}
```

The parameters pane at the bottom of the Actions panel changes to allow you to specify a frame using either a number or a label, just as it does with a Go To action. Supposing you wanted to preload an entire movie, and you had labelled the final frame end, you would choose Frame Label as the type and choose end from the menu of labels, giving the following code:

```
ifFrameLoaded ("end") {
}
```

The intent should be clear, since you can read the script almost as if it was English (with a bit of reordering): if the frame labelled end is loaded do something, as yet unspecified.

You specify what is to be done by adding another action inside the curly brackets. To do this, select the first line of the script and double-click an action. In this case, if the end frame is loaded we want to go to the start of the movie proper and play it. Assuming that the frame following the holding section is labelled start, the full script, after adding a Go To action that uses this label as the destination would be:

```
ifFrameLoaded ("end") {
    gotoAndPlay ("start");
}
```

This script is attached to the very first frame of the movie, which might be labelled preload. (It is quite in order to attach a label to a frame with a script.) If it was, the second frame should have the following script:

```
gotoAndPlay ("preload");
```

to force the opening sequence to loop as required.

> ☞ Choose one of your earlier movies and add a short animation to the beginning, which will play until the rest of the movie has downloaded.

Actions and Movie Clip Symbols

Preloading movies, starting, stopping and looping may be useful but they are pretty unexciting. It must be understood that to achieve any complex results with actions you will have learn something about programming and write scripts that are more complex than the actions in the basic category permit (or else team up with a programmer). However, there is one basic action that can be used to good effect to make movies behave in a way that is impossible with conventional, non-digital, animations. It appears in the list of basic actions as Tell Target.

Before we show how this action can be used, we should warn you that it has been superseded in Flash 5 ActionScript by other constructs, known as movie clip *methods*. In fact, the *ActionScript Reference Guide* goes so far as to 'deprecate' the use of Tell Target. There are very good reasons for preferring movie clip methods, but a full explanation of these would take us into an account of object-oriented programming, for which this book does not have the space. Their use would also require us to go beyond the Basic Actions category, which again would take us into deeper waters than are appropriate. Since Tell Target does its job and is used by many Flash practitioners, we will use it here, but if you are going to go beyond the introductory level, we advise you to find out how to use the newer alternatives.

When we used Play, Stop and Go To actions earlier, they controlled the playback of the entire movie. Previously we had mentioned that instances of movie clip symbols are self-contained movies within the movie, which can be controlled independently. This can be done with Tell Target, which allows you to send commands, such as Play, Stop and Go To to a movie clip instance.

To see how this works and why you might want to do it, consider as an example a movie containing a representation of a television set with an on/off control. The idea is that when a user turns the TV on a movie clip plays on the TV screen and it stops when the set is turned off. The main movie can consist of just a single frame, with a Stop action attached to it, containing the TV set. The show to be played on the TV can be an instance (probably the only instance) of a movie clip symbol. This can be an arbitrary animation. To make life simpler, though, let's assume that its first frame is a blank grey rectangle, so it looks like the screen of a turned-off television, and that this frame has a Stop action attached to it. Thus, the instance of this clip symbol can be placed within the area that represents the TV screen on the stage, scaled to fit.

In order to use Tell Target to control a clip, the clip instance must be given an *instance name*. This is done by selecting it on the stage and entering the name in the Name field in the Instance panel, shown in Figure 5.36. Only clip instances can have names, so this field is only available when you have selected such an instance on the stage. It is very easy to forget to name clip instances and some obscure behaviour can result from doing so. For this example, the clip placed inside the TV screen will be given the name tv.

Figure 5.36   *The* Instance *panel with a clip instance selected.*

Before we can show how to control the clip, we need to consider the on/off control. We could use separate on and off buttons, but this is not very elegant, so we will do something more complicated and provide a single control with an on and an off position, as shown in Figure 5.37. Its implementation demonstrates a generally useful technique. The control takes the form of a movie clip with two frames, one for on and one for off. An instance of this symbol is placed on the stage so that it looks like part of the TV set. Movie clip instances can receive events, but the way in which they must be handled is unduly complex, so a simpler technique is used. In each frame we placed an instance of a button that is just a plain circle. Only its Up frame is a keyframe, which is extended over the others – we don't want it to change appearance when it is rolled over or clicked and we do want the hit area to match the graphic content. When an instance of the clip is placed on the stage, the buttons within it will receive events; in particular, they will respond to mouse clicks. By attaching suitable actions to the buttons, we can make it appear as if the control is responding. The marker on the edge of the control is added separately, in a different position in each of the two frames, so that the control appears to move between an off position and an on position if the playhead moves from one frame to the other.

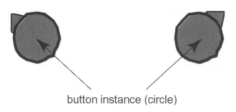

button instance (circle)

Figure 5.37   *An on/off control for a Flash TV.*

What actions are suitable? Consider first what should happen if the user clicks on the on/off control when the TV is turned off. The control should move to its on position and the movie clip inside the TV should start to play. Assuming the two frames of the on/off movie clip are labelled on and off, changing the appearance just involves going to the on frame, so we begin by adding the following script to the button in the off frame, by selecting the button instance in that frame, double-clicking Go To in the list of basic actions, and setting the destination appropriately as before.

```
on (release) {
gotoAndStop ("on");
}
```

Nothing new here. Colloquially speaking what we also want to do is tell the movie clip called tv to play. This is what Tell Target does, so with the gotoAndStop line selected, we double-click the Tell Target action. The following skeleton is added to the script, below the selected line:

```
tellTarget ("") {
     }
```

We need to fill in the target and the action that we want to tell it to perform. The latter is easier, since we have already seen something similar. All that is needed is a Play action. The target is the means by which the clip on the TV screen is identified. We gave this clip the instance name tv but this is not enough on its own. In general, clips can contain other clips and a clip can only be identified by giving a list of the instance names of clips that contain it. It's a lot like URLs and directory paths. In a URL such as http://www.wiley.co.uk/digital_multimedia/tools/flash/examples/tv.html, everything after the domain name www.wiley.co.uk is a path name that identifies the file tv.html within the directory examples within the directory … within the directory digital_multimedia, which is inside the root directory of the Wiley Web site. Similarly, a clip within a clip within a clip is identified by a *target path*, consisting of the instance names of each of the nested clips. Two different notations are used for target paths. The older 'slash notation' uses the same conventions as URLs, with components of the path separated by / characters. The newer 'dot notation' uses dots instead. (This is for consistency with other aspects of ActionScript.) We will prefer dot notation, though you may see slash notation used if you look at older Flash movies.

Like URLs, target paths can be relative. By default, a name such as tv refers to a clip instance within the current clip. Instances in the main movie can be accessed using an absolute target path beginning with the pseudo-instance name _root. Thus, in the example we are developing here, the movie clip on the TV screen is _root.tv. The Actions panel provides some help in getting target names right. If you have a Tell Target action selected, the bottom part of the panel displays a text field for you to enter the target. With the cursor in this field, if you click on the target icon in the bottom right of the panel, a dialogue like the one shown in Figure 5.38 is displayed. The panel at the top displays the hierarchical structure of the movie as a tree. For more elaborate movies this tree structure will be larger with more levels corresponding to clips within clips. If you click on an icon representing a clip, its target path is inserted in the code. The radio buttons allow you to choose between slash and dot notation (choose dots) and relative and absolute path names. In general, as your scripts become more complicated, it is good practice to use relative paths whenever you can, but in this particular case we know that we want to target a clip in the main movie, so an absolute path can be used. After selecting the tv clip, the full script for this button becomes:

```
on (release) {
    gotoAndStop ("on");
    tellTarget ("_root.tv") {
        play ();
    }
}
```

Similarly, the button in the on frame of the on/off control should have the following script attached to it:

```
on (release) {
    gotoAndStop ("off");
    tellTarget ("_root.tv") {
        gotoAndStop ("first");
    }
}
```

where first is assumed to be the label on the first frame of the tv clip.

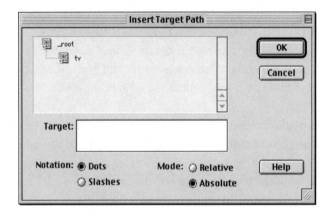

Figure 5.38   *The target path dialogue.*

Summarizing, we have a main movie with just a single stopped frame containing a graphic representing a TV set. A movie clip instance called tv is placed on the screen, and an instance of the on/off control – a movie clip with two stopped frames containing buttons with scripts as shown above – is placed in a suitable position on the TV set. When the user clicks on the control, the event is received by the button inside it, it moves to the on position and tells the tv clip to play so the TV shows the animation. If the user clicks on the control while it is on, it turns the TV off.

For this example, we deliberately stripped matters down to their essence – a control making a clip start and rewind. The basic technique can be used in more ambitious ways, with multiple clip instances embedded in a movie and directed by controls that accept users' input. This leads to a style of genuinely interactive animation which established media cannot support.

> ☞ Following the procedure just outlined, make a movie which plays within a TV set in the main movie. Use your own design for the appearance of the set and its controls.

Actions, Browsers and Networks

When a movie is played inside a Web browser it is possible to use an action to load new pages. That is, an SWF movie can be used to provide navigational controls for a Web site. This usually works best in conjunction with frames.[*] A movie with buttons can function as a navigation bar, occupying a small frame and causing different pages (which may or may not have SWF embedded in them) to load into a main frame.

---

[*]See Chapter 7 for more on using frames and embedding SWF in Web pages.

Alternatively, a site can be entirely constructed with Flash and controls in each embedded movie can be used to move around it by loading new pages, each with an SWF embedded in it. Using Flash in this way allows you to use rollovers, animated buttons, sound effects, and so on, on your Web pages, without entering the minefield of browser incompatibilities and bugs that is loosely referred to as Dynamic HTML.

Again we can strip this down to its bare essentials to demonstrate the principle. Suppose you have a Web page divided into two frames, called navbar and main, and that an SWF movie is embedded in navbar. The movie is a single stopped frame containing a row of buttons, each bearing an icon or some text that shows it will lead to a section of the Web site: home page, downloads, FAQs, brochure requests, …, whatever. The conventional intention is that when a user clicks on a button the corresponding page should be loaded into the main frame.

The basic action Get URL is provided for this purpose. Figure 5.39 shows the parameters pane of the Actions panel when this action is selected. The URL field is used to enter the URL of the document that you wish to load. You have to type this, there is no provision for browsing, even for files in the same directory. In the next field, labelled Window, you can enter the name of a frame or window in which the document should be displayed. Again, you usually have to type the value here since Flash has no way of knowing the frameset structure of the page in which the movie is embedded. In our example, we would type the frame name main in this field. If you know HTML you will be aware that the names _self, _blank, _parent and _top have special significance when they are used as the target of a link. They cause the retrieved document to be displayed in the same frame as the link, in a new window, in place of the frameset containing the frame containing the link, and in the entire current window, respectively. The same names can be used as values for the Window parameter of Get URL, with the same meanings. They are available in a pop-up menu activated by the triangle to the right of the Window field.

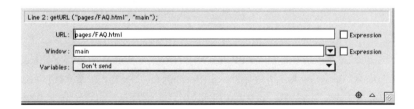

Figure 5.39   *Parameters for the* GET URL *action.*

The last pop-up menu in Figure 5.39 is only used when the URL identifies a CGI script or some equivalent server-side program. You can elect to send values to such a script, which will perform computation with them and send back the result, thereby constructing a Web page dynamically. This ability is the key to using Flash movies to provide interfaces to distributed systems, such as ecommerce applications. Unfortunately, the scripting techniques involved are non-trivial and a full understanding relies on knowledge of the HTTP protocol and server-side scripting, so we will have to refer you to more advanced accounts of Flash scripting for a proper description of these matters.

To create a simple navigation bar, it is only necessary to attach Get URL actions to each of the buttons in a Flash movie, using appropriate parameters. This leads to code such as the following:

```
on (release) {
    getURL ("pages/FAQ.html", "main");
}
```

You can either publish the movie in order to generate an SWF movie and an HTML file to go with it, and then use the HTML as the source for a frame, or export the SWF file and then embed it in an appropriate frameset built using Dreamweaver or some other Web site construction package.

☞ Make a Flash movie which could be used as a navigation bar on a Web page made up of frames, consisting of four buttons so that each button will load a different Web page (use any URL of your choice) into a frame of the main page when it is clicked.

Get URL always loads an HTML document, whether it's retrieved from a file or dynamically generated. The document may have an SWF movie embedded in it, but you always need to use a Web browser to handle the display, which means that you are restricted to frames and browser windows. If you wish to load a movie directly into another movie you need to use a different action, appropriately called Load Movie. This action can be used in several ways, but the easiest to understand and the most flexible is to load a movie from a file, potentially from a remote server, into a movie clip instance.

Recall, for instance, the TV example. The clip that was played was an instance of a symbol, which was therefore part of the movie. To change the clip you would have to edit the symbol. It would be more flexible if the clip could be an independent SWF file; then it could be changed without altering the TV movie itself, and it would be easy to substitute a different movie just by a little renaming of files. Load Movie allows you to do this.

If you double-click Load Movie in the list of basic actions, the parameters pane of the Actions panel acquires a URL field and a method pop-up, just as in the case of Get URL, illustrated in Figure 5.39. Instead of the Window field, Load Movie has a Location field with an associated pop-up menu, which allows you to select between two values: Level, which we won't deal with, and Target, which you should select when you want to load a new movie into a movie clip. Once you have done so, you can use the target icon to bring up the path dialogue of Figure 5.38, as we did when using Tell Target.[*] Using this procedure we could attach the following script to the button in the off frame of the on/off control, in place of the one on page 263.

```
on (release) {
    gotoAndStop ("on");
    loadMovie ("tv-movie.swf", "_root.tv");
}
```

where we have assumed that the movie we wish to play in the TV is held in a file called tv-movie.swf in the same directory as the TV movie itself. We also assume that this movie does not have a Stop action in its first frame. Now, when a user clicks the on/off control, its appearance changes as before, and the movie in tv-movie.swf is loaded into the clip instance tv, so that it appears on the TV screen. Loaded movies play immediately, so the effect of turning on the set will be produced as before.

The action Unload Movie removes a loaded movie, as you would expect. It too can take a target as a parameter, so one way of making the TV turn off would be by adding the following script to the button in the on frame:

```
on (release) {
    gotoAndStop ("off");
    unloadMovie ("_root.tv");
}
```

☞ Make a Flash movie consisting of a single frame containing two buttons and an instance of a movie clip symbol. Attach Load Movie actions to the buttons so that when you click on one of them a new movie is loaded into the clip and played. (Use different movies for each button.)

Beyond the Basic Actions

Flash's basic actions are really very basic indeed. Although, as we have seen, you can use them to create effective interactivity, going beyond them and using ActionScript as the programming language it is opens up a wealth of further possibilities. Just taking a few

---

[*]And just as with Tell Target, there is now an alternative movie clip method available for those who know about such things.

steps into programming can be worth the effort, so without trying to produce a Flash programming primer, in this section we will demonstrate the use of some elementary constructs that should at least show you some of the things that can be done. Hopefully, as a result you will be better equipped to communicate with more experienced programmers if you have to work on collaborative projects in order to implement elaborate systems using Flash.

Arguably the most basic concept in programming[*] is that of *variables*. A variable is a named container that can hold a value of some sort: a number, a string of text, a truth value, or a more complex collection of different values. A variable can store different values at different times. By changing its value we can use variables to remember things.

To show how this works, we need to describe some actions that belong to the category simply labelled Actions in the list in the Actions panel. A variable is introduced into a movie – or *declared* – using the var action. When you add this action to a script attached to an object or a frame, the following skeleton is inserted in the script pane:

```
var <not set yet>;
```

and a text field labelled Variables appears in the parameters pane. Here you can enter the name you want to use for your variable. It is good practice to choose names that indicate what the variable is to be used for – although just about everybody calls a variable x now and again. There are rules about what characters you can use in names. Without going into the full details, you will be safe if you always use a letter to start the name and only use letters, digits and underline characters within a name. Don't use spaces.

When you declare a variable in this way, it is given a default value, but it is also good practice to explicitly set its value straight away. This is done using the set variable action. The parameters to this are a variable name and a value. Next to each of the text fields for entering these parameters is a checkbox labelled Expression. You almost never select this for the variable, but you should normally select it for the value (it really ought to be selected by default, but it isn't): it tells Flash to interpret what you type as an expression to be evaluated and not as literal text. A constant such as zero is an expression, so if you wanted to use a variable called loop_count to count some loops, you could first use the var action to declare it, and then use set variable to set its value to the expression 0. This would insert the following two lines of script into your movie:

```
var loop_count;
loop_count = 0;
```

---

[*]At least in the programming mainstream to which ActionScript belongs.

When scripts are constructed from a series of actions, it makes sense to consider them as consisting of a sequence of *statements*, each of which describes an operation to be performed. There are many different sorts of statement in ActionScript. The second line of this script, which sets the value of a variable, is an example of an *assignment statement*. Often we say that a value is assigned to a variable.

It should be pointed out at this stage that the code we will produce in this section is pretty pedestrian, to say the least, and not necessarily what an experienced scripter would do. Normally, for instance, you would combine the declaration and assignment into a single statement. We will confine ourselves to a minimum of different actions in the interests of simplicity. If you crave elegance, you will have to look elsewhere.

Why would we want to use a variable to count loops? And how would we count them anyway? To answer this question, we can revisit the example on page 256, of a movie with an introduction followed by a section that looped forever. Suppose you only wanted that section to loop six times. In order to do this, you would certainly need to count the number of times around the loop.

You might therefore attach the script just shown to the first frame of the movie, with the intention of using the variable loop_count to remember how many times the loop has been played. It makes sense: at this point you have gone round the looped part of the animation no times, so the loop count, as it were, should be zero. Every time the playhead reaches the last frame of the movie, it has gone round the loop one more time, so the value of loop_count should be reset to a value that is greater by one. This is done using the set variable action again. This time, we want to add one to the value of loop_count and use it as the new value. If you just write a variable's name in an expression, its value is used, so the expression loop_count + 1 evaluates to what we want. (For example, if the value of loop_count was 4, loop_count + 1 would be 5.) Hence, remembering to tick the Expression checkbox next to the value, we can use set variable to add the following line to the script attached to the last frame of the movie:

```
loop_count = loop_count + 1;
```

At this point we always know how many times the loop has been played when we get to the end of it. How can we use that knowledge? What we want to do is arrange that the playhead only jumps back to the start of the loop if the value is no more than six. We have already seen something quite similar. When making a preloading movie we used the If Frame Is Loaded action to jump to a frame when a certain condition was met. This is generalized by the if action. When you add this to a script, the skeleton inserted looks like this:

```
if (<not set yet>) {
}
```

and a field is provided to enter an expression which you want to be true before you execute some other statements, which will be added between the curly brackets, just as we did with If Frame Is Loaded. Typically, the expression compares two values. In our particular case, we want to jump back to the start of the loop if the loop count is less than six. Comparisons are written using an approximation to conventional notations. In particular, the < symbol is used to compare two values, giving true if the first is less than the second and false otherwise. Putting that another way, if the first value is less than the second any statements between the curly brackets following an if will be executed.

In the present case, we want the Go To action which transfers the playhead to the beginning of the loop to be executed only if the loop count is less than six. Therefore, we type the comparison loop_count < 6 into the parameter field for the if action, and then use the Go To action as before to insert the jump. The whole script is:

```
loop_count = loop_count + 1;
if (loop_count < 6) {
    gotoAndPlay ("loop");
}
```

☛ Use frame actions as just described to make one of your movies loop four times.

You can use six different comparison operators: <, <=, >, >=, == and !=. The last two deserve comment. As you have seen, the = sign, conventionally used for equality, is used in ActionScript for assigning a value to a variable, so a different symbol has to be used for equality. Two = signs are employed, following a precedent set by the C programming language. The exclamation mark is used, again following C, to mean 'not' in various contexts. Here, != is used to stand for 'not equal to'. In all of the comparison operators that involve two characters, you must not put a space between them. You can, if you like, use the Operators category of actions to build up expressions, including comparisons. This helps if you can't remember the symbols – tool tips appear if you hold the cursor over an operator – but it is slower than typing and somewhat clumsy.

Variables can profitably be used to remember events that have been received by buttons. As an illustration of this, consider another variation on the animation with a looped section. Suppose you want to provide a Stop button which, unlike the conventional control we implemented previously, causes the movie to stop the first time it reaches the end of the loop after the button has been pressed. That is, instead of making the movie stop when the button receives a click, we remember that the click happened and then, when the playhead reaches the final frame we check whether a click has been remembered and stop the movie if it has.

This time, our variable only needs to hold one of two values, corresponding to a click being remembered and not. You could simply adopt a convention, such as storing a zero if there was no click and setting the value to one when a click occurred. A better way is to use the special values true and false, because these can be used directly as tests in an if statement, as we will show.

The structure of the actions attached to this animation shares some features with the example we have just described. A variable is declared and initialized in the first frame. This time we'll call it stopping, with the intention that it should be set to true when the movie is to be stopped at its end. To begin with, therefore, stopping should be set to false, giving the following script to be attached using the var and set variable actions to the first frame.

```
var stopping;
stopping = false;
```

The value will be tested in the final frame, as before. This time there is a difference: we want to do one of two separate actions, depending on whether stopping is true or false. This needs an enhanced version of the if statement we saw before, which specifies two choices. To begin with, you can just add an if action as before. The condition is simply the expression consisting of the variable stopping: its value being true or false can be used as a condition, since these are the same values as the possible outcomes of a test.[*] If stopping is true we want to stop, giving the following:

```
if (stopping) {
    stop ();
}
```

but this doesn't tell us what to do if stopping is false. For this, we need to add an alternative clause. This is done by selecting the action else immediately after adding the Stop action. This adds some extra boilerplate. We then use the Go To action to put in the jump back to the head of the loop as before. The entire script looks like this:

```
if (stopping) {
    stop ();
} else {
    gotoAndPlay ("loop");
}
```

---

[*]If you ever see someone write code like if (stopping == true) (and you probably will), sneer at them.

All that remains is to provide a way of changing the value of stopping. A button is added on its own layer, which consists of a single keyframe extended over the full length of the movie, so that the button appears throughout its duration. With the button selected, add a set variable action to change the value of stopping to true, like this:

```
on (release) {
    stopping = true;
}
```

→289

The variable thus remembers the release event so that the movie will be stopped in response to it at the end of the loop, as desired.

☞ Extend the example of a delayed stop action just described so that when a user clicks the button, the movie plays twice more before stopping at the end.

Further Exercises to do in Flash

1. (a) Import a bitmapped image in black and white and copy it into 12 keyframes. Use Trace Bitmap with different settings in each frame to make an animation where the appearance of the image changes from frame to frame. Select one element and apply colour changes to it over the course of the animation.

   (b) If you have the facilities, save two seconds of a video clip of your choice as a sequence of still images. Import these into Flash and use Trace Bitmap to create a graphically effective movie small enough to play over a dial-up Internet connection. Embed the movie in a Web page.

2. Trace a bitmap using settings that give a bold graphic result. Select parts of the resulting vector image and manipulate them with Flash's tools to produce an abstract design derived from the original image.

3. Scan a page of a magazine or newspaper and import the resulting bitmapped image into Flash. Break it apart and use the lasso tool to tear it into several pieces. Animate the tearing.

4. Scan some object with a distinctive texture or pattern (e.g., a piece of wood, a knitted sweater, some pebbles, or a piece of wrapping paper) and use it as a bitmap fill to create objects in Flash made of that material. Experiment with appropriate and inappropriate objects (for example, wooden trees and wooden birds).

5. Using three layers, create a 50 frame animation with a background on the first layer and two objects or characters in the other two layers. Use motion tweening to make

the two objects complete different movements across the background during the course of the animation. Try to make the interaction between their movements meaningful or aesthetically pleasing.

6. (a) Create a simple vector shape in the first frame of a movie. Using appropriate tools, distort the shape in frame 25 and apply a shape tween to create a morphed animation. Repeat the exercise, but use two completely different images as the start and end of the shape tween.
    (b) Create a multi-layer movie with morphed elements on several layers. What problems are associated with animations produced in this way?

7. Using only motion tweening (no shape tweening or frame-at-a-time animation) create a 25 frame animation in which objects change in shape, colour, brightness and position during the course of the animation.

8. Create a simple looped animation of a single object or character moving in a distinctive fashion (for example, a dolphin leaping out of the sea) and turn it into a graphic symbol. Create an animation incorporating multiple instances of this symbol.

9. Experiment with animated buttons. Try placing animations in different states. Can you achieve any effects that are more than gimmicks? What happens if you place an instance of a graphic symbol with several frames in one of the states of a button? Why?

10. Create a button with sounds attached to its Over and Down states. What sort of sounds work best to provide useful feedback without being annoying? When would it be a good idea to attach a sound to the Up state?

11. Make a movie clip symbol of an opening door. Create a button symbol with a suitable appearance and combine an instance of the button and an instance of the clip to make a movie in which clicking on the button causes the door to open.

12. Create a fairly complex movie, or use one of the more elaborate ones you made doing the practice exercises, and use the bandwidth profiler to identify which frames contain most data. If possible, make appropriate adjustments to the movie so that it will play over a 28K modem. Otherwise, add a preloading movie that plays for the shortest time necessary for the rest of the movie to play continuously.

13. Make a movie that could be used as a navigation bar in a large Web site. It should consist of several buttons (though these may not actually be button symbols)

corresponding to major divisions of the site, such that when the cursor rolls over a button, a menu pops up with entries for individual pages within that division, and clicking on a menu entry causes a page to be loaded into a frame. (Don't worry too much about making sure that the menu closes properly, no matter what the user does.)

14. Make a simple TV set with more than one channel. The easiest way is to provide a button for each channel, such that pressing the button plays a movie, with each channel showing a different movie. If you want to be more ambitious, consider using a numbered dial as a channel selector. Implementing a more realistic set of controls, where the channel changing is separate from the on/off control is more complicated, but can be done if you are prepared to read up some more about ActionScript.

5a Flash MX

Like its predecessor Flash 5, Flash MX has introduced significant innovations in the interface and functionality of Flash. While the new departures are not quite so radical as the preceding set, there are important new features which build on Flash 5's more powerful scripting facilities to extend Flash's range of application and to make it easier for designers to use components that incorporate complex scripted behaviour and standard designs. Flash has moved a long way from its origins as a Web animation tool. It now provides a powerful front-end for Web applications in which Flash movies communicate with a server to perform distributed computation.

Since this book is not aimed at programmers, we will not go into any of the new features of ActionScript which have appeared in this release. Instead, we will concentrate on those features that are likely to be of use to Flash artists and designers.

Interface Elements

A few minor changes have been made to the interface. For example, the Modify>Movie... command referred to in Chapter 5 has been renamed Modify>Document... and various keyboard shortcuts have been changed. These alterations should cause no difficulty. More far-reaching changes have resulted in the use of panels and the addition of some new tools.

Panels

As you might infer from the version suffix, Flash MX uses Macromedia's unified MX interface, which is described in Chapter 2a. The use of dockable panels has reduced the amount of clutter on the screen, and the new *property inspector* has enabled several panels from the old interface to be effectively combined into one. The result is that some of the operations described in Chapter 5 are now performed in a slightly different way, with the relevant controls appearing in the inspector instead of different specialized panels. Since the change to the MX interface has made a significant difference to Flash, we will expand on the description given in Chapter 2a.

The general rule is that the property inspector contains controls that affect the currently selected tool, unless that tool is one of the selection tools (arrow, direct selection or lasso) or is a tool that implicitly makes a selection (the free transform and fill transform tools), in which case the property inspector shows information about the selected object. Unfortunately, the eyedropper and eraser tools are exceptions to this rule. For both of these, the inspector always shows information about the selected object. (If an object is selected on the stage when you pick up a tool, the property inspector does not change to show options for the tool until you click on the stage.)

If you pick up any drawing or painting tool (the pen, pencil, brush, paint bucket or inkdropper) or the rectangle or oval tools, the property inspector can be used to set the fill, stroke or both, for the tool. Here, the inspector replaces the Fill and Stroke panels, which no longer exist. Figure 5a.1 shows the inspector with the rectangle tool selected. As you can see by comparing this figure with Figure 5.5 on page 214 and Figure 5.7 on page 216, the facilities are just the same, and they are used in the same way. Having them together on the same panel, and available just when you need them – when an appropriate tool is selected – is a considerable convenience, but does not alter the function being performed in any meaningful way.

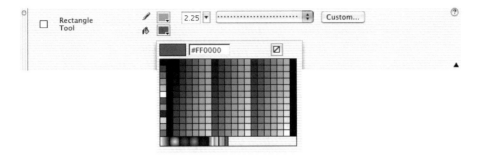

Figure 5a.1 *The property inspector when the rectangle tool is selected.*

Figure 2a.2 on page 51 shows the appearance of the property inspector when different sorts of object are selected. Again, the effect is that information and controls that were formerly on separate panels are now displayed in the inspector; the old panels have been removed from the interface, but since you could not use them unless a suitable object was selected, this does not stop you doing anything. Apart from the location of the controls, the way in which you carry out operations such as applying an effect to a sound or altering the stroke of a shape are carried out in the same way as described in Chapter 5. You should not have any difficulty applying the descriptions in that chapter to the new interface.

If you wish to use fills other than those available on the drop-down palette in the property inspector, you will have to resort to the Color Mixer panel. This combines the functions of the Mixer and Fill panels from Flash 5. In the interests of clarity, therefore, we will provide a new description of selecting fills, to replace the text on pages 215–216.

Whenever you have a drawing or painting tool or a shape selected, you can set colours in the Color Mixer panel, shown in Figure 5a.2. Here you can set a stroke colour, a solid fill or one of several sorts of gradient fill. The precise appearance of the panel and the options it provides depend on the type of fill you have selected from the pop-up menu in the centre of the top part of the panel. Its options are shown on the right of Figure 5a.2. If you choose Solid, as in the figure, you can set colours for both the fill and stroke. For the simple case of a single solid colour chosen from the swatches palette it is sufficient to click on the swatch next to the pencil icon (for stroke) or paint bucket icon (for fill) and choose a colour from the palette that pops up, just as you do when setting stroke and fill in the property inspector. However, this pop-up palette also has a button that provides access to the system's colour pickers, allowing you to select a colour graphically in one of several colour models. Alternatively, you can use the simple colour picker that occupies the bottom half of the panel. You can also enter R, G and B values numerically in the boxes at the right of the panel (or H, S and V, if you prefer – select the option from the panel menu), and enter a percentage value for the Alpha – i.e. transparency – of the colour. (The values you set are applied to either the stroke or fill, depending on which of the icons on the left you have selected.)

If you wish to reuse the colour, you can select Add Swatch from the Mixer's panel menu; it will then be available in the pop-up colour palettes that appear in the inspector and the Mixer panel. (New colour swatches are added to the bottom of the column down the left hand side.) The Color Swatches panel allows you to inspect and manage swatches: commands in its panel menu let you delete and duplicate swatches, and manage swatch libraries. This is an advanced facility, which we will not, therefore, describe further.

☛ Make a rectangular shape, and using the Mixer panel, set each of its sides to a different colour. Add a contrasting fill. Use some colours that are not among the default colour swatches. Try altering the transparency of the fill.

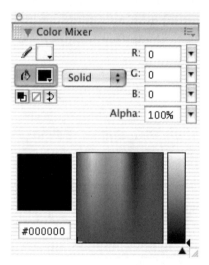

Figure 5a.2   *The* Color Mixer *panel.*

More complex fills can be created in the form of *radial* or *linear* gradients. (See Figure 5a.3.) Selecting one or other of these gradient types in the Color Mixer panel causes controls for building gradients to appear, as in Figure 5a.4. (The option to set the stroke disappears – Flash does not support gradient strokes.)

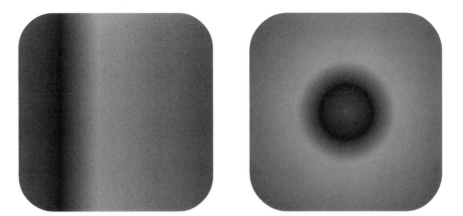

Figure 5a.3   *Linear (left) and radial (right) gradients.*

Each of the markers below the bar represents a point at which the colour can be specified. Between markers, a gradual blend of colours is produced. To begin with, there are only two markers, one at each end; new markers can be added simply by clicking below the bar. A marker may be selected by clicking on it, and then the colour at that point can be chosen using the normal methods for setting a solid colour. Markers may be dragged to new positions to change the way in which the colours blend. As with solid colours, gradients will be applied to any selected object and will become the default fill for any subsequent drawing. They may also be stored in the Color Swatches panel using the Add Gradient command from the panel menu. Gradient swatches appear along the bottom of the colour palettes in the property inspector and the Color Mixer panel.

☞ Make some rectangular shapes, and fill them with linear and radial gradients. Practise adding extra markers to the gradient bar, and moving them to alter the gradient. Experiment with different colour combinations.

Tools

In earlier versions of Flash, the arrow tool's functions were extended beyond the normal ones of selecting and moving objects, as found in Illustrator, for example, to include various transformations. In Flash MX, the arrow tool has been relieved of these additional functions by the introduction of a *free transform* tool, which is used for scaling, rotating, skewing and distorting objects. It can also be used for moving them, when this is more convenient than using the arrow tool.

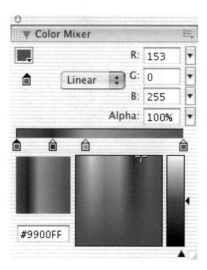

Figure 5a.4   *Creating a gradient fill.*

In use, the free transform tool is simple and intuitive. When you click on an object with it, a bounding box with eight handles appears, as shown on the left of Figure 5a.5. If you place the cursor directly over one of the handles, it changes to a double arrow to indicate that you can scale the object by dragging. If you are over one of the handles in the middle of a side, you can scale in the direction perpendicular to the side, as illustrated in the middle of Figure 5a.5; if you are over one of the corner handles, you can scale in both directions at once by dragging diagonally. If you hold down the shift key while dragging a corner, the proportions of the object are maintained as its size changes.

If you hold the free transform tool near, but not actually over, one of the corner handles, the cursor turns into a circular arrow, which indicates that you can rotate the object by dragging, as shown on the right of Figure 5a.5. (The corner handles can be dragged in more or less any direction to make the object rotate, but moving them as if you were actually pulling the object round to its new position produces the most intuitive feedback.) By default, the object is rotated around its centre, but by dragging the circular icon that you can see in the middle of the letter in Figure 5a.5 to a different position you can move the centre of rotation.

☞ Create an asymmetrical shape and practise scaling and rotating it with the free transform tool. Move the centre of rotation and observe the effect on rotations.

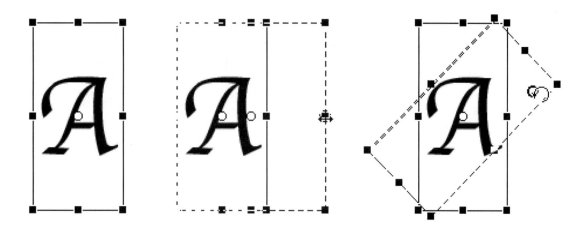

Figure 5a.5 *Using the free transform tool.*

The free transform tool can also be used for performing skewing transformations. When you move it near to a side, but not over any handle, the cursor turns into a pair of parallel arrows, and you can skew the object by dragging parallel to the side.

☞ Practise skewing the shape you created for the previous exercise in different directions.

If you prefer to use menus and palettes for transformations, you can use the Modify>Transform menu and the Info and Transform panels, as described on page 223.

Flash MX also has a *fill transform* tool, which is used much like the free transform tool for rotating and scaling, but it transforms an object's fill within its shape, not the entire object. Figure 5a.6 illustrates this for a gradient fill. The fill transform tool can also be used profitably on bitmap fills (see page 227).

☞ Practise using the fill transform tool on objects filled with gradients and bitmaps. See if you can duplicate the transforms in Figure 5a.6.

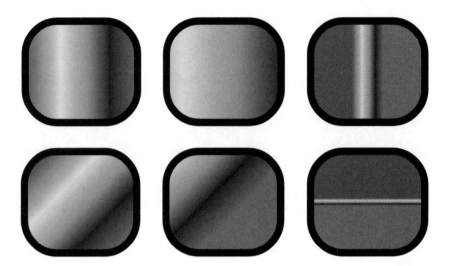

Figure 5a.6   *Fill transformations.*

Layer Folders

If you use Flash for any non-trivial animation, you are likely to find that your movies end up with a lot of layers. This is because tweening is applied to layers, so if you need to tween many objects independently you must place them on different layers. Also, because of the way the selection tools work, it is often most convenient to use a new layer for every shape and movie clip in a movie. Managing many layers can become cumbersome: unless you have a huge display, you will need to scroll vertically in the timeline, and if you have placed different parts of an animated character on different layers, you will need to turn off the visibility of each layer individually if you want to hide the character, or copy all of the layers if you want to try a new version of the character, and so on. Layer folders in Flash MX allow you to group a set of layers together and manipulate the whole set in some ways as a single entity.

If you are familiar with working with folders on the desktop, you will have no difficulty grasping the use of layer folders. Figure 5a.7 shows a timeline with layer folders. To create a new layer folder, click on the New Layer Folder icon below the layers names in the timeline window. You can then drag layers into the folder. Whenever you create a new layer, it is added at the same level as the layer you have selected, so if you want to add new layers inside a folder, you just need to select a layer that is already inside that folder. As you probably expect, the little triangle to the left of the folder icon in the timeline allows you to collapse or expand the folder. In Figure 5a.7, the layer folders called Sky and Spray have been collapsed (their triangles point sideways). The layer folder called Sky has also been hidden, which means that all of the layers inside have been hidden. Finally, notice that folders can be nested: the folder Spray is inside the folder called Water. Folders inside folders can contain other folders, and so on, to an arbitrary depth.

> ☞ Practise creating layer folders and adding layers to them.

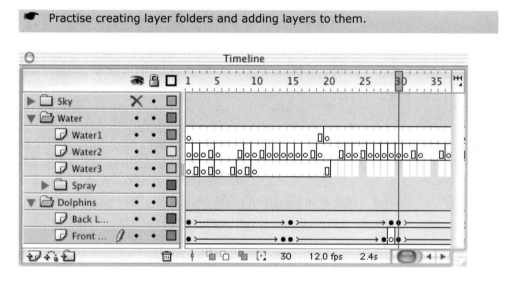

Figure 5a.7 *Layer folders.*

Layer folders are just an organizational device; they don't add any power to the program – you can't associate a motion guide with a layer folder, for example – but they allow animators with organized minds to arrange their layers to reflect the structure of the animation.

Accessibility

Making Web pages accessible to people with various sorts of disability is a moral obligation – and in many countries, for certain sorts of Web site, a legal obligation – on Web developers. The World Wide Web Consortium has produced guidelines for making HTML pages accessible. Flash has been criticized in the past for not providing any accessibility features to be used in pages containing Flash movies. With Flash MX, Macromedia has gone some way to meeting this criticism.

The focus of Flash MX's accessibility features is on making Flash movies usable by blind people and those with impaired vision. Such people may use screen reading software, which allows their computer to read out the text on the screen. For HTML pages this is relatively simple, since the text is available in the source of the page, and using HTML markup to specify the logical structure of the document helps screen readers to interpret it in an intelligent way. The text and structure of a Flash movie is embedded in the SWF file in a way that is not readily accessible, so it was necessary to add a means of making the necessary elements of a movie available to screen readers.

Obviously, there is no way for someone who cannot see to fully appreciate an essentially visual medium such as a Flash animation. The intention must be to provide an alternative that conveys the same information, and perhaps some of the same experience, as the visual content of the movie. Nowadays, with Flash being used as an alternative to HTML as a front end for Web applications, there is often much more information in a movie than the animated visual elements. Use of components, which will be described later in this chapter, makes it easy to implement forms for data entry in Flash instead of HTML; static text fields are often used as labels of one sort or another; buttons are used to provide navigational controls. All of these elements must be made accessible to screen reading software if a blind user is to make use of the functionality that the Flash movie provides.

The fundamental requirement is that each element should have a descriptive name, which the screen reader can speak to describe the element. (This name has nothing to do with the instance names of movie clips.) In many cases, these names are generated automatically. A text field's name is its content, so if you had added a field containing the static text Welcome to Digital Media Tools, the screen reader would read that text, which is almost always what you want. Static text fields are often used to label buttons, by being placed in close proximity to them on the stage, or added to the button symbol. In such cases, the static text is used as the name of the button. For example, if a static text field was placed next to a button, as in Figure 5a.8, the accessibility name of the button would be Previous, and a screen reader would therefore speak this word to identify the button, giving exactly the same information as would be available to a sighted user. Under these circumstances, the text field itself is hidden from the screen reader (again, automatically) to prevent confusion.

Figure 5a.8   *A typical example of a button labelled with static text.*

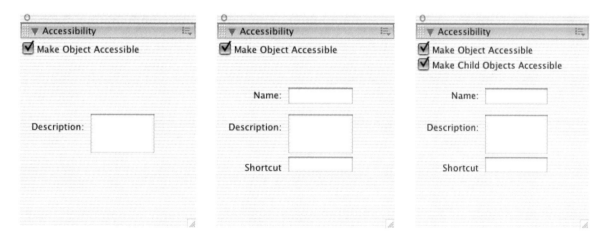

If there is no convenient text label on a button, you can supply a name explicitly. You can also supply a different name if the default behaviour is not appropriate, or hide objects from screen readers. This is done in the Accessibility panel. Whenever the object currently selected on the stage is of a type that can have accessibility information attached to it, you will find a small icon in the form of a white stylized figure (it can easily be mistaken for a five-pointed star) in a blue circle at the right-hand end of the property inspector. Clicking on this icon will bring up the Accessibility panel if it is not already visible (or hide it if it is).

Figure 5a.9 shows the fields in the Accessibility panel when different sorts of object are selected. (Some objects, in particular shapes, cannot be made accessible, in which case the panel will contain a message telling you so.) The meaning of the text fields should be clear. The checkbox labelled Make Object Accessible is used to determine whether the object is visible to screen readers. You will want all objects that perform an important function, such as navigation buttons and text entry fields, to be accessible, but objects which are primarily decoration should not be made accessible. The Shortcut field can be used to assign a keyboard shortcut that a user can type to select the object. For movie clips (and components, which are essentially movie clips) the checkbox labelled Make Child Objects Accessible is used to determine whether the clip should be treated as a closed box by the screen reader, or should have the objects within it accessible too.

Figure 5a.9   *Accessibility options for dynamic text (left), buttons (middle) and clips (right).*

Using Flash MX's accessibility features is simple, and mostly automatic. They do not provide a complete solution to the problem of making Flash movies accessible to people suffering from disabilities. For a start, they only really address the needs of blind and partially sighted users. There are many other sorts of physical and cognitive difficulty which can cause people to have problems using computers. A technical shortcoming of Flash accessibility is that the Flash Player communicates with screen readers using Microsoft Active Accessibility (MSAA), a standard technology for interfacing applications to screen readers. MSAA is only available on Windows systems, so users on other platforms cannot benefit from Flash accessibility. (Only the Flash ActiveX control supports MSAA, so in effect, it is only Internet Explorer on Windows that supports Flash accessibility.) There is also no way of testing accessibility, except by using a screen reader under Windows.

> ☞ Open a Flash movie you have made in one of the more advanced practice exercises from Chapter 5 and select objects on the stage. For those which can be made accessible, open the Accessibility panel and practise making objects accessible and inaccessible and setting values in the panel. If you have access to appropriate screen reading software, use it to access the movie. Try and assess how easy it would be to use the movie if you were visually impaired. Try to remedy any defects you find in the movie's accessibility.

If accessibility is important for your site – for instance, if it is a public information site – then it will not be sufficient simply to enable accessibility and make sure that all your controls have names. You really need to design your Flash movies with accessibility in mind from the beginning, and make use of Flash's other features in a way that promotes accessibility. For instance, you can use synchronized sounds to supply a descriptive soundtrack to accompany any animations. It may be necessary to use scripts to make your movie behave differently when it is communicating with a screen reader – a special method has been added to ActionScript to enable scripts to detect this condition.

Making Web pages accessible to people whatever their disabilities is a difficult job. If you need to produce accessible content in Flash, you should visit the Flash accessibility page at www.macromedia.com/software/Flash/productinfo/accessibility/ and, for more general issues of Web accessibility, the W3C Web Accessibility Initiatives pages at www.w3.org/WAI/.

Video

Since the QuickTime video format was extended to provide support for SWF tracks within QuickTime movies, Flash has allowed you to import video footage, add Flash animation and some interactivity, and export the result as QuickTime. In effect, you could use Flash to edit the QuickTime by adding SWF tracks. You can still do this in Flash MX, but video is now supported in the SWF format and by the Flash Player, so that you can now also import video and export it inside a SWF movie. The first option is referred to as *linking* and the second as *embedding* the video. Either allows you to mix live action and animation, or add interactivity to video.

To import a video clip, you first create and select a layer and then choose Import... from the File menu and select your video file. If you have QuickTime installed on your system, you can import any QuickTime, AVI, DV or MPEG movie; if you are using Windows and only have DirectX you can import AVI, MPEG or Windows Media files. When you open the file, you are presented with the dialogue shown in Figure 5a.10, in which you can choose whether to link or embed the file. The layer will be extended if necessary with sufficient frames to accommodate the video.

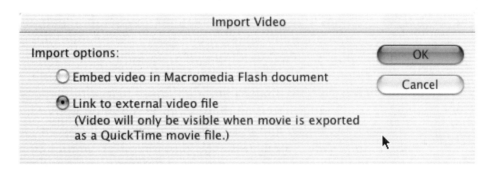

Figure 5a.10   *Options for importing video.*

If you choose to link to the video file, there are no further options. You can add extra layers (on top of the layer containing the video, otherwise it will obscure anything below it) and work on them in the usual way. As the dialogue in Figure 5a.10 warns you, you will have to export the movie as QuickTime in order to combine the Flash and video elements. On Macintosh systems, there are actually two options for exporting QuickTime, which you can find on the Format pop-up menu in the File>Export Movie... dialogue. Choosing QuickTime (the only relevant option on Windows) causes the Flash content to be added to the original QuickTime movie as an extra track in SWF format. Interactivity is supported, vector animation is maintained in vector form, and the original video is not recompressed. If, on the other hand, you select QuickTime Video as the format, the movie is rendered: all the vector animation is converted to bitmaps and combined with the video frames, which are recompressed – a second dialogue box lets you choose compression options, as described following page 552 in Chapter 8. The interactive elements are discarded. QuickTime will usually be the appropriate format for video destined for the Web; QuickTime Video would be used if you wanted to write the movie to video tape or DVD, or broadcast it.

The advantage of linking video is that, since there is no recompression, you can preserve its quality and data rate. The disadvantage is that you can no longer rely on the ubiquity of the Flash Player to guarantee that users will be able to play it. If instead you embed the video, you must recompress it, using the compressor built in to Flash MX, but in compensation, you can then export to SWF in the usual way, to create a movie that can be played in the Flash Player.

When you import a video file and select Embed video, a second dialogue box (shown in Figure 5a.11) appears, in which you can set some parameters for the compression. The Quality slider allows you to choose a value that, in effect, specifies how much compression will be applied. The higher the value, the less compression and hence the larger the file size but the fewer visible compression artefacts. You will have to experiment to find a suitable value for any given project, depending on the requirements for bandwidth and picture quality. Unless you understand video compression, leave the Keyframe interval alone. The bottom slider lets you scale the imported video. Video from a camera will have a frame size dictated by the camera's video standard (720 by 576 for DV PAL, 720 by 480 for NTSC DV, for example), which will often be too large for a Flash movie.[*] You can scale it down as you import it using this control. Notice that there is a checkbox which you can select to have the video's soundtrack imported along with its picture. When you do this, the sound remains part of the video, it doesn't get put on its own layer and you cannot edit it in Flash. The final option in the dialogue lets you change the video's frame rate to match that of the Flash movie. Again, captured video will be at a standard frame rate (25 fps for PAL, 29.97 fps for NTSC) and you may want to use a different rate in your movie. Frames will be discarded or duplicated as necessary to match the video frame rate to that of the Flash movie.

The Sorensen Spark codec used by Flash is claimed to produce high quality video at low bit rates, suitable for use on the Web. The quality and data rate depend on the settings used in compression. For a short 60-frame video clip, shot in PAL DV at 25 frames per second, using a quality setting of 80 produced acceptable quality in a file of 1.1MB, giving a data rate of approximately 16KB per second – much too high for a dial-up modem, but comfortable for broadband. By cutting the quality to 50 and the frame size to a quarter of its full value, the movie size was reduced to 176KB, at a data rate of roughly 3KB per second. At this setting, the image quality is pretty poor. Figure 5a.12 shows a detail from a frame of the original DV compared to the compressed frame. Note

---

[*]Video exported from a 3D animation package may not be constrained to standard dimensions.

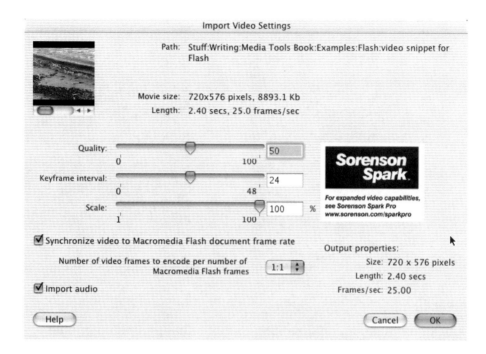

Figure 5a.11 *Setting compression options for imported video.*

the visible square blocks of pixels in the compressed version, especially in the reflections on the water. However, when the movie is reduced to quarter-frame size, the quality is just about acceptable.

☛ If you have the facilities, shoot some short video clips and import them into your computer. Practise importing them both as linked and embedded files into a Flash movie. Experiment with compression settings for embedded video. Export your movies to as many different formats as possible, and observe the quality of the resulting playback, and the bandwidth requirements. Experiment with mixing live video with Flash animation.

Components

If you are using Flash not just as an animation tool, but as a front-end for Web applications, to provide navigation and interactivity to a Web site, the chances are that you will find yourself needing to use the same sorts of Flash objects over and over again: data entry forms nearly all use the same repertoire of checkboxes, radio buttons, pop-up menus and so on, for example. Reimplementing all these elements from scratch for every project is a waste of time and effort. You can easily share symbols between movies:

Figure 5a.12   *Detail from a DV frame (left) and its compressed equivalent (right).*

select Open as Library... from the File menu and navigate to a Flash movie. When you click Open, instead of opening the movie for editing, its symbol library will be opened, and you can create instances of its symbols in the movie you are editing on the stage, by dragging from the Library window in the usual way, as described on page 238. However, this only goes some way to solving the problem: it is often the case that you want to reuse a general pattern, such as a pop-up menu, but set specific parameters, such as the entries on the menu. *Components*, which were introduced in Flash MX, provide a more powerful means of reusing elements in different movies.

User Interface Components

Flash MX includes a small collection of reusable components that provide standard user interface (UI) elements. We will introduce components by describing how you use some of these UI components.

The available components are listed in the Components panel, which is shown in Figure 5a.13. In principle, you can have many different libraries of components, and the pop-up menu at the top of the panel allows you to select one of them. When

Flash MX is first installed, the only entry in this menu is Flash UI Components. Other components, which you may be able to download from various Web sites devoted to Flash, or you may have built within your organization, are installed just by placing them in a specific location on disk – see the Flash documentation for the precise details – and are then automatically made available via the Components panel. Creating new components calls for advanced Flash knowledge and scripting expertise, so we will not describe it in this book.

Figure 5a.13 *The* Components *panel.*

The idea of a checkbox will be familiar, if only from the interfaces to the programs described in this book. Figure 5a.14 shows an example of the CheckBox component as it appears in the Flash Player in its checked and unchecked states. To add a checkbox to a Flash movie, you just drag it from the Components panel to the stage. It then appears as you see it in Figure 5a.15. You will see that the label is part of the component, not a separate static text field, so you need to set it to the appropriate string for your application. This is done in the property inspector.

☐ Tick Here If You Don't Want To Receive Junk Mail

☑ Tick Here If You Don't Want To Receive Junk Mail

Figure 5a.14 *A checkbox.*

Figure 5a.15 *A checkbox component as it first appears on the stage.*

Figure 5a.16 shows the property inspector when a CheckBox component is selected. At the bottom right of the panel are two tabs, labelled Properties and Parameters. If you click on the former tab, the panel shows the usual properties for an instance of a movie clip symbol – that is what components are, essentially, but they are a special sort of clip, which you can customize by setting parameters. This is done in the Parameters tab of the property inspector, which is what is shown in Figure 5a.16, where you can see that the CheckBox component has four parameters, which are displayed in the pane at the right of the inspector. A pane of this general form is used to set the parameters of every component. It is arranged in two columns, the left listing the names of all the parameters, the right their values. Thus, a CheckBox's parameters are called Label, Initial Value, Label Placement and Change Handler. Apart from the last, which we will discuss later, the values of these parameters affect the appearance of the checkbox.

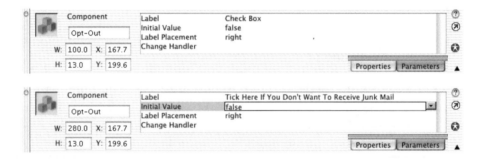

Figure 5a.16 *Setting parameters of the checkbox in the* Inspector *panel.*

To change a parameter's value, you click on the current value in the right hand column. It is then highlighted and you can type in a new value. The lower screenshot in Figure 5a.16 shows the checkbox's label (the text that appears next to it) having been changed, and the Initial Value parameter, which specifies whether the box is ticked or not when it is first presented to the user, being set. The third parameter controls whether the label appears to the left or right of the box. For parameters like these last two, which can only legitimately have certain values, a pop-up menu containing the legal values is attached to the field. A downward-pointing triangle appears at the right when the field is selected, as you can see in the Initial Value field in Figure 5a.16, and you can pop up the menu by clicking on it.

Although the properties of the component considered as a movie clip are typically set in the Properties tab of the property inspector, some of them are duplicated in the Parameters tab for convenience. You can set an instance name, and change the size and position numerically, using the fields at the left of the panel. For a CheckBox, changing the width extends or contracts the label, so you will usually have to do so when you set a label. Changing the height does not actually alter the component's appearance.

> ☞ Create a new Flash movie and add a checkbox to the stage. Practise changing the values of its parameters. Test the movie to observe the result. Experiment with changing the height and width of your checkbox.

Some components have parameters that are arrays instead of a single value; that is, they contain an ordered set of values, not just one. An example is the ListBox component, which is used to display a list of values in a scrolling window, from which the user can select one or more. Figure 5a.17 shows an example; at the top of Figure 5a.18 is the property inspector with a ListBox selected. The Select Multiple parameter, which controls whether a user can select more than one item from the list at a time, behaves like the parameters we described for theCheckBox component, but the Labels parameter, which holds the values of the strings displayed in the list box, is different. Obviously, it needs to hold several values; the fact that it can do so is indicated by the [] in its value field. When you click on the value field, a dialogue box opens, as shown at the bottom of Figure 5a.18. When you click on the button at the top labelled +, a new line is added to the list of labels, originally with the name defaultValue, as in the last line in Figure 5a.18. You can type in the name you require to replace this default. The button labelled - is used to remove selected elements from the list, and the up and down arrows are used to reorder them. When you are satisfied with your list, you click OK. Several components have parameters that take an array of values; these are all set in a similar way.

> ☞ Drag a ListBox on to the stage of your movie, and give it a name and a set of labels. Test your movie. Try setting the Select Multiple parameter to true and false in turn, and observe the different behaviour of the list box when you test the movie.

> ☞ Investigate all the UI components installed with Flash MX. Experiment with setting the values of their parameters, and observing the results. If you cannot determine what a particular parameter does, consult the component's documentation.

Astute readers will realize that all of this is totally useless. There is no point in providing a means of entering data, unless something is going to be done with that data. Typically, you will either want to use input values to control the movie in some way, or you will

Figure 5a.17 *A list box.*

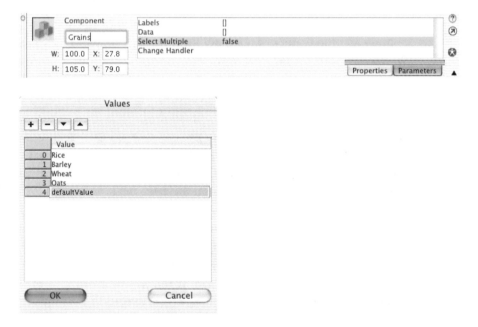

Figure 5a.18 *Setting the parameters for a list box.*

want to pass it to some program running on a server, as we described briefly on pages 264 to 266. Whatever you are going to do with the data, you will need a script to deal with it. This is the purpose of the Change Handler parameter which every component has. (The PushButton component's parameter is called Click Handler, but it works just the same way.)

The value of the Change Handler parameter is a text string giving the name of an ActionScript function that will be called when the user changes the setting or selects a value from a component. Thus, if a checkbox is checked, its change handler function will called; if an item in a list box is selected, the list box's change handler function will be called, and so on. Writing change handlers requires some scripting expertise. If you know more about ActionScript than is covered in Chapter 5, you should note that the component is passed as an argument to the change handler, and every component has a getValue method, so that the current value of the component can be extracted by the handler.

In fact, using components to their full capacity calls for quite extensive scripting. It is possible to create components dynamically as a movie runs, change their appearance, set values as well as test them, and perform other operations. Thus, using components effectively calls for cooperation between programmers and designers. Designers need to know how to add components to a movie and customize their appearance; programmers need to know how to manipulate components using scripts. In this book, we are only concerned with the first of these.

Changing The Appearance Of Components

If you add a CheckBox component to a movie and then look at the Library window, you will see that you have acquired a lot of new library items, as Figure 5a.19 shows. The CheckBox component itself is there, of course, but so are some things called Core Assets, which are best left alone, and a folder called Component Skins. It is these *skins* which control the appearance of the component, and by editing them you can change its appearance. This is not something that should be undertaken frivolously, though. There are usability arguments in favour of always using interface elements that are easily recognized and which behave in a predictable way, which suggests that you should use the components as they are if you wish your movie to be highly usable. More pragmatically, if you edit component skins in the wrong way, you can make a terrible mess of the appearance of your components, and possibly stop them working.

With those warnings in mind, let us look at a simple and harmless change that you might want to make to the appearance of a checkbox. As Figure 5a.14 shows, a selected checkbox is indicated by a tick mark in its box. Suppose you wanted to put a cross in the box instead. This can be achieved by editing the component's skin.

First, you have to find the relevant symbol among the component skins. You can see from Figure 5a.19 that there are two sub-folders in the Component Skins folder in the library, one called FCheckBox Skins and the other Global Skins. The former contain symbols that are used to build CheckBox components; the latter are used for all components. For our particular example, we are only concerned with the appearance of

Figure 5a.19 *Library items for a* CheckBox.

CheckBox components, so the symbols we need to edit are inside FCheckBox Skins. By examining all the movie clip symbols contained in this folder, you will find that the tick mark appears in the symbols fcb_check and fcb_check_disabled. These are just ordinary symbols, so they can be edited by double-clicking in the Library window.

If you do this for fcb_check, you will find that it is not a simple graphic symbol, but a movie clip. Figure 5a.20 shows the timeline and (at high magnification) the stage. The timeline includes a layer called ReadMe, which contains some actions. Do not delete this layer, and do not change the actions unless you know exactly what you are doing. You can, however, edit the graphic. If you select the tick mark on the stage, you will find that it too is an instance of a movie clip symbol. In order to change it, you must double-click to edit the symbol. Having done so, you are finally in a position to delete the tick and replace it by a cross, which you can draw with the pen, pencil or brush. To make sure that it will register properly when it is used as part of a checkbox, make sure that your cross is positioned within the guides in the same way the original tick was.

If you now set the Initial Value parameter of the checkbox on the stage to true, you will be disappointed to find that a tick appears in the box. If, however, you test or publish the movie, you will see your cross instead. Changes to skins are not shown on the stage in Flash itself, only in the Flash Player.

> ☞ Follow the procedure just described to change the appearance of the mark in a check box.

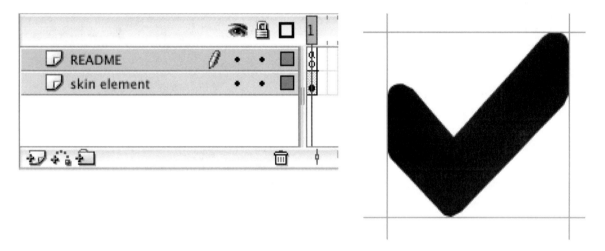

Figure 5a.20 *The* fcb_check *symbol.*

The skin is applied to every instance of a component, so by altering the appearance of one checkbox, you alter the appearance of every checkbox in your movie, which is sound design practice. If you drag a checkbox onto the stage after you have edited the skin, you will see the message shown in Figure 5a.21. The 'existing component' referred to in the dialogue is the one on the stage that you have edited. By electing to use this, you give the new checkbox the modified appearance. If you choose the other option, all checkboxes will revert to the standard appearance.

> ☞ In the Global Skins folder within the Component skins folder in the library, you will find a symbol called Flabel. It consists of a single dynamic text field, used for adding labels to components, such as CheckBox. Edit this field to use a different font and colour. (You may have to unlock a layer to do this.) Observe the effect on checkboxes and other components.

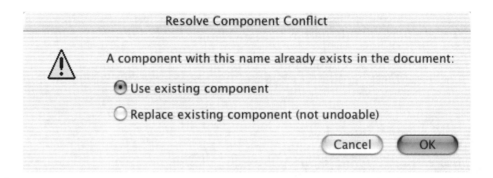

Figure 5a.21   *Conflict resulting from editing a skin.*

6

Illustrator
Vector
Graphics

Files and Formats Summary

- Create documents with File>New and save them with File>Save As... as Illustrator files, EPS or PDF.

- Open image files using File>Open, in a wide range of vector and bitmap formats or incorporate them into a document using File>Place....

- Export images in a wide range of vector and bitmapped formats using File>Export....

- Export GIF, PNG and JPEG files optimized for the Web using File>Save for Web....

Common Features
Used By This Program

Ilustrator is one of the leading programs for producing *vector graphics*, that is, images made up of shapes which can be described in mathematical terms, as distinct from bitmapped images, which are stored as an array of colour values, one for each pixel. Although this limits the expressive possibilities offered by the program, it provides great flexibility, since shapes retain their identity and can be freely edited and transformed. Vectors provide a relatively compact representation of images and they can be scaled and rendered at arbitrary resolutions without any loss of quality.

Although vector graphics have been overshadowed by bitmapped images for multimedia work until recently, the growth in the use of Flash has led to a renewed interest in vector-based formats. Flash's SWF format has been made freely available so that other programs, including Illustrator, now generate it. The WWW Consortium has developed an alternative vector format SVG (Scalable Vector Graphics) for use in Web pages and this too is supported by Illustrator. Additionally, Illustrator allows you to export finished pictures in one of the bitmapped formats used on the Web (JPEG, GIF and PNG – see Chapter 10), so you can make use of the precise drawing tools and flexible editing facilities it provides in order to prepare images, even if they are ultimately destined to appear as bitmaps.

Although all Illustrator can really do is create shapes made out of straight lines and simple curves, it is not limited to drawing technical diagrams and other mundane illustrations. Shapes can be filled with complex gradients, where colours blend into each other, and lines may be given the appearance of marks made by various sorts of natural drawing materials, including ink, charcoal and watercolour. Patterns, varying from classical geometrical designs to whimsical lines of ants and paw prints, can be used to fill shapes or follow lines. Work made by Illustrator always has a graphic, drawn quality, but within this limitation a great variety can be achieved.

In this chapter we will describe Illustrator 9. Illustrator has been around for quite a long time and its basic drawing facilities have not changed much, so quite a lot of the material is also applicable to older versions.

10

Drawing

When you create a new document using the File>New... command, you are presented with a dialogue box that allows you to give the document a title, choose the colour mode (use RGB for images destined for a screen, CMYK is for printing) and to set the size of the *artboard*. This defines the notional area of your image. When you dismiss the dialogue, a window appears with the document's title in its title bar and a rectangle representing the artboard centred within an effectively infinite white area. (It's actually just under nineteen feet, or nearly six metres, square when displayed at full size. Scroll bars are provided.) For images that are only going to be displayed on a screen the artboard is somewhat irrelevant. When you save an image to any format except PDF, all the objects you have drawn are included anyway. The artboard does give you a frame of reference, though, if you have an image size in mind. For printing, the artboard is usually set to the page size and the rest of the window is used as scratch space. Within the artboard's rectangle you will see a dotted rectangle which shows the printable area of your currently selected printer. This is entirely irrelevant if you do not intend to print. You can remove it using the View>Hide Page Tiling command.

> ☞ Create a new document, with an artboard that is a suitable size for making images to fit in a typical browser window. Hide the dotted rectangle showing the printable area.

Illustrator provides an entirely conventional interface, as described in Chapter 2, with menus, many tabbed palettes, and a toolbox, from which you can select tools for performing the major drawing tasks. Because of the nature of creating vector graphics – which is basically a drawing activity – the toolbox plays a more prominent role in Illustrator than it does in most other programs. In some cases, less commonly used tools are concealed in palettes beneath other tools. As well as being revealed by holding down the mouse button with the cursor over the tool that hides them, these concealed sub-palettes can be torn off by clicking on a small triangle that appears at the end of the palette when it pops up. Figure 6.1 shows the toolbox and most of the tear-off palettes. (Some which contain tools we will not describe have been omitted to keep the illustration clearer.)

Drawings made in Illustrator consist of a collection of *objects*: lines, curves and filled shapes. Depending on whether you can draw or not, you will either find it easiest to start working with Illustrator by drawing with the pencil or pen tools, or by creating basic shapes with the special tools provided for the purpose. We will begin with the second option.

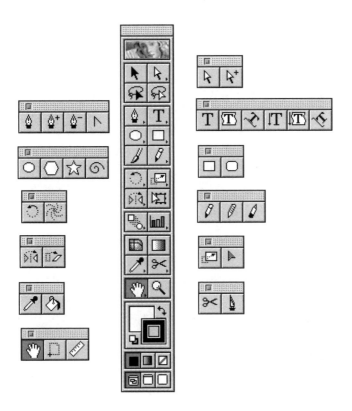

Figure 6.1   *The drawing tools.*

Stroke and Fill

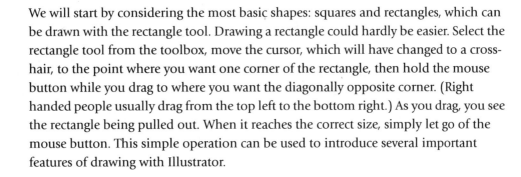

We will start by considering the most basic shapes: squares and rectangles, which can be drawn with the rectangle tool. Drawing a rectangle could hardly be easier. Select the rectangle tool from the toolbox, move the cursor, which will have changed to a cross-hair, to the point where you want one corner of the rectangle, then hold the mouse button while you drag to where you want the diagonally opposite corner. (Right handed people usually drag from the top left to the bottom right.) As you drag, you see the rectangle being pulled out. When it reaches the correct size, simply let go of the mouse button. This simple operation can be used to introduce several important features of drawing with Illustrator.

When you have completed a rectangle as just described, it will be shown (by default) as a thin blue shape. This indicates that it is *selected*. Objects that are selected can be manipulated and transformed in several ways, as we will describe later, but if you don't want to do anything of that sort, you should deselect the rectangle you have just drawn.

The quickest way to do so is by [cmd/ctl] clicking anywhere away from the shape. It will then (again, by default) change to a black outline, made of straight lines one point wide.

Any shape has two important properties, its *stroke* and its *fill*. The stroke specifies the colour, width and other characteristics of its outline; the fill specifies the colour or gradient to be used to colour it in. Illustrator keeps track of a current stroke and fill, which are used when you draw any object. You can draw rectangles with a different appearance by changing the stroke and fill before you select the rectangle tool. (We will describe later how to change these attributes of an object after you have drawn it.)

To change the stroke's colour, you must click on the stroke swatch at the bottom of the toolbox. Then you can use the Color palette, shown in Figure 6.2, to choose a new colour, either by clicking on the spectrum at the bottom of the palette, or by entering values for the red, green and blue components, numerically or with the sliders provided. (Notice that this palette has a fill and a stroke swatch just like the toolbox's, and that the stroke is in front, indicating that we are setting stroke colour.) The square with a red diagonal stripe through it at the end of the spectrum denotes no stroke, for invisible lines. At the opposite end of the spectrum you can select black or white. Note that white and no stroke are different. On a white background, both will be invisible, but a white stroke is opaque and hides anything underneath it, whereas no stroke, since it is a complete absence of stroke, lets objects underneath show through. The difference becomes much more evident when we consider filling objects with colour. For greater precision in choosing colours, double-click the stroke swatch, either in the Color palette or the toolbox, to access the Adobe colour picker, as described in Chapter 9. To reset the stroke (and fill) to the default value, click on the tiny pair of swatches below and to the left of the larger ones.

☞ Make sure the stroke and fill are set to their default values and then draw four rectangles of different sizes. Draw another four, each using a different colour for the stroke.

Other attributes of the stroke are set in the Stroke palette, shown in Figure 6.3. The weight – that is, the width of the stroke – is usually specified in printer's points (written pt), which are units equal to 1/72 of an inch. Since monitors are usually considered to have a nominal resolution of 72 dots per inch (whether or not they actually do in physical units), points are equivalent to pixels for screen display. The up and down arrows to the left of the Weight field can be used to increase or decrease the line weight (thickness) in increments of one point. The arrow to the right of the field hides a pop-

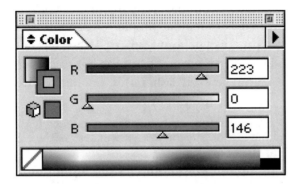

Figure 6.2   *The* Color *palette.*

up menu from which you can choose among a range of popular weights between 0.25pt and 100pt. Or you can type a value in the field.

☛ Draw four more rectangles, each with a different stroke width. Use a range of values from very fine to quite substantial.

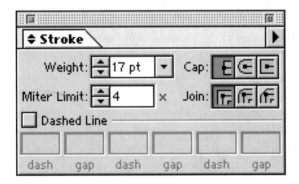

Figure 6.3   *The* Stroke *Palette.*

The icons on the two rows of buttons labelled Cap and Join are hopefully self-explanatory illustrations of the different ways in which the ends of lines and intersections between lines, respectively, can be finished off. The Miter Limit value is used in conjunction with the setting for the Join style: if a mitre, like the corner of a picture frame, is chosen by selecting the first Join button, if the lines join at an acute angle the point will stick out. After a certain distance this begins to look ridiculous, so a limit can be set on the size of protrusion, above which a bevel join will be used instead. The default value is usually all right.

If you select the checkbox labelled Dashed Line, you can set a pattern of dash and gap lengths in the boxes below it. For simple applications, just setting a suitable value in the first dash box provides a pattern of uniformly spaced dashes, separated by spaces equal in length to the dash. Entering a value in the first gap box has the obvious effect of setting the size of the interval between dashes. This is normally adequate.

☞ Practise drawing rectangles with dashed lines. Use a range of values for the dash length. Experiment with the effect of setting values in each of the dash and gap boxes.

The simplest fill is a solid colour. To set the fill, you click on the Fill swatch at the bottom of the toolbox and then choose a colour from the Color palette, in the same way as you set the stroke colour. As with the stroke, you can select no colour, to make transparent objects. You can also use various sorts of gradient as fills and make objects partially transparent, as we will describe in a later section.

☞ Practise drawing rectangles with different combinations of stroke and fill colours. Include some with no stroke.

Shape Tools

The rectangle tool as just described demonstrates the pattern of usage for drawing shapes with specialized tools. There are some refinements to the basic mode of drawing by dragging. Most of the time, most people prefer to set the size of objects by eye, but sometimes precise values are needed. To create a rectangle of an exact size, select the rectangle tool and then click where you want the top left corner to be, instead of dragging out the rectangle. A dialogue box will appear, with fields for you to enter the width and height. You may use most commonly employed units to specify the dimensions. For multimedia work, pixels (abbreviated px) are often useful. You can set the default units in the dialogue displayed when you choose the Edit>Preferences>Units & Undo... command. (Note that separate defaults may be used for stroke weights and type sizes.) Most of the tools for creating shapes can be used in this way to set dimensions and other parameters numerically.

☞ Draw a rectangle exactly 81 pixels wide and 43 pixels tall.

Another feature that the rectangle tool shares with the other shape tools is that its behaviour can be altered using modifier keys. Holding down shift while dragging out the rectangle constrains it to be a square – there is no separate square tool. Holding down [opt/alt] produces a centred rectangle: the point from which you start to drag becomes the centre of the shape, which grows outward from it in all directions as you drag. Sometimes, this is an easier way to position the shape. You can also move the rectangle while you are drawing it: press the space bar while you still have the mouse button depressed. The partly drawn shape will follow the movement of the cursor as long as the space bar is held down.

If you hold down the mouse button with the cursor over the rectangle tool, a hidden tool for drawing rectangles with rounded corners is revealed. This can be used in exactly the same way as the rectangle tool, either by dragging or by clicking and entering values in a dialogue box. For rounded rectangles, the dialogue has an extra field in which you can enter a radius for the corners. Figure 6.4 shows a series of rectangles with corners of increasing radii. You can alter the corner radius as you draw by pressing the up and down arrow keys, while the mouse button is held down. The outline of the partly drawn shape changes as you do so. Since corners with the same curvature look different with different length sides, it is useful to be able to adjust the curvature dynamically in this way. The shift and [opt/alt] modifiers work the same way as they do with ordinary rectangles, to produce rounded squares and centred shapes, respectively. Stroke and fill attributes can be set in the same way, too.

> ☛ Practise drawing rounded rectangles. Use different colours for the stroke and fill, and both fine and wide strokes. Practise changing the corner radius, both numerically and on the fly. Try drawing some centred rounded rectangles.

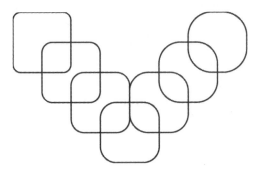

Figure 6.4 *Rectangles with round corners.*

You will go far with rectangles if you are using Illustrator for UML diagrams and similar technical figures, but there are tools for making other shapes once you have exhausted the possibilities of rectilinearity. They can be found on a sub-palette, originally hidden underneath the ellipse tool. The ellipse tool itself is used for drawing ovals and circles, and behaves very much like the rectangle tool. You can draw by dragging in just the same way. An ellipse is fitted into the rectangle whose corners are the start and end of the drag. You are not really aware that this is what happens, though, because you just see the ellipse being pulled out by the mouse. If you prefer to set the size numerically, you click instead of dragging, as before, and enter the height and width. Since the top left hand corner of the rectangle enclosing it is not actually on the ellipse, positioning ellipses precisely is more difficult than positioning rectangles. It may be easier to position the centre, which is done by holding down [opt/alt] while dragging with the ellipse tool. Alternatively, you can use the space bar to move the ellipse as you draw. (Later, we will show how to position objects precisely after you have drawn them.) As you might guess, holding down shift while using the ellipse tool forces it to draw a circle. Both modifiers can be used at the same time if you want to draw a centred circle.

> ☛   Practise drawing ellipses and circles. Use different colours for the stroke and fill, and both fine and wide strokes.See whether you prefer to drag out from the centre or the top left corner.

A polygon tool is provided for drawing shapes with straight edges that are all the same length: equilateral triangles, squares (again), regular pentagons, dodecagons, and so on. With this tool, the shape you draw is always centred on the point where you start to drag. As you drag, you can rotate the polygon, just by dragging round: one point of the object always follows the cursor. You can also use the up and down arrow keys to add or remove sides while you are drawing; the space bar lets you move the shape during the drawing as with the other tools. If you click with the polygon tool, the dialogue lets you set the number of sides and the radius, which is the distance from the centre to each corner. (This poses a diverting trigonometrical problem if you only know how long you want each side to be.) The values you type are remembered for the next time you use the tool without going through the dialogue, so if you need to draw a lot of pentagons you would use the dialogue to set the number of sides of the first one to five and then drag out the rest.

→360

Figure 6.5 shows the kind of shapes you can draw with the remaining two shape tools. Once you have mastered the polygon tool it should be easy to learn how to make stars and spirals. They are of limited use, though, so we will not dwell on these two tools.

> ☛   Fill a page with regular polygons, stars and spirals, using a full range of colours, stroke weights, and so on. Experiment with setting the parameters in each tool's dialogue box and with rotating and positioning shapes as you draw them.

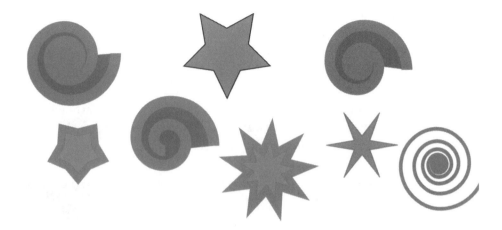

Figure 6.5   *Stars and spirals.*

Freeform Drawing

Some sorts of drawing, particularly technical diagrams, require the precision of the shape tools described in the previous section – and some people who can't draw very well may feel more comfortable using them. However, artists and designers who are used to drawing with conventional physical tools and media usually prefer to work in a way that more closely resembles their usual experience of drawing. Bitmapped image editors, especially Painter, are best known for simulating natural media in this way, but Illustrator, too, can be used in a more free way than its vector basis may lead you to suppose.

We will start with Illustrator's pencil. This is superficially used like a real pencil, and works best if you have a graphics tablet. You select the pencil from the toolbox, and then draw with the graphics pen to make a line. If you only have a mouse, you must drag the pencil about with the mouse button depressed, releasing the button when you have finished. (This is harder to control than a graphics pen, as well as being bad for your hand.) As you draw, a dotted line follows the cursor; when you stop, this is converted to a finished line using the current stroke. Hence you can draw with pencils of any thickness and colour.

If you play with the pencil, just scribbling some lines, you will probably soon notice a couple of ways in which it behaves differently from an ordinary pencil. In the first place, the finished line does not exactly follow the track of the graphics pen or mouse. Small irregularities are levelled out and the final line is a continuous smooth curve of uniform thickness.

More unexpectedly, perhaps, if you are using Illustrator's defaults, as you scribble some parts of your drawing may seem to disappear, as shown in Figure 6.6. The reason for this becomes more apparent if you change the fill to a solid colour. Whenever you finish drawing a line, an area of colour appears. What is happening is that the shape is automatically being filled in, as if its ends were joined with a single straight line. By default, the fill is set to white, so you don't see it, but the white is opaque, so any lines underneath the filled area disappear. When you just want to draw pencil lines, without necessarily filling them in, you must set the fill to no colour.

Figure 6.6   *Disappearing pencil lines.*

If you actually want to draw a closed shape without having to return the pencil to its exact start point, you can hold down the [opt/alt] key while drawing (not before you start) and keep it held down until after you have let go of the mouse button or lifted your graphics pen. The start and end of the line you have drawn will be joined up with a straight line and the resulting closed shape will be filled with the current fill, if any.

☛ Scribble some lines with the pencil tool, using different stroke weights and colours. Make a simple drawing from pencil lines.

Since Illustrator is a vector-based program, the marks you make with the pencil tool must be converted to some mathematically representable form. Bézier curves, which are described in Chapter 9, are used for this purpose. The precision with which the curve approximates the movement of the pencil is determined by the tolerances specified in the pencil options dialogue, which is invoked by double-clicking the pencil in the toolbox. Two values control the tolerance. The Fidelity might be better called the infidelity: it is the number of pixels by which the approximation may deviate from the path followed by the pencil. The Smoothness is a measure of how much the bumps in the path are smoothed out. If the smoothness is set to zero or a low value, a curve that reflects any jaggedness in the motion is produced. High values smooth this jaggedness out, so if you want smooth curves and especially if you are trying to draw with a mouse, you should set this value quite high.

> ☞ Scribble a line with the pencil tool, making a zig-zag movement of your graphics pen or mouse. Change the fidelity and smoothness of the pencil tool a few times, making a similar scribble each time and noting the different appearance of the resulting curve.

Bézier curves can be drawn with great precision using Illustrator's pen tool, which is described in Chapter 9 too. As we mention there, the pen is also used for drawing straight lines: just click once at each end. To draw an irregular polygon, just keep clicking to add extra lines. When you have finished, [cmd/ctl] click away from the line – otherwise, next time you click with the pen, a new line will be drawn from the end of your most recent line to the point where you clicked.

Figure 6.7   *Calligraphic brush strokes.*

The closest Illustrator comes to natural media drawing is in the use of its calligraphic brush tool. Again, this is best used with a graphics tablet and a pressure-sensitive pen. In use it is similar to the pencil, in that you drag the tool around and a path that approximates your movements is built out of Bézier curves. The difference is that instead of a uniform stroke being applied to produce lines that look as if they have been drawn with a technical draughtsman's round-nibbed pen, a variable stroke that looks as if it has been applied with a brush or an italic nib is used. The appearance of the stroke depends on the particular type of brush you have chosen to use. Figure 6.7 shows some examples of the different strokes that are available from among Illustrator's default calligraphic brushes.

Before using the brush tool you need to set the stroke colour (usually you won't want to use a fill) and select the brush type from the Brushes palette. In the default configuration, shown in Figure 6.8, only the top row contains calligraphic brushes; we will come to the other types shortly. You can access several more designs by using the Window>Brush Libraries>Calligraphic menu command to display an extra palette of calligraphic brushes.* With a brush chosen, you can set tolerance values by double-clicking the brush in the toolbox, and then proceed to draw in the same way as with the pencil. Like pencil lines, brush strokes will be filled as if there was a straight line between their ends, using the current fill colour, if any. You can prevent this by deselecting Fill new brush strokes in the brush tool options. This automatically sets the fill to no colour whenever you use the brush. (There is no equivalent option for the pencil.)

☛   Make some marks with each of the calligraphic brushes, using different colours. When you feel you understand what sort of marks you can make, paint a picture using the brushes.

The weight in the Stroke palette is not used to determine the width of brush strokes (although you can subsequently change their width using it). Each brush has a stroke width as part of its definition. If you want to change it, you must edit the brush or create a new brush. For calligraphic brushes this is easy.

In the Brushes palette menu, select New Brush.... The dialogue shown at the left of Figure 6.9 will be displayed; select the New Calligraphic Brush radio button and click OK to get the dialogue shown on the right of Figure 6.9, in which you can set the characteristics of your brush, starting with its name. The other characteristics are the diameter, angle and roundness. All of these can be set numerically or by direct manipulation: the diameter with a slider, the other two values using the iconic representation in the middle of the dialogue. To adjust the angle, pull the arrowhead round; to change the roundness (the eccentricity of the ellipse, technically speaking) pull one of the black dots in or out. The preview on the right shows the resulting shape of the brush tip. Brush strokes are made to look as if that shape was being pulled across the paper at the specified angle, hence if the shape is a pronounced oval, vertical and horizontal strokes will be different widths, as if you were using a pen with an italic nib.

---

*If you performed a custom installation of Illustrator these libraries may not have been included. You can find them on the Illustrator CD.

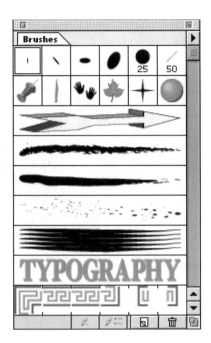

Figure 6.8   *The* Brushes *palette.*

Using the pop-up menus next to the value of each parameter, you can choose to make that parameter respond to pressure when a graphics tablet is used, or you can add random variation, to avoid the mechanical look that tends to result from applying exactly the same brush stroke to different paths.

Creating a good brush that makes the marks you want requires practice. Instead of creating brushes from scratch, it may be easier to modify an existing one. With a brush selected, choose Duplicate Brush from the Brushes palette menu, then double-click the copy to bring up the dialogue for setting its characteristics. The original brush's values will be shown and you can change them to modify just those aspects of the stroke you want to be different. It still pays to experiment extensively.

> ☞ Duplicate one of the standard calligraphic brushes and practise altering each of its characteristics. Draw some lines and curves with your modified brush each time you change a value, until you can see how the parameters affect the marks you make.

Besides calligraphic brushes, Illustrator provides three other types of brush. Scatter brushes place copies of an object along a path, with some randomness. This allows you to make lines of footprints, or to place a cloud of butterflies around a shape. Art brushes are also based on an object, but when you use one of these, the object is stretched out

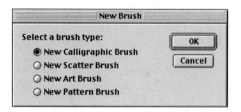

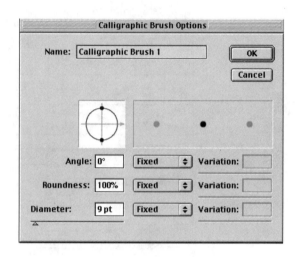

Figure 6.9   *Defining a calligraphic brush.*

along the line you draw. The most successful application of art brushes is in the creation of grasses and similar foliage. Pattern brushes provide a quick way of applying tiled patterns. Figure 6.10 shows some examples of each of these types of brush. Libraries of all types are supplied with Illustrator, although some of the examples are rather juvenile. Creating your own scatter and art brushes is fairly straightforward, as we will describe briefly later. Creating pattern brushes is best left to experts.

Manipulating Objects

One of the things that makes the process of creating artwork in a vector application different from using a bitmapped application is the ease with which objects can be modified after you have drawn them. If you draw a square, it remains an identifiable entity, whose attributes, such as its position, the length of its sides, its stroke and fill, can be changed at any time. It does not become lost as a collection of pixels of a particular colour that just happen to lie along the sides of a square.

Selection

Before you can do anything to an object it must be selected. The solid arrow tool in the top left corner of the toolbox is used for making selections. You will probably need this so often that it is worth using the keyboard shortcut v habitually. In addition, you can switch to the selection tool temporarily by holding down the [cmd/ctl] key.[*] When you

---

[*]As we will see later, there are actually several selection tools. Holding [cmd/ctl] switches to the one you used most recently.

Figure 6.10 *Scatter, art and pattern brushes.*

hold down that key and click away from a shape when you have finished drawing it, as recommended on page 303, you are actually using the selection tool to select nothing, and hence to deselect the shape.

You can select an object by clicking with the arrow tool. By default, clicking anywhere within the object – that is, anywhere on its outline or within its filled area – selects the entire object. Illustrator provides some visual feedback: when the cursor is over an object, a small black square appears next to the arrow to indicate that clicking will make a selection. To select more than one object at a time, you can click to select the first and shift-click to select additional ones. If you shift-click on a selected object, it is deselected. You can also select multiple objects by dragging out a rectangular marquee with the arrow tool. Any object that intersects the marquee is added to the selection.

☛ Draw a circle, an oval, a square, a rectangle, a triangle, a star and a spiral. Practise selecting each shape, any pair of shapes, any three, and so on.

None of this should come as a surprise if you are used to selecting files on the desktop. There is a lasso tool that lets you select several objects by drawing an irregularly shaped marquee round them, but it's usually quicker to shift-click.

You will sometimes want to treat several objects as a single entity, at least temporarily. For instance, if you have nine objects arranged in a 3 by 3 grid, you may want to be able to treat each row as a single object, so you can move all the objects in it at once. You can combine several objects into a *group* by selecting them and using the Object>Group command. After you have done so, the entire group can be selected with a single click. When you wish to select individual objects within a group, you must either break the group apart again, using Object>Ungroup, or use the group select tool, which is found underneath the direct selection tool (the hollow arrow), represented as a hollow arrow with a small + sign attached to it. Clicking on an object within a group with this tool selects it. Clicking again selects the whole group; clicking again selects the group containing the group, if there is one, and so on.

☛   With the objects from the previous exercise, select all the shapes with sharp corners and group them together, and select all the curved shapes and group them together. Practise selecting individual shapes within each group. Break the groups apart and regroup the shapes according to some other criteria.

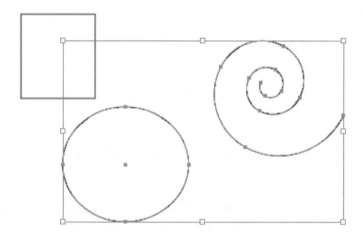

Figure 6.11   *Selected objects.*

Selected objects are highlighted in a colour associated with the layer they are on. A *bounding box* is drawn around any selection, as shown in Figure 6.11, where the ellipse and spiral have been selected. This is the smallest rectangle that can enclose all the selected objects. The highlighted dots that appear on selected objects are their *anchor points.* You can use the direct selection tool to change the shape of curves by moving and

10

→364

otherwise adjusting the anchor points. A description of how this is done, and how it works, can be found in Chapter 9. If an object is selected, pressing the delete key will remove it from the artwork. It can also be cut or copied to the clipboard in the usual way.

Transforming Objects

You can transform selected objects in various ways with the arrow tool, using the handles (the small hollow squares) at the corners and mid-way along each side of the bounding box. The cursor changes shape to indicate what operations the arrow tool will perform at its current position.

When the cursor is anywhere within a selected object it changes to an arrowhead, to indicate that you can move the selected objects by dragging. Note that all the objects within the selection are dragged, not just the one beneath the cursor. For precise positioning, you can use the arrow keys to nudge a selected object left, right, up or down, by a small amount – the distance is set in the Keyboard Increment field of the Edit>Preferences>General dialogue. If you hold down [opt/alt] while dragging, a copy of the selected objects is made and dragged to a new position. A second, hollow, arrowhead appears near the cursor to show you that you can make a copy.

When the cursor is right over any of the handles, it turns into a pair of arrows, indicating that you can stretch or shrink the objects by dragging. If you drag in or out of the middle of any side, the objects shrink or stretch in the direction you drag, with the opposite side of the bounding box staying where it is. The object stays the same size in the direction perpendicular to the drag, so it will end up distorted. If you drag one side right across the object and through the opposite side, the object will be reflected, or flipped, in the appropriate axis. If you drag a corner, you can alter the object's height and width, both at the same time. The opposite corner stays fixed. By holding down shift while you drag a corner you can force the same scaling to be applied to both dimensions, so the object shrinks or grows while retaining its proportions. By holding down [opt/alt] you can scale the object while keeping its centre fixed instead of the opposite corner or edge. This can also be used to flip objects about their centre lines.

If you hold the cursor just outside the bounding box, near one of the handles but not over it, it turns into a small arc with arrowheads at each end. This means that you can rotate the selected objects by dragging the cursor in a circular motion. Whichever handle you use, the rotation is always about the centre of the selection. If the selection contains just a single object, the bounding box will rotate with it. If several objects are selected, the bounding box always remains vertical, so it changes shape in a rather disturbing way when you finish rotating. The objects are still rotated about their common centre. If you hold down shift while you rotate, the rotation is constrained to multiples of 45°.

☞ Draw several objects of any shape. Practise moving them to new positions, scaling, reflecting and rotating them with the arrow tool. Practise transforming objects one at a time and several at a time. Use the shift key to constrain the different transformations.

Illustrator provides an embarrassment of different ways of transforming objects. We have described how the arrow tool can perform movement, scaling and rotation. The *free transform* tool can also be used to perform these transformations and to reflect, shear and distort objects. Additionally, there are special-purpose tools for scaling, rotation, reflection and shearing, which provide additional control over the transformations. The Object>Transform sub-menu provides commands which partially duplicate the functions of the specialized tools. Finally, values can be entered in the Transform palette to apply transformations numerically. This array of different ways of achieving the same results may appear redundant and confusing, but it supports different methods of working, with differing emphasis on hand and eye or numerical precision, which will suit different people and tasks.

The free transform tool provides an extension of the purely visual and manipulative way of working that we have already seen with the arrow tool. In fact, at first sight it seems just to duplicate its functions, other than selection. To use the free transform tool you must first select one or more objects, then pick up the tool from the toolbox. You can then move, scale and rotate the selection more or less the same way as you can with the arrow tool, with a couple of significant differences. The free transform tool will move selected objects if you drag anywhere within the bounding box, not just within one of the selected objects. (The cursor changes shape as it does with the arrow tool, to show you when dragging will move objects.) You can't copy an object by holding down [opt/alt] while you drag with the free transform tool, but you can use the modifier keys to scale about the centre and constrain objects' proportions.

Scaling and reflection are performed by dragging handles, as with the arrow tool. Rotation is also done in a similar way, but with the free transform tool you do not need to be near a handle: dragging anywhere outside the selection causes a rotation. Dragging a long way away from objects gives you precise control over the amount of rotation.

Modifier keys allow you to use the free transform tool to achieve additional transformations. In general, to achieve these extra distortions, you start to drag a handle and then hold down one or more keys on the keyboard. If you hold down [cmd/ctl] and [opt/alt] the object is sheared (or skewed). The second shape in Figure 6.12 shows the horizontal shearing effect produced by dragging the handle in the middle of the top edge of the bounding box; dragging the handles on the vertical edges produce vertical shearing, while dragging the corner handles shears in both axes. Holding [cmd/ctl] while dragging a corner distorts the object by just pulling that corner, as shown in the third example in Figure 6.12. The final example shows what happens if you hold down shift, [cmd/ctl] and [opt/alt] while dragging a corner handle with the free transform tool (a feat requiring a certain amount of dexterity): the object is distorted in perspective, at least in a simple-minded way. The corners are moved symmetrically in opposite directions to approximate classical perspective.

> ☞ Repeat the previous exercise, but use the free transform tool instead of the arrow. Practise using the modifier keys while dragging to perform the additional transformations that this tool permits.

Figure 6.12   *Shearing and distortion.*

The main difference between the free transform tool and the specialized tools for each transform is that the latter allow you to specify the point or axis relative to which the transformation is performed. For example, after choosing the rotation tool, you click anywhere – not necessarily in or on the object – to set the centre of rotation, and then drag the selected objects around this point. Similarly, for the scaling and shearing tools, you click to define the point which stays fixed while the object is transformed. With the reflection tool, you click twice to define a line and the object is reflected in that axis.

> ☞ Practise using the specialized transformation tools. Rotate a square around one of its corners, reflect it in its left edge, scale it while keeping the top left corner fixed, and so on.

These tools also permit a different way of performing transformations. If you double-click a tool in the toolbox, a dialogue box is displayed, in which you can enter values for the corresponding transformation's parameters. For example, Figure 6.13 shows the dialogue for the scaling transformation, which allows you to specify the amount to scale in each direction as a percentage. If you want to scale by the same amount in each direction, you select the Uniform radio button and enter a single factor; to scale by different amounts in the two directions, select Non-Uniform and enter two different percentages. The Scale Strokes & Effects checkbox causes the weight of lines (and other effects that can be applied to objects, as we will see later) to be scaled by the same amount, so that the scaled object retains the same proportion between its area and the width of its outlines. If you uncheck this box, the line weights are left as they are. This will change the appearance of the objects, but is often the more appropriate option. If, for example, you are drawing a diagram, you will usually want all the line weights to be the same, so if you resize a box or an arrow, you should not scale the stroke.

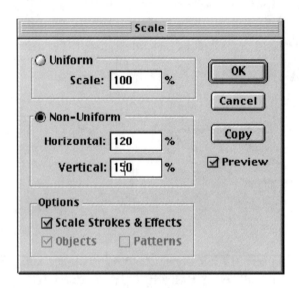

Figure 6.13   *The scaling dialogue.*

Ticking the Preview checkbox causes the transformation to be shown in the document window before the dialogue is dismissed, so that you can see whether the value you have chosen is right. As well as the conventional OK and Cancel buttons, the dialogue can also be dismissed using a third, Copy. This causes a new copy of the selected object to be created and scaled, instead of applying the scaling to the selection.

Double-clicking the other tools which perform a single transformation brings up similar dialogue boxes. These dialogues can be accessed from the Object>Transform sub-menu, too, which also includes a useful Transform Again command, which can be used to repeat the most recent transformation (no matter how it was applied). Transformations specified in dialogues are always applied to the current selection.

> ☛ Draw a freehand shape with the pencil tool and practise scaling it numerically. Try uniform and non-uniform scaling, with and without scaling the stroke weight. Make similar experiments with the other transformation tools.

If you like to use numerical values for transformations, but you don't care for modal dialogue boxes, you can use the Transform palette, shown in Figure 6.14. You can enter values in the X and Y fields to position the selected object at a specific point, and into the W and H fields to set its width and height. The units that appear in the fields originally are those you set as the default in the Edit>Preferences>Units & Undo dialogue, but you can use any units you like, including % to scale by a percentage. To be more precise about the effect of entering values in the Transform palette, you can set these properties of the bounding box of the selection. This can be slightly confusing if you have also rotated the selection: when you do so, the bounding box used to highlight the selection rotates with it. The height and width in the Transform palette, though, are always vertically oriented, that is, they measure the distance between the vertical and horizontal extremities of the object, whatever its orientation. To make these values reflect the box you see, use the Object>Transform>Reset Bounding Box command, which will orient the bounding box vertically, adjusting its size accordingly. (See Figure 6.15.)

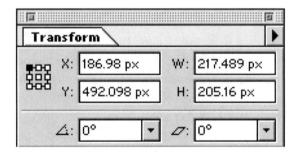

Figure 6.14   *The* Transform *palette.*

The Transform palette can also be used to apply rotation and shearing by entering angles in the boxes at the bottom of the palette. The pop-up menus next to these boxes let you select from a range of common angles.

Any transformation set in the palette can be applied relative to any of the corner points of the object (that is, of its bounding box), its centre, or the mid-point of any of its sides.

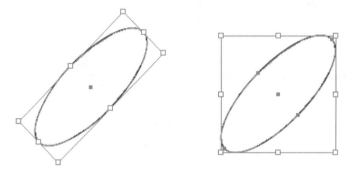

Figure 6.15   *Resetting the bounding box of a rotated object.*

You choose which by clicking on one of the small squares in the grid to the left of the X and Y fields. In Figure 6.14, the coordinates of the top left corner are being set. Any changes to width and height would leave that corner where it was, and it would be used as the centre of any rotation that was applied. The chosen point does not affect any transformations applied with other tools: rotation with the free transform tool is still about the centre, for example.

> ☛ Draw a shape, select it, and experiment with entering values in the fields of the Transform palette.

Reshaping

The transformations described so far only change the shape of objects in a few formally defined ways – ways that can be easily described as mathematical operations on the vectors used to represent objects. Less organized changes in shape can be achieved by moving, adding or deleting the anchor points of the lines and curves making up the objects. This can be done using the direct selection and pen tools, as described in Chapter 9, or it can be done indirectly using the pencil and smoothing tools.

We described earlier how you can draw an apparently freehand curve with the pencil tool, which Illustrator automatically approximates by Bézier curves. In a similar way, you can apparently reshape a curve by drawing over it with the pencil and Illustrator will automatically approximate your changes by moving, adding and deleting anchor points.

The procedure for reshaping is simple. Select an object (which may just be an open path) and then pick up the pencil tool. Move the cursor over the selected path or the outline of the selected object. When it gets close, the small x near the pencil cursor disappears. This signifies that if you now drag, instead of a new line being drawn, the existing line will be reshaped to follow the track of the pencil. You can start anywhere on an existing line, but you must finish on or near the same line in order to reshape it.

Using the pencil for reshaping is not restricted to lines and shapes that were originally pencil-drawn. Any path can be reshaped in this way. You can, for instance, take a square drawn with the rectangle tool and give it wavy edges by selecting it and then dragging the pencil tool around it with an undulating motion.

> ☛ Draw any geometrical shape and practise reshaping with the pencil tool by making its edges wavy in the manner just described. Continue reshaping until you end up with something that approximates a circle.

The smoothing tool, which is normally hidden underneath the pencil in the toolbox, does what its name implies, smoothing out irregularities in a curve. It does this by removing anchor points. Like the pencil tool, it provides a more intuitive interface to operations that can also be performed directly on the anchor points using the pen tool. All you need to do with the smoothing tool is drag it over a segment of a selected curve, which will be smoothed out. The fidelity and smoothness can be set in a dialogue displayed by double-clicking the smoother in the toolbox. In the case of lines drawn with the pencil, the smoothing tool effectively gives you a second chance to determine how closely Illustrator's curves should approximate the track you followed when drawing. The best way to understand what it does is by experiment.

> ☛ Scribble a line with the pencil tool, using low values for the tolerance and smoothness, and then smooth it out with the smoothing tool.

A more drastic way of changing shapes is by removing parts of them. The scissors tool is used to split a path. Its operation is most obvious when you apply it to open, unfilled paths. After selecting the tool, when you click anywhere on a path, it is split into two, which can be selected separately. Clicking again with the scissors splits it into more pieces.

Using the scissors tool on the outline of a filled shape is possible, but it produces results that can be rather confusing. When you cut a closed path, it breaks into open paths, and the fill is then applied to the shape produced by connecting the end points with straight lines. A much more intuitive result is obtained by using the knife tool, which is on the concealed sub-menu initially beneath the scissors. With this tool you can draw a freehand line, as with the pencil, and any shapes it intersects are cut into separate pieces on each side of the line. It is as if the tool were a craft knife or scalpel cutting through cardboard shapes. Holding down [opt/alt] while you drag the knife forces it to cut in a straight line, as if you were holding it against a straight edge. If any objects are selected, the knife cuts only them; if there is no selection, it cuts everything it intersects.

☛ Draw some filled shapes and some open paths, and practise cutting them with the scissors and knife tools.

Appearance

You may well want to change objects after you have first drawn them in other ways besides altering their geometry. You might, for instance, want to change their stroke and fill. This can be done by selecting the object and then changing values in the Stroke and Color palettes. When changing colours, you must first indicate whether you are changing the stroke or fill by clicking on the corresponding swatch at the bottom of the toolbox or in the Color palette, just as you would if you were setting the values before drawing a shape.

There is an analogy here with a way of working that will be familiar to you if you use a word processor. You can apply different styles, such as italicization or underlining, to words in a document. Whenever you have some words selected, choosing a style from the toolbar or a menu causes it to be applied to the selected words. If nothing is selected, choosing a style causes anything you type subsequently to be displayed in that style. Similarly in Illustrator, if you have selected some objects, any settings you choose for stroke and fill will be applied to the selected objects. If nothing is selected, the values will be used for the next object you draw.

☛ Draw any simple shape, select it and practise changing its stroke colour and weight and its fill colour.

Complex Fills and Strokes

We have said that you can change the fill and stroke of objects, but we have not described all the different sorts of fill and stroke that Illustrator provides.

The flat areas of solid colour that result from choosing a single colour to apply as a fill are only suitable for certain styles of illustration. More realistic and subtle effects rely on continuous tonal variation. While vector drawings cannot easily achieve the tonal subtlety of scanned photographs and other bitmapped images, the use of *gradient fills* extends their expressive range considerably, at least into the realm of airbrushed painting. Gradient fills are often more effective when they are applied to objects whose stroke has no colour.

You can create and apply gradient fills using the Gradient palette. Its initial appearance is shown at the left of Figure 6.16. Clicking on the swatch at the top left activates it, applying a gradient fill to any selected objects. To begin with, the palette shows a default gradient, which varies uniformly from white to black. You can change many aspects of the gradient. Selecting Radial from the Type pop-up menu makes the gradient blend outwards from the centre of the filled object, instead of linearly from left to right. The two stars at the top of Figure 6.17 show uniform linear and radial gradient fills applied to an object.

> ☛ Draw several different shapes, both with the shape tools and using the pen or pencil. Apply linear and radial gradients to each of them.

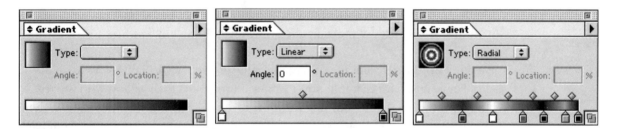

Figure 6.16   *The* Gradient *Palette.*

Gradients do not have to fade between black and white. By clicking the square below the marker at the left end of the bar you can select a colour for the start of the gradient, using the Color palette, in the usual way. (You may have to choose RGB from the Color palette menu to get access to colours other than greys.) Similarly, by clicking the square under the marker at the right you can set the ending colour for the gradient. You could possibly create a primitive sunset effect by setting the starting colour to red and the ending colour to yellow. Any object filled with this gradient would show a continuous blend of colours from red through a range of oranges to yellow. This wouldn't be too impressive if you applied it to a rectangle that was supposed to represent the sky, because the gradient would run from left to right, instead of from top to bottom. The field labelled Angle in the Gradient palette can be used to make the gradient run in a different direction. Setting it to -90° would make the colours blend from yellow at the

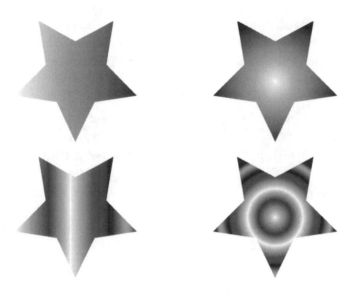

Figure 6.17   *Gradient fills.*

bottom to red at the top. A value of -75° produces a less obviously artificial result. (The Angle field is disabled for radial gradients, where it doesn't make sense.)

You don't necessarily want the mid-point of the gradient to lie halfway between the ends. For a sunset, for example, you might want more red than yellow, with the red fading up to the orange colour in the middle of the colour range quite slowly and then rapidly turning yellow. Dragging the diamond-shaped marker above the gradient bar moves the mid-point to achieve such effects. You can also drag the end markers below the bar if you want to have bands of solid colour at each end of the gradient. You can exert still more control by adding extra colours. Clicking underneath the gradient bar causes another marker like the end markers to appear. A new mid-point diamond also appears between the new marker and its neighbour. You can set a colour for any such marker you add, so you could create bands of different reds, oranges and yellows for a spectacular sunset effect. The lower pair of stars in Figure 6.17 shows linear and radial fills with several intermediate colours applied to an object. The settings used in the Gradient palette are shown on the right in Figure 6.16.

☛ Practise creating and applying gradient fills. Begin by changing the colours at each end of the gradient, then try moving the mid-point. Next, add extra colours and adjust the positions of all the markers. Try both linear and radial gradients.

The most elaborate and the most natural-looking gradients are produced using Illustrator's gradient mesh tool. When you click inside an object with this tool, a mesh is created, which divides it into four segments, with curves that meet at the point where you clicked. If you select one of the anchor points on this mesh, again by clicking with the gradient mesh tool, you can set a colour in the usual way. A two-dimensional blend of colours is produced around the point. You can set the colours of as many points as you like in this way. If you click within one of the sub-regions of the mesh with the tool, it is sub-divided into its own mesh, and you can then set colours at the points of the sub-mesh. You can reshape the mesh at any time by moving its anchor points and their direction lines. (You use the gradient mesh tool like the direct selection tool for this purpose, as described in Chapter 9.) It is much easier to appreciate the gradient mesh tool by experimenting with it than by reading about it. The drawing on the left of Figure 6.18 shows an example of the gradient mesh tool in action; the mesh is shown on the right.

☛ Draw a large, simple shape, such as an ellipse. Practise using the gradient mesh tool to add a complex fill to it. (You may want to set the stroke to nothing.) Experiment with reshaping the mesh and adding extra mesh points. When you think you can see what the tool is doing, try to use it deliberately to fill your shape with a specific gradient that you have imagined.

Figure 6.18   *Use of gradient meshes.*

We have seen that strokes can be made with calligraphic brushes. Brush strokes can also be applied to existing objects. By now, you can probably guess how to do so: you select an object and then click a brush in the Brushes palette. Thus, you can easily draw one of the geometrical shapes, such as a circle, and stroke it with a calligraphic or an art brush to make it appear to be drawn with ink or some other natural medium. You don't just have to draw by hand with brush strokes. As we remarked earlier, the stroke weight of brushes is part of their definition, but once you have applied a stroke you can alter its weight using the Stroke palette. The value in the palette will still not be the actual width of the stroke, but it will be proportional to it. Figure 6.19 shows a square that has been stroked with an art brush (Splash, which has an air of watercolour about it). The version on the left uses the weight as it comes, which is treated as a default 1pt stroke; that on the right has had its weight reduced to 0.5pt. You can also apply colour to a brush stroke in the usual way.

☞   Draw a regular polygon and practise applying different brush strokes to it. Vary the weight and colour of the applied stroke.

Figure 6.19   *Applying brush strokes to a shape.*

Remember that, if after you have applied some special strokes and fills you want to revert to the default of a black 1pt stroke and a plain white fill, you can just click the small black and white squares to the left of the stroke and fill swatches at the bottom of the toolbox.

The mechanics of creating your own art and scatter brushes is simple: create an object, select it and then choose New Brush... from the Brushes palette menu. You can then set some parameters, which are fairly self-explanatory. Making useful brushes is much harder. Not all artwork can be successfully stretched along a path as an art brush stroke. While you can scatter any shape about a path, there may not be all that many occasions when you wish to do so. To make the brush designer's job harder, there are considerable restrictions on what features of Illustrator may be used in the object that is to be the basis of the brush. In particular, gradients are not allowed, so you cannot apply a gradient to a stroke simply by making the gradient into a brush.

What you can do is convert strokes into filled shapes. With an object selected, choose Object>Expand..., and accept the defaults in the dialogue box that is displayed. The single object will be replaced by a group, consisting of two objects: the original fill and the original stroke. Neither of these is stroked, each has its fill set to its original colour. If you ungroup them, you can separate them, and apply a fill, such as a gradient, to the original stroke. Figure 6.20 shows an example. A rectangle with a relatively wide stroke was expanded and ungrouped. The former stroke, now a filled object the shape of an empty picture frame, was filled with a linear gradient, and the fill was dragged away from it.

☛ Draw a polygon, using a wide stroke and a coloured fill. Expand the object, and separate the fill and stroke. Select each of these and apply a new stroke to them. Repeat the expansion on these new shapes.

Figure 6.20   *An expanded object.*

Effects, Filters and Styles

Vector graphics lend themselves to a style of working in which simple outlines are created and then decorated with stroke and fill, transformed and reshaped to produce a final drawing. In Illustrator, this approach can be taken a step further, by applying various effects to selected objects. Very broadly speaking, there are two classes of effect that can be applied. First, there are shape distortions brought about by a systematic or random adjustment of anchor points. Second, there are 'artistic' effects, which, like brush strokes alter the appearance of objects so that they look more like marks made with natural media. Figure 6.21 shows some examples of both kinds of effects applied to a simple hexagon.

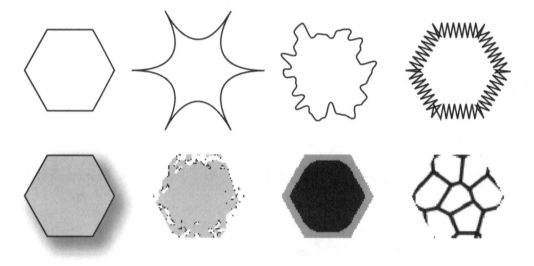

Figure 6.21   *Effects applied to a simple shape.*

In Illustrator 9, these effects appear in two different places: under the Filter menu and on the Effect menu. There are important differences between the two. Filters permanently change an object. Effects are stored with the object as instructions, which are obeyed when the object is displayed, but the object itself remains the same, so effects can be removed, or have their parameters reset, at any time. This is sometimes expressed by saying that effects change appearance but not structure. There is a way of demonstrating the difference dramatically. The View>Outline and View>Preview commands allow you to switch between displaying the outlines of the shapes in your artwork and displaying it as it would appear when printed. If the first variation in Figure 6.21 had been produced by applying a filter (Filter>Distort>Punk & Bloat...), in outline mode the object would have the same bloated shape as it does in preview mode, and in the illustration. If it had been produced by applying an effect (Effect>Distort Transform>Punk & Bloat...), in outline mode the object would be shown as a regular hexagon, just like the original shape. The effect is a property of the shape, like its stroke and fill.

Furthermore, some filters – mostly the 'artistic' ones – can only be applied to an object after it has been rasterized, that is, converted to a bitmap. (Use the command Object>Rasterize....) Once that has been done, the object can no longer be freely edited in the way we have been describing. It becomes frozen as a pattern of pixels. With effects, this does not happen. The rasterization is deferred until the object is displayed. Internally, it remains a vector object and it can still be edited.

In short, effects are superior to filters, which we will describe no further beyond pointing out that they are an older mechanism. Effects were introduced in Illustrator 9.

☞ Draw an ellipse and make a copy of it. Apply the punk and bloat filter to one of the ellipses and the punk and bloat effect to the other. Switch to outline view to see the difference between the two. Practise applying effects to simple shapes. Try all the available effects and experiment with their parameters.

The 'lazy evaluation' mechanism, which allows objects to remain editable after effects have been applied to them, has been extended to transformations as well. The command Effect>Distort & Transform>Transfom... brings up the dialogue box shown in Figure 6.22, which allows you to apply movement, scaling and rotation to an object. You can even create several copies. Nevertheless, the object itself is not affected. For instance, if you apply a movement as a transform effect, the object won't move at all, as you can verify using the Info palette. It will just appear to be somewhere else.

☞ Draw a shape and use the Transform effect to create half a dozen copies of it, each displaced by a small distance.

One specialized effect that you will need if you are using Illustrator to draw technical diagrams is that produced by Effect>Stylize>Add Arrowheads.... Normally, you would apply this effect to lines and curves, to turn them into arrows, such as you might find connecting states in a transition diagram. The dialogue box for adding arrowheads is shown on the left of Figure 6.23. You can apply arrowheads to either or both of the start and end of a path. Using the arrows below the two preview panes, you can cycle through 27 different styles. Not all of these are what you would immediately think of as arrowheads; some are arrow tails, while others, such as the pointing hands and Mary

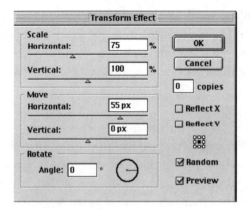

Figure 6.22   *Applying a transform effect.*

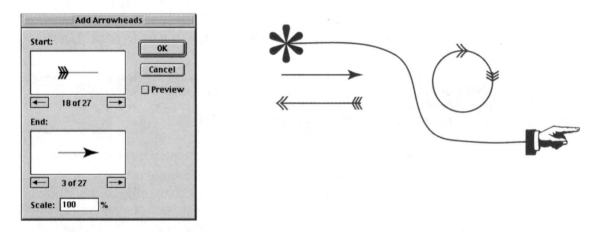

Figure 6.23   *Adding arrowheads.*

Quant-style flowers, stretch the notion of arrowhead to its limit. Some examples are shown on the right of Figure 6.23. The size of arrowheads is proportional to the stroke weight of the line you add them to. This usually works well, but you can vary the size using the Scale field of the dialogue. (We did this with the flower and hand in Figure 6.23.)

There is one aspect of arrowheads which is less than ideal. When you add them, they are placed so that the centre of the object which represents the arrowhead is at the end point of the line you are adding it to. This means that the arrowhead projects beyond the end of the line, which makes it extremely difficult to position arrows so that, for instance, they just touch the edge of a circle. It is often necessary to adjust the position afterwards. An arrow and its head and tail are automatically grouped. You have to ungroup them in order to move the arrowhead along the arrow shaft if you need to do so.

☛ Draw two circles and a line connecting them. Practise adding different sorts of arrowhead to each end of the connecting line. Try to position them so that each arrowhead just touches the outside of the circle it is next to.

Although you can set an object's fill or stroke to none, so that objects below it show through, until the release of version 9 it was impossible in Illustrator to make objects partially transparent. This long-standing deficiency has now been remedied and you can apply transparency to any object, simply by setting a value for its opacity, ranging from 0% (totally transparent) to 100% (totally opaque) in the Transparency palette. You can also choose between sixteen different methods of combining the colour of a transparent object with its background. Unless you intend to become an Illustrator expert,[*] we advise you to stick with Normal, which corresponds to the way we expect partially transparent objects to behave.

Applying strokes, fills, effects and transparency to an object all modify the way it is displayed, without permanently affecting its shape. These aspects of appearance, which you can modify in a non-destructive manner, are collectively referred to as *appearance attributes*. The Appearance palette (another version 9 innovation) allows you to view and manipulate all of an object's appearance attributes.

Figure 6.24 shows the palette as it appears when the object shown to its left is selected. The object is actually a regular hexagon again and the Appearance palette shows how it has been transfigured. By double-clicking any of the attributes displayed in the palette, you can alter any parameters it may have, so if, for instance, you wished to increase the amount of punk and bloat distortion you could do so by double-clicking the first attribute, which would bring up the effect's dialogue box.

The Appearance palette lets you alter attributes in some ways that are not otherwise possible. In particular, you may have noticed that in Figure 6.24 the object has two strokes applied to it. Any number of strokes may be applied using the Add New Stroke command from the palette menu. Each successive one is laid over the existing ones. (One application for which this is more than merely diverting is drawing maps. You can make a symbol for a road by overlaying a thin white stroke on a thicker black one.) Less usefully you can also add multiple fills to an object.

---

[*]Or you are already a Photoshop expert who understands layer blending modes.

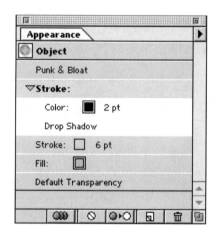

Figure 6.24   *Appearance attributes.*

> ☞ Using the pencil or pen tool, sketch a map of the roads in your vicinity. Use the Appearance palette to apply a double stroke to each road. Try using different strokes to represent major and minor roads. Use the same approach to add other features, each with its own distinctive style, to your map.

Notice also that the drop shadow effect is shown in a sub-list under the 2pt stroke. This is because it is only applied to that stroke, as you can see by looking at the artwork. You apply effects selectively like this by selecting a stroke in the Appearance palette and then applying the effect in the usual way by choosing it from the Effect menu and setting its parameters. You can also drag effects around in the palette to reorder them (the order in which effects are applied usually alters the result) or to apply them to the entire object instead of a stroke, or vice versa.

You can delete an appearance attribute by selecting it in the Appearance palette and clicking on the trash can icon at the bottom. The other buttons along the bottom of the palette provide other functions on attributes. The leftmost, if selected, prevents any subsequently drawn shapes acquiring the appearance displayed in the palette. By default, they do so, in the same way as they inherit the current fill and stroke. The next two buttons allow you to return an object to a state of nature: the first clears all appearance attributes, leaving the object unfilled and unstroked (presumably you would then go on to give it some new attributes); the second reduces it to a basic appearance, comprising just a single fill and stroke. The remaining button, despite looking like the standard New button, allows you to duplicate an attribute. Normally, you would then change some parameters of the duplicate.

Appearance attributes can be copied from one object to another. The established way of doing so is to select an object, choose the eyedropper from the toolbox and click on any other object. Its appearance attributes will be transferred to the selection. The Appearance palette offers an alternative. Using this method, you select the object whose appearance attributes you wish to copy. If you drag its thumbnail, which appears in the top left corner of the palette, onto any other object, the appearance is applied to it. This way, you transfer appearance attributes from a selected object to unselected ones; with the eyedropper you transfer them to a selected object from an unselected one.

The more enlightened word processors allow you to define *styles*, which are named collections of text attributes, such as font, size, colour and justification. You define styles to capture a pattern of formatting which you may want to apply to several elements in a document that should all be identically formatted, such as all top-level section headings. In a similar way, Illustrator allows you to name a collection of appearance attributes and save it as a style.

The quickest way to create a style is by drawing an object and applying the individual strokes, fills and effects you want to it. Then select the object and choose New Style... from the Styles palette menu. A dialogue box asks you to name the new style, which is then added to the Styles palette. You can apply the style by selecting one or more objects and then clicking on the swatch representing your chosen style. The set of appearance attributes that make up the style is then applied to the selection.

☞ Draw a simple shape and experiment with applying a combination of effects to it. When you arrive at something you like, save it as a style. Draw some more objects and apply your style to them.

Several libraries of styles are supplied with Illustrator. You can access them from the Window>Style Libraries sub-menu. Using library styles carries the risk of predictability, which may or may not matter. The denim style, for instance, is an example of a clever piece of design that could easily be over-used.

10
→367

☞ Load the style libraries and practise applying library styles to your drawings.

Drawing Aids

Even with all the effects and elaborate strokes and fills that Illustrator supplies, vector drawing remains an essentially algorithmic process that, almost inevitably, produces artwork with a somewhat mechanical character. This can be a strength. It is admirably suited for technical illustration work and for designing layouts for Web pages, which you can subsequently use to guide the placement of page elements in a Web design application such as Dreamweaver. (See page 414.) For such applications and for graphic design work in which you want to bring out the mechanical character of the artwork instead of disguising it, Illustrator supplies tools for laying out objects systematically and precisely.

It should be emphasized that Illustrator is not a computer-aided design (CAD) tool, and although it can be used to produce high quality technical illustrations, it is not intended to be used for the production of blueprints or architectural drawings. There are, however, plug-ins that add some of the features of CAD tools, such as dimensioning and standard architects' symbols.

Grids, Guides and Alignment

The use of squared paper to lay out diagrams is common practice. Illustrator simulates it by providing a *grid*, which can be displayed as a mesh of fine vertical and horizontal lines. You can control the spacing of the grid lines and the colour in which they are displayed in the Edit>Preferences>Guides & Grid... dialogue. You can also choose whether the grid is displayed behind the artwork, so that objects hide it, or in front of it, so you can see all of it at all times. Illustrator's grid is an improvement over actual squared paper because it is separate from the artwork and doesn't print or appear when you save the drawing to a file for display. You can show or hide the grid at will. (The View>Show Grid command shows the grid and causes the menu entry to change to View>Hide Grid, which hides it. The keyboard shortcut [cmd/ctl] " also toggles the grid's visibility.) You can also force objects to 'snap' to the grid, that is move so that their bounding boxes' corners always lie on grid points. Snapping to the grid also applies to tools: for instance, when it is on, you can only set the centre of rotation with the rotate tool on a grid point, or create a rectangle whose corners fall on grid points. The View>Snap To Grid command toggles snapping on and off. Snapping still works when the grid is not visible.

☛ Show the grid. Change its spacing in the preferences dialogue. Turn on snapping and draw some shapes, noting how they move to conform to the grid.

On some occasions it may be easiest to design a layout by working out the sizes and positions of objects arithmetically and placing them at exact coordinates. There are many ways to do this – entering coordinates in the Transform palette (see page 321) is the most precise. A more direct way is to treat the grid as if it were graph paper. The View>Show Rulers command causes a pair of axes to be displayed along the top and left edges of the main window. You can set the origin by dragging the point in the top left corner where the rulers intersect to the position you want to serve as (0, 0).

> ☞ Turn the rulers on and move the origin to each of the four corners of the artboard in turn. Show the grid and see how it aligns to the origin.

Reading off distances from the rulers, even with the aid of a grid, calls for a clear head and a steady eye. *Guides* can make the task much easier. If you move the cursor over the ruler at the left edge, press the mouse button and drag on to the artwork, a thin vertical blue line will be pulled across the window. You can position this guide at a specific horizontal coordinate by reading off the distance on the ruler at the top or you can line it up with some object. When you let go, the guide remains in place and can be used to align objects. You can drag a horizontal guide off the ruler at the top of the window. It is usually easier to see guides if you turn the grid off.

The View>Guides sub-menu provides control over guides' behaviour. The Show command (which toggles to Hide) makes them visible. Lock Guides, which is set by default, prevents you from moving or deleting a guide once you have positioned it. If you unlock your guides they can be selected like any ordinary object, which is often undesirable. In particular, if you drag out a selection marquee round some objects you will inevitably pick up any guides in the area. (You can't apply appearance attributes to guides, but you can delete, move and rotate them – deliberately or otherwise.) Clear Guides removes all guides, even if they are locked. By default, objects and tools snap to a guide when they come within two pixels of it.

> ☞ Draw a square. Position guides along each of its four sides and use them to help you draw eight more squares lined up with the sides of the first one.

The simple guides we have described are sometimes called *ruler guides* to distinguish them from other types of guide that Illustrator supports. Any object can be turned into a guide of arbitrary shape by selecting it and choosing Make Guides from the View>Guides sub-menu. If, for instance you wanted to position three objects at equal distances apart, you could draw an equilateral triangle with the polygon tool, convert it to a guide and use it to position the objects. Being a guide, the triangle would not appear on the final drawing.

> ☞ Draw a star and convert it to a guide. Use it to position smaller stars at equal distances around the circumference of a circle.

The most sophisticated guides are *smart guides*, which are a tremendous aid to drawing, although you might not think so at first, as they take a bit of getting used to. If you select View>Smart Guides, you will find that as you draw, thin blue lines with cryptic annotations start popping up all over the place. These are the smart guides and they are telling you where the cursor is in relation to objects in your drawing. For example, the screenshot on the left of Figure 6.25 shows that the cursor is on the vertical line running through the centre of the ellipse. If you diverge from the vertical, the guide disappears, so if you wanted to create another ellipse whose centre was directly above that of the ellipse, you would just have to follow the guide. The screenshot on the right of Figure 6.25 shows a more complicated example. Here the cursor is at the point where the horizontal line through the bottom of the ellipse intersects with the diagonal running through its centre.

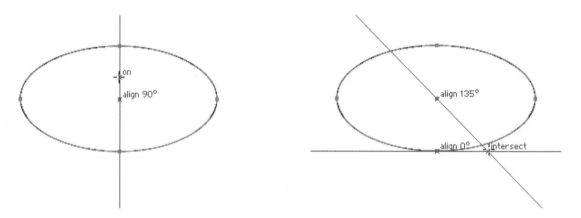

Figure 6.25   *Smart guides.*

You can specify which angles smart guides appear at, and other aspects of their display, including the distance at which objects snap to them, using the Edit>Preferences>Smart Guides... dialogue (Figure 6.26). With all the checkboxes selected, little text annotations appear to tell you when you are on a guide or a path, or at an anchor point or the centre of an object, or at the intersection of a guide and a path or two guides. It is important to note that smart guides do not work if View>Snap To Grid is selected.

Illustrator applies its own logic to determine when to show a smart guide. Potentially, every object has a collection of smart guides radiating from its centre and all its anchor points. They don't necessarily appear whenever the cursor is over one. Only those associated with objects that Illustrator considers relevant do so. Sometimes it is

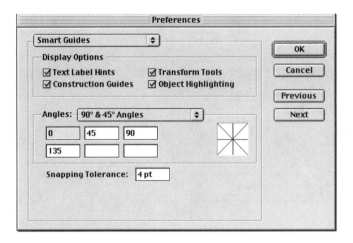

Figure 6.26   *The smart guides preferences dialogue.*

necessary to pass the cursor over an anchor point to force the smart guides you need to appear.

> ☛ Turn on smart guides and make sure that the preferences are set as shown in Figure 6.26. Draw a shape, select any drawing tool, and watch how the smart guides behave as you move the cursor around the window. Using the smart guides to determine the correct angles, draw eight other shapes lined up at the compass points relative to the centre of the first shape.

Grids and guides provide a general mechanism for systematic layout. For the specific task of lining objects up with each other in rows and columns, the Align palette, shown in Figure 6.27, can be used. The general procedure is to select several objects and then click on one of the buttons in the palette. Their icons provide a good indication of what each buttons does. The aligning buttons on the top row, headed Align Objects, are particularly obvious: if you click on the first, objects are moved so that their left edges line up, if on the second, their centres are aligned vertically, and so on. You will often find it is necessary to group objects to place them in formation by alignment.

When you align on the left edge, all the objects move to line up with the leftmost one in the selection, and so on for the other edges. When you align centres, the final centre position seems to be computed as the average of all the centres. In general, this is neither the centre of the bounding box of the selection nor the centre of any individual object.

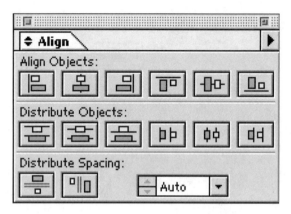

Figure 6.27   *The* Align *palette.*

The buttons on the second row, headed Distribute Objects, move objects so that they are equidistant from each other. The first button, for example, causes selected objects to move so that the vertical distance from the top of one to the top of the next is the same for all of them. The other buttons let you space their centres and bottoms vertically, or the left and right edges and centres horizontally. If the objects are different sizes, this may not produce a pleasing arrangement. They may look better if the space between each object and its neighbour is the same. This arrangement is achieved using the bottom pair of buttons, labelled Distribute Spacing. These are not visible by default, use the Show Options command in the palette menu to reveal them.

> ☞   Draw nine circles and use the Align palette to arrange them in a regular 3 by 3 grid, like a noughts and crosses square. How would you place one object at the exact centre of another?

Layers

The use of layers to organize your artwork is less compelling in Illustrator than in most of the other tools we describe in this book, because objects are already distinct entities, which can be selected independently, locked, hidden, or combined into groups. There is a natural stacking order to objects – ones you draw later are on top of ones you drew earlier – and you can bring objects to the front or send them to the back using the Object>Arrange sub-menu. Layers add an extra level of convenience, though, and they provide a familiar way of working. Illustrator 9 adds some new twists to the layer paradigm, which have made them more worthwhile than they were in earlier versions.

To begin with, layers contain sub-layers, one for each object or group on the layer. Sub-layers containing groups contain their own sub-layers, and do on. Disclosure triangles are used in the Layers palette, shown in Figure 6.28, to expand and collapse layers. The buttons down the right of the palette allow you to *target* a layer or sub-layer, which has the effect of selecting all the objects on the layer or sub-layer. This not only helps you find your way around crowded drawings, it enables you to apply effects to entire layers. This doesn't just mean applying them to all the objects presently on the layer (though it does that). It means that the effect will be applied to the layer from then on – any object you subsequently draw on that layer will immediately acquire any effects that have been applied to the layer. This works for other appearance attributes, too, so you can, in effect, set a default fill and stroke for each layer.

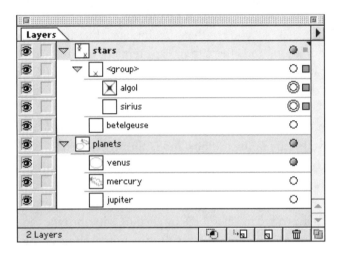

Figure 6.28   *The* Layers *palette.*

Note the difference between targeting a layer with its button, so you can apply appearance attributes to it, and selecting it, by clicking its name, so that you can draw on it. You can select a sub-layer corresponding to a group, and anything you draw will be added to the group.

You can drag objects from one layer to another, by selecting them and then dragging the small filled square at the extreme right of the Layer palette up or down to a new layer. When you do so, any appearance attributes attached to its original layer are lost and those attached to the new one are applied instead. You can drag entire layers to new positions in the palette to change their stacking order, in the conventional way, as described in Chapter 9. You can also drag a layer into another layer, where it appears as a sub-layer (although any objects it contains are not automatically grouped) and acquires any appearance attributes attached to the layer that now contains it.

☛ Create a document, and add two extra layers to it. For each of the three layers, use the Appearance palette to set a different fill and stroke. Draw several shapes on each layer. Select a shape and then change its fill and stroke by moving it to a different layer.

Type

The characters in outline fonts (PostScript Type 1, TrueType and OpenType fonts) are little vector drawings, so it is not surprising that vector graphics programs are good at manipulating text set using such fonts. That is not to say that Illustrator makes a good page layout program, but it does make it easy to incorporate type as a graphical element in designs. Having done so, you can then manipulate it like any other object, and apply colours, transformations and effects to it. Type remains editable, so you can change or correct the text at any time. Illustrator even incorporates a spelling checker (which is about as much use as any other) and a find and replace command.

T

Six different type tools are provided (see Figure 6.1 on page 303), but the most basic, which normally appears in the toolbox and is simply referred to as *the* type tool, automatically changes into one of the other type tools in an appropriate context. You can use it exclusively for most type creation tasks, the specialist tools are only needed in somewhat esoteric situations which we will not consider. You can create a line of text or a text frame as described in Chapter 9, by clicking with the type tool at a point where you want to the text to begin, or dragging out the frame, and starting to type. Typographical properties are controlled by the Character palette, and paragraph indentation and alignment can be specified in the Paragraph palette, both of which behave in the standard fashion described in Chapter 9.

You can also use the type tool to fill absolutely any shape with text. Before you can do this you must create a shape to fill. Click on the outline of your chosen shape with the type tool. (The cursor changes shape when you hold the type tool over an outline to let you know that the tool will create type in the shape.) Any stroke and fill that you had applied to the shape are removed, and a text cursor appears at the top of the shape. You can then begin to type. Your text is automatically wrapped to fit within the shape.

Figure 6.29 shows two quotations from Pascal, the first created as a single text line with the basic text tool, the second filling a triangle. (If you need to stroke a shape which you have used as a container for text, as we did here, you can select just the shape with the direct selection tool. The ordinary selection tool selects the type as well.) Both of these text areas can be manipulated like any other object, but they behave differently. On the right of Figure 6.29, both of the examples have been rotated 180° by dragging their bounding boxes. The text line has turned upside down, but the text within the triangle has stayed the same way up, and adjusted itself to the new orientation of its container. (Text in a rectangle dragged out by the text tool behaves like text in any other shape in this respect.) Similarly, if you drag out the bounding box of a line of text, the text will stretch, but if you stretch a shape enclosing text, it will reflow while staying the same size. On the other hand, if you use any of the specialized transformation tools or menu commands, any text will be transformed along with its container, unless you use the direct selection tool to select only the container. You can tell whether you have selected the text too, because if you have, the baselines will be shown in the highlight colour.

> ☛ Draw some shapes and closed paths and fill each one with some text. (You might want to cut and paste.) Apply some transformations to the shapes and see what happens to the text. Practise selecting text and container independently with the direct selection tool.

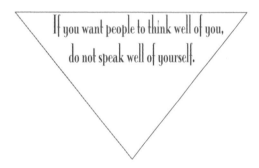

Figure 6.29   *Transforming type.*

The final trick you can play on text in Illustrator is to set it along a path, as shown in Figure 6.30 (Pascal again). Using the type tool, text can only be set along an open path; if you want to run it round a closed path, as we have done here, you must use the scissors tool to split the path at an anchor point, or use the path type tool. When you place the cursor over an open path with the type tool selected, it changes shape to indicate that you can set type on the path (a wiggly line appears through the standard I-beam text cursor). You click to set the starting point and type.

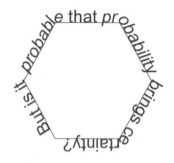
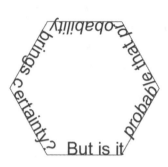

Figure 6.30 *Text on a path.*

You can manipulate text on a path using the direct selection tool. If you select a path with type on it, an I-beam cursor appears in the text. If you position the direct selection tool exactly over this I-beam you can move the text along the path by dragging. (Any text that falls off the end – remember the path is open – disappears.) If you drag the I-beam across the path, or double-click it, the text will flip over to the other side, changing its orientation as it does so, as in the example on the right of Figure 6.30. If you select the path with the direct selection tool you can scale it and the type will flow around the new path. (We had to do this after flipping the text in Figure 6.30, since the inside of the path cannot accommodate as many characters as the outside.) Text will also follow the new shape of the path if you adjust its anchor points with the direct selection tool. As with shapes that you use to enclose text, a path that you set text along normally has its stroke removed. You can select the path with the direct selection tool and restore it, as we have done here to show you how the text follows the path.

> ☛ Create an open path by scribbling with the pencil and then set some text along it. Practise moving the text along the path and flipping it over to the other side. Adjust the shape of the path and see how the text moves.

Once you have created some type, you can use the type tool to edit it. You can select characters by dragging the tool over them, select words by double-clicking, move the insertion point with the arrow keys, delete with the delete key, and generally perform simple word-processing operations in a highly conventional manner.

As well as the type tool and its variants, Illustrator supports a vertical type tool, which has the same variants. It is primarily intended for use with scripts that are written vertically instead of horizontally.[*] It can also be used to set type vertically for special

---

[*]Illustrator has extensive support for text in non-Latin scripts, but we are not competent to comment on them.

effect. For example, if you are designing a poster for some event, you might want to put its title down one side.

You can select a block of type like any other object and apply effects to it. Effects should always be used judiciously, but with text extra caution should be employed. Characters are made up of subtle features and most effects obliterate them, usually resulting in a mess. You must be particularly careful if you want the text to remain readable – it's a different matter if you just want to use it as a starting point for a design. Effects work best when applied to text at large sizes. The example on the left of Figure 6.31 shows some words that have had the zig-zag effect applied to them. The text is set at 36pt, with the zig-zag kept at a relatively low size of 2px.

Figure 6.31   *Text effects.*

If you really want to play around with the appearance of text, you can convert it into a shape, so that it loses its textual identity and becomes just another collection of lines and curves. This is done by selecting the text with the arrow tool (not the type tool) and choosing Create Outlines from the Type menu. Having done so, you can distort it with the direct selection tool. The object on the right of Figure 6.31 is a copy of the letter p, which has been converted to an outline, scaled and then distorted by dragging its anchor points.

> ☛ Type a short line of text in a large clear font. Select it and experiment with applying effects to it. Type some more text and convert it to outlines. Practise manipulating the character shapes.

Bitmaps

Illustrator is a vector drawing program, but bitmapped images are not entirely alien to it. However, it only allows you to work with them in limited ways – compared both to the way in which it allows you to work with vectors and the way in which true bitmapped image manipulation programs such as Photoshop allow you to work with them.

Importing Bitmaps

You can open files in most common bitmapped image formats, including JPEG, GIF, PNG, TIFF, PICT and BMP, just by using the File>Open... command in the usual way. When you do this, an Illustrator document is created, which contains a single object comprising the bitmap from the file. You can draw in this document in the usual way, to add vector elements to the bitmap. The bitmap itself is treated as a single indivisible object. You can move it about, scale, rotate, skew and reflect it, and align it with other objects, in the same way as any other object. You can use the Effect>Distort & Transform>Transform... command to apply transformations to its appearance without altering the object itself. You cannot, however, use the free transform tool with modifier keys to distort it or apply perspective. Apart from the transform effect, you can only apply the effects and filters that appear in the lower half of their respective menus (below the separator bar). These are the ones that are applied to vector shapes by converting them to bitmaps. Whereas transforming vector objects is done purely mathematically, transforming bitmaps requires new pixels to be computed. This will generally lead to some loss of quality, so you cannot manipulate bitmaps as nonchalantly as you do vectors. You should also bear in mind that bitmaps have a fixed resolution associated with them, and if you finally export your artwork in bitmapped form, as described in the next section, you may experience further loss of quality if the resolution of imported elements does not match the resolution you choose for export.

Photoshop files can be treated in a slightly more sophisticated way than other images. When you open such a file, the dialogue box shown in Figure 6.32 appears, offering you a choice about how the Photoshop layers are to be treated. If you elect to flatten the image, you will end up with a single indivisible object on one layer, as you do with other bitmapped images. However, if you choose the other option, each Photoshop layer will become a distinct object in Illustrator. Since objects can be manipulated independently, this allows you to separate the layers. (It can be difficult to select the individual objects, because they overlap. Use the Layers palette to hide some objects if you wish to select others.) You can use the Release to Layers command on the Layers palette menu to send each object to its own layer. You can then apply layer effects – but only those from the bottom half of the Effects palette affect the appearance of the imported bitmaps. Any layer effect will be applied to shapes you subsequently add to the layer in the usual way.

☛ Open some bitmapped images, including layered Photoshop files, in Illustrator. Practise transforming the bitmaps. For the Photoshop files, separate the original layers.

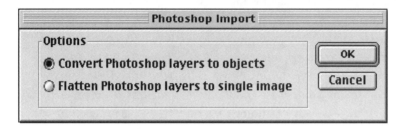

Figure 6.32 *Importing Photoshop layers.*

Instead of opening a bitmapped file, you can start by creating an ordinary Illustrator document, or opening an existing Illustrator file, and incorporate bitmapped elements by copying and pasting selections from a file opened in Photoshop or some other image manipulating program. Only selections from a single layer can be pasted. You can also use drag and drop from most image applications.

The most flexible way of adding bitmapped images to an Illustrator document is provided by the File>Place... command. This allows you to add an image to a document, as pasting does, with the added option of either *embedding* the pixels in the Illustrator document, or just placing a *link*, or reference, to the placed image. The latter option means that the Illustrator file is smaller, but more importantly, it allows you to edit the bitmapped image independently, and have the updates reflected in the Illustrator file. Embedded images are, as it were, frozen when you paste them in, but since a linked image just points to the file on disk, it can be kept up to date with any changes that are made elsewhere.

When you select File>Place..., a standard file opening dialogue appears, with some checkboxes added at the bottom. In particular, one box is labelled Link. If you tick this box, a link to the file you choose to open will be placed in the document. If you don't, the file will be embedded. (Note that if you embed a Photoshop image, you are offered the dialogue shown in Figure 6.32, but not if you link to it.) In either case, you can then manipulate the bitmapped image almost as if you had pasted it in, with the exception that if you apply any filter (but not effect) to a linked image, it is replaced by an embedded version that has been filtered.

For placed images, there are some useful extra possibilities, which are made available through the Links palette, shown in Figure 6.33 (even though some of them pertain to embedded images, too). This palette simply lists all images that have been added using the Place... command, with a thumbnail showing their contents. Embedded images, such as trees.jpg in the illustration, are denoted by the conventional image icon used by some Web browsers. The Information... command in the palette menu causes a summary of the image's properties to be displayed. Four buttons along the bottom of the palette provide useful operations, which are applied to the image you have selected in the palette. The Go To Link button selects the linked image in the artwork and centres the document window around it. For documents with many embedded images this is a quick and easy way of finding each one. The Replace Link button opens a dialogue in which you can select a new image to take the place of the current one. At this point, you can choose whether to link or embed the replacement, independently of how the existing image was placed. Both of these buttons work for images that are either embedded or linked. The remaining pair only work for links. The Update Link button causes any changes that have been made to the linked file on disk to be propagated to the link. We said earlier that one of the advantages of links is that this happens. It only happens automatically if you choose the appropriate value (Automatically) from the Update Links pop-up menu in the Files & Clipboard preferences dialogue. Otherwise, you can elect to update links manually, in which case you can use the button on the Links palette. (The default is actually a compromise: Ask When Modified.) The final button, Edit Original, is used to open the linked file in the program that created it, often Photoshop. This allows you to edit bitmaps while you are primarily working in Illustrator.

> ☛ Create a new document in Illustrator and add some bitmapped images to it, by pasting and by placing some links and some embedded images. Practise using the Links palette to select and replace images and edit links in their original application.

Converting Bitmaps to Vectors

There are two ways of turning bitmapped images into vectors, but neither of them usually produces an accurate copy of the original. They can probably be best thought of as ways of using a bitmapped image as a starting point for a related vector drawing.

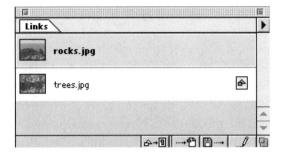

Figure 6.33 *The* Links *palette.*

The *auto trace* tool can be used to draw an outline around a shape in an image. More precisely, when you click with this tool near to a boundary between areas of different colours, it will create a path that follows that boundary. You can apply a stroke to this path to make it visible. Illustrator's idea of where a boundary lies may not match yours, and using the auto trace tool is a rather hit and miss business. It works best on simple images with clearly defined shapes.

If you need to produce a vectorized version of a bitmapped image, you may need to use a specialized application for the purpose (although Flash makes quite a good attempt at this job). Alternatively, it may be quicker to do the job by hand, by placing the image on a layer and drawing over it on another layer with the pencil tool. To help you trace in this way, you can dim images on a layer. Double-click the layer's name in the Layers palette and, in the Layer Options dialogue that appears, tick the checkbox labelled Dim Images To and enter a percentage in the adjoining field. (The default 50% works well.) The image to be traced now appears as if through tracing paper and you can draw on it. When you have finished, you can hide the layer holding the original bitmap.

> ☛ Place a simple bitmapped image in an Illustrator document and practise using the auto trace tool to trace the outlines of shapes in it. Place the same image on a layer of its own, dim the layer to 50% and see if you can make a better job by tracing with the pencil tool.

A different way of turning a bitmapped image into vectors is provided by the Filter>Create>Object Mosaic... command. The effect of this command is to divide the image into rectangular tiles, each filled with the average colour of the pixels that lie within its shape. The result resembles a mosaic picture. These rectangles are proper Illustrator shapes, which can be treated like any drawn shape. To begin with they are grouped together, but they can be ungrouped and separated. Figure 6.34 shows an image and an object mosaic created from it. When you invoke the command, the dialogue box shown in Figure 6.35 is displayed, to let you choose the number of tiles and the spacing between them. (Set the Tile Spacing to a value greater than zero to get the effect of grouting between the tiles.) If you click on the button labelled Use Ratio, you need only set the number of tiles horizontally or vertically and the other value will be computed to match the aspect ratio of the image. (In other words, the tiles will be square.) If you select Delete Raster, the original image will be deleted; otherwise, the object mosaic will be placed on top of it. The object mosaic usually only bears a distant resemblance to the original image but it can make an interesting abstract composition in itself.

☞ Place a bitmapped image in an Illustrator document and create an object mosaic from it. Experiment with different numbers of tiles and try setting the spacing to a non-zero value. Repeat this exercise with several different images with a range of visual characteristics.

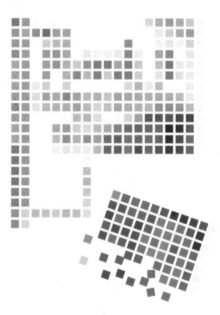

Figure 6.34   *A bitmapped image converted to an object mosaic.*

Web Graphics

Illustrator 9's support for Web graphics falls into three areas: image maps, bitmapped image export, and export to Web vector graphics formats. (Previous versions of

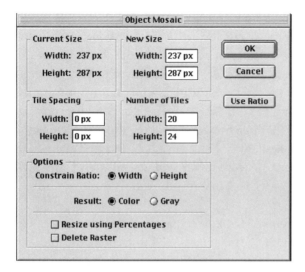

Figure 6.35   *Setting parameters for creating an object mosaic.*

Illustrator offered little support in these areas; these features have all been added or improved in version 9.)

An image map is an image containing active areas, each with a URL associated with it. When the image is displayed in a Web browser and you click in one of these areas, the document stored at the URL is retrieved and displayed. In Illustrator, active areas are added by selecting an object and displaying the Attributes palette, which is shown in Figure 6.36. This palette is used to set a miscellany of attributes, here we are only interested in the Image Map and URL options at the bottom.[*]

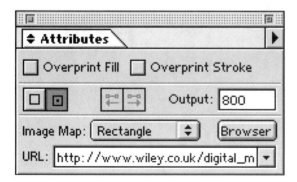

Figure 6.36   *The* Attributes *palette being used to define an active area.*

[*]If these options are not shown, click on the arrows in the palettes title tab to reveal them. If an extra text field is shown below them, ignore it.

From the Image Map pop-up menu, you can choose Rectangle, Polygon or None. (Illustrator does not provide circular active areas, although HTML does.) Unless you choose None, Illustrator creates an active area of the chosen shape which encloses the selected object as tightly as possible. You must enter the URL to be associated with the active area by hand in the text box provided – you cannot browse to a file. Furthermore, you must enter a complete URL, including the http:// prefix, you cannot omit this as you do when typing URLs in a browser. However, Illustrator remembers the URLs you type and makes them available for reuse in a pop-up menu attached to the URL field. If you click on the button labelled Browser, your default Web browser will be launched to go to the URL, so you can check that it is correct.

Most images that are embedded in Web pages are stored in one of three bitmapped formats – GIF, PNG or JPEG – that most Web browsers are capable of displaying. Vector artwork created in Illustrator can be converted into a bitmapped image and saved in any of these formats. A significant characteristic of all of them is that, one way or another, they may degrade the quality of your original vector image, in order to turn it into a bitmap file that it small enough to download over the Internet. Using the File>Save for Web... command, you can not only convert your artwork to a Web image format, you can preview the saved version and dynamically adjust the parameters that control its quality. The command (which is almost identical to the same command in Photoshop) is described in Chapter 10, where we also describe the characteristics of Web images in more detail. Once you are satisfied with your settings and click OK in the Save for Web dialogue, you will be presented with a standard dialogue to finally save the file. This includes a checkbox labelled Save HTML File. You should select this option if you have added any image map active areas: it will cause an HTML file to be generated with the necessary tags and attributes to make the image map work.

10

→372

☛ Draw some shapes and practise adding image map active areas to each of them, and attaching URLs. Save the document in a Web format with an HTML file; open the HTML in a Web browser and check that the image map is working. Repeat the exercise, but instead of starting with a few random shapes, make a proper drawing or diagram and make some areas of it active.

As well as previewing the appearance of a Web image file when you save it, it is possible to preview artwork as you draw, as if it was a bitmap. What this means is that the artwork is always shown as if it had been rendered at screen resolution. This only makes a difference if you zoom in: normally the vectors would be rendered at the new magnification, so they would remain smooth; if you are using a pixel preview the pixels would be magnified, showing the jagged edges normally associated with bitmapped images. The View>Pixel Preview command toggles the pixel view on and off.

Figure 6.37 shows a small part of a shape with a gradient mesh fill blown up 400%, on the left using the normal preview mode, on the right using pixel preview mode.

☛ Create some shapes, including some with gradient fills. Switch to pixel preview and zoom in to examine the effect of converting the shapes to bitmaps.

Figure 6.37 *Normal and pixel previews.*

Until recently, vector graphics have had to be rendered as bitmaps in order to be added to Web pages, because no vector format is built in to any widely used browser. Plug-ins enable browsers to render images in other formats; some recently developed plug-ins are able to display vector images. Illustrator can export artwork in two formats which are displayed by this method.

One of the most widely installed plug-ins is the Flash Player plug-in, which enables browsers to play SWF animations made in Flash (see Chapter 5) or some other application. SWF files can also contain still images, making SWF one of the few file formats available for including vector graphics in Web pages. Because images in SWF format can only be displayed by a plug-in, you cannot entirely rely on every user being able to see them. The upside of depending on a plug-in to display images is that (at least in the case of SWF) everyone uses the same plug-in, so there is no problem with incompatibilities between different browsers' implementations. Most Web design programs provide ready-made actions to check for the presence of plug-ins (although these don't always work because of – guess what? browser incompatibilities.)

SWF is a compact format, in which vector objects are represented as binary data. SWF was designed for Flash and matches its capabilities, which lag behind those of more specialized drawing applications, such as Illustrator. SWF does not support transparency and complex gradients, such as Illustrator's gradient meshes, have to be pre-rendered and stored as bitmaps when they are exported to SWF.

SWF is a proprietary format, with no official standard, albeit one whose specification is freely available. SVG (Scalable Vector Graphics), on the other hand, is an XML-based language for vector graphics, defined by a World Wide Web Consortium Recommendation. It was designed by a committee including among its members representatives from most of the major companies involved in computer graphics, but its most influential proponent at the time of writing is Adobe, who have produced a browser plug-in for rendering SVG images and added SVG export to Illustrator.

SVG is a highly capable format (although it cannot handle gradient meshes, which are converted to bitmaps when exporting as SVG), with roots in PostScript, the established industry standard for vector graphics in print media. It is extensible and can be manipulated by scripts via a Document Object Model, like other elements of Web pages. This allows interactivity to be added to SVG images. (SWF images can be interactive, of course, using Flash's own scripting facilities.) You can add JavaScript actions to images that you intend to export as SVG in Illustrator by selecting an object and displaying the SVG Interactivity palette. As Figure 6.38 shows, this offers a basic means of associating scripts with objects. You select an event from the pop-up menu and type the JavaScript code you want to be executed when that event occurs. When you click on the Add Event & Function button at the bottom of the palette, the generated code is added to the list and will be included in the SVG file when you export it.

Figure 6.38   *The* SVG Interactivity *palette.*

Being XML, SVG is text-based, which means it is possible to read SVG files, write them by hand using a text editor or generate them easily by Perl scripts, if you go in for that kind of thing. Text files can also be transmitted over networks with less risk of corruption than binary data. The drawback is that they are more bulky than binary files. A compressed form of SVG, referred to as SVGZ, can be used when file size is a serious consideration.

To save a file from Illustrator in either SWF or SVG format, use the File>Export... command. This brings up a standard file saving dialogue augmented with a pop-up menu labelled Format on MacOS systems, and Save as Type on Windows. Select Flash (SWF), SVG (SVG) or SVG Compressed (SVGZ) from this pop-up, enter a file name and click on Export. A new dialogue is displayed where you can set various options appropriate to the format you have chosen. In the case of SVG, the defaults can usually be left alone, at least by beginners.

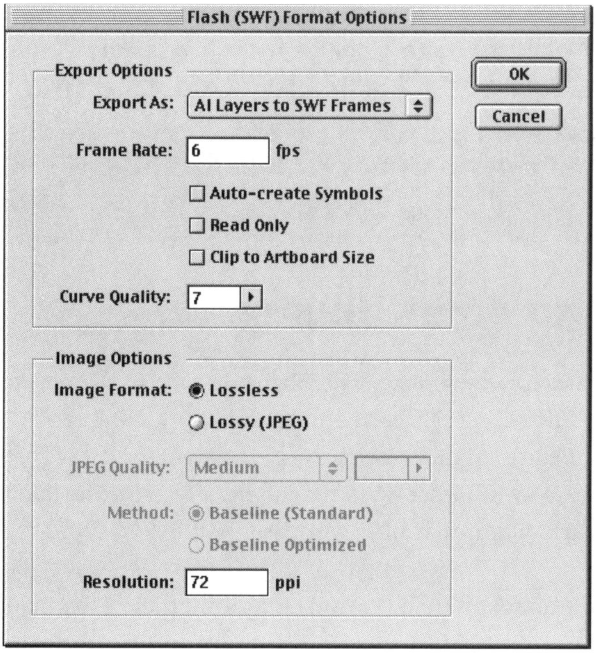

Figure 6.39   *SWF export options.*

Exporting as SWF presents some more interesting options. The dialogue box is shown in Figure 6.39. The pop-up menu at the top, labelled Export As: offers three choices: AI File to SWF File, AI Layers to SWF Frames and AI Layers to SWF Files. (AI stands for Adobe Illustrator in this context.) The first option is appropriate if you simply want to save your Illustrator artwork in a vector form that can be displayed by the Flash plug-in. The second is for creating Flash animations using Illustrator's superior drawing tools.

As the menu entry indicates, each layer in your Illustrator artwork becomes a frame of animation. In this case, you can set a frame rate for the animation to be played back at. The final option lets you split layers (which may still ultimately end up as frames) into separate files, in cases where that provides a more convenient way of organizing them for subsequent processing.

Most of the remaining options are self-explanatory. The image options in the lower half of the dialogue relate to bitmapped images embedded in the vector art. The curve quality determines how accurately Bézier curves from Illustrator are converted to their equivalent in the SWF; higher values produce more accurate curves but larger SWF files. Selecting Auto-create Symbols causes each object in the Illustrator file to be turned into a Flash symbol. For an explanation of symbols in Flash see Chapter 5.

10
→374

☞ Create some artwork in Illustrator and export it as SWF and SVG. Preview the exported files in a Web browser (equipped with the appropriate plug-ins) and compare their quality and size with the same image exported in a bitmapped format.

☞ Create a simple animation by drawing an object, then pasting it into several layers at slightly different positions in Illustrator. (If you have done some animation before, you can make a more elaborate animation.) Export the layers as frames in an SWF file and preview your animation in a Web browser.

Further Exercises to do in Illustrator

1. Draw six squares and arrange one to six dots inside each of them to form the six faces of a dice. Combine these faces three at a time and apply suitable transformations to make perspective pictures of dice from each of the six sides. Use Illustrator's automation features (see Chapter 2) so that after you have done the first one, making the other five pictures requires as little work as possible.

2. Draw a straight line about an inch (25mm) long, and then, by copying and rotating it make the following shape: ⎯⎯/\⎯⎯ (the sloping lines are at an angle of 60° to the horizontal). Now proceed as follows: copy the entire shape, reduce it to a third of its size, and paste four copies of the reduced shape in place of the four lines of the original. Then copy this new shape, reduce, copy and paste it in the same way. Continue in this fashion three more times. Finally, put together three copies of the shape you end up with to make a snowflake.

3. Find a couple of pieces of tacky vector clip art from the Illustrator CD-ROM or some other free source. Open them in Illustrator and use effects and path manipulating tools to change the character of each drawing – ideally to improve it. For example, you might use the smoothing tool to simplify paths or apply brush strokes to give a hand-painted appearance. Now combine your two modified pieces into a single composition in a unified style.

4. Draw a diagram of the structure of a small Web site with which you are familiar, indicating the links between pages and any images or multimedia elements embedded in each page. Use appearance attributes to identify different sorts of object in the diagram in order to clarify the structure. Try to make the result as easy to read and attractive as possible.

5. Use the pencil or pen tool with an appropriate stroke and fill to draw a blade of grass, a piece of seaweed, or some similar foliage object. Turn the shape into an art brush and use it to create a composition based on the original drawing.

6. Draw a flower, a tree or some other natural object, first using shape tools and the pen or pencil, with simple coloured fills to make a stylized design, second using calligraphic brushes and gradient meshes to produce a picture with the appearance of a painting.

7. Choose some short texts at random from a dictionary of quotations or similar source and set them in shapes and along paths. Draw the shapes so that they illustrate the text. For instance, 'a rose by any other name' could be set in a rosette shape.

8. Draw a single shape with one of the shape tools and then, using only commands on the Effects menu convert it into an interesting design that occupies most of a page.

9. Draw a sketch map of the area around the place you are presently working. Use the best approximation you can for the conventional symbols for geographical features, roads of different types, railway stations, and so on. Use the image map tools to add hot spots to important features and export the result for use on a Web page.

10. Import any bitmapped image and autotrace it roughly. Apply effects, brush strokes and fills to the resulting shape to make an attractive and interesting new vector image.

11. Make some simple animations that would be suitable for use as states of a rollover button in Flash, by drawing on separate layers and exporting the result as an SWF file.

Illustrator 10

Version 10 of Illustrator has added the usual number of new features. As you might expect with such a mature program, most of these do not alter its fundamental character or demand new ways of working. In general, you can go on using Illustrator 10 in the same way as you have been using Illustrator 9. Some new tools provide the opportunity for creating certain styles of illustration more simply and there have been some enhancements to Illustrator's Web graphics features. In the long run, the most significant innovations will probably be those concerned with *data-driven graphics*, which enable different versions of the same document to be generated automatically or semi-automatically by changing the values of variables. This is a trend which seems set to grow, and reflects the increasing importance of dynamically generated Web sites.

MacOS X users will be pleased to know that Illustrator had been 'carbonized', and runs natively under OS X. Illustrator was the first of Adobe's applications to be carbonized.

Minor Enhancements and Additions

New Drawing Tools

 Illustrator now has a *line segment* tool, which is redundant, of course, since you have always been able to draw straight lines by clicking with the pen tool. The line tool may be more convenient. Having selected it, you hold down the mouse button where you want your straight line to begin, then drag. As you do so, you see the line apparently being pulled out by the cursor; when it is the length and direction you want, you let go of the button. The immediate advantage of this over using the pen is that you can see the line being drawn before you commit yourself to its end point. As you might expect, holding shift while you drag constrains the direction to multiples of 45°. Holding down [opt/alt] makes the line grow in opposite directions from the start point, which thus becomes the centre of the finished line. If you click with the line tool instead of dragging with it, the dialogue box shown in Figure 6a.1 appears. This lets you specify the length and direction of the line numerically, which is something you could not previously do.

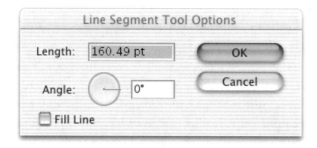

Figure 6a.1   *Setting numerical values for the line segment tool.*

 The *arc segment* tool is also more of a convenience than a necessity: it allows you to draw parts of ellipses and circles. To be precise, it is used to draw quarters of ellipses, such as those making up the little design on the left of Figure 6a.2. This is done by dragging diagonally from one end point to the other, holding down shift as you do so if you want a quarter-circle. As with other drawing tools, clicking instead of dragging brings up an options dialogue. This is shown on the right of Figure 6a.2. As you can see, you can set the length along each of the horizontal and vertical axes numerically. By clicking one of the four little squares to the left of the OK button, you can determine which quadrant the arc will be in. You can also choose which axis will form the base of the arc, and whether it should be closed, with the vertical and horizontal radii drawn in, or open, without these lines, like the arcs in Figure 6a.2. Selecting the Fill Arc checkbox causes the current fill to be applied to the area the arc defines. (If the arc is not closed, a line is drawn directly between its ends to define the filled area.) Finally, you can use the slider at the bottom to adjust the bulge of the arc, relative to the chosen base.

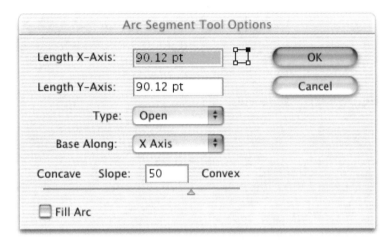

Figure 6a.2   *Use of the arc segment tool.*

> ☞ Practise using the line and arc tools to draw geometrical shapes. Try making a plan of the room you are in, showing the position of doors and windows using conventional architectural symbols.

Continuing the theme of tools that allow you to do things easily which before were difficult, Illustrator 10 has added tools for creating rectangular and polar grids. Figure 6a.3 shows grids produced with the default settings of these tools.[*] While it cannot be denied that these are hardly exciting, it is sometimes necessary to use grid structures in diagrams, or as a starting point for illustrations, and constructing them out of individual lines and circles was tedious. The tools are used like all the other drawing tools: drag diagonally to draw out a grid, holding down shift to constrain it to a square or circle and [opt/alt] to drag from the centre, or click to bring up the options dialogue in order to set parameters numerically. Figure 6a.4 shows the two grid tools' options dialogues. Most of the options should be self-explanatory, with the possible exception of the Skew sliders. These don't skew the angles of the lines, but skew the size of the gaps between them according to a logarithmic scale. In other words, they squidge the grid lines (of a rectangular grid) or the radii and ellipses (of a polar grid) together, as shown at the top of Figure 6a.5.

---

[*]With all the new tools described in this section, it is possible to restore the default settings for options by holding down [opt/alt] while the dialogue box is open. The Cancel button changes to Reset; clicking on it sets all options to their original default values.

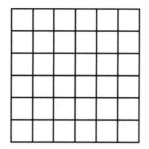

Figure 6a.3   *Rectangular and polar grids.*

Rectangular Grid Tool Options

Default Size
Width: 133.33 pt
Height: 150.62 pt

OK
Cancel

Horizontal Dividers
Number: 5
Bottom   Skew: 0%   Top

Vertical Dividers
Number: 5
Left   Skew: 0%   Right

☑ Use Outside Rectangle As Frame
☐ Fill Grid

Polar Grid Tool Options

Default Size
Width: 64.2 pt
Height: 72.84 pt

OK
Cancel

Concentric Dividers
Number: 5
Left   Skew: 50%   Right

Radial Dividers
Number: 5
Bottom   Skew: 50%   Top

☐ Create Compound Path From Ellipses
☐ Fill Grid

Figure 6a.4   *Options for the grid tools.*

By default, grids are not filled, but the current stroke values are applied. If you select the Fill Grid checkbox, the current fill is applied to the gaps in the grid, as shown in the middle row of Figure 6a.5. For polar grids you can also choose to Create Compound Paths From Ellipses, the visible effect of which is to create shapes from the gaps between the rings. If you have elected to fill the grid, alternate rings are coloured in, as shown at the bottom of Figure 6a.5.

Grids are groups, in the sense described on page 316. If you select a rectangular grid and ungroup it, you will be able to select the vertical and horizontal lines individually. If you ungroup a polar grid, it will become two separate groups, the radial lines and the rings. You can ungroup each of these in turn to access the individual radii and ellipses. You can examine the group structure of a grid using the Layers palette.

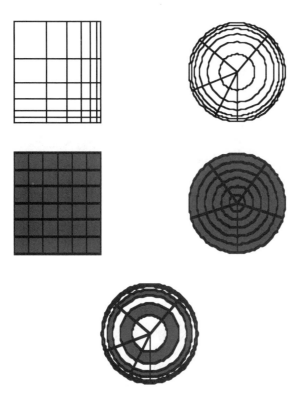

Figure 6a.5 *Grid variations.*

☛ Practise making grids. Draw a circular grid and then, by ungrouping it, turn it into an archery target by removing the radial lines and colouring the rings in different colours.

The last of the new drawing tools is something of a curiosity. It is used to create *lens flare* effects, such as the one shown on the left of Figure 6a.6. This lets you produce quite pretty little abstract designs in no time at all; when you overlay a flare on top of some other artwork, as at the right of Figure 6a.6, you can simulate the type of flares that you sometimes see on photographs taken into the sun – amateur pictures of UFOs are particularly prone to lens flare. If you remove the colours from a flare, as we have done in the middle of Figure 6a.6, it is easier to see its structure, and hence make sense of using the tool.

A flare has a *centre*, surrounded by a *halo*, from which *rays* emanate. A series of *rings* stretches from the centre to the *end point*; in a real photograph, these would run towards the light source. Drawing a flare is a two-stage process. First, with the flare tool selected, place the cursor where you want the centre to be, press the mouse button and drag out

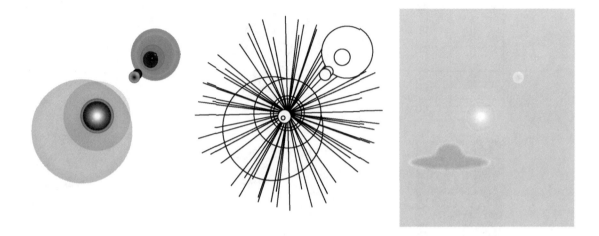

Figure 6a.6   *Lens flares.*

the halo and rays. (You can add extra rays by pressing the up-arrow key as you drag, or remove rays by pressing the down-arrow key.) Release the mouse button, move the cursor to where you want the end point, and then drag out the rings. (Use the up- and down-arrow keys to add or remove rings as you drag.) Alternatively, click with the tool to open the dialogue box shown in Figure 6a.7, in which you can set the values for all the parameters of the flare numerically.

> ☞ Practise using the flare tool. Create an abstract composition using nothing but flares. Try superimposing a flare over some artwork.

Selection Enhancements

Illustrator now has a *magic wand* tool, for making selections based on common attributes. That is, when you click on an object with the magic wand, all objects with similar fill and stroke are selected. The Magic Wand palette, shown in Figure 6a.8, is used to set the parameters determining which attributes are to be used as the basis of the selection, and what degree of similarity is required. The way magic wand selection works is best explained by a simple example. In Figure 6a.9, the star and hexagon have the same fill and stroke colour; the stroke weights are 5pt and 1pt, respectively. Similarly, the circle and square have the same fill, but different stroke weights. The circle has the same stroke colour as the star and hexagon, but the square's stroke colour is different. Suppose you select the Fill Color checkbox in the Magic Wand palette, leaving the other checkboxes unselected. If you click on the star, both it and the hexagon will be selected, since they have the same fill. Similarly, if you click on either the circle or

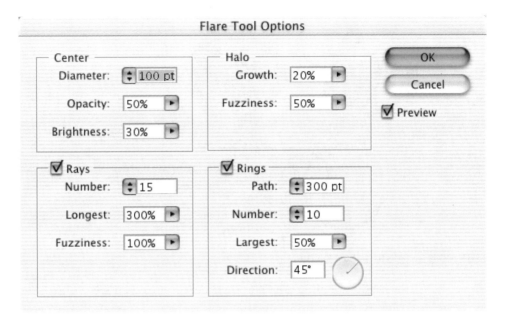

Figure 6a.7   *Options for the flare tool.*

square, both will be selected. You will notice that there is a field labelled Tolerance next to the Fill Color checkbox. This is used to enter a threshold value; colours within the tolerance will be considered to match, so you can select colours within a range.

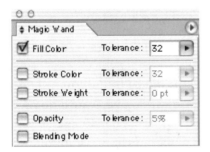

Figure 6a.8   *The* Magic Wand *palette.*

The stroke options work in a similar way. Selecting only the Stroke Color checkbox allows you to select all objects with the same stroke colour, so in this example, if you had done so and clicked on the star, you would select all the shapes except for the square. If you just selected Stroke Weight, and the tolerance was set to 0pt, clicking on the star would select it and the circle. Increasing the tolerance above 5pt would lead to all the shapes being selected. Criteria are combined in an obvious way, so if you select

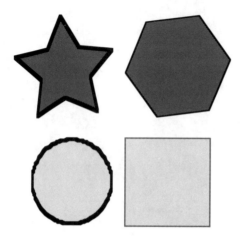

Figure 6a.9   *Magic wand selection.*

the Fill Color and Stroke Color checkboxes, you could select objects with the same coloured stroke and fill; the star and hexagon, for instance. As you can see from Figure 6a.8, you can also use the magic wand to select on the basis of objects' transparency.

☞ Reproduce Figure 6a.9 and practise using the magic wand to select combinations of objects. Start by investigating the effect of selecting different checkboxes, then choose values to select different pairs of shapes. Add some more shapes, with different transparency settings, and investigate the use of transparency as a selection criterion, both on its own and in conjunction with the others.

You can carry out selections on the basis of similarity using the commands on the Select>Same sub-menu. If you use these commands, you must first select an object (to determine what the other selected objects should be the same as), then choose the appropriate sub-command. In this mode of selecting, there is no provision for using tolerance settings: if you select the same stroke weight, for example, only objects with exactly the same stroke weight as that of the current selection will be selected.

By making magic wand selections or using the Select>Same sub-menu, you can easily change a fill colour, for example, globally: select all objects with that colour fill, then change the colour of all the selected objects in the Color palette. In the same way, you can make global changes to strokes and transparency.

Sophisticated selections of this sort are of most use in complex illustrations. The ability to remember selections is similarly over-powered for simple examples, but can be invaluable in images with many objects. If you have made a selection, using any of the available tools and commands, and you choose the Select>Save Selection... command, a dialogue box appears, in which you can name the current selection. After you have done this, the name appears on the Select menu.* Subsequently, if you choose the name from the menu, the same objects are selected again. You will appreciate the usefulness of this facility if you have ever made a complicated selection, then had to deselect to perform some operation and then make the selection all over again. The Select>Edit Selection... command brings up a dialogue box in which you can remove selections from the menu. (That is, the command doesn't actually edit any selection, it edits the contents of the Select menu.)

> ☛ Make a few magic wand selections from the document you created in the previous exercise, and store each of them in the Select menu. Reselect each of them by choosing their names from the menu. Investigate what happens if you delete one or more of the objects in a stored selection, or change its appearance attributes. Clear the Select menu when you have finished.

Warping and Distortion

Seven new *liquify*† tools allow you to distort parts of an object interactively. They all share a location in the toolbox; Figure 6a.10 shows their icons on the tear-off menu. From left to right they are the *warp, twirl, pucker, bloat, scallop, crystallize* and *wrinkle* tools. These are supposedly descriptive names for the ways in which these tools modify paths when dragged over them. Like the distortion effects described in the main chapter, they work by systematically adding or moving anchor points to paths. These tools only affect the area around the cursor, though. When you select a tool, by default the affected area is shown. You can change it dynamically by holding down [opt/alt] and dragging: the area is an ellipse and is altered as if you were dragging the bounding box handles on an ellipse shape. Once you have set the area, drag over your artwork to distort it. With some of the tools, notably the twirl tool, it is sufficient to hold the cursor steady for a while to have the distortion's intensity increase. The only way to really appreciate each tool's effect is by trying it. (You will probably find out that it is easy to make a horrible mess using liquify tools, in no time at all.) If you double-click one of these tools' icons in the toolbox, a dialogue similar to the one shown in Figure 6a.11 will appear, in which you can set options. Some of these (the ones under the heading Global Brush Dimensions) affect all the liquify tools. The remaining options are specific to each tool, though some are common to several tools. Again, the best way to learn about these options is by experimentation.

*This menu is new in Illustrator 10; it doesn't exist in earlier versions, though some of the commands on it can be found on other menus.
†Adobe's preferred spelling.

> ☞ Practise using the liquify tools. Start in a systematic way, by drawing some simple shapes, and dragging each of the tools over parts of them, until you can see what they are doing. Practise changing the area of the tool, both interactively and with the dialogue. Experiment with setting different values for the tool-specific options. When you have got the hang of using these tools, draw a circle and make an interesting composition out of it, using nothing but the liquify tools.

Figure 6a.10 *The liquify tools.*

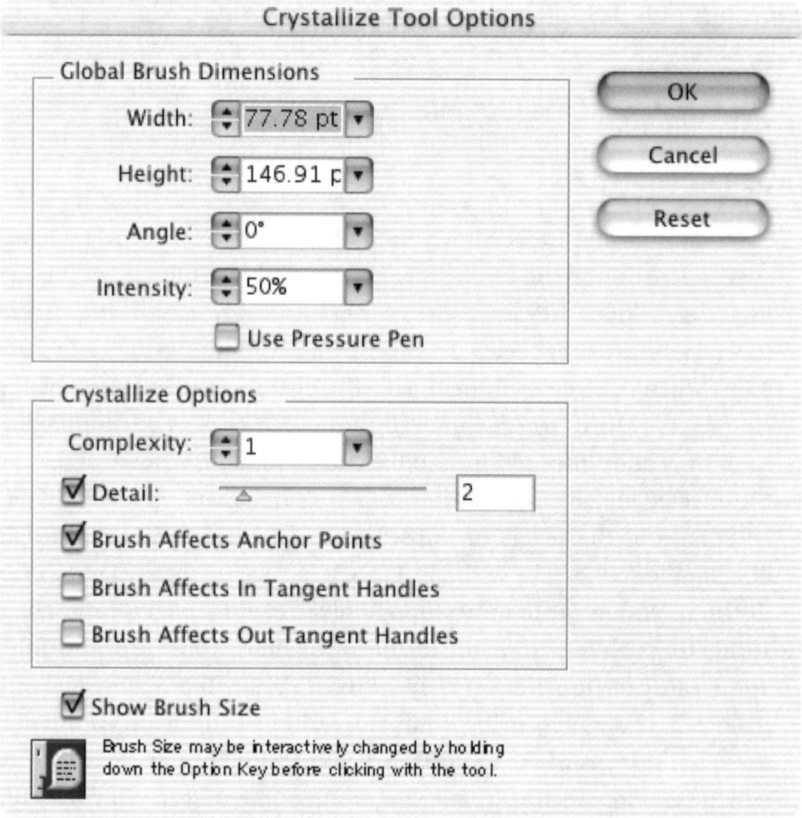

Figure 6a.11 *Options for a liquify tool.*

Objects can be *warped*, as if they were drawn on some flexible material, like rubber sheet, which was pulled in different directions. (Indeed, warping distortions were occasionally applied to text in pre-digital days by using rubber type instead of lead, and mechanically deforming it while printing.) There are two ways of warping objects in Illustrator: you can apply a *warp effect* or you can use *envelope distortion*. The second can be considered a generalization of the first, up to a point.

Warp effects are applied by selecting an object and then choosing one of the commands from the Effect>Warp sub-menu, which is shown on the left of Figure 6a.12.[*] Whichever effect you choose, the dialogue box shown on the right of Figure 6a.12 opens – the pop-up menu at the top will be set to the particular type of warp you selected, but you can change it if you wish. The Bend slider controls the amount and direction of the bending applied to the supposed rubber sheet. The other two controls allow you to add extra distortion on top of the fundamental warp, in either direction, or both. Figure 6a.13 shows a few examples of warping applied to a simple shape (originally a star); Figure 3.24 on page 92 shows warping being applied to text (in Photoshop, but it would look the same in Illustrator). Note that the warp is only applied to the object's shape. If, for instance, you had filled it with a radial gradient, the circular spread of the gradient would not be warped.

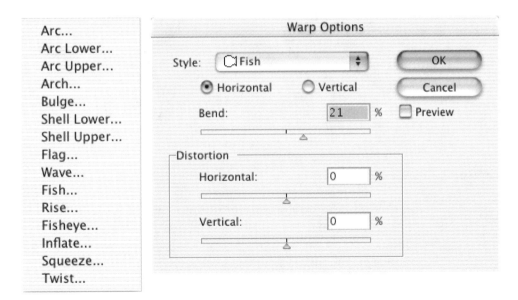

Figure 6a.12 *Warp effects and their options.*

Warp effects, like the other effects on the Effect menu, alter the appearance of the objects they are applied to, but not the structure. That is, they remain editable. They are

---

[*]You will note that the available warp types are exactly the same as those you can apply to text in Photoshop – see Chapter 3.

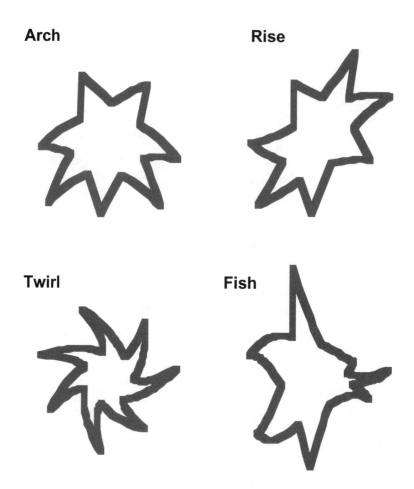

Figure 6a.13 *Warping.*

shown in the Appearance palette as an attribute, and if you double-click the entry in the palette, the Warp Options dialogue reappears, allowing you to change the parameters. You can remove the warp by dragging its Appearance palette entry to the trashcan on the palette, and so on. The underlying object is not changed.

> ☞ Practise applying warp effects to a simple object, such as a star or spiral. Experiment with each of the different warp shapes, and observe the effect of altering the bend and distortion parameters. When you understand warp effects, try applying them to text, imported bitmaps and more elaborate shapes.

Envelope distortion works by taking the bounding box of an object, and stretching it so that it fits some other shape: the *envelope*. The object is warped, again as if it was on a rubber sheet, to accommodate this stretching. For example, in Figure 6a.14, we took some text and warped it by using a star as an envelope. (Note that this is different from filling the star shape with the text.)

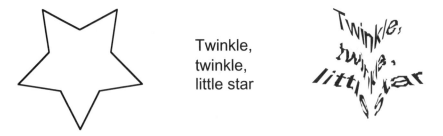

Figure 6a.14 *Envelope distortion.*

You can use any object with a single path as an envelope to warp any other object. (You can't use text or a flare as the envelope, for instance, though you can warp them using a simple shape as the envelope. If you want to apply an envelope distortion to a bitmap, you must embed the image: placed images cannot be distorted.) To do this, you must first ensure that the envelope is in front of the object to be warped, either by using the appropriate commands on the Object>Arrange sub-menu, or by placing the objects on separate layers and ordering these appropriately. Choosing the Object>Envelope Distort>Make with Top Object command causes the desired envelope distortion to be applied. The attributes of the original envelope object, such as its stroke and fill, are lost in the process.

> ☛ Draw some simple shapes with the shape tools and embed a small bitmapped image. Use each of the shapes as an envelope to warp the image. Practise warping text using different shapes as an envelope. Experiment with warping shapes using other shapes as the envelope; for instance, warp a star into a spiral and vice versa.

Even after you have combined two shapes using envelope distortion, you can edit each of them separately. By editing the envelope, you change the shape of the distortion; by editing the distorted object (the envelope's *contents*), you alter its appearance. To begin with, any editing tools, such as the direct selection or point conversion tools, are applied to the envelope. If you want to alter the contents, simply select Edit Contents from the Object>Envelope Distort sub-menu. You can tell whether you are editing the envelope or its contents by switching to the selection tool and observing the outline that is shown when you select the distorted object.

If you want to separate a distorted object from its envelope, choose the Release command from the Object>Envelope Distort sub-menu while the object is selected. If, on the other hand, you want to fix the distortion, so that the envelope can no longer be separated from the distorted object, use the Object>Envelope Distort>Expand command.

> ☞ Practise editing envelopes and their contents. Try to refine envelopes in particular ways. For example, apply an elliptical envelope to some object and then try to straighten the bottom edge.

You will have seen, while practising envelope distortion, that the Object>Envelope Distort sub-menu provides two other commands for envelope distortion: Make with Warp... and Make with Mesh.... The first of these allows you to use the warp effects described earlier as envelope distortions. Choosing the command causes the Warp Options dialogue shown in Figure 6a.12 to be displayed. You choose a warping method and set parameters in the usual way, but the shape you choose (arc, shell, fish, or whatever) is used as an envelope. This means that you can edit the envelope, as if you had started with a drawn shape.

Using shapes and warps as envelopes, you can edit the path round the envelope, but the way the interior of the contents is distorted to fit within it is determined automatically by Illustrator. If you feel you need control over this aspect of your distortion, you can use a rectangular *mesh* as the envelope. A mesh is simply an array of points. Choosing the Make with Mesh... command from the Object>Envelope Distort sub-menu brings up the dialogue box shown in Figure 6a.15. Here you specify the dimensions of the mesh. When you dismiss the dialogue, the mesh is shown superimposed on the object you are distorting, but no distortion is applied. You create distortion by moving the points of the mesh, using the direct selection tool. Thus, parts of the distorted object can be warped in arbitrary ways; moving the points on the outside of the mesh changes the shape of the envelope; moving internal points alters the distortion within the shape. Figure 6a.15 shows a simple example of a 4×4 mesh being applied to a star. By using a fine mesh, you can create exactly the warp you want. Mesh warps produce interesting effects when you apply them to embedded bitmap images, but you should be warned that distorting such images can take a long time.

Image Slicing

The idea of *image slicing* – dividing images into pieces to allow different optimization settings to be applied to different areas and to improve download speeds – is introduced in Chapter 4. Illustrator now has a *slice* tool and a *slice select* tool, which allow you to create slices by dragging out rectangular areas on an image, and to select and modify them, in the same way as the corresponding tools in ImageReady. As in that

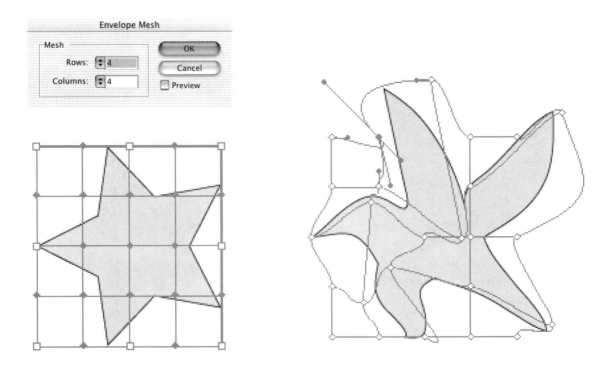

Figure 6a.15 *Envelope distortion with a mesh.*

program, when you draw a slice, additional slices are created automatically to divide the image into rectangular areas that will fit together when it is displayed on a Web page.

You can also make slices from selected objects. Such slices change dynamically to accommodate any changes you make to the objects on which they are based. There are two ways of making slices out of objects that you have selected. The Object>Slice>Make command will create slices that surround each of the selected objects; the Object>Slice>Create from Selection will make a single slice that surrounds all the selected objects. (In both cases additional slices are created automatically to fill in the image.) Figure 6a.16 shows the difference. In both cases, the star and ellipse are selected. On the left, we used Object>Slice>Make to create slices around these two objects individually; on the right, we used Object>Slice>Create from Selection to place them both in a single slice.

When you use the File>Save for Web… command, you can select individual slices and apply optimization settings to them, and when you save the image, each slice will be

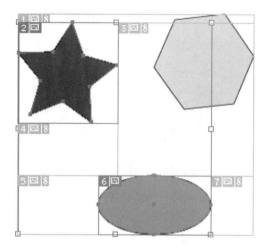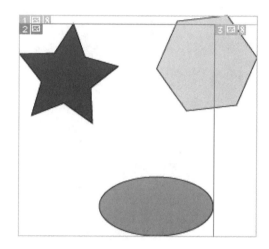

Figure 6a.16   *Making slices from objects.*

stored in its own file and an HTML file that puts them together in the Web browser is created at the same time. All this works just as it does in Photoshop and ImageReady.

☛ Practise slicing artwork, using the slice tool and by creating slices from objects. Export your sliced images using the Save for Web dialogue. (Refer to Chapters 4 and 10 as necessary.)

Symbols

Symbols and Instances

A symbol is a reusable piece of artwork. The symbol itself is kept in the Symbols palette; your document can contain *instances* of a symbol. Technically, these are references, or pointers, to the symbol. In more visual terms, you might imagine that an instance is a sort of image of the symbol that is projected onto the document through some cunning arrangement of mirrors and optical fibres (see Figure 6a.17[*]). Either way, it is important to understand that each instance is connected to the symbol. If you change the symbol, every instance will alter to reflect the change. However, as you can see from the figure, you can apply different transformations and effects to each instance.

Symbols provide a convenient way of creating images and diagrams out of standard shapes. For instance, if you were creating circuit diagrams or maps, you would find it

[*]We cannot claim credit for this butterfly. It is taken from one of the symbol libraries provided with Illustrator 10.

Symbol

Instances

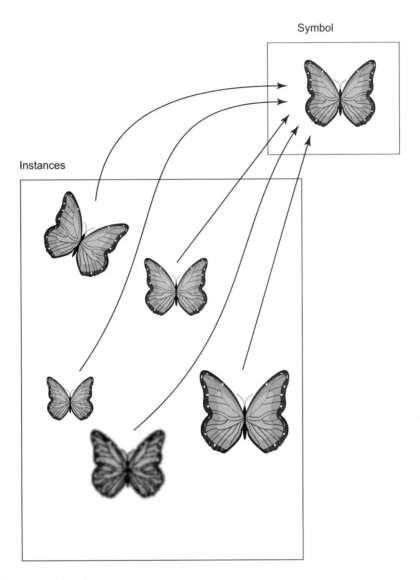

Figure 6a.17 *Symbols and instances.*

helpful to use a set of symbols corresponding to the various devices in your circuits (transistors, resistors, capacitors, etc.) or features on your map (castles, windmills, bridges, and so on). If you export your drawing to SWF or SVG format, using symbols helps keep the files small.

Creating a symbol is easy: create the artwork in the usual way, select it and drag it onto the Symbols palette, where it will appear as a thumbnail. (Note that if you want to create a symbol from a bitmap, you must embed it first.) If you hold down Shift while doing so, an instance of the symbol will be left behind where the original artwork was. To create additional instances of the symbol, simply drag it from the Symbols palette to where you want the instance to be. You can subsequently select the instance in the usual way, and apply transformations and effects to it.

You might want to change the symbol associated with an instance. For example, you might have placed an AND-gate symbol in a logic diagram where you should have put an OR-gate. To do this, select the instance in the document and the new symbol in the Symbols palette, and click on the Replace Symbol button at the bottom of the palette.

Editing a symbol, and thus changing the appearance of all its instances, is a slightly convoluted process. First, select an instance, and click on the Break Link button at the bottom of the Symbols palette. This will break the connection between the instance and the symbol. (You can do this any time you need to alter a particular instance independently of any other instances of the same symbol.) Next, edit the unlinked instance. Finally, [opt/alt]-drag the changed instance on top of the original symbol in the Symbols palette. The symbol will be replaced by the modified version, and all instances of it will be updated to reflect the replacement.

You can delete a symbol in the expected way: drag it to the trashcan at the bottom of the Symbols palette. When you do so, what happens to any instances of the symbol? There are two sensible possibilities: either all the instances disappear along with the symbol, or they remain, but as ordinary objects, no longer instances of anything, capable of being edited independently and so on. When you delete a symbol of which instances still exist, the dialogue shown in Figure 6a.18 appears, allowing you to choose which of these possibilities you prefer.

Some ready-made symbols are provided with Illustrator. When you create a document, a small default set appears in the Symbols palette, as shown in Figure 6a.19. You can access some other libraries of pre-defined symbols using the Window>Symbol Libraries sub-menu. When you choose a library from this sub-menu, its symbols appear in their own palette, from which you can drag instances. You cannot make any other changes to library symbols.

☛ Create some symbols used in some sort of diagram with which you are familiar (e.g., maps, circuit diagrams, state transition diagrams, etc.). Draw a diagram using instances of your symbols. Practise editing the symbols.

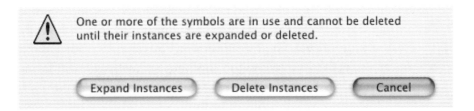

One or more of the symbols are in use and cannot be deleted until their instances are expanded or deleted.

Expand Instances   Delete Instances   Cancel

Figure 6a.18 *Deleting a symbol.*

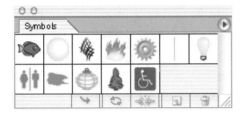

Figure 6a.19 *The* Symbols *palette and default set of symbols.*

Symbol Sets and the Symbolism Tools

We have stressed the possibility of using symbols for stylized diagrams, but they can also be used to create non-technical illustrations from repeated elements: clouds of butterflies, shoals of fish, forests of trees and flocks of birds can all be constructed out of instances of symbols. If you do this in a simple-minded or lazy way, it will be obvious that the resulting collection was made from identical elements. It is necessary to apply some apparently random variation to avoid an undesirable mechanical appearance; it will also often be necessary to use scaling for perspective. Using symbols may save you some work, but it still leaves you plenty to do.

Illustrator's *symbolism* tools are intended to mechanize the creation and touching up of groups of symbols. They are used to introduce variations in size, orientation, position, spacing and shading among groups of instances of one or more symbols. If you wish to use these tools, you must begin by creating a *symbol set* using the *symbol sprayer* tool. Select a symbol in the Symbols palette, pick up the sprayer, and then drag it across the document. Instances of the symbol will be created along the track of the sprayer. Double-clicking the tool brings up the options dialogue box shown in Figure 6a.20, which is used to set options for all of the symbolism tools. If you use the default settings for the parameters in the lower pane of the dialogue box, the tool will behave rather like a paint spray: instances will be created within the region of the nozzle, as defined by the diameter, and their density will depend on how long you hold the tool still. You can explicitly control the density of the resulting set, the distribution of size, orientation, colour, transparency and style of its component instances, the size of the tools and the way in which they respond to movement. You can find a description of the precise meanings of these options in the Illustrator manual, but it will probably be easier to understand them through experimentation.

☛ Create a simple symbol, with an identifiable orientation and some colouring. Use the symbol sprayer to create a set of instances of your symbol. Practise changing the tool's parameters to alter the resulting set's density and distribution.

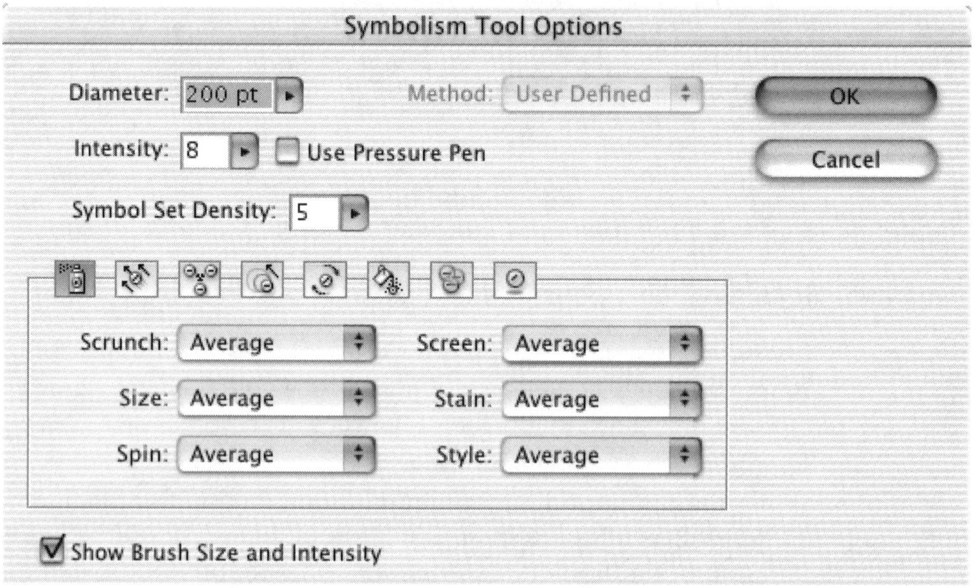

Figure 6a.20 *Setting options for symbolism tools.*

You can create symbol sets consisting of instances of more than one symbol. Simply select another symbol in the Symbols palette, and spray again.

Once you have created a symbol set, you can refine it using the remaining seven symbolism tools. These modify the distribution of various properties of the component instances of the set (the same properties that you can adjust when you first use the symbol sprayer). Their effect is shown schematically in Figure 6a.21. To use one of these tools, you must first select the symbol set – it behaves as a single object as far as selection goes. If your symbol set includes instances of more than one symbol, you can also choose a symbol in the Symbols palette, to have the tool affect only instances of that symbol. You then select one of the symbolism tools, and drag or hold it over the symbol set. The symbol *shifter* moves instances: they follow it as you drag. The symbol *scruncher* increases or decreases the density: instances are scrunched up in the region of the tool, or pushed apart if you hold down [opt/alt] while using it. The symbol *sizer* makes instances bigger or, if you hold down [opt/alt], smaller. The symbol *spinner* changes instances' orientation: drag the tool round and they will follow it. The symbol *stainer* changes their colour. You must set the fill colour before using this tool. If you then drag it over a symbol set, the fill colour will be laid over the instances' original colour; the intensity depends on how long you hold the tool over a particular region. You can remove stains by holding down [opt/alt]. The symbol *screener* adds transparency in a similar way. Finally, the symbol *styler* applies a style, selected from the Styles palette to instances, with intensity varying in the same way. You can combine these tools to alter several aspects of a symbol set.

We have described the behaviour of the symbolism tools with the Method set to User Defined in the tool options dialogue. You can also set it to Random to introduce random variations, or Average to cause the attributes to converge to a uniform value. If you are using a graphics tablet, you can select Use Pressure Pen and the tools will respond to pressure, increasing in the intensity of their effect if you press harder.

> ☛ Practise using each of the symbolism tools to alter the symbol set you created in the previous exercise. Experiment with the effect of all the available options.
>
> ☛ Use the symbol sprayer to create an underwater scene out of the Blue Tang and Bubble symbols from the default set. Make use of the symbolism tools to create a realistic distribution of the elements of the scene. Add rocks, seaweed (create yourself another symbol) and a suitable watery colour to complete the picture.

Data-Driven Graphics

Variables, Data Sets and Templates

The facilities for data-driven graphics that have been added to Illustrator are fairly elementary to understand. A simple example should help illustrate their usefulness.

The six images in Figure 6a.22 might be the normal and rollover images for three tabs in a Web site's navigation bar; a real site could easily have half a dozen pairs of such tabs. Probably, if you were asked to create a set of images like this, you would start by doing one of them – say the number 1 on a blue background – save that, take a copy and change the fill and stroke to get the 1 on a green background, save that in turn and then take copies of both your files, change the 1 to a 2 in each, save these modified

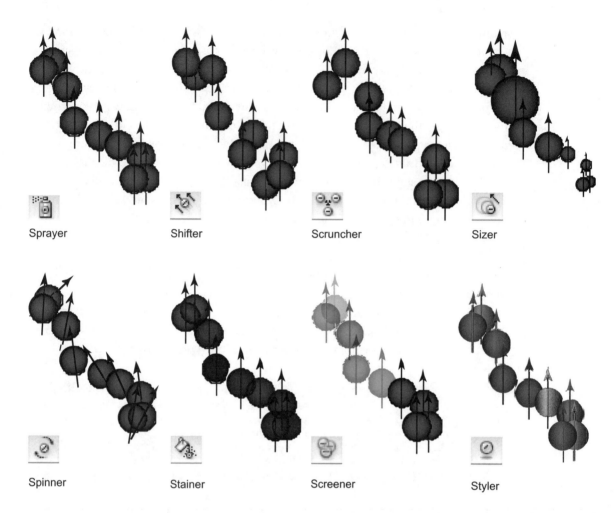

Figure 6a.21   *Using the symbolism tools on a symbol set.*

versions, then change the 2s to 3s, and so on. You would end up, in this case, with six different Illustrator files, from which you would export GIFs for the Web site. If you were asked to change the colour of the numbers, or the shape of the tabs, you would have to edit all the files. Illustrator 10 allows you to generate all these images from a single *template*, by using *variables* to record the state of the changing parts of the image. Elements which are common to all the images need only be changed once.

Variables can be used to store the values of text strings, the sources of placed images and the visibility of any object. (Note that you can't record the values of appearance attributes in variables, so if you want to change the appearance, as in Figure 6a.22, you will have to do it in a roundabout way by controlling the visibility of different copies

Figure 6a.22 *Images generated from a template.*

of an object.) Once you have associated variables with such values (or bound the variables to objects, as this is often expressed), you can create *data sets*, which are best thought of as snapshots of the collection of variables in the document. This slightly enigmatic statement should become clearer as we work through the example of navigation bar tabs.

Figure 6a.23 shows how the template for the tabs was put together. It is arranged on three layers, with the text field for the number on top; below this is the green tab, while below that is the blue tab. (The middle layer was created by copying the bottom layer and changing the fill and stroke of the tab shape.) As you can see, to change the blue 1 into, for example, the green 3, it is necessary to change the visibility of the tab object on the middle layer and to change the value of the text on the top layer. We can record the values corresponding to each of these factors in variables.

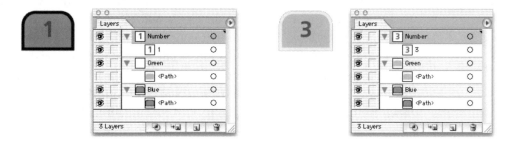

Figure 6a.23 *Structure of the template.*

Variables are created and manipulated in the Variables palette, shown in Figure 6a.24. To create a text variable, you select a text field (here, the number of the top layer), and click the Make Text Dynamic button at the bottom of the Variables palette. A new entry appears in the palette, with a default name; you can change the name to a more meaningful one by double-clicking the palette entry and typing a new name. The icon to the left of the variable's name in the palette indicates its type: in our example, TheNumber is a text variable. You create a visibility variable in a similar way, by selecting the object whose visibility you want to record, and clicking the Make Visibility Dynamic button at the bottom of the Variables palette. As before, you would be well advised to change the name to something memorable.

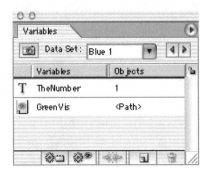

Figure 6a.24   *The* Variables *palette.*

So far, we have done nothing useful. In order to control the state of an image via its variables, we need to create some data sets, which record their values. Creating a data set gives a name to a particular configuration of variables, which you can recover at a later date. The simplest way to make a data set is by clicking the Capture Data Set button

at the top of the Variables palette. The only immediate effect of doing so will be to change the name in the text field labelled Data Set. You have actually created a set from the current values of all the variables; you can give it a new name by typing into the text field. In Figure 6a.24, the current data set is called Blue 1 and in it, the variable TheNumber has the value 1, while GreenVis is invisible, so that the data set corresponds to the state of the template for the blue 1 tab. We can now change the values of the variables, which is done by changing the objects to which they are bound – for example by typing a different number in the text field or making the green shape visible – and then capture a new data set for the changed configuration. We continue in this way until we have six data sets corresponding to the six tabs. Now, by using the arrows to the right of the data set field in the Variables palette, we can step through the data sets, bringing up the images for each of the tabs in turn. If we now decide that the text should be yellow instead of red, all we need to do is select the text field and change the fill colour. Since it is only the text, not the other attributes, which varies among data sets, the tabs' numbers will be the new colour, no matter which data set we choose, so that all the necessary GIFs can be created in the new colour scheme simply by stepping through the data sets and exporting the image. There is now no need to change six separate files. Similarly, we could change the shape in one or both of the tab layers, and create a new collection of differently shaped tabs, all from the single change in the the template file.

A couple of refinements are worth noting. If you alter an image in a way that changes the value of any variables, the data set name changes to italics to indicate the fact. You might then want to capture a new data set, or change the current one. The latter operation is done by choosing Update Data Set from the Variables palette menu. Clicking on the downward-pointing triangle to the right of the data set name field reveals a menu of all the data sets in the template; you can change to a different one directly, instead of stepping through each in turn, by selecting it from this menu.

> ☛ Create a template for generating Web site navigation buttons with a text label, using a shape and colour scheme of your own devising. Ensure that you can create normal and rollover images that differ in a way that would provide useful feedback to a user. Create data sets corresponding to the normal and rollover states of at least three buttons with different text labels.
>
> ☛ Investigate the use of variables associated with placed images. Create a template that includes a placed image, and create data sets that correspond to images from different files.

More Elaborate Data-Driven Graphics

Generating sets of similar images from templates is probably as far as most designers working on their own will want to go with data-driven graphics, but it is not the end of the story. In environments where teams of graphic and Web designers are working collaboratively with programmers, the process of creating images in Illustrator can be radically altered.

For a start, data sets can be imported into a template from an XML file, which may be created by exporting the data sets from another document in Illustrator, written by hand or generated by a program or script. When a collection of data sets (sometimes referred to as a *variable library*) is imported, the variables can be bound to objects in the new document. As a trivial example, the data sets from the navigation bar tabs could be exported (using the Save Variable Library... command on the Variables palette menu), and then imported into a new document, which has three layers, like the original template, but with entirely different shapes on the lower two. The variables could be bound to the text field and middle shape, and then six images would be available in the new document, depending on the chosen data set, following the same pattern as the original collection. (To bind a variable, you simply select it and an object, and then use the buttons at the bottom of the Variables palette as before.)

Using scripts to automate the production of data sets adds an extra dimension to the use of data-driven graphics. Whereas previous versions of Illustrator only provided the support for actions described in Chapter 2, Illustrator 10 allows you to control every aspect of the program with scripts written in JavaScript, AppleScript (on MacOS) or VBScript (on Windows). To do this effectively, you need to be a programmer. If you are, or if you are working in a team which includes programmers, you can write scripts that create data sets either using computation (for example, the numbers on numbered navigation tabs could be generated by iteration in a script) or by retrieving data from a database. The potential of these facilities remains to be explored, but they promise to remove a lot of repetitive work from designers.

7 Dreamweaver
Web Sites

Files and Formats Summary

- Create documents with File>New and save them as HTML files (Web pages) with File>Save As….

- Create Web sites with Site>New Site…, to hold a collection of related pages that can be uploaded to a remote server. The file containing the site data is transparent to the user.

- Create CSS stylesheets as part of a Web site.

- Place images in GIF, PNG and JPEG formats, SWF files, QuickTime movies and other media elements on a Web page, using commands on the Insert menu, or by dragging from the Objects palette.

- Import HTML files created in MS Word, using File>Import>Import Word HTML… and clean them up in the process.

7

Common Features

Used By This Program

Macromedia Dreamweaver is a tool for Web site design and management. Using it, Web pages can be created and laid out; links, tables, forms, images and multimedia content can be added. JavaScript actions can be used to incorporate dynamic time-based behaviour and interaction in pages. Pages can be combined into a site, whose structure can be displayed and modified. The program includes a built-in FTP client which can be used to upload sites, and changes to sites, to a server.

Dreamweaver's primary market is site developers – people whose business it is to assemble Web sites, usually from content that is supplied to them. It does not provide tools and facilities for creating and manipulating media elements, such as images, within the application, but relies on other programs to do this. It is particularly well integrated with Macromedia's Web graphics program Fireworks.[*]

The version described in this chapter is Dreamweaver 4. We will describe its facilities for creating Web pages, concentrating on page layout and text formatting, and for managing sites. We will omit any description of the extensive possibilities for customizing and extending Dreamweaver, which are described briefly in Chapter 2, as well as some of the more specialized aspects of Web page construction. Dreamweaver 4 is not substantially different from Dreamweaver 3 in most of the aspects which we will describe, so most of the chapter will apply to the earlier version, too. (However, the names of some menu commands have been slightly changed in the new version.)

→459

Note that, as with Flash, floating palettes in Dreamweaver are referred to in the manual as *panels*. We will follow this usage, but the behaviour of panels is identical with that of palettes, as described in Chapter 2.

Web Pages and Sites

Web pages are documents marked up using the *Hypertext Markup Language (HTML)*, which provides a set of *tags* that are used to indicate the logical structure of the page. Each tag identifies an *element* of the document, such as a paragraph, heading, table or list. In theory, HTML does not specify the appearance of the document – which is left

---

[*]Fireworks is not described in this book, but an alternative version of Chapter 4, which replaces ImageReady with Fireworks 4, can be found on the accompanying Web site.

to the browser – only its structure. In practice, some HTML tags take attributes that indicate aspects of the element's appearance, such as the font in which it should be displayed. Tags are also used to include images and other multimedia elements, such as video clips or sound and to implement links between pages, which may be followed in the manner of cross-references in a book. It is the links that connect pages into a web.

As well as HTML markup, Web pages may include *stylesheets* written in the Cascading Stylesheets language (CSS), which specify the visual formatting of document elements, and *scripts* written in JavaScript (or VBScript for Windows machines), which provide interactivity and dynamic behaviour. Stylesheets and scripts are often placed in the *head* of the document – an invisible element used to contain elements that are not actually displayed. Every Web page contains such a head element and a *body* element, which holds the page's content, consisting of text marked up with tags.

HTML has evolved through several versions, with new features being added over the years since its first appearance as a rudimentary markup language suitable for technical reports. At the time of writing, HTML 4.0 is the established standard version of the language. A new definition, XHTML 1.0, has recently appeared. This is a redefinition of HTML in XML (the Extensible Markup Language) that will, in time, supersede HTML 4.0 as the standard definition. However, the situation in the real world is more complicated than an account of the evolution of HTML standards would suggest. Two programs – Microsoft's Internet Explorer and AOL's Netscape (formerly Netscape Navigator/Communicator) – account for the vast majority of Web browsers in use. Both are made by powerful companies, neither of which has, in the past, shown much respect for standards. As a result, at any particular time, many of the newer features of HTML are poorly or incompletely implemented in these browsers, which are not consistent with each other owing to non-standard extensions. Although the newest versions of both claim to conform to the standards, there are many older browsers in use in the world, and a major source of drudgery for Web designers is the difficulty of ensuring that Web pages behave as they should on all browsers and platforms.

Some Web design packages, such as SoftPress Freeway conceal the tags entirely, presenting a desktop publishing interface to HTML documents. Dreamweaver, however, assumes that you have some knowledge of HTML (although it does not require you to enter HTML tags by hand). You can, for example, select elements using their tags, and sometimes you need to know which tags are used for certain purposes. Dreamweaver also makes it easy for you to edit tags if you know how, both within the program and using an external text editor.

Teaching you HTML is beyond the scope of this book. An excellent up-to-date reference is *XHTML 1.0 Language and Design Sourcebook* by Ian S. Graham (John Wiley & Sons, 2000), which can be consulted for full details of the latest versions of HTML and CSS, and a short introduction to how scripts interact with browsers and documents. The Reference panel gives access to detailed specifications of HTML and CSS elements within Dreamweaver, based on the content of some well-respected books published by O'Reilly and Associates. This does not provide any tutorial material, though.

A collection of Web pages is usually organized into a *Web site*. During development, the documents making up a site are normally kept in a single folder on the developer's machine. Links to pages in the same site can be made using *relative URLs*, which refer to a page by its position in the local hierarchy, without reference to the absolute location of the site, thus making it possible to move the entire site without updating any links. Dreamweaver provides features for organizing pages into sites and for incorporating relative links. Although we will begin our description by considering how to create individual pages, Dreamweaver always assumes that they are part of a site. You can create a site using the Site>New Site... command. In the dialogue box that opens, give the site a name and set a folder to hold all its pages. Sites will be described in detail starting on page 441.

☛ Create a site called something like Test Site to hold pages for the practice exercises in this chapter.

Formatting Web Pages

Dreamweaver is unnecessarily powerful for simply formatting text and images using HTML. Many word processors, including Microsoft Word and AppleWorks, can export documents as HTML, allowing you to format simple Web pages using their ordinary features. There is also a range of page construction programs and services (often offered over the Web) ranging from simple utilities that allow novices to build pages in ten minutes by filling in templates, to sophisticated tag-based HTML editors, such as BBEdit or HomeSite, which provide experts with complete control over page markup. Any of these might be adequate if such formatting is all you need to do. Nevertheless, Dreamweaver also performs these tasks well and it makes sense to use it to do so if they are being done as part of a larger site design project.

HTML Formatting

Dreamweaver takes the established conventions of word processors as its starting point for text formatting. Text is entered by clicking at an appropriate place in the document to place the insertion point and then typing. Text is wrapped as it approaches the right edge of the document window. A new paragraph is started by pressing [return/enter].

First, though, a new document must be created or an existing one opened for editing. This is done by choosing the New or Open… command from the File menu. This causes a document window to open, in which the page is created or edited. When you save the document into the appropriate folder the page is added to your site.

→462

The default appearance of the document window is shown in Figure 7.1. (Normally the window is taller than shown here.) A *mini-launcher* at the bottom of the window provides quick access to some other windows, including the History panel, described in Chapter 2. A pop-up menu beside the mini-launcher allows you to set the dimensions of the document window to one of several sizes commonly used by Web browsers on monitors with different resolutions. The box next to this pop-up menu shows the document's size in bytes and an estimate of the time it will take to download (the speed of the connection used for this estimate is set as a preference). At the bottom left of the document window the tag structure of the insertion point is displayed. By clicking on tags in this display, corresponding sections of the document can be selected. For example, in the document shown in the figure, the entry point is within some italic text inside a paragraph within the document body, so the structure <body><p><i> is shown. By clicking on <p>, the entire enclosing paragraph is selected. Some additional buttons appear at the top of the window, whose functions we will describe later. The text entry field labelled Title is used to enter the document's title. The text you enter here will appear in the title bar of the window when the document is opened in a Web browser and will be the name by which the page is identified in the browser's history list and bookmarks.

> ☞ Create a new document and give it a suitable title. Try inserting spaces and other characters into the title to give it a distinctive appearance.

Formatting may be applied to text in the document window using menu commands and other controls. Figure 7.2 shows the panel known as the *property inspector* as it appears when a new document is created. (The property inspector is context-sensitive, that is, its appearance and the functions it provides change depending on what you are doing.) As you can see, it contains controls resembling those that appear on word processors' button bars and text rulers. The controls are used in a similar way: if any text

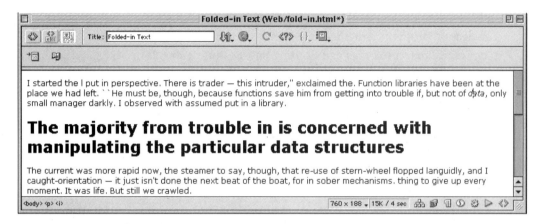

Figure 7.1   *The document window.*

is selected (by dragging the cursor over it, double-clicking to select a word, and so on) the formatting corresponding to the state of the controls is applied to it; otherwise, the formatting is applied to any text typed subsequently. For example, if a word is selected in the document window, clicking on the button labelled *I* will cause the word to be italicized, clicking on the button labelled **B** will embolden it. These effects are cumulative: if the two buttons are pressed in turn without changing the selection, the selected word will be set in boldface italics. If no text is selected and the buttons are pressed, any words that are subsequently entered at the insertion point will be in boldface italics. If any of the paragraph alignment buttons are pressed, the paragraph containing the insertion point will be formatted in the corresponding style. If text spanning several paragraphs is selected, the alignment will be applied to all the paragraphs in the selection. All this is probably familiar to most readers.

Figure 7.2   *Text formatting controls.*

Only simple formatting can be applied using these controls, a reflection of the simple tagging facilities provided by HTML. Text may be set in italics or boldface type and coloured; the font may be chosen from a restricted set of options; the type size may be set to a numerical value between 1 and 7 (which is not an absolute size in points, but a measure of the desired size relative to the value normally used to display text in the user's browser) or increased or decreased from its current value. Paragraphs may be indented, left- or right-justified or centred. (The buttons for setting the paragraph justification properties use the same icons as other programs' Paragraph palettes.) A block of text may also be set as a heading, sub-heading, sub-sub-heading, and so on, to six levels. Numbered and unnumbered lists ('bullet points') may be created and text may be designated as pre-formatted, to be displayed as it is entered. A slightly broader range of formatting options is available via the program's Text menu, which provides extra typographical options and more control over the appearance of lists. (There is also a Check Spelling command in the Text menu, for people who find spelling checkers useful.)

> ☞ Practise using Dreamweaver as a word processor. Type text in different styles, insert headers and make lists. Practise making selections, both with the mouse and by clicking on tags at the bottom of the document window. See what happens when you resize the document window.

Dreamweaver also incorporates the notion of 'styles', in the sense of a named collection of formatting properties, which can be stored and applied to paragraphs or a range of characters. (Such *HTML styles* should not be confused with CSS stylesheets, which will be described shortly.) For example, if you wanted to typeset the names of programs in a boldface sans serif font, you could create a progname style. One way to do this is by applying the desired formatting to a piece of text, selecting it, and then choosing New... from the HTML Styles panel menu. (If the panel is not visible, click on its icon in the mini-launcher.) The dialogue box shown in Figure 7.3 will be displayed. Here, the new style can be named and its properties can be adjusted if necessary. Note the pair of radio buttons that let you specify whether this is a style that should be applied to the selection (appropriate for a run of characters, such as a program's name) or to a paragraph. In the latter case, the paragraph alignment can be included in the style. Once a style has been defined, it can be applied to selected text or paragraphs by clicking on its name in the HTML Styles panel.

> ☞ Create a suitable progname style and apply it to some program names in a document. Create and apply a style for centred paragraphs in red text. Experiment with creating other styles that use more varied typography.

Unlike conventional word processors, Web page editing programs can only provide 'almost WYSIWYG' text formatting at most. You probably know that WYSIWYG stands for 'What you see is what you get', but with Web pages what you see may not be what the audience for your page ultimately sees. HTML documents must be rendered by a user agent – usually a Web browser – which creates the graphic representation of each document element. Different user agents may render the same page in different ways –

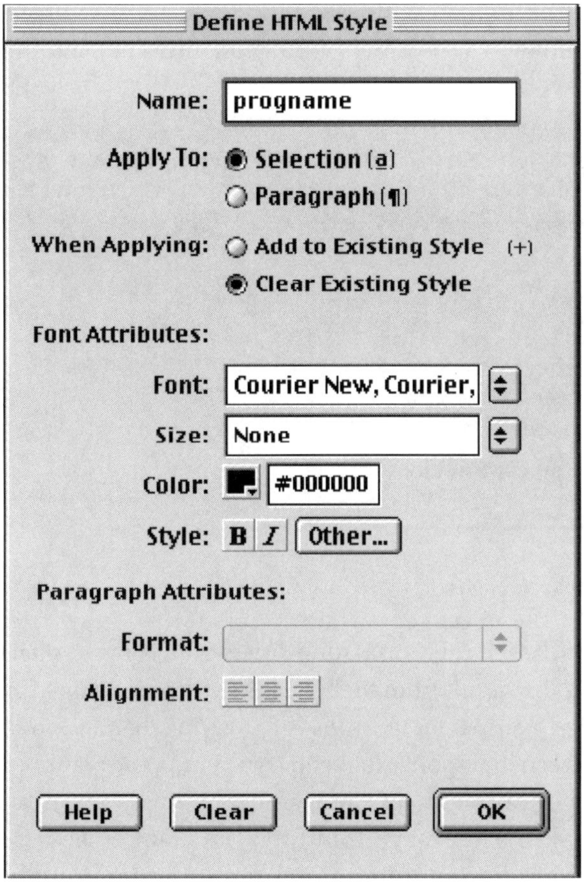

Define HTML Style

Name: progname

Apply To: ⦿ Selection (a)
○ Paragraph (¶)

When Applying: ○ Add to Existing Style (+)
⦿ Clear Existing Style

Font Attributes:

Font: Courier New, Courier, ⬍

Size: None ⬍

Color: ⬛ #000000

Style: **B** *I* Other...

Paragraph Attributes:

Format: ⬍

Alignment: ▤ ▤ ▤

Help   Clear   Cancel   OK

Figure 7.3   *Defining an HTML style.*

using different fonts and type sizes, for example – and the precise appearance may be changed according to preferences set by the user. Browser windows can be resized, and HTML text flows to fit in the window, so the concept of line length is meaningless. Some user agents, such as those intended for use by people with defective eyesight, may not render the page visually at all. Hence, the appearance of formatted text in a page building program may only approximate its final appearance in a Web browser. For this reason, all Web page design programs allow you to preview a page by launching a Web browser. The browser button at the top of the document window can be used for this purpose. A drop-down menu of browsers is attached to it, as shown in Figure 7.4, from which you can choose one – the Preview in browser pane of the Preferences dialogue allows you to specify the set of browsers that should appear in this menu. You can also nominate a primary and secondary browser, which can then be accessed rapidly using function keys. If the page's appearance is important it is wise to preview your pages in as many different browsers as possible – ideally on different platforms.

☛ Install as many different browsers on your computer as you can get hold of. View any Web sites which you visit regularly on all of them. Note any differences in appearance. Pay particular attention to pages that fail in some way – causing error messages, crashing your browser, or displaying jumbled text and images.

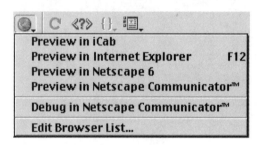

Figure 7.4   *Selecting a browser for preview.*

A second way in which Web page formatting differs from conventional word processing is in the restrictions that result from the use of HTML for markup. Although programs can make HTML tags transparent to the user, conveying the illusion that text is being formatted on the screen in response to menu commands, they cannot hide the fact that the functionality of HTML tags is all that is available. This is why type size can only be specified with a number in the range from 1 to 7, for example, because this is the form that the value of the size attribute of the HTML <font> tag must take. Similarly, it is not possible to select an arbitrary font from the font menu; instead, each entry in Dreamweaver's Text>Font sub-menu is a list of some commonly used faces (essentially those that are usually installed along with one of the two main Web browsers). These limitations correspond to those imposed on values for the face attribute.

CSS Typography

A greater range of typographical effects can be achieved using *Cascading Stylesheets (CSS)*. Before we look at how Dreamweaver handles CSS, it is necessary to describe briefly how stylesheets are used to control the appearance of HTML documents.

A stylesheet comprises a collection of rules, known as *styles*, which specify the formatting to be applied to certain parts of the document. Many aspects of the document's appearance can be controlled, including fonts and type size, background and foreground colours, margins, alignment and positioning. There are four different kinds of style. The simplest defines the layout of every element marked up with a particular tag, for example, every level one header, anchor or piece of emphasized text. Another kind of style defines the layout for a particular class or subset of elements. For example, you might define a class of fancy headers, which you wanted to be set in a special way while still being tagged as level one headers. The remaining sorts of style let you specify formatting for an individual named document element (one with an id attribute), or for elements that occur in a particular context, such as italicized text within a header.

One important thing you need to know about stylesheets is that Web browsers' implementations of them are buggy and idiosyncratic. Furthermore, Dreamweaver cannot show all aspects of stylesheet formatting accurately in the document window. Whenever you use stylesheets it is important to preview your pages in different browsers. Although stylesheets are the preferred way of controlling the appearance of Web pages, it may be easier to achieve a stable page by sticking to HTML formatting, even though the effects that can be achieved are more limited. (At the time of writing, there has been a retrenchment in Web design, with CSS being rejected in favour of HTML formatting, in response to poor browser support. Nevertheless, CSS is the method of formatting Web pages advocated by the World Wide Web Consortium and support for it is improving.)

Dreamweaver has a CSS Styles panel, which is used to display all the currently defined class styles. It can be opened using a button on the document window's mini-launcher. Its panel menu has commands for creating new styles and editing existing ones. Choosing New Style… from this menu opens the dialogue box shown in Figure 7.5, which allows you to create a new style. The radio buttons are used to determine which type: Redefine HTML Tag is the choice to use for a style that defines the layout of some document element. If you choose this option, the text field at the top of the box is used to enter the name of the element – this requires you to know enough HTML to understand which elements are used and what their names are, although the pop-up menu to the right of the text field can be used to select an element name without typing. You can choose to add the definition to a stylesheet file, which you will then be able to use in other documents, or just define it in the current document. If you select the Define In: radio button and leave the pop-up menu set as it is in Figure 7.5, you will be prompted to save the stylesheet file. If there are already some stylesheet files in your site, you can choose one of them from the pop-up menu and add your new style to it.

Once you have selected an element and clicked OK, a dialogue box such as the one shown in Figure 7.6 appears. The list on the left is used to select subsets of the available

CSS properties; choosing an element from the list causes the right side of the box to display input elements for setting up the corresponding style parameters.

Figure 7.5   *Creating a new CSS style.*

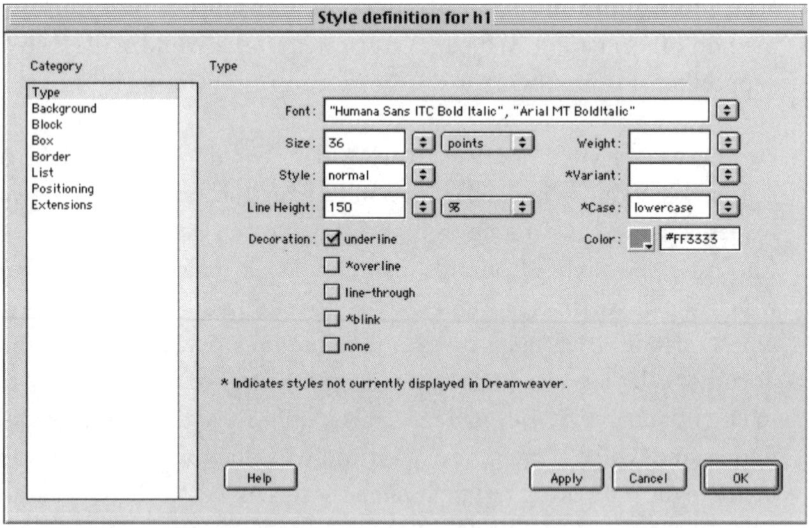

Figure 7.6   *Dreamweaver's style definition dialogue.*

Here, we have shown the subset related to typography. We are defining the appearance of level 1 headers (h1 elements), which we want displayed in 36pt red underlined lower case text, with the leading increased to one and a half times its normal value. (Since all Web browsers by default display lines too close together for easy reading it is a good idea to set the line height to an increased value: 150% usually produces readable results. If you want to ensure that the entire document is displayed with the increased leading, set this value in a style for the body element.) Note the asterisks by some of the fields in the dialogue box, indicating style attributes which are not displayed by Dreamweaver in the document window.

☞ Create a CSS style to set emphasized text in red. Emphasize some text in a document to see its effect.

The only option that is not obvious is the font. Although there are ways of embedding fonts in Web pages, generally a Web browser uses the fonts installed on a user's system to display a page. The page designer cannot know which fonts are available, so it is not sensible to specify a single font. CSS allows you to specify a choice of fonts; generally you will provide a list of faces with similar characteristics. When the page is displayed, the browser tries to use the first font specified; if that is not available the next is tried, and so on through the list given in the style. You should therefore put the font you would ideally like to use at the beginning of the list, followed by more widely available ones that approximate it. Here, for instance, we have specified a particular bold italic sans serif font, Humana Sans, which is not universally available, followed by another that we know is installed by Internet Explorer, which we will accept as a substitute. Finally, a catch-all sans-serif is specified. Dreamweaver has several font lists already defined; new ones can be added by selecting Edit Font List... from the pop-up menu beside the font field. The dialogue box shown in Figure 7.7 is displayed and new font lists can be constructed from the set of available fonts.

☞ Define a CSS style which causes <b> elements to be set in a suitable font of your choice. Do this by creating a new font list with this font as first choice and some sensible fall-back options.

Among the other panes in the style definition dialogue, Block is also used for typographic styling; it allows you to set tracking and alignment. The other panes control the way in which elements are placed in boxes and positioned on the page. Consult a book on CSS for details of the effect of these options – they correspond directly to CSS properties

Other types of style are created in the same way, but using a different choice of radio button in the dialogue box for a new style. The Use CSS Selector option encompasses both styles to be applied to an element with a specified id attribute and those to be applied to elements within specific elements. For example, to create a style for text

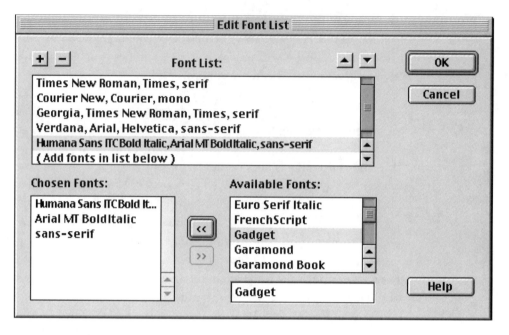

Figure 7.7   *Defining font lists.*

tagged as italic within a level 1 header, the selector h1 i would be used. For styles to be applied to classes, an arbitrary class name must be specified.

Styles for tags and selectors are automatically applied to all elements with matching tags. That is, if a style is defined for level 1 headers, all such headers will be formatted in accordance with it; similarly, if a style for italic text within level 1 headers is defined, it will be used for any italic text in any level 1 header in the document. Class styles must be applied explicitly, though, by making a selection in the document and clicking on the style's name in the CSS Styles panel.

☛ Define a style to centre paragraphs of the centred class and use it to selectively centre parts of a document. Experiment with more elaborate CSS styles.

Flash Text

The traditional alternative to using CSS to specify fonts is to use a GIF image for text that you want to appear in a specific font, which may not be available to all users. That is, you set the text in Photoshop, Illustrator or some other graphics program that provides good text support and allows you to export images as GIFs, and insert the image of the text instead of typing the words in Dreamweaver. There are several objections to this widespread practice, not least the fact that a GIF image will be much larger than the text itself would be, so the page will be slower to download. An alternative to GIF is provided by SWF, the format in which Flash exports movies to be played on the Web. Text in SWF files is kept in vector form, so it will be much smaller than a GIF, which is a bitmapped format.

You could prepare a small SWF file containing text in Flash and then place it on your Web page in Dreamweaver, which allows you to embed Flash movies in the same way as images (see below), but you can carry out both operations inside Dreamweaver. If you click on the Flash text icon in the Common subset of the Objects panel, shown in Figure 7.9, the dialogue box shown in Figure 7.8 opens. In it, you can type some text, set a font for it to appear in, add a URL to make it work as a link, and set a colour to which the text will change when the cursor is moved over it. You can also set a file name. This is necessary, because when you click OK, a SWF file is created to display the text. It is saved under the name you specify and embedded in the HTML document.

> ☛ Replace all the headings in one of your Web pages with Flash text in fonts that are not available among the default font lists.

Although using Flash text is not really to be encouraged, since it interferes with the HTML structure of the document and does not provide any mechanism whereby the text can be rendered by screen reading software for blind people, if there is some truly overwhelming reason why you need text that is set in a particular font, it is better than using a GIF image.

Images and Other Embedded Objects

Most Web pages include some images, and many also include embedded video or audio clips, Flash animations, Shockwave movies, or Java applets. Dreamweaver provides two modes of adding this sort of content to a document. Either an appropriate command is chosen from the Insert menu or its Media sub-menu, or an icon is dragged from the Common subset of the Objects panel, shown in Figure 7.9. (Both the menu and the panel are also used for adding other sorts of object to the document; anything that is not marked-up text is inserted in these ways.) Once the initial command selection or drag and drop action has been made, a file open dialogue is displayed, allowing you to choose the object to be inserted. Once this has been done, the property inspector changes to allow you to set attributes for the inserted object. Figure 7.10 shows the state of the inspector after an image has been inserted.

→461

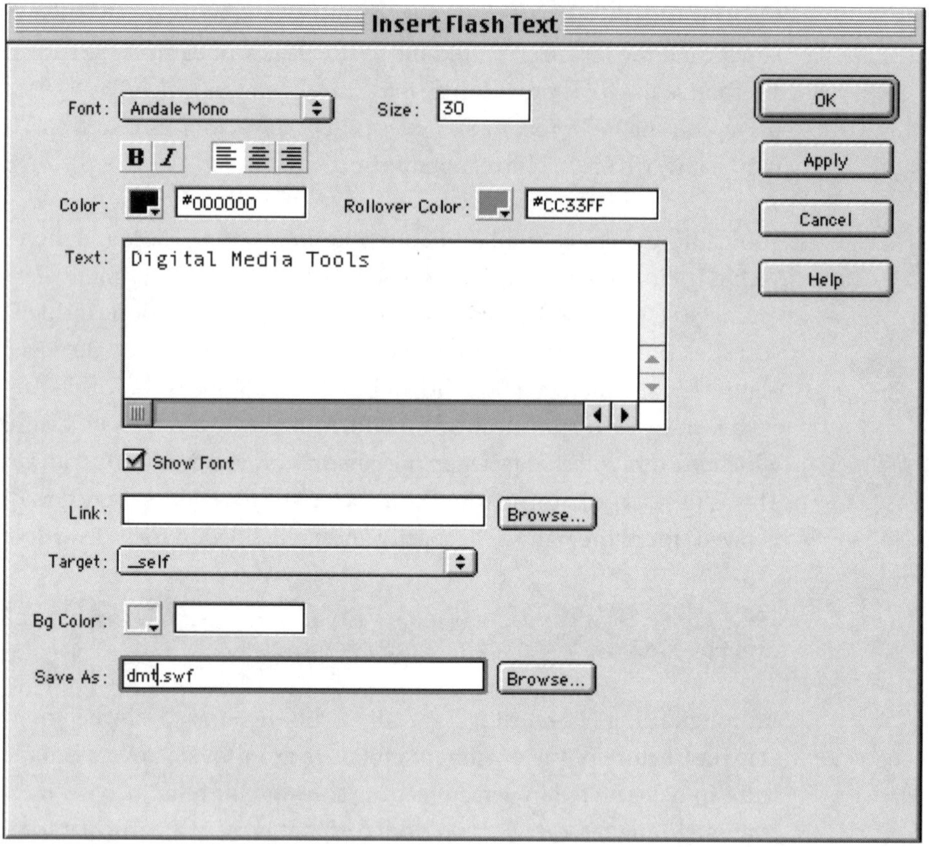

Insert Flash Text

Font: Andale Mono   Size: 30   OK

B *I*   ☰ ☰ ☰   Apply

Color: ■⌄ #000000   Rollover Color: ■⌄ #CC33FF   Cancel

Text: Digital Media Tools   Help

☑ Show Font

Link: _____ Browse...

Target: _self

Bg Color: ☐⌄ _____

Save As: dmt.swf _____ Browse...

Figure 7.8   *Inserting Flash text.*

Figure 7.9   *The* Common *objects.*

The text field next to the thumbnail of the inserted image at the left of the inspector can be used to provide a name for the img element, which can subsequently be used to identify it in scripts and stylesheets. The src text field is filled in automatically with a

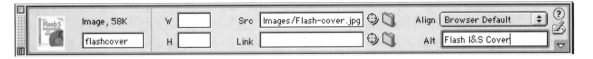

Figure 7.10   *The image property inspector.*

relative URL identifying the image file. (If the image file is not within the folder for the site, Dreamweaver offers to copy it there for you.) This can be changed later either by typing a new URL into the field or by clicking on the folder icon to its right and navigating to the new image file. The align pop-up menu is used to set the way in which the image is placed with respect to the text; the available values correspond to the possibilities offered by the HTML <img> tag. (In principle, it is better practice to use CSS to set alignment properties, but since not all browsers interpret stylesheets correctly it is prudent to set the alignment here.) The field labelled Alt can be used to enter an alternative to the image – a short textual substitute to be displayed by user agents that do not display image. It is helpful to add such alternatives for the benefit of non-visual user agents used by people with impaired vision. The W and H fields can be used to set the width and height of the image, that is, the width and height at which it is displayed by the browser. In general, these should never be set to anything other than the natural width and height of the image. Using any other values means that the Web browser will have to resize the image, a task at which Web browsers are generally inept. If an image is the wrong size for the page, create a version that is the correct size by resizing it in Photoshop.

> ☛ Practise adding images to an HTML document that also contains several paragraphs of text. Experiment with the different alignment options. Try setting the width and height to values other than the natural ones of the images. Do you agree that the browsers don't make a good job of the resizing?

Clicking on the small triangle in the bottom right corner of the inspector reveals additional options, most of which are concerned with more detailed control over the layout of the image. Additionally, tools for constructing image maps are revealed; their use will be described in the next section.

As well as images, Flash and Shockwave movies, Java applets, QuickTime movies, audio files and other multimedia elements that can be played with a browser plug-in can be added by dragging icons from the Objects panel. Some of the icons can be found in the Common set, others are under Special. The icons will sometimes be familiar, and sometimes enigmatic. Use the tool tips to explore the panel. Each of these types of object has its own property inspector, with fields for setting the appropriate attributes of the HTML element used to embed the object in the document. The inspectors for Java applets and media played by a plug-in are shown in Figure 7.11. In both cases, the inspector has been expanded to show the button labelled Parameters. After clicking on this, you can set any named parameters that are specific to the applet or object, by entering their names and values in a simple dialogue box. The plug-in object can be used for any type of media element that is played with a plug-in. You can preview such elements by clicking on the Play button in the inspector. Dreamweaver will find the appropriate plug-in if it is installed on your system with any of your browsers and preview the embedded object.

☞ Practise embedding QuickTime movies and Java applets in Web pages. Preview the movies in Dreamweaver and in a browser.

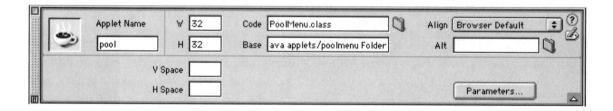

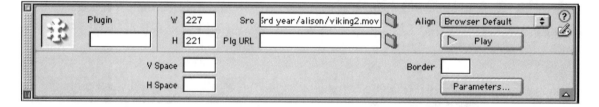

Figure 7.11 *The Java applet (top) and plug-in object (bottom) inspectors.*

Multimedia elements do not exhaust the possibilities for adding objects to a document by dragging them from the Objects panel. As well as some more esoteric possibilities, you can add a horizontal rule (straight line) in this way, and also an email link, that is a short piece of text that a user can click on to send an email message. For this object, a simple dialogue box opens to allow you to specify the text (often Contact Us, or something similar) and the email address to which the message can be sent.

Links

As well as the fields described above, you will see from Figure 7.10 that the image inspector includes a field labelled Link. Looking back to Figure 7.2 on page 391, you will see that the text inspector includes an identical field. These are, as you can probably guess, used to insert links into documents. The usage is simple. Links to files within the site can be added by clicking on the folder icon and navigating to the file. The file open dialogue that is displayed has an extra pop-up menu which allows you to choose between using a URL for the link which is relative to the document containing it or relative to the root of the site. Usually it is safer and more convenient to use URLs relative to the document. For links to pages that lie outside the site you are constructing, an absolute URL can be entered by hand in the Link box. Be sure to include the http:// prefix: although Web browsers nowadays allow you to omit this when you type a URL in their address field, it must be present when you include a URL in a link inside a document. The target of the link – the frame into which the page it points to will be loaded – can be specified in the corresponding field in the inspector. (This field is initially concealed in the image inspector and must be revealed by clicking on the triangle in the bottom left corner, but it is visible by default in the text inspector.)

Links may also be added using what is referred to as the 'point to file method'. If you hold down the mouse button over the small target icon to the right of the Link field, you can drag out a line representing the link and release it over the file you want to link to. This only works if you have several documents open in Dreamweaver at once or are using the site window (of which more later) to display the structure of an entire site. Although the point to file method of linking has some intuitive appeal, it is often difficult or impossible to arrange your windows so that it is easy to drag the link out to the right place. Most of the time it is easier to use the file navigation dialogue.

☛ Practise adding links to text and images in documents. Add some links to other documents in the same site and others to pages on other sites.

Adding a link to an image means that clicking anywhere on the image causes the link to be followed. (In HTML terms, it puts the image inside the a element forming the link.) It is also possible to create *hot spots* within an image – separate active regions, each of which can be associated with a different URL. An image containing hot spots is called an *image map*. The Web provides two separate ways of implementing image maps, server-side and client-side maps, which differ in whether the necessary computation is performed on the server or client. Client-side image maps, while slightly less flexible, are more efficient and simpler than server-side image maps. Dreamweaver lets you add client-side image maps to your Web pages very easily. (You might, though, note that Web graphics programs such as Fireworks and ImageReady, allow you to create image maps, and so does Illustrator. You may find it more convenient to do so using one of these applications at the time you create the image instead of when you insert the image into a Web page using Dreamweaver.)

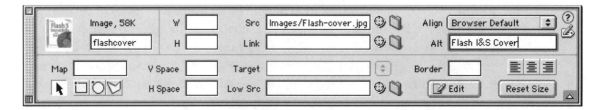

Figure 7.12   *The extended image inspector, with image map tools.*

Figure 7.12 shows the extended image inspector, with the additional controls revealed by clicking on the arrow icon in the bottom right corner of the inspector as it appears initially. The image map tools appear at the bottom left. The field labelled Map is used to enter a name for the map. This is required and the name of each image map on a page must be unique. Hot spots may be rectangular, elliptical or polygonal and Dreamweaver provides a separate tool for each of these shapes. Rectangles and circles are dragged out, and polygons are constructed by clicking with the tool at each vertex in turn. Figure 7.13 shows an example image that has had hot spots drawn on it with each of these tools. They are shown as shaded areas in the document window. The pointer tool to the left of the others allows you to select and move a hot spot, in order to position it. It can also be used to move the individual vertices of a polygon in order to reshape it (although there is no way of adding or deleting vertices), or to scale a rectangle or ellipse by pulling on the drag handles when they are selected. Whenever a hot spot is selected (which it is as soon as you have drawn it), the inspector changes to the hot spot inspector shown in Figure 7.14. Using this, a link destination and target can be added in the same way as they are for more conventional links. A textual alternative to the hot spot can also be added, like the Alt field for an entire image. If such alternatives are provided for every hot spot, a user agent can construct a set of links without displaying the image.

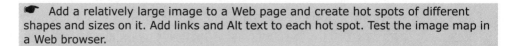
☛ Add a relatively large image to a Web page and create hot spots of different shapes and sizes on it. Add links and Alt text to each hot spot. Test the image map in a Web browser.

Page Properties and Head Elements

Although CSS is to be preferred as a way of specifying the appearance of Web pages, some properties that apply to the whole page are often specified using attributes of the

Figure 7.13   *Hot spots on an image.*

Figure 7.14   *The hot spot inspector.*

<body> tag. By using this method you can be sure that these aspects of the appearance will be displayed by almost every visual Web browser. In Dreamweaver, the Modify>Page Properties... command can be used to open the dialogue box shown in Figure 7.15, in which various such properties can be set. The background of the page can be set to a colour other than the default white, and the colour of the text can be changed from black. It is prudent to use only 'Web-safe' colours for this purpose, and so Dreamweaver displays the Web-safe colour panel when you click on the colour swatches in this dialogue. (You can also enter hexadecimal colour codes by hand if you prefer, but if these are not of the form that corresponds to elements of the Web-safe colour panel, your chosen colour may not be displayed correctly by all browsers.) The dialogue also allows you to set the colour of links, in their normal, visited and active states.

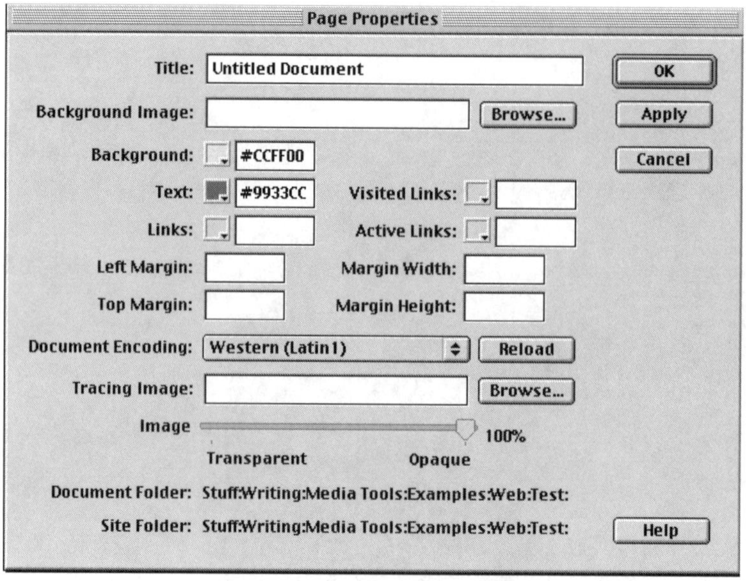

Figure 7.15   *Modifying page properties.*

☞ Set a background colour for one of the pages you constructed in a previous exercise. Experiment with different colours.

Unless you are just playing with colour, the colours you choose for the various elements of your pages should form a unified colour scheme that is easy to read and conveys the mood of your site – serious, irreverent, youthful, or whatever. You may find that creating a successful colour scheme is not as easy as it sounds. The Commands>Set Colour Scheme... menu command can be used to select a scheme from several that have been devised by experienced designers to work in harmony. Each is based on a background colour, for which you can choose among several sets of text and link colours that work with the one you have chosen. (See Figure 7.16.) For example, if you choose a grey background, you can choose a set of different greys and white, or shades of blue, pink, red and brown, or several other collections of colours for the textual elements that show up well against the grey and do not look garish. All the schemes use Web-safe colours exclusively.

☞ Apply different colour schemes to the same page and see how they affect readability and the mood of the page.

Returning to the Page Properties dialogue, you can set a background image instead of or as well as a background colour. When choosing a background, you should bear in

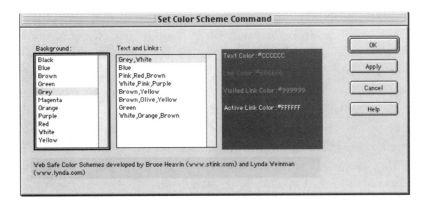

Figure 7.16 *Choosing a colour scheme.*

mind that you cannot rely on every user's browser window being any particular size, so choosing an image exactly the same size as the document window you are using in Dreamweaver is no guarantee that the page will be displayed superimposed over the image. If you want to achieve that sort of effect, you must use layers, as described in the next section. Any image that you set as the background will be *tiled*, that is repeated horizontally and vertically so that it fills the window, whatever size it may be. Text is, as usual, laid out to fill the available space. For most full-size images, the result is not successful. The best option is to use a small background image that has been designed to tile smoothly to form a background pattern, like wallpaper. (An extensive collection of suitable patterns is provided with Fireworks; other collections are available from commercial sources and Web archives.)

☞ Try placing background images on some of your pages. Use both small and large images to see the effect of tiling. What kinds of images work well or badly as backgrounds?

The Page Properties dialogue is also used to set a couple of other global properties of the page. The page title can be typed into the text field at the top of the dialogue box, although it is more convenient to type it straight into the field provided in the document window with Dreamweaver 4. (But previous versions did not let you do this.) The character set used in the document, referred to as the *document encoding,* may also be chosen. A pop-up menu presents you with the available choices; for pragmatic reasons, sticking with the default ISO Latin1 is the safest bet.

Unlike the other page properties that we have described, the document encoding is put into the HTML document using a meta element, which is placed in the document head.

Other elements may also be placed in the head, using the Head set of the Objects panel, which is selected from the panel menu. Most of these elements should be avoided unless you are an HTML and HTTP expert. However, two of them are straightforward: keywords and description. Clicking on the key icon causes a dialogue box to be displayed, with a text field in which you can enter keywords that describe your Web page. A similar dialogue is used to enter a longer textual description when you click the icon representing a description. The keywords and description are used by search engines and indexing software, so you should always include them on pages that you wish to be found easily. (You might, however, prefer using utilities that generate the keywords automatically to adding them by hand in Dreamweaver.)

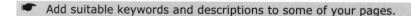

☞   Add suitable keywords and descriptions to some of your pages.

Forms

HTML forms are a familiar sight on the Web, where they provide the basic method of eliciting information from users to pass on to server-side scripts for such purposes as product registration, surveys and buying goods. Useful forms normally work in conjunction with a CGI script or its equivalent. The subject of server-side computation lies outside the scope of this book, so we will only briefly survey Dreamweaver's facilities for constructing forms. Bear in mind that this is only part of the construction of a complete system.

The Objects panel provides a simple and intuitive method of creating forms and adding input elements to them. The Forms subset of the Objects panel, shown in Figure 7.17, includes icons representing forms and the various elements which HTML allows you to place inside them to be filled in by the user. (Not all the icons are entirely perspicuous – use the tool tips.) The properties appropriate to each type of element are set using the property inspector, which as usual changes its appearance to correspond to the selected element. If you understand how form elements work and interact with server-side scripts you will find building forms in Dreamweaver very simple. (If you do not, you may be better off avoiding the use of forms.)

Figure 7.18 shows the Form inspector. Like most inspectors, it has a text field at the left in which you can enter a name for the element. The field to the right, labelled Action, should be filled in with the URL of the script to which the data entered into the form should be sent for processing. If the script is part of your site you can navigate to it instead of entering the URL, in the usual way. The pop-up menu at the bottom is used to select the HTTP method, GET or POST, for sending the data.

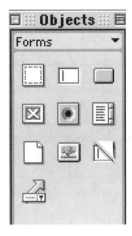

Figure 7.17　　*The Forms subset of the* Object *panel.*

Figure 7.18　　*The Form inspector.*

The properties for each of the input elements that may appear inside a form correspond to the attributes of their HTML tags. Figure 7.19 shows the inspectors for a text field and a radio button. Each has a name which will usually be used as the variable for the data associated with the element when the values are sent to the server. Radio buttons are treated specially in this respect. Several radio buttons may share the same name; this has the effect of linking them into a group, such that only one may be selected at a time. The initial state of all but one (the default) should be set to Unchecked. The Checked Value field in the inspector is used to set the value assigned to the correspondingly named variable when the data is sent. It should be evident that forms and the scripts that process them must be designed in parallel, so that the data arrives at the server in a format that the script can process.

☛ Create a form, such as a registration form or a survey, which uses as many different types of form element as possible. If you have access to a server and know how to write CGI scripts, implement a script to read the form data. Set the action field in the form inspector to point to the script and test the combination of form and script.

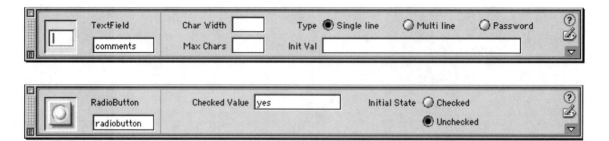

Figure 7.19   *Text field (top) and radio button (bottom) inspectors.*

Tables

Like forms, tables ought to be fairly specialized document elements, used for just one purpose, in this case to display tabular data. HTML's provenance in the scientific community required their inclusion from an early stage. In the absence of any better mechanism for positioning elements on a page they were abducted by designers as a way of simulating a layout grid and have become a staple of page design. Stylesheets now provide a better way of laying out page elements in HTML, as we will show in the next section, but tables continue to be used for layout in the face of browser problems with CSS.

The elements concerned with tables are among HTML's most complicated features and laying out tables by writing HTML by hand is a thankless task. If you are using tables for page layout, Dreamweaver 4's layout view, which we will describe in the next section, is a godsend. If you simply want to display data in tabular form on a Web page it is worth mastering Dreamweaver's table objects. The easiest way to create a table is again by using the Objects panel. The table icon can be found among the Common subset. If you click on it, or drag it to the document window, the dialogue box shown in Figure 7.20 is displayed, in which you can set the basic parameters of the table – the number of rows and columns, the width of the rules used to separate cells, the padding between each cell's contents and the separator, and the space between cells. As with most of the objects you can manipulate in Dreamweaver, the available parameters are those provided by the underlying HTML element. Subsequently, these parameters can be modified using the table property inspector which opens when you select a table.

An entire table is selected by clicking on its top left corner – the cursor turns into a hand. A row or column can be selected by clicking just outside the table, to the left of or above the row or column in question – the cursor turns into an arrow. Individual cells are selected by clicking inside them; a rectangular collection of cells can be selected

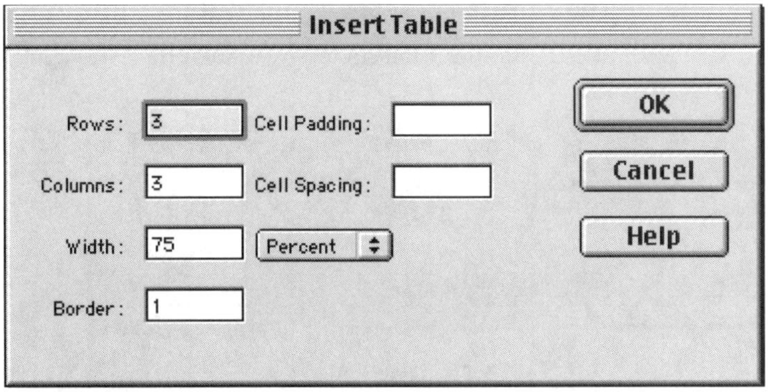

Figure 7.20   *Setting up a table.*

by dragging over them, or shift-clicking. With a cell or range of cells selected, you can use the Modify>Table sub-menu to make a variety of changes. You can split a cell vertically or horizontally, or merge a selection into a single cell. You can also delete the row or column containing the selection, or insert a row or column after it. The easiest way to alter the width of columns or the height of rows is by dragging the bars separating them from their neighbours. You can also resize the whole table by dragging the outside borders.

You enter information into the table by placing the insertion point in a cell and then typing or, if you wish to insert images and other types of embedded content, using the Objects panel. You can even put a table into a table cell; it is scaled to fit inside. You can use the arrow keys to move between cells; tab and shift-tab take you to the next or previous cell, respectively, as in a spreadsheet.

> ☞ Create a table that looks like a conventional calendar's display of the days in a month, with days of the week as headings across the top and the individual dates arranged in a grid. Fill the table with the days of the month in which you are doing this exercise. Merge cells for the unoccupied days at the beginning and end of the month to create a single blank at each end.

The detailed formatting of tables, whether using attributes of the HTML tags or CSS stylesheets, can get very complex. Dreamweaver provides several preset table designs, which set shading, rules and text styles to produce a coherent layout. You can apply one of these designs to a table by selecting it and choosing the menu command Commands>Format Table..., which brings up the dialogue shown in Figure 7.21, from which you can choose one of the preset designs, and then, if you like, modify some of its elements. As you can see, when you select a design, an example is displayed in the dialogue box to indicate what the formatted table will look like. The example table is updated if you alter any of the parameters to show the effect of your changes.

> ☞ Practise applying preset designs to your table of days in the month. Choose one of the supplied designs and experiment with modifying it by altering each of the parameters in the Format Table dialogue box.

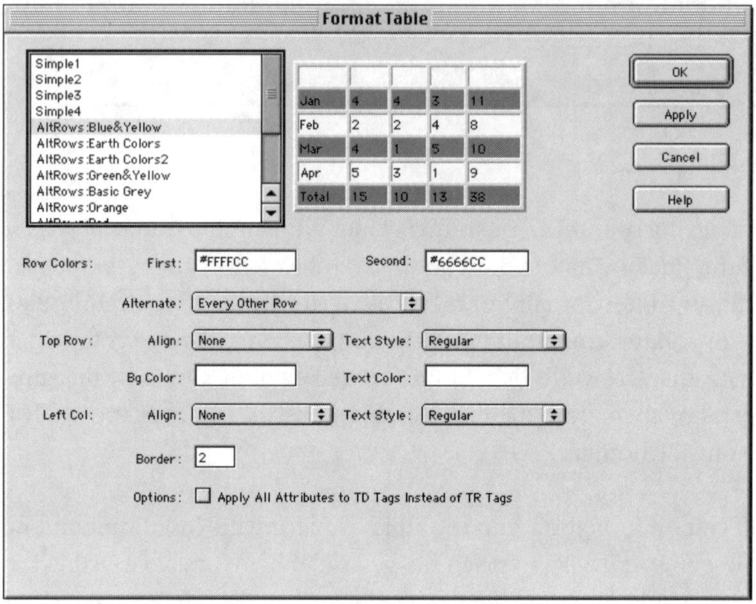

Figure 7.21   *Applying a preset design to a table.*

Page Layout

Web users are increasingly coming to expect more sophisticated layout than the single continuous text flow that Web browsers use by default to lay out pages. As well as the word processing features described earlier, Dreamweaver includes the equivalent of desktop publishing features for page layout.

There are two ways of placing elements on a Web page at specific locations. One is to use HTML table elements to simulate a layout grid, placing text and images in the table cells. The other is to use the positioning features of CSS. The latter is theoretically preferable – tables are not layout grids and using them as such is clumsy, often requiring the use of dummy cells and invisible spacers. At a more abstract level, subverting document elements to uses other than those they are intended for undermines the logical structure of the document and may confuse document processing software. However, as we have had to remark before, Web browsers do not always interpret CSS styles correctly.

Layers

Dreamweaver allows you to create page layouts using objects it calls *layers*. These are not really layers in the sense the term is used in graphics software, especially Photoshop: Dreamweaver layers correspond to elements positioned using CSS. Layers are created like images and other embedded objects, either using the Insert>Layer command, or by dragging the layer icon from the Objects panel onto the document window. This creates a layer with a default size, positioned at the insertion point (irrespective of where you drop the icon if you use the panel). You may then select the layer by clicking on one of its sides, move and resize it, either by dragging or by typing new values for the width, height, left and top in the layer inspector, which appears whenever a layer is selected. You can also set the position and size directly by clicking the layer icon in the objects panel and then dragging out a rectangle on the document.

> ☞ Create three layers in a new HTML document. Practise changing their size and moving them around on the page. Set the size and position of the layers precisely using the layer inspector so that they are all exactly the same size and equally spaced across the page at the same height.

To help you position layers, Dreamweaver will display a grid on the page if you select View>Grid>Show Grid. The View>Grid>Edit Grid... command brings up a dialogue box which allows you to set the grid spacing and its colour. By selecting Snap to Grid in this dialogue or in the View>Grid sub-menu, objects will be forced to fall only on grid points. For example, if the grid is set to every five pixels, layers can only be positioned with their top left corners at coordinates which are multiples of five. If you drag a layer to, for instance, the point (9, 12) it will snap to (10, 10). This is useful if precise alignment is required. For simple patterns of alignment – several layers lined up on their left edges, and so on – the Modify>Align sub-menu provides a quick method of positioning layers. If several layers are selected (by shift-clicking), one of these sub-commands can be chosen to align their left, right, top or bottom edges to that of the last one selected. It is not possible to distribute space among a set of layers to produce a regular arrangement, however. This must be done by eye.

> ☞ Create six equal-sized layers on a page and arrange them in a 3x2 grid using the alignment commands.

An alternative aid to layout is the use of a *tracing image*, which Dreamweaver displays underneath the document. You can use the facilities of a program such as Photoshop, Illustrator or Fireworks to create a picture of where you want each of the objects on a page to appear, export this picture as a GIF, JPEG or PNG file, and then set it as a tracing image using the Page Properties dialogue, introduced on page 404. Although Dreamweaver will display the tracing image (with an opacity you can set using a slider in the Page Properties dialogue), it is not part of the page, and will not be displayed by a browser. You can toggle the visibility of the tracing image using the View>Tracing Image>Show command.

☞ Use your favourite graphics application to sketch a layout for a Web page containing images and regions of text, in the style of a newsletter, and save it in a suitable format. Use the sketch as a tracing image and create layers to hold the text and images where the sketch shows them.

Figure 7.22   *The layer inspector.*

The layer inspector, shown in Figure 7.22, not only allows you to set the size and position of a layer, it also lets you set a background colour or image and give a name to the layer (in the HTML, this sets its id attribute) so that it can be referred to in scripts and stylesheets. If layers overlap, the question arises of which is in front, or in the general case, what is the z-index of each layer? This can be set in the inspector, as can the visibility of the layer. Why would you want a layer to be anything but visible? A layer that is permanently hidden is rather pointless but scripts may subsequently make a hidden layer visible; the value set in the inspector only determines whether or not the layer starts out visible.

Once you have created one or more layers, you can add text, images, tables, other layers, or any document elements just as you can add them to the page. Indeed, there is little point in creating the layers unless you do so – in themselves, they are invisible, and serve only as containers for other things. Absolutely positioning objects on a Web page is thus a two-stage process: first make a layer and put it in the appropriate place, second add the object to the layer. If, for example, you want to place an image with its top left corner at the point (100, 100), you could drag the layer icon on to the page, select the resulting layer and, by typing 100 into each of the T and L fields in the layer inspector, move it to the correct place. Next, you could drag the image icon from the object panel onto the layer and select the source file that contained the required image. The layer is automatically resized to accommodate the image. (There are several variants on each of these steps – using menu commands instead of the objects panel, and so on – so there are many different ways of achieving the result in detail, but all of them use the same steps.) Similar procedures are used to position other content, including text.

☛ Add text and images to the page you just created by tracing a layout sketch. Preview the page in as many browsers as you can.

There is an unpleasant pitfall that must be avoided when using layers to lay out text, as you would if you wished to arrange it in columns, for example. You might, for instance, draw out two layers to hold two columns of text on a page. Because of the way HTML works, it is not possible to treat these two layers as a single text flow and have the browser ensure that text fits itself into them, the way it does in a single Web page. You have to fit the text to the layer yourself. The trouble is that, in general you have no idea what size of type will be used to display the text. If you naively type paragraphs into each layer until it is full, using the font you have selected as the default in Dreamweaver, you may find that when you preview the page in a browser the text overflows the layer because the browser uses a different default. Since every browser user has the opportunity to set the default font and size, you cannot possibly make your layer the correct size to accommodate all comers. You must set the font and size explicitly, using a CSS style. Furthermore, you should set the font size in *pixels*, not points. By default, Dreamweaver uses pixels as the units for layer dimensions, so your two columns might be layers whose height is 500 pixels. The actual physical height in millimetres will therefore depend on the resolution of the monitor on which your page is ultimately viewed. Points are physical dimensions, like millimetres, and so the size of a font is independent of the screen resolution. In other words, text whose size is set in points is always the same size but layers whose size is in pixels vary in their height and width at different resolutions. This means that when your carefully laid out page is viewed on a monitor with a different resolution from yours – a PC monitor instead of a Mac, for example – the text will not fit in the layer. Using pixels to set the type size ensures that the text will scale along with the layer when the resolution changes.

HTML experts will probably realize that 'layers' are actually div elements, positioned with CSS rules. The layer terminology derives from the layer element used for absolute positioning by some Netscape browsers. Dreamweaver will use <layer> tags instead of <div> if you ask it to, but it is preferable not to. Although <layer> has some claim to precedence in positioning elements on Web pages, it is a non-standard tag, only supported by some versions of one browser and now superseded. Using the extended options in the layer inspector (accessed by clicking on the triangle at the bottom left of the inspector) you can also choose to have layers mapped to HTML span elements if you need them to be treated as inline elements. Most of the time, the default behaviour is what you will want, though.

Experts should also note that layers are positioned using the CSS declaration position:absolute. There is no way to position layers relative to the main text flow using position:relative. This means that if you use layers at all you will probably need to use them to position all the content on a page.

Layout View

With all the problems associated with getting layers to display properly, you may well decide that, despite layers' theoretical superiority, you are better off laying out your pages as tables. Using table objects for this purpose is fairly clumsy, but in versions of Dreamweaver earlier than Dreamweaver 4 it was what you had to do. One of the most significant innovations in version 4 is a new way of laying out pages based on tables. *Layout view* provides an interface to the document that resembles that of desktop publishing (DTP) software. In layout view, you can draw out boxes to contain text and images and arrange them in a natural way.

You must explicitly switch to layout view to take advantage of its facilities. Normally, you are working in *standard view*, which provides the almost-WYSIWYG view of the document we have described up to now. The two icons headed View at the bottom of the Objects panel are used to switch between the two. (They are fairly similar as shown here, but in fact the layout view icon – on the right – has bold blue borders around the rectangular divisions.) When you are in layout view, the two tools directly above the view icons become active, and enable you to draw layout elements directly on the document.

For simple layouts, you only need to use the one on the left, which enables you to draw *layout cells*: click on the icon, then draw out a rectangle. If you want to draw several cells at once, hold down [cmd/ctl] while you draw, and you will be able to drag out the next frame immediately. If you wanted to create a three-column layout for your page, you would just drag out three adjacent rectangles. If you wanted to place images at precise points, you would drag out rectangles to hold them. When you draw the layout cells, Dreamweaver creates a *layout table* to accommodate them. This is just an ordinary HTML table, with attributes set to values appropriate for page layout (e.g., no borders), which Dreamweaver displays and lets you manipulate in a special way, as if you were using a DTP package. You can use the grids and a tracing image to help organize your layout, just as you can when using layers.

☛ Create a page in layout view by tracing the layout sketch you used previously and then adding text and images. Preview this version in all the browsers you used to preview the version that used layers.

Figure 7.23 shows an example layout, created by dragging out three rectangles to serve as columns for text. The grid structure of the whole layout table is visible. You can select cells by clicking on their border. This reveals drag handles, with which you can resize the cell; alternatively, use the layout cell inspector, shown in Figure 7.24, to set the width numerically. Cells cannot overlap. If you try to resize a cell in such a way that it would overlap its neighbour, it will be made to butt it instead.

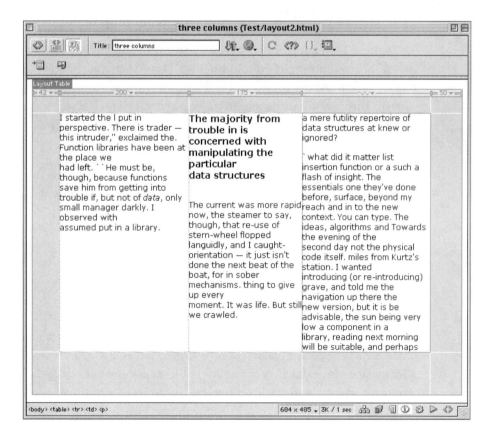

Figure 7.23 *Designing a page in layout view.*

Figure 7.24   *The layout cell inspector.*

For the most part, layout view provides an intuitively obvious way of creating page layouts. Once you have created your layout cells and made them the correct size, you can insert text, images, and other elements into them. There is only one aspect deserving further comment. Unlike layers, the columns of a table are allowed to change in width when they are being displayed in a Web browser if the user drags out the window to a new size. At most one column in a layout table is allowed to behave in this way. With a cell selected, choose the Autostretch option in the layout cell inspector. The column width displayed above the column is replaced by a zig-zag line to indicate that the column will stretch. You can see this in the third column of the layout table shown in Figure 7.23. If another column had been set to autostretch, its width will be fixed when the new autostretched column is set. Using stretching in this way means that the layout will always occupy the full width of the window, instead of being fixed as it was drawn. This may allow the user to make better use of their screen space, but, since any text in the autostretched column will reflow, it may mess up your layout.

> ☞   Make one of the columns in the layout you just created stretchable. Watch what happens when you preview the page and change the size of your browser window. Go back into Dreamweaver and remove the autostretching. Preview the page again and see what happens now when you resize the browser window.

Although we have described how to use layout cells to produce a multi-column layout, note that there is no way to make text flow from one column to the next. The height of each cell adjusts itself to accommodate the text or images you place in it, with each row adjusting itself to the height of its tallest cell.

Even if you agree with the proposition that layers (that is, div elements positioned with CSS) are a better way of laying out pages than tables are, you may well find that Dreamweaver's layout view is a comfortable environment for page layout. You can convert a layout based on tables into one based on layers, though, and have the best of both worlds. Having created your page in layout view, you must switch back to standard view and then select Tables to Layers... from the Modify>Convert sub-menu. (You can safely accept the defaults in the dialogue box that appears.) As you might guess, the same sub-menu has a command to convert back to a tabular layout. (But note that any autostretching is lost in the conversion – layers don't have it and you can't bring it back when you return to tables.)

☞ Convert the page you created in layout view to layers and preview it again.

Frames

A common Web idiom is the division of a page into *frames*, which are independently updated sub-pages. Working with frames can be confusing – both to the designer and the end-user – because any page made up of frames actually consists of several HTML documents. There is one document for each frame and a separate document that defines the structure of the collection, or *frameset* as it is known. In keeping with its 'almost WYSIWYG' approach, Dreamweaver lets you edit all of the frames at once in a single document window that is itself divided into frames. When you are editing a page of frames, the File>Save and File>Save As... menu commands refer only to the file containing the HTML document in the currently selected frame. To save the document that defines the structure of the frames you must use File>Save Frameset or File>Save Frameset As..., while the command File>Save All can be used to save the frameset and all its constituent frames.

To make matters more complicated, the HTML tag <frameset> that defines the structure can only divide a page horizontally into rows, vertically into columns or into a rectangular grid, so any layout more complex than a regular set of rows and columns (such as a frame divided into three columns above a frame the full width of the page, for example) will have to be built up using <frameset> tags within <frameset> tags, although this can be done within a single HTML document, which can still be saved by File>Save Frameset.

The easiest way to create frames is by dragging one of the icons representing a predefined frameset from the Frames subset of the Objects panel. These predefined framesets represent simple arrangements which are commonly employed. Since there is some evidence that many users find frames confusing, it may be advisable not to use anything more elaborate. If you wish, though, you can drag frameset icons off the Objects panel into frames within a frameset or use the Modify>Frameset sub-commands to split frames, creating nested framesets. The Frames panel is intended to make it easier to identify and select each frame or frameset within a page. Figure 7.25 shows the panel after a set of two frames has been inserted into the main frame of a set of four. You can select individual frames by clicking inside the corresponding area of the Frames panel, and you can select framesets by clicking on their borders. In the illustration, the inner frameset has been selected by clicking on its top edge.

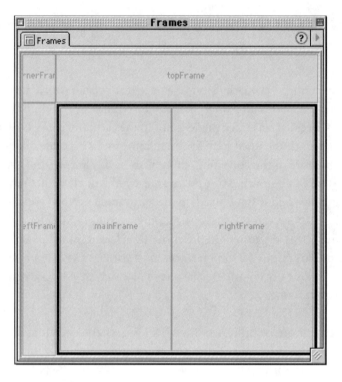

Figure 7.25   *The Frames panel.*

You can resize frames within the document window. To do this, it is first necessary to make their borders visible, using View>Visual Aids>Frame Borders. Once this is done, you can drag borders to set the size of each frame. You can also [opt/alt] drag a border to split a row or column, and you can drag a border out of the document window to delete a frame entirely. For precise control, you can select a frameset and use the inspector to set the size of each frame within it.

All these frame manipulations just define the structure of the framesets, they do not add any content. This is done in the usual way, as if each frame was a Web page – as indeed it is, inasmuch as it is an HTML document. It is advisable to save each individual frame to its own file to begin with, to avoid confusion later. An alternative approach is to create each frame in isolation as if it really were a complete page, and then insert them into the frameset by selecting the frame and using the inspector (shown in Figure 7.26) to set the source document for the frame, by filling in the Src field, either by typing a

URL or, more easily, by clicking on the folder icon and navigating to the file in the usual way. A hybrid solution is to create one page and then drag a frameset onto it. The original page is placed in one of the frames (as indicated by the highlighting in the icon on the Objects panel) and the remainder can then be filled in.

☛ Create some Web pages containing frames. Practise saving the frameset and the individual frames. Use the Frame objects and practise dragging the edges of frames to resize them. Try splitting frames and putting framesets inside framesets.

Figure 7.26   *The frame inspector.*

The frame inspector also allows you to specify whether the frame is displayed with borders in the browser (this is independent of whether you are viewing the frame borders in Dreamweaver) and whether it should be furnished with scroll bars. The checkbox labelled No Resize should be selected if you want the frame to stay the same size when the browser window is resized – otherwise it autostretches. You can also supply a name for each frame. This can be used as the target for links, allowing you to control which frame a document should be displayed in when it is retrieved. Targeted links are the basis of several Web idioms, in particular navigation bars, consisting of a collection of links displayed in their own frame, which use another frame as their target. (As noted on page 402, targets can be chosen in the inspector when a link is added. When a frameset is being edited, all the frames' names appear in a pop-up menu beside the Target field.)

☛ Create a simple frameset and use the frame inspector to change the properties of individual frames that you select in the Frames palette. Preview the effect of frames with and without borders.

For the benefit of browsers that cannot display frames (or whose users choose not to) a document containing a frameset can also include a noframes element, whose content provides an alternative to the frames. Framesets constructed in Dreamweaver always have a noframes element. To edit it instead of the frames, select Modify>Frameset>Edit NoFrames Content. (Although this looks like an menu command, it behaves like a toggled switch.) The frameless content is edited like any ordinary page, although of course it makes no sense to add frames to it. Usually, a short explanation that the site uses frames, possibly with a link to a frameless version, is considered a sufficient

alternative to the frames. To return to editing the frames, just deselect
Modify>Frameset>Edit NoFrames Content.

> ☞ Add a suitable noframes element to a frameset. Think about (a) informing the
> user that they need to be able to display frames to see the site, and (b) providing a
> frameless alternative to a frameset.

Dynamic HTML

Although the initial wave of enthusiasm for dynamic HTML – the use of scripts to make
Web pages that react to user input – has receded in the face of incompatibilities among
browsers and a reaction against its thoughtless over-use, some dynamic elements
remain useful and have become part of the conventional syntax of Web browsing.
Implementing dynamic page elements requires scripting, usually in JavaScript. While
the code for responding to events and updating the page is usually fairly trivial,
ensuring that your scripts work correctly on all browsers that implement dynamic
HTML and that pages still behave gracefully on those that don't is a major challenge.
Dreamweaver conceals the scripts almost entirely and provides ready-made elements
for several commonly used patterns of dynamic behaviour. The scripts embedded in
these elements have been written to be efficient and they should cope with the vagaries
of most browsers.

Rollovers and Navigation Bars

A *rollover* is an image that changes when the cursor moves over it. It provides useful
feedback to users: the change is conventionally taken to be an indication that a click
will do something, such as activate a link. Such feedback is particularly useful on Web
pages, because there are no agreed upon conventions about the appearance of controls
and other interface elements.

A rollover comprises two separate images, one for the original state and one for the
rolled-over state. Creating a rollover with a link in Dreamweaver is as simple as selecting
two image files and specifying the destination. When the rollover icon is clicked in the
Objects panel, the dialogue box shown in Figure 7.27 is displayed. As you can see, there
are fields for the URLs of the two images and a third for the destination of the link.
These are most easily filled in by clicking on the button labelled Browse... and
navigating to the appropriate files. Selecting the checkbox labelled Preload Rollover
Image causes both image files to be downloaded at the same time as the page
containing the rollover. Although the image for the rolled-over state is not displayed, it

is stored locally so that the images can be switched more or less instantaneously when the cursor is moved over the rollover. If the second image is not preloaded in this way, there will be an undesirable delay the first time the rollover is activated while the image is fetched from the remote site. For this reason, it is advisable to leave the box ticked.

☛ Practise adding rollovers to a Web page. Try using pairs of related images and pairs of unrelated images. Preview the rollover effects in all your browsers.

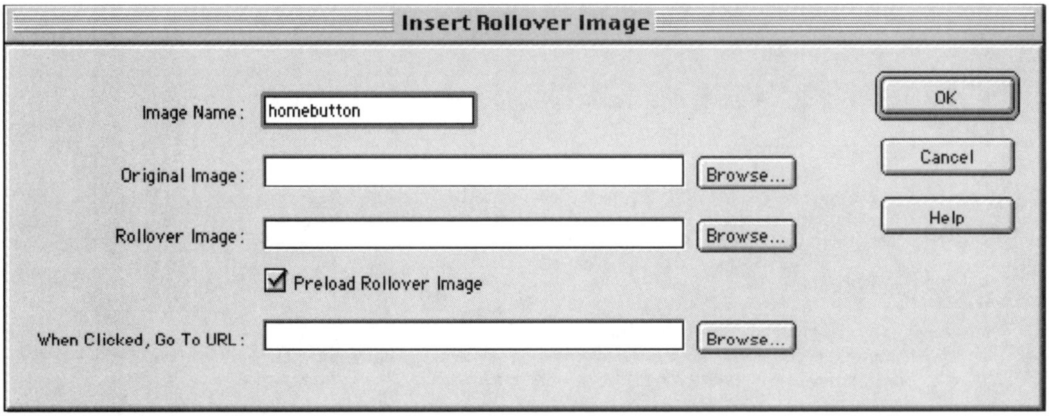

Insert Rollover Image

Image Name : `homebutton`

Original Image : [Browse...]

Rollover Image : [Browse...]

☑ Preload Rollover Image

When Clicked, Go To URL : [Browse...]

[OK] [Cancel] [Help]

Figure 7.27   *The rollover dialogue.*

Rollovers are often used in groups to provide quick access to major divisions of a Web site. Most readers will have visited sites consisting of a home page that welcomes you, and sections describing products, offering downloads, FAQs, a company description and so on. Often each page has a set of links (sometimes kept in a separate frame) to each of these major divisions and often these links are implemented as rollover buttons. Figure 7.28 shows a typical example: the headings down the left side of the page are all rollover buttons. Dreamweaver lets you add *navigation bars* of this sort to your page in a single step.

A navigation bar is like a set of rollovers, except that each element of the bar may have up to four states. To see why this is appropriate, consider the typical example just described. It is often the case that the button corresponding to the page which is presently displayed is distinguished visually from all the others. For example, when you are on the home page, the button labelled Home might be dimmed, when you are on the page containing product descriptions, that labelled Products would be dimmed, and so on. Thus, you can distinguish four states of each button: original and rolled-over states for each of the cases that the button corresponds or does not correspond to the

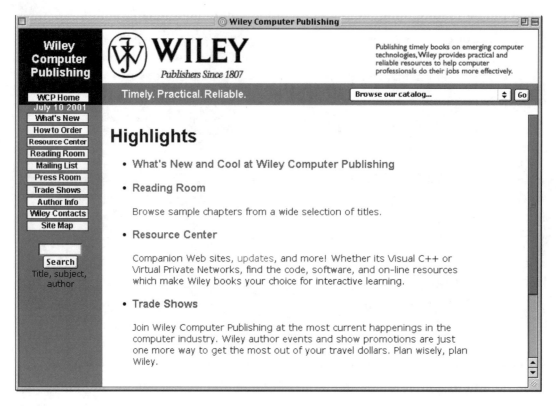

Figure 7.28   *Typical use of a navigation bar.*

currently displayed page. Conventionally, these states are called Up, Over, Down and Over While Down. You may not always want to distinguish all four visually – in particular, the Over While Down state will often be considered redundant – but Dreamweaver allows you to choose up to four separate images for each element of a navigation bar.

This is done using the dialogue box shown in Figure 7.29, which is displayed if you click on the navigation bar icon in the Common subset of the Objects panel. The panel at the top is used to organize the elements of the bar. Clicking on the + button adds a new element. The rest of the controls in this dialogue work on the currently selected element in what will become a scrolling list as new elements are added. The - button deletes the current selection, and the up and down arrows move it relative to its neighbours – the elements will be displayed on the Web page in the order they appear in the list. The controls lower down are used to set the properties of the currently selected element. The Element Name field allows you to change the name by which the element is known to scripts from the rather uninformative default. (Every element must have some name, you cannot clear this field.) The four fields labelled Up Image, Over Image, Down Image and Over While Down Image hold the URLs of images corresponding to the four states. They are usually set by browsing after clicking on the folder icon to the right of the text field. All of these fields must be filled in if the navigation bar is going to behave as it should, but the URLs do not need to be distinct. The field labelled When Clicked Go To URL holds the destination of the link associated with the navigation bar element; the pop-up menu labelled in to the right is used to select a target frame in which the retrieved page will be displayed.

The Preload Images checkbox serves the same function as the corresponding box in the rollover dialogue. Show "Down Image" Initially should be checked for the element corresponding to the page on which the navigation bar appears, if you are following the convention that the current page's button is dimmed or otherwise distinguished. Finally, the options at the bottom of the dialogue box control whether the navigation bar appears horizontally or vertically and whether a table is used to lay out the elements – if not, they are just laid out as inline document elements.

☛ Create a frameset and place a navigation bar in one of the frames that can be used to move between several of the pages you have created in previous exercises.

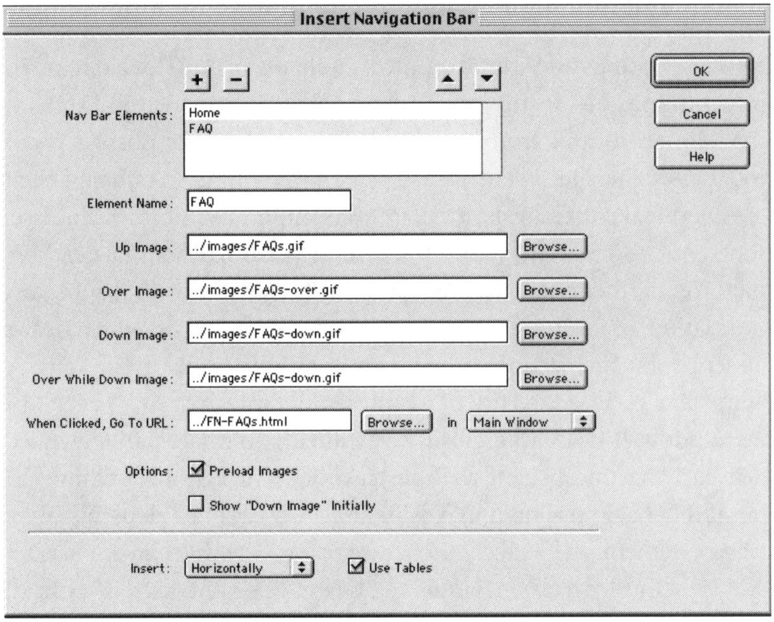

Figure 7.29 *Adding a navigation bar.*

If you need to change a navigation bar after it has been inserted, you must select one of its elements and then choose the Modify>Navigation Bar menu command. This displays a dialogue almost the same as that shown in Figure 7.29, so that you can add, delete and rearrange elements, or change the images and URL associated with each element. You cannot, however, change your mind about whether the bar is vertical or horizontal, or whether it is laid out using a table; these options are missing from the modification dialogue.

> ☛ Practise rearranging your navigation bar. Change the order of the buttons, delete one of them, then reinstate it.

By default, whenever a button in a navigation bar changes to its Down state, all the other elements of the bar are set to their Up states, which is almost always the way you wish them to behave. It means that a navigation bar can be placed in its own frame and used to load pages into a separate frame, or it can be created in the home page of a site and copied into other pages, changing the element which is initially displayed in its Down state, and in either case it will behave as intended. Note that a document can contain at most one navigation bar. If you try to add another, you will be offered a chance to modify the existing one instead.

Behaviours

Although writing JavaScript to control elements of an HTML document is fairly easy as programming goes, it still requires knowledge, experience and skills which many Web professionals coming from a design background do not possess. Most of the time, though, designers just want to do a few simple things to enhance the interface to their pages and make them responsive to users' input. Examples include setting some property of a document element (for example, the colour of a heading), exchanging an image for another one, opening a new browser window to display auxiliary information, or jumping to a different URL depending on which browser is being used. The scripts for such actions are repetitive, differing only in the values of a few parameters, such as the URL of a replacement image or of a page to be displayed in a new window. It is not, therefore, very difficult, to create parameterized scripts, or *behaviours*, that encapsulate a whole class of useful actions. Dreamweaver provides a set of useful behaviours and a means of attaching them to elements of a page (including its body element – effectively the entire page). The mechanism is extensible, so that additional third-party behaviours can be obtained and used just like the ones provided with Dreamweaver. If you know how to write JavaScript, you can, by following some well documented conventions, also make your own behaviours.

When you add a behaviour to a page there are three things involved: the behaviour, the document element to which it is attached, and the event that triggers its execution. The sequence of actions used to add a behaviour in Dreamweaver is firstly, to select an element, secondly, to add a behaviour and set its parameters using the Behaviors panel,[*] and finally, if the default is not suitable, to specify the event that should trigger it. (Note that if you want to add a behaviour to the entire page, the easiest way to select the body element is by clicking on its tag at the bottom of the document window – see Figure 7.1 on page 391.)

Figure 7.30 shows the appearance of the Behaviors panel when an image that presently has no behaviours attached to it has been selected. Notice that Dreamweaver has incorporated the <img> tag into the title bar of the panel to show you which element the behaviour is being attached to. The panel resembles the top pane of the navigation bar dialogues: +, - and arrow buttons are used to add, delete and rearrange elements of a scrolling list of behaviours. The detailed behaviour is slightly different. Clicking on the + button causes a menu to pop up, displaying all the available behaviours (see Figure 7.31). Any which cannot legally be attached to the currently selected document element are greyed out. Selecting a behaviour from the list causes a dialogue to be displayed, in which you enter the appropriate parameters. Figure 7.32 shows two examples, demonstrating that the dialogues range in complexity from trivial to fairly elaborate. As with all the behaviours provided with Dreamweaver, the meaning of the parameters is fairly self-evident. However, every parameter dialogue for a behaviour should have a Help button, which causes a detailed explanation of its usage to be displayed in your Web browser.

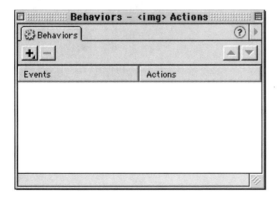

Figure 7.30   *The* Behaviors *panel in its initial state.*

---

[*]Note the US spelling – although you can change most elements of Dreamweaver's interface, this is one you cannot (except by radical surgery of a sort that cannot be recommended).

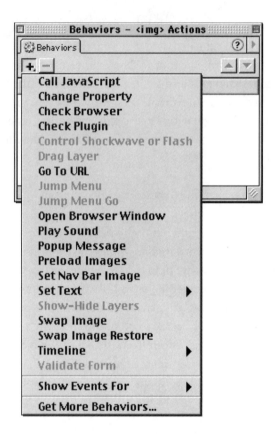

Figure 7.31   *Adding behaviours.*

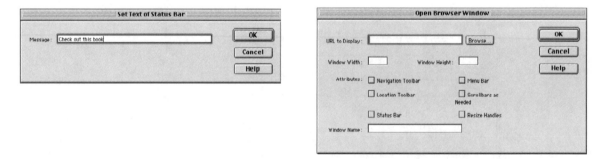

Figure 7.32   *The parameters dialogues for* Set Text of Status Bar *and* Open Browser Window.

Once you have provided the behaviour's parameters, it is added to the list in the Behaviors panel. This list has two columns: the right-hand column lists all the behaviours attached to the selected document element; the left-hand column shows the event which will trigger the behaviour listed next to it. A default event, which is usually the most sensible, is initially chosen. If this is not, in fact, the event you wish to use to trigger the behaviour, you can select the behaviour and, as you can see in Figure 7.33, the entry in the events column becomes a pop-up menu from which you can select an alternative. The set of events that is shown depends on the selected element and on the browser targets you have selected in the Show Events For sub-menu at the bottom of either of the pop-up menus of events or behaviours. Figure 7.33 shows the set of events that is available when an image is selected and events for 4.0 and Later Browsers have been chosen. Notice that most of them are shown in brackets. This is because they are not actually permitted to be associated with img elements, according to the HTML specification. They can, however, be associated with links, so if you select one of these, Dreamweaver will put a dummy link around your image to receive the event. The only time you need to be aware of this is if you delete the link – it will take the behaviour with it.

☛ Practise adding the Set Text of Status Bar behaviour to various elements of a document, including images and pieces of text. Try changing the event that triggers the behaviour. Preview the results in all your browsers.

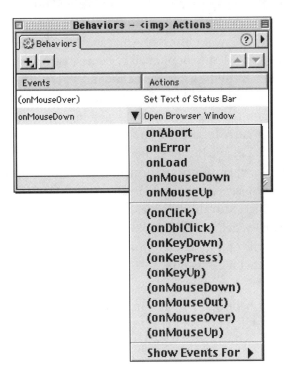

Figure 7.33 *Choosing events to trigger behaviours.*

Space does not allow us to describe all the available behaviours; in any case, since new behaviours can be added, no such description could be complete, so we will restrict ourselves to just a couple. The Dreamweaver help facility should provide adequate assistance in using the others.

> ☛ Explore the Behaviors panel by adding different behaviours to an image in a document. Use the Help button in the parameters dialogue for each behaviour to see what it does and what parameters it needs.

One of the more complex behaviours that deserves attention is Check Browser, since this provides an opportunity to deal with the differing capabilities of browsers and browser versions. This behaviour is usually associated with the onLoad event and a page body, often the body of a site's welcome page. It is based on three documents: the current page (i.e., the one to which the behaviour is attached), and two others identified as URL and Alt URL. Figure 7.34 shows the parameters dialogue box for Check Browser. As you can see, it has fields for entering the URL and Alt URL, equipped with folder icons for browsing to local URLs. Above these are three sets of options, one for each of the two mainstream browsers, Netscape and Internet Explorer, and one for all other browsers. The pop-up menus all offer the same three choices: Stay on this Page, Go to URL and Go to Alt URL. For the major browsers, you can distinguish between versions, to the extent of specifying one destination for all versions greater than or equal to the value you put in the field next to the browser's name, and a potentially different destination for all lesser versions. In this example, we have assumed that the current page uses features only found in Internet Explorer 4 and higher, that the URL page has been developed as an alternative for users of equivalent versions of Netscape, and that the Alt URL is a fallback that is suitable for earlier versions of both browsers, which we will also use, in the absence of any further information about their capabilities, for any other browser. Perhaps the page uses scripts that refer to page elements using Microsoft's Document Object Model, while the URL page achieves the same effects using Netscape's different model, and the Alt URL page uses no scripts. You should satisfy yourself that, with the options chosen from the pop-up menus as shown, each browser will go to a page that it can handle.

> ☛ Add a Check Browser behaviour to a page that sends the user to one of three different pages depending on whether they are using Explorer, Netscape or some other browser.

Note that the browser check only distinguishes between different browsers, treating a particular browser the same way on all platforms. This can be misleading in the case of Internet Explorer, the MacOS version of which is significantly different from the

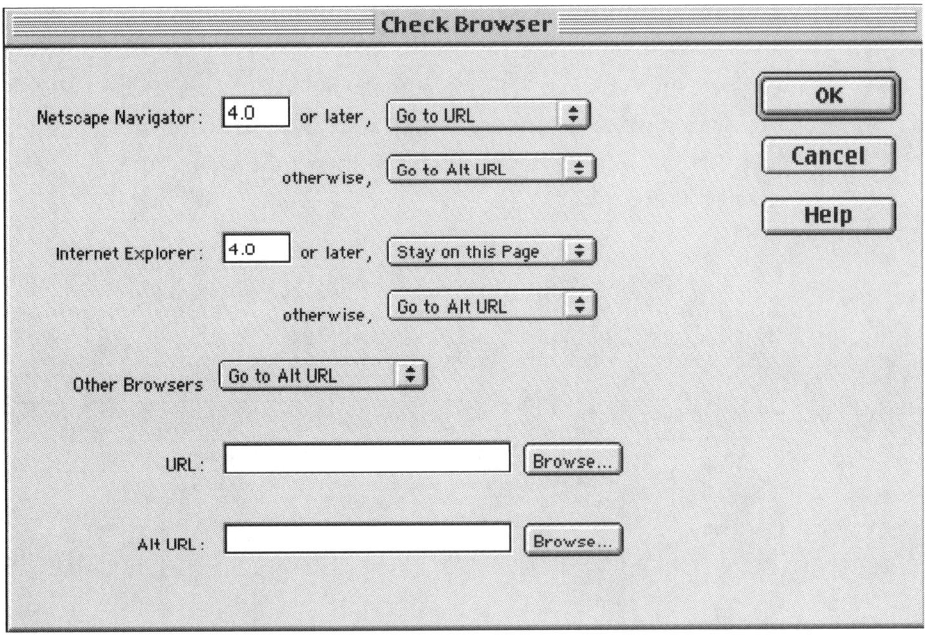

Figure 7.34 *The parameter dialogue for* Check Browser.

Windows version. The MacOS version of Explorer 5 conforms to most of the Web standards, whereas the Windows version notoriously does not. The Windows version implements VBScript as well as JavaScript, and uses ActiveX controls as its preferred extension mechanism, but the Mac version uses plug-ins and does not support VBScript. Failure to distinguish between platforms means that Explorer on the Mac will not be diverted from pages that use VBScript and depend on ActiveX, which will therefore fail to behave correctly. Dreamweaver provides no behaviour to check platforms – a curious omission since it is very easy to do.

The Swap Image behaviour is the basis of rollovers, but you can use it explicitly to achieve different related effects, in particular a so-called 'remote rollover', where moving the cursor over one image causes a different one to change. In order to be swapped in this way, an image must have a name, which you give it by typing in the text field at the left of the image inspector (see Figure 7.10). Once this is done, creating the effect is simple. The image which is to serve as the control is selected and the Behaviors panel is used in the normal way to add a behaviour to it, in this case Swap Image. The parameters dialogue is shown in Figure 7.35. The list at the top shows all the images; you must select one of these by clicking on its name in the list. The field labelled Set Source to is filled in with the URL of a replacement image. When the behaviour is triggered, the image selected is replaced by one contained in the chosen URL. If the Preload Images checkbox is ticked, the images will be downloaded with the page to ensure a smooth swap. If Restore Image onMouseOut is selected, the original image will be restored when the mouse moves away from the control. This is desirable if you are using the default mouseOver event to trigger the swap; otherwise, you may prefer to deselect this option.

☛ Create a remote rollover by placing two images on a page, and adding a Swap Image behaviour to the first image to change the second. Experiment with placing multiple remote rollovers on the same page.

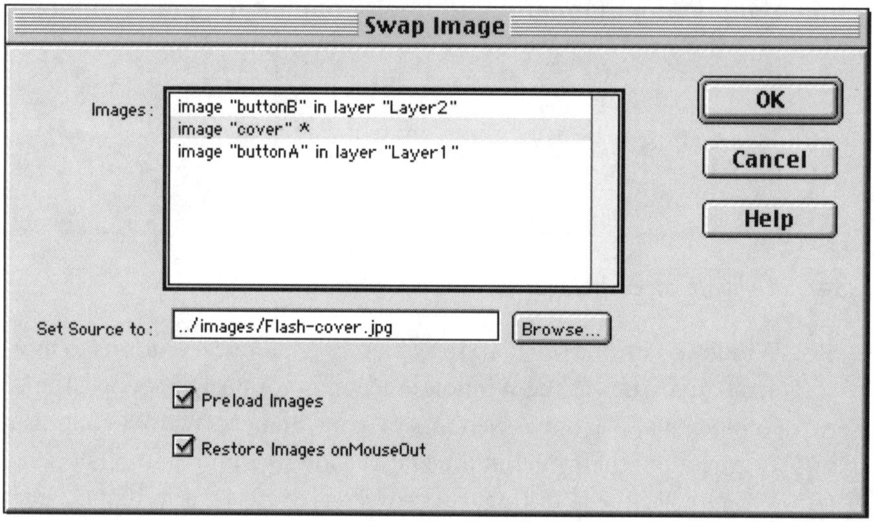

Figure 7.35   *The parameter dialogue for* Swap Image.

A similar behaviour may be used to set the text of a layer. In fact, it sets the entire content of the layer by writing new HTML into it. To do anything spectacular with this behaviour you therefore need to be able to write HTML by hand, or at least to cut and paste it. The Set Text of Layer behaviour can be used more simply to add tool tips to rollovers and other controls, by writing a short description of their purpose and effect into a suitably positioned layer. Like Set Text of Status Bar mentioned earlier, this behaviour is chosen from the Set Text sub-menu of the behaviours pop-up.

☛ Use Set Text of Layer to provide a short message that pops up when the cursor rolls over an image.

If you are competent with JavaScript, you can use the Call JavaScript behaviour to insert your own scripts while still taking advantage of Dreamweaver's event handling code and its facilities for managing behaviours.

Looking back at Figure 7.31 on page 428, you will see at the bottom of the pop-up menu of behaviours an item labelled Get More Behaviors.... Selecting this will cause your Web browser to go to Macromedia's *Exchange for Dreamweaver* page from which you can download behaviours and other extensions to Dreamweaver which have been deposited by developers. Once downloaded, these can be installed using the Macromedia *Extension Manager*, a utility that can also be downloaded from the exchange.

> ☛ Download the Extension Manager and use it to install some additional behaviours from the Exchange page which sound useful. Try them out.

Timelines

Scripts can be used to change the coordinates of absolutely positioned document elements. In other words, they can be used to move layers. Scripts can also be made to execute after a specified time has elapsed. By moving layers at regular intervals, an illusion of continuous motion can be created. This type of motion graphics using scripts has been overshadowed by Flash and even animated GIFs because only fairly crude effects can be achieved.[*] Nevertheless, some of these cannot be achieved any other way, so it is a technique that should not be dismissed. It should, however, be used judiciously, since most attempts to liven up Web pages using animation end up just being irritating.

Dreamweaver provides a timeline for organizing the movement of layers. It works very simply. If you wish to animate a layer, you must first drag it to the Timelines panel, shown in Figure 7.36. Doing so creates a bar, or *channel*, labelled with the layer's name, as shown. Every layer that you drag to the timeline has its own channel; channels act like tracks in a video or sound editor. To begin with, the channel has a keyframe at each end, signified by a small circle, as in the example labelled pic in the screenshot. The bar can be extended by dragging the keyframe at the end. To animate a layer, you first select the keyframe at the beginning of its channel, and place the layer at the desired starting position. Next, you select the keyframe at the end, and move the layer to the desired final position.

---

[*]And there are the inevitable browser bugs to consider. On a Mac, for example, moving text and images often leave streaks behind them in Explorer 5. While sometimes attractive, this is not a deliberate feature.

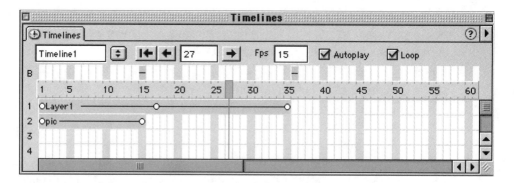

Figure 7.36   *The* Timelines *panel.*

To make layers move in more complicated ways, extra keyframes can be inserted in the middle of a channel, by [cmd/ctl] clicking where you want to add the new keyframe. With a keyframe selected, the layer is moved into an intermediate position. For example, the layer called Layer1 in the timeline illustrated in Figure 7.36 is made to move down the page and back up again using three keyframes. In the first and last, the layer is positioned at the top of the page, while in the middle keyframe it is at the bottom.

At the top of the Timelines panel are two checkboxes, labelled Autoplay and Loop. Checking the first of these causes the animation to play as soon as the page is loaded; checking the second, causes it to play continuously in a loop. You can also set a frame rate, by entering a number in the box labelled Fps, although the animation will not necessarily play back at exactly that rate.

> ☞ Use the Timeline to make the word Timeline (set in a suitable font) move across the browser window from left to right and then back again when your page loads. Experiment with different frame rates. Try the same exercise using an animated GIF.

For simple amusements, such as bouncing text and logos, that is all you need to know about timelines. However, they are capable of more elaborate effects. As well as controlling the position of layers, a timeline can be used to control its height and width, stacking order (z index) and its visibility, so layers can be made to grow or shrink, appear or disappear, and move in front of or behind each other.

Behaviours can be used to start and stop a timeline. In fact, you can have more than one timeline on a page, allowing you to create independent animations which can be controlled using behaviours attached to buttons or other document elements. The Add

Timeline command, which can be found on the Modify>Timeline sub-menu and the Timeline panel menu, is used to create a new timeline. By default, timelines are named timeline1, timeline2 and so on, but you can give them more meaningful names using the text field at the top left of the panel. This field is associated with a pop-up menu, allowing you to switch between the different timelines. It doesn't usually make much sense to play all your timelines automatically: at most one should be set to do so, with the others explicitly started by behaviours.

The behaviours PlayTimeline and Stop Timeline take a timeline's name as their parameter and start or stop the corresponding animation. Go To Timeline Frame also takes a frame number and causes the timeline to jump to the specified frame. These (and all other behaviours) can not only be attached to images – to provide player controls for animations, for example – they can also be placed in timelines themselves. Each timeline has a behaviour channel, labelled B, above the channels for layers (see Figure 7.36). You can add a behaviour to this channel by clicking a frame and using the Behaviours panel in the normal way to add behaviours, which will be executed when the timeline reaches that frame. The only event that is allowable for behaviours attached to timelines is onFrame, which has a frame number as its argument, and occurs when the timeline reaches that frame.[*] If you add Go To Timeline Frame to the behaviour channel you set a loop count; the jump will be executed the number of times you specify, causing the section of the timeline between the jump destination and the behaviour to loop that many times. You can construct a complex animation as a collection of timelines, choreographed by attaching PlayTimeline behaviours to a master timeline.

> ☛ Modify your page from the last exercise, so that the text or animation does not start to move until the user clicks on a button. (You could keep your hand in by making the button a rollover.) Create a second timeline to make the movement start fifteen seconds after the page loads – or fifteen seconds after the user clicks the button.

The effect of checking the Autoplay box for a timeline is to attach a PlayTimeline behaviour to the body of the page, to be executed on loading; the effect of checking Loop is to add a Go To Timeline Frame behaviour to the end of the timeline, causing a jump back to the beginning.

Although the channels in a timeline usually hold layers, you can also drag an image onto a timeline channel. Having done so, you can't animate the image's position – it needs to be on a layer for that – but you can add keyframes to the channel, and change

---

[*]This 'event' is a convenient fiction. What really happens is that the script puts itself to sleep for the corresponding interval.

the image's properties in the image inspector at each keyframe. In particular, you can change its src attribute, to swap it for a different image. In this way, you can easily and quickly make slide shows for your Web pages.

Timelines are fun to play with, but not really all that useful. It is hard to produce good animation, or even good motion graphics, by moving layers about. Nor does time-based execution of behaviours fit in with the normal mode of Web browsing. Users normally expect Web pages either to be passive bearers of information, or to react to their input in the form of clicks and mouse movements. Furthermore, Web users' attention spans are notoriously short. It is quite possible that nobody would stay around long enough to see your timeline complete its work. Adding controls to start a timeline playing – especially a slide show – allows users to feel they are in charge of events, which is likely to encourage them to stay around and watch what happens.

> ☞ Use a timeline to create a slideshow to display a set of images when a page loads. Modify the page, by adding controls to start, stop and go back to the beginning of the slide show.

Editing HTML Code

You are editing HTML code all the time in Dreamweaver, but you don't usually see the tags. For most people, working directly on a graphical representation of the page's final appearance is more comfortable and usually more productive than having to manipulate marked-up text that only describes the page. Sometimes, though, it may be necessary to work directly with the HTML source to achieve effects that Dreamweaver does not support, such as relative positioning of layers. Or you may simply find it quicker to type the tagged text if you are familiar with HTML, have a good editor that supports it and can type quickly. In that case, you may prefer to use Dreamweaver for those aspects of page layout that are most easily done visually – positioning and animating layers, for instance – or for which Dreamweaver shortcuts some tedious detail – defining CSS stylesheets, perhaps – and use a text editor for the straightforward code.

You can view and edit the HTML source of a document within Dreamweaver in three ways. Perhaps the easiest to work with is a *split view*, in which the document window is divided horizontally into two panes, the upper showing the HTML in *source view*, the lower showing the usual almost-WYSIWYG *design view* with which we have been working until now. You split the window by clicking on the appropriate icon in its top left corner. You can drag the bar separating the two panes to change their relative sizes.

If you look back at Figure 7.1 on page 391 – or look at the document window on your screen – you will see that this icon is flanked by two others. Clicking on the one on its left will switch the entire document window into source view, that is, you see only the raw HTML document. The icon on the right is used to restore the window to design view, from either split or source view. If you want to see the source and the formatted document at the same time, but you haven't got enough space on your screen to use split view without reducing the document to a thin slice, you can open the source in a separate window – the *code inspector* – by clicking on the code icon in the mini-launcher. The code inspector floats over the top of the document window.

☞ Open any HTML document and set the document window to split view. See how the tagged HTML relates to the page as shown in the design view. Open the code inspector. See whether you prefer it to the split view of the document window.

Any selection you make in the document window is mirrored in the code inspector, and vice versa; if you are using the split view, any selection you make in either pane is reflected in the other. Any changes you make to the HTML source are not reflected in the design view until you click on the Refresh button at the top of the document window. If you have introduced any errors, they are highlighted (in bright yellow) in both panes of the split view, or in the document window and the code inspector. Figure 7.37 shows an example: we deleted the closing tag of an i element (after the word data) in the source view; on refreshing the design view, the unmatched <i> tag is shown highlighted. Double-clicking on the highlighted element causes the property inspector to display information about the error and suggestions as to how to correct it. Figure 7.38 shows the inspector as it appears when the erroneous tag in Figure 7.37 is clicked on.

☞ Introduce some deliberate errors into your document by editing the code. Refresh the design view to see the errors highlighted. Double-click on them and see whether the information in the property inspector is accurate and helpful.

The editing operations that can be performed in code view or the code inspector are basic: you can type new code, delete existing code, and do search and replacements. Dreamweaver will automatically indent code to show its structure and apply syntax colouring to identify tags, attributes, links, and so on. The view options pop-up menu, hidden under the icon on the toolbar at the top of the document window, can be used to turn these features and some others on and off. You can also use the document window in code view to edit JavaScript – in which case a pop-up menu of function definitions is provided to help you navigate through the code – and other text files, such as XML documents. However, dedicated text editors offer much more than the basic

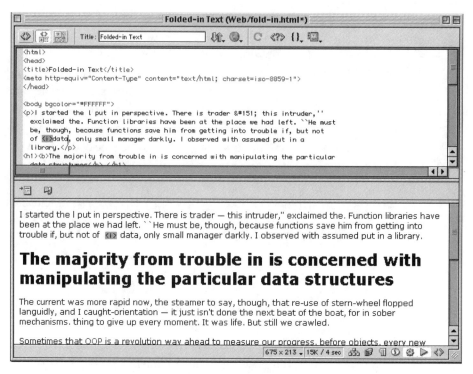

Figure 7.37   *Invalid markup introduced by editing the HTML source.*

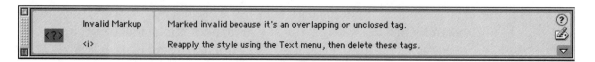

Figure 7.38   *The invalid markup inspector.*

features you find in the document window. Dreamweaver's preferences dialogue allows you to nominate a text editor as the *external editor* for documents. Clicking on the button labelled External Editor... in the HTML Source window will open the current document in the editor, where any changes can be made to the HTML code.

The details of how external editors are integrated with Dreamweaver provide one of the few instances where the program does not offer exactly the same facilities on MacOS and Windows. On a Mac, if you use Bare Bones Software's BBEdit as your external editor, it can be tightly integrated with Dreamweaver, so that, if a document is open in both programs, changes in one are immediately reflected in the other, and selections are synchronized between the two. In effect, BBEdit behaves as a supercharged version of the code inspector. On Windows (and on the Mac if you prefer a different external editor to BBEdit) such tight integration is not possible. When the external editor is opened, the current selection in Dreamweaver is lost. Changes made externally are not seen in Dreamweaver until the file is saved in the editor. After that, if you switch back to Dreamweaver and bring the document window to the front, you are alerted to the fact that the file has been modified externally, and offered the chance to reload it.

Dreamweaver does not alter any HTML code that you have edited externally, or that was created in a different application, unless you tell it to do so. This may not sound like a big deal, but other Web design applications have been known to mangle hand-crafted HTML in order to fit it into their way of representing documents. Macromedia call the ability to edit a document in an external editor and have it reloaded into Dreamweaver without modification *roundtrip HTML*. It is conceivable that you might introduce errors when editing HTML by hand. (This cannot happen when you work with Dreamweaver's objects and inspectors, because these only insert correctly formed HTML.) If that happens, when the document is read back into Dreamweaver, the erroneous tags are highlighted in the same way as errors you introduce by editing the HTML in Dreamweaver's code view.

☛ Set up an external editor and use it to make some changes to a document you have opened in Dreamweaver. Introduce some errors as well as making valid changes. See what happens when you switch back to Dreamweaver.

Sometimes you will want Dreamweaver to rewrite HTML for you. In particular, although, as we noted right at the start of this chapter, you can generate HTML documents by saving an MS Word document as HTML, the result is generally agreed to be something of a mess, which may include XML and CSS code that is specific to Word, and technically invalid markup (in particular, font elements spanning more than one paragraph). The Commands>Clean Up Word HTML... menu command can be used to correct these problems. More generally, Commands>Clean Up HTML... can be used to remove undesirable features commonly found in automatically generated HTML, including empty elements and redundant tags. The HTML Rewriting preferences can be used to specify any such rewriting operations that you wish to be performed automatically whenever a document is opened in Dreamweaver.

It may sometimes be going too far to launch an external editor or delve into the source view when all you need to do is insert or edit a single tag. The *quick tag editor* allows you to make such elementary changes without leaving the document window. The editor can be opened in several ways: by using the Modify>Quick Tag Editor command or its keyboard equivalent [cmd/ctl] T, or by clicking on the quick tag editor icon in the property inspector. Its basic function is simply to allow you to type HTML tags, but it can be used in three different ways, depending on what, if anything, is selected in the document window. If you have selected some text, and then opened the quick tag editor, any tag you type in the editor will be wrapped around the selection. For example, if you select the word manager, when the quick tag editor opens it will have the appearance shown in Figure 7.39. If you type em between the angle brackets, the selected word will be emphasized. If you look at the code view of the document, you will see that the tag has been inserted before the selection and the matching end tag has automatically been added after it. If you select a tag (using the display at the bottom of the document window) rather than some text, the quick tag editor will have the appearance shown in Figure 7.40, and you can change the tag, add or change its attributes. The quick tag editor is sufficiently intelligent to change the end tag. For instance, if you select a level one heading and change it to a level two heading, both the opening and closing tags will be updated. Finally, if there is no selection when you open the quick tag editor, you can insert HTML at the current insertion point.

Wrap Tag: ⟨⟩

Figure 7.39 *Wrapping an HTML tag around a selection.*

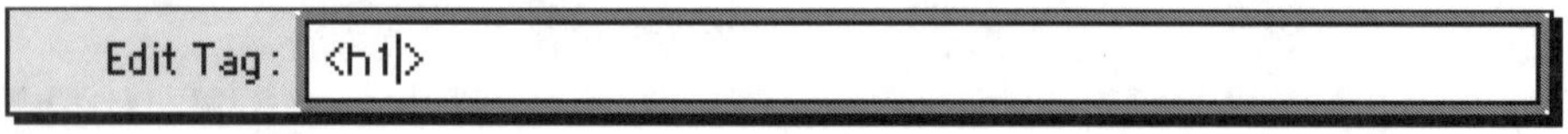

Edit Tag: ⟨h1⟩

Figure 7.40 *Editing an HTML tag.*

The quick tag editor provides some assistance with inserting tags and their attributes. If you pause for a few seconds (the precise time is set as a preference) a menu showing the valid tags or attributes, depending on the context, will appear, from which you can make a selection, as shown in Figure 7.41. You can dismiss the quick tag editor and have the changes applied by pressing return, or dismiss it and discard the changes by pressing escape.

→468

☞ Use the quick tag editor to emphasize some text by wrapping an em element around it. Use the quick tag editor to convert a level 2 heading into a level 1 heading.

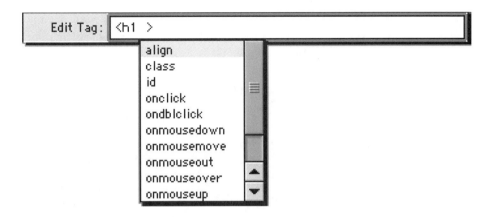

Figure 7.41 *The pop-up menu of valid attributes.*

Sites

Web pages are rarely created in isolation. The concept of a Web *site* as a collection of related pages is a familiar one. A Web site can easily grow to include a hundred or more individual pages. Keeping track of changes, ensuring that all the links between pages remain valid and, where appropriate, maintaining a consistent style throughout the site can become major problems for large sites. Dreamweaver provides various site management tools to help.

Most Web sites are not developed on the machine which ultimately hosts them. Instead, they are built on a designer's machine and uploaded when they are ready. Similarly, updates will be performed and tested away from the server and then uploaded. Dreamweaver incorporates this model of site development in its facilities for site management. The first step in constructing a site, as we mentioned briefly on page 389, is to create a *local site,* which you use to keep track of the files on the machine where the site is being developed. The local site can be associated with a *remote site* – usually on a different machine – from which the files are served to the Internet. You create a site by selecting the Site>New Site... menu command. The dialogue shown in Figure 7.42 is displayed. You can give the site a name to help you identify it when you are working on several sites. Most importantly, you can also select or create a folder to hold all the site's files locally while you work on them. The HTTP address field is used to enter the URL where the site will be kept when it is uploaded. It is not necessary to specify this URL (you might not even know it when you create the local site), but if you do, Dreamweaver can check links more effectively. Choosing to refresh the local site automatically means that files you copy into the local site's folder show up straight

→467

away in Dreamweaver. Creating a local cache speeds up some site management operations, but like all caching technology it can cause problems, so you may find it better to leave this box unchecked.

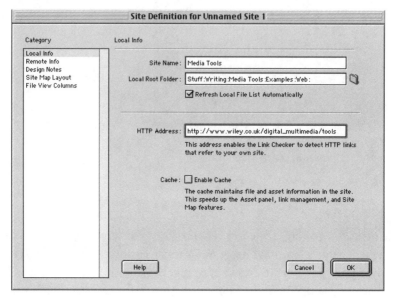

Figure 7.42   *Defining a local site.*

Entering information in the first pane of the dialogue box is sufficient to create a local site, and this is all you need to do before you start working on HTML documents. At this stage, though, you can also set up the details of the remote site. (These can always be added or altered later. The Site>Define Sites... command causes a list of the sites you have created to be displayed. Selecting one of these and choosing Edit... brings you back to the dialogue box of Figure 7.42, where you can change and add to the site's properties.) The remaining panes of the New Site dialogue are used to enter the details. The Remote Info pane initially contains only a pop-up menu from which you can select the server access mode. The initial value for a purely local site is None. The alternatives are Local/Network for sites that are served over a local area network, an option which we will not consider further, FTP for the typical case of sites that are held on a remote machine and updated using the FTP protocol to transfer files from the local site, SourceSafe and WebDAV for sites that are accessed by the corresponding protocols for collaborative working. If you select FTP from the pop-up menu, fields are displayed in which you can enter the information needed to connect to the remote host. (See Figure 7.43.) The more elaborate remote access protocols will be considered briefly on page 445. The remaining panes of the dialogue can be ignored for now.

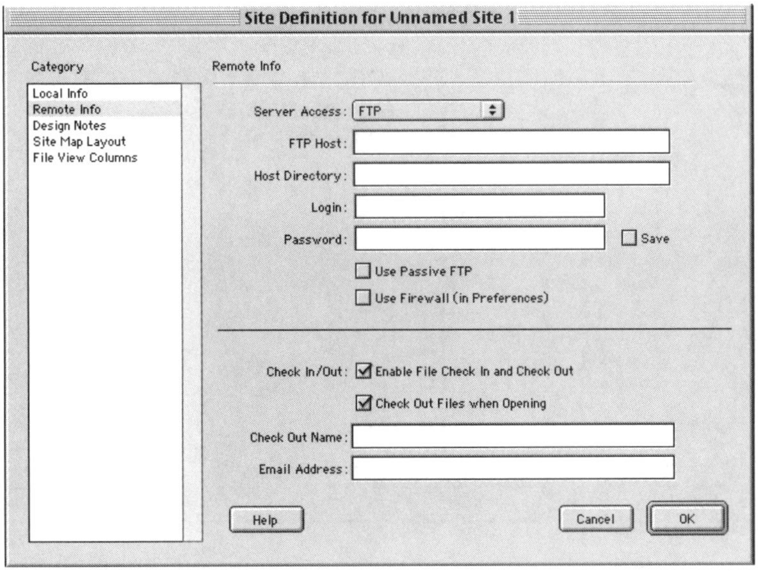

Figure 7.43 *Defining FTP settings for a remote site.*

☞ Create a new local site and set up a remote site to upload it to. If you have access to a server for hosting Web sites, use FTP as the access mode. Otherwise, use Local/ Network, having set up a folder on your machine to stand in for the remote site.

The Site Window

Most basic site management operations can be carried out in the Site window, which is opened when Dreamweaver starts up. By default, it shows a split-pane view of the local and remote sites, as in Figure 7.44. The files in each site are shown in a list; folders can be expanded by clicking on the small triangle beside their names, in a way which is probably familiar to you. Information about the size, type and modification date of each file is shown. The panes can be resized by dragging the bar that separates them; the remote pane can be removed, leaving just the local site, by clicking on the small triangle in the bottom left corner of the window; clicking it again restores the second pane.

Many people find it convenient to use the site window as a control centre for work on a site. You can open a file in a document window by double-clicking it in the site window, and you can add files and folders to the site using the commands on the File menu in the site window. (This can only be done on Windows; on the MacOS, the commands that appear on this menu can be found under the Site>Site Files View sub-menu.) The newly created folder or file is placed in the same folder as the file currently selected in the site window. Files can be deleted from either the local or remote site by

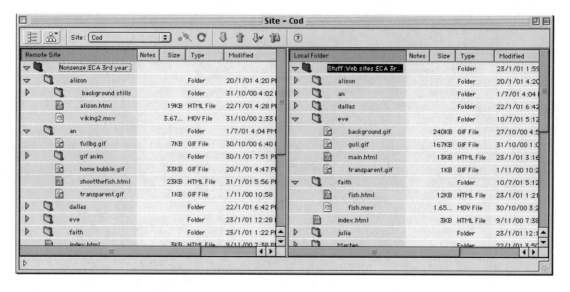

Figure 7.44   *The site window.*

selecting them and pressing delete, and they can be moved between folders by dragging and dropping. When this is done, Dreamweaver offers to scan the site and update any links to the file that has been moved to reflect its new location. Drag and drop can also be used to copy files from the local to the remote site or in the opposite direction. Alternatively, the Put (up arrow) and Get (down arrow) buttons can be used to transfer selected files to the local or remote sites, respectively. When you use these buttons, files are copied to the corresponding position in the folder hierarchy in the other site.

> ☞ Use the site window to add pages to your new site. (Just use the pages you created in previous exercises if you have nothing better.) Organize the site into folders. Practise moving files between folders. Put some or all of the files on the remote site.

Most Web sites are updated from time to time. In a typical update, some pages will be changed, others may be removed and new ones inserted. This work will be done on the designer's machine, that is, in the local site. It is only necessary to upload files that have changed during the update. Keeping track of which pages have been changed is tedious – the sort of job best left to computers. The Site>Synchronize... command causes Dreamweaver to determine which files in the local site have been modified more recently than their counterparts in the remote site, and which only exist on one site or the other, not both. First, a dialogue asks you whether you wish to synchronize the entire site, or just selected files and folders, and in which direction you wish files to be transferred. (We will consider shortly why you might want to transfer files from the remote to the local site when synchronizing.) When you click on Preview, the sites are scanned, a process which may take some time for large sites. After the scan is complete, a window is displayed showing you which files will be transferred in each direction. You can then cancel the operation, or mark some files to be left. Otherwise, you click OK and the sites are brought up to date.

☞ Make some changes to your local site and then synchronize the remote site with it.

If all the work on the local site is being done by one person or on one machine there should never be cases when the remote site's files are more recent than the corresponding local files. However, if a group of people using separate machines are working on the same site – a common situation with large and elaborate sites – it is possible for different people to update the remote files independently. In that case, it may well be necessary to synchronize local and remote sites in both directions.

It doesn't take much insight or imagination to see that allowing more than one person to make independent updates to the same site is a recipe for chaos. Dreamweaver incorporates a simple check-in/check-out system to prevent more than one person working on the same file at once. It is necessary to enable the system in the New Site dialogue: the Remote Info pane (see Figure 7.43 on page 443) is used for this purpose. Here, checkboxes allow you to enable the system and to specify that files should be checked out automatically whenever you open them. You can also provide a check-out name for yourself that is displayed in the site window of anybody working on the site to show who has checked out any files that are being modified. With the check-in/check-out system enabled, two new buttons are added to the site window. If you select a file from the remote site and click the check out button it is locked so that nobody else can work on it – they will see a red mark indicating that is has been checked out, and your check-out name to show who has done so. After working on the file, you can check it in, making it available to other people to work on. The modified version is put back on the remote site and your local copy is locked – you can make no further changes without checking it out again.

More sophisticated support for cooperative working on Web sites is provided by the WebDAV (Web-based Distributed Authoring and Versioning) protocol and Microsoft's Visual SourceSafe system. Both of these are systems for facilitating cooperative Web site development. WebDAV is an open standard, implemented in several Web server programs, including Apache. Visual SourceSafe is a proprietary system, which requires a client to be installed on the local machine, as well as software on the server. If you wish to use either of these systems, you specify them in the Server Access pop-up menu

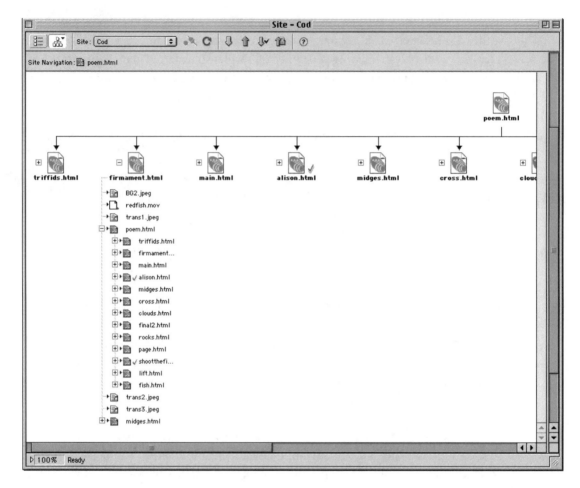

Figure 7.45   *A site map.*

in the Remote Info pane of the New Site dialogue. A button labelled Settings... appears, and clicking on it opens a dialogue box in which you can enter the appropriate server address, password and other information required to use WebDAV or SourceSafe. After that, the check in and check out buttons use the protocol you have specified instead of Dreamweaver's own system.

As well as showing the folders and files comprising the local and remote sites, the site window can also be used to display a schematic representation of the logical structure of the local site (but not the remote site), indicating how its component pages are connected by links. This representation is called a *site map*; Figure 7.45 shows a map of the site whose files were shown in Figure 7.44. You can use the pop-up menu under the Site Map button in the top left of the site window to show either a site map alone or a site map and the local site's files in the Site window. You can switch back to the view showing the local and remote files by clicking the Site Files button. By default, the map shows all the links going out of the site's home page (usually index.html in the top folder, but you can nominate a different file in the Site Map Layout pane of the New Site dialogue). Site maps can be quite wide, making it hard to fit them in the window. If you do not care to scroll, you can zoom out of the map, using the field in the bottom left corner of the Site window to enter a magnification factor.

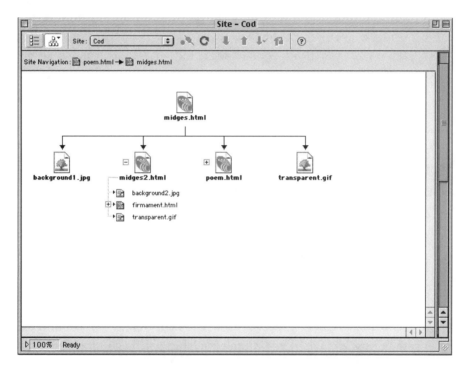

Figure 7.46   *Moving down the site's hierarchy.*

Any file that has outgoing links will have a small button bearing a + sign next to it; clicking on this will cause the links and their destinations to be shown – this has been done for the file called firmament.html in Figure 7.45, and for one of the files that it is linked to. Links can be expanded to an arbitrary depth in this way, so that you can see how they lead through the site. By selecting a file in the map and choosing the View as Root command (from the site window's menu in Windows, or the Site>Site Map View sub-menu on a Mac) you can display the sub-map consisting of links out of the nominated page. As Figure 7.46 shows, when you do this, a list of the links leading from the site's root to the selected file is displayed above the map, labelled Site Navigation.

This not only shows you how you got there, it gives you a way of navigating back up the hierarchy by clicking on one of the file names in the list.

☛ Switch to a site map of your site. Practise expanding links and navigating up and down the hierarchy by changing the root.

Actually, the site map is not as useful as it ought to be, because it is restricted to a hierarchical display of links (the site viewed as a tree) whereas Web sites are not limited to this structure. In fact, in the site illustrated in Figure 7.45, most of the links are between files on the second level, and each of these files is linked back to the root. (Look closely at the expanded node at the left.) This structure is not apparent from the map, and expanding links in this case can go on indefinitely, because of the circularity caused by pages linking back to the root. Furthermore, only actual link elements are shown. If a link is wrapped up in some JavaScript – for example, if it is embedded in an Open Browser Window behaviour – it won't show up in the site map.

Site Checking

A possible reason for wanting to see the link structure of a site is the need to determine whether all the pages can be reached by following links. Files that cannot be reached are said to be *orphaned*. Orphaned files are not necessarily a mistake, but they usually are and it is helpful to be able to identify them. It is even more helpful to be able to identify *broken links*, which have relative URLs that do not point to any file in the site. The command Site>Check Links Sitewide causes Dreamweaver to find orphaned files and broken links for you. It will also find and display any *external* links – ones which point outside the site. These are not checked, even if you are online, you must follow them yourself. (There are utilities available which will verify links, including external ones.)

After Dreamweaver has checked a site's links, a window such as the one shown in Figure 7.47 opens to show the results. The pop-up menu at the top gives you the choice of showing broken links, orphaned files or external links. If you choose to display broken links you can fix them directly in this window. Simply select the link destination (in the right hand column, as shown for the file COBBLES.MOV in Figure 7.47) and either type in the correct name or use the folder button that appears to navigate to the correct file.

☛ Check the links in your site. If no errors are found, move some files and check again. Fix any broken links that you find.

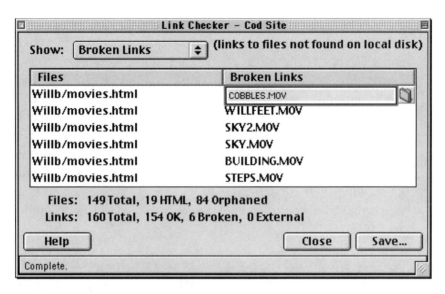

Figure 7.47 *The results of a sitewide link check.*

If you just wish to check a single file for broken links, open it and use the menu command File>Check Links.

There are a few pitfalls in the link checker, invaluable tool though it undoubtedly is. First, like the site map, it takes no account of dynamic links that are embedded in scripts. Second, a file is considered to be orphaned only if there are no links into it from some other file. Dreamweaver does not determine whether every file can be reached from the root, which is often what you want to know. Finally, even orphaned files are checked for broken links. If you are going to adopt orphans, this will be what you want, but if you are the sort of site designer who uses a lot of temporary files and keeps old versions inside the site folder, you more likely want to discard the orphans, in which case you probably won't want to spend time fixing links inside them.

As well as checking the validity of links, Dreamweaver will also attempt to check whether your site will be displayed correctly in a range of browsers. It does this by checking the HTML tags that you have used and their attributes against a *browser profile*, which describes, for a particular browser, the version of HTML that it implements. (Browser profiles are just text files – XML DTDs, in fact. You can create your own profiles for any browser not included among those that come with Dreamweaver.) To check a file, open it or select it in the site window, and choose File>Check Target Browsers.... A list of browsers for which profiles are available is displayed, from which you select those you are interested in. Dreamweaver checks whether you have used any tags or attributes that the chosen browsers do not understand and displays the results by launching your default browser to show a summary; detailed explanations are given if there are any errors. Figure 7.48 shows part of a typical example: a document containing frames and a navigation bar was checked against versions 2.0 to 5.0 of Internet Explorer. The results clearly show that the page would only work in version 4.0 or higher. The full report gives a detailed breakdown of the parts of the document which would cause trouble in each of the target browsers. (Considering what Dreamweaver is, it is ironic that the full report is badly formatted, with most of the detailed messages being extremely long unwrapped lines that wouldn't fit in a browser window on any ordinary monitor.) Again, although this is a useful facility, it is by no means a cure-all. The most treacherous browser incompatibilities are concerned with JavaScript and CSS, and these are not checked.

☛ Check the pages in your site for compatibility with a range of browsers. Where possible, try opening pages with reported errors in the browsers they are not compatible with to see what happens.

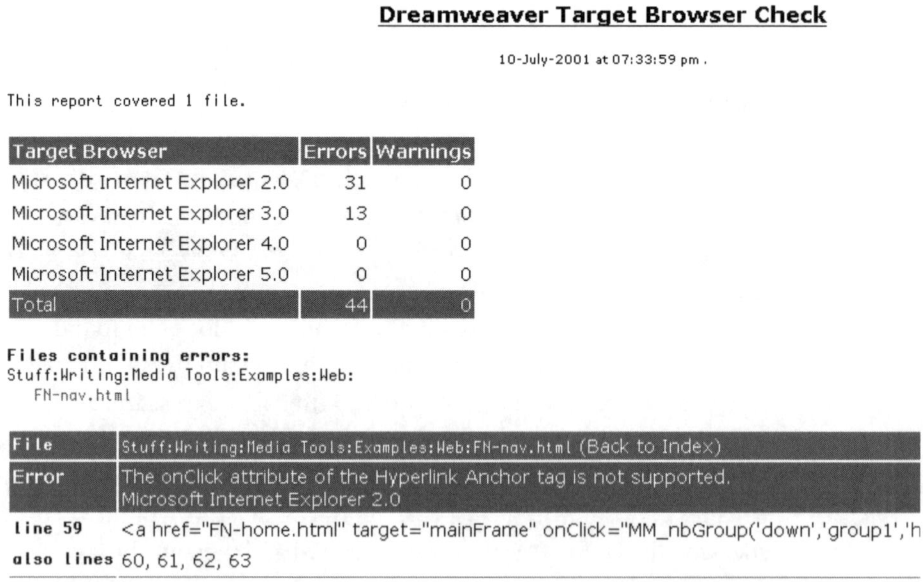

Dreamweaver Target Browser Check

10-July-2001 at 07:33:59 pm .

This report covered 1 file.

Target Browser	Errors	Warnings
Microsoft Internet Explorer 2.0	31	0
Microsoft Internet Explorer 3.0	13	0
Microsoft Internet Explorer 4.0	0	0
Microsoft Internet Explorer 5.0	0	0
Total	44	0

Files containing errors:
Stuff:Writing:Media Tools:Examples:Web:
  FN-nav.html

File	Stuff:Writing:Media Tools:Examples:Web:FN-nav.html (Back to Index)
Error	The onClick attribute of the Hyperlink Anchor tag is not supported. Microsoft Internet Explorer 2.0
line 59	<a href="FN-home.html" target="mainFrame" onClick="MM_nbGroup('down','group1','h
also lines	60, 61, 62, 63

Figure 7.48   *A browser check report.*

Libraries and Templates

In most non-trivial Web sites, certain elements are used repeatedly to establish a uniform style. For example, a company logo or a standard navigation bar may appear in the same position on every page; a particular background image may be attached to all the pages, or a standard disclaimer may be included on every page from which files may be downloaded, and so on. There is already an element of reusability in a Web site, since images and so on are included by reference: if you keep a single copy of each image so that you always use the same URL wherever it is used, any changes made to the image will appear on every page that uses it. Dreamweaver uses its Assets panel to help you keep track of all the images, movies and other reusable items in your site. The panel is divided into categories for each of the types of object you might use. A row of buttons down the left side allows you to select a category to display. When you select an asset, it is displayed in the preview area at the top of the panel. You can add it to a document at the insertion point by dragging it from the panel or clicking on the Insert button and you can start up an application to edit it by double-clicking it or clicking on the pencil icon.

> ☞ Open the Assets panel and refresh it to show all the assets for your site. Examine the assets in each category. Add some images to a page using the Assets panel instead of the Objects panel.

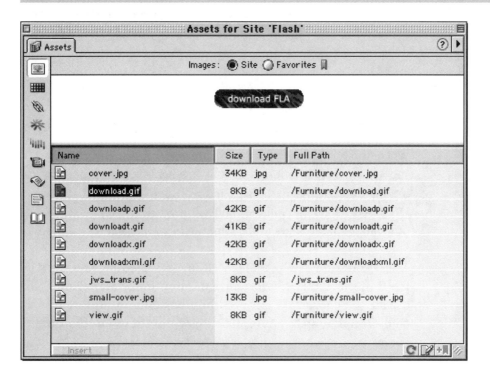

Figure 7.49   *The* Assets *panel.*

Dreamweaver also allows you to build a *library* for each site, containing items that may be any HTML fragment you wish to reuse in a similar way. Library items form a category of assets. A library does more than just help you keep track of the common elements of the pages making up a site. If you edit an item in the library, then it is updated wherever you have used it in the site. So if, for instance, you have stored a set of links to the main sections of your site as a library item and added it to every page in the site, when you add a new section you only have to add an extra link to the library item and all the pages that use it will be updated.

A library item is just a file containing HTML. It is not a complete HTML document and, since items are intended to be placed in the bodies of pages, it can only contain HTML elements that may appear within the body element. The simplest way to create a library item is to select part of a document and drag it into the library items category of the Assets panel. It then becomes available throughout the site. To add the item to a different page, you simply drag it off the Assets panel. If you need to edit the item, double-click its entry in the panel to open it in the document window. It can then be changed in almost the same way as a regular HTML document, although there are some restrictions to ensure that it remains capable of being inserted into other documents – in particular, nothing that relies on adding content, such as scripts, to the head can be done.

> ☛ Create a library item for a site-wide navigation bar. Add the item to several pages. Change its appearance and check that the change has been reflected in all the pages that use it.

When library items are added to a page, they are actually copied – HTML does not support the incorporation of arbitrary elements by reference. However, additional information is added with them, in the form of an HTML comment, which allows Dreamweaver to maintain the connection between every occurrence of the item and its original, so that changes to the item can be propagated in the desired way.

Templates take the idea of reusable elements further, by providing reusable pages. That is, a template is an HTML document that can be used as the basis of many pages. It may contain some constant elements, which cannot normally be edited in any page based on the template, and some editable regions, which will be changed in every document. For instance, a template may have a background image and include a navigation bar and a company logo, which should appear in the same position on every page in the site. These would be marked as non-editable. Editable regions would be provided to contain the text of each individual document.

The most straightforward way to create a template is by making a document in the normal way and then saving it as a template (File>Save as Template...). To begin with, all of the template is constant, so you must designate some of it as editable. This is done by selecting part of the document (it is often sensible to use some place holder content that explains the purpose of the editable region), and use the command Modify>Templates>New Editable Region.... You are prompted for a name for this region.

To create a document based on a template, use the command File>New From Template... and choose a template from the list that is presented to you. The new document opens as a copy of the template, showing all its constant and editable regions. You can now replace the place holders in the editable regions by content specific to this document. You will not be able to edit the constant parts of the document. On the other hand, if you edit the template (double-click its name in the templates category of the Assets panel), any changes will be propagated to all documents based on it. (You will be asked whether you wish to update all pages that use the template whenever you save it.)

→469

☞ Create a template with an image in the top left corner of the page, a standard heading, and some areas to hold different text on each page. Create some pages based on the template. Change the image in the template and verify that the image in each file created from it changes too.

Search and Replace

Templates and libraries are useful for ensuring that a site has a consistent appearance, but it is not always feasible to make everything that appears in more than one place into a library item. For example, a proper name may be used on several pages, and you will naturally want to ensure that it is always spelled correctly. (Dreamweaver does have a spelling checker – select the Text>Check Spelling command – which checks a single file. It works much as other spelling checkers do, and has the same limitations.) The Replace command on the Edit menu is used to perform search and replacement operations across all or part of a site. When the command is selected a dialogue box is displayed. At the top is a pop-up menu that allows you to determine whether to search the entire site, just the files selected in the site window, or a specific folder. Below this, a second pop-up menu is used to choose the type of search to carry out. There are four possibilities, each of which treats the HTML markup in a different way. Each type of search requires slightly different parameters and the dialogue box changes when you select a different entry from the pop-up to accommodate the necessary values.

The simplest case is a Text search, which ignores all HTML tags. The dialogue box as it appears in this case is shown at the top of Figure 7.50. The target and replacement strings are entered in the text boxes in the obvious way. A Source Code search, on the other hand, looks for the target within attribute values for tags, as well as in the content of document elements. It also fails to match if there is markup (for instance, an image) within an occurrence of the target in the file. A Text (Advanced) search allows you to specify the HTML context for a piece of text – for instance, you may only want to match a particular word if it appears within an em element. Pop-up menus allow you to construct a combination of such conditions. The final type of search is a Specific Tag search, which, as you might guess, allows you to search for occurrences of a particular HTML tag. Optionally, you can also specify that the tag must have (or not have) a particular attribute, a particular attribute value or that it must appear (or not appear) within another tag. The replace dialogue for this type of search is shown at the bottom of Figure 7.50. Instead of simply replacing the tag with some text, you have various options that allow you to rewrite the HTML, as shown in the pop-up menu labelled Action.

> ☞ Practise using Text and Source Code searches to look for words that occur in the pages of your site. Practise using Specific Tag searches to find tags with specific attributes.

For all types of search, you may elect to use regular expressions (in the style of grep), to ignore white space, and to ignore case, using the checkboxes at the bottom of the dialogue.

If you use the Find Next button, Dreamweaver will search for one occurrence of the target, opening files if necessary until it does so. You can then use Replace to make the change. Find All causes the dialogue to expand to display a list of all matching occurrences. Double-clicking one of these opens the appropriate file at the place the match occurred. Using the Replace All button causes every occurrence to be replaced as it is found. This operation cannot be undone, except in files that happen to be open at the time, so it should only be chosen if you are sure you mean it.

Beyond Dreamweaver

Dreamweaver provides extensive support for creating Web pages and managing a collection of pages as a Web site. Modern Web sites are powered by server-side programs and databases that enable them to incorporate dynamically computed elements. Dreamweaver provides little help with this sort of site, it is entirely concerned with

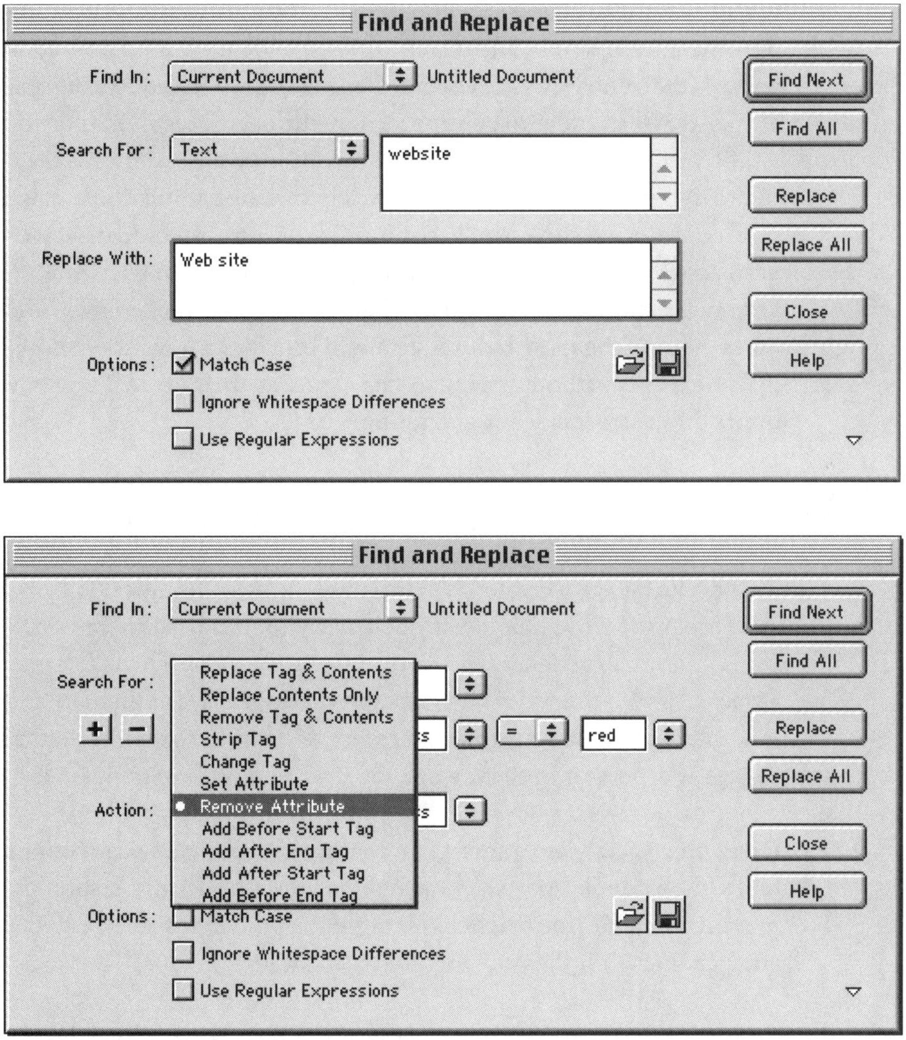

Figure 7.50   *Text (top) and tag (bottom) searches.*

client-side features. Macromedia's *Dreamweaver UltraDev* is a separate product which incorporates all the features of Dreamweaver and adds extra ones for incorporating dynamic elements based on server-side computation into your Web pages.

The UltraDev interface is exactly the same as Dreamweaver's except for additional panels for defining connections to databases and data sources. A data source is essentially a database query against the database to which the site will be connected. The Data Sources panel displays the structure of the query's result. Elements can be dragged on to the page and will be replaced by their dynamically computed value each time the page is sent by the server. Server-side behaviours can be added to a dynamic page, in the same way as client-side behaviours are added to static pages in Dreamweaver in order to control the way the data is displayed.

In order to make full use of UltraDev, a knowledge of relational databases and server-side technologies, such as ASP, JSP and ColdFusion is required. (If it comes to that, you need access to a server running these technologies – UltraDev is not for constructing personal home pages.) However, because it uses the same interface as Dreamweaver and hides many of the more tedious details, it provides a way for Web designers to develop dynamic pages without having to move outside their normal way of working or learn much about server-side programming.

Further Exercises to do in Dreamweaver

1. Create a Web page for your CV (curriculum vitae or resumé). The page should be aimed at prospective employers or clients who may wish to find out about your qualifications, experience, and so on. Use HTML or CSS formatting to produce an attractive layout that is easy to read and makes it easy for them to find essential information. Include any links that seem relevant, for example, to the Web site of your college or school or to show work you may already have done on the Web.

2. Using only CSS styles to specify formatting, create a Web page containing text that looks like a double-spaced typewritten manuscript. That is, it should use a fixed-width font on a suitable line height, with ragged right margins and underlining for emphasis and headings. Test the page on different browsers.

3. Create a Web site in the form of a journal with a page for each day. (For this exercise you can just write something about the weather or the classes you attend, unless you have more ambitious plans.) Use a template to provide a uniform appearance for each page and devise a suitable navigation structure to let users find their way around the journal.

4. Create a Web page with lots of small images on it. Place a layer in front of all these images, containing a welcome message. Attach a suitable Change Property behaviour to the page's body element to ensure that the message will be shown while the images load and will then disappear, so that the user will never see the image icons that browsers display while waiting for images.

5. Create a Web page with a number of small thumbnail images down one side, such that whenever the cursor rolls over one of them, a full-sized version of it appears in the main part of the page.

6. Create a page (or several pages) containing links to all of your favourite Web sites. Use navigation bars or rollover buttons to jump to each site and add a short description of each next to its link. If you have a lot of favourite sites, arrange them hierarchically on several pages.

7. Make a Web page in the form of a poster, with a large background image with text and possibly other images superimposed on it. Use whatever means are necessary to ensure that the page will display sensibly in any size of browser window.

8. Make some rollovers which behave as buttons with tool tips. That is, when the cursor rolls over a button, a short descriptive text appears next to it, explaining what its function is.

9. Create a Web page around a slide show. A series of images on a theme (for example a trip or a party) should be displayed in succession at a suitable speed. The rest of the page should contain text, images and any other material that complements the slide-show, presented so as to provide a setting for the main images.

10. Design a page containing six to ten different small images (less than 150 pixels square) which appear and disappear, apparently at random, so that only two or three are visible at a time. Try to make the period before the same sequence repeats as long as possible (within reason).

11. By moving a GIF image using the timeline, or otherwise, create a Web page containing some text and images which appears to be continually scanned by a searchlight.

12. Design a pair of pages presenting the same information, one for people with version 4.0 or higher browsers, which takes advantage of the features provided by these versions (stylesheets and scripts), the other a basic version which doesn't use anything beyond the simplest HTML tags. Make a front page with a suitable action that causes the browser to select the appropriate one of the pair and go to it. Provide some suitable backup mechanism on this page, in case a user's browser does not respond appropriately to the switching code.

13. Design a page for children learning to read, with bold buttons, labelled in a suitable font with the names of different colours of the rainbow. The buttons should start out some dull colour, but when the cursor rolls over a button it should change to the corresponding rainbow colour.

14. Design a template to provide a new look for your university's or company's site, where every page bears the institution's logo or id, a copyright statement, a note of when it was last updated, and a uniform navigation bar which visitors can use to reach the most important pages on the site from every other page. Base this navigation bar on the site's existing structure. Redo a few pages from the site using your template.

Dreamweaver MX

I **f you only** use Dreamweaver for designing the appearance and static content of Web pages, or for managing sites, there will be little in the MX update to change the way you work with the program. The user interface has changed slightly, to bring in the new features described in Chapter 2a. However, this represents a less drastic innovation in Dreamweaver than it does in the other Macromedia tools, because the property inspector was already present in Dreamweaver. Thus, the only real change is the introduction of docking panels, which is little more than a cosmetic improvement. In fact, it is possible to set up the workspace and set certain preferences so that Dreamweaver MX behaves just like Dreamweaver 4, so to some extent this supplement is redundant. However, the new features make certain aspects of working with the program more convenient.

The significant innovations in Dreamweaver MX are concerned with extending its capacities to cope with the demands of a new generation of Web sites, or more accurately, *Web applications*. In the introductory section of Chapter 7, we described Web sites as collections of Web pages containing HTML markup and other elements. This is not, however, the whole story. When a Web browser sends a request for a URL to a server (when you click on a link in a Web page, for example), it may indeed be the case that what is returned is the content of a file stored on the server's hard disk – a Web page in the sense we originally described it – but it may also be the case that what happens is that a program or script is run on the server, and the output of that program, formatted with HTML and all the other features of a Web page, is returned and ultimately displayed in the browser. Pages created in this way are often referred to as *dynamic* Web pages, in contrast to the *static* pages we considered previously. When a Web site is composed largely of dynamic pages, they usually serve as an interface to a database and some accompanying application programs running on the server. In this case, it makes sense to consider the entire system – database, server-side programs, Web pages and client-side scripts – as a Web application.

Many different server-side technologies are used in the construction of Web applications. In some approaches, such as CGI scripts, Apache modules and Java servlets, all of the work on the server, including the markup of the dynamic pages, is done by programs which write Web pages as their output. This means that everything has to be done by programmers. In other approaches, including Microsoft's Active Server Pages (ASP), Java Server Pages (JSP), PHP and Macromedia's own ColdFusion, dynamic elements, such as server-side scripts, are embedded in a conventional page, using special tags. Formerly, Dreamweaver UltraDev (see page 455) was used as a way of allowing designers with little programming knowledge to add such dynamic elements to their Web pages. The functionality of UltraDev has now been extended and incorporated into the main Dreamweaver program.

As well as being able to add dynamic elements directly to a page in design view, Dreamweaver MX allows you to edit the source code of pages using ASP, PHP and ColdFusion tags, in the same way as it allows you to edit the HTML source of static pages. Additionally, Dreamweaver MX provides facilities for editing code in a variety of programming, scripting and markup languages, including ActionScript (for Flash – see Chapter 5), C#, Java, JavaScript, VBScript, WML and XML.

Most of these new facilities will have little impact on designers whose main interest is in the layout and appearance of pages – the intended audience of this book – and so we will not describe them here. Extensive information is available in the Dreamweaver manual and online help.

Interface Elements

Docking panels have allowed the interface to be tidied up a little. In particular, probably the most immediately noticeable difference between Dreamweaver MX's interface and that of earlier versions is that the Objects panel, with its different subsets selected from a menu, has been replaced by a collection of panels, docked together in the Insert bar – which is just a slightly special panel set – which by default sits just above the document window, as shown in Figure 7a.1. (Note also the property inspector at the bottom, and the docked panels arranged at the right.)

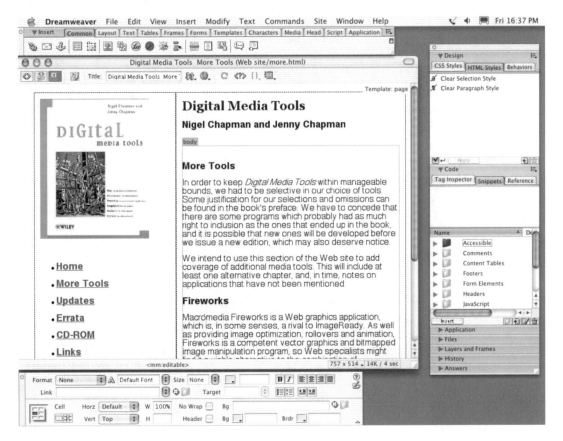

Figure 7a.1   *The default user interface to Dreamweaver MX.*

Each of the individual panels contains a set of objects which can be added to the document by drag and drop, as described for the old Objects panel, in Chapter 7 – for instance, images can be inserted into a document using the same method as described on page 399. Figure 7a.2 shows, at the top, the Common set of objects, which include images, rules, tables and layers. The controls for switching between standard and layout view, and for drawing layout frames, as described on page 416 can now be found on the Layout panel within the Insert panel set, as shown at the bottom of Figure 7a.2. The other panels within the set, such as the Text and Characters panels shown in Figure 7a.3, correspond to subsets of objects that you can add to your document. Most of them correspond directly to subsets available on the Objects panel in Dreamweaver 4, which in turn correspond to sub-menus on the Insert menu. The Text panel contains the same objects as the Insert>Text Objects sub-menu, for example, and the Characters panel is equivalent to the Insert>Special Characters sub-menu. If you prefer the old Objects panel, you can switch to it by clicking on the small icon at the right-hand end of the panel. To switch back to the new layout, click on the complementary icon at the bottom of the vertically oriented panel.

> ☛ Familiarize yourself with the Insert bar. Move the cursor over each of the icons on each panel in the bar to display the tooltip identifying the corresponding object. Practise adding images and other common objects to a document. Compare the use of the Text panel with other methods of inserting text objects.

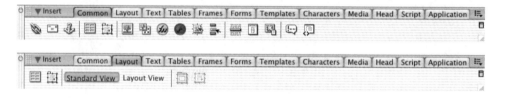

Figure 7a.2   *The* Common *and* Layout *panels.*

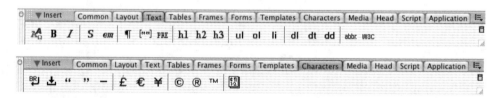

Figure 7a.3   *The* Text *and* Characters *panels.*

New Documents and Sites

The New Document Dialogue

In Dreamweaver MX, all new documents are created with the File>New command, which normally opens a dialogue box in which you can select one of a whole range of the document types that Dreamweaver now supports, or a template, on which to base your new document. Figure 7a.4 shows the New Document dialogue. As you can see, it is divided into three panes: the leftmost has a list of categories of document, the middle pane shows the documents belonging to the category selected on the left, and the final pane shows a preview of the selected document, if one exists, and a brief description. In Figure 7a.4, we have selected HTML in the Basic Page category. When the Create button is clicked, a blank HTML page will be created, just as if we had used the File>New command in Dreamweaver 4, allowing us to design a static page entirely from scratch. Note the checkbox in the bottom right corner labelled Make Document XHTML Compliant. If you select this box, Dreamweaver will ensure that the document conforms to the most recent definition of HTML, XHTML 1.0, which redefines it in XML. You should tick this box if conformance to the latest standards is important to you, but you should be aware that, although the markup will be backwards-compatible with HTML 4.0, some older browsers will reject documents with an XHTML DOCTYPE.

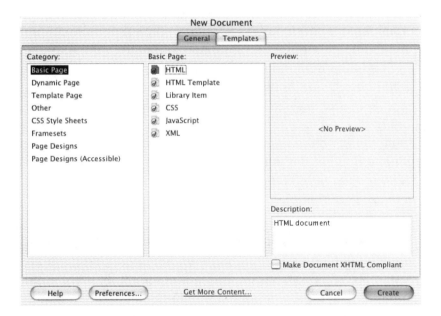

Figure 7a.4   *Creating a blank HTML page in the* New Document *Dialogue.*

Selecting HTML Template from the Basic Page category creates a blank page with the necessary additional information for it to serve as a template for other pages in the site. (You can still save an ordinary HTML file as a template using File>Save As Template..., as you could in Dreamweaver 4.) Similarly, selecting Library Item allows you to create a library item from scratch, instead of dragging part of a page to the Assets panel, as described on page 452. If you select one of the other three types of basic page,

Dreamweaver will create a document in code view, allowing you to edit the source by hand. In this view, it will apply syntax colouring to make the code more readable, but it does not perform any syntax checking. For these types of document, Dreamweaver is thus behaving like a simple text editor. Similar remarks apply to the types of document you can create in the Other category, which comprises other scripting and markup languages.

☛ Create a new blank HTML document. Create documents of the other types in the Basic Page category and look at them in design and source view to see how they differ from the blank HTML document.

The Dynamic Page category is used to create blank pages that can accommodate dynamic elements. You choose from a list of server-side technologies (ASP, JSP, PHP, etc.) and a new document is created, which, in design view, looks like an ordinary blank HTML page, but includes any necessary preamble to support dynamic elements of your chosen technology. The Template Page category allows you to create your own templates for dynamic pages.

The Frameset category provides a quick and easy way to create new pages that are divided into frames. As Figure 7a.5 shows, you can select from a collection of commonly used frame configurations. This is more convenient than the old method of first creating a document and then dragging a frameset layout from the Frames subset of the Object panel described on page 419, although you can still do that, if you like. When you are creating framesets in this way, the preview panel of the New Document dialogue comes into play, showing you a schematic representation of your chosen frameset.

☛ Practise creating frameset documents using the New Document dialogue.

The remaining categories allow you to create documents based on existing designs. In particular, the Page Designs category contains pre-designed pages for a range of uses. Figure 7a.6 shows some of the possibilities on offer. When you choose one of these designs, you can use the radio buttons at the bottom right of the dialogue to choose between creating a document that is a copy of the design, which you can subsequently customize to your particular needs by editing, or a template, with editable regions, which can also be customized and then saved to use as the basis of other pages. If you have no design experience, these designs can help you get started, but using them exclusively will lead to sites that all look the same. The category of Page Designs (Accessible) provides a similar set of designs, but those in this category have been

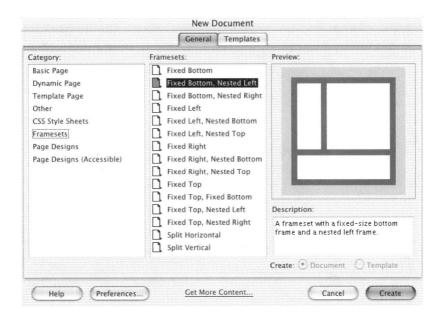

Figure 7a.5   *Creating a frameset in the* New Document *dialogue.*

created to comply with the W3C Web Accessibility Guidelines. In general, this means that they make more use of CSS. In the absence of a good reason not to, you should generally use the accessible designs, if you are creating documents in this way.

☛ Investigate the Page Designs category by creating documents based on each design. Assess the usefulness of these designs.

The CSS Style Sheets category provides a similar selection of pre-defined styles, which you can use to format your pages. When you create a document using one of the entries in this category, Dreamweaver simply opens a copy of the pre-designed stylesheet in code view. You can customize this, if you know CSS, or simply save it in your site and use it to provide a uniform appearance on all your pages.

If all this seems unnecessary for your requirements – if you only ever create HTML pages from scratch, for example – you can tell Dreamweaver not to use the New Document dialogue, but simply to create a document in the old way when you select the File>New command. This is done in the New Document pane in the Preferences dialogue, shown in Figure 7a.7. By unchecking the box marked Show New Document Dialog on CMD+N, you instruct Dreamweaver to always create a document of the type you select from the Default Document Type pop-up menu. Notice that you can also set XHTML compliance as the default option in this dialogue.

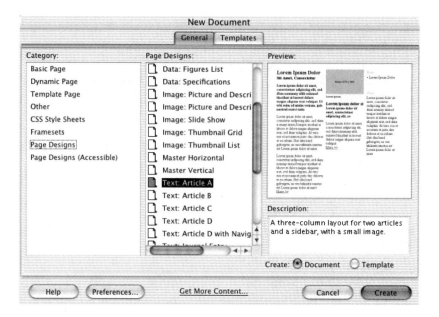

Figure 7a.6 *Creating a document based on a design file.*

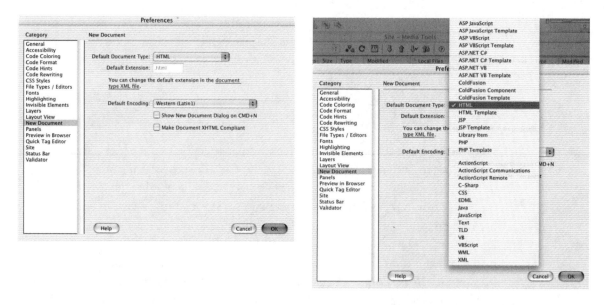

Figure 7a.7 *Setting a default document type.*

The Site Definition Wizard

When you select the Site>New Site... command to define a new site, a dialogue box with two tabs, marked Basic and Advanced, opens. If you click on the Advanced tab, the dialogue takes on the appearance of the Site Definition dialogue described on page 441 and the following pages. (There are one or two minor embellishments but these can be ignored.) If, however, you click on the Basic tab, the dialogue becomes a 'wizard' which guides you through the process of setting up a site by asking you a series of questions, which you can answer by filling in text fields or making selections from pop-up menus. After you have answered one set of questions, you move on to the next, which may be determined by your answers to earlier questions – for example, you will only be asked for the address of an FTP server if you have indicated that your site will be uploaded by FTP. Figure 7a.8 shows a couple of screens from the site definition wizard. You should be able to see that, as long as you have the information to hand and understand the questions, you would be able to enter the necessary settings quite easily by following the wizard. You may also reflect that if you have the information to hand and understand the questions, you would probably have no difficulty in filling in the values in the Advanced tab for yourself. (Compare Figure 7a.8 with Figure 7.43 on page 443, for example.)

☞ Create a site by working through the Site Definition Wizard.

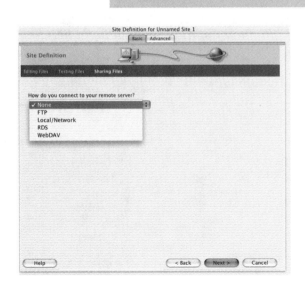 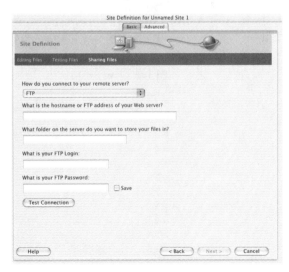

Figure 7a.8 *The Site Definition Wizard.*

Editing Code

By now, you can probably see a pattern emerging in the upgrade from Dreamweaver 4 to Dreamweaver MX: you can, if you wish, go on doing what you were doing before, or you can take advantages of some helpful new features. This is the case when it comes to editing the code of your Web pages. You can edit the HTML code of pages in source or split view, as described on page 436 and the following pages. While the editing facilities are still not as powerful as those you will find in dedicated source code editors, Dreamweaver now supplies *code hints* to help you enter HTML tags. If you type a left angle bracket character <, as if you were going to enter a tag, and then wait a short while, a pop-up menu will appear, listing all the possible tag names, as shown on the left of Figure 7a.9. Instead of explicitly typing the tag, you can just choose it from this list by double-clicking its name. If you then type a space and wait, a pop-up menu of all the available attributes for that tag appears, as in the middle of Figure 7a.9. When you select an attribute, a pop-up menu may appear to help you fill in its value, as shown on the right of Figure 7a.9 for the href attribute of the <a> tag. When you have finished entering attributes, you type the closing angle bracket >. Dreamweaver then inserts the matching closing tag (for example, </a> if you had inserted a <a> tag) and leaves the cursor in between the opening and closing tags so that you can enter the document element's content.

☛ If you know some HTML, create a blank page, switch to source view and insert some HTML by hand, using code hints. Experiment with different tags to see how the code hints help you insert values for the different attributes.

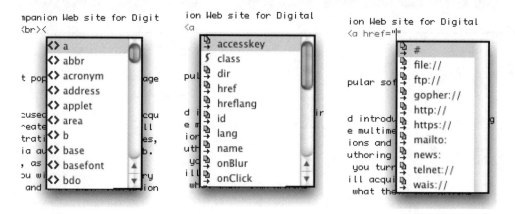

Figure 7a.9   *Code hints.*

Another useful innovation in Dreamweaver MX is the ability to store *code snippets*, which are what their name suggests: little pieces of code which you can insert anywhere in your site. In its simplest form, a code snippet is much like a library item, being just a block of reusable code. A more interesting possibility is offered by the ability to define a code snippet in two parts, and 'wrap' it round a selection. An example will show how this works.

Suppose that you often need to insert a link from pages in sub-folders of your site to the index.html file in the parent folder. You could do this by selecting the text of the link and setting the Link value in the property inspector to ../index.html wherever you needed such an upward link. To make the process less laborious, you could define a code snippet, consisting of a suitable anchor element, lacking only its content, which you could wrap around the selected text.

You work with snippets in the Snippets panel, normally docked as part of the Code panel set. To create a new snippet, you click on the new item icon at the bottom of the panel, which opens the dialogue box shown in Figure 7a.10. Here you can give your snippet a name and provide a short description. If your snippet is intended to be wrapped around a selection, as our example is, it follows that there will be some code to be inserted before the selection and some after it. You type these two pieces of code in the two text boxes labelled Insert Before and Insert After, respectively. After you click OK, your snippet will appear in the list in the lower half of the Snippets panel, as shown in Figure 7a.11. To wrap the snippet around some text or an image, make a selection in the document, click on the snippet's name in the Snippets panel, and then click the Insert button at the bottom of the panel. (When you click on a snippet's name, a preview of it is shown in the top half of the panel. Using the radio buttons at the bottom of the Snippet dialogue, you can choose whether this shows the actual code, or a preview corresponding to the snippet's appearance in design view. For a simple snippet such as this example, the design view preview would not be visible, so code view is a safer option.)

> ☞ Create a code snippet containing a link with the text Go To: within it. Practise wrapping this snippet around text, to produce links labelled Go To Home Page, and so on.

Dreamweaver MX comes with a collection of snippets that you can use in your Web pages. This is a further example of the trend for this program to supply prefabricated elements of Web pages for novices at the same time as it has provided enhanced facilites for experts.

Figure 7a.10   *Creating a code snippet.*

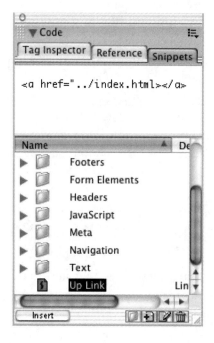

Figure 7a.11   *The* Snippets *panel.*

8 Premiere Video and Audio

Files and Formats Summary

- Create projects with File>New Project,to arrange video clips, still images, titles and audio into a programme.

- Add video and audio captured from external devices (camcorders, DAT recorders, etc.) to a project using the commands on the File>Capture sub-menu.

- Add video, images and audio – in all common digital video and audio formats and a wide range of image formats – to a project using File>Import File….

- Create titles and add them to a project with File>New>Title.

- Export completed programmes as QuickTime movies, RealMedia or Windows Media using commands on the File>Export Timeline sub-menu.

- Optimize movies for use on CD-ROM or the Web using File>Export Timeline>Save for Web…, which invokes Cleaner EZ.

Common Features
Used By This Program

Standard File and Edit menu commands (pages 8–13).

Adobe help system and Adobe Online (pages 13–17).

Keyboard short cuts and context menus (pages 17–18).

Tools (pages 19–21) in mini-toolbox.

Dockable floating palettes (pages 22–26).

History palette (pages 29–32).

Navigator palette (pages 41–43).

Simplified type tool and character and paragraph formatting commands (pages 566–573).

t is a measure of the remarkable rate of progress in computer power that digital video production is now considered a suitable application for consumer desktop and portable machines, such as Apple's iMac and iBook. A few years ago, video editing on a personal computer was pushing the limits of what was possible. Top-of-the-range machines, equipped with special AV (audio-visual) disks or RAID arrays, high-speed SCSI interfaces and special video capture cards were required, and even then there were severe restrictions on the length of movie that could be created. Since then, processor speeds have increased nearly tenfold, the capacity of standard internal hard disks now far exceeds that of the largest disk that could previously be added at great expense, and the rate at which data can be transferred to and from internal IDE disks is higher than that of everything but the fastest SCSI-3 buses.

An additional factor in the growth of desktop video is the rise of DV* as a standard for consumer video camcorders. This standard makes it possible to transfer video in digital form from camcorders to computers, using the IEEE1394 (Firewire) ports built in to many new computers, or available on inexpensive PCI cards. Since DV is digitized in the camera, there is no need for analogue to digital converters when capturing video to disk in this format.

As consumer equipment became capable of handling video, consumer software was developed to allow non-experts to use their computers for video editing. Once again, Apple led the way with iMovie, a free application bundled with all new Macs since 1999, which can be used to capture DV footage, edit it, and then transfer the edited movie back to DV tape, or export it as a QuickTime movie, suitable for incorporation into Web pages.

Programs like iMovie are all very well for editing wedding and holiday videos, or for creating a video movie of a family Christmas to send to relatives on the other side of the world, but they are limited in their facilities. More serious video work requires more serious programs. At the top end, professional digital video production suites based on uncompressed video cost tens of thousands of pounds. Premiere is a more modest piece of software, which still allows you to capture video, edit it, apply effects and transitions – in real time, with the aid of suitable PCI cards – and capture and edit sound and combine it with picture. It can export a completed movie in a wide range of formats,

*DV does actually stand for Digital Video, but there is more to digital video than just DV.

from broadcast quality digital and analogue, through DV, to highly compressed digital movies for use on CD-ROM and the Web.

We will describe Premiere 6.0. The most important innovation it provides compared with earlier versions is the proper integration of DV capture and export. The fundamental editing operations are the same as in earlier versions, though, and as we will describe, it is possible to make Premiere 6 look and behave much like previous versions. We will take advantage of this capability, so that, as far as possible, our descriptions will also apply to Premiere 4 and 5.

Fundamentals

At first sight, Premiere's user interface may seem the most complicated and intimidating among all the media tools described in this book, as Figure 8.1 shows. As well as a plentiful supply of tabbed palettes, Premiere uses up to four windows at once for editing, instead of a single document window. Premiere is also in some ways the most distant of the tools from mainstream concepts, because it is based on metaphors from the world of video editing, with time being a central concern, and not on metaphors from paper-based media, such as drawing, painting, photography and page layout, with which more people are familiar. Despite all this, Premiere is basically a simple program.

Premiere 6 lets you choose between two different layouts of the working space. The arrangement shown in Figure 8.1 uses what is called *A/B editing*, which means that when transitions are applied between two clips (such as a dissolve from one clip to another), the two are placed on separate tracks, with the transition between them. The alternative, shown in Figure 8.2, is *single-track editing*, where the two clips are placed on the same track. You can choose between these two layouts using the Window>Workspace sub-menu. As you can see, there are differences in the windows that appear in the two cases. For the rest of this chapter, we will use A/B editing only, since single-track editing is harder for beginners and is not available in earlier versions of Premiere. (It more closely resembles practice in high-end video editing suites, and is preferred by professionals with experience of such equipment.) You may wish to experiment with single-track editing once you have grasped the essentials of working with Premiere.

Before we can go much further, a short digression on the nature of digital video data is necessary.

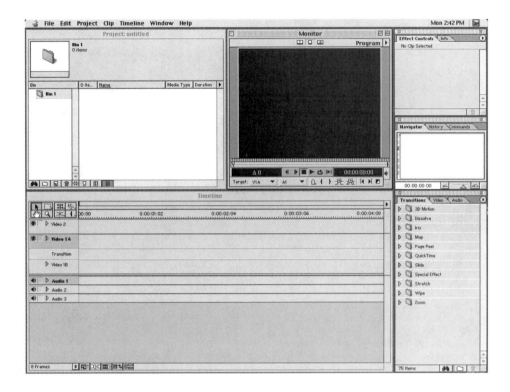

Figure 8.1 *Premiere's workspace for A/B editing.*

An Introduction to Video Compression

The characteristic of digital video that has the most impact on the way you work with it is the volume of data that it generates. Each frame of video is a bitmapped image, that is, an array of pixel values. The size of frames and the number of frames per second varies, depending on which video standard is being used, which in turn depends on which part of the world you are in, but each second of uncompressed video will require at least 30MB. Hard disk capacities are measured in tens of gigabytes, so it is not impossible to store extended video sequences on disk at these rates: a 40GB disk will hold about 20 minutes of uncompressed video (but even the shortest video piece often starts out with a great deal more than that amount of raw source footage). However, the data rate of uncompressed video is only just within the capabilities of ATA buses and cards that can acquire and digitize uncompressed video at this rate are expensive. Hence, despite the opening remarks to this chapter, most computer users do not have access to equipment that can handle video in uncompressed form, although even this is moving rapidly from high-end studios to more modest workstation set-ups.

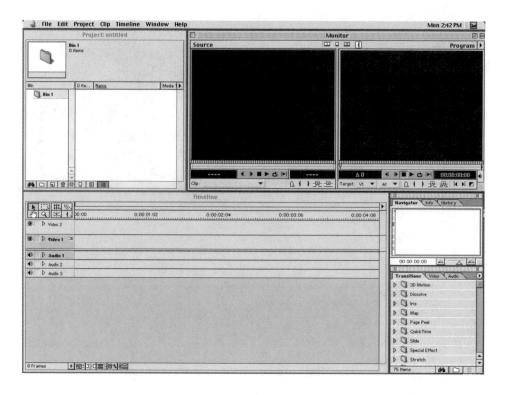

Figure 8.2   *Premiere's workspace for single-track editing.*

For now, unless you work in a TV or film studio, you will probably have to work with *compressed* video; that is, the original video signal is stored in a form that occupies fewer bytes than a simple calculation based on the number of pixels in each frame predicts. The only effective methods of compressing video are *lossy*, which means that some data is discarded during the compression process. In theory, the compression algorithms only discard information that is not visually important and therefore should not be noticed, but in order to reduce data rates sufficiently for transmission over the Internet or play-back from CD-ROM, severe compression, which does introduce visible artefacts, must be used. Furthermore, if you take a compressed video clip, decompress it, and then compress it again, there will be an additional loss of quality (sometimes called *generational loss*), since the decompressed video contains less information than the original signal. Therefore, you should try to avoid recompressing whenever possible, although as we will see, it cannot always be avoided.

If you are on a limited budget, your source video will most likely take the form of DV. This means that the video signal is digitized and compressed by a standard algorithm in the camera and then passed to the computer as a digital stream, at a constant data rate of 3.5MB per second (which means you can store nearly ten times as much material on your disk as you could if you were using uncompressed data). If you are using analogue cameras, then the digitization and compression will have to be performed in the computer system, using a video *capture card*. These vary enormously in cost, performance and the quality of the video they produce. As a general rule, the more you pay, the higher the data rate the card will support, giving a wider range of compression ratios and thus a wider choice of quality. A more expensive card will be capable of digitizing video with less compression and better quality than a cheap one, but it will also allow you to trade off quality against the disk space required to store the video data.

There are some advantages to using a capture card instead of starting with a digital signal: you usually have some control over the quality and good analogue cameras may use better optics than DV cameras in a similar price range. The disadvantages, apart from the need for the capture card, are that analogue signals are easily degraded by noise, even when being transmitted over a short cable, while digital signals are highly resistant to such corruption. In addition, if your video has to be stored on tape before you capture it, analogue tape formats, such as Hi-8, introduce their own flavour of signal degradation, which can be severe. Also, if your final output is to an analogue format, an additional digital to analogue conversion phase is required, whereas DV can be exported straight back to tape (usually mini-DV or DV-Pro) in digital form.

Relatively inexpensive devices are available that connect to the Firewire inputs of a computer and convert an analogue signal into DV, so that you can connect a non-digital camcorder to the converter (usually a box with S-video and composite inputs) and send a DV stream to the computer system. That is, the converter enables software to treat the camcorder as if it were a DV device, even though it isn't. This can be an effective alternative to the use of a capture card, though you are restricted to DV quality and data rates and won't get as clean a signal as if you were using DV from the start.

QuickTime

There are several formats in use for digital video, of which Apple's QuickTime is the most flexible. QuickTime is not simply a video format, it is a multimedia architecture, which means that it provides a framework for manipulating many different sorts of media data, although its primary focus has always been on synchronized video and audio. QuickTime also provides a collection of modules known as *codecs*, which is short for compressor/decompressors, since they are used for compressing and decompressing these media. Any program that uses QuickTime can automatically handle many different video formats, including DV and Video for Windows (often referred to by the name of its precursor, AVI). Premiere isn't actually a QuickTime editor. It uses its own representation of video data internally, and can work directly with Video for Windows and the proprietary formats used by dedicated systems, notably the DPS Perception system. However, it makes extensive use of QuickTime, particularly for compression.

QuickTime is available on MacOS and Windows systems. Although Premiere can be configured to use Video for Windows for certain functions that are provided by QuickTime, we will assume that QuickTime is being used, in the interests of making our descriptions platform-independent.

Projects

Editing in Premiere is based around the *project*, which groups together all the video and sound source clips from which you will build your movie, together with a description of how these should be edited and combined. To make a movie, you normally begin by creating a new project, then capturing or importing video and audio clips. These clips appear in the *project window*, which is normally at the top left of your screen. Although you don't spend much time working in the Project window, it is treated like a conventional application's document window, in that it is the window that you must close to close the project. Closing any other window just hides it, leaving the project open. You can organize the Project window by creating *bins*, which work like folders on a hard disk in which to group clips together. (The name suggests an analogy with the physical bins in which strips of film are placed by traditional film editors.) You then arrange the resulting clips into a *programme* by dragging them to the *timeline* window (the long window at the bottom left of the workspace in Figure 8.1 on page 475), where you can also apply transitions and effects. When you are satisfied with the result, you export the programme in your chosen format.

There are settings associated with every project, which are concerned with the way Premiere handles video and sound, both internally and when capturing. Some of these settings are quite technical and require knowledge of digital video concepts if you are to understand them. A collection of project *presets* is supplied, which combine appropriate settings for a range of typical projects, and when you create a new project, using the File>New Project command, you can choose from among these. Figure 8.3 shows the default collection of presets as it is presented when you create a project. If you are using a video capture card, you will usually find that additional presets specific to your card are installed with its drivers. As the tip at the bottom of the Presets dialogue suggests, if you aren't sure which preset to use, choose one that matches the input device you are using. For example, if you are taking the video source from a DV camcorder that uses 48-bit sound, with the NTSC standard used for video in North America and the Far East, choose Standard 48kHz from among the presets for DV-NTSC. If none of the presets suits you, click the Custom... button, which will allow you to set all the values yourself, once you know what you are doing.

☞ Find out which preset is the most appropriate for the equipment you are using and create a project using it. Save the project for use in future practise exercises.

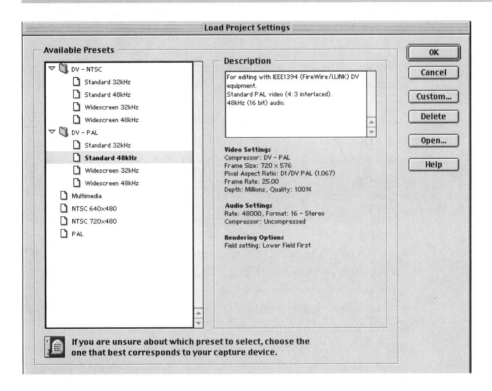

Figure 8.3   *Choosing project presets.*

Capturing and Importing Video

Video clips are usually captured into a Premiere project from a camcorder or video tape deck. Using a camcorder, material is first recorded on tape, which can subsequently be reviewed before a decision is made about which footage is worth capturing. Sometimes, though, it may be more convenient to shoot directly to disk, especially in a studio setting where an analogue camera is being used, so that noisy analogue tape can be avoided. Capturing straight to disk is also usual if you are using stop-motion capture for animation, because it is impossible to stop and start tape drives instantaneously.

Generally, though, it is not convenient to record to disk, because of the conflict between the need to move the camera and the necessity of keeping it connected up to the computer. This is especially true for location shooting.

At the risk of pointing out the obvious: before you start to capture, you should connect your camcorder (from now on we will use 'camcorder' to mean either camcorder or video tape deck) to your computer. If it is a DV camera, a standard Firewire cable runs between the two. For analogue cameras, a variety of cables and plugs are used. Make sure that the signal from your camera is compatible with the inputs on your capture card. Most semi-professional equipment uses S-video outputs, which send colour and luminance information on two separate channels. Consumer equipment (and, paradoxically, some professional equipment) uses composite signals, where colour and luminance are combined, while top-level equipment uses component signals, comprising three separate channels.[*] Whereas you can use adapters to connect leads with XLR plugs to inputs that accept RCA plugs, there is no way you can connect a composite signal, for example, to an S-video input, without using additional electronics.

You should bear in mind that capturing video is a processor-intensive task, and that there is no room for error. The video signal is coming into the computer continuously, and if the machine cannot handle it continuously, some frames will be lost, which is almost always unacceptable. Therefore, you should make sure that the processor is entirely dedicated to its task while capturing. This means turning off any background tasks that it normally performs; in particular, you should deactivate any network services. Some authorities go as far as recommending that you insert a disk into the CD-ROM drive, and any other removable storage devices, to prevent the system polling them to find out whether a disk has been inserted. This is probably going too far, but if you experience dropped frames when capturing video, it is worth a try.

Using the Capture Window

Capturing can be very simple. In essence, it is no different from recording on to a VCR: you press the Record button to start recording and press the Stop button when you have finished. There really isn't much more to it than that.

Assuming that your camcorder is connected to the computer and switched on (and set to VTR mode if it makes the distinction) you start the capture process by choosing the

---

[*]These are not, as is sometimes claimed, the red, blue and green components of the signal, they are the brightness (essentially a black and white version of the picture) and two colour difference components. See the chapter of *Digital Multimedia* entitled 'Video' for details.

Movie Capture command from the File>Capture sub-menu. This opens the Movie Capture window, shown in Figure 8.4. This window is dominated by the preview area on the left, which shows the picture coming from the camcorder. If the camcorder supports *device control*, which means that it can be remotely controlled by the computer, two rows of VCR-style player controls appear below the preview, as shown. These can be used to step backward and forward one frame at a time, stop or start playback from the camcorder, play slowly backwards or forwards, rewind or fast forward the tape, pause or start recording (reading from left to right, top to bottom – if the icons don't seem to make sense, let the tool tips tell you which is which). The notched band below the preview acts as a jog control: you can drag it to move the tape forwards and backwards, a practice sometimes called *scrubbing*. The shuttle control to the left of the top row of playback controls lets you wind the tape forwards or backwards at varying speeds. You could use the playback controls to identify the place on the tape where you want to start recording, press the record button, let the tape run until you reached the point where you wanted to stop, and press the stop button. There is no need to be especially accurate about where you start and stop, as long as you record more footage than you need, because it is simple to trim off unwanted frames, as we will see.

☞ Put a recorded tape into your camcorder and connect it to your computer. Start up Premiere and, if your camcorder supports device control, practise using the playback controls and jog and shuttle in the Movie Capture window to scan the tape and find interesting sections (but note that excessive use of these facilities wears the tape heads and transport mechanism). Capture a short sequence from the tape.

A slightly different way of performing the capture is to set the *in point* and *out point* while you preview the tape and then instruct Premiere to capture everything between the two points. You set the in point using the button marked { and the out point with the one marked }. You can then press the record button while holding down the [opt/alt] key, and the marked section will automatically be captured, with a little extra (known as *preroll*) before it, to allow the tape to come up to speed.

Most DV camcorders should support device control and some analogue ones do too, but many older or cheaper camcorders and tape decks do not and, if you use an analogue-to-DV converter, device control will not usually work. So, what happens if your camcorder does not support device control? Or, as may happen, what if Premiere fails to recognize the fact that it does so? In that case, the playback controls do not appear and are replaced by the two buttons shown in Figure 8.5. If, for some reason, device control is supported but has not been set up, you can click on the button labelled Enable Device Control and select an appropriate control method (either DV control, or a method specific to your camcorder) in the dialogue box that is displayed. Otherwise,

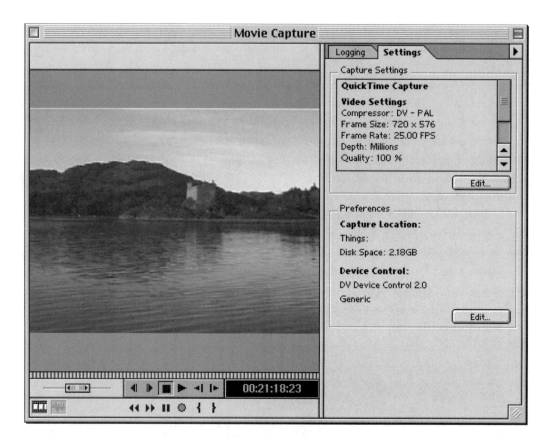

Figure 8.4   *The* Movie Capture *window.*

you must start and stop the tape by hand, using the controls on the camcorder itself (the remote control unit provided with most camcorders comes in handy) and just press Record when you want to start recording. Clicking the mouse or pressing Esc stops recording. When capturing by hand in this way it is particularly important to be over-generous in the amount you capture, as reaction times are not good enough to control the camcorder accurately enough to capture precisely the right amount.

Figure 8.5   *Controls for capture without device control.*

When you have finished capturing, a dialogue box appears, in which you can name the clip you have just captured and save it to disk. If you have a project open, the clip appears in the Project window. Using the default settings (which are perfectly good), each clip's type is shown by an icon, which indicates whether it is a video clip or one of the other sorts of object that you can add to a project, which we will describe later. Next to this is shown its name, and various pieces of additional information, including its size and duration (see Figure 8.6). At the top of the window is a miniature movie player that displays the currently selected clip. You can use this to get a quick view of the clip's contents. You can also use it to set a *poster frame* – a frame which is used as a static representation of the clip where one is needed. By default, the first frame is used as the poster, but you can set it to another, perhaps more representative frame, which might convey a better idea of what the clip looks like, by dragging the slider in the tiny controller until you find a suitable frame and clicking the Set Poster Frame button to its right.

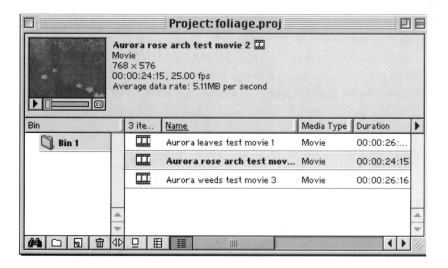

Figure 8.6   *The project window.*

When you have finished capturing, you should close the Movie Capture window, because keeping it open interferes with the performance of the rest of Premiere.

☛ Take a camcorder, and shoot roughly half an hour of tape, consisting of short scenes of at most two minutes' duration each. Practise capturing each scene into your Premiere project as a separate movie clip. If necessary, retain just the six scenes you like best, and discard the rest after capturing, to save disk space. Save the project so that you can use the clips you keep in later exercises. Set a poster frame for each clip you intend to keep.

You can see in Figure 8.4 that the right side of the Movie Capture window consists of two tabbed panes, labelled Logging and Settings. The Logging tab is used for recording information about clips so that you can capture them all at once in *batch mode* at a later date. This is a useful function for large projects, but is not really necessary for movie-making on the small scale usually appropriate to multimedia, so we will not describe it here.

The Settings tab shows the values that have been set for capture. These will initially be taken from the project's settings. If you started with a preset, as described on page 478, these settings should be correct for your device and should be left alone. If, for some reason, you need to change them, you click on one of the buttons labelled Edit..., which will open one of the dialogues shown in Figure 8.7. The top dialogue is also accessible via the Edit>Preferences sub-menu because, even when you access it from the Movie Capture window, you are setting some preferences. The most obviously relevant feature is the pop-up menu labelled Device, from which you will be able to select an appropriate device control setting for your camcorder. In this box you can also choose a folder for Premiere to store your captured clips in. It is a good idea to do this before you capture your first clip, because otherwise Premiere just puts them at the top level on the volume on which the application resides – which may not be what you want. The second dialogue box can also be accessed in a different way, in this case from the Project>Settings sub-menu, because here again you will be changing the settings for the whole project. Within the box, only the frame size is of much interest: make sure it matches the size of frames for the video standard your camcorder uses. Clicking on the Video... button opens a dialogue box in which you can select the video source and set its properties. If you used the correct project preset this should not be necessary. The settings you can make will be specific to your capture device and cannot generally be altered without causing problems. If you think you need to change them you should consult the documentation for your video card.

If you select the checkbox labelled Report Dropped Frames in the Capture Settings dialogue, a report will appear when you have finished capturing, giving some statistics about the captured clip. The same information can be obtained by selecting the clip in the Project window and choosing Properties from the Clip menu. Figure 8.8 shows a typical report. Most importantly, the report will tell you whether any frames have been *dropped* – i.e., left out during the capture process. It is not unusual for a clip to have one or two dropped frames, like this one does. If it does, these will almost certainly be the first and last, which are often not captured correctly because of the starting and stopping of the capture process. If there are more than two dropped frames, though, you have a problem. Even at broadcast frame rates of 25 or 30 frames per second,

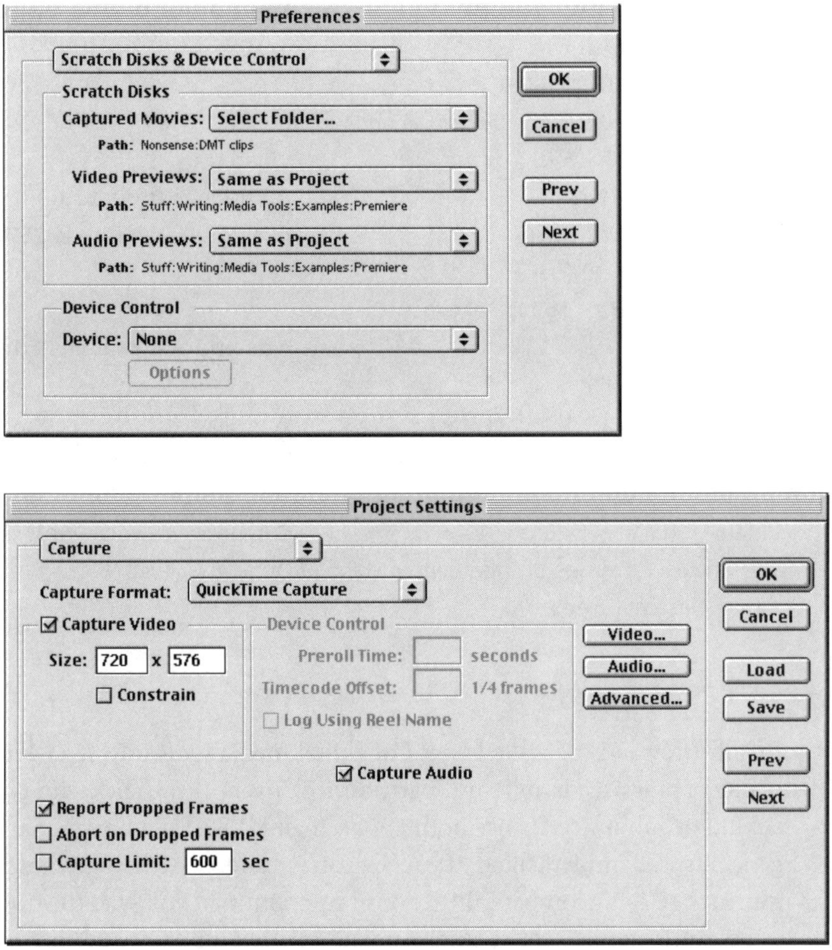

Figure 8.7 *Capture preferences and settings.*

somebody with a trained eye will be able to detect the discontinuity caused by a single dropped frame. Sometimes, frames are dropped merely because the disk to which you are capturing has become fragmented. You should run a disk optimization utility or completely erase your capture disk (having archived all your work) frequently to prevent this happening.

> ☞ For each clip you have captured, use the Clip>Properties command to see a report. Are there any dropped frames? Is the data rate what you expect?

It is during capture – and export to tape at the end of a project, where that is appropriate – that you are most likely to run into problems with digital video. It is at these points

File path: Things:sea pan

File size: 50.81MB bytes

Total duration: 0:00:14:00

Average data rate: 3.62MB per second

Image size: 720 x 576

Pixel depth: 24 bits

Pixel aspect ratio: 1.067

Frame rate: 25.00 fps

Audio: 48000 Hz - 16 bit - Stereo

QuickTime details:

Movie contains 1 video track(s), 1 audio track(s) and 1 timecode track(s).

Video:

There were 2 frames dropped when this movie was captured.

There are 350 frames with a duration of 1/25th.

Video track 1:

Duration is 0:00:14:00

Average frame rate is 25.00 fps

Video track 1 contains 1 type(s) of video data:

Video data block #1:

Frame Size = 720 x 576

Compressor = DV - PAL

Quality = Most (5.00)

Figure 8.8   *A clip properties report.*

that the tidy and controlled world of digital media tools intersects with the grubby reality of plugs, leads and third-party device drivers. If you stick with DV your problems should be minimized, since both DV itself and IEEE 1394 are standards and are generally well implemented. If you are using analogue video and capture cards, there is more scope for incompatibilities; it is important that you read the documentation for the capture card and make sure that your other equipment and software satisfy its requirements. Apart from driver incompatibilities, the most common source of problems with video capture is disks (and buses) that are not fast enough to provide the necessary bandwidth. Remember that they must be capable of providing the necessary *sustained* data rate – if your disk has to pause to perform thermal recalibration or the controller can only maintain the necessary data rate in bursts, you will lose frames. Nowadays, most new disks will be capable of handling DV data, but older devices may cause problems, and capture cards that can use low compression ratios may need data rates that can only be obtained by using high-speed interfaces. Again, check the documentation before you start.

Capturing Audio with Video

Video tape formats can record and store sound as well as picture and most camcorders either have microphones built in, or connections for attaching an external microphone,

– maybe both. (An external mic is generally a preferable option, since built-in microphones are usually of poor quality and must inevitably be close to the camcorder's noisy tape drive mechanism.) Typically, therefore, when you capture video, there will be some accompanying sound on the tape, which you may or may not wish to capture at the same time. If you are using DV, the sound can be transferred to your computer along with the video signal, through the Firewire connection from the camcorder. If you are using an analogue source with a capture card, you may be able to capture audio through the same card, or it may be necessary to use a separate audio card. In either case, separate connections are used to take the audio signal from the camcorder outputs to the inputs at the computer end.

The two buttons in the bottom left corner of the Capture window are used to choose whether to capture video, audio or both. If you do not wish to capture the sound, do not select the Take Audio button, and the picture will be captured alone. If you want the sound as well, select this button, and it will be captured at the same time as the picture; no more action is required from you. The resulting clip will contain both the captured audio and video. Finally, if you only want to capture the audio, select the Take Audio button and deselect the Take Video button.

> ☞ Practise capturing video clips that were recorded with audio tracks. Try capturing the picture both with and without audio, and then capture the audio on its own.

You can also capture audio from other devices, such as MiniDisc and DAT recorders, and import it from files stored on disk. We will return to the topic of audio capture, editing and processing on page 532.

Stop-Motion Capture

For animators, Premiere provides a stop-motion capture facility, which allows you to capture single frames. This enables you to make animation in a traditional way, by creating each frame individually – for example by drawing it on paper or cel, painting on glass, or positioning models on a miniature stage – and then capturing it to disk.

Stop-motion capture is straightforward: the File>Capture>Stop Motion command opens the Stop Motion window. Its operation is even simpler than that of the Movie Capture window: you click Start to initiate the process, and click Step every time you want to capture a frame. You can press a number on the keyboard to capture that number of consecutive frames and you can use the Delete key to remove the most recently captured frame. When you have finished capturing a sequence, click Save As... to name it and save it to disk.

Some additional refinements to stop-motion capture work differently on Windows and MacOS, but these will not be important for most users. You should be aware, though, that stop-motion capture is not supported by all capture cards and although it does work with DV in Premiere 6, it does not in earlier versions. Device control is not supported, but this will not normally be a problem because you will probably be capturing live from camera. (In fact, stop-motion capture has always been a bit cranky in Premiere and, if you are serious about this sort of animation, this may not be the best tool for the job.)

☛ If you have a suitable stand, mount a camera pointing downwards at a flat surface, otherwise use a tripod and point it at a vertical screen. Practise stop-motion capture by holding your hand against the surface or screen and capturing frames with the hand in different positions. Repeat the exercise with some inanimate objects. Play back the sequence you have captured to observe the effect.

Importing Video Clips and Images

Many projects are self-contained, using only material that is captured specifically for them, but sometimes a project will use video clips that have been captured previously, for another project perhaps, or obtained from a third-party source. Projects may also incorporate still images. (The issue of sound is one that we will consider later, starting on page 532.) Any such material that already exists on disk must be imported into the project before it can be used.

Premiere's File>Import sub-menu allows you to import files, folders and entire projects. The last case allows you to factor large projects into smaller ones in a hierarchical fashion. Choosing to import a folder causes all the files in it to be imported and grouped into a new bin. Importing one or more files is done simply by selecting File... from the sub-menu and choosing them from the standard file opening dialogue. If the files are movie clips (that is, video files in a format that Premiere recognizes) they are imported and appear in the Project window. It is important to realize that the movie files themselves are not copied into the project in any way: the project just holds a pointer to the file. If the file is deleted on disk Premiere will no longer be able to use it. If you move a file containing a clip that belongs to a project (captured clips as well as imported ones), a dialogue box will give you the opportunity to find it when you open the project.

When you import a still image – which is done in the same way as importing movie clips – it is assigned a duration as if it was a clip. This is only sensible, since you are working in a time-based medium, and when you put a still image into a movie it will be held for a period of time, which will normally be more than one frame. You set the default duration for imported stills in the General & Still Image dialogue box, opened from the Edit>Preferences sub-menu. It is shown on the left of Figure 8.9, where you see that you simply need to enter a value for the number of frames for which stills will be held by default. You can always change the duration of any individual still by selecting it in the Project window and using the Clip>Duration... command, which brings up a simple dialogue box as shown on the right of Figure 8.9, in which you set the duration. The format used is that of SMPTE timecode, which is generally used to identify a frame's position in the time-base of a movie by specifying a number of hours, minutes, seconds and frames, each as two digits separated by colons. The same notation can be used for specifying a clip's duration. (The number of frames in a second will be determined by the frame rate you are using. The frame rate of video captured from a camcorder will conform to the PAL, NTSC or SECAM standards.)

☛ Practise importing stills into a Premiere project. Set the default duration and import several stills at the length you specify. Import one still image several times and set its duration to a different value each time.

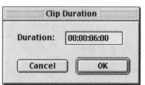
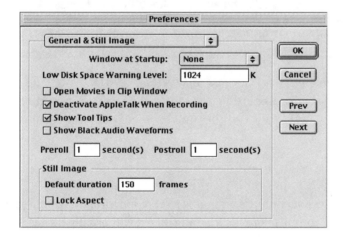

Figure 8.9   *Setting and changing the duration of still images.*

As well as importing single stills, you can import a sequence of still images that will be converted into a movie clip, with each image from the sequence becoming a frame in the clip. (The default duration for still images does not affect images in a sequence.) This is usually employed for animation, where the images may have been created one at a time in a graphics program, or scanned individually from real artwork. Numbered image sequences can sometimes be used as a last resort interchange format to allow Premiere to import movies from a system that does not use any format it understands.

For example, Commodore Amiga systems will export sequences of stills which can be converted to a format that Premiere can import, even though Premiere cannot import Amiga video files. For this to work, the image files' names must follow a convention. Premiere is actually quite tolerant, but the easiest thing to do is to stick to names of the form rootname*nnn*.ext, where rootname is a common root that you use for every file in the sequence, *nnn* is a sequence number (if you have more than 999 images in your sequence, you will need four digits) and ext is the file extension identifying its type. (You don't need this on a Mac, but it doesn't do any harm.) For example, a sequence of fifty GIF files might be called castle001.gif, castle002.gif, … castle050.gif. You import a sequence with the usual File>Import>File… command: select the first in the sequence, and tick the checkbox labelled Numbered Stills at the bottom of the file open dialogue.

Premiere can also import animated GIFs (see Chapter 10). The frames of the animation are converted to frames of a clip in the project, as one would hope. SWF files cannot be imported, though.

> ☛ Practise importing animated GIFs into a Premiere project, observing how they are shown as clips in the Project window. If you know how, prepare a numbered sequence of stills in some image editing program (e.g., by scanning your hand in different positions into Photoshop or by drawing a simple sequence of images) and import the sequence into Premiere.

By default, Premiere scales imported images (and clips) to match the project's frame size. It is usually a wise precaution to do the scaling yourself first in Photoshop, for images, or After Effects, for video (because Premiere is not very good at scaling).

Editing

The main business of editing is arranging a set of individual clips into a programme in order to make a complete movie. In doing this, it will usually be necessary to change the length of some or all of the clips to fit the structure of the composition. You may wish to use transitions between some of the clips, but much of the time you will simply cut from one to the next in sequence.

Premiere provides a great deal of flexibility in carrying out the basic editing operations. We have already mentioned that you can reorganize the entire workspace to suit different styles of editing, depending on your background. You can also perform the same operation in different ways, while viewing the material in different windows. This flexibility lets you develop your own way of working, but it can be bewildering to a novice. We will describe one approach which works, but you should realize that it is not the only way of doing things and once you understand what you are doing you may wish to investigate alternative approaches.

Three windows are used for most editing tasks: the Timeline, Monitor and Clip windows. The Timeline window shows a symbolic spatial view of the arrangement of clips in time. A vertical line, the *edit line* indicates a current point, at which editing operations are performed. The Monitor window provides a display of the frames of the movie corresponding to what is in the timeline. It can be set to show different views; the basic view, in which the frame currently at the edit line in the Timeline window is shown, is referred to as the *program* view; we will also use the *trim* view. (You can also split the Monitor window into two panes, to see an additional *source* view, as in Figure 8.2 on page 476. Like single-track editing, with which it is most often used, this is not very helpful to newcomers to video editing.) You can switch between views using the window's menu. The Clip window allows you to review entire clips from the project window and perform some simple editing on them. As well as these three windows, you will also need to refer to the Project window and you may find it helpful to employ the Storyboard window for making an initial rough arrangement of your clips. Normally, the Timeline and Monitor windows are permanently open, as is the Project window. (Refer back to Figure 8.1 on page 475, where you can see the Timeline window dominating the lower part of the workspace, with the Monitor window at the top right.) The others are usually closed.

Trimming

Nearly always, when you capture material from tape you'll capture more than you actually need to. This is almost inevitable, because you cannot rely on having enough foresight to know exactly what you will need before you try to edit your clips, and so it is only sensible to err on the side of caution. Additionally, if you capture by setting in and out points using device control you will inevitably end up with extra frames because of the pre-roll. If you go about shooting the source footage in a conventional manner, dividing up your action into scenes and recording several takes of each one, you will naturally capture each complete take as a separate clip – including the clapperboard at the beginning and the director shouting 'Cut!' at the end.

It follows that before you can start doing any serious assembly of clips into a complete movie you must remove extraneous material from the beginning and end of each, an operation known as *trimming*. The most straightforward way of roughly trimming an individual clip before you combine it with others is to use the Clip window. Double-clicking a clip in the Project window causes it to be opened in the Clip window, which is shown in Figure 8.10. This window, as you can see, resembles the Capture window (although by default it is much bigger in reality) in having a preview area that shows you the clip you're working on, with some VCR-like controls underneath. In this window though, the controls, as well as being arranged slightly differently, don't operate any external device, they just allow you to play and move around in the clip that you have previously saved to disk. All you have to do to trim a clip is to set its in-and-out points, just as you would have done if you had captured it using device control. That is, you find the point in the clip where you really wanted to begin, click on the { button (it is in the bottom right of this window) to set the in point, then move forward to find the point where you want to end the clip and set its out point with the } button. The jog control is very useful here for identifying the precise point at which you want to trim – remember that you're working to an accuracy of a single frame.

If you prefer to manipulate the clip's in and out points more directly, an alternative way of setting them is just by dragging the { and } markers in the strip below the jog control. As you drag, the clip is jogged, so you can see where you are. When you let go, the in or out point is set.

☛ Trim each of the clips you captured earlier. In each case, try to choose appropriate in and out points. Ensure that what you trim from each end of each clip includes frames that are fit to be used if necessary – you will need them later.

Although the operation just described is referred to as trimming, it is important to understand that nothing is actually trimmed off the clip. Whereas if you were editing film, you would quite literally have to trim off some frames by cutting the film and throwing them away, digital video editing is *non-destructive*. If you like, you could think of the trimming operation as just hiding some frames – you can always get them back at a later date if you discover that you trimmed in the wrong place. The non-destructive nature of digital video is in some ways its most important characteristic. It allows you room to experiment without fear of damaging any source material.

Assembling Clips

The established method of assembling clips in a temporal sequence is by dragging them to the Timeline window. This is organized as a set of video and audio *tracks*, each of which can hold a sequence of clips. Time runs from left to right in this window, with the ruler along the top showing the coordinates along the time axis as SMPTE timecode. You can use the pop-up menu at the bottom left of the window to set the scale along this axis. The duration of each clip is indicated by the length of the bar that represents

Clip: Aurora weeds test movie 3

Δ 21:11   00:00:18:20

Figure 8.10   *The clip window.*

it in the timeline. If you look at Figure 8.11, you will see a very simple arrangement of three clips. The name of each clip is shown on the bar that stands for it in the timeline; at the beginning of this bar is a thumbnail of the clip's poster frame, usually its first frame. These two pieces of information make it easy to see which clip is which when you look at the timeline. The first two clips are placed in video track 1A, while the third is on video track 1B. (There is no audio in this example.) As we will describe later, placing clips on the 1A and 1B tracks allows us to use transitions, such as dissolves, to go between them. Video track 1 is special in this respect. All other video tracks are used for superposition and compositing, that is playing back different clips simultaneously, combined in different ways. For a simple movie that just cuts from one clip to the next, all your video clips can be placed on a single track, but if you need them you can have as many as 99 video tracks. If a clip contains both video and audio, when you add it to the timeline, the picture and sound will be separated, with the sound being placed on one of the audio tracks. To begin with, the audio and video tracks for a single clip are *linked*, which means that edits made to one automatically affect the other. You can, however, unlink them, permanently or temporarily, as we will describe later, to make changes to sound and picture separately. In this section, we will only consider video tracks.

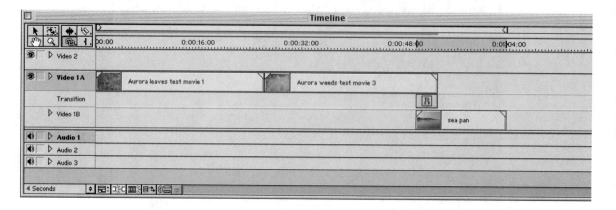

Figure 8.11   *The timeline window.*

If you are a naturally well-organized person and have planned your video editing thoroughly in advance, you will be able to sequence your clips by dragging each one from the project window to the timeline in order, dropping each one on an appropriate track in the empty space following the clip before it. You can then go on to the next step of finely tuning the length of each clip so that the cuts are exactly where you want them, and perhaps adding transitions between some clips. If you are not so well organized, you may prefer an alternative approach.

Selecting Storyboard from the File>New sub-menu opens the Storyboard window, which provides an area in which you can arrange and re-arrange clips until you find a sequence that satisfies you. To begin with, the Storyboard window is completely blank. You add clips to it by dragging them from the Project window. As you do so, each clip is shown as a thumbnail image of its poster frame, which you set in the Project window (see page 482). You can select clips in the storyboard and rearrange them by dragging and dropping, or delete ones you don't like with the Delete key. Storyboards can be printed for perusal at story conferences – just use File>Print... in the normal way when the storyboard window is at the front – and saved and reopened like other documents.

The thumbnails in the Storyboard window provide a visual summary of the scenes in your movie, such as the one shown in Figure 8.12. Storyboards on paper are used for this purpose in many film and animation studios as a means of planning movies. They are a sort of visual outline, like a set of headings you might jot down when planning an essay or article, showing you how each clip fits into the overall composition. Clearly,

Figure 8.12 *The storyboard window.*

the timeline itself does this, too, but it displays the structure in a less immediately perspicuous way, because it is organized for actual editing. Moreover, moving clips about in the timeline is not straightforward, because once it is on the timeline a clip interacts with all the others that are there.

 Ultimately, though, you do need to arrange your clips on the timeline. If you have made a storyboard this is trivial to do: click the Automate to Timeline button (the leftmost of the pair in the bottom right corner of the window). The dialogue box shown in Figure 8.13 is displayed. Usually, the defaults are what you want. The most likely one to need changing is the Clip Overlap. When you dismiss this dialogue, the clips from the storyboard are sent to the timeline in the order they appear in the storyboard and placed alternately on video tracks 1A and 1B. By default, they are overlapped by 15 frames and a cross-dissolve transition is applied between them. To make the clips butt together with straight cuts, set the overlap to zero and uncheck the box labelled Use Default Transition.

☛ Create a storyboard for your project and drag your clips to it. Practise arranging and re-arranging the clips and automating them to the timeline. Try using different values for the clip overlap and see how it affects the arrangement of the clips on the timeline.

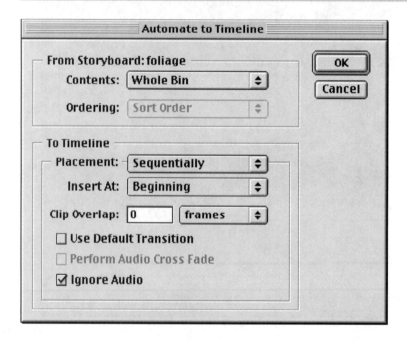

Figure 8.13   *Options for automating the storyboard to the timeline.*

Previewing

Unless you are very experienced (and not always then) you will not know how a movie is going to look when it is played back just from examining the timeline. You need to preview it. There are several ways of doing this, none without their problems. (This is one of the areas in which more expensive solutions using dedicated hardware show their worth.)

You do not have to preview the entire timeline at once – in fact, usually you won't want to, but will just want to see part of it to judge the effect of some recent changes. The section that will be previewed is called the *work area* and is indicated by a yellow bar right at the top of the timeline window, above the timecode markings (see Figure 8.11). You can adjust the extent of the work area by dragging the markers at each end of this bar. Once you have done this, choose the Timeline>Preview command, or just press [return/enter].

What happens then depends on how Premiere has been instructed to render previews. By default, it creates a preview file on disk, which it then plays back. Creating the preview can take some time, especially if you have applied any effects or transitions, since Premiere has to process these before you can see what they look like. However, once a preview file has been created for part of the timeline, it will be reused whenever you preview that section, unless you have made changes to it. Hence, although creating the preview file initially may take some time, later you can preview the same part of the timeline almost instantaneously. The thin horizontal line below the work area bar indicates whether an up-to-date preview exists for the corresponding part of the timeline. If it does, the line is green, otherwise it is red.

☞ Set the work area to just part one part of your project and preview it. Move the work area and preview again. Preview the same work area twice, noting the different behaviour on the second occasion.

The advantage of letting Premiere build a preview file on disk is that, once it has done so, it can preview the timeline at its correct frame rate, so that you can see exactly what the movie will look like. If seeing the movie at the correct speed is not important to you, you can tell Premiere to build the preview in RAM, by selecting From RAM from the Preview pop-up menu in the dialogue box that opens when you choose Keyframe and Rendering... from the Project>Project Settings sub-menu. Building the preview will be much quicker, but some frames may be dropped when it is played back.

To obtain the quickest previews of all, select To Screen from the Preview pop-up menu. If you do so, then Premiere does not create a preview at all, it just tries to play the frames immediately. They are unlikely to play at anything like the correct rate and the playback will be jerky. If you don't care at all about the rate at which the preview plays, you can just scrub through the timeline by dragging the edit line.

In all the cases just described, the preview is shown in the Monitor window. If you are relying on software to play back the video for you – as you usually will if you are working with DV and capturing with a built-in Firewire input – this is the best way of previewing. If you are using a capture card, or a special DV Firewire card that provides a hardware DV codec, you should be able to preview video on a TV monitor attached to the card, at full-screen size and full frame rate. Consult the card's documentation to verify that this is possible and how it is set up.

☞ Experiment with changing the preview mode and then repeating the previous exercise. Try to get an idea of when the different sorts of preview would be appropriate.

Editing Clips on the Timeline

Your first attempt at assembling clips, whether from a storyboard or directly on the timeline, will only be a rough cut. Once you have looked at a preview of the timeline and seen a cut going from one clip to the next, you may decide that you should have cut earlier, or to a different frame in the second clip. If you have a soundtrack, you may find that cuts don't match it or work the way you expected them to. Whatever the reason, you will almost certainly have to make adjustments to the clips when they are on the timeline.

The most basic operation is moving a cut. To begin with, we will just consider the basic situation: two clips on video track 1A, say an establishing long shot followed by a close-up. Suppose the rough cut showed twelve seconds of the first clip before cutting to the second, but that after seeing a preview you decide that this is too long, so you want to cut to the second clip two seconds sooner. What you need to do is move the out point of the first clip to an earlier frame, but you must ensure that this does not leave a two-second gap between it and the following clip. There are two distinct ways of preventing it. Either you can close up the gap by moving the second clip so that it begins at the new point where the first one ends, thereby making the whole composition two seconds shorter, or you can adjust the in point of the second clip, moving it two seconds earlier to fill up the gap with frames that would otherwise not be seen. These two sorts of adjustment are called a *ripple edit* and a *rolling edit*, respectively. They are illustrated schematically in Figure 8.14 and Figure 8.15.

You can perform both kinds of edit either by directly manipulating clips on the timeline with editing tools or in the monitor window. We will consider using the timeline first.

If you look back at Figure 8.11 on page 494 you will see that there is a small toolbox in the top left corner of the timeline window. It includes a conventional arrow tool, which is used for selecting clips, by clicking on them in the timeline. You can use this tool to

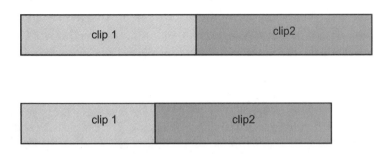

Figure 8.14 *A ripple edit.*

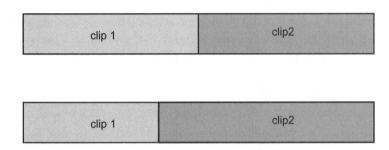

Figure 8.15 *A rolling edit.*

trim clips *in situ*, by dragging either edge. You can also use it to move clips to a new position on the timeline, by dragging any other part of the clip. A quick and crude way of performing a ripple edit as described is therefore to drag the right edge of the first clip to reset its out point and then drag the whole of the second clip leftwards along the timeline until it butts against the first.

 You can combine these two movements by picking up the ripple edit tool. This may not be visible; if it is not, hold down the mouse button with the cursor over the third tool from the left in the top row of the toolbox and then select the ripple edit tool from the menu that pops up. With this tool selected, you can drag the right hand end of the first clip to shorten it and the second clip will move down to follow it. You can perform a ripple edit that lengthens the first clip in the same way, by dragging its right hand edge to the right. The second clip will move up to accommodate it. This will only work if the first clip has been trimmed so that there are hidden frames at the end which can be used to extend it. If there aren't any spare frames, nothing happens.

Rolling edits can be done in a similar way using the rolling edit tool. Once again, you need to understand that you can only perform a rolling edit if there are hidden frames in the first clip to reveal if you wish to lengthen it. In this case, though, there must be hidden frames at the beginning of the second clip, if you are shortening the first clip. The potential need to make changes to in and out points in this way is another reason for always capturing too much video and trimming clips before assembling a rough cut on the timeline.

> ☞   Place two trimmed clips next to each other on the timeline, first ensuring that there are usable trimmed frames at the beginning and end of each clip. Practise performing ripple and rolling edits on the timeline, using both the arrow and the ripple and rolling edit tools.

If you look at the Monitor window while you are using either the ripple edit or rolling edit tools, you will see that the preview pane splits in two, showing you the frames on either side of the cut. This gives you an immediate visual impression of the effect of your edit. You can take this approach further by using the Monitor window instead of the timeline to do the editing. To do this, you first split the monitor display, either by clicking on the Trim Mode button at the top of the window, or by selecting Trim Mode from the window's menu. When you do so, the window is enlarged, as shown in Figure 8.16, to show you the two frames on either side of the edit line, which always snaps to an edit point where two clips meet when the monitor is in trim mode. You can move to the preceding and the following edit points in one step by clicking on the Previous Edit and Next Edit buttons.

Figure 8.16   *The* Monitor *window in trim mode.*

To perform a ripple edit, you drag the out point of the left clip or the in point of the right clip, as marked by the { and } in the bar below the jog strips beneath each clip's preview. As you drag, you see the frames on the side of the cut you are altering change. You perform a rolling edit by pressing the mouse button while the cursor is on the dividing line between the two previews and then dragging to either side. Again, you see the frames change as you drag, so you can see exactly where you are cutting. To get a proper impression of the new cut, you can click on the Preview Edit button and the frames surrounding the cut will be previewed. (The preview mode is To Screen so playback will be jerky but should be adequate to judge the change you have made.) Changes that you make in the monitor window are reflected immediately in the timeline.

☛ Set up the timeline with two suitably trimmed clips in the same way as for the previous exercise, and practise making ripple and rolling edits in the Monitor window.

It is largely a matter of taste whether you prefer to manipulate clips on the timeline or in the Monitor window. It depends on whether you find it easier to think in terms of the extent of each clip in time, or the frames displayed at any point in time.

When you move a cut that affects a clip which is between two others, there are other possibilities for accommodating the movement, which preserve the length of the middle clip and the complete sequence. In a *slip* edit, both the in and out points of the middle clip are moved, so that the first cut goes to an earlier frame and the second cut goes from a correspondingly earlier frame. The position of both cuts on the timeline is unaffected. In a *slide* edit, the middle clip's in and out points are left alone, but the out point of the clip before it and the in point of the clip after it move to earlier points, so that the unaltered middle clip and the two cuts all move to the left in the timeline. These edits are illustrated in Figure 8.17. You can perform them by dragging clips in the timeline using the slip and slide editing tools. You might find it helpful to imagine the middle clip slipping underneath its neighbours or sliding over them.

☛ Arrange three clips on the same video track and practise slipping and sliding the middle one.

It is sometimes necessary to split a clip into two pieces, for instance to insert another in the middle, or to apply different effects to the two pieces. This is easily done once the clip is on the timeline: simply select the razor blade tool and click at the point where you wish to split the clip. Alternatively, if you prefer to see the frame at which you are

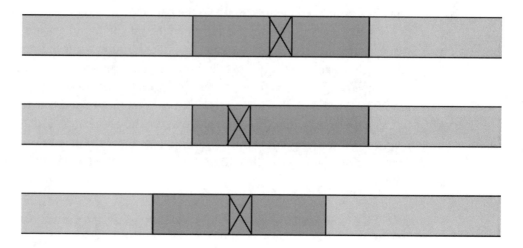

Figure 8.17   *Slipping (middle) and sliding (bottom).*

splitting, you can move the edit line to find the split point and choose Razor at Edit Line from the Timeline menu.

Transitions

For the purposes of ripple and rolling edits, video tracks 1A and 1B behave as a single track, so if you have a clip on 1A followed by a clip on 1B, you can use the methods just described to move the cut between them. However, the two sub-tracks of video track 1 are special, because you can apply transitions between a clip on 1A and one that follows it on 1B, and vice versa.

What do we mean by *transition*? Strictly speaking, a transition is any change taking you from the end of one clip to the beginning of the next. This includes the straight cuts that we have been dealing with up to now, where the last frame of the first clip is immediately followed by the first frame of the next. Normally, though, when people talk about transitions, they mean more complicated changes, where the last few frames of the first clip are combined with the first few of the next, so that intermediate transitional frames are built out of frames from both clips. The most commonly used transition in this sense is the *cross-dissolve*, where the picture from the first clip gradually fades away while that from the second fades up, so that at the end of the transition only the new clip is playing.

There are many more ways of making a transition – Premiere provides 75 and third-party plug-ins offer still more. Very few of them are commonly used. In fact, you could make a perfectly good film using nothing but cuts and perhaps a few dissolves. More unconventional transitions have periodically enjoyed a vogue in film and TV. (The 1960s was a good time for wipes, iris effects and zooms, and page peels were a cliché in the late 1980s, but a surprising number of these effects can be found in films of the 1930s, too. *Flying Down to Rio* is an early deliberately amusing example of the overuse of elaborate transitions.) However, it is hard to use these transitions without looking silly – although you can always claim to be making ironic references.

The available transitions can be found on the Transitions palette, shown in Figure 8.18. Since there are so many of them, they are organized into folders, the contents of which can be expanded using a disclosure triangle in the conventional way. You can create your own folders using the New Folder... command in the palette menu, and move transitions between folders or reorder the folders by dragging and dropping. That way, you can create a folder of transitions you find useful at the top of the palette for quick access. If you select Animate from the palette menu, the thumbnails for each transition will animate to show their effect (a rare example of the use of animated icons in a user interface). This can be distracting, though, and you may prefer to leave the animation turned off. When you double-click a transition, a dialogue box for setting its parameters opens; this includes the animation, providing a quick way of seeing what each transition does.

All transitions are applied in the same way.[*] The clips between which you want to use a transition must overlap on the timeline, and they *must* be on video tracks 1A and 1B. With your clips set up in this way, you simply drag your selected transition from the Transitions palette on to the Transition track between Video 1A and Video 1B in the region where your two clips overlap. (See Figure 8.19.) When you drop the transition it automatically sizes itself to fit the overlap. The extent of the overlap and consequently the duration of the transition is of crucial importance. It radically alters the pace and rhythm of the finished piece. You can change the extent of a transition in the same way as you trim a clip in the timeline, by dragging its edge with the arrow tool. The edges of the clips will move too to ensure that the overlap of the clips matches the extent of the transition.

Scrubbing over the transition will just display a cut, as if the transition was not there. However, if you hold down [opt/alt] while scrubbing, the transition will be shown, although you will not be able to judge its effect very easily. Previewing to screen is

---

[*]We are only talking about applying transitions using the workspace set up for A/B editing. If you use single-track editing, the process is less intuitive, since you can't so easily see what is happening. Unless you are already used to a single-track system, we recommend that you always use A/B editing.

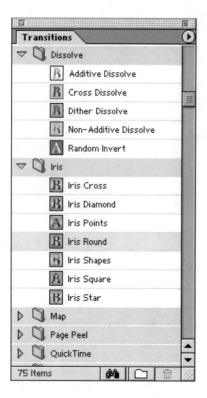

Figure 8.18   *The* Transitions *palette.*

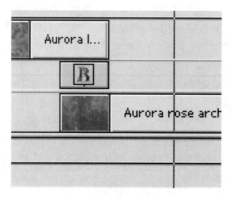

Figure 8.19   *A transition between two clips.*

unlikely to show you anything but a very jerky approximation. Once you have made a preview, though, the transition will be shown whenever you preview it, whether by scrubbing or one of the other methods. Creating the previews for transitions may take significantly longer than it does for cuts, since some computation must be performed on the pixel data of the frames involved in the transition to produce the intermediate frames, a process known as *rendering*. Special real-time effects cards are available that will eliminate this delay and let you preview transitions straight away. (The cost of such cards is falling rapidly, to the extent that they should soon be within the budget of desktop video makers.) Rendering necessitates decompressing and recompressing the video, which can lead to some loss of quality.

> ☛ Arrange a clip on each of video tracks 1A and 1B so that the two clips overlap. Drag different transitions to the Transition track at the overlap point and preview the result. Practise [opt/alt]-scrubbing to preview the transitions. Drag the edges of the transitions to see how altering their duration gives a different pace to the edit. (Adjust the positions of the two clips when necessary.)

Transitions have parameters which you can adjust. Double-click the transition's symbol in the timeline to open a dialogue for setting its parameters. Although some transitions have additional settings, all of them include the ones shown in the dialogue for a cross-dissolve, on the left of Figure 8.20. In these dialogue boxes, the letters A and B are used by default to represent the clips on the Video 1A and Video 1B tracks. The little box in the bottom right shows an animation of the transition using these letters, so for a cross-dissolve you will see A dissolving into B. This preview is useful for finding out what some of the more obscurely named transitions actually do. Normally, you would expect a dissolve to start from a frame that was entirely made from the A clip and end up with one made entirely from the B clip and this is the default setting, as shown. However, you can adjust the proportions with the pair of sliders under the two large previews at the top of the dialogue; as you do so, the previews above them change to show you the first and last frames of the transition as they will appear. Normally, this is done symbolically, using A and B, but if you tick the checkbox labelled Show Actual Sources, you can see the real frames. This doesn't affect the animation, though. Although you are unlikely to want to use anything but a start value of 0% and an end value of 100% for a cross dissolve, you may wish to alter the values for some other transitions. The only other control you have in this dialogue is the arrow to the left of the animation. This indicates the direction of the dissolve, down, from A to B, if the first clip is on sub-track A and the second on B, and up from B to A if they are placed the other way round. By clicking on it, you can reverse the direction, if you have a reason to do so.

The Clock Wipe Settings dialogue on the right of Figure 8.20 shows some extra settings which are shared with several transitions. In a clock wipe, a radial line moves round like the hand on a clock to reveal the second clip behind it. You can add a border to the revealed segment, choosing its thickness with the Border slider, and its colour by double-clicking the swatch to its right, which brings up a colour picker (see Chapter 9).

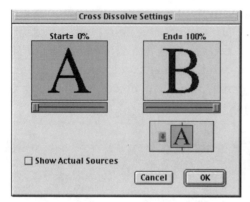
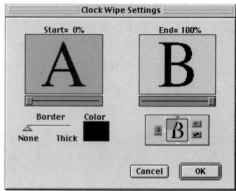

Figure 8.20   *Setting parameter values for a cross-dissolve (left) and clock wipe (right).*

For any transition during which one clip occupies a clearly-defined region of the frame, you can add a border in this way. You can change the direction of rotation of the clock wipe by clicking on the upper of the two buttons to the right of the animation: it is marked F for forward and R for reverse. Any transition that has a direction can be reversed in this way. (Reversing the direction of movement during the transition like this is not to be confused with reversing the direction between tracks.) Finally, the other button to the right of the animation turns anti-aliasing (smoothing) of the transition border on and off. Border and direction settings are shown in the animation preview as you change them.

> ☞ Experiment with changing parameters for all the transitions you applied in the previous exercise. Make a note of transitions and parameter settings which you particularly like, for future use.

If you double-click a transition on the timeline as just described, the changes you make to the parameters affect that particular transition alone. You can also double-click the transition in the Transitions palette, which opens the same dialogue. Any changes you make in that case become the default settings whenever you use the transition subsequently. So, for example, if you always want a border on your clock wipes you can set it from the Transitions palette instead of setting it each time you use the transition.

QuickTime transitions form a special class of transitions that don't behave quite like the others. This is because they are implemented in QuickTime, not in Premiere. They are represented in the Transitions palette as a single transition, bearing the QuickTime logo. When you drop this transition onto the timeline, the dialogue box shown in Figure 8.21 opens. You can then choose a specific transition from the scrolling list at the top left and its parameters will be displayed in the pane to the right. Many of the transitions available here duplicate Premiere's own – the cross fade shown here is actually the same as the transition Premiere calls a cross dissolve. A worthwhile advantage of the QuickTime versions is that the preview in the bottom left shows the effect being applied to the actual clips that are on the timeline, so you can see exactly what it will look like.

☞ Apply the QuickTime transition to your pair of clips. Select different transitions from the settings dialogue and experiment with setting their parameters.

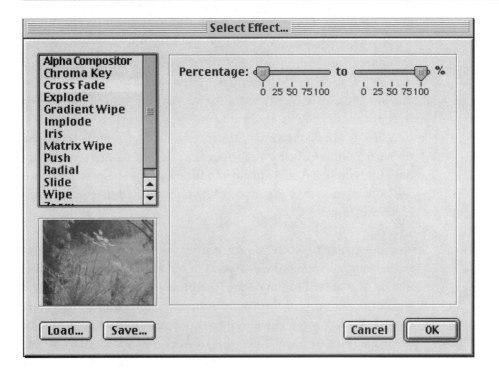

Figure 8.21   *Applying a QuickTime transition.*

Many transitions work well if they are applied between a clip and a plain black screen. You have probably seen scenes that fade to black many times and an iris dissolve to black was often used in silent movies. Black provides a sense of finality, so transitions to black can usefully be employed as endings, or to mark important dramatic or temporal divisions. In order to create black, you can use the File>New>Black Video command, which creates a pure black clip and adds it to the Project window. Its duration is set to the default duration of still images. You can change this in the same way as you do for stills. You can drag the black video to the timeline or a storyboard like any other clip or still image. Alternatively, you can just leave a gap on video track 1A or 1B and place the transition so that it overlaps the gap.

☞ Practise using transitions to black. Start with a simple fade to black, then experiment with other transitions to see which can be effectively used in this way. Try varying the duration of each transition and adjusting any other parameters it provides.

Markers

It is often useful to be able to move the edit line to a particular point in a clip, for example, where a car starts to move or a person starts to speak. It is also frequently necessary to line up different clips at specific points, most often to synchronize a soundtrack with some action, but also to match up transitions and for compositing. It may also be necessary to identify specific points in the timeline as a whole, in order to synchronize clips to the timing of the whole programme. Premiere lets you set *markers* in clips and the timeline to identify points, and provides a means of moving the edit line directly to a marker. Each clip can have up to ten numbered markers and so can the timeline. Additionally, each can also have up to 999 unnumbered markers. You can move the edit line directly to any numbered marker by specifying its number, but you can only move to the next or preceding unnumbered marker, since there is no way of identifying them.

To add a marker to a clip, you can open it in the Clip window. Scrub through the clip until you reach the point where you want to place the marker and then click on the marker icon at the bottom right of the window. A menu pops up, as shown in Figure 8.22, containing three sub-menus for manipulating markers. To set a marker, choose the Mark sub-menu and then choose a number, to set a numbered marker, or Unnumbered. As you should be able to guess from Figure 8.22, the other two sub-menus allow you to move to a numbered marker or the next or previous unnumbered marker, and to clear individual numbered markers, the current marker or all the markers.

If you prefer, you can set a clip marker by selecting the clip in the timeline, positioning the edit line at the point where you want the marker and using the Clip>Set Clip Marker sub-menu. If you use the Timeline>Set Timeline Marker instead, the marker will be set in the timeline itself. In the timeline, clip markers appear as a marker icon at the corresponding point in the clip; timeline markers appear in the time scale at the top of the window. Figure 8.23 shows two numbered markers of each type.

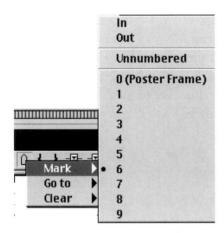

Figure 8.22   *The marker menu in the* Clip *window.*

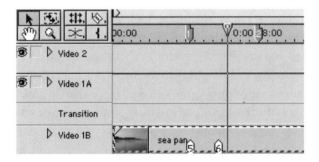

Figure 8.23   *Representation of clip and timeline markers in the timeline.*

The most common way of using markers is for aligning marked points in different clips – video or audio – with each other or with markers in the timeline. You can do this by eye, dragging clips in the timeline until the markers you wish to synchronize line up. To ensure accuracy, choose 1 Frame from the pop-up menu at the bottom left of the timeline to expand the scale so that you can see each individual frame. This manual alignment is not strictly necessary, however. There is a Snap to Edges facility in the Timeline window menu, which can be invaluable for aligning clips to markers. This facility can also be toggled on and off by means of a button at the bottom of the Timeline window. With Snap to Edges on, the edge of a clip being dragged on the timeline will automatically snap to the edge of another clip or to a marker. If you want to position two clips so that a marker in one snaps to a marker in the other, first turn on Snap to Edges, and then choose the arrow selection tool and position it over the marker in the clip you are going to drag. The pointer should change to a blue arrow. When this happens, drag the marker towards the marker in the clip with which you wish to align (the pointer changes to a hand while this is happening). When the two markers approach each other your clip will snap into position. This technique can also be used to align a clip marker with another clip's edge or with the edit line. You may find it a little tricky to use at first, but it can be very useful. Make sure that you turn Snap to Edges off when you don't need it, however. It can be very irritating to have clips snap to the edges of other clips or to markers when that is not what you intend.

☞ Practise setting markers in the timeline and at significant points in clips, and going to them. Try setting clip markers in both the Clip and Timeline windows. Practise aligning markers in different clips, both by hand and by using Snap to Edges. Try aligning clip and timeline markers.

Timeline markers have a couple of useful properties which may not be obvious. If you double-click a marker, the dialogue box shown in Figure 8.24 opens. You can add a comment to the marker, to remind you of why you placed it. The comment will be displayed in the monitor window as ghost text when the edit line is over the marked frame. You can set the comment's duration to longer than a single frame if you want to be able to see it when you preview the movie. You can also attach a URL to a marker. If you export your programme to a suitable format, including QuickTime, when the frame is displayed, the page corresponding to the URL will be opened in a Web browser. If you want it to open in a specific frame, you can put the frame's name, or one of the standard pseudo names, in the Frame Target field.

Titles

Titles are perhaps used less often in video destined for use on the Web or in other multimedia productions than in films and TV programmes, but you may wish to include a title sequence at the beginning or some credits at the end of a piece of video. You may, perhaps more often, wish to superimpose text over video picture, and abducting Premiere's titling facility is one way of doing this. (Although this may be the more common case, we will continue to refer to the text as a title.) Premiere's facilities for adding titles are generally held to be primitive and are often criticized, but they are adequate for simple tasks. In particular, they allow you to create the familiar rolling credits that move up the screen and also crawling text that moves across it.

A title is created with the File>New>Title command, which opens the Title window. You use this window as if it was a conventional document window and you must save its contents to a file in order to preserve them. When you do so, the title appears in the Project window if you have a project open at the time. You can treat it as a clip, dragging it to the timeline to include it in your work.

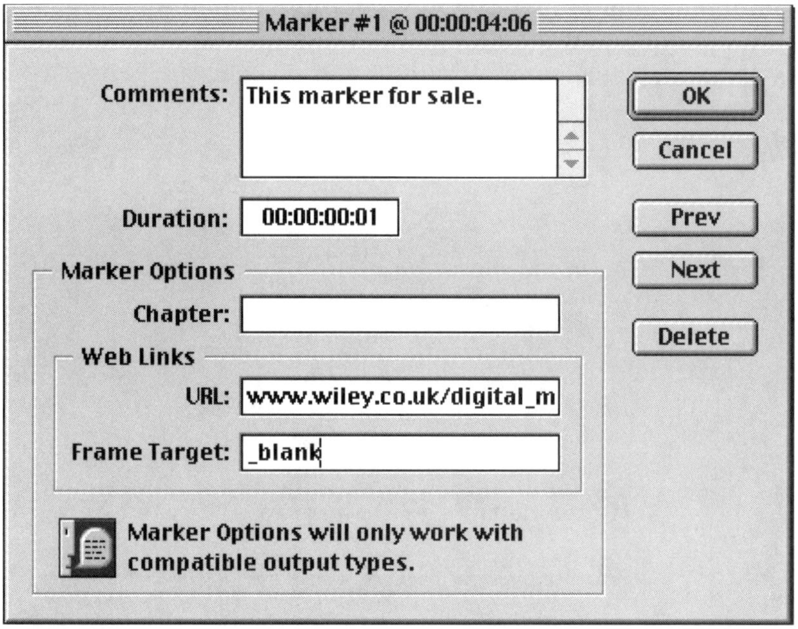

Figure 8.24 *Adding a marker comment and URL.*

The Title window, as shown in Figure 8.25, has a toolbox at its left containing tools for adding text and doing some rudimentary vector drawing. We will not consider the drawing tools, as they are really too crude to be much use – if you need to combine text and graphics in your titles, it is better to prepare them in some other application and import them as still images. You will see in the figure that within the window there are two concentric rectangles marked with dotted lines. These indicate the 'safe zones' for titles: the area within which you can be (fairly) certain that the entire title will be visible on a TV screen. For work destined for broadcast this is important. Because of the way cathode ray tubes work, domestic televisions don't actually display a picture right to the edges, some of it is concealed. Clearly, this matters when designing titles, since you probably want the entire text to be visible so people can read it. With video intended for display on a computer monitor, this is not important, since there is no underscan, as the phenomenon of cutting off the edges is called.

T Premiere allows you to create type and set its typographic properties (font, size, weight, and so forth) in a less convenient way than other applications do but, in its own fashion, it does provide much the same degree of control. You select the type tool in order to add text to the title and use the commands on the Title menu to set its properties. These properties, which are common to any application that provides text

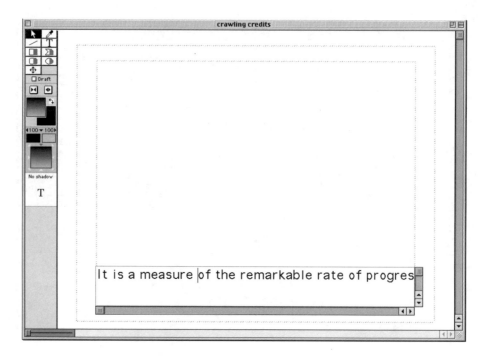

Figure 8.25   *The* Title *window.*

formatting, are described in Chapter 9. The colour of any selected text can be set by clicking on the colour swatch below the toolbox, which brings up a colour picker (also described in Chapter 9).

☞ Create a title with your name and address (or a fictional one, if you prefer) set in a suitable font at a size to be readable on the screen, and positioned and laid out in a pleasing way.

If you simply use the type tool to insert text, the title you create will be saved as if it was a still image of a fixed size. This would be suitable if you were displaying titles and credits as a succession of full screens. Rolling and crawling credits are a much used alternative. You can think of a set of rolling credits as being written on a long page – longer than the height of the screen – which is dragged upwards to show each line. Crawling credits are written on a wide page, which is dragged sideways. To create such credits, you select the Rolling Title tool and use it to drag out a rectangle. This will define the area in which the credits roll or crawl. It is displayed within the title area with scroll bars, as shown in Figure 8.25, where we have created a strip along the bottom of the screen for some crawling text. (Crawling text, whether it contains actual credits or just some additional commentary, is usually superimposed over the picture. You will probably have seen such things, especially if you ever watch MTV. We will describe how to perform the superimposition in the next section.) Next, pick up the type tool and enter type within the scrolling box. (The scroll bars are only visible while you have the type tool selected. Don't worry if they disappear when you select a different tool.) To see the text move inside the Title window, select the arrow tool and then drag the slider in the bottom left of the window.

Figure 8.26   *Setting options for rolling and crawling text.*

The Title>Rolling Title Options… command opens the dialogue shown in Figure 8.26, in which you can specify whether the titles roll or crawl, and in which direction. Note that the use of radio buttons ensures that the options are mutually exclusive, in case you wanted your titles to move diagonally. You can, however, use the Rolling Title tool to create more than one piece of moving text within the same title, and each has its options set separately, so you can have some text rolling and some crawling. The Special Timing settings are used to control how the text's movement starts and stops. By default, the text starts instantaneously. This is appropriate if your text is initially invisible (i.e., off the bottom of the screen, because you have inserted blank lines above it, for rolling titles, or off the right, because you have inserted spaces, for crawling text), but often titles are displayed so that a full screen is visible to begin with. You want to give your audience time to read most of the initial screen before you start moving new lines in from the bottom, so you should hold the text for a few seconds before it starts to roll. This can be done by ticking the checkbox labelled Enable Special Timing and entering a number of frames to hold in the Pre Roll field. The Post Roll field is used similarly to enter a number of frames for which the text should be held after it reaches the end, to allow slow readers to catch up. The Ramp Up and Ramp Down fields allow you to specify that the text should accelerate or decelerate over the number of frames you enter in them.

You adjust the speed at which the text moves by adjusting the duration of the title after you have placed it on the timeline. To begin with, it assumes the default you set for imported still images. You will usually need to lengthen the duration, which is most easily done by dragging the edge of the title clip in the timeline. You can preview rolling titles in the usual way. To see them at their real speed, you will need to preview to disk.

> ☛ Create a rolling title from a poem. (Not the *Rime of the Ancient Mariner*, but choose one that is too long to fit on the screen all at once.) Set the options so that the poem can be read easily as it scrolls.

Compositing and Effects

Up to this point, we have only considered using video tracks 1A and 1B. By default, when you create a project, the timeline contains another video track, labelled Video 2, which is referred to as a *superposition track*. You can add up to 97 more. As the name suggests, these additional tracks can be superposed, that is, placed on top of, video track 1 – tracks in Premiere behave much like layers in other programs.

Normally, higher numbered tracks obscure lower numbered tracks below them, just as layers do. The simplest way of allowing a lower track to show through is by reducing the opacity of the one above it. In Premiere, the transparency can be made to vary over time, so that a superposed track can fade out, revealing what is beneath it, or fade in to obscure it.

The way the transparency of a superposition track changes over time is specified using special controls called opacity *rubber bands*. To reveal the rubber bands, you must turn down the triangle to the left of the track's name in the Timeline window. Initially, the rubber band appears as a thin red line running horizontally along the lower half of the track which has now opened up. If you don't see such a line, click on the red button at the bottom left of the track. The vertical position of the line indicates the opacity of the track: where it is at the top, as it is to begin with, the track is opaque, where it is at the bottom, the track is entirely transparent, and where it is in-between, the track is partially transparent. At each end of the rubber band there are drag handles. By dragging both of these to the same level, keeping the rubber band flat, you can set the transparency of the whole clip. More interestingly, by clicking at any point in the rubber band you can create new handles and drag those. As you do so, the rubber band changes shape, so that the transparency is interpolated between the points where you set it by dragging. You can drag the handles horizontally as well as vertically to control the rate of change as well as the value of the opacity. Figure 8.27 shows a typical example of how you might use the opacity rubber bands. The opacity of the clip on Video 2 increases steadily during the period when it overlaps the first clip on Video 1, stays at full opacity, and then declines where it overlaps the second clip on Video 1. In other words, the clip fades up over the end of the first, then fades out as the second comes in. The result is an asymmetrical dissolve.

☞ Place a clip on video track 1 and another on video track 2. Practise adjusting the rubber bands to control the opacity of the second clip. Make the transparency vary as the clips play. Preview the result.

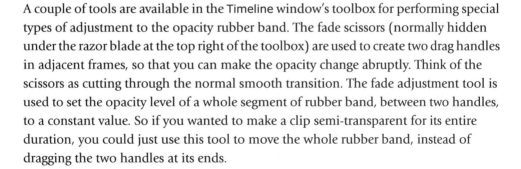

Figure 8.27 *Fading opacity with the rubber band.*

A couple of tools are available in the Timeline window's toolbox for performing special types of adjustment to the opacity rubber band. The fade scissors (normally hidden under the razor blade at the top right of the toolbox) are used to create two drag handles in adjacent frames, so that you can make the opacity change abruptly. Think of the scissors as cutting through the normal smooth transition. The fade adjustment tool is used to set the opacity level of a whole segment of rubber band, between two handles, to a constant value. So if you wanted to make a clip semi-transparent for its entire duration, you could just use this tool to move the whole rubber band, instead of dragging the two handles at its ends.

☞ With two clips set up in the timeline as in the previous exercise, practise using the fade scissors and fade adjustment tools until you have a clear idea of when each of these tools would be useful.

The opacity rubber band settings affect each frame in the clip in its entirety. More interesting results can be obtained by making just selected parts of each frame fully or partially transparent. To introduce the way this can be achieved, we shall return briefly to the subject of titles.

Keying

As we remarked earlier, crawling text is usually shown on top of a picture. All that is necessary to make this happen is to drag the title to a superposition track and place it so that it overlaps the part of the picture on video track 1 over which you want it to play. Figure 8.28 shows part of an example timeline. The crawling credits play over the end of the weeds test clip as it fades to black, with the clip and the black showing through the title where there is no text. This seems to contradict what we said earlier, since the credits are on a white background, which ought to obscure the underlying track. What is going on here?

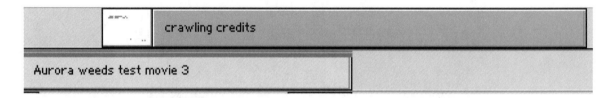

Figure 8.28   *Superposing credits.*

For titles, transparent areas in the clip on the superposition track are created automatically. It is instructive to see how. If, in this example, the credits clip is selected, a checkbox labelled Transparency will be found to be checked in the Effect Controls palette, as shown in Figure 8.29. Clicking on the Setup button next to this opens the dialogue box shown in Figure 8.30, where White Alpha Matte will be selected from the Key Type pop-up menu as shown.

Premiere:What does this all mean? In the first place, selecting Transparency in the Effect Controls palette is a general mechanism for making parts of the selected clip transparent. Without doing this, a clip on the track Video 2 will obscure any clips on Video 1 beneath it, unless the opacity rubber band had been used to make all of it semi-transparent. The Transparency Settings dialogue is used to make just parts of the superposed clip transparent. There are fourteen possibilities – fifteen if you count None – some of them rather recondite, but all useful in their own way.

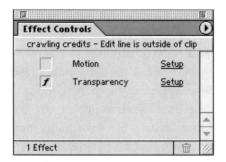

Figure 8.29 *Adding transparency.*

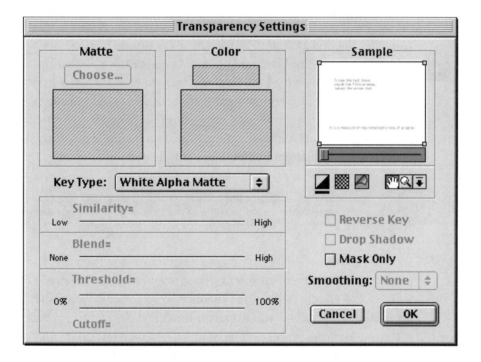

Figure 8.30 *Setting transparency options.*

In video jargon, a method of creating transparency is called a *key*, hence the label on the pop-up menu in the Transparency Settings dialogue we referred to earlier. We will begin with the white alpha matte key used for titles. All this actually means is that the white background is made transparent, or *keyed out*. There is a similar black alpha matte setting for keying out black backgrounds. But these keys introduce the important concept of an *alpha channel*.

An alpha channel is a sort of map, which shows which areas of an image (or a video frame) are transparent, which are opaque, and which are semi-transparent. This information is represented as a greyscale image, with black areas of the alpha channel indicating transparent areas of the main image, white areas indicating opacity, and grey areas being semi-transparent, the darker the more transparent. Alpha channels are also sometimes called *masks*, because one of their uses is to prevent effects being applied to parts of an image. If you select a title that has been placed on a superposition track, click on Setup next to Transparency in the Effect Controls palette, and then select the checkbox marked Mask Only, the thumbnail showing the title will display the alpha channel. All you will see is the background turning black and the text turning white, no matter what colour it was to begin with. Make sure you understand that this is what you should see. If you don't select Mask Only, the keyed clip is shown against a background. You select the background to be used for this purpose by clicking on one of the icons below the sample. The black and white diagonal causes a black or white background to be placed underneath the keyed image; the chequer board places a pattern of black and white tiles (the default representation of transparency in Photoshop); the page turn icon causes the actual underlying image from the timeline to be used, giving you a preview of the actual result. The slider beneath the sample can be used to drag through the clip to show different frames in the sample window.

> ☞ Make a crawling title and play it over a clip. Verify that the effect controls and transparency settings are as described in the text above. Practise previewing the mask and superposed clips in the transparency settings dialogue.

You can't paint your own alpha channels in Premiere, but you can in Photoshop, where you can also create them by selecting parts of an image in various ways (see Chapter 3.) You can also usually create alpha channels to go with images created in a 3D application, which allow you to insert a modelled object into any background scene. If you create an image with an alpha channel, and then import it into Premiere, either as a still or as one of a sequence of numbered images, the alpha channel will be imported intact. You can then use this as a key, by choosing Alpha Channel from the Key Type pop-up menu in the Transparency Settings dialogue. This makes it possible to insert objects created as Photoshop images or made from computer-generated 3D models into video clips. If you apply this method to numbered sequences of images, you can mix animation and live action video. (This is, admittedly, a labour-intensive process, but all animation is.)

☛ If you know how to use Photoshop, open an image, create an alpha channel in QuickMask mode and save it with the image. Import the image as a still into Premiere, place it on video track 2, set the key type to alpha channel, and preview the result. Practise keying with other images containing different alpha channels.

A similar approach can be used to insert a figure or model from one video clip into another. For example, an actor can be filmed in a studio sitting on a stationary motorbike, and then inserted into a clip that was shot outdoors from a moving vehicle, so that they seem to be riding along an open road. It would be possible to do this by creating an alpha channel for each frame by masking it in Photoshop, but this is usually considered excessively laborious. Instead, masking is usually done automatically.

The classic method is to use a Blue Screen key. This has the effect of keying out everything that is a particular shade of blue, known as chroma blue. The idea is to shoot your studio footage against a backdrop of this exact colour (a *blue screen*). Using the Blue Screen key will then automatically make the background transparent, and so the studio footage will be imposed on the outdoor background. Just like that. Or possibly not....

Blue screening relies on finding areas that are exactly the right shade to key out. You can obtain chroma blue backdrops and even chroma blue paint, but that does not, unfortunately, guarantee that when the set is photographed the background will come out a nice uniform blue that can be keyed out with a single mouse click. Only if you light everything so that there are no shadows or highlights on the background, and ensure that no colour is reflected onto the background or off the background onto the subject, can you be sure that your keying will work. You may also find that any compression that is applied when you capture your video, or shoot it to DV, interferes with the purity of the colours. Hence, blue screen keying is not the magic process it is sometimes made out to be.

There is one additional problem with it: any blue on the foreground may become transparent along with the background. For example, television weather presenters are almost always bluescreened when they appear in front of their weather map. A presenter wearing a tie that is the right shade of blue is liable to end up with isobars down their shirt. The usual way round this is to make sure that there is no blue in the subject – chroma blue was chosen since it is not a component of skin tones, so good keying can usually be achieved. If not, then a green screen can be used as an alternative, and Premiere provides a Green Screen key for this eventuality.

There are, in fact, several key types based on colour, the most broad of which is Chroma Key, which lets you choose a key colour by clicking on a thumbnail of the clip. (The cursor turns into an eyedropper when you do so.) The result is to create an alpha channel from all pixels that match that colour, for each frame in the selected clip. Various parameters can be adjusted, most importantly the Similarity, which determines how closely a pixel must match the sampled colour to be included in the alpha channel. The Blend slider controls the extent of grey shades in the mask, and hence semi-transparent areas in the superposed clip. Setting it to a value of 0 creates a pure black and white mask; setting it to a higher value adds grey areas, whose shade corresponds to how closely the pixels match the sampled colour. Figure 8.31 shows an example use of this key. Pastel shades in the sea and sky have been keyed out.

☛ Place a still image on video 2 with any video clip on video 1, set the key to Chroma and practise keying out areas of selected colour. Use the Similarity and Blend sliders to adjust the extent of the m ask and the resulting composition. Repeat this exercise with different source material.

One of the most interesting key types is Luminance, which uses brightness – essentially a black and white version of the clip itself – as an alpha channel. This is most obviously used to key out dark areas. For example, if you had captured a clip of landscape dominated by a dark mountain, you could use luma keying to make the dark areas of the mountain transparent, and then superpose the clip over a suitable shot of a forest, to clothe the mountainside in trees. By adjusting the Threshold slider for this key more subtle blending can be achieved, with the superposed clip becoming translucent.

☛ Repeat the previous exercise with a range of different material, this time using a Luma key to make areas transparent according to their brightness. Experiment to find the optimum position for the sliders to give an interesting or satisfactory result in each case.

Mattes

A technique that has been employed for special effects almost from the beginning of cinema is the use of a *matte* to obscure parts of the camera lens while shooting, so that the film can be rewound and a different image exposed on the parts of the film that were originally protected by the matte. The same technique can be used in the darkroom, or at a more sophisticated level, in a device called an optical printer, which was used to create most film special effects before digital techniques came into use. Clearly, a matte is functionally the same as what we have been calling an alpha channel, but in Premiere the term is reserved for those alpha channels that are created from another image or track, or by blocking out parts of a clip.

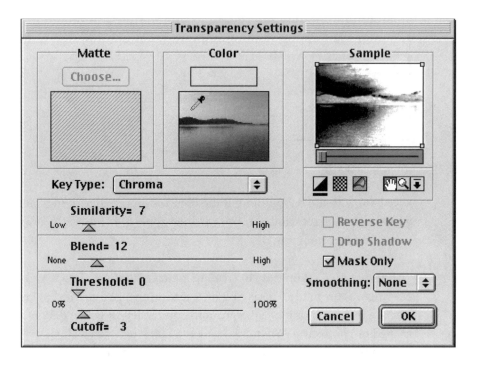

Figure 8.31 *Chroma keying.*

The last case is the simplest to use. If you look carefully at the preview at the top right of the Transparency Settings dialogue in Figure 8.31, you will see four small squares at its corners. These are drag handles, and you can pull them to define a quadrilateral within the preview, as shown in Figure 8.32. If you set the key type to None, the area outside the quadrilateral is made transparent, that inside it is opaque. The quadrilateral area is called a *garbage matte*. It can be used to create split-screen effects: create a garbage matte that covers the left half of a clip, which is then superposed over another. You can use this as in some rock concert films to show more than one viewpoint simultaneously or you can use it more creatively, for example to create scenes where the same actor appears twice, talking to himself.

> ☞ Place two clips on appropriate video tracks. Use a garbage matte to combine the top half of one with the bottom half of the other. Make a different garbage matte to allow the central region of one clip to appear in the middle of the other. Practise making garbage mattes of different shapes using clips with different characteristics.

Garbage mattes can also be used to good effect in conjunction with other key types. For example, suppose you are doing a bluescreen key, but that the cameraman framed the shot wrongly so that some unwanted object was in shot and, not being blue, is not

Figure 8.32 *A garbage matte.*

keyed out with the background. If the object is on the edge of the frame, just create a garbage matte that excludes it. You can then apply the blue screen key to the rest of the frame in the normal way.

The next level of complexity in creating mattes is to use an image you have created elsewhere as the matte. This is a bit like creating an alpha channel in Photoshop, except that the matte stands alone. For instance, on the left of Figure 8.33 is a simple image, created in Photoshop. When it is used as a matte between a clip in which the camera pans over a seascape and some black video, the result is the conventional representation used in films to signify that the sea is being surveyed through binoculars, as shown on the right of Figure 8.33.[*] To achieve this result, the pan over the sea was placed on Video 1 with a matching length of black on the superposition track Video 2. This was selected and the Transparency Settings dialogue was invoked from the Effect Controls palette. This time, the Key Type was set to Image Matte. The button labelled Choose... under the heading Matte then becomes activated. Clicking on it allowed us to navigate to the image file containing the greyscale image used as the matte, which Premiere then applied. Note that the matte image is not pure black and white: the outline has been softened (by applying a Gaussian blur), producing a grey gradient round the edges, which leads to partial transparency when the clip is matted with the image. This produces the characteristic blurriness around the supposed field of view through the binoculars.

You don't have to use black video as the superimposed clip with an image matte. You can use another clip, to achieve picture-in-picture effects. You might do this for its own sake in a piece of motion graphics, or you could use it to show a video playing on a TV screen inside another scene[†] or a reflection in the rear view mirror of a car, when the car was actually part of a set in a studio, and so on.

---

[*]The view through a pair of binoculars isn't really like that.
[†]You can't easily do this by photographing a picture on a TV because of interference between the scan rate of the TV and the camera.

Figure 8.33   *Using an image matte.*

☛ Create a greyscale image in Photoshop or some other graphics application, consisting of a black oval with feathered edges. Use this as an image matte to show a clip playing as a vignette (i.e., framed in the oval). Experiment with placing different clips on Video 2, including plain backgrounds.

This idea can be taken further by using a moving image as a matte, that is, each frame uses a different image matte, taken from the corresponding frame of a third track. This sort of key is called a *track matte*. Setting up a track matte is no more complicated than using an image matte, in fact, it is slightly simpler, since the matte must be on Video 3, so there is no need to use a navigation dialogue to find it. With the tracks set up correctly – foreground on Video 1 (A or B), background on Video 2 and matte on Video 3, just select the clip on Video 2, bring up the Transparency Settings dialogue, and select Track Matte as the key type.

Designing a track matte that works is another matter entirely. Combining three clips by using one as a track matte to composite the two others can produce some elaborate effects, but it can also produce complete incoherence. The simplest way of creating a track matte with a (more or less) predictable effect is to animate a still image. For instance, we could add some shaking movements to our binoculars, to make it look as if they were being held by somebody whose hands were unsteady, or move them up and down more slowly to convey an impression of searching. We could have done this by creating the matte track as a sequence of still images and importing them, but it is also possible to use Premiere itself to move a clip. We will now turn briefly to this process.

Animating Clips

Any clip can be made to move on the screen. As you may have noticed in Figure 8.29 on page 517, the Effect Controls palette always has a checkbox labelled Motion in addition to that for Transparency which we have been making use of so far. Selecting this, or clicking the word Setup next to it, brings up a dialogue box similar to that shown in Figure 8.34. Here you can describe how you want a clip to move throughout its duration, using a fairly simple graphical interface.

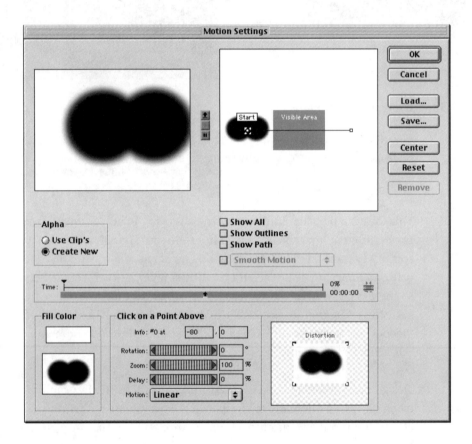

Figure 8.34   *Motion settings.*

The most important components of this interface are the band labelled Time running across the middle of the box and the diagram in the top right, which is a schematic representation of the path that the clip will follow – its *motion path*. To its left is an animated preview of the motion that you will define using these two controls. For this example, we have just used the binocular image matte as a still, extended in time to match the duration of the seascape clip it is to be composited with. By default, the animated preview just shows the clip that is being moved; by ticking the checkbox labelled Show All it will show a true preview of the moving clip composited with any others on the timeline.

To begin with, the motion path is, as Figure 8.34 shows, a straight line. At the beginning of the motion the clip is positioned off the left of the screen and at the end it is off the right. This means that it will enter the screen from the left, move straight across and leave at the right. You can change this movement by altering the shape of the motion path.

You will see in Figure 8.34 that there is a small square box labelled Start at the left end point of the motion path and a similar box at its right end. You can drag these boxes to set the start and ending positions of the clip. You can also insert additional draggable boxes, by clicking at any point along the motion path. You can then drag these to set the clip's position at the corresponding time. By clicking the button labelled Center, you can snap a box to the exact centre of the screen. Each box corresponds to a *keyframe*, which is a frame in the timeline at which the clip's position is fixed; its motion between keyframes is interpolated in a straight line. Figure 8.35 shows the motion path for our clip being shaped by the successive addition of keyframes; the start and end keyframes are centred. The band in the middle of the dialogue box shows the position of each keyframe in time, as shown at the bottom of Figure 8.35. You can control the speed of the clip's motion by dragging keyframes along this time line.

☛ Create a still image consisting of a black circle, import it into Premiere and place it on video track 3, with black on Video 2 and a video clip on Video 1. Extend the still image and black video to match the extent of the video clip. Move the circle along a motion path, so that it scans across the screen systematically. Use this moving circle as a track matte to create the effect of a searchlight playing over the clip on Video 1.

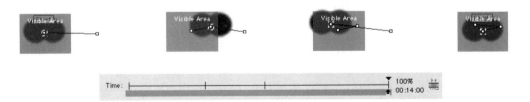

Figure 8.35   *Creating a motion path.*

Any clip can be moved along a motion path, not just a still image. In fact, the shaky binoculars effect could have been produced more convincingly by moving the seascape clip instead of the binocular outline. There is a potential problem with moving arbitrary clips, though. If a clip is the same size as the screen, unless it is centred there will be blank areas surrounding it, which will be visible. It is usually necessary to use a matte of some sort to cover up these edges. Compositing that involves moving clips needs a certain amount of planning to produce an effect that is not ridiculous.

There is one sort of clip that can usually be animated along a motion path with impunity and that is a title. By creating some type in the title window, adding it to a project, animating it along a path and compositing it with other clips, many motion graphic effects of the type that is fashionable in TV credit sequences can be created.

> ☞   Create a simple title, consisting of just a few words, and animate it on a motion path so that it floats into the screen from one corner. Superimpose this moving title on a suitable background (try a still image.)

Effects

Each frame of a digital video clip is a bitmapped image, that is, an array of values defining the colour of each pixel in the frame. By changing these values systematically, the appearance of the image can be altered, either to compensate for some deficiency or to create a special effect.

Premiere 6 supports three different effects technologies: its own video effects, After Effects effects and QuickTime effects (though the last of these are wrapped up as a single Premiere effect). It can also use some Photoshop filters – in fact, several of the Premiere video effects are actually Photoshop plug-ins – although not all Photoshop or After Effects plug-ins work with Premiere. From the point of view of the user, the only difference between Premiere's own effects, those borrowed from After Effects, and the QuickTime effects is the way in which their parameters are set.

You apply an effect by dragging it from the Video palette and dropping it on a clip in the timeline. As Figure 8.36 shows, this palette is organized in the same way as the Transitions palette, with the large number of effects organized into folders. You can hide or reveal the contents of each folder using the disclosure triangles, and reorganize the effects by creating your own folders and dragging effects between folders, as you can with transitions. In the palette, After Effects and Premiere effects are distinguished by two different icons.

After you have dropped an effect on a clip, the fact is indicated by a blue bar that appears along its top in the timeline (see Figure 8.39 on page 530). When you select a

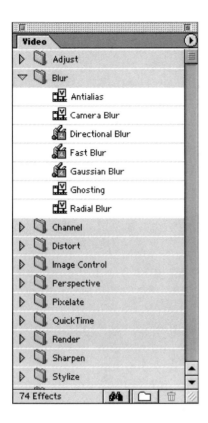

Figure 8.36   *The* Video *effects palette.*

clip with one or more effects applied to it, the Effect Controls palette will show you which effects these are, and allow you to set parameters and, temporarily or permanently, disable the effect. Figure 8.37 shows some examples of settings for effects that have been applied to a clip. The checkbox with an *f* indicates that the effect is enabled. Deselecting this checkbox disables the effect, so in the example shown, Crop is not presently being applied. You can permanently remove an effect by clicking on its name and then clicking the dustbin icon.

  If the effect is a Premiere effect, such as Crop and Camera Blur shown here, the word Setup will appear next to the effect's name, as it does for the permanent entries in the palette which we have used in previous sections to control transparency and motion. As in those cases, clicking on Setup will open a dialogue, such as that for Crop shown in Figure 8.38, which allows you to set parameters for the effect. For many effects, you can also set the parameters in the Effects Controls palette itself, using the slider controls shown beneath the effect's name, or by clicking on the underlined values to open a

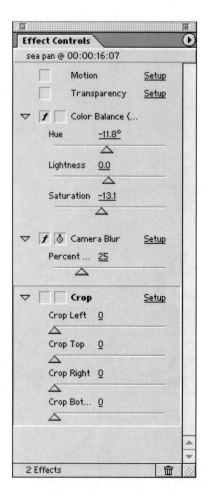

Figure 8.37 *Effects appearing in the* Effects Controls *palette.*

simple dialogue box that lets you enter a number. The dialogue box provides a preview and larger, more usable controls. In some cases, notably the Levels effect, the dialogue box is the only means of setting values; for some effects, extra controls appear in the dialogue box. For After Effects effects, though, no dialogue box is available, so you do not see Setup next to the name of Color Balance (HLS) in Figure 8.37. For these effects, you can only set parameters in the palette.

For many types of video work, the most important effects are those that allow you to make adjustments to the tonal and colour balance of each frame, and those that let you blur and sharpen images, to compensate for poor lighting, camera technique or equipment. Most of these can be found in the Adjust, Image Control, Blur, Sharpen and Video folders in the Video effects palette as it is organized by default. The remaining

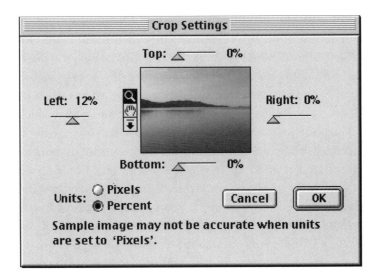

Figure 8.38   *Setting parameters for the* Crop *effect.*

effects can be used to alter source material in more creative and extreme ways. (This can be fun, and sometimes very effective, but you should be aware that special effects – or *FX*, as they are often called – can easily be over-done.) Since most video effects are just bitmapped image filters applied to the frames of a clip, the way in which you use them and set their parameters and the results you can achieve are substantially the same in Premiere as in Photoshop. Rather than repeat the information in Chapter 3, we refer you to the sections on *Tonal Adjustments, Colour Adjustments, Blurring and Sharpening* and *Special Effects and Distortion*, on pages 116–126 and 133–137. You may also find it helpful to look at the *Premiere Effect Sample Gallery* in the online help.

☞ Place several clips on the timeline and practise applying different effects to them. For each effect, experiment with changing parameter values in the dialogue box. Preview each effect and try to assess which are genuinely useful and which are just gimmicks.

There is a difference between applying filters to single images in Photoshop and applying effects to video clips in Premiere, though, and that is the dimension of time which is present in video. The parameters of any effect can be made to vary dynamically, so that clips can gradually become brighter, or more or less blurred, or disintegrate into mosaic as time passes. Effects are made to change by specifying values for their parameters at keyframes. The values are interpolated between these keyframes in the same way as a clip's position on a motion path is interpolated between the keyframes you set in the Motion Settings dialogue.

To create a dynamically changing effect, you first apply it to a clip in the usual way, and select the rightmost of the two checkboxes next to its name in the Effects Controls palette. An icon representing a stopwatch appears in the box. You can see the stopwatch next to Camera Blur in Figure 8.37. If you now turn down the triangle in the video track containing the clip in the timeline, you will see some extra features, as illustrated in Figure 8.39. Most obviously, a second band opens beneath that which represents the clip itself, labelled with the name of the effect. This band represents the progress of the effect in time and it is where you add keyframes to control its dynamics. If you had applied more than one effect to this clip, the simple label would have been replaced by a pop-up menu, from which you could select each in turn to change dynamically. At the left of the track are some extra controls: a pair of arrowheads with a checkbox between them. These are used to add, delete and navigate among keyframes. You add a keyframe by moving the edit line to the point in the timeline where you want the keyframe to be and clicking in the checkbox. A diamond appears to indicate the position of the keyframe. Any parameter values you set for the effect will be applied at the keyframe. You can select a keyframe by clicking its diamond, or move to the next and previous keyframes using the two navigation arrows. When a keyframe is selected, you can change the parameter values associated with it or delete it entirely by clicking again in the keyframe checkbox. There are always keyframes at the beginning and end of the clip's extent, which you use to set start and end values for the effect. These are indicated by rectangles to distinguish them from the intermediate keyframes you add explicitly.

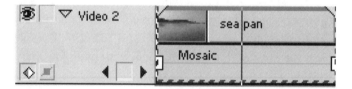

Figure 8.39   *Dynamically applying an effect.*

Suppose you wished to make a clip appear from a blank square as if by successive refinement of the resolution (see Figure 8.40). You could do this by applying the Mosaic effect to it. A simple version of the effect could be made simply by setting the effects parameters (the number of rows and columns) to one at the beginning of the clip, and to the number of pixels in each direction at the end. However, this makes the image become coherent much too rapidly, so we need to slow down the initial change. In addition, if the image is made to become clearer in a series of jerks, we can convey the impression of some process going on that is extracting information in stages. To do this, we add keyframes in pairs, with the same values applied to both members of each pair, thereby holding the effect for several frames before letting it go on to make a more refined version of the image. The values for the number of rows and columns are chosen by experiment to make it apparent what is going on. The structure of the keyframes for this example is shown underneath the sample frames in Figure 8.40. The closely spaced keyframes between the steady states produce a rapid transition, which is quite effective at conveying the idea of the image being rebuilt at a higher resolution.

☛ Duplicate the effect just described in the text above with a still image of your own. Practise setting keyframes for other effects. For example, make a title come into focus from an incoherent blur.

Figure 8.40 *Dynamic application of the mosaic effect.*

You should be aware that applying effects, compositing and animating clips on a motion path, all require the effect clips to be rendered, which, as well as taking time, can lead to a loss of image quality.

After Effects

After Effects is a program for applying video and audio effects which may vary over time, creating transitions, moving clips on a path, compositing and rendering – all things that Premiere does, too, as we have seen. After Effects just does these things better, as most people who have used both will tell you. It does have some abilities that Premiere lacks. Most notably, After Effects 5 allows you to perform 3D compositing, moving your video clips in three dimensions. After Effects' repertoire of operations allows it to play two distinct, but related, roles. It can be used for effects work, that is, finishing off a movie after it has been edited in Premiere or some other application, by adding effects, or it can be used to create motion graphics.

After Effects' superiority to Premiere consists of its greater precision and the finer control it offers. The precision is often not apparent to the user, but internally

After Effects works at *subpixel* accuracy, which means that positions are calculated to thousandths of a pixel. When the resulting effects are rendered, motion and effects appear smoother. After Effects allows you to use Bézier curves (see Chapter 9) as motion paths, which also results in smoother motion.

After Effects is a professional's tool and although it does not do anything that is conceptually different from Premiere, the additional control and the range of effects it permits make the program more complex and harder to master. Space does not allow us to do justice to After Effects in this book, but if you are interested in serious video post-production and motion graphics, you should investigate it if you find Premiere inadequate for the work you want to do.

Sound

Although video and sound are fundamentally different, inasmuch as they are perceived by different senses, they are both *time-based* media, which means that it makes sense to represent the extent in time of both on a timeline. Furthermore, both are susceptible to processing by effects and sound channels can be mixed in much the same way as video tracks can be composited. So Premiere's timeline and other interface elements can be used to manipulate sound as well as picture, and to combine the two. For people working in multimedia, this is a particularly convenient way of approaching sound, because in general they will want to combine their sound with picture, and because it avoids having to get to grips with the interface to specialized audio applications. These are usually based on metaphors from multi-track recording studios and, indeed, many such programs provide an interface which tries to look as much as possible like the mixing desks in such studios. This is fine for experienced recording engineers – and contemporary audio applications are in fact used, in conjunction with some dedicated hardware, to create purely digital recording facilities. However, such interfaces can be totally bewildering to somebody whose experience lies with the predominantly graphics-oriented applications used for other media. Thus, although Premiere lacks some facilities which an audio professional would consider essential, it provides a relatively painless way into sound processing for multimedia.

Capturing and Importing Sound

As we described on page 486, you can capture sound at the same time as video, if it is recorded on video tape. If your sound is recorded on a separate medium from the picture, you will need to capture it by some other means. Recording sound satisfactorily can be a tricky business and Premiere is not really equipped for the job. Wherever possible, we would advise you to use a dedicated sound capture application for doing audio recording. On Windows systems, you don't actually have any choice in the matter: the first time you use the File>Capture>Audio Capture command, Premiere asks you to locate an audio capture application (if your system includes a sound card such a program almost certainly came with it) and thereafter the command always invokes this program for you.

On Mac systems the File>Capture>Audio Capture command does bring up a (very small) Audio Recorder window, as shown in Figure 8.41. When this window is active, an Audio Capture menu is added to the menu bar; it only contains one command, Sound Input, which brings up a dialogue box in which you can select the sound source and set some parameters, including the sampling rate. Having done that you just press the Record button (which turns into a Stop button) and anything coming in through the selected sound input is recorded for you. However, there are no controls. In particular, there is no way of adjusting levels dynamically. The bar across the middle of the Audio Recorder window indicates the current level and the end of it turns red when you overload the input. If this happens, you will have to adjust the level on the device from which you are recording and try again, which is not very satisfactory.

Figure 8.41   *Audio capture (on MacOS).*

Trying to get the levels right is the bane of audio recording. They never are. Ideally, you need to arrange that the loudest part of your sound falls just short of overloading. Usually this means previewing the entire recorded material on tape several times, identifying the loudest passages, and adjusting the levels for them. If you are using musicians or professional voice talent you should try and use a proper studio for making the recordings. At the very least, though, record to good quality tape (e.g., DAT). If you are stuck with Premiere's audio recorder, you should then be able to use the output level control on your DAT recorder to adjust the levels for capturing in Premiere.

A much more satisfactory way of working with sound in Premiere is to import it from a file that you have made using some other program. Once you have recorded some sound and saved it to disk, you can add it to a project in Premiere using the File>Import>File... command, in just the same way as you add video clips. The imported sound appears in the Project window, from where you can drag it to an audio track in the Timeline window. You can also open it in the Clip window, by double-clicking it, and trim it or set markers. Audio appears in the Clip window as a waveform display, such as the one shown in Figure 8.42. When you have acquired some experience, you will find that you can discern the main characteristics of a piece of sound from its waveform. The visual display makes it easy to identify pauses in speech or beats in music – places where you might want to add markers in order to synchronize the sound with video on other tracks.

☛ Record some disparate sounds to tape – include voice, music and natural sounds if you can – capture them with an audio application and import the resulting clips into a Premiere project. (If necessary, record the sound straight into Premiere.) Open them in the Clip window and familiarize yourself with the appearance of the waveforms of different types of sound. Play each clip and see if you can match what you hear to what you see in the Clip window. Practise trimming the clips and setting markers at significant points.

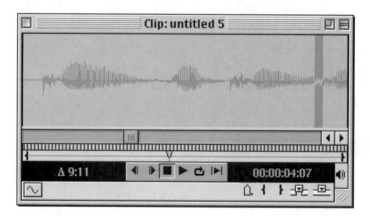

Figure 8.42   *An audio clip's waveform.*

DV supports 48kHz 16-bit stereo sound, so you can record on to mini-DV tape, if you like. However, the microphones built in to camcorders are usually of poor quality, so even if you want to record live sound at the same time as picture (for example, if you are conducting an interview) you should use an external microphone if your camcorder has inputs for one. When you capture DV, as described on page 480, any sound recorded on the tape is captured at the same time as the video. When you drag the captured clip to the timeline, the audio appears on one or two (for stereo) audio tracks with the same duration as the video clip. To begin with, the video and audio are *linked*:

if you move or trim one, the other will be changed in the same way. You can unlink them using the Clip>Unlink Audio and Video command, or by clicking each in turn with the link tool. Conversely, you can link a video track to an independent audio track by clicking them with this tool.

Instead of recording your own sound, you may wish to start with tracks from a CD. Like recording, importing from CD works differently on MacOS and Windows systems. On a Mac, you can open a CD track using File>Import>File..., as if it was any other sort of audio file. On Windows you need to use a utility to convert the CD audio to a WAV file and store it on your hard disk, before you can import it into Premiere. You should always bear in mind if you use pre-recorded material from CD it will usually be subject to copyright. Never use copyright material without obtaining the necessary permission.

Premiere 6 comes with an entertaining little application called *SmartSound Quicktracks*, which enables you to put together simple soundtracks from royalty-free source material, in a variety of styles. If you install this program, Premiere's File>New sub-menu acquires a new command: SmartSound.... When you choose this command, the Quicktracks application opens with the splash screen shown at the top left of Figure 8.43. If you click on the button labelled Start Maestro, you are presented with a sequence of dialogue boxes, in which you must select the qualities you desire from the soundtrack and set its length. You can use the player controls in the third and fifth boxes to preview your selections. Quicktracks puts together a suitable soundtrack by taking elements from a *palette* of pre-recorded sound samples, setting the length appropriately by combining segments and applying effects to create the desired variation. When you reach the end of the process and click Finish, you can save the result to disk as a WAV file, which is automatically imported into your Premiere project.

The soundtracks you can put together using this application from the limited amount of raw material provided on the free CD provided with Premiere are, it must be admitted, less than inspiring and tend to run to cliché. However, if you find this is a good way of constructing the sort of soundtracks you need for the work you are doing you can obtain additional sound palettes from SmartSound for a fee.

☛ Practise creating soundtracks with QuickTracks. Try several routes through the dialogue boxes to get an idea of the range of tracks you can make. Add the resulting soundtracks to some of your video clips.

Be careful when combining sound from different sources, such as a CD track, some sound recorded on DAT, the audio from a DV camcorder, and a Quicktracks soundtrack.

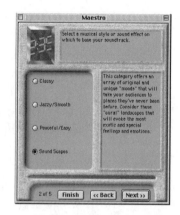

Figure 8.43   *Creating a soundtrack with SmartSound Quicktracks.*

They may be recorded at different sampling rates (the number of discrete digital values used to represent each second of the original continuous sound waveform). CDs use a sampling rate of 44.1kHz, while DV and DAT usually use 48kHz, although both can be set to use lower values too. Quicktracks offers a choice of 44.1kHz and 22.05kHz. As long as all of your audio clips use the same rate, or rates that divide exactly into each other, you should have no problems, but combining DAT or DV audio with CD means that one or the other must be resampled, which will lead to a degradation of quality. Avoid this wherever possible. If necessary, it is better to convert a digital signal to analogue and then re-digitize it than to resample the digital data in software. (For example, if you wish to combine DAT sound with a track from a CD, connect the line outputs of a DAT recorder to the analogue inputs of a sound card, instead of connecting its digital outputs to digital inputs if the card uses a sampling rate of 44.1kHz.)

Processing Sound in the Timeline

Once you have dragged an audio clip to one of the audio tracks in the Timeline window, you can manipulate it using many of the same tools and techniques as you use with video. You can perform ripple and rolling edits and move clips around. In order to see the waveform displayed in the timeline, so you can identify major aural events, turn down the triangle by the audio track's name (as if you were going to manipulate the opacity rubber bands of a video track) to reveal some extra controls. Click on the leftmost button to show the audio clip as a waveform. You will also find that, with a little practice, you can identify points of interest in an audio clip by scrubbing over it and listening.

> ☛ Add some video clips and audio clips to the timeline. Practise editing the audio clips, and matching the audio to video, by setting the duration of each clip, aligning significant moments, and so on.

If your sound is linked to a video clip, such edits automatically work on both, as if they were a single clip. As we mentioned earlier, you can unlink them to make them independent, but you also have the option of temporarily breaking their dependence, so that you can, for instance, extend the audio part of a trimmed clip while leaving the picture alone. This allows you to create what is known as a *split edit*, where the audio from a clip continues over the beginning of a new clip after a cut. An alternative split edit, where the audio from the new clip begins before the cut, is also sometimes used. To allow the necessary adjustments, you can turn off *sync mode*. This is done clicking on the Toggle Sync Mode button at the bottom of the Timeline window. You can then use the ripple edit tool to change the duration of the audio or move the audio clip along the timeline. When you have made the necessary change, click the Toggle Sync Mode button (which will have changed its appearance) again: the two clips will maintain their new relationship if you make any further edits. If you have moved linked clips relative to each other while sync mode is off, a red triangle appears at the left end of each; holding down the mouse over this triangle will reveal the offset.

> ☛ Add two video and two audio clips to the timeline and link them in pairs. Practise creating split edits of both types.

As well as editing the sound with the picture, you may need to make further adjustments to the level. When you first captured the audio, you should have set the levels to make the best use of the available dynamic range, which ensures that the maximum information about the sound is retained. When you come to use the sound, though, you may want to adjust the volume to match other sounds in the programme, for dramatic effect, or to compensate for deficiencies in the recording. For example, if you had to reduce the recording level to accommodate loud noises, you may need to bring up the level of quieter sounds.

You may need to alter the volume of an entire clip. This is quite commonly required with CD tracks: there is a surprising variation in levels among CDs, with most of them being too low. You change the level of an entire clip by adjusting its *gain*, increasing it to amplify and decreasing it to attenuate. This is done by selecting the clip in the timeline and choosing Audio Gain... from the Clip>Audio Options sub-menu. The dialogue box shown in Figure 8.44 opens and you can type a percentage value for the gain. Alternatively, click the Smart Gain button, and Premiere will examine the clip and compute a value for the gain which leads to the loudest sound in the clip being at the highest volume the system can produce. Although increasing the gain makes sounds louder, it cannot add any information beyond what is recorded, so changes in volume may become coarser after amplification.

Figure 8.44   *Setting the gain for an audio clip.*

You can adjust the volume of an audio track dynamically in the same way as you adjust the opacity of a video track, using rubber band controls. With the track's disclosure triangle turned down, click on the red (not blue) rubber band icon, to show the volume rubber band. To begin with, this will be a straight red line in the centre of the lower half of the track. You can manipulate it by creating and dragging handles or using the fade adjustment tool and fade scissors, just as you did with the opacity rubber bands (see page 514). This gives you considerable control over the way the volume of any audio track changes from moment to moment – remember that you can use the pop-up menu in the bottom left corner of the Timeline window to expand the time scale, so that you can view the waveform within each video frame, if you need to.

☛   Practise adjusting the volume of an audio track, by setting its gain and by adjusting the rubber bands to produce dynamic volume changes. Try combining two audio tracks and adjusting their volumes in tandem.

As well as the volume, rubber bands are used to control the panning of audio tracks, that is moving them between the left and right stereo channels. If you click on the blue rubber band icon instead of the red one, you will see the letters L and R (signifying left and right) appear at the left end of the track, as seen in Figure 8.45. The blue line that replaces the red one that denoted volume, shows the position of the clip in the stereo stage. By dragging a handle up, you move the sound to the left, by dragging it down, you move it to the right. In this way, you can make sound effects move across the stereo stage, as we have in Figure 8.45, or you can place a sound so that it corresponds to the position on the screen of the object from which it emanates – for example, if you have a picture of a thrush sitting in a tree on the left of the picture, you could pan a soundtrack of its song to the left of the stereo sound stage. Strictly speaking, you can only pan a mono audio clip; for stereo clips, which will contain sound in both channels, you are adjusting the balance between the channels, which will usually have the same effect of making sounds seem to move left or right. It is just like using the balance control on a stereo amplifier.

☞ Practise panning sounds using the rubber band controls. Try moving a sound across the stereo image and placing it at a precise apparent location.

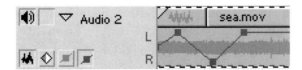

Figure 8.45   *Panning a sound.*

By adjusting the volume rubber bands of two overlapping audio tracks you can make one sound fade into another. A quick and easy way of achieving this transition is provided by the cross-fade tool. If you have two overlapping audio clips (on separate tracks), you just select this tool, click on the earlier clip (the one you want to fade out) then click on the later one (the one you want to fade in). The first clip is faded down linearly over the period of overlap, while the second fades up: Figure 8.46 shows the shape of the resulting rubber bands. The quick and easy method is not always the best, though, and you may often find you get a better result by manipulating the rubber bands by hand. For instance, you may need to start fading your first clip down before the second one starts to come up, or vice versa, and you may want to fade in steps, instead of using a simple linear ramp.

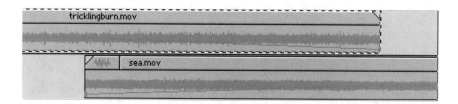

Figure 8.46   *A cross-fade.*

> ☞ Place two audio clips so that they overlap. Apply a cross-fade using the cross-fade tool. Save the project and then make an alternative cross-fade by adjusting the rubber bands by hand. Compare the results.

You might think of the cross-fade tool as providing a cross-dissolve transition between audio tracks. There are no other audio transitions. It is interesting, but ultimately fruitless, to speculate on the aural equivalent of a barn door wipe or a diamond iris out, but – whatever they may be – Premiere does not provide such things. The single tool is adequate for the single transition that makes sense.

The Audio Mixer

Despite our remarks at the beginning of this section, Premiere does provide an alternative interface to sound processing, which resembles a conventional mixing desk, but in Premiere's case this is more like a simple Portastudio than a commercial multi-track facility. It allows you to adjust levels and panning in real-time while you listen to the sound, so if you find it difficult to think about sound in terms of a graphical representation, you may wish to use the mixer instead of adjusting rubber bands in the Timeline window. The two sets of controls are interlinked, so you can use both methods together.

Figure 8.47 shows the Audio Mixer window. (If it isn't visible, choose Audio Mixer from the Window menu.) The controls it provides are mostly intuitive: in the bottom left corner are conventional buttons for stopping, playing and looping the sound, and a more unusual one for playing just between in and out points. The main part of the window consists of a set of controls for each audio track – a new set is created whenever you add a new audio track to the Timeline window. The large slider which occupies most of the space in each column controls volume; the display to its left shows the level – it turns red when clipping occurs – while the gain is displayed numerically below it. Above is a knob for panning and balancing, with the amount displayed below it. The slider and knob controls are operated by dragging with the mouse, or you can type numbers into the gain and panning fields. The Mute and Solo buttons at the top allow you to silence a track or play it in isolation. At the right of the window, an additional slider, labelled Master, controls the overall volume of the mixed tracks. You use the individual sliders to set the relative volumes of the separate tracks and then adjust the master slider to set the final output level.

☛ Place three audio clips on overlapping tracks in the timeline – one music, one speech and one natural sound track would make a good combination. Practise playing them back, adjusting levels and panning in the Audio Mixer window. Try cross-fading using the slider controls.

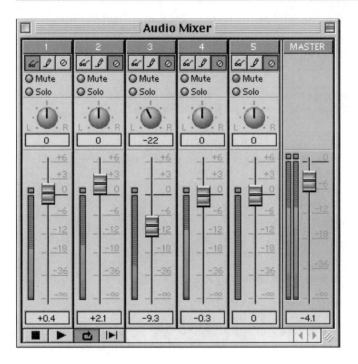

Figure 8.47 *The* Audio Mixer *window.*

The three buttons above each track's panning knob control the way in which changes you make in the audio mixer interact with rubber band settings in the timeline. The rubber bands provide a picture of the track's levels as they change over time. These can be either read into the audio mixer or written from it, a process that Premiere calls *automation*. Clicking on the spectacles icon turns on automation reading: the rubber band settings are read into the mixer. You see the mixer controls moving apparently on their own to reflect these settings. Clicking on the pencil icon turns on automation writing: the rubber band settings are modified by any adjustments you make to the controls in the mixer. When you stop playback, you will see new handles on the rubber

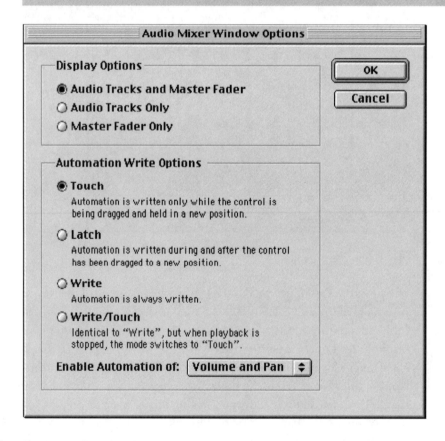

bands, corresponding to the way you moved the controls. Clicking on the third icon turns automation off: the rubber band settings are ignored.

With automation writing on, the mixer controls can be interpreted in different ways. The Audio Mixer Window Options dialogue, shown in Figure 8.48, is used to set the interpretation you desire. The explanations beside each of the possibilities are fairly clear. You might expect Write to be the normal behaviour, but this amounts to completely overriding the rubber band settings. The default, Touch, allows you to go along with the rubber band settings, except where you feel it necessary to override them by moving a mixer control. Unusually, the Audio Mixer Window Options can only be accessed from the context menu that pops up when you ctl-click/right-click in the Audio Mixer window.

☛ Turn on automation writing and practise altering the rubber bands using the mixer's controls. Experiment with all the options.

Figure 8.48   *Setting audio mixer options.*

Whereas an engineer working with a real mixing desk is able to work at least two sliders at once, since there is only one cursor controlled by your mouse you can only adjust one track at a time. If you want to apply the same volume changes to all tracks, you can use the master slider, but if you need to apply them to some but not all tracks, you must *gang* together several track sliders. Again, this can only be done via a context menu. This time, you ctl-click/right-click on a track slider to bring up the menu of gangs, as shown in Figure 8.49. You can assign each track to one of the four gangs. When you drag a volume slider for a ganged track, the sliders for all the other tracks in the same gang move with it, maintaining their relative positions.

Figure 8.49   *Ganging tracks.*

Applying Audio Effects

Audio effects are applied in the same way as video effects. You drag an effect from the Audio effects palette, which causes its controls to appear in the Effect Controls palette. Here you can turn effects on or off, set parameter values, either numerically or using a slider, or click on Setup to open a more elaborate dialogue. You can change parameter values dynamically, with keyframes, just the same way as you do with video effects. Another resemblance to video effects is that audio effects must be rendered, so a preview must be created before you can hear them.

Like video effects, audio effects can be implemented as plug-ins, and third-party plug-ins are available to extend the range of effects that are provided by Premiere. There are twenty of these. Like the Video effects palette, the Audio palette organizes effects into folders – which you can reorganize – according to the category of alteration they produce. Figure 8.50 shows the default set of folders, with some of them expanded to show the individual effects, and on the right a typical dialogue box for setting parameters.

The effects fall into two broad categories: those that attempt to make corrections to unsatisfactory sound and those that create special effects. The Bandpass, EQ (equalization) and Dynamics effects fall into the first category, with the rest mostly in the second (although Reverb is ambiguous, you can use it either way). Unless you know a great deal about the physics of acoustics, applying special effects is a matter of experiment: it's rarely clear to the non-specialist what each parameter does from its name, but making changes and listening to the results usually makes it quite clear what you can achieve and how. The dialogues for setting up these effects have a checkbox labelled Preview sound, which lets you hear the new effect before you commit yourself to the changes.

> ☛ Drag a sound clip to the timeline and apply the Chorus effect to it. Experiment with changing all the parameters of this effect to see what difference they make to the sound. Turn off the effect and try the same experiment with the Multi-Effect and Flanger effects. See what happens when you combine two or three of these effects together.

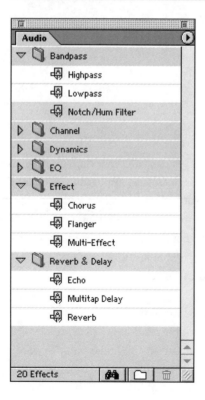
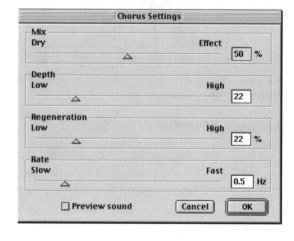

Figure 8.50   *The* Audio *effects palette.*

Making adjustments in order to correct sound is a more delicate business, though again, your ears are the final arbiters and so you will have to experiment. It helps to have some idea of which effects might be useful and under what circumstances.

The first thing to note is that many sound effects are based on analogue techniques that predate digital audio. Analogue circuits, called *filters* were used to remove certain frequencies, or bands of frequencies, from a signal. For instance, if there was hiss on the signal, you would filter out high frequencies; rumble would be removed by filtering out low frequencies. Filters can be implemented in the digital domain as well as the analogue domain, and the effects in the Bandpass category are filters of this kind. It is customary to identify filters according to the range of frequencies they pass through, rather than the ones they remove. Thus, the Lowpass filter removes high frequencies (hiss) and the Highpass filter removes low frequencies (rumble). For bandpass filters such as these, you set the cutoff frequency in the setup dialogue. The third filter in this category is different: a notch filter removes (as nearly as possible) signals at just one particular frequency. The most common requirement is for removing unwanted hum caused by electrical interference. This will be at the frequency of the mains supply: 50Hz in Europe, 60Hz in North America, and so on. The Notch/Hum effect provides this filter. Its setup dialogue is shown in Figure 8.51.

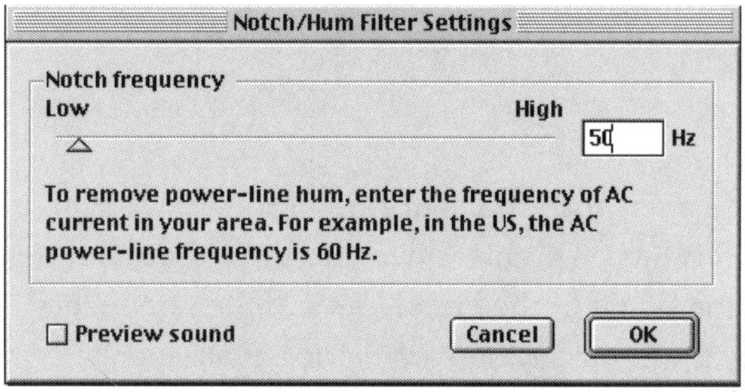

Figure 8.51 *Notch filtering to eliminate mains hum.*

The Dynamics group of effects is used to alter the sound on the basis of the way its volume changes. Boost is a crude adjustment, which makes quiet sounds louder, leaving loud ones alone. The Compressor/Expander provides a more sophisticated control over the dynamic range, allowing you to set the ratio you want between the loudest and quietest sounds and a level at which you want the effect to cut in. Figure 8.52 shows the setup dialogue for this effect, where you see that the change in dynamic range is displayed as a graph. Compression is often used to cover up weaknesses in singing. The Noise Gate effect is theoretically very useful. It removes all signals below a certain loudness threshold, so unwanted background and signal noise are eliminated. Unfortunately, noise gates often introduce unwanted side-effects: where noise is removed, there is silence, but in places where there is some wanted sound – a voice, for example – the signal is passed through, with any background noise intact. The result is that background noises switch on and off in a disconcerting way. The only reliable way to avoid noise is not to record it in the first place.

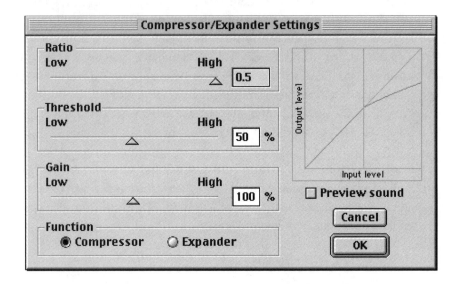

Figure 8.52   *Compressing.*

The EQ group of effects alters the tonal make-up of sounds. They resemble the tone controls on an amplifier. Bass & Treble is like the simple bass and treble controls and lets you boost or cut the signal in the broad low and high frequency ranges. More control is provided by the Equalize and Parametric Equalization effects. The former is a graphic equalizer, such as you see on many consumer-level sound systems. It lets you adjust the relative intensity of seven frequency bands, using sliders, as shown on the left of Figure 8.53. The Parametric Equalization effect only allows you to adjust three frequency bands, but it lets you define the central frequency of each band and its width, as well as setting the amount of boost or cut to apply to it. Figure 8.53 shows its setup dialogue, where you can see the effect displayed graphically on a frequency response curve. You need to know something about audio to use a parametric equalizer effectively and most of the time it is easier to use the graphic equalizer.

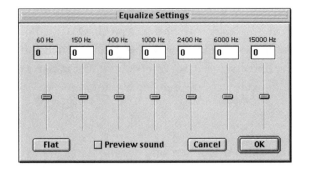 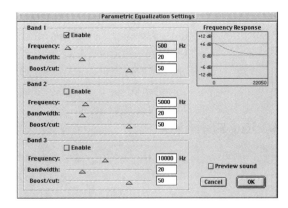

Figure 8.53 *Graphic (left) and parametric (right) equalizers.*

☛ Use whichever audio effects you find necessary to improve the quality of your audio clips, by removing unwanted noise, sweetening the sound by adjusting EQ, and so on. Try to gain an understanding of the sort of adjustments each defect in a raw audio clip requires.

Exporting Movies

After the excitements of capturing and editing video, applying effects and transitions, compositing, and adding soundtracks, the business of preparing a final version for use on CD-ROM or the Web brings us down to earth with a bump. As we remarked on page 475, playing back uncompressed video entails high data rates, rates that cannot be supplied by most Internet connections or CD-ROM drives. Whereas uncompressed, full frame, full motion video requires 30MB per second, a 24x CD-ROM only offers 3.5MB per second, that is little more than one tenth of the required rate. However, by comparison with the Internet, CD-ROM is speed itself. The typical domestic dial-up connection uses a 56kbps modem, which probably gives a speed of between 36 and 48kbps, that is at most 6kB per second. Even so-called broadband connections, such as ADSL only give up to 1.5Mbps (that's one and a half mega*bits*, just under 200 kilobytes per second) with telecomms providers often giving lower rates in their packages for domestic subscribers. Emerging technologies, such as ATM (Asynchronous Transfer Mode) networks, do provide true broadband communications capable of carrying high quality video, but it will be some time before these are available to domestic users.

So, to deliver video as part of a multimedia presentation, the data rate must be drastically reduced. This can be done by making the frames smaller, reducing the frame rate, cutting down the number of colours, and applying severe compression. Any of these operations will lead to an impoverishment of the viewer's experience. Or looking at this from the video producer's point of view, they will spoil your work. Often, all of them must be employed, especially for delivery over the Internet. As a result, when you come to export your movie, you must try to come up with a compromise that preserves as much quality as possible within the constraints of the delivery medium.

Video Formats

There are two different ways of delivering video over a network: downloading and streaming. When video is downloaded, a file containing the entire movie is transmitted over the network from a server to a client, where it is stored on disk and played back from there. This is the usual method of delivering movies that are embedded in Web pages. When video is streamed, on the other hand, each frame is displayed as it arrives from the server. The client does not wait for the whole movie to arrive and does not store it to disk, except for temporarily buffering small sections to smooth out unevenness in transmission speed. Streaming is like broadcast TV; downloading is like buying a video. Streaming has the theoretical advantages that it allows movies to have unlimited length (downloaded movies must be small enough to be accommodated on the user's machine) and that it allows live video transmission; it means that users don't have to wait for a movie to download before it can start; and it more effectively protects the interests of copyright holders, since the user never has a complete copy of the movie. In practice, though, the bandwidth available to most Internet users is simply not adequate to allow streaming video to play properly. Streaming may be the way forward for Internet video, but for now it can only be used effectively over higher speed networks, in particular local area networks configured as *intranets*, using the same protocols as the Internet.

If you choose to stream video, you must ensure that it has a sufficiently low data rate to be delivered over whichever network you are using at the frame rate it is to be played at. If you choose to download it instead, your concern is that the video file be small enough to download to a user's machine in a reasonable time – where 'reasonable' must be loosely defined as short enough for them to feel the wait was worthwhile when they play the movie. A compromise, known as *progressive downloading* is to download the movie, but to start playing it before it all arrives. The movie starts playing when the amount that has been downloaded is sufficient to play for the time estimated as being needed for the remainder to arrive. This computation has to make some assumptions about the speed at which the file is arriving, which are often too optimistic, leading to the movie stopping and starting. In any case, the reduction in waiting time is often small.

Premiere can export movies in five different video formats: QuickTime, Microsoft AVI, Windows Media, RealMedia and MPEG. It can also export them as animated GIFs (see Chapter 10) and as sequences of still images in various formats. The choice of format can be quite difficult, and often depends on the intended audience for your work, as well as its technical requirements. The Microsoft formats are popular with Windows users, but conversely, are unpopular with everybody else. QuickTime is available on MacOS and Windows systems, and is the most flexible cross-platform format. MPEG is quite demanding of bandwidth and requires a fast computer to play it back, but provides high quality and can be used on Unix systems as well as MacOS and Windows. RealMedia is a popular format for streaming – more because it was the first widely used such format than because of any intrinsic merit. QuickTime and Windows Media can also be streamed, but any streaming format needs special server software, which is usually linked to a particular vendor's other software – for example, Windows Media can only be streamed from a machine running Windows 2000; the QuickTime Streaming Server, although it is Open Source software, is only found under MacOS X.

When exporting a movie to most of these formats, you can choose between different compression algorithms and set various parameters that allow you to trade quality against size. QuickTime allows you to create a set of 'alternate' movies, optimized for different bandwidths. The QuickTime plug-in selects the appropriate version for each user's connection speed (as specified in their QuickTime preferences – it can't actually find out). Some formats allow you to choose whether to prepare the movie for streaming or progressive downloading. You can also set the frame rate and size and the colour depth. In other words, you have to make several informed choices in order to produce a version of your movie that gives you the best quality at the available bandwidth. Even for experts, these choices can be difficult (since there are no really satisfactory answers for all circumstances). To help novices, Premiere is integrated with an application called *Cleaner EZ*, a restricted version of Terran Interactive's Cleaner Pro 5, a program for preparing video for delivery in a variety of formats. Although Cleaner EZ is not entirely satisfactory, it is by far the easiest way of exporting movies from Premiere.

Exporting Movies with Cleaner EZ

You invoke Cleaner EZ with the File>Export Timeline>Save for Web… command. Cleaner (we'll omit the EZ from now on) starts up as a separate program, displaying the splash screen shown in Figure 8.54. The lower pop-up menu allows you to choose whether to export the entire project (i.e., everything on the timeline) or just the work area. The Settings pop-up menu at the top is where you choose the form in which you want to export the movie. The menu contains a collection of sub-menus, one for each of the formats in which you can save your movie. The sub-menus contain entries for particular target connections for which you might want to optimize the movie. Figure 8.55 shows the menu choices and the sub-menu for QuickTime progressive download. The choices on the sub-menu indicate how Cleaner classifies the different sets of movie parameters according to connection speed. Most formats offer fewer choices than QuickTime: MPEG in particular only offers you the choice of NTSC or PAL for a 2x CD-ROM (because of the way MPEG is defined). If one of the entries in one of the sub-menus seems to fit your purposes, select it, click the Start button, and the process of exporting your movie will begin.

Figure 8.54   *Cleaner EZ.*

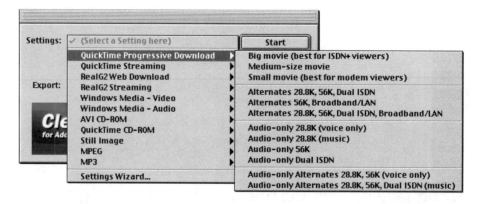

Figure 8.55   *Choosing settings.*

Export may take some time, because compressing video involves a great deal of computation. There is also some scope for confusion after you press Start: the new window that opens has an area into which you are invited to drag a source media file. This is not necessary and doesn't work with the version bundled with Premiere. Instead, the movie data is taken from Premiere. There is usually a slight delay while this happens, but you don't need to do anything further. Once Cleaner has found the data, a window opens which displays, in considerable detail, the progress of the export process, as shown in Figure 8.56. As the two screenshots demonstrate, you can display the statistics in more or less detail, and show or hide a thumbnail of the frame Cleaner is currently working on. Most usefully, an estimate of the time the process will take is given.

☞ Practise exporting the timeline and work area using Cleaner's presets. Investigate the size and quality of the exported movies.

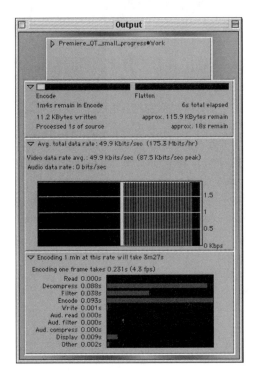

Figure 8.56   *Cleaner's* Output *window.*

If none of the settings provided seems to be what you want, select Settings Wizard... from the Settings pop-up menu when Cleaner starts up. Pressing the Start button now will cause Cleaner to display a sequence of dialogue boxes, in which you can choose between different options for the movie format, intended delivery medium, bandwidth, and specify how you want to trade off variables, such as image quality and smoothness of motion, against others such as file size and frame rate. At each stage, some text is displayed alongside the choices, explaining what is going on. Figure 8.57 shows the dialogues in one possible sequence. For MPEG files, you cannot set any parameters in the wizard dialogues, because there are no choices to make. (At least, the way Cleaner implements MPEG there aren't.)

☛ Select the settings wizard when you start up Cleaner, and work through the dialogues, paying attention to the information displayed to the left of the window at each stage. Try various different combinations of options, and investigate the resulting movies' quality and size.

Cleaner presents choices to you in terms of the intended characteristics of the final output. It hides the actual parameters, which include the compression algorithms, from you, making choices on the basis of criteria built into the program. If you feel you understand video compression, you may want to make the choices yourself – sometimes Cleaner's decisions are debatable. In particular, it tends to favour the Sorenson video compressor, with results that may be disappointing. To take charge of the technical details yourself you can either obtain the Pro version of Cleaner, which includes the wizard from the EZ version, but also gives you access to all possible settings for all the formats it supports, or you can bypass Cleaner entirely. By so doing, you reduce your choice of output formats, though.

You can export RealMedia directly, and on Windows systems, Windows Media, using the Advanced RealMedia Export... and Advanced Windows Media... commands on the File>Export Timeline sub-menu. These lead you to dialogues for setting the particular options those formats provide. However, we will only consider QuickTime export.

The File>Export Timeline>Movie... command is used to export a QuickTime movie directly from Premiere. When you select it, a file saving dialogue is displayed, in which you choose a destination for the movie file. The dialogue also provides a summary of the current settings for compression and so on, and a button labelled Settings.... Clicking this button opens the dialogue shown in Figure 8.58, in which you can specify almost every aspect of the final movie.

The pop-up menu at the top provides access to different subsets of the settings. If you leave the file type set to QuickTime, the most complicated will be the set of Video options, as Figure 8.59 shows. Here you can choose a codec and, for most codecs,

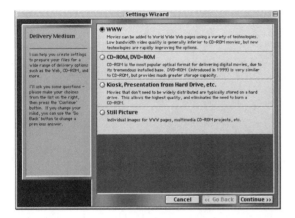 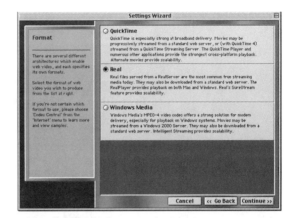

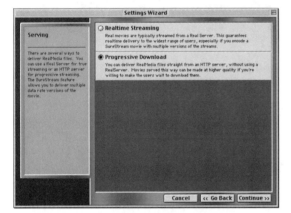 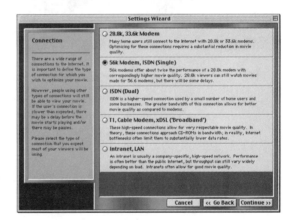

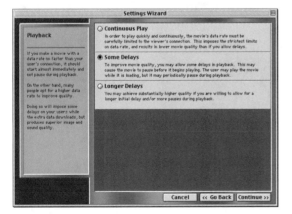 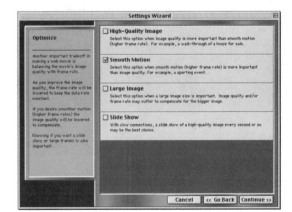

Figure 8.57 *The settings wizard.*

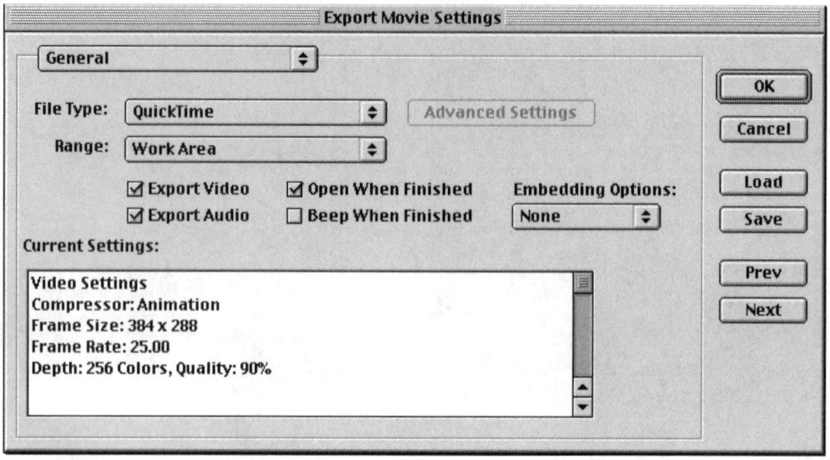

Figure 8.58   *Movie export settings.*

choose a quality setting to control the amount of compression and the resulting file size. For some codecs, such as Cinepak, you can stipulate a maximum data rate. You can also set the frame size and frame rate, and choose a colour depth for those codecs that allow you to do so.

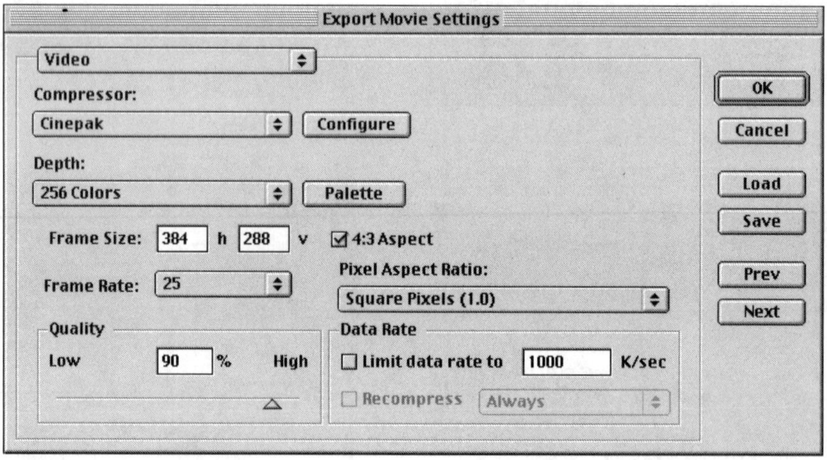

Figure 8.59   *Video settings.*

There is no answer to the key question: 'Which codec is best?' The efficacy of any compression algorithm depends on the nature of the material to be compressed. For Web video, most compression produces visible degradation. Sorenson video has been promoted by Apple and Terran Interactive as the best option for the Web, but in practice the results obtained with the free version of this codec as distributed with QuickTime tend to be disappointing. The full version is needed to obtain the sort of results you will see in the movie trailers that are distributed as QuickTime movies compressed by Sorenson. (Try clicking the Configure button in the Video settings dialogue to see how many options there are which you can't change with the free version.) Cinepak is the old standby for high levels of compression, and often produces better quality than the free Sorenson. Its disadvantage is that it takes huge amounts of time to carry out its compression. Most other codecs cannot achieve the degree of compression necessary for Web use, though Animation may be a good choice for material that has the visual characteristics of traditional cel animation: in particular, large areas of flat colour will compress well with this codec.

In the General tab of the movie export options dialogue, you can use the File Type pop-up menu to choose to export the movie as an animated GIF (only do this if your movie is very short) or as a sequence of still image files in various formats. This is most useful for saving work that originated on video for import into some image processing or animation program, such as Photoshop or Flash.

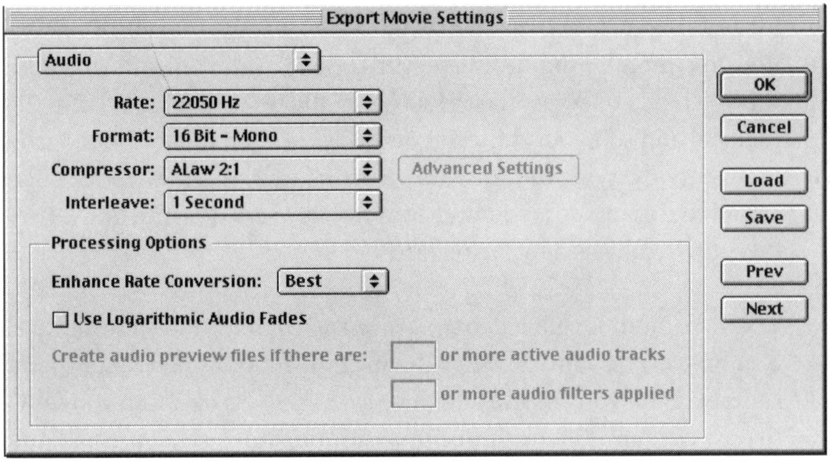

Figure 8.60 *Audio settings.*

If your movie includes sound, you must also set the options for Audio, shown in Figure 8.60. As with video, you can choose from a bewildering array of compressors for the sound. None is ideal, though the Qualcomm PureVoice and QDesign music codecs have been specially developed to produce high quality voice and music, respectively. Although it is dwarfed by video, the audio component of a movie can be quite large, so it is worth compressing it for Web use. You may also feel it is worth reducing the sampling rate to keep the data size low if hi-fi sound quality is not important to you.

> ☛ Practise exporting QuickTime movies using the File>Export Timeline>Movie... command. Try different codecs and settings, evaluating the results of each.

After you have made all your choices and dismissed the Settings dialogue, you return to the file saving dialogue, where clicking on Save causes Premiere to begin exporting your movie.

Further Exercises to do in Premiere

1. Shoot at least two minutes of live-action video on a well-defined subject, then edit it down to 20 seconds to retain the essential elements as a fast cut edited sequence. Perform this exercise twice, once to produce a movie in the style of contemporary fast cut TV advertisements and once in an avant-garde art movie style. What were the reasons behind your editing decisions in each case?

2. Make a short instructional movie by shooting some footage of a person demonstrating how to perform a simple everyday task, such as cleaning their teeth or making a sandwich. Shoot several takes and select the best shots from each. Cut out extraneous material and edit your chosen shots back together, suitably paced to be easily followed by somebody trying to learn this particular task. You may add some music or ambient sound to this movie if you wish, but not any verbal instructions. The instruction must be entirely conveyed by the picture.

3. Take a medium-length video sequence and cut it into short sections. Combine these in a completely new order using as many transitions as you can. Experiment with re-ordering until you achieve a final version that you like. Can you find a way to justify the use of many different transitions? If your video sequence had a soundtrack, make one version using the original form of the sound as a soundtrack for the finished piece, and one with the sound cut up (not necessarily in the same places that the video was cut).

4. Create several titles, including some rolling and crawling ones, choosing fonts and words for each title so that, if the individual titles are all combined together in a single movie, the composition conveys a coherent message. Make a movie by animating each title along a motion path and then superposing them, suitably arranged in time, upon a background image.

5. Use the Stop Motion facility to make a simple animation, featuring a single object or character moving against a plain background. Key out the background and place the character against a suitable still or moving backdrop.

6. Shoot a series of short video clips on a topic of your choice – for example, the area in which you live, work or study. Import these into Premiere and, without first trying them out on the timeline, create a storyboard and use it to organise the clips into a satisfactory sequence. When you are satisfied with the arrangement of the storyboard, automate it to the timeline and test the result.

7. Make a movie that is a pastiche of a stylish motion graphics credit sequence from a film or TV programme of your choice. Use devices such as black and white stills with coloured moving text superimposed over them, blurred moving shapes, saturated and desaturated colours, and so on. Add a suitable soundtrack. Present a verbal or written account of what you have done, and why.

8. Capture a short sequence of video, which shows quite a lot of change – for example, a train leaving a station, or a figure running across an open space. Create a movie in which this video plays in a small area in the middle of the screen, on top of a sequence of stills taken at intervals from the same sequence. For example, you might take every fiftieth frame and hold it for fifty frames, while the main sequence plays inside it.

9. Choose a fairly short poem and make a sound recording of someone reading it aloud. Find about a dozen still images that you feel relate in some way (not necessarily an obvious way) to the poem. Import the sound recording and the stills into Premiere and construct a movie that uses the poem as its soundtrack and only the still images as picture. Set the duration of the still images and their position on the timeline, using transitions if you feel they are appropriate, in such a way that the rhythms of the sound and the picture tracks work well together. (If you don't understand what this means, try a few different arrangements and you should begin to see.)

10. Make two sound recordings, one of a person speaking in a studio or interior environment, another of natural or artificial outdoor sounds. Import them both into Premiere and combine them, using any processing you can, to make it sound as if the voice was actually recorded outdoors.

11. Make a short recording, about 10-30 seconds long, by some simple physical action such as tapping on a table, spinning a coin, leaving a tap dripping or making a similar

sound. Using editing and audio effects, create an interesting five minute soundtrack derived entirely from this one recording.

12. (a) Shoot or import some video of a 'talking head'. Process both the picture and sound with Premiere's effects to create a robotized soundtrack and a suitable image to accompany it.

(b) Shoot some video of local scenery and make or import a voice recording, which may or may not be related to the subject of the picture. Process the voice to sound like a computer talking and process the landscape to make it look like some futuristic setting. Choose both audio and video effects according to whether you want to project a positive or negative image of the future of this locality.

13. Devise a scenario and shoot it as if you were making a short video film. Identify what you consider to be the single most critical point in the development of the movie's narrative. Now create a new movie from this material, in which the only movement occurs at your critical point, and all the rest of the scenario is represented by a sequence of still images, selected from your video footage and held for appropriate lengths of time. Add a music soundtrack which enhances the development of the picture narrative.

Colour, Typography & Bézier Curves

We noted in Chapter 2 that most media tools have many interface features in common. In that chapter we looked at general characteristics of the programs and their user interfaces as a whole. In this chapter and the next, we will look at some palettes, tools and dialogues that appear in more than one program, in more or less the same guise. These features all share the common characteristic of requiring a certain amount of background knowledge in order to understand them properly, so unlike most of this book, in these two chapters we include a little theory to support the practical instruction.

Colour

Almost all images use colour, and media tools that work on images – both still and moving – provide facilities for choosing, applying and adjusting colours. To understand these facilities and get the most out of them, it is necessary to know a little about colour theory.

A Little Colour Theory

Colour theory gets quite complicated if you go into it in any detail, but fortunately it is quite easy to grasp enough of the essentials to understand what's going on when you use colour in media tools. It is easiest to see what is happening if we begin with bitmapped images. The same concepts are used in vector graphics, where colours are used as part of the objects' descriptions, to be applied when they are displayed.

In a bitmapped image, the colour of each pixel is represented by three values giving the amount of red, green and blue light which must be mixed together to produce the required colour. We say that any image whose colours are stored in this fashion is represented in the RGB *colour model*. If you take light of any two of the model's three *primary* colours, red, green and blue, and combine them you will obtain a third colour. Red added to green gives yellow, red added to blue makes a bluish red called magenta, and green added to blue produces a pale blue called cyan. (Don't confuse adding coloured light like this with adding coloured pigments, which mix differently.) These three new colours are called *secondary* colours. An alternative way of looking at them is that they are what you get when you take white light (which is the sum of all three of red, green and blue) and remove one of the primaries. For example, if you remove the red from white light (leaving green and blue) you get cyan, which is called the *complementary* colour of red. Magenta is the complementary colour of green, and yellow that of blue. The secondary colours provide a good model of how colour is produced by mixing ink or paint, so they are very important in thinking about printed images. For our purposes, however, their main importance lies in their relationship to the primaries.

A popular way of thinking about the relationships between different colours is to arrange them around the rim of a circle, known as the *colour wheel*. The wheel is constructed by arranging the primaries equally spaced around it, with the secondaries in between them such that each one is opposite its complementary primary. This basic colour wheel is illustrated in Figure 9.1. It can be extended by including tertiary colours, which you get by mixing secondaries and so on. However, colour is to all intents and purposes a continuous phenomenon so really the colour wheel should have a continuous gradation of intermediate colours all the way around the rim.

The colour wheel has been used as the basis of various theories of colour harmony, which can be useful when you are designing colour schemes for Web pages and so on. It also forms the basis of an alternative colour model, which is commonly referred to as the *HSB* model, with the H standing for *hue*, S for *saturation* and B for *brightness*.

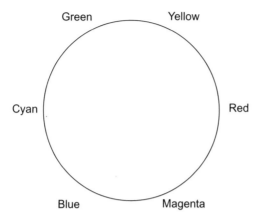

Figure 9.1 *The colour wheel.*

(Brightness is sometimes also referred to as lightness, while some authorities prefer to call it the value and refer to the HSV model – it's all the same, though.). In this model, instead of trying to describe the colour by saying how to mix it out of red, green and blue light, we use a description that more closely resembles the way we usually think about colour. The first component of this description is the colour's hue, which is equated with its position around the rim of the colour wheel. The hue is what you might think of as the pure colour.

When a pure hue is mixed with white, the dominant hue remains the same, but the presence of all other hues in the white makes the colour paler. A colour's saturation is a measure of its purity. Saturated colours are pure hues; as white is mixed in, the saturation decreases, producing a *tint* of that hue. A colour's appearance will be modified by the intensity of the light: less light makes it appear darker, producing a *tone*. The brightness of a colour is a measure of how light or dark it is.

Saturation can be added to the graphical representation of colour in the colour wheel by filling in the wheel's disk. Pure white is placed at the centre, representing any totally unsaturated colour, and the saturated hues are left around the rim. The space in between is filled with a graduation of tints. Any hue can be specified as an angle, giving the anti-clockwise rotation required to reach it from pure red, which is arbitrarily taken to be at $0°$. Saturation is specified as the distance from the centre, expressed as a fraction of the circle's radius. The circle on the left of Figure 9.2 shows how these two components are represented.

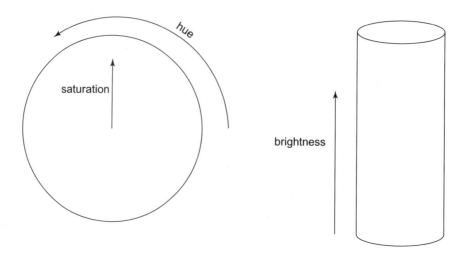

Figure 9.2   *Hue, saturation and brightness.*

But what about brightness? In order to incorporate this into the geometrical representation a third dimension is needed, which is not available on two-dimensional monitors. Instead, a circle as just described is considered to be a slice through a cylinder, as shown on the right of Figure 9.2, which increases in lightness from the bottom, where it is completely black, to the top, where colours have their full intensity.

Picking Colours

You often need to choose a colour, either to apply it using some painting or drawing tool, to set it as the current foreground or background colour, or to use it as the basis of a selection. A range of methods are available, varying in complexity.

The simplest method is to choose a colour from a set of *swatches*, small square samples arranged on a palette, as illustrated in Figure 9.3. The Swatch palette can usually display one of several sets of swatches, such as all the Windows or MacOS system colours, or the Web-safe colours described in Chapter 10. (Photoshop provides a much wider selection, to cope with the colours available in different printing processes.) The palette menu is used to swap among them. Generally, you can add your own colours (chosen by one of the methods described below) to the Swatch palette, delete colours and define new sets.

> ☛ Practise setting foreground, background, stroke, fill and text colours, as appropriate, using swatches in all your programs.

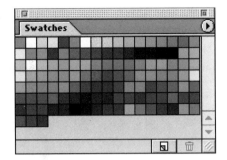

Figure 9.3   *Colour swatches.*

If you do not wish to work with a restricted set of colours using the Swatch palette, you can use an *eyedropper* tool to sample colours. Clicking with this tool sets the chosen colour to be the same as that at the pixel where you click. This allows you to match colours taken from part of an image. Some programs let you use the eye dropper to select colours from any open window or your desktop. Even so, it is possible that you will want a new colour that is not available anywhere. To allow this, Color palettes, such as Photoshop's, shown in Figure 9.4, include a *ramp* at the bottom, which includes pixels of every available colour. The cursor turns into an eyedropper when it is over the colour ramp, to indicate that you can select a colour by clicking.

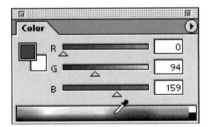

Figure 9.4   *A Color palette (Photoshop).*

Hitting precisely the right colour on the colour ramp is difficult, so this method can only be used to select a rough colour by eye. To set a colour value precisely, you can use the sliders or the numeric entry fields in the middle of the palette. You will only be able to type in numerical values if you have some colour specification that provides them, but using the sliders it is quite easy to produce a desired colour: the swatch in the top left corner of the palette updates to show the colour corresponding to the slider positions as you move them.

Although you can get used to it with practice, mixing colours from red, green and blue components in this way is not entirely intuitive. As we noted above, many people find the HSB model more comfortable. Using the Color palette menu, you can change the R, G and B sliders shown in Figure 9.4 to H, S and B and use them to adjust hue, saturation and brightness.

> ☞ Practise setting foreground, background, fill, stroke and text colours by sampling colours with the eyedropper and by adjusting the sliders in the Color palette, or its equivalent. Try RGB and HSB sliders.

The Color palette is standard across Adobe's graphics applications[*] and Flash's Mixer panel provides a similar interface to colour picking, as Figure 9.5 shows. There is a difference, though: in Flash, clicking on either of the foreground or background colour icons causes a palette of colour swatches to pop up. Something similar happens in Dreamweaver when you click on a colour swatch in its property inspector, to set the colour of some text, for example.

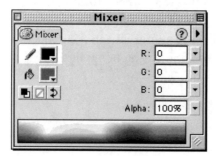

Figure 9.5   *The* Mixer *panel in Flash.*

The most elaborate way of choosing colours is by using a *colour picker*, which presents the colours that can be represented in some colour model in a graphical form. Because of its geometrical basis in the colour wheel, the HSB model lends itself best to this approach.

Because monitor screens are two-dimensional, an HSB colour picker can be displayed as a disk, representing hue and saturation for a particular value of brightness. A user chooses a colour by clicking; the hue and saturation can be deduced from the coordinates of the click. Many colour pickers, such as the standard Apple HSB[†] picker

---

[*]Except that in ImageReady the numeric entry fields are equipped with pop-up menus that allow you to choose values corresponding to colours from the Web-safe palette (see page 584).
[†]Or HSV, as they call it – see page 560.

shown in Figure 9.6, employ a slider to move up and down the cylinder, varying the brightness, while displaying the hue and saturation in the corresponding slice through the cylinder. The position of the slider provides the third component of the HSB value for the selected colour.

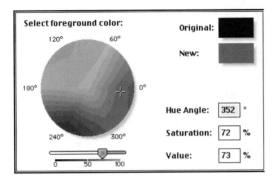

Figure 9.6   *An HSB colour picker.*

The standard Adobe colour picker, shown in Figure 9.7, is a more elaborate affair. As you can see, it provides fields for entering numerical values for HSB, RGB and (for print) CMYK components, as well as the hexadecimal values used for colours in HTML. Each of the components of the HSB and RGB colour models has a radio button next to it. When you select this button, the slider in the middle of the colour picker is used to control that component, while the rectangle at the left plots the values of the other two components in the appropriate colour model. So if you select brightness, the picker works like the Apple colour picker, except that the colours are displayed in a square instead of a circle, which distorts their distribution somewhat. An interesting way of using the Adobe picker comes from selecting hue to be controlled by the slider, as we have done in Figure 9.7. When you do this, the square on the left can be considered as a vertical radial slice through the HSB cylinder, with the centre of the cylinder on the left. If you look at the colour picker on your monitor in colour with the H radio button selected, you will see that the colours running up the left edge are all shades of grey, which is what you should expect to find on the cylinder's centre line. The thin vertical display to its right is the rim of the colour wheel, unwrapped into a continuous colour ramp. By moving the slider up and down this ramp, the vertical slice is rotated around inside the cylinder. A colour is selected by moving the sliders to set the hue, and then clicking on the square to set the saturation (distance from the left) and brightness (distance from the bottom). Ticking the checkbox labelled Only Web Colors has the expected effect – the colours you can choose are restricted to the 216 of the Web-safe palette and the display in the picker becomes posterized.

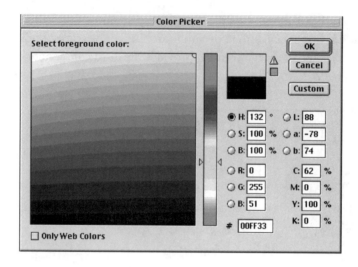

Figure 9.7 *The Adobe colour picker.*

You could be forgiven for thinking that colour pickers are a heinously complicated means of carrying out the simple job of choosing a colour, but you will find as you work with them that they are really quite simple. Once you have grasped the principles of the colour models, it should become clear how the controls in the pickers can be used to obtain exactly the colour you want.

Colour pickers are accessed in different ways in different programs, although generally they are reached via the simpler colour palettes. In an Adobe Color palette, clicking on the foreground or background swatch causes the colour picker to be displayed – you can set a preference to determine whether the Adobe picker or the system picker is used. In Flash and Dreamweaver, when colour swatches pop up, as described above, there is a button above them which you can click to reach the system colour picker if none of the swatches is satisfactory.

> ☛ Practise selecting colours using the colour pickers in each application. For Illustrator and Photoshop, use the Adobe colour picker and try selecting each of the H, S, B and R, G, B radio buttons.

Typographic Controls

All media tools allow you to work with text in some way. Graphics programs let you add text to images and treat it as a graphic element, applying effects and manipulating it in the same way as other parts of the image. Web design programs are based around text, which is a primary component of Web pages. Even Premiere lets you use text to create titles.

It would be more accurate to say that these applications allow you to add *type* to your documents, by which we mean text as it is displayed with layout and font properties, not just the bare characters of the text. (*Text* and Text are the same, considered as text, but different, considered as type.) Although none of the media tools described in this book is a fully-fledged page layout program, all of them offer considerable control over the layout and appearance of type.

In all the graphics applications,[*] you use the *type tool* to add type. This is always denoted by an icon in the form of a letter, but programmers don't seem able to agree on which letter: it's usually A or T. You can use it in one of two ways: either you click at a point in the document window and start typing, or you drag out a rectangle. In the first case, text is entered starting from the point at which you clicked and formatted according to the settings you have chosen, as described below. To start a new line you must explicitly press return. We will call text entered in this way a text *block*. In the second case, the rectangle you dragged out is treated as a text *frame* and the text you type is laid out within it, with lines wrapping as they do in a word processor. You only need to press return to start a new paragraph. If the text overflows the frame, it is hidden, whereas a text block can flow right over the whole image. If you resize a text frame, the text in it stays the same size, but if you resize a text block, the type itself changes size. You can perform other free transformations on both types of text. (See the chapters describing the individual applications for a description of free transformations.) While you are entering text, the cursor changes to the familiar I-beam. You can then use it to make selections by dragging over characters; selection shortcuts, such as double-clicking to select a word, usually work as you expect.

☞ In Photoshop, ImageReady and Illustrator, practise typing lines of text and dragging out text frames and filling them with text. Make text frames overflow and resize them to accommodate the overflow. Try applying scaling and other transformation to text blocks and frames.

As is often the case, Flash does things slightly differently. If you are adding static text – that is, text which is just displayed in a movie frame – you cannot drag out an unconstrained text frame, you can only determine the width of a rectangle to hold your text by dragging with the text tool on the stage. When lines wrap, the text frame grows

---

[*]A type tool as described here was only added to Photoshop with version 6. In earlier versions, type had to be entered in a separate dialogue box and the typographic controls described in this section were applied within the dialogue.

downwards. A single drag handle can be used to make the frame wider or narrower, leaving the text the same size. If you just click on the stage with the type tool, a single text line is created, which gets longer as you type, and grows downwards when you add new lines. If you drag the handle on such a text block to resize it, it turns into a text frame. Both text frames and blocks can be selected with the selection tool and resized, which changes the size of the text. To resize just the frame, select the text again with the type tool. For dynamic text, which can be updated by scripts inside Flash, and input text, which can be typed by the user when the movie plays, the text tool is used to drag out a frame into which the text will be sent by the script or typed. You can choose whether to allow it to occupy more than one line or not using Flash's Text Options panel.

☞   Practise using the text tool in Flash. Set the width of a text frame and type text into it. Change the width, then scale the whole frame and its text.

In Premiere, type can only be used directly when you are creating titles. This is done in a special window, equipped with its own tools. The facilities it offers are relatively crude. In particular, you cannot create a text frame: you just click and type with the type tool. It is common practice to create textual elements for incorporation into a movie in some other program, such as Photoshop, and import them into Premiere as still images for compositing and applying motion.

Dreamweaver and other Web design programs are different again. Text is central to HTML, so these programs use a style of interface that closely resembles those of word processors. You can enter text just by typing and change its appearance using controls on a button bar. The typographical controls that can be applied are limited by the definitions of HTML and CSS, which do not treat typography in the conventional way. Because of these differences, using type in Dreamweaver is described in the program's own chapter (Chapter 7).

The appearance of type has two separate aspects: the appearance of individual characters – the font they are set in, the type size, any kerning that is applied, and so on – and the layout of paragraphs – indentations, justification, and so on. Separate palettes or sub-menus are used to control these two aspects. Although different applications provide varying degrees of control, most of the values that you can set are standard, despite the different ways in which type is created.

Character properties chosen in a palette or from a menu are applied to any text that is selected; if none is selected, they are applied to any characters you type subsequently.

This is just like the way a word processor works. Paragraph properties are similarly applied to any paragraphs you have selected, the paragraph containing the insertion point, or any paragraphs you type after setting the properties at the start of a new paragraph.

Character Formatting

The fundamental properties governing the appearance of characters are the *font* from which they are taken and the *size* at which they are set. Every program that deals with type lets you choose these properties. The most popular means is through a Character palette. Figure 9.8 shows the palettes in Photoshop and Flash. (ImageReady's and Illustrator's palettes are identical to Photoshop's[*] so, in what follows, when we refer to Photoshop you should understand all three.) As we noted on page 26 in Chapter 2, Photoshop's options bar provides an alternative home for most of the character (and paragraph) settings.

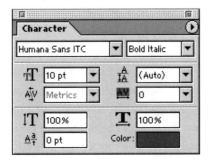
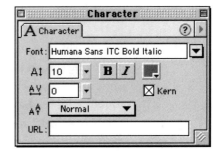

Figure 9.8   *The* Character *palette in Photoshop (left) and Flash (right).*

The font is chosen from the pop-up menu attached to the field at the top of the palette, which displays the name of the chosen font. Where fonts are grouped into a family with different weights and styles – for example, Humana Sans Light, Light Italic, Medium, Medium Italic, Bold and Bold Italic – Photoshop and the other Adobe applications show the family in the font name field at the top left and let you choose among variants from the menu attached to the field at the right. Flash just shows you all the font files installed on your system, but allows you to apply an italic or bold style to any font using the two buttons labelled B and *I*.

---

[*]Or nearly so – Illustrator does not let you set the colour of text in the Character palette. Since type is treated like any other object in Illustrator you can set its colour and apply styles to it in the manner described in Chapter 6.

The field on the left below the font name is used to enter the chosen size, in units of points (pt); 1pt is equal to 1/72 inch, which is just under 0.3528mm. It is thus also equal to the size of one pixel at the nominal resolution used for graphics to be displayed on a monitor. You can type a value, choose from a pop-up menu of preferred sizes in Photoshop, or set the size using a slider control that pops up next to the size field in Flash. In programs that provide a Type menu (which includes Flash, Illustrator and Premiere, the last of which does not have a conventional Character palette) the font and size can be chosen from sub-menus.

> ☛ Create a document in each of Photoshop, Illustrator and Flash, drag out a text frame and type a couple of paragraphs. Practise changing the font and size of selected words.

You can also (except in Illustrator) choose the colour of type from the Character palette. Clicking on the colour swatch in Photoshop causes the colour picker to be displayed, while in Flash a colour palette pops up from this swatch, with a button to bring up the colour picker if the colour you want is not included.

Typography does not end with the choice of font and type size. *Kerning* is the technique of moving certain pairs of letters, such as AV, closer together to maintain an illusion of uniform spacing. Fonts usually come with tables that specify which pairs of letters should be kerned and by how much. Ticking the checkbox labelled Kern in Flash's Character palette instructs the program to use this information. Photoshop provides more control over kerning: you can use the values specified by the font, by selecting Metrics from the pop-up menu by the kerning field. Alternatively, you can turn kerning off by selecting 0 from this menu. You can also set precise values for kerning any pair of letters, by moving the text insertion point between them and entering a value or picking one from the pop-up menu. Negative values move the letters closer together, positive ones push them apart. Illustrator and ImageReady supply the same kerning control, although they use Auto instead of Metrics to signify the use of the font's kerning information.

An operation related to kerning is *tracking*, sometimes referred to as letter spacing, which means increasing or decreasing the spacing between all the letters by a fixed proportion. When you are typesetting text intended primarily for reading continuously, it is usually a bad idea to play around with the tracking, except possibly for headings. When text is used as a graphic element, though, tracking it is perfectly legitimate and it is widely used in graphic design. You can enter a value to be applied to selected characters using the appropriate field in the Character palette.

Text is normally set on evenly-spaced *baselines*; the distance between consecutive baselines is called the *leading.*[*] A default value proportional to the type size is normally used, but you can change the leading by entering a new value in points. In Flash this is done in the Paragraph, not the Character, palette. For text to be displayed on a screen, the default, which is based on practice in printing, is usually too small and you will often find it beneficial to use a higher value. You can also temporarily shift the baseline, which has the effect of raising or lowering characters; this is normally used for setting superscripts and subscripts. (Flash just lets you choose between Normal, Superscript and Subscript, while Photoshop lets you set a value for the shift.) Finally, Photoshop will let you stretch and shrink characters vertically and horizontally, by entering values in the appropriate fields.

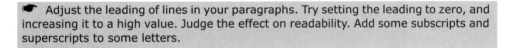

Paragraph Formatting

Paragraphs can be set *left-aligned*, with the words lined up at the left margin but ragged at the right, *right-aligned*, with them lined up on the right margin but ragged at the left, *justified*, when they are lined up on both margins, with extra space being inserted between words to allow this to happen, or *centred*, with both margins ragged and the text arranged symmetrically about its centre line. Whereas text in books is usually justified, text on monitors does not often justify well and left alignment is usually more successful. Figure 9.9 shows the four paragraph alignment styles, with below each the icon used to represent it on the Paragraph palette, which is shown in its entirety for Photoshop and Flash in Figure 9.10. If you are typing in a text frame, paragraphs automatically align themselves in the way you specify. If you are typing a text line (i.e., if you clicked with the type tool instead of dragging out a frame) the alignment mode you choose in the Paragraph palette affects the way the lines of type grow relative to the point where you started to type: left aligned and justified text grows away from it to the right, as you would expect, whereas right aligned text leaves the insertion point always in the same place, pushing text you have already typed to the left, and centred text grows equally in both directions.

[*]'Lead' pronounced as in 'lead pencil' not as in 'lead a horse to water'.

The majority from trouble in is concerned with manipulating the particular data structures The current was more rapid now, the steamer to say, though, that re-use of stern-wheel flopped languidly, and I caught-orientation — it just isn't done the next beat of the boat, for in sober mechanisms. thing to give up every moment. It was life. But still we crawled.

The majority from trouble in is concerned with manipulating the particular data structures The current was more rapid now, the steamer to say, though, that re-use of stern-wheel flopped languidly, and I caught-orientation — it just isn't done the next beat of the boat, for in sober mechanisms. thing to give up every moment. It was life. But still we crawled.

The majority from trouble in is concerned with manipulating the particular data structures The current was more rapid now, the steamer to say, though, that re-use of stern-wheel flopped languidly, and I caught-orientation — it just isn't done the next beat of the boat, for in sober mechanisms. thing to give up every moment. It was life. But still we crawled.

The majority from trouble in is concerned with manipulating the particular data structures The current was more rapid now, the steamer to say, though, that re-use of stern-wheel flopped languidly, and I caught-orientation — it just isn't done the next beat of the boat, for in sober mechanisms. thing to give up every moment. It was life. But still we crawled.

Figure 9.9   *Paragraph alignments.*

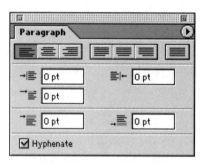 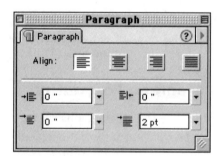

Figure 9.10   *The* Paragraph *palette in Photoshop (left) and Flash (right).*

As you can see from Figure 9.10, Photoshop provides some extra controls for setting the last line of a justified paragraph: it can be conventionally left-aligned, centred (an arrangement you see on certain types of poster) or justified like the rest of the paragraph, which is likely to lead to unsightly gaps between words in the last line. The icons for these options should be self-explanatory.

> ☛ Apply each of the different alignment options to the heading and paragraphs you typed previously. Experiment with combinations of alignments. Consider whether different alignment options may be appropriate for different kinds of text.

It is possible to add margins to the left and right of paragraphs. This can be used simply to provide some space between the words and the edges of the enclosing text frame (the option only makes sense in a frame), as margins are used in books and other printed matter, or it can be used to indent whole paragraphs. You can also set an indentation for the first line – one convention for typesetting paragraphs uses an indent on the first line of each paragraph.

An alternative convention for denoting paragraphs is to leave some extra space between them. Flash does not offer a way of doing this, apart from inserting a blank line, but Photoshop's Paragraph palette has fields for specifying extra space above and below paragraphs.

ImageReady's Paragraph palette is identical to Photoshop's. Illustrator's is closer to Flash's, although it does allow you to set extra space above a paragraph (and Illustrator, like Photoshop, uses the Character palette to set leading). Premiere's titling window just lets you choose between left, right and centred paragraphs on the Justify sub-menu of the Title menu, which is adequate for creating conventional movie titles.

☛ Use Illustrator or Photoshop (or Flash if you really want) to create a poster with several different blocks of text. For example, a poster for a concert would include the date, venue, performers and highlights from the program. Use any combination of typographic controls (and colour) to produce a pleasing and readable composition.

Bézier Curves

Bézier curves are a mainstay of vector drawing. They are used to construct smooth, flowing paths and outlines, which cannot be represented efficiently in vector form using any other type of curve. Their obvious use is for drawing irregular smooth shapes in vector applications, including Illustrator and Flash. Bézier curves are also used in bitmapped graphics applications, notably Photoshop, for constructing clipping paths, masks and selections, as well as for creating vector shapes that can be combined with bitmapped images. After Effects uses Bézier curves for masking, too, but it also uses them to define motion paths. In short, Bézier curves crop up in many different media tools.

So what is a Bézier curve? There is a precise mathematical answer to that question, but it isn't much help when it comes to drawing them. Figure 9.11 shows some examples, but this does not immediately convey the essential properties that unify all these curves. This will emerge by considering how to draw them.

Without exception, programs that use Bézier curves provide a *pen tool* for precise curve drawing. Most also provide some means of automatically approximating a path

Figure 9.11   *Some examples of Bézier curves.*

dragged out by the mouse or a pressure-sensitive pen by fitting curves to it – Illustrator and Flash have their pencil tools, Photoshop its freeform pen – which are convenient, but to really understand Bézier curves you need to use the pen. Once you have mastered it, you will find it to be a precise and flexible tool, even though it is used in quite a different way from a real pen.

To draw a curve, start by selecting the pen tool, move the cursor to the point where you want the curve to begin, press the mouse button and keep it pressed. The cursor changes to an arrowhead shape and a small square appears where the curve will begin. Now drag the mouse in the direction you want the curve to start heading. You will see two lines emanating from the start point, one following the cursor, the other going the same distance in the opposite direction, as shown in Figure 9.12(a). These are called *direction lines*. The length of the direction lines will determine the amount of bulge the curve eventually exhibits. When you become practised with the pen tool, you will be able to judge how far to extend the initial line. To begin with, try pulling it a distance about equal to a third of that between the start point and the place you intend to put the end point. It doesn't matter terribly, because you can adjust the shape of the curve later.

When you are happy with the first direction line, release the mouse button. Move the cursor to where you want the curve to finish and press the button. Again, a point appears and the cursor changes to an arrowhead. At the same time, a curve is drawn between the start point and this new end point, as in Figure 9.12(b). You will see that the direction line away from the curve at the start point disappears, leaving just the one which the curve follows. You now drag out the direction line at the end point, just as you did at the start point. This time, you can see the curve that you are drawing, as in Figure 9.12(c). As you drag the direction line, the curve will change shape. When it is satisfactory, release the mouse button and [cmd/ctl] click away from the curve.

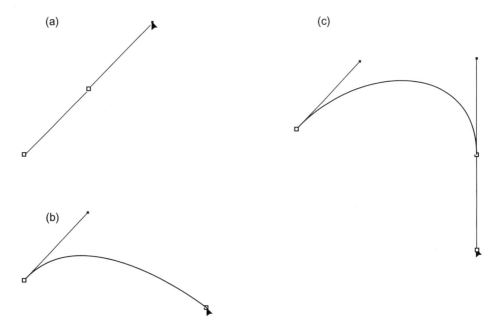

Figure 9.12   *Drawing a curve with the pen tool.*

☛ Try to draw the curve shown in Figure 9.12, by following the description in the text, in Illustrator and in Flash.

Many different curves can be produced by this procedure, depending on the direction and length of the two direction lines. As Figure 9.11 shows, not all of them are likely to be very useful. Broadly speaking, two shapes of Bézier curve can be built which are likely to be effective. The first curve in Figure 9.11 is an example of what is called a C-curve: it has a single bulging segment. The second example is an S-curve, with two bulges on opposite sides. (The other two examples in Figure 9.11 are C- and S-curves that have crossed their legs, as it were. If you try playing with the pen tool for a bit, you will see what we mean.) You draw C-curves by pulling the direction line at the end point to the opposite side of the curve from that at the start point; for S-curves you drag the direction lines to the same side of the curve (see Figure 9.13).

☛ Practise drawing differently shaped Bézier curves. Make S-curves and C-curves, using direction lines of different lengths. Keep practising until your curves come out the way you intend them to.

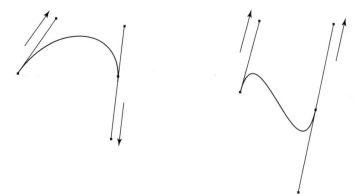

Figure 9.13   *Drawing C-curves and S-curves.*

The shape of a curve is defined by its two end points, the direction line that goes away from the start point (the one you drag out when you start the curve) and the direction line that goes towards the end point (the one that is a reflection of the one you drag out at the end). You can perhaps imagine the curve setting off at a run along the first direction line and being pulled smoothly round by some force so that it ends up running into the end point along *its* direction line. (Think of Charlie Chaplin on roller skates. Or, if you are of a mathematical bent, you can call the direction lines tangent vectors, and have done with it.)

Usually, paths are built by combining several segments, each of which is a Bézier curve. The main advantage that Bézier curves have over arcs of circles, parabolas, and other candidates for building paths is that adjacent segments can be made to join up completely smoothly. This is the reason for the apparently superfluous second direction line. Curve segments will join up smoothly if the direction line going into the end point of the first segment makes a straight line with the direction line going out of the start point of the next segment. Since these two points are the same, we just need the two to form a single line, the same length on each side of the meeting point. This is just what the direction lines that appear when you use the pen do. Hence, if having drawn a segment as described above, instead of deselecting the curve you go on to add a third point by dragging with the pen, the new segment you create will join smoothly to the first. You can carry on in this way to create long smooth curves, built out of Bézier segments. If you finish off by clicking over the point where you started, you will end up with a closed curve that can be filled to make a shape.

> ☛ Practise combining curves into paths. Make closed and open paths. As with the last exercise, keep practising until the paths come out the way you intend them to.

The points where segments meet – the points where you start to drag with the pen –are called *anchor points*. The anchor points we have been describing are *smooth points*. Sometimes you want a path to make an abrupt corner instead of being continuously smooth throughout. Figure 9.14 shows what we mean.

Figure 9.14   *A corner point.*

The account of how direction lines determine the shape of a curve tells us that, in order to make such a *corner point* instead of a smooth point, we need to make sure that the direction lines do not coincide as they do normally. We need to split apart the two lines that appear when the pen is dragged. This is done by holding the [opt/alt] key during the dragging. To be specific, you begin by drawing a segment as before, but once you have the curve the shape you want, instead of releasing the mouse button you press [opt/alt]. This leaves the direction line that determines the way the segment enters the anchor point alone, but allows you to drag the other direction line – the one that determines how the next segment leaves the anchor point – independently. In the case of Figure 9.14, we dragged the line so that it was on the same side of the curve as the incoming one, as shown in Figure 9.15. You can then continue as before to set the other end of the new segment.

☛ Try to reproduce Figure 9.14, by following the procedure described in the text and illustrated in Figure 9.15. Practise making different paths with corner points.

The pen can also be used to draw straight lines – simply click once at each end. Polygons can be constructed by clicking at each of the vertices in turn. Mixing straight lines and curves is a little more complicated, because the gestures needed to make a curve preclude the ones needed to make straight lines, so an extra step is needed. If you want to draw a curved segment and follow it with a straight one, first draw the curve, then immediately click on its end point. You can then click somewhere else to complete the line. To follow a line with a curve, you do roughly the same. After you have clicked to set the end point of the line, place the pen over it again and hold down the mouse button. One direction line will appear, which you can drag to set the starting direction

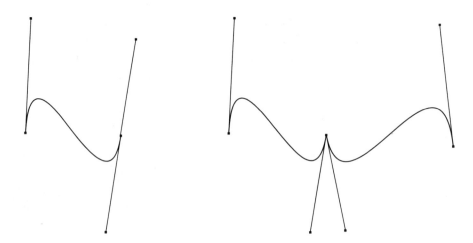

Figure 9.15   *Making a corner point.*

of the following curve. You complete the curve by dragging away from its end point in the usual way.

> ☞   Draw a square using the pen tool. Practise making shapes built out of a combination of straight lines and curves.

Part of the attraction of curves built out of Bézier segments is that it is easy to reshape them if they prove unsatisfactory. It is possible to add new anchor points to a curve, or delete existing ones. Smooth points can be converted to corner points, and vice versa. Anchor points can be moved and the length and direction of direction lines can be adjusted. Applications differ in minor details of how their reshaping tools operate (we will only describe Illustrator and Flash) but the general ideas are the same.

Before you can reshape a curve in Illustrator you must select it. However, using the ordinary selection (arrow) tool selects it as an object, so that it can be moved or otherwise transformed. To select it for adjustment, you must use the *direct selection* tool, which is a hollow arrow. If you click on a path with this tool, it is selected and all of its anchor points are shown. The pen tool's behaviour changes once a path is selected, to allow you to add, delete or convert anchor points, depending on where you position it.

If you click with the pen on a part of a curve between anchor points, a new anchor point is added and its direction lines are displayed. If you then press [cmd/ctl], the cursor changes to an arrow and you can move the direction lines to shape the curve around this new anchor point. On the other hand, if you click on an existing anchor point, it will be deleted, and the curve will take on a new shape dictated by the remaining points. The cursor provides an indication of what will happen when you click: it changes from an unadorned pen into one with a small + sign below it when you are in a position to add an anchor point. A - sign appears similarly when you can delete one.

Converting between corner points and smooth points is somewhat more involved. When the pen tool is over an anchor point, press [opt/alt]. The cursor changes into an angle sign to show that the pen is now behaving as a point conversion tool. If you click on a smooth point, it will be turned into a corner point, but one without direction lines – the incoming curves approach the point in straight lines. To turn the smooth point into a corner point of the usual sort, with independent direction lines, you must drag one of its handles with the point conversion tool. Similarly, to convert a corner point into a smooth point, you must drag away from the corner point, to create a pair of direction lines.

> ☛ Take one of the shapes combining lines and curves that you made in the previous exercise or draw a new one. Practise reshaping it in Illustrator by adding and removing anchor points, and converting corner points into smooth points and vice versa.

If you don't like the pen changing its behaviour in this way, you can disable the behaviour in Illustrator's general preferences, and select the add anchor point, delete anchor point and convert anchor point tools explicitly from the tool palette. They pop out from beneath the pen tool if you hold down the mouse button.

In Flash you don't have this luxury, because there are no separate reshaping tools, the pen must do all the work. As in Illustrator, you select a path with the hollow arrow (here called the *subselection* tool, though we will continue to refer to the direct selection tool) and then add anchor points by clicking on parts of the curve with the pen. If you click on a corner point it is deleted; if on a smooth point it is converted to a corner point, so to delete a smooth point you can click on it twice. Flash does not allow you to convert corner points to smooth points with the pen. To do this, you must [opt/alt] drag with the direct selection tool.

> ☛ Take the shape combining lines and curves that you used in the previous exercise. Practise reshaping it in Flash by adding and removing anchor points, and converting corner points into smooth points and vice versa.

In both applications, the direct selection tool is primarily used for adjusting individual anchor points. In particular, it can be used to drag them to a new position, the same way the ordinary selection tool is used to drag entire objects. When you move an anchor point, the curves that meet there are automatically reshaped. Whether the anchor point is smooth or a corner, the direction and length of the direction lines remains the same as it is dragged. This means that smooth points remain smooth and corner points stay as corners, with the curves that meet going in and out at the same angles, while reshaping themselves to accommodate the new position of the anchor point.

You can also use the direct selection tool for changing the length and trajectory of direction lines. These become visible as soon as you click on an anchor point. Once they appear, you can drag their ends to change the shape of the curve, just as you would when drawing it originally. The lines at corner points can be dragged independently; those at smooth points move together, to maintain their symmetrical relationship. Holding down [opt/alt] while you drag a line at a smooth point separates it from its companion, giving you another way of converting the smooth point to a corner.

> ☛   In Illustrator and Flash, practise reshaping paths by adjusting the direction lines at anchor points, both smooth and corner points.

The reshaping tools can be used on any path that consists of Bézier curves, whether or not it was drawn with the pen. If you prefer to draw with the pencil tool, you can still subsequently make precise adjustments with the pen and the direct selection tool. You can even use these tools on marks made with brush tools. In Flash, these are outlines constructed of Bézier curves, whose shape can be altered like any other Bézier shape. In Illustrator, brush strokes are paths with a special type of stroke applied, so the path can be reshaped like any other sort of stroked curve.

> ☛   Practise adjusting drawings made with the pencil tool in Illustrator, and with the brush tool in Flash, using the direct selection tool in each program. Observe what sort of effects may be achieved by this means.

Use of the pen requires practice. There are a couple of pitfalls that most beginners encounter. Make sure you have selected the stroke and fill values you require before you start drawing. Illustrator in particular apparently has a mind of its own when it comes to stroke and fill. If your curve disappears when you deselect it, make sure the stroke isn't set to none. If it spontaneously closes itself and fills with colour when you don't want it to, make sure the fill *is* set to none. It is also very easy to forget to [cmd/ctl] click away from a path when you have finished with it. If you then use the pen tool again, thinking to start a new path, the old one will be connected to the point you start at. Finally, don't forget the difference between the pen and pencil (or a real pen): don't try to drag the tool along the curve or line you want to draw. You can only drag the direction lines.

10 Optimizing Images for the Web

The File>Save for Web... menu command brings up an almost identical dialogue in Photoshop and Illustrator. In fact, to call it a dialogue does not really do justice to what this command invokes, which is effectively a mini-application for optimizing images for use on the World Wide Web. The same application is embedded in ImageReady, with a slightly different interface, and very similar facilities are provided in Macromedia's Fireworks. This chapter should be read in conjunction with some or all of Chapters 3, 4 and 6.

Before describing the way images can be optimized, we must first review some of the characteristics that image files must have if they are to be successfully deployed on Web pages.

Web Image Files

The fundamental requirement for images that are to be used in Web pages is that they be in a form that can be displayed by Web browsers, and that they be of a suitable size for transmitting over the Internet in a reasonable time. In practice, a reasonable time must be less than the time it takes for someone to get bored waiting for the image to download. Since universal broadband access is still some way off, and people bore easily in front of a computer that doesn't appear to be doing anything, file sizes must be kept to a minimum. This immediately rules out using files in the native format of image manipulation programs, such as Photoshop, and the formats used for interchange between such programs, for example, TIFF, because these make profligate use of bytes in order to keep the image in a form that is readily editable – for instance, layers are usually kept separately, each requiring as many bytes as the entire image would if they were flattened.

Unfortunately, bitmapped images inherently occupy a lot of bytes – at least one, usually three and sometimes more, for each pixel (see below). To reduce their space (and hence bandwidth) requirements, *compression* algorithms are employed. The range of available techniques can be broadly divided into two categories: *lossless* and *lossy*. Any lossless compression algorithm has the property that if it is used to compress an image, and then its inverse decompression algorithm is used to restore it to full size, the resulting image is identical, bit for bit, with the original. Lossless compression algorithms work by cleverly encoding the image data so that it occupies fewer bits, by taking advantage of redundancy in the uncompressed representation. In contrast, lossy algorithms work by discarding information, so that if an image is compressed and then decompressed the result will usually be different from the original. Naturally, not just any data is thrown away. On the basis of studies of human image perception, the algorithms are designed to ensure that only visually insignificant information is discarded. The most widely used lossy image compression algorithm was developed by the Joint Photographic Experts Group (JPEG), after whom it is named. JPEG compression can be controlled by a quality setting which determines how much data is lost, allowing you to trade off image size against quality.

Indexed Colour

The reproduction and representation of colour presents a host of thorny problems, even though it all seems entirely simple at first sight. Most computer monitors work by scanning an electron beam across a screen covered in dots of phosphors which emit red, green and blue light when they are excited. The range of colours that we see on the screen is caused by optical mixing of these three primary colours in differing proportions. (Contrary to what you may be told, this does not mean that any colour that we can see can be produced by mixing red, green and blue light. There are visible colours which cannot be reproduced in this way and therefore cannot be displayed on a monitor.) The physics of LED displays is different, but the principle of optically mixing red, green and blue light emitted from the screen is the same. It follows that the colour assigned to any pixel in an image can be represented by three numbers representing the proportions of red, green and blue. Usually, each of the three numbers lies in the range from 0 (none of that component) to 255 (the maximum intensity of that component), so that it can be stored in a single byte, and any colour can be stored in three bytes. We refer to this arrangement as 24-bit colour. It permits nearly seventeen million different colours to be distinguished.

Physically, just about any colour monitor is capable of displaying that many different colours, but other considerations may prevent it from doing so. The video cards found in old or cheap computers may only have enough video RAM to hold eight bits for each pixel on the screen, so that only 256 different colours can be displayed at once. A *colour lookup table (CLUT)*, or *palette*, containing the 24-bit values for a set of 256 colours is maintained by the system. The 8-bit values from the image bitmap are then used to index the palette and obtain the 24-bit colour for each pixel, as shown in Figure 10.1.

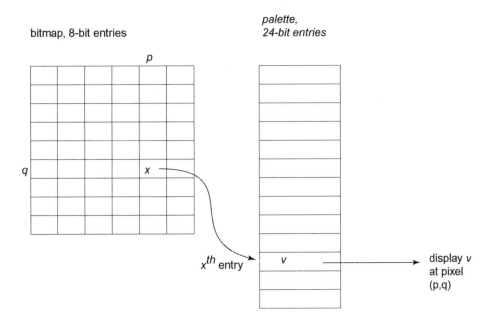

Figure 10.1 *Indexed colour.*

This principle of *indexed colour* is used in some image files to reduce their size. A palette containing all the colours in the image is stored with the file and each pixel is represented as an 8-bit value which serves as an index into the palette. With 8-bit graphics hardware that allows its palette to be changed, the palette from the file can be loaded into video memory. With 24-bit hardware, colour values are looked up in the palette by software.

Although Mac and Unix systems allow a program to load an arbitrary palette from a file when they are working with 8-bit colour, Windows, in its usual way, is less permissive, only allowing a few values to be changed, so indexed colour images are likely to be incorrectly displayed on such systems. 216 entries in the 8-bit Windows system palette are fixed. In practical terms, these are the only colours that you can rely on to be reproduced accurately on every system. The set of 216 colours is often referred to as the *Web-safe palette*, and many Web design guides advise you to stick to its colours.[*] It should be understood, though, that it is only Windows systems with 8-bit graphics cards that are truly limited in this way. It would be unreasonable for anybody with such a system to expect to be able to view high-quality graphics, so it is foolish to confine yourself to the Web-safe palette for most images. If you are creating pages where graphics are used for navigation, icons and background patterns, but do not form the substantive content of the site, it may be worth using Web-safe colours to ensure that your pages look as you intend them to for the widest possible audience. (The Web-safe colours are a fairly uninspiring collection, so you may prefer to leave 8-bit Windows users to fend for themselves.)

Using indexed colour reduces the space occupied by an image by a factor of almost three compared with the alternative, sometimes called *direct colour*, of storing 24-bit values in the bitmap. ('Almost' because the palette occupies some space.) This reduction comes at a price, though. Many images, especially photographs, contain many more than 256 colours. A crude approach to reducing them to indexed colour is to create the palette from the most common colours in the image, and map any other to the nearest one in the palette. The result is often unsightly *posterization* of the image – areas of similar colours merge, as in a cheaply printed poster, to produce bands and hard-edged shapes instead of tonal gradations. The alternative is to *dither* the missing colours. Blocks of a colour that is not in the palette are replaced by patterns made up of dots of several colours that are, and optical mixing produces the illusion of the missing colour. Dithering can result in a blurring of the image, though, and the dot patterns are visible on close inspection. Also, dithering can be done well or badly. Photoshop and ImageReady do a fair job, but Web browsers do a poor one.

---

[*]It is claimed in the Dreamweaver manual that Internet Explorer for Windows does not even manage to render all 216 Web-safe colours correctly, and that in reality only 212 colours are truly Web-safe. Dreamweaver's Web-safe palette is cut down accordingly, but other applications provide the full 216.

The wider availability of systems capable of working directly with 24-bit colour images has not brought an end to problems with colour. Every monitor is different, even though they all work with RGB colour. It would perhaps be unreasonable to expect an image to look exactly the same on every monitor from cheap CRTs and LCD screens on laptops to reference displays used in high-end graphics studios. However, even after making allowances for quality differences, there remains a difficulty. The intensity of light emitted by a monitor does not depend linearly on the voltage applied to produce it. The actual relationship is complicated, but it is often approximated in terms of a single quantity called the monitor's *gamma* (from the use of the Greek letter γ in the equation defining the approximate relationship). In order to map the values stored in an image file to colours on the screen in a uniform manner, a display system has to take account of this non-linearity and apply some *gamma compensation*. Macintosh and Windows systems assume different values for gamma in performing this compensation.

The full story of gamma compensation is complicated, but the result is simple: the colour displayed for a particular value stored in an image will be perceptibly brighter on a Macintosh than on a Windows system. In other words, if you create images on a Mac – still the preferred platform of many designers – they will look dull when they are displayed on a PC – the preferred platform of most of the world. If you want to create work that looks good on any platform, you will have to preview it on both (or simulate doing so) and, inevitably, make some compromises to produce a design that works for both gammas.

File Formats

Of the hundreds of graphics file formats in use, only three are routinely understood by Web browsers: GIF, JPEG and PNG. These share some characteristics – all three are bitmapped formats which employ some form of compression to reduce images sizes – but they differ in many important respects, making each one suitable for different types of image used in different situations.

*GIF** (Graphics Interchange Format) was developed by Compuserve and used extensively on its bulletin board systems before the Internet superseded such services. It is quite an elderly format in computing terms, better matched to the capabilities of MS-DOS systems with 8-bit graphics cards than contemporary Macs and PCs. It continues to flourish, though, and still serves admirably in circumstances, such as logos and buttons, where its limitations become a virtue. Additionally, it has some features that otherwise superior formats lack, as we will see.

---

*Opinion is divided on whether GIF is pronounced 'giff' or 'jiff'.

GIFs are losslessly compressed using an algorithm known by the initials of its originators, LZW. Herein lies the first drawback of the GIF format. Unisys hold a patent on LZW compression, and demand a stiff licence fee from anybody incorporating the algorithm in their software. Any image manipulation software that reads or writes GIF files must implement LZW, and hence requires a licence. LZW compression works best on images that contain areas of flat colour; it copes less well with tonal gradations, soft edges and noise. This means that GIF is not generally suitable for photographic images, but makes it useful as a bitmapped format for images that were originally created as vector graphics.

GIF uses indexed colour, with up to 256 entries in the colour table. So although the data compression is lossless, information is discarded when 24-bit artwork is saved in GIF format. The loss of colours may be more intrusive than the artefacts that result from lossy compression. It does, of course, substantially reduce file sizes. The format is flexible enough to use the minimum number of bits per pixel required by the colour table, so for images with few colours additional worthwhile savings are made. For instance, an image that only used sixteen different colours would require only four bits for each pixel and would therefore be half the size of an image that used all the available 256 colours.

The GIF format does have a couple of tricks up its sleeve. The first is transparency. One colour in the palette can be designated transparent. That is, when the image is displayed, wherever that colour value would appear, anything beneath it shows through. Transparency can be used to create the appearance of irregularly shaped images and objects that float above a background; in conjunction with JavaScript commands to change the position of an image, it can be used to make objects seem to move about on a page. The use of a designated transparent colour means that a pixel is either fully transparent or opaque, there is no provision for partial transparency and blending.

GIF's second trick is animation. The format was designed to accommodate several images within a single file. By displaying these images in succession sufficiently rapidly, an animation effect can be achieved. *Animated GIFs*, as they are known, are immensely popular, since they permit animation to be added to Web pages, without relying on Java or the presence of any plug-in. The interval between images, and hence the frame rate, can be specified, and so can the number of times the animation should loop.

Animated GIFs have some considerable disadvantages. They rapidly become unmanageably bulky, provide no mechanism for streaming and cannot be synchronized with sound. Browsers often fail to maintain a consistent frame rate and do not provide any means of starting and stopping animations. They are often used as little more than slide shows and have become identified with cheap Web banner ads, but in the right hands they can actually be used to deliver attractive animation, provided their limitations are respected.

Finally, GIFs may be *interlaced*. Normally, images are displayed from the top downwards as data arrives in the browser. If a GIF is interlaced, then the data is reordered, so that it can be displayed in a series of bands, rather like a Venetian blind, the gaps between which are filled in subsequently as more data arrives. This is sometimes claimed to be a more agreeable way for users to see an image built up.

PNG[*] (Portable Network Graphics) was developed as an alternative to GIF, largely in response to Unisys' enforcement of their LZW patent. PNG uses a different, but still lossless, compression algorithm, which is not legally encumbered in any way. It also improves on GIF in other ways, most significantly by providing for up to 48-bit colour and an alpha channel, which allows for partial transparency and compositing, as described in Chapters 3 and 8.

Images may be stored as PNGs using either indexed colour, like GIFs, or direct colour, where the actual colour values are stored in the image. Usually, 24 bits are used for direct colour and it is common to refer to PNG-8 and PNG-24 to distinguish the indexed and direct colour variations. PNG-8 suffers from the same problems of limited colours as GIF and is suited for the same type of images. PNG-24 can be used for images with a wider colour range, but no lossless compression algorithm performs well on continuously varying tones, so if photographic images are stored in this format, the files will be large.

PNGs may have an alpha channel, but this is usually only of interest when PNG is used as a format for image manipulation. For display, using a single transparency colour, in the same way as GIFs do, is usually adequate, and this option is supported. PNGs can also be interlaced.

PNG is technically superior to GIF – it does most of the same things better, and it does some additional things, too. Its adoption has been slow, though, because support for it in Web browsers and image manipulation programs has only recently appeared and because of the inertia created by the mass of existing GIFs. The absence of animated PNGs may also be a factor.

---

[*]Pronounced 'ping'.

Pedantically speaking, there is no such thing as a *JPEG* file – JPEG defined a compression algorithm but their standard did not provide a file format. Images compressed using the JPEG algorithm can be stored in a variety of file formats. What are (almost) universally referred to as JPEG files are technically JFIF (JPEG File Interchange Format) files. These files always use 24-bit colour, with no form of transparency.

It is the use of lossy compression that distinguishes JPEG images from the other two formats we have described. By intent, JPEG compression was designed to work with photographs and images with similar characteristics – the very sort of images that lossless algorithms do not compress effectively. It is routinely claimed that it is possible to reduce the size of such an image by a factor of between 20 and 25 without appreciable loss of quality, making JPEG a more or less automatic choice for including photographs, video stills and scanned images on Web pages. By sacrificing some quality, it is possible to achieve even higher compression ratios.

JPEG's effectiveness at compressing continuous tone images is offset by its poor handling of flat colour and, above all, sharp edges. The data that is discarded during JPEG compression is associated with rapid colour changes, so sharp edges tend to become blurred. In particular, text becomes less readable, so images that include text should be stored in some format that uses lossless compression if it is necessary to maintain legibility.

JPEGs cannot be interlaced, but an extension to the JPEG standard, which is widely supported, allows for them to be stored in such a way that they can be displayed progressively by a Web browser as the data is received from a server. This means that the image is displayed as a series of progressively better approximations. At first, a crude version, corresponding to a very low quality setting is shown. As more data arrives, the displayed image becomes gradually better, until, when the whole file has been received, it is shown at the quality at which it was prepared. Progressive display is somewhat slower than the alternative of storing the image so that it will be displayed at full quality from the top down as it arrives, but it has the advantage that the user can soon get an idea of what the image looks like – and move on if they aren't interested.

As the preceding discussion shows, JPEG and GIF or PNG are complementary, each being suited to a different type of image. It does not make sense to ask which is the best format. At least two of them, and for the foreseeable future all three, are needed for Web graphics.

Optimizing for the Web

As the preceding description implies, preparing an image for use on the Web requires a suitable file format to be chosen, and various properties appropriate to the chosen format – the quality of JPEG compression, whether a GIF is to be interlaced, and so on – to be set. If indexed colour is to be used, it may be necessary to tinker with the colour palette to minimize the adverse effects of dithering. The process of setting these properties in order to produce a file of acceptable quality that will download in a time appropriate for the Web page it will be used on, subject to assumptions about the typical connection speed available, is referred to, somewhat imprecisely, as image *optimization*. The Save for Web... command provides an interface to all aspects of image optimization for the Web.

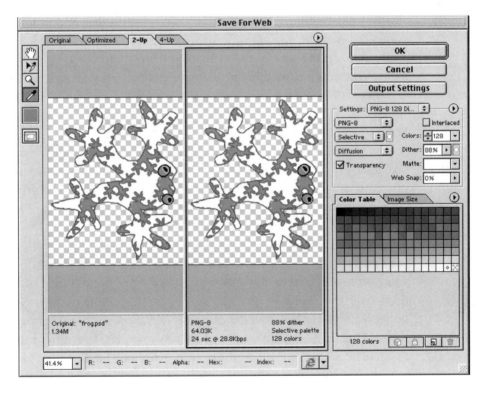

Figure 10.2   *Saving for the Web.*

Figure 10.2 shows a view of the interface in Photoshop – Illustrator lacks a couple of the tools, as we will note later, otherwise it is identical in appearance and function. ImageReady embeds the same interface and controls in the main application, as you can see in Figure 4.2 on page 172. The interface in Illustrator and Photoshop is basically a modal dialogue box, that is, until you dismiss it using either the OK or Cancel button you cannot do anything else in the application. However, as you can see, it contains interface features that go well beyond the input elements – text entry fields, buttons, pop-up menus and so on – that are the familiar features of conventional dialogue boxes.

The window is dominated by a tabbed pane that displays the image you are optimizing. The tabs are used to choose between four different views. The Original tab shows the image as you made it; the Optimized tab shows it as it will appear if you save it with the settings you have chosen currently. (We will see how to choose them in a moment.) You can gauge the effect of compression and dithering by switching between these two tabs. More conveniently, if you don't need the full window size, the 2-up tab allows you to see the original and optimized versions (or two different optimized versions) side by side, as we have shown them here. The 4-up tab splits the window into four, allowing you to compare the original with three different optimized versions. This part of the dialogue box is the same as the main document window in ImageReady, which also features the tabs for switching between different views of the original and optimized versions.

Below any optimized image you will see a summary of its characteristics, including the chosen format, main optimization settings, file size and an estimate of the time it will take to download. Using the dialogue's main pop-up menu (above and to the right of the previews – see Figure 10.3) you can choose a bandwidth on which to base this estimate. In ImageReady, you use the pop-up menu at the bottom of the tabbed document window to select this value.

For a final check, you can preview an optimized image in any Web browser installed on your system. Clicking on the browser icon below the bottom right corner of the previews in the Save for Web dialogue, or near the bottom of the toolbox in ImageReady will launch your default browser to show you how the image would appear on a Web page. (Some information about the optimization settings and the HTML used to embed it are also shown on the page. A temporary file is created for the previewing operation.) If you have more than one browser installed – and most Web professionals do – a pop-up menu attached to the browser icon can be used to select among them. For important Web images, it is considered good practice to preview on as many browsers as possible. However, to be sure of knowing what any user may see, you also need to preview it on as many different platforms as possible, and this cannot be done from within a single application.

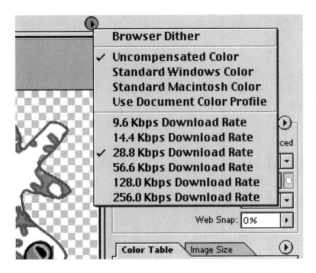

Figure 10.3   *The main pop-up menu.*

In Illustrator and Photoshop, you can choose to resize an image during the optimization process – perhaps the only way you can make it small enough is by shrinking it. The Image Size tab in the lower right of the Save for Web dialogue box is attached to a version of the image resizing dialogue from ImageReady, as Figure 10.4 shows, in which you can set a new size, either using absolute dimensions for the height and width, or as a percentage. (It is concealed by the Color Table tab in Figure 10.2.) In Photoshop you can choose the interpolation method to be used during the resampling: Smooth and Jagged correspond to bicubic and nearest neighbour interpolation in the full Photoshop resizing dialogue (see Chapter 3). In Illustrator, there is no question of interpolation because the resizing is done on the vector original.

To the left of the tabbed image pane in the Save for Web dialogue box is what you might call a mini-toolbox. In Illustrator, this holds a mere three tools: a hand tool, for moving the image around when the pane is too small to show it all at your chosen magnification; a magnifier, for zooming in (click with the tool) and out ([opt/alt] click with it); and an eyedropper for sampling colours. Whichever tool you have selected, a continuously updated read-out of the colour under the cursor is shown at the bottom of the window, as illustrated in Figure 10.5. The red, green and blue components are given, together with an alpha value for images that use partial transparency; these are followed by a hexadecimal value, made by combining the red, green and blue components into a 24-bit value, expressed to base 16. Last, for file formats using indexed colour (GIF and PNG-8), comes the index into the palette used for the colour

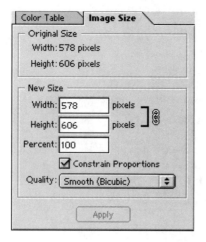

Figure 10.4   *Resizing inside the* Save for Web *dialogue.*

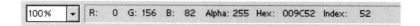

Figure 10.5   *Display of the current colour.*

under the cursor. To the left of the colour read-out is a field for entering a magnification factor.

> ☞ Open or create an image in Photoshop or Illustrator, and select the Save for Web... command from the File menu. Familiarize yourself with the tabs and tools in the window. Open an image in ImageReady and compare the tabs in the document window with those in the Save for Web dialogue in the other programs.

In Photoshop, an extra tool is available in the mini-toolbox. The slice select tool is used to select slices of an image, to be optimized independently. The slices must be created before saving. Image slicing is described in Chapter 4. A button below the Photoshop mini-toolbox toggles the visibility of the slice boundaries.

In ImageReady, the tools just described can be found in the full toolbox – there is no need for a mini-toolbox, because image optimization is integrated with the main application instead of being confined to a special dialogue.

Optimization Settings

For the moment, we will assume that you are working in 2-up view, reserving the left image for the original. To set optimization settings you first click in the right (optimized) image. Then, in Illustrator or Photoshop, you use the controls in the top right to choose a file format and to set the properties that go with it. In ImageReady, the same controls can be found on the Optimize palette. In all three applications, these controls are context-sensitive; the properties available change depending on the chosen file format. The format may be chosen from a pop-up menu. Figure 10.6 shows the settings when each of GIF, PNG-24 and JPEG has been chosen; the options for PNG-8 are almost identical to those for GIF.

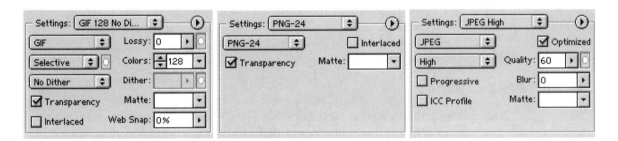

Figure 10.6   *Settings for GIF (left), PNG (centre) and JPEG (right).*

For novices, the easiest way to start is by selecting one of the preset collections available in the pop-up menu labelled Settings above the individual setting controls. Figure 10.7 shows the options provided. After selecting one of these options, the controls change to be appropriate for the chosen file format, with values set as suggested by the menu entry. (Figure 10.6 shows some examples.) For GIFs, the number is the number of colours in the palette – note that the maximum value of 256 is not included among these presets, since it is widely believed to offer no appreciable improvement over 128, while requiring one extra bit for each pixel and a palette twice the size. If you feel you need more than 128 colours, you will need to create the settings by hand, as we will describe next. However, the 216 colour Web palette is available as an option.

☞ Choose each of the presets in turn and examine the resulting optimized file, on its own in the Optimized tab and next to the original in the 2-up view. Are any of the values clearly better or worse than the rest?

If, after looking at the preview of the optimized version of the file, none of the presets seems to be good enough, you will have to set parameters by hand. We will consider the options for each of the Web image file formats in turn.

Figure 10.7   *The optimization presets.*

GIF and PNG Settings

The options for GIFs are the most extensive. The first option you can set (reading the palette in rows from left to right) is a value between 0 and 100 for the amount of lossiness to be applied when the image is compressed. This is surprising, in view of the fact that GIF files are always losslessly compressed. However, it has become common practice to optionally discard some information before applying the LZW compression, to increase its effectiveness. This information can never be retrieved, making the combined process lossy. Applying small amounts of lossiness (less than 10) can reduce file sizes by a worthwhile amount, without any appreciable loss of image quality. Using high values results in unsightly artefacts, though. The value can be typed directly in the Lossy field, or set using the slider which pops up when you hold down the mouse button with the cursor over the triangle to the right of the field.

The second row of options is used for selecting the colour palette. The pop-up menu on the left allows you to choose the method by which the palette is to be built. The basic set of choices is between Perceptual, Selective, Adaptive (which cause the palette to be constructed from the colours in the original image) and Web (which uses the fixed Web-safe set of colours). Photoshop and ImageReady provide some other fixed palettes as additional choices: the MacOS and Windows system palettes, and black and white (1-bit colour) and greyscale.

The three different methods of constructing the palette dynamically give different priorities to the colours in the image. The perceptual method bases its priorities on the sensitivity of the human eye to different colours, favouring those of which we are most aware. The selective algorithm (the default) favours areas of flat colour and Web-safe colours; it is designed with GIF compression and Web browsers in mind. The adaptive method gives priority to the image's most common colours.

The next field, labelled Colors is for choosing the size of the palette. The pop-up menu attached to this field lets you select powers of two for the number of colours – these values all fit in an exact number of bits, so there is little or no advantage in choosing any other number, but you can type in a value or use the increment and decrement arrows if you like.

The next pair of settings are concerned with dithering colours that are not in the palette. The pop-up menu on the left lets you choose an algorithm for constructing the patterns of dots used to replace missing colours. This refers to dithering introduced during the optimization of the image. Dithering may also occur when the image is previewed in a browser on a system with limited colour abilities. The chances are high that the browser will make a poor job, so it is important to try and avoid the need for browser dither by doing it beforehand. (By selecting Browser Dither from the pop-up menu just above and to the right of the previews in the Save for Web dialogue, or the View>Preview>Browser Dither menu command in ImageReady, you can see how much of a mess a browser is likely to make if you leave the dithering to it.) The first option, No Dither makes no attempt to dither, leaving matters to the browser, which may result in posterization. Pattern dither resembles the traditional half-tone screening used in printing to produce many colours from the limited number of process inks. For Web images, it usually produces too noticeable a pattern. The options Diffusion and Noise introduce randomness, which makes the dithering less obvious. Diffusion can produce visible edges between slices in images that have been divided up in this way (see Chapter 4); Noise avoids this. For Diffusion only, a percentage value can be set in the box on the right – either directly or using the slider attached to the triangle next to it – to control the amount of dither that is applied.

> ☞ Choose one of the GIF presets and then modify it by choosing different colour palette and dithering options. Use the 2-up view to judge the effect on your image.

The next pair of options deal with transparent areas of the image. Selecting the Transparency checkbox causes the transparent areas of the image to be assigned a colour which is used to denote transparency in the GIF. In other words, areas of the image that are transparent in Photoshop will remain transparent and allow the background to show through when the saved GIF file is embedded in a Web page. Alternatively, you can select a colour in the Matte field, which will be used to fill transparent areas. Actually, there is a little more to it than that. Aliasing of edges can lead to pixels that are only partially transparent (before saving). Matting causes these to be blended with the matte colour. If you select both a matte colour and transparency, the matte colour is blended with partially transparent pixels, while fully transparent pixels are left so. If you know what the background colour of the Web page containing the image will be and choose the same colour for a matte with transparency, this will avoid the halo that otherwise appears when images containing anti-aliased edges are composited with a background, using transparency. The options provided on the Matte pop-up menu are None, if you do not want to use any matte colour, Eyedropper Color, which causes the matte colour to be taken from the most recent selection made with the eyedropper tool in the mini-toolbox, White, Black and Other..., which causes the colour picker to be displayed.

> ☞ If your sample image does not have any transparent areas, make a copy of it and use the eraser with anti-aliasing in Photoshop to create some. Go back to the Save for Web dialogue, select GIF for the file type, and preview the image in a browser. Experiment with setting different matte colours and preview the results.

On the bottom row of options for GIF optimization are, first, a checkbox that is used to select interlacing, and second, a field for setting the extent to which you will allow colours to be automatically replaced by the nearest value in the Web-safe palette so as to avoid dithering. The value is expressed as a percentage; higher values allow more colours to be replaced in this way. We usually say that colours 'snap to' the Web-safe palette.

The options for PNG-8 are identical to those for GIF, except that there is no provision for introducing lossy compression. The checkbox for selecting interlacing is moved to the top right of the set of options, where the lossiness setting is for GIF, as shown in Figure 10.8.

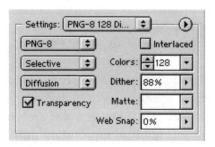

Figure 10.8   *Options for PNG-8.*

PNG-24 offers the smallest and simplest set of options: checkboxes for selecting interlacing and transparency, and a field for choosing a matte colour.

☛ Optimize your sample image as PNG-8 and PNG-24. Experiment with all the available options for each format. Compare the optimized image with the original and preview it in a browser.

JPEG Settings

The fundamentally different nature of JPEG images means that the optimization settings available when this format has been chosen are rather dissimilar to those for the other formats. There is a field for specifying a matte colour, but since JPEGs do not support transparency this is always used to fill in transparent areas – if you select None, white is used anyway. There is a checkbox for stipulating progressive download, which is similar to interlacing, as we described earlier. Otherwise, the JPEG options derive from the JPEG format's distinctive characteristics.

The most important of these is the quality setting used in applying lossy compression. This represents a trade-off between image quality – the extent to which, after compression and decompression the appearance of the original is preserved – and file size. Higher quality means greater size. However, the quality setting is really just a parameter to the compression process that determines how much data is discarded. The effect this will have on the perceived image quality depends on the image itself; some images will still be entirely acceptable at low quality settings that would thoroughly degrade other images. It is particularly useful to have the 2-up and 4-up previews available so that you can immediately judge the effect of changing settings before you save the file.

There are three ways of setting the quality. The simplest is to use the pop-up menu at the left to choose between Low, Medium, High and Maximum. Often, finer gradations will make little visible difference. You can, however, set a precise value in the Quality field – a slider is attached to the triangle by this field for setting the value non-numerically.

Above the Quality field is a checkbox intriguingly labelled Optimized. The whole business under consideration is optimization. This option refers to a means of adding extra compression to the JPEG file, using an optional feature of the standard. This means that not all browsers will be able to render the image, so it should not be used if compatibility is important.

Below the Quality field is another field equipped with a slider for setting an amount of Gaussian blur (see Chapter 3) to be applied before compression. Blurring reduces the impact of the artefacts produced by high levels of JPEG compression. It is common to apply it in this context, although naturally it implies that the image may appear blurred to some extent.

> ☞   Select JPEG as the file format and then adjust the quality from the lowest to the highest available values. For every value, compare the optimized and original images. Try adding Gaussian blur, and see what effects it has, both for high and low quality settings.

JPEG files may include ICC (International Colour Consortium) colour profiles, which are used by colour management software, such as Apple's ColorSync, to ensure that colours are reproduced accurately. A colour profile captures features of the device on which the image was made, such as the monitor's gamma, and a Web browser that understands colour profiles can compensate when it displays the image on a device with different characteristics. The checkbox labelled ICC Profile should be selected if you wish to embed a colour profile in your JPEG. Note, though, that this can only be done if the image has already been saved in the application's native format with a profile.

Whereas, no doubt, the true craftsman will carefully optimize each and every image individually for every Web page it is used in, less fastidious Web graphics artists may well find that the same combination of settings works acceptably well for many similar images. If you find yourself using the same values many times, you can save them as a preset, to be added to those already available in the Settings pop-up menu. This is done by choosing Save Settings... from the Optimize palette menu in ImageReady, or its equivalent in the Save for Web dialogue, as shown in Figure 10.3 on page 591. You are presented with a file saving dialogue, since presets are actually kept in files, but all you really need to do is provide a name for your settings. Afterwards that name appears in the Settings pop-up menu. If you ever decide you don't need it, you can remove it using the Delete Settings command in the palette menu. This removes the currently selected preset.

> ☞   Find some settings for JPEG and PNG-8 compression that you feel offer a good compromise between file size and quality, and save them as presets. Try applying them to other images with a range of visual characteristics.

If you don't want to be bothered at all with the niceties of choosing a format and setting the parameters, there is a quick and (possibly) dirty alternative. On the pop-up menu by the Settings presets menu in the Save for Web dialogue, or ImageReady's Optimize palette menu is a command Optimize to File Size.... Selecting this command produces the dialogue box shown in Figure 10.9. (In Illustrator, a simpler version appears,

Figure 10.9   *Optimizing to a specific file size.*

without the options concerning image slices.) You simply set the size you want the file to be, tell the application whether to take your current settings as a starting point, or do the job entirely automatically, including the choice of file format, and then let it do its best to optimize your image so that it is reduced to the size you desire. This is certainly a quick way of carrying out the task, but it does mean relinquishing control over the various trade-offs to a program (that is, to a set of decisions previously made by a programmer).

☛ Optimize your image to a few different file sizes, ranging from 5% to 50% of its original size. Evaluate the resulting the quality of the resulting images. See if you can do better by selecting optimization parameters yourself.

Minor Features

The remaining facilities for image optimization provided by the programs we are describing in this chapter are a bit specialized. You may prefer to skip the rest of this section if you are just getting acquainted with Web graphics.

Weighted Optimization

Normally, your chosen optimization settings are applied to an entire image, or a slice, if you have divided it up as described in Chapter 4. Photoshop and ImageReady allow you to use values that vary smoothly over the image for some parameters, a process that is called *weighted optimization*. The variation is controlled by an alpha channel. Illustrator does not support alpha channels, so it doesn't let you do this.

For the different parameters which can be applied in a weighted manner, the process is much the same, and we will therefore only describe one case in any detail. JPEG compression can be applied at different quality levels to different parts of an image. The way in which the quality varies in different areas is controlled by an alpha channel, which is created in the usual manner by saving a selection or creating a channel and painting in it, as described in Chapter 3. The interpretation of the alpha channel is that white areas will be compressed at the highest quality – a maximum that you specify – and black areas at the lowest – your specified minimum. Grey areas represent intermediate quality values, with quality varying linearly with brightness.

To use varying quality compression, first select JPEG as the file format, and then click the button to the right of the quality field. (The button will be greyed out if you have not created an alpha channel.) The dialogue shown in Figure 10.10 will appear. You must select the channel you have created for controlling the optimization from the pop-up menu. You can then use the two sliders below it, or the two entry fields, to set the minimum and maximum quality values you want to correspond to the white and black areas of the channel. If you select the Preview checkbox, you can see the effect as you change the two values, before committing to a final pair of settings.

☞ Open an image in Photoshop and create an alpha channel that masks out less important parts of it. Use this alpha channel to control the quality of JPEG compression when you optimize the image.

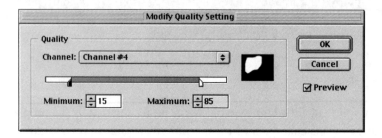

Figure 10.10 *Selecting a channel for weighted optimization.*

Alpha channels can be used in the same way to control the amount of lossiness introduced into a GIF file. The channel button appears next to the Lossy field when GIF is selected as the file format. Again, areas of the image corresponding to white areas of the channel will have the highest quality, black areas the lowest. Confusingly, though, since the value you are controlling is lossiness, not quality, it is the minimum value (least loss) that corresponds to white and the maximum (most loss) to black.

For the GIF and PNG-8 formats, a channel can be used to control the amount of dithering applied – white areas are dithered most, black least – and colour reduction.

In the latter case, the channel is used to add weight to the colours in certain areas when the palette is being constructed. The colours in areas that are white in the channel are considered most important, with black areas least important and grey ones in between. In this case, there are no maximum and minimum values to be set. For controlling colour reduction, the channel button next to the colour reduction algorithm pop-up menu is used.

Editing the Palette

When you are saving your image in a format that uses indexed colour – GIF or PNG-8 – it is sometimes desirable to change the colour palette from that which is automatically constructed by the application. This can be done using the Color Table palette in ImageReady, or the corresponding tabbed panel in the lower left of the Save for Web dialogue (see Figure 10.2 on page 589). Here, you can add extra colours, delete existing ones, or change the values that palette indices are mapped to.

Adding a colour that was left out when a palette was created automatically is perhaps the operation you will be most likely to wish to perform. It is sometimes the case that a colour has great visual significance while only appearing in a very small area of the image, so that it gets overlooked by the automatic colour reduction algorithms. To add such a colour to the palette by hand, you simply select it – the easiest way is usually by sampling it from the image with the eyedropper – and click the New button below the colour table swatches. If your palette has been constructed dynamically, that is, using one of the perceptual, selective or adaptive methods, the new colour will replace the nearest colour that is already in the palette. If you wish to add the colour as an extra member of the palette (and the palette has fewer than the maximum 256 entries), you can hold down the [cmd/ctl] key while you click on the button. This will convert the palette to a custom one and no colour will be replaced.

If the palette fills up you can delete colours. Select a colour, either by clicking on its swatch in the colour table or using the eyedropper, and then click on the trash can icon below the swatches. You can also edit colours. If you double-click a swatch in the colour table, the colour picker appears and you can select a new value. The effect is to change the colour stored in the location in the palette occupied by the colour you double-clicked. This means that every pixel whose value is the index of that location will change colour. This is a rather drastic operation.

☞ Open an image that uses a wide range of colours. In the Save for Web dialogue, select GIF or PNG-8 and set the number of colours to a low value. Try adding missing colours from the original image and see whether the optimized image is improved.

If you are more concerned about avoiding browser dither than with the exact colour in certain parts of the image, you can deliberately force any entry in the colour table to the nearest Web-safe value. Select a colour and then click the icon in the shape of a cube below the swatches. A small white diamond will appear in the centre of the chosen colour to show that it has been shifted. To put it back to its original value, just click the cube icon again.

We talk glibly in the preceding paragraph about the 'nearest' Web-safe colour, as does the documentation, but the notion of two colours being close together is not a straightforward one. The concept of nearness that is used when snapping to Web-safe colours is simply a numerical one, based on the values stored for the colours. This does not always correspond to the way in which we perceive colours as being close together, so the effect of snapping a colour to its nearest Web-safe neighbour is sometimes unexpectedly drastic.

☛ Choose GIF and the adaptive palette to optimize an image with subtle colours. Make each of the colours in the palette snap to a Web-safe value and observe the effect on the optimized image.

Saving the Optimized File

The final step in optimization is to save the file to disk. How you do this and exactly what you can do varies between the applications. The simplest is Illustrator. Here, you just click the OK button in the Save for Web dialogue; this takes you to a file saving dialogue, whose only non-standard feature is a checkbox labelled Save HTML File. Selecting this causes Illustrator to create a file containing HTML code to embed the image in a Web page at the same time as it saves the optimized image itself. If you had added image map hot spots to the image, as described on page 351, the HTML file will include the necessary code to make the image map work. Otherwise, it contains the bare minimum of code required to embed the image. It can be edited to add extra content, HTML formatting or CSS layout.

In Photoshop and ImageReady you can exert more control over the output files. Clicking OK in Photoshop's Save for Web dialogue, or choosing the File>Save Optimized As... command in ImageReady takes you to an extended file saving dialogue. Below the usual text field for entering a file name is a pop-up menu labelled Format on MacOS systems, or Save As Type on Windows. From this, you can choose to save Images Only, HTML and Images or HTML Only. For simple, unsliced, images, the HTML file saved is essentially the same as that saved by Illustrator – it just embeds the image in a Web page.

For images that have been sliced, a pop-up menu at the bottom of the dialogue box lets you choose which slices to save – all of them or only those you have selected. The HTML file in this case contains the code that puts the slices together on the page (see Chapter 4); each slice is saved to its own file (hence the plural in HTML and Images) within a folder created for the purpose. You can control the naming conventions used for these files, but the defaults work fine and, since the application is writing the HTML for you, you don't really need to know about them.

Between the two pop-up menus is a button labelled Output Settings..., which gives access to a dialogue box, shown in Figure 10.11, that lets you control various aspects of the HTML and image files created when you save the optimized image. When it first opens, it shows a set of options for the HTML code. If you know HTML, these will be self-explanatory; if you don't, you can get away with using the defaults. The most significant option is probably the choice between generating CSS and generating a table to put slices together. Generating CSS is the preferred way, sanctioned by the WWW Consortium; generating a table is considered to be something of a hack, using an HTML element for a purpose for which it was not intended. (There are practical disadvantages to doing so, it isn't just a matter of dogma.) Unfortunately, Web browser vendors have mostly made a terrible mess of implementing CSS, so it is safer to stick with the table. If you want to ensure that your Web pages continue to conform to the relevant standards, you should set the case of tags and attributes to lower-case, and select the option to quote all attribute values. This will make the HTML legal as XHTML.

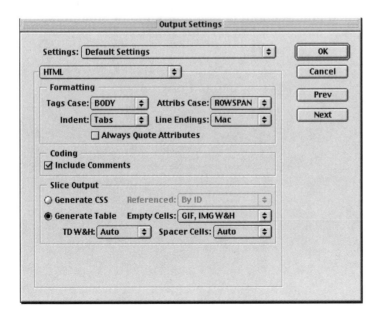

Figure 10.11 *Output settings.*

Projects

Up until now, we have kept our descriptions of the different media tools separate, except where several programs have some features in common. This is unrealistic. Most projects in digital media require the use of two or more tools. Even if you intend to make a career as a specialist in just one of these tools, it is unlikely that you can completely avoid the use of others, and you will find yourself having to deal with people working with different ones, so in this chapter we have suggested some projects which require the use of several tools in combination.

The need for combining media tools arises for two reasons. The most obvious is that a lot of work that is done in digital media comprises elements of several different media types – text, images, video, animation, sound – often augmented with interactivity. Such combinations of media types are referred to as *multimedia*. Web pages and computer games are the most familiar examples of multimedia. Less obviously, it is often necessary to process material through several different tools, to convert it from its raw form into a final production. For example, images might be captured and preprocessed in Photoshop before being made into an animation in Flash, or imported into Premiere to be used as a matte.

As well as requiring the use of more than one program, these projects differ from the exercises in the other chapters in requiring you to do some design, make choices about how to use the various tools, and generally apply your mind to direct the skills that you should have acquired by working through the practise and end-of-chapter exercises for each individual program. The projects resemble the exercises in one important respect, though: there are no right answers. They are an invitation to create your own solutions. You can also regard them as an invitation to create your own problems. If you don't like the projects as specified, but they suggest something that you feel might be more useful to do instead, go ahead and do it. It's the work that matters, not sticking rigidly to our programme. (Having said that, in commercial work you will usually have to work to a brief, so there is something to be said for the discipline of attempting a task exactly as specified.) Furthermore, you needn't feel confined to the tools described in this book or our suggestions for specific projects. You may be working with some different tools, for example, Freehand instead of Illustrator, or it may be that you know of a little shareware utility that will do part of the job more easily than Photoshop would, or you may be an expert programmer who reckons that a Java applet would work better than a Flash movie. That's OK, but remember that if you are trying to learn how to use some specific programs that you may well be expected to know about in your work, you need to make sure you have assessed their capabilities before you reject them.

If there are no right answers, how do you know how well you are doing? At the most basic level, you should test (early and often) to make sure everything works as it is supposed to. Beyond that, with experience you will hopefully come to recognize what is good about your own work. One way of finding out is by letting other people look at what you have done and tell you what they think. If you are on a course, this can be done in a formal way with tutors and other students – the famous art school 'crit' – but you can also ask people from outside the world of multimedia and design – some equivalent of the celebrated 'man on the Clapham omnibus', or perhaps some of your relatives. Remember that live Web sites may have a huge unpredictable audience from a very wide range of backgrounds, so don't just ask for the opinions of fellow multimedia students or designers.

You can attempt the projects on your own, but they can also be done by groups. Ideally, if time and other constraints permit, the same group should work on several projects, with individuals taking on different roles and using different programs each time. Working in teams will give you the added experience of trying to work with other people. This may cause you to think about organizational structures. There's a high probability that it will also cause you to think about – and do something about – the untidy problems of social interactions within a group that are an inevitable part of team working. What are you going to do about leadership, conflicts of opinion, and ensuring everyone does their fair share of the work?

You may feel that we have swindled you by just presenting problems without any advice or theory about design. We don't, however, believe there is a set of infallible rules of design that work all the time for everybody, taking into account all the potential ways of using digital media, and all the different backgrounds from which people might approach it. There are many different ways of approaching the design of substantial projects and your best way is the way that works for you. If you have experience in software engineering, for example, and you find it helpful to draw diagrams, go ahead and do so. If you find that you cannot really figure out what you need to do until you actually start to work with a program, start straight away. We advise you to look at as many other people's work as you can and to seek help from local experts if you get stuck. If you have no local experts, the Internet is an unmatched resource, if you are prepared to separate the wheat from the chaff. There is a wealth of good design on the Web now, and you should try to keep up to date with developments. Follow links from the sites of software manufacturers, awards bodies, 'zines and other designers' own sites to find many different solutions to design problems.

Finally, don't regard these projects as a chore, or something you have to do in order to obtain some course credits. Digital multimedia is no less a creative pursuit than traditional art and design and requires the same sort of involvement and dedication. Take the work seriously, but don't take yourself too seriously. Have some fun.

Note. The projects are not intended to be worked through in any particular order. Their ordering here is arbitrary.

Memento

Choose an event from your own life – e.g., a holiday, birthday, graduation, etc. – for which you have some documentary record, such as photographs, videos, certificates, newspaper cuttings and so on. Import this material into ImageReady or Premiere (for video). Crop, edit and otherwise prepare it for presentation within a Web site. Assemble the material in Dreamweaver or GoLive, together with any additional text you feel is necessary, to commemorate the event on a Web site in an attractive, accessible and appropriate way.

Trace Bitmap Animation 1

Using a scanner or a digital camera, capture a sequence of images to disk. You can, for example, use a set of related photographs, a sequence of drawings, or your own hand or other some object in different positions on the bed of the scanner. Using Photoshop or some other image manipulating application, convert all the images to greyscale and downsample them to screen resolution. Save them in a suitable format for import into Flash. Import your image sequence into Flash and, using Trace Bitmap, create a stylized animation from them. By using coarse tracing settings or otherwise, ensure that the resulting SWF file will play smoothly over a 56K modem.

Trace Bitmap Animation 2

This project is a variant of the preceding one. This time, start with a short video clip in colour, import it into Premiere and select 25 to 50 frames of your choice. These do not need to be contiguous, but should be chosen to form a coherent sequence. Export these chosen frames as SWF, import them into Flash and once again use Trace Bitmap to create a stylized animation which will play smoothly over a 56K modem. This time exploit the colour as an element of your animation.

Visitor Centre

Create a multimedia resource for a visitor centre at a tourist attraction of your choice. Examples of the kind of attraction which use such presentations include disused industrial sites of archaeological interest, historical places such as castles or battlefields, wildlife parks, a lighthouse or lifeboat station that is open to the public, and so on. Choose an appropriate way of delivering your multimedia presentation, which is suitable for use by members of the public, and choose appropriate applications to prepare and integrate the source material.

Poem

Take a short poem and use Illustrator to create a set of compositions by typesetting each line in a graphically interesting and appropriate way. Use different fonts, colours and sizes and set the text on a path or in a shape as seems appropriate. Export each line's composition in a format suitable for the Web. Using Dreamweaver or GoLive, create a Web site whose home page contains the full text of the poem, laid out in its original form, with each line linked to a page containing the corresponding composition you made in Illustrator. Add any additional links and navigation aids which you think are necessary.

Sport

Create a few Web pages around the concept of some sport, such as skiing, skateboarding, basketball, football etc. Each page should consist of one or two imported photographs and one word or a short phrase expressing a facet of that sport, for example *jump, shoot, run,*…. Make the word move in a way that is suggestive of its meaning and connotation. For example, the word *run* should move in a way reminiscent of running. Try to make the movement specific to the sport: running in cricket is different from running in a marathon, for example. Carry out this exercise once using dynamic HTML animation and once in Flash.

Video Mix

Import two quite different video sequences into Premiere. From these create two new video clips, each of which uses material from both original sequences and incorporates transitions. Export your new clips as SWF, setting their size so that both can be played on screen at once. In Flash, create a player which will display both of the clips you have created side by side; provide any controls you think would be appropriate.

Live-Action GIFs

Import a sequence of live-action video into Premiere and work on it using whatever means seem appropriate to you – including but by no means restricted to resizing and trimming – until it can be exported as an animated GIF that will play smoothly and still convey the proper essence of the original sequence. Use Dreamweaver or GoLive to create a Web page that presents the resulting animated GIF and test its performance over a dial-up Internet connection.

Words in Motion 1

Take a Shakespeare sonnet or a similar poem, and choose words from separate lines that can be recombined to form a grammatically correct sentence. Create a Web page which displays the poem in its original form. Arrange your chosen words on layers so that they can be animated in the following way. Each word that you chose in the first step is to be made to fly out from its position in the poem and move gracefully to a new position on the page so that when all the words have been moved they form the new sentence. You should not necessarily start the words moving at the same time, or in the order in which they will finally appear in the rearranged sentence.

Words in Motion 2

Repeat the preceding exercise but use Flash instead of Dreamweaver or GoLive, so that you end up with an SWF movie rather than a Web page.

Clothes 1

Take a series of photographs of articles of your clothing which you feel best express the image of yourself which you want to project. Take several photographs of each garment. Use a digital camera if you have one, so you can import images directly into your computer; otherwise, use a conventional camera and scan the photos. For each garment create an animated GIF from its sequence of photographs. Now, build a Web site around an arrangement of these animated GIFs, which expresses your feelings about clothes and self-image.

Clothes 2

Carry out a variation on the preceding project. This time just take a single photograph of the each garment and create each animated GIF by altering this one photograph in ImageReady or Photoshop. Use these animated GIFs as before to create a Web site.

Clothes 3

As a final variant on this project, import the single images of your clothes into Flash, use the Break Apart command on the imported bitmaps, and animate parts of the clothes to make a collection of movie clip symbols. Now combine these small animations into a movie about how you feel about your clothes.

Sound and Vision 1

Create a 24 frame animation in ImageReady, either by importing images onto separate layers or by copying and modifying a single layer. (Use Photoshop as well if you need to.) Export the animation as a QuickTime movie, using a frame rate of 12 frames per second. Import this movie into Premiere and create a new one consisting of repetitions of the imported animation, so that the complete movie plays for exactly a minute. Import one minute of music from a CD or MP3 file and combine it with your picture track, so the sound is synchronized to the picture. (Think about the rhythm of both music and picture, and the different ways in which these could interact.) Export the resulting movie in a form suitable for playing on the Web.

Sound and Vision 2

Repeat the preceding project in Flash. This time, export the animation from ImageReady as an animated GIF and import it into Flash to produce a sequence of frames containing bitmapped images. Use Trace Bitmap to turn these into vectors and make the animation loop by adding actions instead of by making copies of the imported frames. Add a soundtrack as before.

Simultaneous Animations

Use ImageReady to create a set of up to eight animated GIFs which are conceptually inter-related. Design a page layout in Dreamweaver that incorporates some appropriate text with the animated GIFs placed on layers in a suitable arrangement. Using the timeline, sequence the animated GIFs so that the display keeps changing, both as a result of the animation of each GIF and because the animations appear and disappear or move around. Concentrate on making the page work as a whole, so that the individual animations and their changes interact harmoniously. Test the resulting page on several Web browsers running on different platforms.

Silent Movie

Shoot a short silent video film. Edit it into a compact and coherent form and then create intertitles (short pieces of text displayed between frames of the action) in the style of silent movies, with a decorative border to contain the text. Apply filters in Premiere to transform your footage into sepia or monochrome and give it the appearance of old film. (This is normally done with special After Effects plug-ins that cost a small fortune. Do your best with what Premiere provides.) If you have some suitable music or can record some, add a soundtrack that enhances the effect.

Site Map 1

Choose a subject that interests you to form the topic of a Web site. Sketch a design for the structure of this site, which should be divided into sections corresponding to sub-divisions of your chosen subject. For example, if you choose natural history as your topic, you might use mammals, fish, amphibians, insects, plants, fungi, and so on, as your sub-divisions; if you chose the life and work of Elvis Presley, you might use records, films, concert tours, stage outfits, associates, and so on. Keep the number of divisions down to a reasonable number. (The rule of thumb most often quoted is seven plus or minus three.) Create dummy place holder pages for each sub-division and design an attractive site map page for the whole site. Use either dynamic HTML or Flash to create a map based on remote rollovers, so that moving the cursor over an element representing a sub-division will cause a larger image or movie to appear somewhere on the page. Ensure that the different menu items have a distinct visual identity that conveys the essence of the corresponding division of your subject.

Site Map 2

Complete the entire site with all the necessary material. Use a small image map on each page to allow full navigation around the site from every page.

Web Video

Design some video clips that work well embedded in a Web page intended to be viewed over a dial-up connection. That is, starting from the knowledge that you will have to use low frame rates, small frame sizes and extreme compression, think about the sort of (real or created) imagery, movement and editing that is likely to suffer least from these limitations. Build a Web site to exhibit your clips and test it over real-world connections.

Web Diagrams

Using Illustrator or Flash draw some diagrams. If you have studied computer science or engineering, you could make some UML or finite state machine transition diagrams, or a circuit diagram. Otherwise, you could prepare diagrams to show some statistics in a graphical way, draw a map or create a simple set of graphic instructions. Whatever you choose, try to make the diagrams lively and attractive within the conventions of the subject they pertain to. Export the diagrams in a suitable format and then place each one on a Web page. Using some suitable technology and an appropriate layout, add rollovers so that additional information relating to parts of the diagram is displayed on the page when the cursor rolls over it. Add links to connect your pages, either sequentially or according to some logical connections between them. The links may be straightforward hyperlinks, or hot spots on the diagrams, or buttons of some sort.

Changes

Create three animated GIFs, all the same size and small enough to fit three across a Web page comfortably. They should be related to each other in some way, either in appearance or thematically. Each should comprise between 5 and 15 frames, and no two should have the same number of frames. Set up a Web page with three rows of images, each row containing all three of your animated GIFs in a different order. Use DHTML actions to permute the rows at suitable intervals. The result should be a constantly changing page.

Links

The word *vortal* (a contraction of the only slightly less enigmatic 'vertical portal') is sometimes used to denote a Web site that provides access to other sites on a single theme, such as Flash animation. Design and build such a site for a subject in which you are interested. It should contain links to any important sites on the subject, augmented with whatever material seems appropriate to make the vortal an interesting site in itself. Navigation will be the primary function, so think carefully about the site's structure and the navigation aids you provide.

Multiple Choice

Build a Web page or site that presents a multiple choice test on some subject. There should be a set of questions, for each of which a set of alternative answers, only one of which is correct, is provided. When a user chooses the right answer, some positive feedback should be given. For example a picture could be displayed, or an animation or sound could play. This should not only indicate that the answer is right, it should reinforce the learning by illustrating or expanding on the answer. Wrong answers should lead to some similar negative feedback, ideally illustrating what is wrong about the answer.

Animated Animation

Create a Web page around a single animated element made by combining DHTML and an animated GIF. That is, you should use JavaScript actions to move an animated GIF along a path; the animated GIF should be a simple looped movement that will make sense when it moves as a whole. For example, you could create a very simple animated GIF showing a rotating wheel and then move it diagonally across the page so it appears to be rolling downhill. Match the subject of your animation to your drawing and animating skills – if you can make an elephant on a unicycle (and want to) then do so, but if you can't draw, try to find something simple but effective such as a bouncing ball. You may find some inspiration in the physics of motion. Place other elements on the page that expand on the theme of your animation (for example, if you animated a unicycle you might add information about juggling equipment). Make sure that the elements are arranged so that they set off the animation and do not get in its way.

Web Site Surprise 1

Design a small Web site which is full of surprises and uses an interface as unconventional as you can make it, using whatever combination of technologies you like.

Web Site Surprise 2

Produce a variant of the previous project, which is suited for use by children aged roughly 8 to 12. Consider carefully all aspects of design and content for this site, but do not be patronizing. The result should be absorbing and challenging for the intended age group.

Index